St. Olaf College Libraries

*Gift of the
Freeman Foundation*

FINANCIAL GLOBALISATION AND THE OPENING OF THE JAPANESE ECONOMY

FINANCIAL GLOBALISATION AND THE OPENING OF THE JAPANESE ECONOMY

James D. Malcolm

CURZON

First Published in 2001
by Curzon Press
Richmond, Surrey
http://www.curzonpress.co.uk

© 2001 James D. Malcolm

Typeset in Stempel Garamond by LaserScript Ltd, Mitcham, Surrey
Printed and bound in Great Britain by
Biddles Ltd, Guildford and King's Lynn

All rights reserved. No part of this book may be reprinted or reproduced or utilised in any form or by any electronic, mechanical, or other means, now known or hereafter invented, including photocopying and recording, or in any information storage or retrieval system, without permission in writing from the publishers.

British Library Cataloguing in Publication Data
A catalogue record of this book is available from the British Library

Library of Congress Cataloguing in Publication Data
A catalogue record for this book has been requested

ISBN 0-7007-1472-3

To Luke

To think is to forget differences, generalize, make abstractions
– Jorge Luis Borges, *Labyrinths*

Contents

List of Figures	xi
Preface	xv
Glossary	xvii
Glossary of Frequently Used Japanese Terms	xx

Introduction   1

Part One
Financial Globalisation in Theory and Practice

1   Beyond Partisan Agendas   11
    1.1   The Political Economy of Economic Globalisation   11
    1.2   The Empirical Reality of Financial Globalisation   29
    1.3   Implications for National Institutional Convergence   42

Part Two
The Case of Japan

2   Financial Deregulation 'Japanese Style'   59
    2.1   The 100-year Development of a Modern Financial System   59
    2.2   Change and the Japanese Financial System   70
    2.3   Case Study: The Japanese-Style 'Big Bang'   110

3   'Awkward Convergence' in the Financial Sector   129
    3.1   The Internationalisation of Japan's Financial Sector   129
    3.2   The Rise and Fall of Japanese Firms as Global Competitors   148
    3.3   Big Bang: Paving the way for Institutional Convergence?   163

4	Societal Implications of a 'Gradualist' Approach	195
	4.1 The Macroeconomic Effects of Gradualism	195
	4.2 The Microeconomic Effects of Gradualism	217
	4.3 Case Study: The Societal Implications of Big Bang	245

Part Three
Lessons for Global Theorists and 'Japanologists'

Conclusion	265
Epilogue Entering the Twenty-first Century: Beyond the Big Bang	275
Notes	284
Appendix 1 Moves to Break up the Ministry of Finance (1/94–9/98)	347
Appendix 2 Economic Stimulus Measures (1/91–9/98)	354
Bibliography	366
Index	385

List of Figures

Chapter 1
1.1	Financial Deregulation in Selected Countries	31
1.2	Size of Eurocurrency Market	33
1.3	Annual Growth of International Financial Markets (net activity)	40
1.4	Size of International Financial Markets (outstanding stocks)	40
1.5	Global Derivatives Market (nominal amounts outstanding)	41
1.6	Daily Foreign Exchange Market Turnover	41

Chapter 2
2.1	Segmentation in the Postwar Japanese Financial System	66
2.2	Conceptions of Regulatory Reform	71
2.3	The Yen-Dollar Agreement	81
2.4	The Bubble Economy (Nikkei 225 and land price indices)	86
2.5	Financial Failures in the 1990s	99
2.6	Itinerary of the 'Japanese-style Big Bang' Proposal	112
2.7	Main Points of the 1998 Financial System Reform ('Big Bang') Law	123
2.8	Direct Causes of Financial Regulatory Change in Postwar Japan	128

Chapter 3
3.1	Number of Domestically Licensed Banks	130
3.2	Japanese Banks' Domestic Offices	131
3.3	The Internationalisation of Japanese Banks	132
3.4	Distribution of Japanese Banks' Overseas Offices (by type of bank)	133
3.5	Distribution of Japanese Banks' Overseas Offices (by geographical region)	134
3.6	Domestically Licensed Securities Companies	134

List of Figures

3.7	The Internationalisation of Japanese Securities Companies	135
3.8	Distribution of Japanese Securities Companies' Overseas Offices (by size)	136
3.9	Distribution of Japanese Securities Companies' Overseas Offices (by region)	137
3.10	Foreign Financial Institutions' Expansion in Japan	138
3.11	Foreign Financial Institutions in Japan (1995)	139
3.12	Foreign Banks in Japan (1995)	139
3.13	Foreign Securities Companies in Japan (1995)	139
3.14	Japanese Banks in Worldwide Rankings by Assets	140
3.15	Japanese Banks in Worldwide Rankings by Tier One Capital	141
3.16	Japanese Banks in Worldwide Rankings by New Measures of Strength	141
3.17	Proportion of New International Bank Lending by Japanese Banks	142
3.18	International Banking Assets Held by Japanese Banks	142
3.19	Position of Japanese Banks as Lead Managers in International Syndicated Lending	143
3.20	Position of Big Four Firms in Eurodollar Bond Underwriting Tables	143
3.21	Position of Big Four Firms in Euroyen Bond Underwriting Tables	144
3.22	Position of Big Four Firms in Underwriting Eurobonds with Warrants	144
3.23	Position of Japanese Firms in Annual *Euromoney* Global Financing Polls	156
3.24	Personnel Cuts by Major Japanese Financial Institutions (9/91–9/96)	158
3.25	Japanese Firms' Rankings in Euromoney Polls of Professional Opinion	162
3.26	Examples of Recent Personnel-Cost-Reduction Initiatives	165
3.27	Examples of Recent Internal Restructuring Initiatives	167
3.28	Examples of Recent Strategic Retrenchment Initiatives	169
3.29	Examples of Recent Foreign Firm-Japanese Firm Tie-ups	171
3.30	Examples of Recent Japanese Firm-Japanese Firm Tie-ups	175
3.31	Examples of Recent Specialisation Initiatives	188
3.32	Domestic Retail Sales Potential (1996)	190
3.33	Examples of Analysts' Predictions for Financial Sector Consolidation	192

List of Figures

Chapter 4

4.1	Comparative Annual Rates of Economic Growth (nominal GDP)	197
4.2	Comparative Stock Market Performance (1990 = 100)	198
4.3	Comparative Rates of Unemployment (seasonally adjusted)	198
4.4	Real Economic Growth (seasonally adjusted)	200
4.5	Overall Business Conditions (from 'Favourable' to 'Unfavourable')	201
4.6	Corporate Bankruptcies (firms with debts over ¥100 million)	202
4.7	Year-on-year Changes in Personal Consumption	203
4.8	Public Works Spending	204
4.9	Major Economic Stimulus Measures During the Heisei Recession	205
4.10	Changes in Selected General Budget Items (1990 = 100)	206
4.11	Real GDP Growth Forecasts Versus Actual Results	206
4.12	Outstanding Government Debt (ratio to GDP)	207
4.13	Central Government Fiscal Balances (ratio to GDP)	208
4.14	Official Discount Rate and Money Supply	210
4.15	Banks' Interest-related Earnings and Expenses (as a percentage of income)	221
4.16	Annual Government Debt Servicing Expenses	222
4.17	Changes in Profit for Manufacturers Versus Nonmanufacturers (1990 = 100)	223
4.18	Sectoral Business Conditions (from 'Favourable' to 'Unfavourable')	224
4.19	Changes in Annual Profit by Firm Size (1990 = 100)	224
4.20	Manufacturers' Business Conditions (from 'Favourable' to 'Unfavourable')	225
4.21	Nonmanufacturers' Business Conditions (from 'Favourable' to 'Unfavourable')	226
4.22	Year-on-year Changes in Annual Profits for Selected Sectors	227
4.23	Changes in Corporate Finance	227
4.24	Financial Position by Firm Size (from 'Easy' to 'Tight')	228
4.25	Companies Hiring Temporary Workers	232
4.26	Employment Contracts at Listed Firms	233
4.27	Year-on-year Changes in Household Income	236
4.28	Year-on-year Changes in Worker Household Income and Expenditure	237

List of Figures

4.29	Key Unemployment Indices	238
4.30	Changes in Unemployment by Age Group (1990 = 100)	239
4.31	Unemployed Persons by Reason for Redundancy	239
4.32	Temporary Staff Registered with Agencies	240
4.33	Personal Bankruptcies	241
4.34	Personal Financial Asset Growth and Ratio to GDP	242
4.35	Average Household Savings Rate	242
4.36	Currency and Bank Deposits as a Percentage of Personal Assets	243
4.37	Insurance and Pensions as a Percentage of Personal Assets	243
4.38	Securities Holdings as a Percentage of Personal Assets	244
4.39	Balance of Postal Deposits to Total Cash and Bank Deposits	245
4.40	What Do You Expect from Financial Liberalisation?	245
4.41	What Characteristic will you Prioritise when Investing?	246
4.42	Which Products do you Intend to Invest in?	246
4.43	Impact of New Financial Products and Services by Sector	260
4.44	Distribution of Benefits from Big Bang	261

Preface

This book was conceived in the early summer of 1995 as a way to bridge and develop longstanding interests in the esoteric worlds of finance and Japan. My timing was incredibly fortuitous. Having spent a year at the University of Sheffield developing ideas and working on a theoretical framework, I came to Japan in October 1996 to begin two years of fieldwork at the University of Tokyo. Barely two months later, Prime Minister Hashimoto announced a radical programme of financial sector deregulation measures – the 'Japanese-style Big Bang' – which has proved to be the most significant development in this sphere in at least half a century. Thus, I was privileged in having the opportunity to watch close up its progress and various repercussions.

My postgraduate studies were made possible by scholarships from the University of Sheffield, its School of East Asian Studies (SEAS), the Japanese Ministry of Education, Culture and Science (*Mombushō*), and the International Center for Comparative Law and Politics at the University of Tokyo. I thank, first and foremost, my supervisor and friend Professor Glenn Hook, for his boundless encouragement, confidence and efficiency – which I have blessed and cursed in equal measure. For their help and support, I am also particularly grateful to Professor Takahashi Susumu, my sponsor at the University of Tokyo; Professor Ian Gow, director of SEAS; Mrs. Gill Goddard, SEAS librarian; and Dr. Hugo Dobson, a fellow Sheffield/Tōdai researcher and partner in crime. Finally, I am immensely indebted to my wife, Genevieve, who patiently put up with my long hours of work and seemingly endless frustrations, and then proofread draft upon draft of the book. As to errors, the usual disclaimers apply.

Following convention, Japanese names appear surname first, macrons are used to denote long vowels, and Japanese words are italicised. The exceptions to this rule are where a publication cited is in English, when a Japanese author has chosen to render his name in an alternative Romanized form, and the place name Tokyo, for which macrons are omitted because it is widely known. Dates for newspaper articles follow British convention –

i.e. 1/9/98 refers to September 1, 1998, as does spelling, apart from where it appears otherwise in quotes and book/journal/article titles. Dollars refers to US dollars, and whole numbers under 100, with the exception of dates, are spelled out.

Glossary

ABS	asset-backed security
ARC	Administrative Reform Committee (Japan)
ATM	automated teller machine
BAC	Business Accounting Council (Japan)
BIS	Bank of International Settlements (Basel)
BOJ	Bank of Japan
C–20	Committee of Twenty (IMF)
CAPM	Capital Asset Pricing Model
CBOE	Chicago Board Options Exchange
CBOT	Chicago Board of Trade
CD	certificate of deposit
CFEOT	Council on Foreign Exchange and Other Transactions (Japan)
CIP	covered interest parity
CMA	cash management account
CME	Chicago Mercantile Exchange
CP	commercial paper
CPA	Certified Public Accountant
DIC	Deposit Insurance Corporation (Japan)
DPJ	Democratic Party of Japan
DTB	Deutsche Terminböurse
EC	Economic Council (Japan)
EMTN	euromedium-term note
EPA	Economic Planning Agency (Japan)
FRC	Financial Reconstruction Commission
FRN	floating rate note

Glossary

FSA	Financial Services Agency (Japan)
FSRC	Financial System Research Council (Japan)
FTC	Fair Trade Commission (Japan)
GDP	gross domestic product
GSA	general securities account
G–3	Group of Three (the US, Germany and Japan)
G–5	Group of Five (G–3 plus the UK and France)
G–7	Group of Seven (G–5 plus Italy and Canada)
G–10	Group of Ten (G–7 plus Belgium, the Netherlands and Sweden; also known as the Paris Club)
G–30	Group of Thirty
HLAC	Housing Loan Administration Corporation (Japan)
IBF	international banking facility
IC	Insurance Council (Japan)
IDB	inter-dealer broker
IMF	International Monetary Fund
IMM	International Money Market (Chicago)
IOSCO	International Organisation of Securities Commissions (Montreal)
IPB	International private banking
IPE	International Political Economy
IR	International Relations
JCP	Japan Communist Party
JFBA	Japan Federation of Bankers' Associations
JGB	Japanese government bond
JOM	Japan offshore market
JSDA	Japan Securities Dealers' Association
LAN	local area network
LDP	Liberal Democratic Party (Japan)
LIBOR	London inter-bank offer rate
LIFFE	London International Financial Futures Exchange
M&A	mergers and acquisitions
MAI	Multilateral Agreement on Investment
MATIF	Marché à Terme des Instruments Financiers (Paris)
MBA	Master of Business Administration
MHW	Ministry of Health and Welfare (Japan)

Glossary

MITI	Ministry of International Trade and Industry (Japan)
MOC	Ministry of Construction (Japan)
MOF	Ministry of Finance (Japan)
MOFA	Ministry of Foreign Affairs (Japan)
MPT	Ministry of Posts and Telecommunications (Japan)
NASDAQ	North American Securities Dealers Automated Quotation system
NIE	New Institutional Economics
NIF	note issuance facility
NTA	National Tax Agency (Japan)
NYSE	New York Stock Exchange
ODR	official discount rate
OECD	Organisation for Economic Cooperation and Development
OPEC	Organisation of the Petroleum Exporting Countries
OSE	Osaka Stock Exchange
PCA	prompt corrective action
PEP	personal equity plan
PER	price-earnings ratio
PIT	Portfolio Insurance Theory
PKO	price-keeping operation
ROA	return on assets
ROE	return on equity
RUF	revolving underwriting facility
SCAP	Supreme Commander for the Allied Powers
SDPJ	Social Democratic Party of Japan
SEAQ	Stock Exchange Automated Quotation system (London)
SEC	Securities and Exchange Council (Japan)
SESC	Securities and Exchanges Surveillance Commission (Japan)
SIMEX	Singapore International Monetary Exchange
SPV	special purpose vehicle
TSE	Tokyo Stock Exchange
USTR	United States Trade Representative
WTO	World Trade Organization
WWI	World War I
WWII	World War II

Glossary of Frequently Used Japanese Terms

amakudari	bureaucratic retiree gaining lucrative second-career post in public or private sector as result of former regulatory contact (literally, 'descent from heaven')
chō-endaka	ultrahigh yen
eigyō tokkin	money-in-trust
endaka	high yen
gaiatsu	external pressure
gensaki	repurchase agreement ('repo')
Heisei	the period 1989–present (named after the current emperor)
jûsen	housing loan companies
Keidanren	Japan Federation of Economic Organizations (the largest big business interest group)
Keizai Dōyûkai	Japan Association of Corporate Executives
MOF-tan	MOF-watcher (an elite post in private financial institutions with responsibility for maintaining good relations with the Ministry of Finance)
Nikkeiren	Japan Federation of Employers' Associations
shingikai	deliberative committee (organised under each government ministry to discuss policy changes)
shinkin	credit bank
sōkaiya	corporate racketeer
tobashi	a 'creative' accounting manoeuvre involving the shifting of liabilities to affiliates with different financial reporting dates based upon an implicit agreement to repurchase the liabilities at a later date
yakuza	underworld/Japanese mafia
zaitekku	financial engineering (usually derivatives-related)

Introduction

Globalisation was *the* 1990s buzzword. It attained almost universal currency in media, business, political, and academic circles as shorthand for an emerging era of transnationalisation made possible by new computer and communications technologies. Used most often in relation to developments in the economic sphere, it also applied to the worldwide spread of ideas such as democracy, capitalism, and basic human rights. Scarcely can one pick up a major newspaper or watch television today without coming across the term in a news story. The business world is now overflowing with 'global' jargon, from companies' annual reports to the latest management publications, and from journalism to the MBA programmes where tomorrow's aspiring leaders are equipped. Globalisation also permeated the political world to its highest echelons, headlining the G–7 Lyons Summit of June 1996 and figuring prominently in subsequent meetings.[1] In the academic world it became the hot, *fin de siècle* topic for debate and research, as evident just from the proliferation of books using the term in their titles.[2]

For all the hype, however, globalisation remains a nebulous concept for most people.[3] Loose usage and overinflated claims have occluded much of its analytical potential and explanatory promise, with the result that the focus of debate has shifted towards contesting the concept on two fronts. First, in regard to what it purports to describe, its semantic appropriateness is questioned on the basis of evidence presented to show that the present era is not fundamentally different from the recent past (e.g. Hirst and Thompson 1996). Second, with regard to its ideological function, the term's rhetorical role is highlighted by others who seek to draw attention to the fact that it may function as part of a political project to foreclose certain viable policy options (e.g. Youngs 1996). In this regard, globalisation has been called a 'euphemism' (Gill *et al.* 1992, p. 3), but thinking of it as a *metaphor* is actually more useful because this encourages us to take it seriously, while at the same time permitting us to question its descriptive appropriateness and potential for rhetorical appropriation.

Introduction

(i) Why Study the Impact of Financial Globalisation in and on Japan?

Financial globalisation is an interesting area for research because of its tremendous real-world implications and empirical possibilities. It is in relation to finance that globalisation is commonly held to have progressed furthest, and it is in this context that policymakers have often invoked globalisation as a reason for pushing radical deregulatory programmes. The Asian financial crisis which began in July 1997 provides the most recent and vivid case in point, highlighting afresh the massive economic, political and social repercussions and tensions associated with financial globalisation.[4] Moreover, in spite of its esoteric nature, financial globalisation is an area in which the basic issues at stake are not technical or abstract but are highly amenable to concrete investigation.

A considerable amount of empirical research already has accumulated on different aspects of financial globalisation. Scholars tend to concentrate their analyses in one or two specific areas, although their work usually has broader implications as well. Examples of important contributions to date include work on the current reality and extent of financial globalisation (Reinike 1995; Thompson 1997; Goldblatt *et al.* 1997), the mechanisms and history of financial globalisation (Walter 1993; Helleiner 1994), its implications for the state in terms of autonomy, regulatory convergence and democratisation (Frieden 1991; Moran 1991; Goodman and Pauly 1993; Pauly 1995; Cerny 1993, 1997), its implications for geography (Corbridge, Thrift and Martin [eds.] 1994), and the rise of new nonstate forms of governance and authority (Strange 1988; Stopford and Strange 1991; Porter 1993; Kapstein 1994; Sinclair 1994a; Coleman 1996). The impact of financial globalisation also has been documented empirically in comparative studies of the US, UK and Japan (Moran 1991; Sobel 1994; Vogel 1996) and of North America and the EU (Coleman 1996); and in single country/group of countries studies of the EU (Underhill 1997), Germany (Story 1997), France (Coleman 1997), Eastern Europe (Rodkey 1997), and Korea and Taiwan (Bernard 1997), among others.

This book investigates the impact of financial globalisation in and on Japan. The case of Japan provides arguably the most interesting single-state study on financial globalisation because of the country's core position in the world economy – evidenced by its position in the G–3 and Tokyo's place alongside New York and London as the three leading international financial centres – in spite of its heritage of considerable institutional differences from leading Western states.[5] As yet, no in-depth study on the impact of financial globalisation in or on Japan has been published. The existing work which addresses financial globalisation in Japan even indirectly is written by Western political scientists who have tended to focus narrowly on the country's record of regulatory reform (Pauly 1988; Moran 1991; Sobel 1994; Vogel 1996). This relative dearth of applied theoretical analysis is related in part to the fact that Japan is less accessible to Western social scientists because of its geographic, linguistic and cultural attributes.[6] However, the fact that Japan has been badly misunderstood in the past by nonspecialists who have attempted to include it in their broader work (e.g. Helleiner 1994) probably is not insignificant either.[7] Moreover, since major recent developments – namely, the 'Japanese-style Big Bang' – await systematic analysis, it is argued that even the limited work in existence stands in need of being brought up to date.

Hereby, the mandate adopted for this research is to map the main economic, political and social implications of financial globalisation in and on Japan. As will be clear from the framework established in Chapter One, these implications can be examined in reference to the notion of institutional convergence upon an emerging dominant model which is close, if not identical, to the Anglo-American paragon.

(ii) A Pluralist Approach

This book adopts a pluralist theoretical approach (Smith 1995a), following in the footsteps of a growing body of work which addresses globalisation. The reason for this is that while approaches derived from competing theoretical traditions may claim universality or a privileged perspective, each remains subject to certain limitations. For example, while (neo-) Marxist approaches are particularly suited to identifying structural changes (such as globalisation) and theorising their broad social implications, they are not helpful in shedding light on competitive developments *within* a particular sector of the economy;[8] (neo-)Liberal approaches, by contrast, are well suited to analysing competitive developments within a particular sector of the economy, but they tend to be insensitive to the exercise of structural power in social relations and unable to theorise long-term historical change; and (neo-)Realist approaches, which are useful in analysing narrow political developments, will often ignore major structural and cultural factors which are not amenable to the pseudo-scientific reductionism which is integral to its model-making methodology (see, for example, Gill and Law 1988). There is an obvious advantage to be gained from seeking to draw on different bodies of work.

Nevertheless, an important preliminary issue which any pluralist approach must address is how diverse approaches can be integrated when their epistemological methods and ontological roots are different. Some scholars maintain, for example, that approaches which prioritise agency over structure are incommensurate with those which do the opposite (e.g. Krasner 1994). Two points can be raised to counter such concerns, one factual and one theoretical. First, different approaches were not always considered incommensurate. Classical political economy drew freely on scholarship in a wide range of disciplines in its pursuit of knowledge (see Redman 1997). But it was only from the latter part of the nineteenth century, and particularly since the Second World War, that the idea of exclusive scholarly traditions became entrenched. This was the product of a fashion for universal 'scientific' approaches which was boosted by the ideological polarisation imposed by the Cold War. Such approaches relied heavily on positivist dualities (e.g. right/wrong, national/international, economic/noneconomic), but have been recognised increasingly as reductionist and bounded. The proliferation of counter-currents in many disciplines during the 1980s was an inevitable reaction against the strictures imposed by orthodoxies which were unable to make sense of the real world in all its complexity. The end of the Cold War and the rise of Postmodernism freed up new space for pluralist ventures, making possible a return to cross-disciplinary work in the vein of classical political economy (see below).

Second, an awareness of the meta-theoretical issues at stake is vital if the researcher drawing on a range of approaches is to recognise the potential dangers of such an exercise. Here, the distinction which Robert Cox draws between 'problem-solving theory' and 'critical theory' is enlightening. Recognising that theory is always for someone and for some purpose, Cox emphasises that different approaches employ theory as either (i) a problem-solving device to help correct specific dysfunctions that occur within an existing social context or order, or (ii) as a means of appraising the very framework or problematic (i.e. order) which problem-solving theory accepts as its parameters (1981, pp. 128–9). He goes on to point out that, consequently, problem-solving approaches tend to work within a synchronic framework of analysis, and critical approaches within a diachronic one. Essentially, this suggests no good reason why someone should not adopt one or other type of approach according to the particular needs of their research. Indeed, as Cox makes explicit in later writings (1995), critical theory need not be required to supplant problem-solving theory because each performs a different function. Problem-solving approaches, such as variants of realism, need not be totalising in their reductionism just as critical approaches, such as variants of Marxism, need not be totalising in their determinism. Provided that users are aware of the meta-theoretical issues involved – i.e. the practical limitations and implications of each approach – no good reason exists as to why researchers should not draw upon both according to the exigencies of their investigation. Susan Strange is one example of a scholar who has been doing this for years, and she has openly called for more academics to join her in going beyond 'protestant parsimony' to embrace 'catholic complexity' (1994, p. 218).

Globalisation studies is an area where such 'catholic' approaches are relatively well established, at least in part due to the transdisciplinary nature – indeed, 'global-ness' – of the topic. As globalisation has attained prominence, work in a range of different social science disciplines has begun to problematise it from different perspectives. According to their professional and personal interests, economists, political scientists, sociologists, and geographers have highlighted different aspects of globalisation, and since disciplinary boundaries are artificial and porous, a growing cross-fertilisation of ideas has taken place. Sub-disciplines such as international political economy (IPE) within international relations (IR), various approaches under the umbrella of new institutional economics (NIE), economic and political geography, economic sociology and cultural studies among others find their *raison d'etre* in going beyond the narrow confines of orthodox approaches within their disciplines. In recent years, several more formal attempts have been made to put together an open analytical framework which draws on related insights from such counter-currents. Two such projects which have particularly inspired this book's pluralistic approach are 'heterodox' or 'inclusive' IPE (*RIPE* 1994; Danemark and O'Brien 1997) and 'new political economy' (Gamble 1995).[9]

Epistemologically, this book seeks to combine the historical and institutionalist analysis of structure with rationalist analysis of agency. It draws on plural ontologies (e.g. state and nonstate actors, individuals and classes, corporations and economic sectors) used across a range of relevant literatures in order to construct a broad and inclusive approach necessary for examining wide-ranging (e.g. global) issues which, by nature, transcend the boundaries of any single discipline or body of knowledge. Recognising the social and cultural embeddedness of markets avoids the clinical separation of economic and noneconomic processes; simultaneously, emphasising structured as well as nonstructured action provides for a nonteleological approach.

In addition to these methodological concerns, the other risk for a pluralist approach is that seeking to accommodate alternative perspectives may result in vague analytical practice and the loss of a distinct 'voice' to the dominant interpretive frameworks in scholarship. In this regard, this book proceeds upon the calculation that in the particular context of the current globalisation debate, the benefits of pluralism outweigh its disadvantages. The rationale underlying this judgment is explored in greater detail in Chapter One.

(iii) The Structure of this Book

Freed by its pluralist orientation, this book's methodological framework is determined simply by its mandate of investigating the economic, political and social effects of financial globalisation in and on Japan. And unlike comparative studies, there is no need for its research agenda to conform to a prespecified framework for analysis.

In a nutshell, this book sets out to do three things: (i) establish an understanding of the substance of financial globalisation and (ii) identify the state of the current debate concerning its impact on national regulatory, corporate and social structures, before (iii) empirically mapping the case of

Japan in each of these three areas. Rather than compiling anecdotal evidence in support of a particular understanding of financial globalisation, it seeks to investigate, in the consciousness of existing global structural dynamics, the effects which changes in the worldwide financial services industry are exerting upon Japan. Hereby, it aims to shed light on financial globalisation's contentious link with the notion of convergence among diverse national institutional structures.[10]

Chapter 1 begins by reviewing the theoretical background of globalisation, as furthered by its leading proponents, in order to show that a coherent problematisation of the concept is both logically possible and empirically sustainable when applied to recent developments in the economic arena. Drawing on secondary and original research in the field of finance, it goes on to map the reality of financial globalisation by examining the processes and products by which it has progressed. Against this background, it becomes possible to review the conclusions which scholars have made thus far concerning the current state of financial globalisation and its impact upon hitherto diverse national systems of political economy. This impact can be set out in terms of financial globalisation's effects on (i) state regulatory structures, (ii) national financial systems, and (iii) domestic social orders in order to provide an agenda for the book's empirical research which occupies the three subsequent chapters.

Chapter 2 examines the effects of globalisation on financial policymaking in Japan. It starts with an overview of the history of Japan's modern financial system, and goes on to examine its regulatory transformation over the 1970s, 1980s and 1990s. It ends with a detailed analysis of the country's latest and most radical financial deregulatory programme since the Occupation, the Japanese-style 'Big Bang' which was announced in November 1996. It concludes that in spite of considerable evidence to suggest that financial regulation in Japan is converging on an Anglo-American model, the country's regulatory environment continues to express, albeit less explicitly than before, most of the particularistic institutional structures which have historically characterised it.

Chapter 3 examines the effects of financial globalisation on Japan's financial services sector. It reviews the internationalisation of Japanese financial institutions in the postwar period, and examines their meteoric rise to global dominance in the 1980s and subsequent retrenchment in the 1990s. It ends by charting their responses to the Big Bang in a detailed case study, and concludes that there is considerable recent evidence in support of the convergence hypothesis. For the foreseeable future, however, it is clear that Japanese financial institutions will continue to exhibit many of their particularistic institutional characteristics, partly because they are physically incapable of following the lead of top Western financial institutions, and partly because their senior management are loath to abandon several of their traditionally 'Japanese' traits.

Chapter 4 investigates the effects of financial globalisation on Japanese society more generally. It sets out the macroeconomic effects of Japan's nonconvergence in the past, and examines how national political and institutional structures have hampered the Japanese economy's performance in the 1990s. It then turns to examine the microeconomic effects of financial globalisation as they have impacted the corporate and household sectors of the economy, primarily via the actions of the state and financial institutions. A case study of key aspects of the Big Bang anticipates the implications which current developments will have for Japanese society, and the chapter concludes that convergence is taking place, but at a significantly retarded pace.

The book's Conclusion relates its empirical findings to the state of the debate outlined in the first chapter. It confirms that as a result of its continued record of 'gradualism' in financial modernisation (Endo 1996a), Japan is still 'converging awkwardly' with the world of Western capitalism (Asher 1996a). Hereby, it finds little evidence to support the notion of the state being radically transformed by financial globalisation into the sort of proactive and undemocratic 'competition state' identified by some theorists in the West (Cerny 1990; 1997). Recent deregulation associated with Big Bang gives the impression that sweeping changes are afoot, but the substance of the country's convergence turns out to be considerably less than first appearances suggest. A systematic study shows that structural trends of continuity are still at least as strong as those for change in many areas of the financial system. Essentially, the country is continuing to seek a 'middle way' between the traditional Japanese financial model and a cutting-edge Anglo-American financial model. This does not bode well for the international competitiveness of the Japanese economy, but this is what the country's political system has produced to date. Financial globalisation is hereby confirmed to be a powerful structural development to which policymakers and financial institutions in Japan are responding, but it has yet to attain a level of ascendancy which would allow us to consistently predict, even retrospectively, the responses of these actors.

Thus, this book refines our understanding of the concept of globalisation by incorporating evidence from a the world's most economically advanced nonwestern state. It also adds to our understanding of contemporary Japan by systematically documenting the way in which the state and private actors have reacted to contemporary global market developments. Finally, it is hoped that the empirical research gathered constitutes a contribution to the data available to scholars seeking to understand Japan's political economy in general, and the country's current Big Bang programme of financial deregulation in particular.

Part One

Financial Globalisation in Theory and Practice

Chapter 1
Beyond Partisan Agendas

Introduction

This chapter sets out to establish an understanding of financial globalisation both in theory and in practice. It draws on work from a variety of disciplines to create a holistic picture of financial globalisation.

The first section reviews the current state of the economic globalisation debate and makes use of a foundational conception of globalisation to get beyond the intransigence of much recent work in the field. It argues that the term globalisation is applicable to recent developments in the economic sphere, and highlights the way in which the process has progressed in the context of new technological possibilities via a complex dynamic of deregulation and competitive innovation. The second section proceeds to analyse developments in the financial sector in order to construct an empirical picture of the mechanics and current state of financial globalisation. Key deregulatory moments and competitive innovations are reviewed and quantitative indicators of current levels of integration are surveyed. The third section explores the implications for institutional convergence. Recent developments in the regulatory regimes, financial systems and social structures of advanced capitalist states are examined. Evidence of institutional structures becoming more similar in significant and unprecedented ways is unearthed.

1.1 THE POLITICAL ECONOMY OF ECONOMIC GLOBALISATION

A properly conceived notion of globalisation can provide a valid and useful framework for examining contemporary developments in the economic sphere. The staleness of much of the current debate on globalisation can be circumvented by employing a back-to-basics working definition of the concept. This, in turn, can provide a means of reconciling many competing observations about economic globalisation.

(i) An Intransigent Debate

The economic globalisation debate is in deadlock. Rodrik has described it as 'a dialogue of the deaf' (1997, p. 20), and there are at least three reasons as to why contributors do not hear each other. First, participants appear disinterested in establishing foundations for the debate. A lack of general agreement on even the most basic point of reference – namely, a minimal definition of globalisation – is the foremost impediment to real dialogue. To the extent that contributors insist on asserting, explicitly or implicitly, arbitrary definitions to bolster preconceived theses, they argue at cross purposes. However, as the next section shows, a very adequate, broad and nontotalising framework of reference already exists. It can be speculated that participants do not avail themselves of this aid out of ignorance/ laziness, or wariness that it would lead them closer to those they oppose than they wish to be, a consideration which might lessen the force of their platform. Unfortunately, of the few that have grounded their work in such foundations, a failure to make this explicit has encouraged reviewers to brush away their efforts as lightly as the ungrounded efforts of others.[1]

Second, participants tend to oversimplify the field in their eagerness to carve out a space for their own contribution to the debate. Reducing the field to nice, neat and oversimplified taxonomies from which one can proceed by a banal form of dialectical method is poor scholarship. But in this case, failing to engage with the debate in its complex totality exacerbates the existing impasse in dialogue since opponents' positions are parodied to the point of absurdity. Ironically, it is the Critical Theorists and others on the Left who, for all their avowed metatheoretical consciousness and rejection of reductionism, tend to be most culpable.[2] Through their critiques, Ohmae's (1990) *Borderless World* has attained a status in political science out of all proportion to its status as a popular work by a Japanese management theorist written in hyperbolic tone. In many cases, such potshots across disciplinary (and national) boundaries serve no purpose other than to detract from an author's failure to engage with the more complex and topical real 'meat' of the debate. By contrast, many on the Right tend to avoid this trap only by default, largely ignoring the fact that globalisation is a contested concept at all. In both respects, Cox's (1981) observations about theoretical perspective – in particular, the distinctions he draws between 'problem-solving theory' and 'critical theory' mentioned in the introduction to this book – shed light on why this may occur.

There are several ways around this dilemma, but most are less than satisfactory. Jones (1995) stresses the complexity of the concept of globalisation as a multilayered and multilevel process which can be easily misconstrued by the unwary. He shows that it cannot be captured adequately by parsimonious approaches which tend to be excessively 'rationalistic' or by unduly optimistic approaches which tend to be 'functionalistic'. Instead, he suggests that a 'constructivist' or 'structurationist' approach is better but, by failing to conceptually differentiate globalisation from interdependence, his framework for analysis can only be applied to globalisation as a rhetorical critique. Hirst and Thompson seek to dodge the problem of reductionism by admitting up-front their strategy of interrogating 'an extreme and one-sided ideal type' of the globalisation thesis (1996, p. 7). Out of their concern that the rhetoric of globalisation may destroy the political will to seek a means to maintain output, employment and social equality in advanced countries to the detriment of long-term economic performance, they imply that this is a legitimate way to illuminate a more complex reality (pp. 15–16; see also Hirst 1997, p. 410). However, their effort is contrived since it involves assembling considerable empirical and intellectual resources to overwhelm what they themselves recognised was only ever a straw man. Others, mostly older and (presumably) wiser scholars, tend not to get involved in the debate at all. Rather, they forge ahead with their own projects which sooner or later become recognised according to the merit they deserve (e.g. Susan Strange and Phil Cerny).

Third, the sheer size of the topic tends to magnify and entrench the repercussions of the first two obstacles. The pool of empirical data from which researchers can draw evidence is bottomless; even without resorting to misrepresentation it is possible to fortify almost any reading of globalisation. Thus, it is not so much that 'globalisation becomes a "horse for every course"' (Amoore *et al.* 1997, p. 182), but rather that globalisation becomes a course for every horse. Each author is able to heighten and lower the hurdles and construct the track in such a way as to predetermine the outcome of the race for whichever 'horses' he/she chooses to mount. Of course, it is to be expected that scholars in a range of fields will approach globalisation from different disciplinary angles, using different tools, and subject to various professional and personal interests and agendas. But to the extent that these considerations are not recognised, commentators who seek to reduce the field to a single dimension and make direct comparisons about the truth-value content of one approach versus another court reductionism in their efforts.

Yet this is not to suggest that one cannot legitimately divide up the field in order to make it navigable. A sensitive approach can discern, for instance, a spectrum of understandings of globalisation from 'malign' to 'benign' (Jones 1997, p. 50), on which some, but by no means everybody's, readings can be plotted. At the malign extreme fall those of the far Right as well as Left: for example, the outspoken American broadcaster Chuck Harder, who has condemned globalisation as 'TREASON' (cited in Rupert 1997, p. 110, 113), and Gills, who in a recent editorial of *New Political Economy* special issue on globalisation outlines their mission to 'expose the "litany of sins" of globalisation discourse' (*NPE* 2:1, 1997, p. 12).[3] Both examples ultimately reject the concept: Harder dismisses it summarily as 'globaloney', and the various *NPE* contributors conclude that it is too misleading a concept to be of any analytical or explanatory value (see also Marshall 1996, p. 214). Other popular ways of dividing up the field are between those who offer 'stronger' or 'weaker' versions of the thesis (e.g. Weiss 1997, pp. 5–6); between accounts which are based in conservatism and liberalism (e.g. Scholte 1996, pp. 49–53); and between those who support an extreme version of the globalisation thesis, the 'hyper-globalisation school', and those who reject the term categorically, the 'globalisation skeptics' (Perraton *et al.* 1997, pp. 257–8). As most of these divisions remain unqualified – little attempt is made to account for the variety of contributors' viewpoints which do not fit neatly into such simple taxonomies (see again work by Strange and Cerny, among others) – they can serve only as a broad and introductory framework for orientation, and must be discarded as soon as they begin to hinder rather than help our understanding of the field.

(ii) Invoking Precursor and Postmodern Theories of Globalisation

For all its torpid postmodern jargon, a now substantial body of literature in Sociology which theorises globalisation itself offers a highly practical and ready-made touchstone for the economic globalisation debate. It provides for a nontotalising working definition of the concept. Such an exercise has more than semantic significance. By measuring contemporary economic developments against a theoretical structure which can highlight and systematise potentially new and significant changes, a nuanced understanding of globalisation promises to provide a new perspective on the state of late-modern capitalism.

In his literature review of precursor and postmodern theories of globalisation, Waters (1995) shows how theorisation of the social and political implications of modern supranational economic issues developed, for much of the Twentieth Century, within the field of international relations (IR). Reflecting the classical debates of the discipline,[4] three precursor theories emerged – American Functionalism, World Capitalism, and Transnationalisation – tracing their genealogies back to the work of Durkheim (1984), Marx (1977) and Weber (1978), respectively. From a realist perspective, Bell (1976) stressed the emergence of competing 'postindustrial societies'; from a Marxist perspective, Sklair (1991) emphasised the role of transnational corporations (TNCs) in promoting the emergence of a new capitalist class; and from a liberal perspective, Rosenau (1980) pointed to how the spread of transnational economic relations heightened patterns of interdependence. Recently, this embryonic issue-area has been revolutionised by the emergence from other disciplines, principally Sociology, of various full-blown conceptualisations of globalisation. These have not rendered earlier approaches in IR obsolete, but they have paved the way for convergence in the way in which Western social science understands the direction in which late-modern capitalism is heading. The following brief synopsis of the contributions of five key figures in this debate demonstrates this by highlighting areas of general consensus.

First is Robertson (1992), who holds possibly the strongest claim to paternity of the concept of globalisation. For him, globalisation 'refers to both the compression of the world and the intensification of consciousness of the world as a whole ... both concrete global interdependence and consciousness of the global whole in the Twentieth Century' (1992, p. 8). By pointing out how military/security issues today are redefined in terms of 'world-order', economic issues in terms of 'world booms' and 'global recessions', religious issues in terms of ecumenism, citizenship in terms of 'human rights', and environmental crises in terms of 'saving the planet', he shows that individual phenomenologies are increasingly addressed to the entire world rather than to the local or national level. Modernisation, he asserts, accelerates this inherent process, but what separates globalisation in the contemporary era from its earlier manifestations is its dialectical reflexivity. That is, people now conceptualise the world as a whole and so they reproduce it as a single unit. For Robertson, globalisation follows its own inexorable logic: by bringing differences into sharp contrast it provokes a response, but it is impossible to predict into what shape the single system will metamorphose.

Second is Giddens (1990), another sociologist and Robertson's main rival for the mantle of parent of the concept. For him, globalisation represents a 'radicalising of modernity' characterised by 'the distanction of time from space' (1990, p. 64). Time and space become liberated from each other as a direct consequence of two 'disembedding mechanisms' of modernity: 'symbolic tokens' and 'expert systems'. Money is the archetypal symbolic token because it can transfer value from context to context and thus make social relations possible across great expanses of time and space, while repositories of technical knowledge become expert systems which can be deployed across a wide range of actual (spatial) contexts. As a result of new technologies, social relations are freed increasingly to transcend their local contexts, although some are, of course, better placed to exploit opportunities than others. Thus, globalisation is full of contingency, and is likely to fragment just as it coordinates.

Third are Lash and Urry (1994), who also use the notion of time-space distanction, but draw more vivid conclusions. Whereas Giddens posits current transformations to be a continuation of modernity, they insist on postmodernism being understood as a fundamental disjuncture. They assert that the previous era of 'organised capitalism', in which production was tightly arranged in time and space by firms and states, is being progressively eroded by the increasing velocity of flows of information and goods, made possible by new technologies. For them, globalisation involves the 'dematerialisation' of objects which are reproduced symbolically as 'a decentred set of economies of signs in space' in a new world order (1994, p. 280).

Fourth is Harvey (1989), a geographer who adopts similar concepts, but argues that the objectification and universalisation of the concepts has allowed time to annihilate space. He argues that history proceeds by short and intense periods of technological change, such as the Industrial Revolution, which provide for 'time-space compression', effectively shortening the time needed to accomplish things and reducing the experiential distances between different points in space. He asserts that the Telecommunications Revolution, which he dates to around 1970, has substantially eroded spatial barriers and essentially transformed the world into a single field of action within which capitalism can operate.

Fifth is Beck (1992), a sociologist who places risk at the centre of his analysis of contemporary social change. He asserts that today most of the industrialised world lives in a 'post-scarcity society' in which our priorities must increasingly address the side effects of our own modernisation. New risks like radioactivity and global warming are qualitatively different from the hazards of the past in that often they are imperceptible to the senses and no longer tied to their local origins. Such risks globalise because they universalise and equalise, and both our realisation of their consequences and search for possible solutions reinforce our consciousness of the global whole.[5]

From this exercise it is possible to draw out, irrespective of numerous outstanding points of debate, a five-point canon of how globalisation is currently understood by its leading theorists.[6]

- Globalisation is *at least* contemporaneous with modernisation;
- It involves the systematic integration of social ties such that, in a fully globalised context, no given relationship or set of relationships can remain isolated or bounded since each is linked to all others and systematically affected by them;
- It describes a phenomenological process that alters the scaler appearance of the world measured in time and space, and this is at least partially a result of the application of new technologies;
- Its phenomenology is reflexive and self-fulfilling, as people individually and collectively orient their thoughts and actions to the world as a whole;
- It affects social relations concretely because of its implications for risk and trust.

This canon can be applied to the economic globalisation debate where it provides a means of resolving, or at least circumventing, the existing logjam.

Specifically, the problematic issue of whether or not economic globalisation is a new phenomenon, which some have argued should be the fundamental point of departure for the debate (e.g. Piven 1995, p. 109), can be left to one side. Theoretically speaking, this issue parallels the ongoing debate noted above of whether or not globalisation represents a continuation of, radicalisation of, or disjuncture in modernisation. Thus, one can assert a basic requirement of economic globalisation being understood as at least contemporaneous with economic internationalisation – i.e. interdependence (see Jones 1995) – to deal minimally but satisfactorily with the issue.[7] This manoeuvre, however, should not be taken as scholarly sleight of hand, opening the door to an 'anything counts' definition of economic globalisation. To fulfil the proper requirement that the term be distinguished from others in order to make it analytically useful, the following three assertions represent a minimal definition and working guidelines for the term's application:

- Economic globalisation describes a phenomenological process of socio-economic integration;
- It cannot be used to describe a mere *quantitative* progression in the degree of international interconnectedness, but must be understood to engender a *qualitatively* different structure of integration within the world economy;
- It should only be applied in the case where a new, structurally different and highly significant pattern of interconnection within the world economy can be identified as largely superseding the hitherto dominant pattern of world economic exchange, which was organised internationally.

The question thus becomes an empirical one: Are contemporary developments in the economic sphere sufficiently *new* and *significant* as to make application of the term 'globalisation' appropriate? Proving this one way or the other is somewhat problematic. Apart from the difficulties already noted which the sheer size of the topic presents, the fact that qualitative change is to be considered at least as significant as quantitative change means that, as Perraton *et al.* note, economic globalisation 'cannot simply be read off' from quantitative indices of trade, investment, and so on. (1997, p. 259).[8] While Section 1.2 grapples with this problem in regard to financial globalisation, here it is sufficient to note that Perraton *et al.* have reviewed already a considerable amount of evidence for economic globalisation with such criteria in mind. They broadly assert that qualitative as well as quantitative changes are notable in three areas: (i) world trade flows today are more extensive and intensive than ever before, (ii) world financial flows also are more extensive and intensive than ever, and (iii) the role of multinational corporations in world trade, finance and politics is concomitantly more significant than ever.[9]

It should be noted that commentators who reject the existence of economic globalisation on the basis of empirical evidence generally do so on the grounds that (i) it is not new, (ii) the benefits to corporations prophesied by some proponents have not materialised, and (iii) it has not proved universal and worldwide in scope (e.g. Hirst and Thomson 1996; Weiss 1997). None of these reasons stand up as objections against a theoretically grounded understanding of the concept such as this. The issue of the newness of globalisation has already been dealt with, and the notion of globalisation totally transforming corporate life rests upon a transparently selective reading of the thesis and a highly subjective interpretation of the evidence. However, the idea that globalisation equates with a state of totality and uniformity deserves more explicit comment. At the risk of stating the obvious, the etymology of the word globalisation suggests that it should be understood as a *process* of transition rather than an end-state or destination. In this regard, Perraton *et al.* observe that 'the conception of global markets is often conflated with perfect markets, so that, when international markets do not operate as textbook perfect markets, this is erroneously taken as evidence against globalisation' (1997, p. 258). Moreover, the claim of a nuanced version of the globalisation thesis that the phenomenon of distance (measured in time and space) is being rendered less relevant does not imply automatically that geography is becoming less important or that development is becoming universal and even. A large body of theoretically grounded literature in economic geography attests to the fact that under globalisation, specific 'places' are, if anything, becoming more important. Work on international financial centres, for example, shows the increasing importance of 'agglomeration economies' for hard- as well as soft- (i.e. social) infrastructure (e.g. Sassen 1991; Thrift 1994; Budd 1995).

The next subsection corroborates this by showing how economic globalisation exaggerates patterns of unevenness and inequality in many areas. It also explodes a related myth – that globalisation implies the end of the nation-state.

(iii) A Nuanced Conception of Economic Globalisation

Economic globalisation is ultimately nothing more than an umbrella term employed as a convenient way of framing a host of recent and interconnected developments which relate to the economic sphere but are thought to be significant for the ramifications which they also entail for social and political life. In examining how economic globalisation progresses and what it actually implies, three areas are particularly noteworthy: (i) the impact of technology on competitive innovation and economies of scale and scope, (ii) the ascendance of financial and knowledge structures and their exploitation by transnational elites, and (iii) the repercussions of these developments for state-market relations.

Competitive innovation and economies of scale and scope

Economic globalisation is frequently associated with new computer and communications technologies but, as Cohen points out, technological innovation *per se* cannot account for it because 'any approach that causally links an outcome (globalisation) to its own defining characteristics (competition and innovation) borders on the tautological' (1996, p. 275). Rather, technological developments must be seen as having *facilitated* a number of new developments in the way economic relations are structured by firms and governments, though they have no agency role in and of themselves. In this regard, one author designated technological change as the 'main independent variable' in the process of economic globalisation (Cerny 1994, p. 319).

Firms' exploitation of new technologies since the 1970s has been captured under at least two blanket concepts: the introduction of post-Fordist production methods, which tend to emphasise the spread of new organisational forms, and the Third Industrial Revolution, which highlights the transformative impact which information technology has had on all areas of business.

The widespread adoption of 'flexible' post-Fordist manufacturing systems is seen as having contributed significantly to a qualitative transformation in the productive process.[10] In management studies, post-Fordism is associated with small-batch production of a variety of products, the use of 'flexible' machinery, the physical reorganisation of factories to stress reduced inventories and defect rates, the decentralisation of manufacturing-related decision-making to workers on the shop floor, and the application of microelectronics to product and process design and to production machinery. Aware of the concept's theoretical roots, Bernard argues that post-Fordism is better understood not as a specific set of practices, but rather in terms of *links* between various production units and the institutional contexts in which they are located (1994, p. 220): the now dominant 'networked' production structure serves to encourage inter- and intrafirm links across national borders which can better exploit local comparative advantage structures. As a result, the power of labour and the state relative to capital is weakened, and productive relations are restructured into a transnational core-periphery model.

The notion of a Third Industrial Revolution (Castells 1989/Cerny 1995) engenders considerable overlap with post-Fordism. New computational and communications technologies have paved the way for 'flexibalisation' in the production and marketing of goods and services, enhanced employee and customer monitoring systems, facilitated 'lean' management, and fostered decentralised and networked organisational structures. As with the previous industrial revolutions, there have been serious and wide-ranging social repercussions, the most significant of which are outlined below.

One way in which leading firms have sought to exploit these new opportunities has been pursuing economies of scale and scope on a supranational basis. Driven by self-perpetuating competitive pressures, economic globalisation in the 1980s and 1990s was not so much a smooth, linear, quantitative spatial progression as a qualitative change in the dominant wisdom concerning corporate strategy. During the 1980s, management literature reflected new competitive possibilities, and therefore pressures, by conveying the message that firms would have to 'go global' if they were to survive in the new environment. A spreading awareness of tumbling crossborder transaction costs highlighted not only the possibility of gaining access to a larger market, but heralded the onset of unprecedented levels of competition as national markets became increasingly difficult to protect against entry by foreign competitors. The heightened price sensitivity of financial markets added significantly to the intensification of these competitive pressures, and the exploitation of marginal differences in rates of return became more important in almost all sectors of the economy. Against this background, the hunt for competitive advantages took on added urgency and, in accordance with classical economic theory, the pursuit of economies of scale and scope were seized upon as being of paramount importance.

In retrospect, the 'high growth 1980s' were characterised by corporate strategies which focused upon aggressive domestic and international expansion and the maximisation of market share.[11] Cut-and-thrust management action in the form of takeovers and divestitures were rewarded by the financial markets, and multinational conglomerates such as Hanson Trust epitomised the definitive industrial structure of the decade – large, predatory, cash rich, and heavily diversified. In this sense, management literature, corporate strategy and financial market rewards began to act in concert to reinforce the idea that the best firms were those thinking 'globally'. By contrast, the more sober 1990s saw significant amendments to this 'common sense'. Management theorists peddled new euphemistic concepts such as 'reengineering', 'downsizing', 'consolidation', and 'de-merger' in order to help businesses purge themselves of their excesses and implement leaner, fitter corporate structures. More generally, the emphasis shifted from crude size and capital gains to profitability and shareholder value, from market desegmentation to resegmentation and even microsegmentation; and from economies of scale to economies of scope and flexibility. Inevitably, skeptics saw these changes as another short term anomaly, but many accepted them as a more fundamental adjustment.[12] Either way, this reverse course is important to note because it highlights the fact that globalisation is more than the physical process of transnational corporate expansion or even operation. Economic globalisation takes place when the physical capacity for integration is reflected in the subjective consciousness of individuals who reflexively and ever more widely orient their thoughts and actions towards a globally integrated economy in a self-fulfilling dynamic. Conceived as such, it is unlikely that economic globalisation has receded with the retrenchment in corporate operations in the 1990s. Empirical data serves only as a crude and anecdotal general indicator of a deeper, structural-level process.[13]

In sum, the accelerated pace of innovation and technological change since the 1970s has facilitated an unprecedented degree of transnational capital and factor mobility. Crossborder investment and economic operations are physically easier, quicker and cheaper than ever before as new technologies have facilitated a phenomenological restructuring of corporate time and space. Such possibilities have fostered a qualitatively different structure of economic relations as actors became increasingly reflexive (i.e. globally conscious) in their decisionmaking and actions. Globalisation proceeds as the objective reality of new technological possibilities permeates and is reflected in the subjective strategies of producers, consumers and regulators.

Financial structures, knowledge structures and transnational elites

Economic globalisation necessarily has significant repercussions for social relations because it entails changes to who gets what, i.e. the question *cui bono*? which Strange suggests should lie at the heart of all political economy (1988, p. 234). Drawing on the work of various political economists and economic sociologists, Strange's (1998) concepts of the financial structure and the knowledge structure provide a framework for analysing the changes in social power relations associated with economic globalisation.

The financial structure refers to the power conferred by control over credit in a modern economy. Marxist approaches are especially well placed to theorise such relations because they understand capital in social terms – capital exploits labour by extracting a surplus. Moreover, they show how the unique mobility and of money makes control of the financial structure a central feature of the power of the capital class over labour (see Dodd 1994). However, important theoretical contributions have also been made in the elitist tradition (Mills 1942) and the corporatist tradition (Lindblom 1977),[14] such that a synthesis of insights from all three schools is evident in most recent work which addresses the privileged position of internationally mobile finance capital in the contemporary world economy. A representative example is Cerny's assertion that '[m]oney is not merely an economic phenomenon; like ideology, it is also a cultural phenomenon. Finance thus constitutes an intellectual challenge different in kind from most other structural issue areas in international relations' (1993a, p. 5). This power operates at both the behavioural and structural levels, and with the division of the globe into rival states, the ascendance of internationally mobile finance over states, labour, and nationally constrained capital is dramatically increased thanks to the many new opportunities for investment arbitrage, i.e. profitably exploiting price differentials which may exist in seperate but bridgable markets.[15]

At the macro- or interstate level, the power of the financial structure is affected by the international politico-legal framework which is in place at any given time. The New Liberal Order which has emerged since the 1970s has dramatically strengthened the ascendance of the financial structure over both states and firms. Its institutionalisation was a result of successive policies of competitive deregulation undertaken by core states following the collapse of the Bretton Woods framework of fixed exchange rates (Helleiner 1994). Floating exchange rates meant that, by selling certain currencies short,[16] financial markets were able to exert discipline much more easily on governments which pursued policies that were collectively deemed unsustainable; the deregulation of capital controls meant that capital could flow overseas much more easily to take advantage of relatively more attractive investment opportunities. Systematic analyses by scholars in IPE, as well as considerable anecdotal evidence, suggests that hereby, states have become increasingly constrained in their policy options. Strange (1987) shows that some states are more constrained than others, with the US benefiting from its own form of structural power within the system, due to its size, position at the forefront of deregulation and other reasons. Kurzer's (1993) comparative work on state responses to international capital market discipline in Austria, Belgium, the Netherlands and Sweden during the 1980s demonstrates the vulnerability of smaller states. She found that

> [a]s business and finance became more mobile, their power resources increased and those of labour decreased ... the greater mobility of capital and deepening financial integration corroded social concertation ... Consequently, governments have lost the ability to carve out national strategies and sustain social accords (1993, p. viii).[17]

To these, numerous high-profile policy reversals can be added which increasingly appear to confirm Margaret Thatcher's famous maxim that 'you can't buck the markets!': the UK pound and the Italian lira being forced out of European Exchange Rate Mechanism (ERM) in 1992, and the French franc in 1993, and the recent Asian currency crisis of 1997, which is engendering much larger social and political consequences (Henderson 1998). Accordingly, Frieden asserts that finance has become 'the pivot around which the world economy twists and turns, and it affects politics and economies in every nation' (1987, p. 1), and Cerny postulates that

> [g]overnments, international regimes and regulatory authorities within governments will increasingly come to be 'whipsawed' by different sectors and firms in the financial services industry seeking the most

amenable regulators and the most permissive rules – what is called 'regulatory arbitrage' or 'competition in laxity' – as states themselves are increasingly fragmented and constrained by the imperatives of international financial competition (1993, pp. 15–16).[18]

This is not to say that capital's veto is absolute. Cohen, for example, gives three reasons why the power of the financial markets might not be as great as it is often assumed to be (1996, pp. 282–3). First, there are limits to just how much can be accomplished by independent fiscal and monetary policies, even in the absence of a high degree of capital mobility.[19] Second, international financial integration is far from seamless and, as Maxfield has pointed out (1990), not all international investors are quite so highly sensitive to monetary and fiscal differences between countries. Third, a tradeoff still exists between currency stability and policy autonomy.[20] That is, domestic economic policies need not be fatally compromised as long as governments are willing to tolerate a degree of currency volatility abroad.[21] In sum, Cohen's citation of Pauly (1995) is instructive:

> Capital mobility constrains states, but not in an absolute sense ... Analysts should therefore be cautious when interpreting the current dimensions of international capital flows as constituting an exogenous structure that irrevocably binds societies or their states (1996, p. 276).

At the micro- or intercorporate level, the power of the financial structure is also affected by endogenous change in the capital market itself. Work within Economic Sociology, a subdiscipline of NIE, examines the changing relationships between financial and nonfinancial institutions and finds that the power wielded by the financial sector over the nonfinancial sector has increased in recent years.[22] Financial control theorists have shown how a general increase in firms' reliance on external capital irrespective of business conditions has led to a sharp rise in external control by financial institutions since 1970 (e.g. Stearns 1990).[23] Hegemony is exercised both structurally and behaviourally, via a combination of financial institutions' control over access to the pool of capital for investment, their substantial stock holdings, and their centrality in the network of interlocking corporate directorates. Stearns argues that firms' increasing risk-averseness in investment decisions, and their prioritisation of short-term profits often at the expense of long-term viability, is a direct consequence of the exercise of such power. This concurs with claims made by scholars in other fields, such as Cerny's observation that under globalisation, financial markets have come to epitomise the structural ascendance of nonspecific assets over specific assets (1995, p. 617), and Cox's pronouncement that '[f]inance has become decoupled from production to become an independent power, an autocrat over the real economy' (1992a, p. 29).

If one accepts this trend of the financial sector's ascendance over the nonfinancial sector, it is necessary to explain periodic examples of intersectoral cooperation and intrasectoral discord. As to the former, social class theorists argue that cooperation between financial and nonfinancial institutions may be possible if it can be secured by exploiting asymmetrical power relations, or where a network of ties between corporate leaders allows them to overcome, at least episodically, the major conflicts of interest which tend to exist between sectors. Soref and Zeitlin's (1987) investigation of interlocking directorates in the US suggests the emergence of a new group of finance capitalists who lead both financial and nonfinancial corporations. Hereby, they explain, major divisions are often successfully suppressed in order to facilitate coordination of the business community as a whole.[24] As to the latter, Mintz and Schwartz (1990) invoke a Gramscian-inspired theory of financial hegemony to shed light on the issue of episodic intrasectoral cooperation. They declare that cohesion within the financial sector is significantly enhanced by the high level of structural interdependence that exists between different institutions. This tends to mute competition and contribute to a united financial community which, although fragile at times, tends towards a similarity of interests in the long run. This claim is buttressed by evidence of firms acting in concert to determine the direction of capital flows, an action which is directly related to the dominant knowledge structures which are in place at any given time (see below).

The rapid progression of global financial market integration over the past twenty-five years, which the next section documents, has resulted in a new ascendance of the financial structure. Using Rosenau and Czempiel's (1992) term, it has come to constitute an emergent form of 'governance without government' in which nonstate actors – i.e. financial institutions – exert significant influence over global sociopolitical and economic affairs. Stopford and Strange (1991) propose that it is possible to interpret these changes using a 'triangular diplomacy' model to represent the emerging power relations between states, firms and markets. They argue that governments *as a group* have lost bargaining power to multinationals, but that more than anything else this is a result of intensified competition between states. At the same time, they maintain that the power of individual firms over the factors of production has also fallen as the result of intensified competition between firms. Herein, the market itself exerts increased power over firms. On a note of caution they conclude '[o]ne needs to separate the power to influence general policy from the power to insist on specific bargains' (p. 216).

The knowledge structure refers to the power conferred by control over knowledge in a modern economy. Such power has long been emphasised by scholars in the elitist tradition (e.g. Kirkpatrick 1979), but more recently it has become popular to adopt insights from the structuralist philosophy of

Foucault (1972; 1980) and others (e.g. Sinclair 1994a; 1994b).[25] Theoretically, this necessitates adding a second dimension to the concept of 'information elites' popularised by Drucker (1993) and Reich (1991). Such work draws on a Weberian concept of power – power accrues from the coordinating and gate-keeping positions occupied by key decision-makers and specialists in an organisation or society. By contrast, the idea of 'knowledge elites' is broader: it encompasses those who are able to set the normative parameters for what information is considered to be relevant to decisionmaking *per se*. Whereas information shapes action at the behavioural level, knowledge shapes ideology at the structural level because knowledge is a social construct. Thus, knowledge elites are able to (re-)define what is understood to constitute 'knowledge' in a given society.

Clearly, the increasing power of the financial structure noted above will accrue to those who benefit from the way in which the relationships between creditors and debtors, savers and investors are structured in the present economic environment. This means, first, those who coordinate and regulate economic decisions in terms of determining and communicating what is socially understood to constitute value (or 'de-value'), and, second, those who have or can potentially gain access to information which is likely to be deemed 'valuable'.

Two examples illustrate the point in regard to the former category. First, in the field of Economic Sociology, Montagna's (1990) work on accounting rationality highlights the role which public accountants play in bringing about the homogenisation of values, dispositions and orientations among private, state and professional organisations through a process of 'normative isomorphism'. Second, in the field of IPE, Sinclair's (1994a; 1994b) work on credit rating agencies illuminates their increasingly central function in the global capital allocation process. Both are cases of dominant knowledge-producing institutions which occupy a key position and work to shape and extend economic globalisation.[26]

Similarly, two examples illustrate the point in regard to the latter category. First is Nelson's (1995) work on the US, which relates the increasing professionalisation of management to heightened levels of social polarisation. In contrast to most current work in management studies, which focuses on the way in which business is increasingly structured around the dissemination of ideas and how knowledge has become a central aspect of competitive advantage (Peters and Waterman 1982; Porter 1985; Drucker 1993), Nelson juxtaposes his work against Chandler's (1977) classic statement of how the 'managerial revolution', contributed to postwar affluence in America. Second is Gill's (1990; Gill *et al.* 1992) identification of a broad category of 'transnational elites' who benefit directly from the new ascendance of the financial and knowledge structures associated with globalisation.[27] Gill shows how an informal alliance of intra- and interclass factions has formed among those holding positions in key strategic locations in TNCs, universities and research institutes, the media, government and international organisations. Members are highly geographically and professionally mobile, and their frequent interaction consciously and subconsciously works to promote the spread of neoliberalism and other ideas which are congenial to economic globalisation.

Cumulatively, this work highlights the way in which social relations are being altered through the oblique institutionalisation of new knowledge structures. As Thrift observes, this process is a significant contributor to, and consequence of, the dynamic of globalisation:

> ... it seems clear that the production, distribution and exchange of knowledge is a crucial element of the global economic system on a scale unknown in the previous international system. As with the fiscal structure, owing to the enormous inter-penetration of know-how and scientific culture between nation states and the rise of communications, media and information technologies, the knowledge structure is becoming less and less tied to particular national and local circumstances, after it has been released from its original context. (1994, pp. 366–7)

The reconfiguration of state-market relations

The changing nature of the state has been widely commented upon in recent years. Many of these changes can be linked to the aforementioned developments, as several theorists demonstrate. One example is Cerny (1990; 1997), who observes that a new kind of state – the 'competition' state – is emerging in advanced industrial economies. Another is Jessop (1993; 1994), who frames the changes in terms of a replacement of the postwar Keynesian welfare state with the neo-Schumpeterian workfare state. Of the two, Cerny's conception stresses more heavily the functional rationale underlying the change, and Jessop's the role of technological development in transforming the state's relationship with its citizens. Both agree that the state's role in society is changing rather than diminishing *per se*. That is, although the appearance is of the state's shrinkage and hollowing out, its withdrawal from investment and ownership in national economies tends to require compensation by a stronger role in the regulation of competition and, in sectors with monopolistic tendencies, of prices.[28] Hereby, the state cannot be considered purely as a casualty of economic globalisation; invariably, it has been also the agent of its own transformation through 'competitive' as well as 'defensive' deregulation.

> The net effect of globalization on governments will be to focus their efforts on a smaller set of more critical tasks. This implies a shrinkage of their optimal size (in terms of government employees; not

necessarily as a share of GDP) and an upgrading of the technical expertise of civil servants responsible for monetary, tax, social, and regulatory policies. These policies provide a key advantage (or handicap) to domestic firms in the global marketplace. They constitute part of the strategic assets (or liabilities) that create a firm's competitive edge. Speed is a critical determinant of this edge. Governments with rapid regulatory processes, carried out by expert professional staff, able to take account of international as well as domestic considerations, and efficient at providing the social services they choose to keep in the public sector, will be those whose firms have the best chance of competitive success in a globalized world. (Julius 1997, p. 468)

Cerny's work draws attention to the fact that the state's metamorphosis into a 'quasi-enterprise association' has been justified by a subtle change in the way gains from economic interaction are understood to accrue in the new global environment. Informed by recent work in business strategy (e.g. Porter 1985; 1990), the traditional Ricardian idea of 'comparative advantage' has been replaced with a notion of 'competitive advantage'. But as Krugman (1996) has pointed out, the former posits a positive-sum payoff from the economic interaction of states, whereas the latter involves a zero-sum payoff from the interaction of firms, the implication being that states are now involved in a Darwinian struggle for survival. It is on such grounds that the World Economic Forum's *World Competitiveness Report 1994* advocates protectionist measures in advanced economies for the sake of protecting jobs from competition from lower wage developing economies (cited in Krugman 1996, p. 75). From the point of international trade theory, Krugman argues, this logic is grotesque. He allows that comparative advantage structures can be positively influenced by government intervention in theory, but suggests that the necessary conditions and possible payoff are so far from being simple to identify and model as to make them irrelevant in practice (1996, p. 108–13).[29] On this point others differ, maintaining that because economic globalisation raises geometrically the payoff from strategic policy failures/successes, and advances the day of reckoning, such attempts are today important as never before (e.g. Julius 1997, p. 466).

Jessop observes that another integral element of this 'supply-side revolution' is the devolution of state powers both vertically – upward as well as downward – and horizontally (1994, p. 264). That is, state powers are transferred to a growing number of supra-, multi-, and international organisations, and to local, regional, and pan-regional bodies. In this way, sovereignty is pooled in a bid ultimately to protect it in an era of economic globalisation. While autonomy is usurped by the market's rise, it is also voluntarily ceded in the hope of matching state capacities to the new environment. Studies on international macroeconomic policy coordination (Webb 1994), and on public, semipublic, and private regimes in international finance (e.g. Porter 1993; Deane and Pringle 1994; Kapstein 1994; Underhill 1995; Coleman 1996), show how this process tends to foster the creation of transnational 'epistemic communities' (Haas 1992) which, in turn, represent new threats to democratic policymaking (see below).

The cumulative result of such changes, Cerny observes, is that the state's ability to create the communal solidarity (*gemeinschaft*) from which Western states have derived their legitimacy is diminished. In what tends to be interpreted as a Catch-22 situation, economic globalisation is taken to increase the demand for social insurance, by inflating levels of social inequality, while simultaneously reducing the ability of governments to redistribute wealth, since they must focus on attracting high value-added investment from TNCs in order to secure future national competitiveness (Rodrik 1997, p. 26). Thus, cutbacks are targeted at 'sunk costs', such as unemployment benefits and welfare, and often spare potential sources of comparative advantage, such as training and development budgets (Scholte 1997, p. 448).

The assumption underlying this doctrine of national competitiveness is that benefits will eventually 'trickle down' to all levels of society. Investment by TNCs creates employment directly as well as indirectly, and technology transfer promotes new comparative advantage structures. Hereby, as national wealth and sustainable tax revenues are maximised, minimum social safety nets will be sustainable in the long run. Hence, the director-general of UNCTAD, writing in a 1996 paper entitled *Globalization and Liberalization: Development in the Face of Two Powerful Currents*, can observe objectively 'the role of governments is progressively shifting towards providing an appropriate enabling environment for private enterprise' (cited in Scholte 1997, p. 446). Work by Strange confirms this shift towards 'facilitative' or 'infrastructural intervention' (1996, pp. 66–87) which Cox interprets bleakly as the state transforming itself into a mere 'transmission belt' for adjusting the national economy to the perceived exigencies of the new global economy (1992a, p. 31).

Gill explains this transition in neo-Marxist terms – inhering in and from the dominance of a 'new constitutionalist ideology' which seeks to establish and institutionalise a framework of legal and political structures favourable to neoliberal capitalism (1992, pp. 167–72; 1995a, pp. 412–8). He suggests that this hegemony has been strengthened by new technologies which present transnational elites with a panopticon of modern surveillance mechanisms to ensure that their interests are prioritised in public and private regimes at all levels of society. In this way, he links a privileged position in the knowledge structure to the extension of economic globalisation.

Unsurprisingly, this gives rise to concerns about a possible democratic deficit. Following Bull (1977), some have used the metaphor of a 'new mediaevalism' to describe the new environment which emerges as a result of the reconfiguration of state-market relations (e.g. Tanaka 1996; Gamble 1997). Such a conception stresses the apparent anarchy of contending and overlapping authority structures, previously the church, state, landlords, and so on, now markets, bureaucracies, networks. Invoking Polanyi (1994), who drew attention to a 'double movement' in the historical cycle of market deregulation and reregulation, scholars in a range of fields have speculated about the possibility of re-subordinating the market to social concerns (e.g. Cox 1992; Gill 1995b; Pauly 1995; Amin 1996; Germain 1997).[30] Opinions range from probable to improbable, and from imminent to remote. Jessop urges caution, arguing that the new state form appears to represent some sort of stable equilibrium since it functions both to resolve significant crisis tendencies of the Fordist state and to consolidate the emerging dynamic of the post-Fordist accumulation regime (1994, pp. 264–6).

In sum, the reconfiguration of state-market relations should be understood to be ushering in a new type of state, rather than the end of the nation-state *per se*. As Goldblatt *et al.* have stated, the state continues to be important both as a key site of political legitimacy and as the locus for considerable enduring powers (1997, pp. 269–70). Under economic globalisation, the competition state/neo-Schumpeterian workfare state represents nothing more than an archetype. Recent empirical research by Palan and Abbott (1996) supports the assertions of Cerny (1997, p. 267) and Jessop (1994, p. 266) that states pursue trial-and-error strategies in their attempts to adjust to their new environment. Even in cases where states are confronted by common problems and seek to implement identical solutions, their capacities to do so will usually be different.[31] This is because the social embeddedness of economic institutions necessarily implies that variation will persist (Boyer 1997).

1.2 THE EMPIRICAL REALITY OF FINANCIAL GLOBALISATION

The previous discussion suggests that the term 'financial globalisation' should refer to a qualitatively different stage of integration in the financial services industry, a new level of progressive enmeshment in which capital allocation decisions increasingly are addressed to the global level. A minimum prerequisite for this is the absence of effective international capital controls, and in this respect, the period 1815 to 1914, as well as the one since 1971, is often designated as an era of 'global finance' (e.g. Helleiner 1994).[32] Hereby, some commentators mistakenly assert that there is nothing fundamentally new about the present era (see section 1.1). The following section outlines the emergence of financial globalisation since the mid-1960s as a historically unique phenomenon which, against a background of new technological possibilities has progressed through a complex dialectic of competitive deregulation by states and competitive innovation by firms.

(i) Competitive Deregulation by States

Figure 1.1 provides a typical summary of major financial deregulatory measures undertaken in selected states in the postwar period.[33] Expressed in this form, no pattern is evident beyond the increasing frequency of deregulatory measures in the 1980s and 1990s. However, a more detailed, politically and economically conscious investigation reveals a clear pattern of competitive deregulation led largely, but not exclusively, by the US (see, for example, Helleiner 1994). A competitive dynamic of financial deregulation in core capitalist states was set in motion by, and institutionalised in, three related developments: (i) the conscious decisions of US and UK authorities not to impose restrictions on the embryonic eurodollar market in the 1960s, (ii) the abolition of capital controls in core states in the 1970s and 1980s, and (iii) the programmes of domestic financial sector deregulation implemented in the 1970s, 1980s and 1990s.

First was the US's tacit allowance of an extraterratorial market in dollars to emerge in London in the late 1950s. In the context of growing international criticism for its exploitation of seigniorage gains accruing from the dollar's position at the centre of the Gold Standard, the US Treasury saw the eurodollar market as a means of securing policy autonomy because the market's growth would remove much of the rationale for other governments to demand the conversion of swelling dollar reserves into gold. The British government did nothing to tax or otherwise regulate the embryonic eurodollar market for equally mercantilistic reasons. The Bank of England urged that an offshore market in dollars could provide a means for the UK to maintain its dominance in international trade financing in the face of the restrictions imposed on the pound as a result of the sterling crisis of 1957.

Once established, the eurodollar market grew rapidly. Nevertheless, under heavy commitments in Vietnam and elsewhere, the US's unabated exploitation continued to outstrip the patience of its allies, and Nixon eventually opted to suspend dollar-gold convertibility in August 1971 rather than compromise on domestic macroeconomic policy. Essentially, the fixed exchange rate regime established at Bretton Woods had been undermined by the existence of a pool of unregulated capital which made large private speculative currency flows possible. Several attempts were made to reestablish cooperative capital controls, including a G–10 central bankers agreement in June 1971 to limit the placement of funds in the euromarket to stem its growth, and a series of C-20 meetings which ended in deadlock in

Figure 1.1: Financial Deregulation in Selected Countries

	Price Liberalisation			Desegmentation					Regulation		
	Interest rates	Securities commissions	Securities transaction tax	Banking/ securities	Banking/ insurance	Short-term/ long-term financing	Trust banking	Interstate banking	Foreign exchange liberalisation	Deposit insurance	Prompt Corrective Action
Canada	1967	1983		1987	1992		1992		1967	1967	
France	1990	1989				1966			1990	1980	
Germany	1967		1991						1961	1966	
Hong Kong	1964								1973		
Italy	1984	1997		1987		1987			1990	1987	
Japan	1994	1999		1992*	1999*	1999	1992	1982	1980	1971	1999
Singapore	1975			1986					1978		
UK	1971	1986	1986						1979	1982	
US	1986	1975	1966		1997*			1994	1974	1933	1992

*indicates partial deregulation

[Source: based on Ministry of Finance (Japan), *Kinyu Jyānaru* 3/98, p. 39]

May 1973. However, with the US unconvinced that its interests would be served by cooperative initiatives, the decision was effectively settled by default. The subsequent OPEC oil price hikes reinforced the *status quo* as petrodollars flooded into the euromarkets. Ironically, governments and private enterprises alike found it expedient to borrow in the market to meet their sudden need for large quantities of hard currency (i.e. dollars) for rocketing energy bills.

Political scientists generally interpret these events as marking a shift in US hegemony, from a benign, cooperative style of leadership of the 'free world' to a competitive, coercive one. In the history of financial deregulation, however, they represent the initial undermining of the postwar public, multinational organisation of international economic management – what Ruggie (1982) terms 'embedded liberalism' – with reversion towards a quasiprivate, market-oriented regime. They began a self-perpetuating cycle of mercantilistic nonregulation which soon spread to other states.

Once the market had been established, UK authorities recognised that any form of unilateral restriction would lead, in all probability, to the euromarket simply migrating to a different location, taking with it all of its attendant benefits. And aware that their own interests were being well served by having abandoned the dollar to the market, US authorities were unlikely to cooperate in stemming the market. This proposition was actually tested in the wake of the dollar crisis of 1978–9, when the Federal Reserve sought to reign in the eurodollar market in an effort to tighten monetary policy. Under strong pressure from the domestic banking community, US policymakers rejected the idea of restricting the euromarket, opting instead to allow regulation-free international banking facilities (IBFs) on US soil from 1981 in the hope of regaining some lost eurodollar business through free-market channels. Other states gradually followed these competitive initiatives; most of their own volition, in recognition of the potential benefits of attracting extraterritorial markets and/or allowing the use of their own currencies, some under coercion from their trading partners (for example, the case of Japan, set out in Chapter 2).

The second type of financial deregulatory development followed from the demise of the Bretton Woods system, and involved the competitive abolition of capital controls. A product of the new mercantilist environment, this paved the way for a vast increase in the volume of international capital flows, enabling new financial products and markets to be used to arbitrage away differences in return across what were once separate markets.

The US was the first to abolish capital controls, eliminating all restrictions on the dollar's convertibility in 1974, and then actively moving to promote similar deregulation abroad.[34] US authorities saw this as a means of drawing overseas investors to its deep and liquid financial

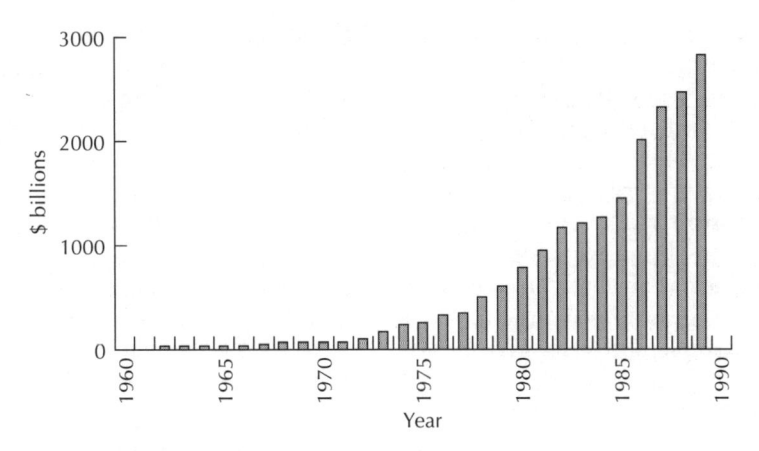

Figure 1.2: Size of Eurocurrency Market
[*Source*: Martin 1994, p. 258]

markets, with obvious advantages: growing budget and trade deficits could be financed while US financial institutions, as the leading players in the market, would gain from increased volumes of activity. The UK followed in 1979, with one of the first projects of the incoming Thatcher administration, in conjunction with the Bank of England, being to abolish capital controls in order to protect and enhance London's status as an international financial centre. Japan followed in 1980. London's proactive move was mirrored by new neoliberal governments in Australia and New Zealand, which came to power in 1982 and 1983, respectively. It also foreshadowed changes throughout continental European and Scandinavian states during the mid-to-late 1980s. Here, the rhetoric of competitiveness was at least as important as that of economic cooperation in justifying the deregulation.

A few states, such as Portugal and Ireland, did not lift their controls until the 1990s, but with the OECD passing an agreement to extend its Code of Liberalization on Capital Movements to cover all capital transactions – including short-term financial flows – in May 1989, the consensus was essentially completed at the turn of the decade for core capitalist states. Periodic attempts have been made to extend capital liberalisation to developing states, but such efforts are highly contentious among economists. In the wake of the 1997 Asian financial crisis, an annual IMF Interim Committee meeting in Hong Kong issued a statement virtually endorsing an eventual move to full capital account convertibility for all IMF members. Bhagwati spoke out against such a move in a recent article, arguing that it represents an elite conspiracy by 'the Wall Street-Treasury complex' (1998, p. 7).

The third type of financial deregulatory development was spurred on by the diffusion of neoliberal ideology in the 1980s. It involved domestic financial sector deregulation, or, more specifically, 'desegmentation' – that is, the dismantling of barriers between different sectors of the financial market. This trend is reflected poorly in the previous table since deregulatory measures were often diverse, involving changes of degree rather than black-or-white liftings of restrictions, as in the case of capital controls. Moreover, the fact that the scope for various types of desegmentation tends to vary from state to state as a result of different national institutional structures makes tabular representation problematic. For example, Germany's traditional universal banking structure meant that there was no barrier between the banking and securities sectors to dismantle.

Most commentators agree that the competitive desegmentation dynamic of the 1980s was set in motion by the US's high profile May Day deregulation of commissions on New York Stock Exchange (NYSE) in 1975. This drew an increasing amount of international business to New York, but it was not until the US abolished taxes on foreign holdings of US securities in 1984 that the British government recognised the dangers to London and set to work on a response.[35] The UK's highly aggressive Big Bang policy of stock market deregulation was implemented in October 1986. Representing 'an almost complete departure from traditional practice' (Hayes and Hubbard 1990, p. 200), it involved both the deregulation of commissions and the opening up of the London Stock Exchange to foreign firms. It was a proactive move in so far as it was intended to put the City in a position to benefit from the contemporary transformation of the financial services industry by securitisation (see below).

In the late 1970s, the US also seized the opportunity to promote the interests of US firms abroad by demanding reciprocal access from foreign governments. Against a background of mounting trade friction, bilateral pressure worked particularly well in Japan where, under the aegis of a Yen-Dollar Committee, the Ministry of Finance (MOF) agreed in 1982 to a long-term programme for domestic financial sector deregulation (see Chapter 2). In Europe, such moves reinforced competitive concerns that financial activity would come to be concentrated in New York, London and Tokyo. Following the US's lead, Germany lifted its taxes on foreign holdings of domestic securities in 1984. It then stepped up deregulation after a leading bank relocated its centre for operations to London. Similarly, competitive pressures from the US and UK were important in prompting deregulation in France (see Cerny 1989) and elsewhere. In this way, the idea that states needed an 'industrial policy' to retain the competitiveness of their financial sectors became pervasive (Helleiner 1994, p. 160).

This dynamic has continued unabated in the 1990s. In the US, restrictions on interstate banking were abolished in 1994 and, although nominally still in tact, the Glass-Steagal Act of 1933 separating the banking and securities industries has been considerably weakened. In Japan, a Big Bang policy of deregulation measures considerably more wide ranging than the UK's was announced in November 1996 in response to the competitive decline of the country's financial sector (see Chapter 2 section 2.3). But, whereas capital controls have been almost universally abolished in the OECD, decompartmentalisation remains a much less even process. This is because deregulation in any form, but particularly desegmentation, necessarily involves domestic political bargaining and conflict. As one commentator concludes from his study of financial deregulation in the 1980s, to the extent that competitive deregulation in core states has proceeded, it has involved state power being used to override vested interests hostile to reform (Moran 1991, p. 1).

In this way, a competitive deregulation dynamic in financial deregulation was initiated and perpetuated among core capitalist states by mercantilistic actions of frontrunner governments. Such moves supplied vital ingredients for the advent of financial globalisation by granting leading firms the space to exploit new technological possibilities and to market revolutionary financial instruments.

(ii) Competitive Innovation by Firms

While the history of financial innovation goes back several thousand years, the innovations of the last thirty or so years make the contemporary period qualitatively different. This can be seen by examining recent developments in process and product innovation – a distinction borrowed from management studies. In regard to process innovation, it is hard to underestimate the contribution to financial globalisation made by the dissemination of computer and communication technologies. While the spread of telephone and telegraph services in the 1920s was important in that it fuelled the proliferation and speed of securities issuing and trading volume and was fundamental to the creation of the eurodollar market, it was the application of computer technologies to finance which radically transformed the nature of the industry during the 1970s and 1980s. Figuratively speaking, by improving the infrastructure through which financial transactions flow, geographical participation in various financial markets increased arithmetically, but the capacity of markets to handle large volumes of contracts quickly, accurately, and cost efficiently was increased geometrically.[36] Early examples of this type of innovation were computer-networked settlement systems, first introduced in the euromarket in 1968 and subsequently reproduced in all national banking systems,[37] and screen-based trading systems, which debuted in over-the-counter (OTC) securities market with the establishment of the NASDAQ (North American Securities Dealers Automated Quotation System) and subsequently were extended internationally.[38] A similar concept was extended globally by Globex, a financial futures trading network, established in 1986.[39] Management at various stock markets are working to develop automated trading capacities;[40] the US government securities market is considering automated trading, and automated order routing and hand-held trading terminals have been or are being developed in both the equities and derivatives markets (Gramm 1992, p. 199).

Concomitantly, there has been a huge increase in the quality and quantity of financial information available to market participants since the late 1960s, in which technology has been instrumental in presenting professionals with new modes of information dissemination and processing. The first screen-based financial information service for subscribers was Reuter's Monitor system, launched in 1973. It proved tremendously successful and encouraged a proliferation of similar services.[41] Since information is the commodity at the heart of the financial industry, it is not surprising that financial institutions are more than willing to subscribe to several service providers in the hope of gaining/securing a competitive advantage over competitors. The impact of this has been to intensify competition in the markets, as better informed investors tend to be more demanding and better informed portfolio managers should be able to secure better returns on investment (Useem 1996).

In regard to product innovation, most of the significant inventions of recent years have been permutations and combinations on a familiar theme, with the impulse for experimentation by market participants stirred by the potential rewards available subject, of course, to some form of regulatory license. Important product innovations fall into one of three overlapping categories. The first category is inventions which directly foster regulatory and tax arbitrage by creating alternative markets for existing products. Led by the establishment of the eurodollar market, offshore financial markets and tax havens gradually sprang up in many places – Paris, Brussels, Frankfurt, New York, Tokyo, the Channel Islands, the Cayman Islands.[42] The eurodollar business was followed by the creation of euromarkets in other currencies, such as deutschmarks, French francs, sterling and yen; then by eurobonds, which offered a cheap way to raise funds and soon developed a large and liquid secondary market in which participants could remain anonymous and, therefore, tax-free; and, more recently, euroequities (Hayes and Hubbard 1990, pp. 193–232). Eurobonds have proved particularly popular and received the tacit approval of many governments since the markets in sovereign and local government debt inevitably developed alongside markets in corporate debt, giving them access to cheaper funding. Eurobonds, in turn, provided benchmark interest rates for the pricing of floating-rate notes (FRNs), and eurocommercial paper (euronotes).[43]

The second category of product innovation is inventions which foster product arbitrage by offering traders and investors close and superior substitutes for existing products. A representative selection of examples of new products in this vein would include new types of instruments which are hybrids of loans and securities, such as note issuance facilities (NIFs) and revolving underwriting facilities (RUFs);[44] variants of existing instruments, such as zero-coupon bonds, convertible bonds, and warrant bonds;[45] and products tailored to appeal to certain groups of investors, targeted by currency, maturity, and special features, such as customised eurobonds – packaged to appeal to OPEC investors in the 1970s, to retail investors in Switzerland and the Benelux countries in the early 1980s ('Belgian dentists'), to Japanese corporate investors in the mid-1980s, and to small-lot Japanese investors in the mid-1990s ('Japanese housewives') – unit trusts (known in the US as mutual funds), and personal equity plans (PEPs)/401(K) savings plans.[46]

The third and most high-profile category of product innovations in recent years is the invention of financial derivatives. They are part of a broader long-term trend in the financial industry known as securitisation – the move away from bank-intermediated financing in favour of raising funds directly through the issue of securities in capital markets.[47] But whereas many of the examples of new products cited above have contributed to securitisation's acceleration in recent years, the creation of derivatives in the 1970s constitutes a *qualitative* turning point in the trend's development. They are unique in that their value 'derives' from that of an underlying financial asset. That is, they are contractual tools which create synthetic markets between real markets to give investors and traders new ways of managing and even exploiting uncertainty in the real markets in which they engage. Essentially, they enable investors and traders to insure ('hedge') or bet ('speculate') against certain occurrences – for example, a rise in interest or exchange rates, or downward movement in a certain market – by creating an intermediate market in risk.[48] Used cautiously, derivatives can reduce risk exposure considerably; used recklessly, they may multiply the original level of risk exposure many times over.[49]

Three innovations made fundamental contributions to the development and proliferation of derivatives, all of which provide clear illustrations of the innovative application of existing technologies or knowledge to the financial industry in the pursuit of competitive gains. The original step was the invention of financial futures in 1972 by Leo Melamed, a Chicago lawyer and trader. Until this time, futures markets existed only in commodities. They represented a speculative insurance market, which provided suppliers (mostly farmers) and consumers of primary goods (wholesalers, retailers and manufacturers) with a cushion against price volatility. Melamed extended this logic to the dollar, which was alleged to be overvalued, and had interested acquaintance Milton Friedman write a paper outlining the potential benefits of currency trading on the Chicago Mercantile Exchange

(CME). Money soon began trading as a commodity on a newly incorporated International Money Market (IMM), and the rapid increase in financial futures trading led to similar markets being established in other financial centres (Melamed 1992).[50] Today, futures contracts are widely available on interest rates and stock indices as well, and commodity futures at the CME account for only about a third of transactions.

The second step was the development of options trading, which took off following the publication of a mathematical model for options pricing by Fisher Black and Myron Scholes in 1973. The Black-Scholes model used new computer technology to process an amended version of Harry Markowitz's Capital Asset Pricing Model (CAPM), a quantitative stock-picking model which used statistical profiles of securities' historical movements.[51] As a result, options trading, which had existed in some form or other for more than a century but had never been widely used because of the difficulty of pricing the volatile contracts, spread rapidly. A Chicago Board Options Exchange (CBOE) was initially established at the Chicago Board of Trade (CBOT) in 1973, but had to move out within a year into its own purpose-built premises because business was so brisk.[52] The American Stock Exchange and Philadelphia Stock Exchange both began trading options in 1975, and markets were established in San Francisco, Los Angeles, Montreal, Sydney and Tokyo the following year. By 1978, over 200 types of options were being traded at the CBOE alone, on commodities, currencies, stocks and bonds and mortgages. In 1990, more than 200 million options contracts were written in the US, and considerably more money was spent purchasing stock options than actual stocks. Thus, the Black-Scholes model has been called 'the most successful theory in economics', and 'the equation around which an entire industry was built' (Kurtzman 1993, p. 140; see also pp. 127–45).

A third milestone was the establishment of Portfolio Insurance Theory (PIT) in 1976 by Hayne Leland, a professor of finance at Berkeley. PIT used a modified version of the Black-Scholes model, and relied on an early supercomputer to analyse simultaneously the statistical profiles of hundreds of products in the options, stock and currencies markets. Essentially, it was the first fully functioning automated method of hedging investment through arbitrage (Kurtzman 1993, pp. 157–60). Recent amendments to PIT have involved the application of 'artificial intelligence technologies' – genetic algorithms, neural networks, and fuzzy logic – and fractal mathematics (used to model crowd behaviour) in order to sift, analyse and replicate market movements and the behaviour of investors (Lederman and Klein 1995). Cumulatively, these developments mean that derivatives have contributed spectacularly to the growth of 'fictitious' capital flows. They have provided for a quantum progression in the interconnectedness and, thus, price sensitivity of hitherto diverse markets.[53]

(iii) Financial Globalisation Today as a 'Halfway House'

Confusion about the state of financial globalisation today is common among nonspecialists and casual observers,[54] yet broad agreement exists among those who study the financial industry that, while financial markets did become much more integrated during the 1980s, they are far from fully integrated. The current state of the financial industry is captured concisely as 'a half-way house, a hybrid structure that is partly a truly global system, and partly still a series of national financial and monetary systems' (Strange 1988, p. 90). Claims that globalisation is either all but complete (e.g. Waters 1995) or, conversely, nonexistent (e.g. Epstein 1996), rest either upon an arbitrary selection and reading of the evidence, a misconception of what financial globalisation involves, or some mixture of the two.

While it has already been stressed that globalisation is fundamentally defined by a qualitative progression in interconnectedness, quantitative statistics still provide useful indicators of the transformation in the financial industry which globalisation has wrought. On the one hand, surveying the growth of international financial activity provides evidence of the significance of new products and markets; on the other, cross-price sensitivity measurements between different markets attest to high levels of integration.

First, statistics collected by the Bank of International Settlements (BIS) reproduced in figure 1.3 show that levels of international financial activity became significant in the 1970s following the abandonment of Bretton Woods. Year-to-year volatility has reflected the ups and downs of the global macroeconomic cycle, but the long-term trend has been one of progressive, almost exponential growth.[55]

Similarly spectacular increases are evident in the global derivatives and foreign exchange markets, as figures 1.4 and 1.5 show, although comprehensive figures are not available for the years preceding 1988 and 1989, respectively.[56]

Calculations also can be made to show the increased significance of these developments in the financial sector relative to developments in the 'real' economy. Recently cited examples include international banking activity (i.e. loans extended) as a percentage of world output – net growth rates from 0.7 percent in 1964, to 3.7 percent in 1972, to 8.0 percent 1980, to 13.2 percent in 1985, and to 16.3 percent in 1991, and gross growth rates from 1.2 percent, to 6.3 percent, to 16.2 percent, to 27.8 percent, and to 37.0 percent for the same periods (UNCTAD figures cited in Perraton *et al.* 1997, p. 266) – compound growth rates for international banking activity versus international trade and foreign direct investment – twenty-five percent versus twelve and ten percent, respectively, for the years 1965 to 1990 (Reinicke 1995, p. 46) – and foreign exchange transactions as a multiple of world trade – up from about ten times in 1980 (i.e. about $100 billion per day) to over fifty times in 1995 (*Banker* 5/96).

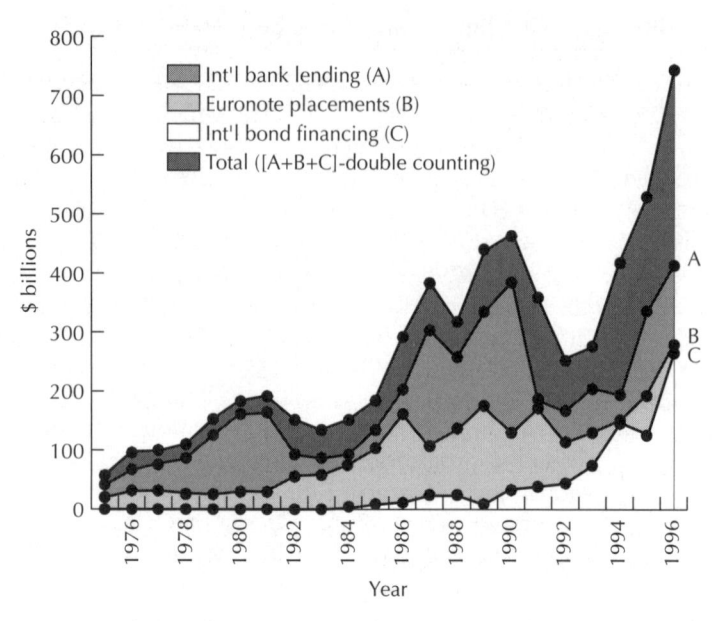

Financial Globalisation in Theory and Practice

Figure 1.3: Annual Growth in International Financial Markets (i.e. net activity)

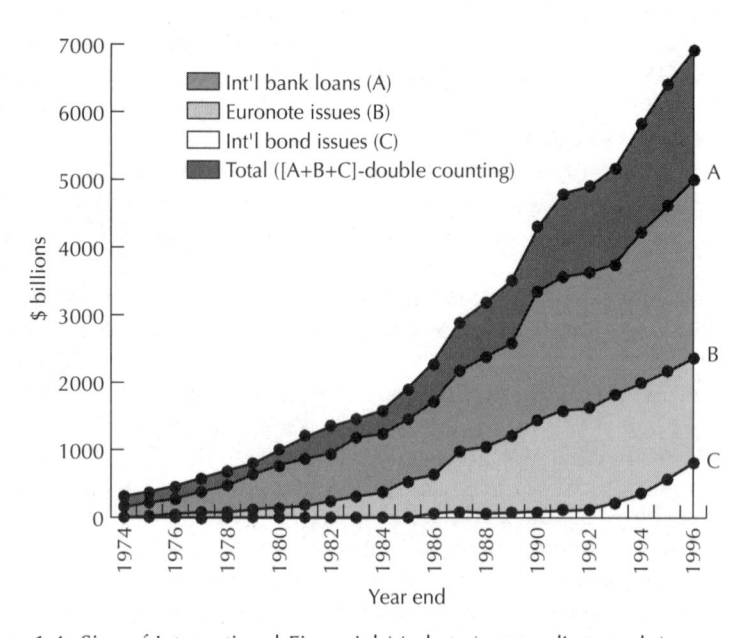

Figure 1.4: Size of International Financial Markets (outstanding stocks)
[*Source*: BIS *Annual Accounts*]

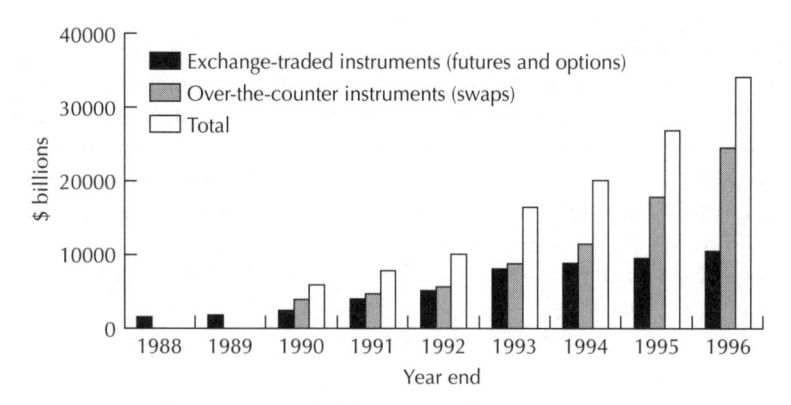

Figure 1.5: Global Derivatives Market (nominal amounts outstanding)

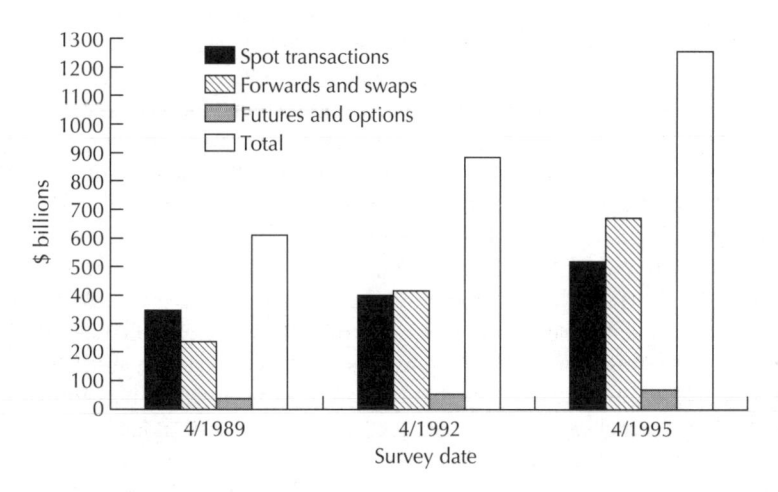

Figure 1.6: Daily Global Foreign Exchange Market Turnover
[Source: BIS *Annual Accounts*]

Second, econometric studies show that levels of financial integration have progressed significantly with the developments of new markets. A host of studies exist for various asset markets (e.g. Zevlin 1992; Bosworth 1993; Frankel 1993a; Obstfeld 1995; and Marston 1995). Findings vary in detail, but broadly accord with the simple logic articulated by Frieden, among others, who has pointed out two reasons why global investment is 'by no means yet a seamless web' (1991, p. 429): first, the movement of capital across borders always involves country and currency risks; and second, forms of capital differ in their inherent degree of geographical specificity. That is, many forms of capital are specific to their current use and cannot easily be transferred from place to place (e.g. technological and managerial knowledge, skills, and networks). Hereby, evidence points to foreign exchange markets being highly integrated for large transactions in major currency pairs (e.g. $:DM, $:Y, $:STG), but less so for smaller, more obscure currencies.[57] Accordingly, they show that bank lending tends to be highly integrated for large denomination, short-term financing (i.e. similar interest rates are available in New York, London and the euromarkets), but less so for longer-term or smaller corporate financing, which is often regional or national, and much less still for personal finance, which tends to be national or local. They show, too, that in the securities markets, bond markets are considerably more integrated than equity markets, which, in turn, are more integrated than venture-capital markets.

Furthermore, Perraton et al. note that there are significant signs of integration progressing among even recently disconnected markets (1997, p. 268). For instance, while investors generally prefer domestic bonds and equities, there is a clear trend towards portfolio diversification among institutional investors in the 1980s and 1990s, and some evidence of convergence in rates of return (e.g. Akdogan 1995). Moreover, the strong correlation between national savings and investment, noted, among others, by Feldstein and Horioka (1980), weakened perceptibly during the 1980s (see, for example, Ghosh 1995). Hereby, significant balance of payments deficits and surpluses have proved more sustainable than was ever imagined – most spectacularly in the US and Japan – because financial integration has worked to distance national financial markets from the performance of their economies. In turn, this has diminished the ability of governments to direct national finance to their own economic priorities (see also Garrett 1995).

None of this automatically implies that the market mechanism is functioning more efficiently or that financial development is becoming more even. The former is a highly subjective and emotive issue,[58] the latter, although debatable, seems easier to answer in the negative. But such considerations do not detract from the evidence of the reality of financial globalisation built up here. The next section seeks to augment the picture by examining in more detail the implications which these developments are understood to engender for state regulatory structures, domestic financial systems, and national models of political economy.

1.3 IMPLICATIONS FOR NATIONAL INSTITUTIONAL CONVERGENCE

Financial globalisation is now held to constitute a powerful force for institutional convergence across states with hitherto diverse national models of political economy. As pointed out by several observers, the issue is not so much whether national governments and financial institutions retain the capacity to be different, so much as on what terms and with what implications (Pauly 1995, p. 385; Perraton et al. 1997, p. 270). Financial globalisation acts as a structural constraint which affects societies' long-term possibilities rather than their short-term options: 'It is a path-dependent process, rooted in real historical decisions, non-decisions and conjunctural turning-points' (Cerny 1997, p. 257). This final section surveys the implications for institutional convergence that are commonly attributed to financial globalisation by the financial press and by major contributors to the debate. In addition to shedding further light on the nature of the phenomenon and the processes by which it progresses, this exercise serves to establish a framework for the rest of the book's empirical investigation of the impact of financial globalisation on Japan.

(i) Regulatory Regimes

Financial globalisation signals a historically unique pattern of convergence among national financial regulatory regimes via the changes which it has effected in leading states. Three areas of *de facto* convergence stand out. The first involves the rationalisation of financial regulation. The previous section indicated that the way in which states have deregulated their financial systems differs considerably — for a host of institutional as well as political and economic reasons, some tend to be more proactive than others. Nevertheless, a remarkable commonality has been the shift towards transparency and codification. This emerging universal regulatory norm is clearly a product of financial globalisation in that it is intended, on the one hand, to respond to new market realities and, on the other, to attract internationally mobile capital ('hot money') from both domestic and foreign investors.

In the former case, the Blair administration's ongoing reorganisation of the UK's financial regulatory structure provides an example. As part of Labour's post-election reform of the Bank of England (see also below), a new Financial Services Authority was launched in November 1997 and will eventually centralise financial regulation in the UK, amalgamating nine increasingly fragmented and competing financial supervisory authorities — which were created, in turn, as a rational response to Big Bang — and combining responsibility for regulating banking, building societies and mutual insurance companies, and the various London stock, futures and commodity exchanges (*FT* 4/11/97). This is a typical case of ongoing rationalisation in regulation supervision for the sake of supervisory, and thus market, efficiency.

In the latter case, the rhetoric of creating an internationally attractive environment for financial investment has become almost universal, though the reality may lag considerably. Many states have initiated a switch to common accounting and disclosure standards to better cater to international finance capital. Moran has pointed out that such 'rationalisation' often amounts to little more than the 'Americanisation' of regulation (1991, p. 1).

Some argue that this is coincidental: the US regulatory regime is inherently more market-oriented than most and is well suited for dissemination because of its high level of explicit codification. Others see it as the upshot of US structural power within the international system (e.g. Strange 1988; Edwards and Patrick 1992). Either way, it is inevitable that US regulators, and firms familiar with their practices, are privileged by such changes.

The second area of convergence involves the depoliticisation of financial regulation. At the broader policy level, this has commonly involved giving central banks greater independence, particularly in regard to monetary policymaking. While some central banks are traditionally more independent than others – the Bundesbank being notorious in this respect – much has been made of recent initiatives to grant the Bank of England, Bank of Japan, and new European Central Bank, among others, high degrees of political independence. The rationale behind such moves is that international investors are more likely to invest in an economy where key areas of economic policy can be guaranteed exempt from domestic political influence.[59]

At the regulatory level, depoliticisation has often involved the devolution of day-to-day regulation to the private sector in order to make greater use of self-regulatory bodies. The logic behind this is that private actors may be in a better position to police themselves, both in terms of having the technical expertise and by virtue of their position at the centre of developments. Much has been written about quasipublic regulatory regimes, such as the Bank of International Settlements (BIS), and quasiprivate regimes, such as the International Organisation of Securities Commissions (IOSCO – Porter 1993; Kapstein 1994; Underhill 1995; Coleman 1996). Both of these organisations have been instrumental in the dissemination of global regulatory norms in finance, the BIS's Basle Concordat of 1975 and Basle Accord of July 1988 representing important landmarks in preventing systemic risk in internationally banking activities,[60] and IOSCO's numerous agreements to prevent international securities fraud in working to strengthen the foundations of the international financial system.[61] Interestingly, it seems that even within the BIS regime, moves are afoot to promote greater self-regulation by relying on heightened disclosure requirements and internal risk-management systems.[62]

The third area of convergence involves the multilateralisation of financial regulation. Andrews (1994) has shown how, under financial globalisation, the very act of participation in interstate regimes tends to channel states' behaviour into conformity with international regulatory norms. As the above examples of the BIS and IOSCO show, at times states have willingly traded individual policy autonomy for collective power in an attempt to maintain some regulatory capacity over the financial industry. The Basle Concordat and Accord demonstrate collective responses to one type of *problematique* – areas which are vulnerable to market failure;[63] IOSCO demonstrates a response to another – areas where the potential exists for regulatory competition in laxity. Many other examples exist along one or other of these lines. The G–5 finance ministers' coordinated intervention in the currency markets under the Plaza and Louvre Accords of the mid-1980s are historical examples of the former, in that they represented multilateral efforts to restore a positive equilibrium where exchange rates had moved damagingly out of line with economic fundamentals (see Funabashi 1988; Volcker and Gyohten 1992). The OECD's January 1998 agreement to work towards establishing guidelines by 2003 for avoiding 'harmful' tax competition in attracting 'geographically mobile capital' (*FT* 24/1/98), and G–7 efforts to combat global money laundering (*FT* 9/5/98), are two ongoing examples of the latter.

A more controversial area of multilateralisation involves the collective extension of regulatory norms where front-runner states and firms derive disproportionate advantages from the changes. In addition to the IMF efforts to remove capital controls (mentioned in the previous section), examples include the OECD's Multilateral Agreement on Investment (MAI), which aims to provide equal treatment for foreign and domestic investors (*FT* 17/2/98), and the World Trade Organization's (WTO) pact on financial services, which was reached in December 1997 (*FT* 14/12/97). The WTO agreement took six years to establish, being held up by a bitter dispute between the US and developing Asian countries over the latter's reluctance to open their markets to the US' highly competitive firms. The agreement, which was scheduled to go into force in March 1999 following ratification in January, was expected to clear away barriers to the expansion of global banking, securities and insurance business. It guarantees gradual access to developing countries' markets and will mean that states breaking their commitments can be taken to international arbitration.

In short, it is clear that globalisation is encouraging convergence in many areas of national financial regulation. The processes by which this is happening are not amenable to reduction to a single category of cause or effect. Some are more benign than others, but all are intrusive to an unprecedented degree. Bretton Woods was a common regulatory framework which mandated common external controls, but it left domestic financial systems isolated and, therefore, regulators were free to pursue their own particularistic regimes. By contrast, financial globalisation has mandated that key aspects of domestic financial regulation be brought into line with emerging global norms.

(ii) Financial Systems

Through the interrelated competitive dynamics of deregulation and innovation, financial globalisation has ushered in a new era of institutional convergence among hitherto diverse national financial systems. For the purpose of analysis, at least three causes of convergence can be identified.

First, national financial systems have been, and are being, transformed by the extension and intensification of global competition. Polarisation takes place, on the one hand, because financial globalisation works to exaggerate the differences between competitive and noncompetitive firms. Thus, within the scope of domestic anticompetitive legislation – which itself is increasingly weakened in order to respond to the perceived exigencies of national competitiveness – a trend towards consolidation is evident in most established and mature market sectors. For example, the number of banks in the US fell by almost thirty percent between 1990 and 1995 (from over 14,000 institutions to under 10,000), and sector analysts expect this trend to continue in the US and be repeated elsewhere (*Banker* 4/96, p. 13).

Polarisation takes place, on the other hand, because financial globalisation encourages firms to specialise in order to survive. Thus, a very small number of truly global financial conglomerates has emerged in recent years to dominate international markets. The remainder of firms are compelled by necessity to specialise in one or a few sectors or geographical areas. In 1995, the top twenty financial institutions already accounted for between forty and sixty of world transactions; three years later this estimate relates to the top ten institutions. These firms include J.P. Morgan, Chase Manhattan, Citigroup (the merger between Citicorp and Travelers Group [see below]), Morgan Stanley Dean Witter Discovery (MSDWD), UBS United Bank of Switzerland (Union Bank of Switzerland and SBC Warburg), HSBC Holdings, Deutsche Morgan Grenfell (DMG), Dresdner Kleinwort Benson, ABN Amro, and ING Barings. Top UK firms such as Midland and Lloyds-TSB both announced in 1997 that they intend to specialise in the UK market, while Barclays and National Westminster abandoned their global ambitions two years previously to seek sanctuary in a limited number of market sectors. In the US, many of the so-called bulge-bracket Wall Street firms have concentrated their focus more narrowly, regardless of whether they are part of a large conglomerate or not. For example, Salomon-Smith Barney concentrates on bond dealing and retail broking, but does little equity underwriting, and Goldman Sachs specialises in wholesale M&A advisory and syndicated loan arrangement services, but does little retail business; (*Banker* 5/95; 4/98).

Second, diverse national financial systems are being transformed by technological innovation. This has promoted convergence both indirectly, through industry consolidation, and directly, by encouraging firms and markets to abandon idiosyncratic practices. The best example of technology-driven consolidation is the global custody sector, where competitiveness is largely a product of the effectiveness of a firm's risk management systems.[64] Many firms (including National Westminster and Lloyds-TSB) exited the market in the mid-1990s, finding that they could not keep up with the intensive investment needed to develop sophisticated computer software programmes in the face of declining commissions margins (*Economist* 21/6/97). Remaining competitors either consolidated themselves through M&A, or sought downstream links with asset management firms in order to secure future business which could justify their massive technology-related investments (*Euromoney* 6/98). Examples include Merrill Lynch's purchase of Mercury Asset Management (MAM) for $5.2 billion, Axa's purchase of Union des Assurances de Paris for $6.1 billion, Salomon Brothers' 1997 tie-up with Fidelity Investments (now in question after Salomon's subsequent takeover by Travelers, merger with Smith Barney and proposed merger with Citicorp), J.P. Morgan's purchase of a forty-five percent equity stake in American Century, the Bank of New York's joint venture with Gartmore Investment Management, and SBC Warburg's merger with Union Bank of Switzerland. With the global custody market having been estimated to reach $50 trillion by 2000, analysts reckoned that there will be only fifteen-to-twenty global firms by the end of the century, with scope for four-to-seven in the long run. Technological expenses are set to rise further with the long-awaited introduction of real-time gross settlement trading (*FT* 10/12/97; *Banker* 12/97; 4/98).

Technology was also given as the rationale behind the megamerger of Citicorp and the Travelers Group.[65] In contrast to the more familiar cost-saving logic underlying most financial sector M&A activity,[66] the rationale for this merger was access to each others' consumer databases, which should provide opportunities for cross-sales of products. In the past such logic has not always translated well into practice – as attempts to cross-sell motor insurance and mutual funds to credit card holders have shown[67] – but in this case there is already considerable evidence that combining retail and investment banking offers considerable synergies.[68] In such an environment, firms which cannot keep up with the pace of change and technological consolidation are left with little choice other than to pursue niche strategies.

One notable exception where technology appears to be lowering some barriers to entry is consumer banking. This sector is seeing increased automation, with more use of telephone, internet and ATM banking services and the development of electronic money (see *Banker* 1/97; 9/97). In a few areas, new technology can translate into lower fixed costs for banks.[69] But as only strong brand names are likely to attract deposits in cyberspace, such developments are likely to benefit large nonbank firms seeking entry into the banking market rather than small firms already in the industry (see below).

Technology is also playing an important role in the convergence of organisational management techniques through the competitive dissemination of 'best practices'.[70] This is evident on several levels. The use of computer-based risk-management systems has become a standard way for banks to measure their risk exposure for any given asset base. This technology has developed from simple value-at-risk models, which use historical data to estimate potential damage to the firm's investment portfolios caused by simulated market movements, to more complex credit-risk models, which factor in the possibility of borrower defaults (based upon credit ratings) to simulate additionally the amounts of potentially recoverable loans (*Euromoney* 12/97). The first firm-wide risk management system was J.P. Morgan's RiskMetrics, launched in November 1994, which was followed by Credit Suisse's CreditRisk+ and another system developed by McKinsey, a management consultancy firm. Rather than following J.P. Morgan in sinking a billion dollars into developing a sophisticated system of their own, many firms have opted to buy an existing system from a pioneer firm.[71] These are sold readily, both to recoup some of their development costs, and because the competitive advantages of such systems are often held to depend more upon the technical capability of staff using them than anything else (*Banker* 11/94; 5/96; 3/97).

In terms of human resource management, the measurement of individual or team performance is increasingly used as the basis for staff renumeration. Moreover, the now common practice of the financial press publishing regular peer ratings of top economists and sector analysts, and performance ratings of fund managers, has contributed to an across-the-board bidding up of salaries for star performers. Firms that refuse to pay competitive rates see individual staff, and sometimes whole departments, poached by their competitors. Lehman Brothers was a victim of this mind-set, losing most of its experienced research staff to Deutsche Bank and others in 1994; two years later Deutsche Bank rocked the industry by buying up ING's entire Latin American research team (*Euromoney* 4/96; *FT* 8/6/96). In conjunction with the increasing technological sophistication of the industry, such developments encourage employees to specialise in a particular area which is not firm-specific for the sake of their future marketability.

Finally, new technology has contributed to the demise of particularistic market features. For example, with the introduction of electronic broking systems like Reuter's Dealing 2000, London's traditional currency market intermediaries, 'inter-dealer brokers' (IDBs) found themselves bypassed in an increasing number of trades. Mirroring the ongoing demise of open outcry traders on the Chicago exchanges, IDBs found themselves able to compete only in large spot trades (over $5 million), where they provide tailored services, and in small volume sectors of the market, such as emerging market currencies. Similarly, the July 1996 introduction of Crest, the London Stock Exchange's electronic share dealing and clearing system, was a further nail in the coffin of small stockbroking firms. Those that survived the competitive pressures of the Big Bang found themselves faced with the prospect of having to install new Crest-compatible systems at a cost of between £250,000 and £500,000 plus staff training (*Euromoney* 5/96).

Third, diverse national financial systems also are being transformed by deregulation and desegmentation. Deregulation has paved the way for much of the consolidation in the industry by rolling back anticompetitive legislation, while desegmentation has removed many of the major barriers to the convergence of national financial systems. The impact of such changes was particularly dramatic in the UK. The Big Bang led to the rapid demise of Britain's traditional merchant banks, which were largely taken over by investment or commercial banks, and ended London's idiosyncratic segregation of stock jobbers (market makers) and brokers. More recently, many building societies have transformed themselves into banks, and now the industry is being transformed by the entry of nonfinancial firms, brand-led conglomerates such as Virgin, and national supermarket chains such as Sainsbury's, Tesco and Safeway.[72]

Likewise, the progressive weakening of the US's 1933 Glass-Steagal Act segregating the banking and securities industries has contributed to considerable institutional change in that market in recent years. After the Section 20 loophole was widened in December 1996, commercial banks rushed to buy up investment banks in order to gain securities distribution capacity.[73] Deals include Bankers Trust's purchase of Alex Brown for $1.7 billion and NationsBank's purchase of Montgomery Securities for $1.2 billion. Furthermore, the weakening of US legislation separating the banking and insurance industries has given rise to so-called bankassurance mergers (*Economist* 16/8/97).[74] Essentially, the blending of banking and life insurance, which are similar in terms of their risk and revenue patterns, the rationale for such tie-ups, as with fund management, is to extend ties downstream.[75] Hence the 1997, $9 billion megamerger between Salomon-Smith Barney and the Travelers Group (which incorporates Travelers [general insurance] and Primordia [life insurance]), and Credit Suisse First Boston's (CSFB) subsequent $8.5 billion purchase of Winterthur, a Swiss insurer (*FT* 13/8/97).

In these and other ways, domestic financial markets are becoming dedifferentiated through public and private competitive responses to financial globalisation. A decade ago it was widely anticipated that the continental European universal banking model would emerge as the baseline corporate structure in international finance. This has not happened. Leading German, Swiss and Dutch financial institutions are instead transforming themselves into US-style global investment banks with substantial domestic banking business on the side. Their historical role was defined by national borders – they accepted domestic deposits, made loans to domestic industry, and acted both as retail brokers and corporate underwriters within the national market. But as elsewhere, this isolated existence has been undermined by globalisation. In the international markets particularly, and to a lesser extent at home, they have been compelled by competitive pressures to concentrate on building up strategic and profitable areas of their business and scaling down in superfluous, less profitable areas (*FT* 11/12/97).

This is not to suggest that the emerging global archetype is simply the US model, or even some sort of Anglo-American-continental European amalgam. Since firms create the archetype and proceed towards it only through trial and error, the target is neither fixed nor predictable. That said, US firms have been consistently at or near the forefront of developments, and so, within the confines of competitive developments, they have some degree of leverage over the direction of the industry's development. This need not imply that financial services firms are about to become indistinguishable according to their national heritage. As one of many studies has noted already:[76]

> Investment banks and securities vendors of various stripes and nationalities are not all uniform in their organisational structures, their internal resources, or their offering of products and services. Our research indicates that national and regional differences are very much influenced by the investment bank's origins, early history, and status accorded them in their home market environments (Hayes and Hubbard 1990, p. 340).

Nevertheless, it must be obvious from the preceding discussion that the increasing amount of transnational and interregional mergers, joint ventures, staff movements and business interaction serves to undermine particular idiosyncrasies to the extent that they undermine firms' global competitiveness. Hereby, many particularistic characteristics of national financial systems which developed both before and during the relative isolation of the Bretton Woods period are being rapidly eroded by financial globalisation.

(iii) Social Structures

Financial globalisation also has contributed to a more general trend of convergence in advanced capitalist states through the repercussions which it engenders in other parts of society. As a structural force, financial globalisation effects societies only indirectly; a primary filter is the regulatory environment provided by the state, and a secondary filter is the actions of financial institutions therein.

At the macroeconomic level, the way in which advanced capitalist states have reacted to changes in the financial sphere has been a central element of their broader responses to economic globalisation. Their responses have varied in kind, because different states embody different models of political economy. However, an endemic development has been the shift towards greater flexibilisation in national economic and social policies for the sake of maintaining some degree of international competitiveness (Gough 1996; Esping-Andersen 1996). This is related to financial globalisation in that internationally mobile capital wields more power than ever over states, both via the exit options which it can exploit where high cost structures exist, and through the financial markets' ability to impose interest rate premia on governments which pursue macroeconomic policies that are collectively deemed unsustainable. Governments are hereby encouraged to create internationally attractive business environments by reducing their levels of business and personal income taxes, by ensuring high levels of transparency in regulation and corporate disclosure, and by making their labour markets more flexible.

Anglo-American states have led the neoliberal shift, curtailing the government's redistributive role in the economy and deregulating proactively in the 1980s. It essentially began in the US with the so-called Volcker shift when monetary policy was sharply tightened in October 1979; since then, economic globalisation has been managed by reliance on supply-side solutions, which attempt to work with the grain of the market, rather than demand management, which attempts to intervene and work against it. Policy measures have aimed to produce labour market and wage flexibility, while universal welfare regimes have been cut back, with greater reliance placed on means-testing, workfare schemes and new emphasis on private forms of social insurance in the fields of pensions and healthcare.

Continental European and Scandinavian states responded more reluctantly. The former are characterised by high levels of social insurance and underdeveloped social services. The labour force reduction route of shorter working hours and early retirement, which they pursued in response to deindustrialisation in the 1970s and 1980s, merely exacerbated their labour market rigidities, and has resulted in relatively high levels of long-term unemployment, particularly among the young. As both high levels of income transfer and large public sector deficits became unsustainable in an era of economic globalisation, continental European states were forced to amend their traditional familialist structure by implementing more flexible labour markets which, for example, made greater use of temporary workers and women.

The latter only emerged as distinct from the continental European model in the 1970s, epitomised by high levels of social insurance *and* comprehensive social services. In creating an egalitarian wage structure both by sex and profession, the public sectors of all Scandinavian states ballooned in absorbing an influx of women, while marginal tax rates were structured to increase sharply in order to pay for the generous benefits and to support high wages in low-skilled jobs. However, under globalisation, growing public sector deficits and crippling tax structures rapidly became unsustainable. Sweden led the way in trimming benefits, revising marginal tax rates (especially for high income bands), placing new emphasis on skills training, and introducing limited workfare measures. Hereby, Esping-Andersen has observed that 'there no longer seems to be a Swedish 'middle way' [between the free market and communism]' (1996, p. 2).[77]

In retrospect, a short-term trade-off between macroeconomic performance and equality clearly occurred. Most macroeconomic indicators attest to the fact that Anglo-American states almost universally have done better than their continental European and Scandinavian counterparts in levels of growth, stock market performance, and unemployment rates, yet have experienced rising levels of social inequality and poverty, while their counterparts' records on the latter front has shown little change. In the neoliberal model the opportunities for social mobility are substantial, but conditional upon adequate skills – unskilled workers have a high chance of remaining trapped. The temptation, at least for cultural relativists, is to dismiss this as a straightforward reflection of different policy preferences being reflected in different institutional models (e.g. Streeten 1996). However, a structural perspective which takes account of the progression of globalisation should warn against complacency in regard to the long-term sustainability of these models. Again, this is not to suggest that all models will converge upon a similar archetype. States differ in their endogenous institutional capacities for strategic action. The challenge for all states is achieving a sustainable and politically acceptable (i.e. pragmatic) balance between marketisation and decommodification (see also Cerny 1997).

At the microeconomic or intercorporate level, financial globalisation has introduced a new and overarching distinction between globally competitive and noncompetitive firms. This is reflected in the realignment of domestic political coalitions according to their support for deregulation (Frieden 1991). It is also evident in the new terms of access to credit which firms encounter.

To the extent that domestic industry is exposed to global competition, financial institutions and markets naturally move to revise the terms under which they extend loans or provide direct financing. Theoretically, firms which are deemed uncompetitive will be forced to pay higher risk premiums, while those which are deemed competitive will gain access to credit at globally competitive rates as a result of competition between domestic and foreign institutions. In practice, however, market imperfections – information asymmetries and bounded rationality – tend to mean that large, well-known firms are placed at a direct advantage over small, less well-known firms, regardless of their creditworthiness. This bias is reinforced by the trend towards securitisation, which can often provide access to cheaper financing for sufficiently large, well-established and well-known firms.

Nevertheless, stock exchange-listed firms face increased pressures as a result of novel developments in the financial markets. Through credit rating and share price changes, the market is able to pass judgment on the quality of a firm's corporate governance, rewarding popular management actions and punishing, ultimately by threat of hostile takeover, unpopular actions or complacency. The market power of institutional investment funds encourages something of a bias towards rewarding certain changes and thus encourages convergence, even when such changes are nothing more than a fad.[78] In recent years, the market has rewarded firms divesting surplus businesses and firing or demoting to temporary status all but core employees, moving towards flatter, decentralised organisational structures which promote autonomy and quicker decisionmaking;[79] using surplus cash for share buyback programmes; and implementing performance-based pay systems for regular employees, and stock option programmes for senior management.[80] Moreover, in markets where Anglo-American accountancy standards are not universal, large listed firms are rewarded by international investors for disclosing information in accordance with these more transparent emerging global standards.

Hereby, the short-term logic of quantitative financial results increasingly pervades all aspects of corporate life as financial globalisation intensifies competition in the real economy through its remaining, albeit increasingly distant, relationship to it. Of course, financial globalisation should not be expected to bring anything near total convergence among diverse corporate structures, because markets will always be imperfect and deregulation is still far from complete. But it will continue to have a substantial impact in encouraging the adoption and implementation of similar patterns of management across hitherto diverse institutional models.

At the individual level, financial globalisation is associated with a common trend of heightened polarisation between the 'haves' and 'have-nots'. This is an obvious consequence of the developments noted above, in so far as heightened levels of inequality are an indirect consequence of economic deregulation, and in so far as grading and rewarding individuals in terms of their contribution to the firm's profitability is an integral part of corporate competitivisation. However, financial globalisation also feeds social polarisation in terms of people's direct relations with financial institutions as lenders and borrowers.

Financial globalisation has led to an explosion in the variety of financial products which compete to meet consumer needs in ever more closely tailored ways. Significant innovations in this regard include products such as mutual funds/investment trusts, cash management accounts/wrap-around accounts and 401(k)s/PEPs (see Chapter 4 for definitions and examples).[81] These offer a vast array of alternative investment choices according to individual preferences of liquidity and risk, and tend to deliver higher rates of return than traditional bank deposit accounts. Deregulation and intensified competition between financial service providers has also led to cheaper prices and better services throughout the industry: securities transaction and foreign exchange commissions have tumbled with the advent of discount brokers, twenty-four hour automated teller machines (ATMs), telephone and internet banking, and electronic money (both in the form of now familiar credit/debit cards and the more novel 'smart' cards) have revolutionised or are revolutionising consumer banking, and insurance policy rates have tumbled in both the life and nonlife sectors. Moreover, a large ancillary service industry has built up around these changes to help investors navigate the vast and often baffling new territory: financial coverage in the media has increased dramatically since the 1970s, as have consumer finance publications, and the growth of the personal financial planning profession.[82]

But while these developments purport to benefit the consumer, it is clear that their advantages are not felt universally. Many financial products and services require large minimum investments or personal net worths for consumers merely to qualify, and even then, the technical intricacies make many products or services beyond the comprehension of many would-be investors. As Chapter Four shows, those in the upper and upper-middle social strata invariably gain disproportionately as a result of having more financial assets and, thus, a greater incentive to come to terms new developments, either personally or by proxy. Correspondingly, those at the bottom of the scale lose in relative, and possibly even in absolute terms, due to their *de facto* exclusion from many new opportunities. Those in the middle are increasingly polarised according to both economic well-being and personal initiative.

Hereby, under the rhetoric of expanded consumer choice, financial risks and returns are privatised according to the implications of freely made and supposedly informed individual decisions. But because financial globalisation results in a more complex interdependence of the whole, risk is paradoxically socialised and universalised at the same time.[83] In short, financial globalisation is thus an inherently social, as well as economic and political, phenomenon.

How one interprets these developments, and the ones in the preceding two subsections, and even those associated with financial globalisation and globalisation more generally, will largely depend upon one's perspective and values as well as particular understanding of the issues involved (see Introduction). Recognising the ultimate incommensurability of cost-benefit calculations, one can do no more than seek to highlight the implications of particular developments as they affect various sectors of society.

Conclusion

This chapter has sought to show that, in addition to the high level of currency which it has already attained in the 'real' worlds of international business and politics, *globalisation* can provide a descriptively apt and analytically useful perspective on contemporary economic developments. Properly conceived, that is, the concept need not be totalising or politically blind. Hereby, it was argued that scholars have a duty to engage with the reality of globalisation in its complex totality.

Through an empirical review, the chapter went on to show that the term 'globalisation' is applicable to the sphere of finance, where, against a background of new technological possibilities, the competitive deregulatory actions of leading states and the competitive innovatory actions of leading firms have transformed the industry in recent years. Finally, it addressed the implications which financial globalisation has for diverse national regulatory regimes, financial systems, and social structures. It found that a proliferation of new and significant points of confluence appear to be balanced by heightened levels of polarisation in almost every sphere. This supports Cerny's assertion that, with globalisation, '[c]onvergence and divergence are two sides of the same coin' (1997, p. 273).

Having hereby constructed a sympathetic and coherent portrait of the general state of knowledge pertaining to financial globalisation, this book can turn to interrogate the thesis constructively. By subjecting it to rigorous empirical analysis, it should be possible to refine our understanding of the concept and explore the limits of its usefulness.

Part Two

The Case of Japan

Chapter 2
Financial Deregulation 'Japanese-Style'

Introduction

The first in a tripartite investigation of the impact of financial globalisation on Japan, this chapter examines the development of Japan's financial regulatory regime during the second half of the twentieth century. It seeks to assess the extent of recent convergence with the emergent norms adumbrated in Chapter 1. Part one outlines the historical development of financial regulation in Japan and shows how key characteristics became institutionalised in the country's postwar financial system. Part two maps the way in which subsequent internal, external and systemic (i.e. market) developments affected the traditional structures and practices of financial regulation. Part three presents a case study of the latest and most radical package of financial deregulatory measures to date, the Japanese-style 'Big Bang'.

2.1 THE 100-YEAR DEVELOPMENT OF A MODERN FINANCIAL SYSTEM

A historical perspective on the Japanese financial system is an indispensable starting point for any study of contemporary changes therein for at least two reasons. As Ito (1995) points out, it cautions against the danger of 'coping' with the system's present complexity by simply adopting a ready-made understanding of the mechanics involved from the findings of a small number of supposedly representative recent studies. While informative in their own right, many of these studies turn out to be incapable of shedding much light beyond the scope of their narrow parameters.[1] For Western observers, such a temptation is often magnified by their misplaced hope that a magical key exists which, once found, will immediately unlock the door to an unfamiliar and occluded Oriental system. These observers would surely be quick to dismiss such a dubious quest were it inferred as a way of understanding their own (more complex?) American or British politico-economic systems.[2]

The Case of Japan

More generally, though, a historical perspective on the development of any national financial system is important because current regulatory institutions and practices tend to be informed by those of the past. This happens to be especially true in Japan's case. Only nominally cognizant of such a consideration, many commentators mistakenly assert the post-World War II reforms as the baseline from which the contemporary Japanese financial system evolved (e.g. Ozaki *et al*.; Noguchi 1995). Whilst this may appear a logical starting point, even the most cursory review of the success of the Occupation reforms to the Japanese financial sector attests to this being far from the case. The financial system that emerged during the 1950s and 1960s, while superficially new, was shaped strongly the prewar system in both its structure and regulatory ideology. A more appropriate starting point is the end of the nineteenth century, the point at which the infrastructure of a modern financial system was first established in Japan (Tsurumi 1991; Tamaki 1995).

Historical Background

Following the Meiji Restoration of 1868, a host of economic, political and social reforms were implemented by the Japanese government in the hope of modernising the state and ensuring its continued independence from colonial rule. As in other areas, the government borrowed heavily, but not indiscriminately, from the West when seeking to establish a modern financial system as the most expedient means of facilitating industrialisation. However, the system which emerged over the following decades was distinctively Japanese in terms of, among other things, its structural bias towards indirect financing, low levels of explicit legal codification, and considerable indirect state involvement in private sector activities.

Japan's financial authorities initially adopted the US banking system as a development model and began to license several private banks to issue the national currency in 1872. But when, after extensive reforms in 1876, the system still had not taken root as envisaged – private banks remained overly dependent on the government – they decided to try a new tack. Under the direction of Finance Minister Matsukata Masayoshi, a new plan was implemented which drew on the experiences of various European states: stock exchanges were established in Tokyo and Ōsaka (the TSE and OSE) in 1879 based upon London's example; a central bank with exclusive currency-issuing rights – the Bank of Japan (BOJ) – was set up in 1882 along the lines of the Belgian model; a new regulatory framework for commercial banking (the Banking Act) went into effect in 1890, informed by the codes of conduct in various European states; and a postal savings system was inaugurated in 1885, ten years after its founding in the UK.

In spite of the appearance of wholesale borrowing from the West, the Japanese financial system began to develop a shape of its own during the remaining years of the Meiji Era (1868–1912). The Banking Act was revised in 1895 to establish a single class of private deposit-taking institutions – 'ordinary banks' (*sōgō ginkō*) – and to set out skeletal rules for their operation.[3] Notably, it omitted to specify guidelines on even such supposedly basic considerations as minimum levels of capitalisation for banks, the maximum proportions of bank loans that could be extended to a single customer, and limits on involvement in nonbanking activities. Consequently, the number of banks in existence proliferated rapidly. By 1901 there were 1,867 institutions, most of which were small, unspecialised, single-unit entities (i.e. having no branches). Unsurprisingly, they were highly susceptible to instability in times of economic uncertainty.

While the government espoused a *laissez faire* attitude towards the internal development of the financial system in public, oblique involvement in the system's development was evident from the outset. It underwrote the stability of the banking system by frequently calling upon the BOJ to extend help to troubled firms. Hereby, it was able to ensure the undisturbed flow of private sector funds to industry. It also sought a direct role in the financial system by establishing government financial institutions to supplement private capital flows. The Yokohama Specie Bank was nationalised and used to finance special trade needs, the Industrial Bank, to finance strategic industrial demands, and the Hypothec Bank of Japan, to finance real estate development.[4] However, the government chose not to replicate its support for the banking system in the country's stock markets, and as a result, they remained comparatively underdeveloped. Due to their volatility, individual investors preferred either postal deposits, which carried an explicit government guarantee, or bank deposits, which at least had a chance of public bailout in the event of a collapse. Nevertheless, considerable concentration did take place in the banking sector, and by 1921 the number of institutions had fallen to about 1,300. Moreover, encouraged by government patronage, four banks at the centre of the country's largest financial-industrial conglomerates (*zaibatsu*) emerged from the World War I (WWI) boom much larger and stronger than their rivals.[5] Such developments, combined with recurrent market crashes, increased levels of competition within the industry and encouraged banks to begin specialising in order to secure market niches and exploit economies of scale.

The 1920s was a decade of heightened economic instability in Japan. The post-WWI recession was exacerbated by the Great Kantō Earthquake of 1923, and investors adopted an increasingly speculative attitude. In the context of traditionally lax bank supervision, such developments proved volatile, and systemic instability was soon triggered when the bankruptcy of a Tokyo bank led to a series of runs in the spring of 1927. The government stepped in quickly to stem the panic with large-scale public bailouts via the

BOJ, and promulgated a new Banking Law in 1928 which incorporated revisions that the MOF had been debating for several years.[6] The new law provided an objective basis for consolidation by establishing minimum capital requirements and banning banks from engaging in nonbanking activities. It also increased the regulatory powers of the MOF substantially, giving the Ministry its first legal mandate to license banks, regulate branching, authorise mergers, conduct prudential examinations and introduce annual reporting requirements. Nevertheless, the new law retained a characteristically skeletal nature in that it still did not specify a maximum proportion of loans that banks could make to a single customer, minimum cash reserves, or loan collateral guidelines. Apparently, such omissions were made out of a desire to maintain the previous system's benefits – its operational and administrative flexibility – whilst responding to the new need for stability.

The 1930s saw Japan's embarkation on the course to a centralised wartime economic structure, and over the next decade-and-a-half, the MOF used the new Banking Law to guide consolidation among private banks in order to improve efficiency. Under the slogan 'one prefecture, one bank', administrative pressure for mergers intensified in 1936, and the number of banks eventually fell from 1,031 in 1928 to sixty-one in 1945 – there are forty-seven prefectures in Japan. Correspondingly, the market share of the big four *zaibatsu* banks grew spectacularly,[7] although their actual influence declined with increasing government control. The state's direct role in the financial system also rose, as it supplemented its existing 'special banks' with new public financial institutions such as the Wartime Finance Bank, as the loans from the Industrial Bank increased by a factor of thirty-seven during the War's final decade, and as stock exchange trading was monopolised by government issues after 1936. In 1937 a Temporary Funds Adjustment Law was enacted to centralise the allocation of industrial credit. To prevent unnecessary loans and reign in speculation, private banks were required to gain MOF approval for all new loans, and stock exchange-listed firms were instructed to seek bureaucratic consent for all dividend payouts. Finally, in 1942 the BOJ Law was revised along the lines of the German Reichsbank Act of 1939 to strengthen state control over the economy, and the National Finance Control Organisation was established, enabling the MOF to coordinate private banking activity with national economic policy. This last development provided the main channel for the issue of government directives relating to the forced absorption of government bonds and the extension of new credit, both of which were carried out with disregard for commercial concerns but underwritten by loans from the BOJ. From this point, it was only a short time before the desperate strains of Japan's war effort led to industrial collapse in 1943, after which crippling inflation engulfed the financial system. At the time of the country's ultimate defeat in 1945 the financial system was in ruins.

The Legacy of Postwar Reforms

Under the rhetoric of democratising Japan, US Occupation authorities set out to 'normalise' the country's financial system by rebuilding it on an idealised US model. This plan was conspicuous for its abject failure on this front: the postwar Japanese financial system which emerged in the 1950s and 1960s retained many of its prewar characteristics.

The Supreme Commander for the Allied Powers (SCAP) initially pursued a three-pronged strategy of financial reform which involved (i) breaking up the *zaibatsu* system, a move legitimised by both US antitrust ideology and the *zaibatsu*'s central involvement in Japan's recent colonial exploits; (ii) reorganising the securities industry along the lines of US reforms in the 1930s, replicating the Glass-Steagal Act and transforming the stock exchanges from private companies into institutions governed by their members; and (iii) restructuring the country's financial regulatory apparatus along US lines, making the BOJ as independent as the Federal Reserve and establishing a separate Securities and Exchange Commission. However, with the exception of Article 65 inserted into Japan's Securities and Exchange Law to segregate the banking and securities industries, the legacy of US attempts to 'Americanise' the Japanese financial system was negligible. The end of the US occupation in 1952 saw first the revival of Japan's 'special banks', institutions endowed by the state with special privileges in return for performing specialised tasks (e.g. foreign exchange transactions). Next, the newly established Securities and Exchange Commission was absorbed into the MOF and replaced by an independent advisory committee with no legal authority. BOJ reform was abandoned altogether, and the strict Antitrust Act of 1947 was soon relaxed by a newly promulgated law which made way for the *de facto* reemergence of prewar *zaibatsu* banks at the centre of postwar *keiretsu* industrial groups. Moreover, the MOF emerged virtually unscathed,[8] and its dominant position over the central bank remained firmly in tact.[9] Thus, the preexisting architecture of the Japanese financial system remained largely in place in spite of the Occupation.

This renaissance was facilitated by several factors. Most important was the 'reverse course' in Occupation policy, by which the policies targeting Japan's democratisation and demilitarisation were subordinated to the country's rapid reindustrialisation and reintegration in the international ('free' world) economy for the sake of responding to the perceived exigencies of communist containment (Sakakibara and Noguchi 1977; Teranishi 1993). However, Tsutsui (1988) argues that this explanation obfuscates the role played by other significant factors such as deficiencies in SCAP's plans, infighting in the US administration, and broader insensitivities to the Japanese situation. Additionally, it is clear that the Japanese authorities did not feel the prewar financial system had been discredited by the War – quite the opposite, in fact – and so little incentive existed for them to persevere with unfamiliar and possibly suboptimal reforms. If anything, their predilection towards intervention was reinforced by the ideological trends of the day – the spread of Keynesian economics and the early successes of the centrally planned Soviet economy.

Japan's new situation, however, necessitated that indirect means of influence over the allocation of capital be resurrected to substitute for direct wartime controls. In the Temporary Interest Rate Adjustment Law of 1947, which provided a basis for the BOJ to set a ceiling on interest rates 'for the time being', the MOF obtained a basis for suppressing lending rates in order to make funds available for economic reconstruction at below-market-clearing levels.[10] Where banks were unable to satisfy demand for funds, the shortage was often alleviated by central bank credit, as it had been during the 1930s and 1940s. The practice of encouraging overlending to certain industrial sectors by 'window guidance' (*madoguchi shidō*) also provided a strategic lever for national development and was used until the 1970s. New public financial institutions were again established to supplement private sector flows and ensure that strategically important sectors received sufficient funding. These included the Reconstruction Finance Bank (1947), the People's Finance Corporation (1949), the Export-Import Bank of Japan (1950), the Housing Loan Corporation (1950), the Japan Development Bank (1951), and the Small Business Finance Corporation (1952). Interestingly, even after the volume of funds handled by these institutions began to decline in the late-1950s, they continued to play a key role in the economy until the early 1960s in that approval of a loan from a government bank was often used as a signal to spur private investment because it could be interpreted as an implicit government guarantee. Other steps were also taken to centralise bureaucratic control over the financial system. Not only were balance sheet, branching and entry regulations all reformulated, but guidelines were established to regulate the income and expenditure of individual financial institutions down to the level of specifying precise ceilings on employee wage levels and share dividend payout rates.

Five Characteristics of Financial Regulation in Postwar Japan

Hereby, a distinctively Japanese financial regulatory regime reemerged in the 1950s and 1960s. It was distinguished by five characteristics, two of which were structural, two administrative, and one contextual: (i) a bias towards indirect finance, (ii) rigid functional segmentation of financial institutions, (iii) administrative guidance, (iv) convoy regulation, and (v) international isolation.

First, the authorities worked to maintain the financial system's prewar bias towards indirect – i.e. bank-intermediated – financing because of the greater discretionary control over credit allocation which this allowed.[11]

That Japan's capital markets continued to be comparatively underdeveloped was not simply the result of bank loans being available at below-competitive market rates. Rather, in the same way that the 1937 Temporary Fund Adjustment Law (abolished in 1948) had provided a basis for restricting bond issuance as part of the wartime mobilisation effort, the MOF continued to influence bond financing in a similar way through the Bond Issue Committee (*Kiseikai*). This meant that the issue and pricing of new securities did not follow market-determined formulae, but were heavily influenced by the administrative guidance (see below) of the MOF in league with big banks.[12] Furthermore, as a result of the Ministry's strict interpretation of the Securities and Exchange Law of 1948, financial institutions were given little room to launch new types of financial products because the MOF defined securities according to prespecified categories, rather than assessing their functional attributes. Supposedly for the sake of protecting 'naive' investors, it prohibited outright the listing of risky or technically complex products.[13]

Second, the MOF reinforced the prewar financial system's structure of compartmentalisation in line with the principle of 'division of labour', as shown in figure 2.1.[14] Not only did financial institutions have their roles defined by the strict segregation of the banking, securities and insurance businesses, but subsectoral segmentation mandated that firms specialise narrowly within each sector. This requirement fostered the institutionalisation of a clear hierarchy of financing relations, with, for example, city banks serving big business, regional and credit (*shinkin*) banks serving small- and medium-sized firms, and long-term credit banks meeting firms' longer term needs. On the one hand, this ensured that funds flowed into areas of the economy which would otherwise have gone short; on the other, it served to prevent the construction of an industry-wide front against the MOF. It resulted in often intense intrasectoral competition, which was largely restricted to nonprice means, but an almost complete absence of intersectoral competition.

Third, administrative guidance (*gyōsei shidō*) became *the* central means by which the MOF conducted financial regulation.[15] The skeletal Securities and Exchange Law of 1948 (amended 1992) and Foreign Exchange Law of 1949 (amended in 1979 and 1997) were added to Japan's existing legal framework for financial regulation – the Banking Law of 1927 (amended in 1982 and 1992). They afforded the MOF broader scope than ever in deriving its own dynamic interpretation of codified statutes, and the Ministry came increasingly to rely upon a range of formal and informal channels for the dissemination and execution of day-to-day regulation. Formally, administrative guidance was transmitted through ministerial ordinances (*shōrei*), regulations drafted by individual ministries on the basis of existing legislation and implemented without the authority of the Diet, notifications (*tsûtatsu*), a form of administrative guidance without any legal basis beyond

The Case of Japan

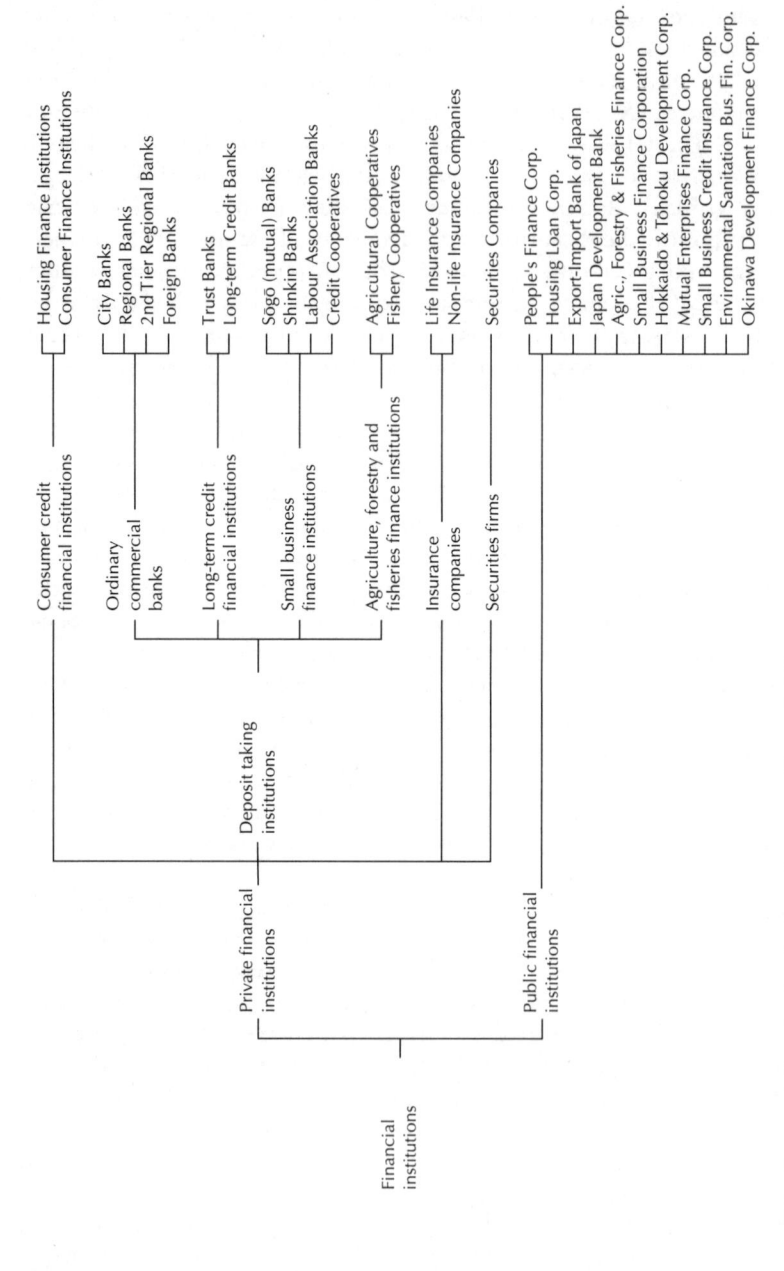

```
Financial
institutions
├── Private financial institutions
│   ├── Consumer credit financial institutions
│   │   ├── Housing Finance Institutions
│   │   └── Consumer Finance Institutions
│   └── Deposit taking institutions
│       ├── Ordinary commercial banks
│       │   ├── City Banks
│       │   ├── Regional Banks
│       │   ├── 2nd Tier Regional Banks
│       │   └── Foreign Banks
│       ├── Long-term credit financial institutions
│       │   ├── Trust Banks
│       │   └── Long-term Credit Banks
│       ├── Small business finance institutions
│       │   ├── Sōgō (mutual) Banks
│       │   ├── Shinkin Banks
│       │   ├── Labour Association Banks
│       │   └── Credit Cooperatives
│       ├── Agriculture, forestry and fisheries finance institutions
│       │   ├── Agricultural Cooperatives
│       │   └── Fishery Cooperatives
│       ├── Insurance companies
│       │   ├── Life Insurance Companies
│       │   └── Non-life Insurance Companies
│       └── Securities firms
│           └── Securities Companies
└── Public financial institutions
    ├── People's Finance Corp.
    ├── Housing Loan Corp.
    ├── Export-Import Bank of Japan
    ├── Japan Development Bank
    ├── Agric., Forestry & Fisheries Finance Corp.
    ├── Small Business Finance Corporation
    ├── Hokkaidō & Tōhoku Development Corp.
    ├── Mutual Enterprises Finance Corp.
    ├── Small Business Credit Insurance Corp.
    ├── Environmental Sanitation Bus. Fin. Corp.
    └── Okinawa Development Finance Corp.
```

Figure 2.1: Segmentation in the Postwar Japanese Financial System
(*Source:* amended BOJ 1995, p. 11)

a ministry's jurisdiction over activities within a particular sector, and administrative notices (*jimu renraku*), less authoritative guidance issued by section chiefs (*kachō*) (Horne 1985, p. 235, note 9).[16] Informally, it has been backed up by an extensive array of established channels of contact between the MOF and individual firms within the financial sector: by personal relationships, through specifically designated *MOF-tan* (usually translated 'MOF-watchers', whose job it was to oversee his firm's relations with the Ministry),[17] and via *amakudari* networks;[18] and between the MOF and firms in a particular area, via umbrella organisations.[19] In the MOF's case, its scope for discretionary action has been particularly large as a product of an unusually broad regulatory mandate which encompassed financial supervision, as well as budgetary, tax, and customs policymaking – functions which in other OECD countries are shared between the central bank and branches of national or local government.

This should not, however, be taken as a suggestion that the MOF was an all-powerful actor in the sphere of financial regulation.[20] Bureaucratic sectionalism makes it misleading to assume the MOF is a unitary actor in that the Ministry's seven bureaus often represent different interests in accordance with specific functional mandates. In spite of interbureau personnel movements, considerable jurisdictional competition exists: the Banking and Securities Bureaus broadly defend the interests of their respective sectors (e.g. Vogel 1994); the International Finance Bureau, the interests of larger, internationally active financial institutions; the Finance Bureau, Japan's public financial institutions, and so on. Interministry competition also curtails MOF power in areas where various ministries which share responsibility for financial regulation compete: when dealing with interest rates, the MOF must consult with the Ministry of Posts and Telecommunications (MPT), which has primary responsibility for the postal savings (*yûcho*) and postal insurance (*kanpo*) schemes; and when dealing with bank supervision and the licensing of new financial products, it must negotiate with the Ministry of International Trade and Industry (MITI), which has primary responsibility for overseeing agricultural financial institutions (e.g. Mabuchi 1995). Moreover, the prospect of conflict with politicians (particularly by those belonging to the Liberal Democratic Party [LDP]) exists in any area of financial regulation which touches upon the interests of powerful lobby groups, issues involving the Post Office, regional/agricultural financial institutions, and the life insurance industry (which employs nearly half a million sales personnel) are notably sensitive areas which touch upon the local support bases of many LDP politicians (e.g. Rosenbluth 1989, pp. 167–208; Horne 1985, pp. 118–41).

This last point draws attention to the fact that the MOF only ever enjoyed autonomy in exercising administrative guidance in unpoliticised areas of financial policymaking. Barring the examples noted above, the LDP has historically maintained a critical distance in most areas of financial policy. However, that politicians generally have avoided overt 'capture' by specific groups of financial institutions is not for lack of funding ties. City banks, for example, have made large contributions to the LDP since its formation in 1955, and their total publicly reported political contributions have consistently amounted to twenty percent of private industry's total contribution (Rosenbluth 1989, p. 188). These donations are made largely to the party itself rather than individual politicians and, hereby, the LDP has been broadly supportive of their interests, yet has managed to avoid involvement in the horse-trading that actual financial policymaking necessitates. The generic explanation for this is that financial policymaking is too technical for nonspecialists to grasp. More convincing, however, is the proposition that the LDP has been eager to avoid upsetting the banks' major rivals, Japan's securities companies, who themselves were large contributors of funds, although reportedly more so through *subrosa* donations to key politicians and via the provision of insider information on 'hot' stock purchases. Rosenbluth contends that, in this case, the money from both sides guarantees a favourable disposition, but 'the LDP shows a strong preference for delegating to the MOF the delicate balancing operations between Japanese banks and their rivals, the securities companies, for fear of alienating either group' (1989, p. 26). Furthermore, Mabuchi points out that the party's general avoidance of involvement in financial policymaking serves another valuable purpose in that it tends to keep opposition parties away from the issue as well, to the benefit of both the MOF and the financial industry, if not the average man in the street (1995, pp. 306–9).

Fourth, the MOF's established 'escorted convoy method' (*gosōsendan hōshiki*) of regulation – in which its administrative powers were exploited to ensure that the financial industry evolved with all firms more or less in step – developed significant immobilist tendencies.[21] Since the 1920s, the Ministry had used branch and product licensing restrictions to slow the pace of leading firms, and the threat of forced mergers to hurry that of lagging firms.[22] But after a spate of mergers between small financial institutions to improve the sector's efficiency following the instability of the mid-1960s, the MOF was forced by political pressure to abandon active support of hostile takeovers for blatantly inefficient firms (Horne 1988, pp. 186–90).[23] By default, this paved the way for greater direct Ministerial intervention in the affairs of weak financial institutions, since industry regulators were left with little choice other than to try to improve their management by other means. When firms encountered difficulties, the MOF used its influence with other financial institutions to prod them to extend support, whilst insisting simultaneously that the troubled firm accept new and (supposedly) skilled senior managers in the form of retiring MOF officials. For the MOF, this also proved to be a useful conduit for retiring staff, but paradoxically the practice worked to increase the new immobilist tendencies in the convoy system brought about by political intervention. As

MOF *amakudari* who 'descended' into troubled firms ironically were seen to make such firms more adept at protecting their own interests *vis à vis* the Ministry's periodic attempts to force their pace of reform, other laggards caught on to the advantages of soliciting MOF *amakudari*. And, mindful of their own post-retirement prospects, many in the Ministry became hesitant to 'burn bridges' by actively promoting consolidation.[24]

Thus, in the 1960s and 1970s the original aims of convoy regulation became perverted: a practice that was intended to both speed the slow and temper the fast for the sake of all increasingly restricted the fast to the pace of the slow. As already noted, the postwar reforms included new controls on licensing, branching and the introduction of new financial products. But both of these tools were invoked to a degree that went beyond either provisions for the maintenance of diversity (i.e. antimonopoly mandates) or basic prudential requirements. They became the main means by which the MOF sought to preserve the essential balance – or, rather, *status quo* – between firms in the financial sector. This was evident in the way in which the MOF played the role of mediator between opposing interests from the late 1960s onwards.

As the introduction of new financial products and technologies threatened to blur the system's rigid boundaries, turf wars flared between firms in different sectors wanting the right to market or utilise them.[25] In such situations, MOF practice was typically to seek out a consensus based on some sort of compromise among the parties involved. In cases where no compromise was possible and a decision could not be deferred, one group was favoured only for its competitors to be favoured on a subsequent occasion. This type of mediation was possible precisely because of the Ministry's exclusive role as the interpreter of Japan's skeletal legal code of financial regulation. It provided for the institutionalisation of a 'no-rule-means-prohibition' custom in which

> ... the non-existence of an 'explicit' legal rule endorsing a certain activity under explicit regulatory conditions is understood to mean that such an activity is prohibited ... Put differently, until a consensus is reached and an explicit rule or administrative guideline is established for a financial device, followed by [sic] a lengthy process, virtually no one creates or markets such a financial instrument (Kanda 1997, pp. 312–3).

Typically, such a consensus is arrived at via the lengthy and complex process of decisionmaking which accompanies most major administrative and legislative policy reappraisals in Japan. Discussions take place in ministerial 'deliberative councils' (*shingikai*), which are made up of representatives of directly affected sectors and the public (usually represented by eminent journalists and/or academics), and testimony from all sides is heard in order to flesh out a reasonable compromise.[26] This procedure is advantageous to both the regulator and the regulated for three reasons. First, since the Ministry selects the panel members, sets the agenda, provides much of the information upon which discussions proceed, and drafts the final *shingikai* report, its view is almost always reflected strongly in the final outcome (see, for example, Ogita 1969; Schwartz 1997). Second, because the *shingikai* system serves as an *ex ante* monitoring mechanism which involves all of the concerned parties, there are almost no subsequent judicial challenges to legislation or administrative rules, unlike in the US (Kanda 1997, p. 314). And third, due to the often lengthy discussions (running to several years in some cases), and thanks to firms' direct participation in the debates, the *shingikai* process gives participants an idea of what changes to expect and gives them a chance to gear up accordingly before being allowed to move forward in convoy. These, it must be noted, though, are not costless. They come only at the considerable price of adding further to the system's already considerable immobilist tendencies, since thorough *ex ante* monitoring can only be achieved by stifling financial innovation and competitive dynamism (see Chapter 3).

Finally, these structural and administrative characteristics of the postwar Japanese system depended fundamentally upon international isolation for their efficacy. As with almost every other state under Bretton Woods, Japan's financial markets were separated from the rest of the world by capital controls. But, Japan's Foreign Exchange Law did more than just provide a basis for controlling the flow of funds into and out of the country in order to prevent speculation and maintain the value of the yen. In securing for the government absolute control over both private and public spheres of financial activity, it enabled the financial system to be tailored to the country's needs for economic rehabilitation and industrial development. Herein, it provided a vital breathing space to nurture an embryonic and unique financial system which would never have become as deeply rooted under terms of international engagement.

2.2 CHANGE AND THE JAPANESE FINANCIAL SYSTEM

Regulatory changes encompass more than legislative amendments. They may also take the form of bureaucratic reinterpretations of nonstatutory codes of practice. In both cases, change can be either proactively led or reactively implemented, as the following stylised taxonomy demonstrates in terms of popular conceptions of the Japanese state (figure 2.2).

By both definitions, the distinctive institutional characteristics of Japan's postwar financial system began to change in the 1970s. Initially, this was a result of the country's transition to economic maturity. International developments and pressure from abroad (*gaiatsu*) took over the role of primary catalyst for change in the 1980s, but in the 1990s it has been market developments associated with globalisation that asserted the strongest

Financial Deregulation 'Japanese-Style'

	Politicians	Bureaucrats
Proactive Leadership	Competition State	Developmental State (e.g. Johnson 1982)
Reactive Implementation	Reactive State (e.g. Calder 1988)	Vested Interest-driven State (e.g. Hartcher 1998)

Figure 2.2: Conceptions of Regulatory Reform

influence in shaping the evolution of the financial system. The following section traces these changes, separating pressures which are brought to bear on the system into three categories for the sake of analytical simplicity: (i) those coming from developments in the domestic arena, (ii) those emanating from developments in the international environment, and (iii) those driven by developments in the financial services industry itself (designated below as 'global systemic developments' and understood in terms of the globalisation thesis set out in Chapter 1).[27]

Domestic Economic Transformation in the 1970s

During the 1970s, the appropriateness of Japan's existing financial regulatory regime was called into question as a result of the slower economic growth rates which accompanied the country's transition to industrial maturity, through repercussions engendered by the country's integration in the international financial system, and via financial institutions jostling to exploit new competitive product and process technologies. Most significant at the time were changes within the domestic economy which began to undermine the broad consensus which had supported the *status quo* in the financial system during the 1950s and 1960s.

(i) Domestic Developments: Economic Maturity and the Impact of the Oil Crises

Two seminal events coincided to levy pressure for change on Japan's financial regulatory authorities during the 1970s. One was the country's transition from a developing to a developed economy around the start of the decade. The other was the externally induced OPEC oil price hikes of 1973 and 1978, which accentuated the country's slowdown in economic growth that was occurring at the time. Together they brought Japan's era of high growth to an abrupt halt, as the double-digit rates of real economic growth the country enjoyed in the 1950s and 1960s fell to 8.3 percent in 1970,

5.3 percent in 1973, and turned negative in 1974. Resulting changes in the domestic flow of funds created significant pressure for financial reform.

In response to the economic downturn and heightened instability, the corporate sector's demand for funds fell rapidly and the personal sector's surplus increased sharply. With the securities market still underdeveloped in terms of opportunities for individual investors, lower rates of income growth and rising inflation made savers more sensitive to marginal rates of return. As a result, the postal savings system, which offered a marginally higher interest rate than banks, saw its deposit base grow rapidly.[28] This meant that banks were caught in a pincer movement between falling demand for funds from their corporate clients and falling supply of funds from individual depositors. City banks, which were hit hardest, led a campaign to press the MOF for substantial deregulation, including the liberalisation of deposit and lending rates, the removal of maturity restrictions, the right to offer new investment products, and permission to diversify their customer bases and portfolio activities beyond the bounds specified in their original mandates.

For its part, the MOF had not been unaware that the end of the era of high economic growth era was nearing. With one eye on the way in which financial markets in the US and Europe were developing, it had already begun to study the prospects for financial regulatory reform in the late 1960s.[29] However, very limited progress had been made as interbureau conflicts had resulted in deadlock.[30] Nevertheless, as a result of the new developments of the early 1970s, the Ministry was able to pull together and put its weight behind the idea of deregulating deposit rates. But after experiencing the extent of the political opposition which the Post Office was capable of mobilising, it switched tack to favour a proposal for the introduction of certificates of deposit (CDs), realising that this represented a less controversial, yet potentially significant change. That is, CDs would not adversely affect the business of politically sensitive smaller financial institutions, yet would provide a new means for larger banks to attract funds. The Bank of Japan was strongly in favour of the proposal, because developing a short-term money market would give it better control over the money supply.

This plan became the beachhead for a broader MOF-led financial reform initiative. Paradoxically, the catalyst came in 1975 when the Socialist opposition in the Diet took up protests by nonfinancial firms to the effect that banks were taking advantage of the unstable and inflationary environment to curtail new loans and hike interest rates on existing ones. Finance Minister Ōhira Masayoshi took the opportunity to commission the FSRC to undertake a comprehensive review of the entire banking system. The MOF subsequently drafted a revised version of the Banking Law which went into effect in 1981. However, it demonstrated its discretionary capacity in that it did not wait until the 1981 Banking Law had been passed in the Diet to begin implementing the changes. As soon as the FSRC's final report had been produced in 1979, the Ministry began taking administrative steps to ease branching and retail deposit-taking restrictions and to improve efficiency in the interbank market. Importantly, the revisions in banking were reciprocated in other areas of the financial system in order to preserve the system's essential balance. Thus, for example, where commercial banks gained permission to issue CDs in 1979, securities firms were given permission to market *chûkoku* (medium-term government bond) funds in 1980 which also bore market-determined rates of interest and offered levels of liquidity near to that of bank deposits.

An even more prominent change in the flow of funds data was the rapid increase in government indebtedness. From very low levels in the 1960s, government borrowing had risen steadily, logging its first deficit in 1965 and overtaking the corporate sector as the country's largest net debtor during the following decade.[31] This was a consequence of two developments, one foreseen and one not. The country's strict adherence to balanced budgets (the 'Dodge Line' – named after the prominent US banker who was instrumental in establishing this norm in postwar Japan) was initially abandoned for pragmatic political reasons and in response to the country's economic maturity. Under Prime Minister Tanaka Kakuhei, government spending on public works and quality-of-life-related investment (e.g. roads, train lines, sewers, parks, medical care, and pensions) was increased massively with the aim of maintaining the LDP's position as Japan's only 'catch-all' political party (Muramatsu and Krauss 1987, pp. 526–36). The sudden oil crisis-induced recession further spiked the rise in spending as many new state-financed projects were commissioned to stimulate growth. Inevitable opposition from the MOF's Budget Bureau was overcome with comparative ease as a result of both the emergency nature of problem and politicians' increasing centrality in the policymaking process.[32]

However, a significant problem arose when the MOF's syndicated banks refused to underwrite such large quantities of Japanese government bonds (JGBs) at the fixed, artificially low interest rates which the existing regulatory structure imposed. In 1975, the BOJ found that it could no longer reabsorb, for fear of fueling inflation, the proportion of the outstanding bonds held by banks that it customarily repurchased prior to maturity.[33] Banks were thus left holding large quantities of the low-yielding bonds until maturity, and in protest, boycotted subsequent placement syndicates on a number of occasions. This forced the MOF to begin deregulating the bond market; politicians were powerless to intervene, having initiated the new spending commitments in the first place.[34] Critically, because rates in the JGB market acted as an anchor to all others, scrapping the artificially low interest rates in this sector immediately put pressure on, or demolished outright, the rigid structures which were in place elsewhere.

(ii) International Developments: Early Attempts to Manage Monetary Instability

A second front on which Japan's financial authorities came under pressure to reform their regime was through the country's newfound involvement in international economic diplomacy in the 1970s.[35] This pressure was indirect but again related to the fact that the Japanese economy was no longer small in comparative terms – it had consolidated its position as the world's third largest economy and was clearly no longer a price-taker in international markets. Essentially, the sympathetic international consensus towards the country's development which the US had underwritten against the backdrop of Cold War politics rapidly waned as Japanese mercantilism became a focus of attention upon which other countries could pin many of their difficulties in the unstable macroeconomic environment. This led to calls for significant liberalisation of Japan's markets in both trade and finance, but centred on the revaluation of the yen.

Serious criticism first surfaced with the events surrounding the breakdown of Bretton Woods. The message for Japan was that it had become closely intertwined with the world economy and insulated policy management was no longer possible. The events, Gyohten notes,

> demonstrated Japan's serious underestimation, even ignorance of the strength of its own economy, and ... the irresistible power of market forces ... [They] also left a strong impression among Japanese that we were under very serious international pressure, particularly from the United States, and unfortunately this impression fortified our defensive posture which remained fixed for years afterwards (Volcker and Gyohten 1992, p. 99).

Refusing to accept the damage which its trade surpluses were doing to the fixed exchange rate system, Japan's monetary authorities participated in negotiations at the Smithsonian Institute in 1971, agreeing only to a bare minimum of concessions in terms of allowing the yen to appreciate.[36] This stance was justified by a belief among Japanese monetary officials that its surpluses were transitory, although most commentators, including ex-BOJ Executive Director Ogata Shijûrō, now concede that this calculation was wrong (1996, pp. 4–10).

Following the first oil shock Japanese authorities participated in multilateral negotiations to reconstruct some sort of managed exchange-rate regime in response to escalating financial instability which had led to two major bank failures, one in the US (Franklin National Bank) and one in Germany (Herstatt Bank).[37] Here, the tone of discussions was more congenial but efforts ultimately failed due to narrowly defined and conflicting national interests. In response, the MOF arranged for a secret five-year bilateral loan facility of $1 billion from Saudi Arabia in 1974 to ensure that Japan's own interests at least would be secure. This facility, however, was never used because the Japanese economy recovered relatively rapidly from the oil crises as manufacturers implemented strict domestic cost-cutting and pursued greater export-led growth in concert with periodic intervention by the country's monetary authorities to dampen the yen's rise.

In light of this unilateral currency market intervention, Japan's export-led recovery drew further international criticism. At the IMF summit of May 1977, British Chancellor of the Exchequer Dennis Healey singled the country out as being responsible for distorting the equilibrium of the entire world economy by its 'dirty float'. The Japanese protested that they were merely protecting their economy, but conceded, in concert with the Swiss and the IMF, to extend credit lines to the US later that year to finance a $30 billion stimulus programme when America finally overcame its long-standing aversion to borrowing internationally under the new Carter Administration. Japan's 'dirty float', however, continued until a serious dollar crisis in March 1978 prompted Prime Minister Fukuda Takeo to instruct the MOF to begin overhauling Japan's restrictive foreign exchange controls.[38] Four months later, at the Bonn Summit, Fukuda went further to placate international criticism, agreeing in principle to Japan's costly participation in the ill-fated 'locomotive' experiment, which soon floundered due to the second oil crisis of December 1978 through a lack of common incentives (Volcker and Gyohten 1992, pp. 152–4).[39]

(iii) Global Systemic Developments: Early Repercussions of the Euromarkets

Wider developments in the global financial system also levied pressure for change on Japan's postwar regulatory regime in the 1970s. The enormous expansion of the eurodollar market indirectly affected Japan's domestic financial system as its domestic banks, which were licensed to conduct foreign exchange business, faced a sharp drop in demand.[40] On the one hand, Japanese multinationals had direct access to these new sources of funding at internationally competitive rates;[41] on the other, their competitors in the domestic foreign exchange business – a small number of foreign banks licensed to provide 'impact loans' (foreign currency-denominated medium-term loans sourced through the euromarkets) – saw the demand for their services rise, spurred by increasingly price-sensitive domestic customers. In response, the Japanese banks pressed the MOF for access to the impact loan business, and their wishes were eventually granted.

Inevitably, this upset the foreign banking community, but their troubles were magnified when a credit squeeze which followed the first oil shock compelled the MOF to grant licenses to more foreign institutions to operate in Japan. The twofold increase in competition narrowed lending margins and eroded what profitable business opportunities had existed in 'their' market sector. From 1976, large US firms began to press the MOF for permission to compete in areas of business open only to domestic banks, and to introduce some of the more sophisticated financial products which they marketed overseas.[42]

Moreover, since the MOF had taken the opportunity only to grant new licenses to foreign banks on the grounds of reciprocity, large domestic banks which had recently expanded overseas soon joined foreign firms in calling for the licensing of more advanced financial products, their expertise in this area having grown rapidly with recent experience.[43] The Ministry managed to limit its concessions to the changes already noted above (i.e. the introduction of a commercial paper market, limited interest rate deregulation, etc.), and proposals to which it was less receptive were bogged down interminably in one or other of its in-house *shingikai*. Furthermore, in order that the international expansion of Japanese banks would not undermine the functional segmentation – and, therefore, essential balance – of the domestic market, the MOF's main financial regulatory organs agreed in the Three Bureaus Agreement of 1974 to enforce a prohibition on Japanese banks' overseas securities subsidiaries acting as lead-managers for any international flotations.[44]

To sum up, the way in which Japan's financial regulatory regime dealt with domestic, international and systemic developments in the 1970s was characteristically reactive and piecemeal. Of the three areas, changes emanating in the domestic arena were by far the most significant in that they led directly to regulatory amendments. By the end of the decade, the financial system had undergone peripheral changes – its rigid interest rate structure had been partially undermined and its high degree of functional compartmentalisation between different financial subsectors had been perceptibly weakened. Nevertheless, the regime's administrative characteristics of bureaucratic guidance and convoy regulation had been exploited effectively throughout the period as a means of reactively shoring up the intricate system wherever it was challenged by internal, external or systemic developments.

Internationalisation in the 1980s

Whereas structural changes in the domestic economy had been the main agent of financial regulatory changes in the 1970s, international developments took centre stage in the 1980s. Framed according to a narrow perspective of what domestic structural transformation necessitated, the reforms implemented during the 1970s had been largely piecemeal and reactive. Little consideration was given to drawing up a blueprint for change which took account of important external developments, and the strains which this had caused were already showing. Thus, it was inevitable that reforms in the 1980s would have to address the issue in terms of bringing Japan's regulatory practices closer into line with international norms.

(i) Domestic Developments: Nakasone's Reform Agenda

Domestic developments were not of themselves important in generating pressure for financial deregulation during the 1980s, but they formed an indispensable backdrop for the changes which did take place by cultivating an atmosphere which was receptive to reform more generally. The domestic political agenda was shaped by the legacy of the 1970s – chronically deteriorating public finances and rising levels of bilateral trade friction – and largely predetermined the core policy initiatives upon which successive administrations were to focus: fiscal reform, administrative reform, and the harmonisation of external relations with Japan's main trading partners (Hayao 1993).

In retrospect, virtually the whole the decade bore the impression of Nakasone Yasuhiro, Prime Minister from November 1982 to November 1987, who also influenced both the previous administration of Suzuki Zenkō, through his chairmanship of the Administrative Reform Research Council, and subsequent administrations, through his status as a party elder and his leadership of a powerful LDP faction. Nakasone was an ardent reformer who developed a relatively unusual top-down style of leadership which combined pragmatism with an unusually forward- and outward-looking policy agenda. He challenged the traditional restraints on Japanese prime ministerial power, circumventing the immobilist tendencies of factional politics and the bureaucracy by appointing private advisory groups made up of sympathetic professionals and academics to formulate his own policy agenda, for which he sought a direct mandate from liberal and internationally-minded metropolitan constituents.[45]

All of Nakasone's main consultative bodies paved the way for a change in the ideology governing Japanese financial regulation by including proposals in their reports for a decrease in the existing level of formal and informal regulation.[46] Most explicitly, the first Maekawa report of April 1986 argued the need for the thorough deregulation of cumbersome government rules under the premise 'freedom in principle, restrictions only as exceptions'. Three of its six proposals were related directly to the financial sector.[47] Framed against a background of yen appreciation and mounting trade friction, these bodies contributed to provoking an intense and long-overdue public debate concerning Japan's international roles and domestic economic responsibilities. As such they were important in preparing the ground domestically for international pressure which was brought to a head as a result of developments in the areas of trade and global monetary affairs.

(ii) International Developments: The Yen-Dollar Agreement and Plaza Accord

The two highly significant international developments that introduced new and irresistible pressures for the reform of the Japanese financial system in the 1980s were the Yen-Dollar Agreement and the Plaza Accord. The first grew out of the systemic pressures for reform in the 1970s noted above, the second out of America's experimentation with a strong dollar policy in the early 1980s.

Bilateral lobbying for financial reform in Japan began in 1978 following a tax dispute between foreign firms and the MOF which had occurred two years previously (Pauly 1988, pp. 66–86).[48] In a series of formal and informal meetings, government representatives began to discuss issues of reciprocity and national treatment of foreign financial institutions operating in Japan. Eager to avoid the politicisation of their sphere of influence, financial authorities in Japan reflexively launched a campaign to disabuse observers of the idea that regulatory policy somehow discriminated against foreigners, and a number of issues of 'misunderstanding' were soon identified and remedied. But having had their interest in the issue roused, foreign governments were not about to let the matter drop so quickly. A US congressional team which was scheduled to come to Tokyo in November 1978 to investigate trade issues had already decided to add to its agenda the issue of whether rigidities in the Japanese capital markets might be a significant factor in the bilateral deficit. Its conclusions, published as the Jones Report, asserted that Japanese regulatory treatment 'discriminated against' foreign institutions in that they were treated differently from domestic banks.[49] The MOF rejected the Report as groundless, a posture fully supported by both opposition and government members of the Diet Finance Committee. However, by the time a US Treasury Department team came to study the US bank treatment the following year, a number of more formal changes regarding the treatment of foreign banks had been slated in anticipation of the new Banking Law.[50] After extensive discussions with the Ministry's Banking Bureau, the US team concluded that Japan was making progress towards opening its banking system to foreigners, but that a 'substantial lack of national treatment and equality of competitive opportunity' existed. Eager to head off further congressional intervention on sensitive trade policy issues, the Carter administration decided to push ahead with bilateral financial diplomacy, but made little progress in the face of an upcoming presidential election.

When unveiled in 1981, it was clear that Japan's revised Banking Law set out a new policy of national treatment for foreign firms and came at least as close to meeting standards of openness as did laws in most other OECD countries (Pauly 1988, p. 80). It provided an explicit code for foreign bank regulation (subject to a preliminary reciprocity test) but nevertheless managed to avoid compromising the strict segmentation of the domestic market. Financial issues appeared to have been extricated successfully from ongoing trade controversies. But even as the new Law was being enacted, many foreign bankers were coming to realise that the technical/legal framework for their operations in Japan was less important than the actual response of the Japanese market to their presence. The administrative burden of detailed reporting to the MOF and close monitoring of the money market by the BOJ remained considerable, but foreign firms realised that without either a strong retail base or fully free capital markets they would never be able to match their domestic competitors for profitability. Thus, the issue of market access came to be associated with qualified notions such as 'equality of opportunity' and 'effective reciprocity'.

In the context of rising bilateral trade imbalances, the new Reagan administration picked up on this point and approached the MOF with a formal list of demands for reforms.[51] In addition to the issue of reciprocity, the move was bolstered by the assertion that the yen was undervalued as a result of Japan's closed financial regulatory structure, and that this conferred unfair advantages upon Japanese manufacturers and financial institutions in international markets.[52] This action provided the administration with a highly visible policy by which it could be *seen* to be addressing America's deficit without having to raise the perennially unpopular issue of tax/interest rate hikes.

The MOF appeared genuinely taken aback. Its officials firmly believed that the newly revised Banking and Foreign Exchange and Trade Control Laws were equivalent in substance to those prevailing in the US, and that ongoing liberalisation would provide more profitable opportunities for foreign financial institutions and, in time, rectify trade imbalances. In an attempt to convey this message, a team of senior bureaucrats and prominent domestic bankers was assembled and sent to the US and Europe on a two-week tour to 'explain' the new regulatory environment. But finding that the US in particular would not be easily placated, the Japanese government nominally agreed to enter into bilateral discussions realising that, if nothing else, this would provide temporary cover from protectionist elements in Congress. The establishment of a bilateral project team, the 'Joint Japan-US *Ad Hoc* Group on Yen-Dollar Exchange Rate, Financial and Capital Market Issues' – colloquially known as the Yen-Dollar Committee – was thus announced at a November 1983 US-Japan summit (Frankel 1984; Tadokoro 1988). It became the first body to formalise foreign demands for Japanese financial reform.

The Japanese team was led by representatives from the relatively progressive International Finance Bureau, but included members of the Banking and Securities Bureaus. It came to the table ready to negotiate with a set of new reform proposals which the FSRC had drawn up eight months earlier.[53] However, it was immediately evident that the US delegation, which was notable for its extreme ideological makeup, was looking for much more radical concessions.[54] A Japanese participant, Gyohten Toyoo recollects that the Japanese side wanted to proceed on a step-by-step basis but that Treasury Secretary Regan, impatient for immediate action, backed up his demands using the analogy of cutting off a dog's tail – doing it in one stroke so as not to prolong the animal's suffering by cutting it off in small pieces (Volcker and Gyohten 1992, p. 250)!

The Committee met six times, and in a May 1984 joint statement by Finance Minister Takeshita Noboru and Regan announced a far-reaching programme for the structural reform of the Japanese financial system. In what was later hailed by the MOF as 'an epochal document', the Committee's report outlined Japan's commitments (i) to deregulate interest rates considerably, (ii) to licence a number of new markets for financial products that had become widely used elsewhere, (iii) to provide greater access to euroyen financing to domestic firms, (iv) to allow foreign banks to participate in domestic trust business, and (v) to open membership of the Tokyo Stock Exchange (TSE) to foreign firms (MOF 1985; see also Hall 1993, ch. 6).[55] Figure 2.3 sets out the Agreement's twenty-two point agenda in chronological order of implementation.

From the table it is evident that reforms undertaken would necessarily undermine the existing structure of Japan's closely regulated and carefully balanced financial system. Three areas are worth highlighting. First, under criticism that the yen's role as a reserve currency in trade and international finance was incommensurate with Japan's position in the world economy, the MOF agreed to promote greater internationalisation of the yen. Measures taken included gradual relaxation of the rules governing the eligibility of participants trading yen products (both by nationality and by type of institution), the permissible types of financial instruments used, and quantitative restrictions on transactions.[56] Second, the MOF agreed to relax rules restricting price competition in domestic market which, the US argued, hindered the competitive advance of foreign firms by violating the norm of reciprocity. Measures taken included the stepped deregulation of interest rate ceilings, floors and maturity qualifications,[57] and the licensing of new control-free capital market instruments such as Money Market Certificates (MMCs). Third, and again invoking the principle of reciprocity, this time to back up US concerns that foreigners were disadvantaged from 'proper' fundraising and investment opportunities in Japan, the MOF agreed to allow the broadening and deepening of domestic financial markets.[58] Measures taken included liberalising the short- and long-term money markets and government bond market in terms of underwriters and issuers (both by nationality and type of institution), issuing criteria, and products traded (both on primary and secondary markets).[59]

While it appeared that the Treasury had been able to dictate the reforms, it had actually encountered substantial resistance in matters which touched

Financial Deregulation 'Japanese-Style'

Item	Date implemented
• Lifting of ban, in principle, on speculative currency trading	4/84
• Lifting of ban on euroyen bond issuance by residents	4/84
• Liberalisation of short-term euroyen impact loans	6/84
• Lifting of ban on converting into yen foreign currency funds raised in the euromarkets	6/84
• Lifting of ban on foreign firms lead-managing debt issues by Japanese firms	12/84
• Liberalisation of floating rate financial products	3/85
• Authorisation of euroyen commercial paper issues	4/85
• Revision of taxes on euroyen bonds	4/85
• Decision to authorise medium- and long-term euroyen loans	4/85
• Lowering of minimum issuing unit for commercial paper	4/84
• Establishment of yen-denominated bankers acceptance market	6/85
• Liberalisation of interest rates on large denomination deposits	10/85
• Authorisation of foreign banks' entry into the trust market	10/85
• Tokyo Stock Exchange membership to be opened to foreign firms	11/85
• Decision to establish a financial futures market	12/85
• Decision to establishment a Japanese Treasury bill market	2/86
• Liberalisation of euroyen issuance by nonresidents	4/86
• Decision to establish a Tokyo offshore market	12/86
• Liberalisation of corporate bond issue terms	2/87
• Decision to allow the establishment domestic bond credit rating firms	7/87
• Revision of short- and long-term prime interest rate system	1/89
• Liberalisation of interest rates on small amount deposits	6/89

Figure 2.3: The Yen-Dollar Agreement
(*Source:* amended from Endo 1996a, p. 19)

core institutions of domestic regulation. Suggestions, for example, that financial openness would be enhanced by completely deregulating all interest rates or abolishing funding restrictions in segmented domestic sectors were rejected outright by the MOF, and other propositions which would challenge powerful domestic interest groups were euphemistically assigned for 'further study'.[60] In fact, most commentators conclude that the MOF was able to exploit *gaiatsu* surrounding a highly politicised issue – increasingly fragile US-Japan relations – to further its own agenda for progressive reform. Bilateral pressure formed a convenient guise for circumventing vested interests and modernising the financial system. And since there were so many US demands, the MOF could almost pick from a menu those which it was willing to make or, at the very least, barter the pace at which it was willing to implement particular reforms. Hereby, relatively uncontroversial issues, such as the establishment of a euroyen market, were executed quickly, while those which would prove more disruptive domestically, such as interest rate deregulation, could be delayed and drawn out.

The sea change in Japanese attitudes to domestic deregulation marked in the Yen-Dollar Agreement was simultaneously evident in a new proactive attitude towards international cooperation in monetary affairs. Proposals in this area proliferated with the severe international monetary instability precipitated by the second oil crisis and in the context of a prolonged 'global' recession punctuated by numerous unilateral interventions to head off speculation against the Deutsche mark, French franc and British pound in particular. In contrast to his predecessors in the 1970s, Nakasone saw Japan's participation in such an exercise as a chance to advance Japan's international stature. However, it was not until the US was willing to climb aboard that any attempt at international macroeconomic management could realistically be attempted (Funabashi 1987; Volcker and Gyohten 1992).[61]

The catalyst was the advent of the second Reagan administration. The new Treasury team under James Baker began almost immediately to make positive noises about coordinated intervention at tentative talks on the coordination of basic economic policies at the June 1985 G–5 summit meeting in Tokyo.[62] This led to a heavily publicised and unprecedented agreement struck at the Plaza Hotel in New York on September 22, 1985. The Plaza Accord called for the 'orderly appreciation' of other currencies against the dollar and promised joint intervention to restrain further rises in the dollar in order that exchange rates might better reflect 'fundamental economic conditions'.[63] Finance Minister Takeshita had surprised the American side by volunteering to permit the yen to go up by more than ten percent, a factor which was crucial to the success of the negotiations because the primary concern of the Europeans was not so much the rates of their currencies against the dollar but against the yen (Volcker and Gyohten 1992, p. 244–5; 254). This good will reflected the Nakasone administration's sensitivity to mounting protectionist pressures in Congress, and it was successful in so far as the Accord succeeded in averting such action.

The intervention to bring down the dollar, however, proved disastrous in that it initiated a seemingly inexorable fall in its value *vis à vis* the yen. Retrospectively, this is explained by the fact that the dollar already had been on a downward trend for six months prior to the agreement, although this was not so clear at the time. Consequently, the coordinated intervention only added to the inertia of the dollar's fall. In Japan, what was experienced as the high yen (*endaka*) consumed the media and sparked infighting within the LDP, as Miyazawa Kiichi led criticism of Nakasone and Takeshita as the plan's prime instigators. For his part Nakasone appealed for patience, and quietly dispatched Takeshita to the US to request help in stopping further yen appreciation. Unsurprisingly, no help was forthcoming since the recent currency movements had made little impact on the US bilateral deficit. Still, back in Japan the general election results of 1986 showed that *endaka* had had surprisingly little affect on public opinion. To some extent, consumers were benefiting from lower prices and increased overseas investment and travel choices. Knee-jerk criticism from politicians and businessmen also abated, partly because Nakasone had strategically replaced Takeshita with Miyazawa, and partly because businesses were able to use *endaka* as an excuse to pursue rationalisation.

By the end of 1986 the effects of the Plaza Accord had run their course. The dollar had depreciated by an average of twenty-five percent, but America's trade deficit had continued its long-term upward trend. The US continued to push for more expansionary policies from Japan and Germany and, in return, was asked to curtail its government deficit. A subsequent exercise in multilateral coordination failed to stop the dollar's slide: the Louvre Accord of February 1987 mandated economic stimuli in Japan and Germany and set up 'reference zones' of target currency ranges for central banks to defend, but the latter were soon guessed and overwhelmed by the markets.[64] Finally, in the wake of the October 19 stock market plunge on Wall Street (Black Monday) later that year, the G–7 issued the Christmas Communiqué in December which sought to assure the markets that central bankers would work together to ensure that further speculation against the dollar came to nothing. This marked the end of a three-year period of intense collaboration to 'manage' the dollar which had cumulated in resignation as to the dollar's level. All that the participants could claim to have achieved was that their efforts had succeeded in intensifying frank, informal dialogue among policymakers (Volcker and Gyohten 1992, pp. 287–310).

(iii) Global Systemic Developments: Regulatory Arbitrage and the Bubble

Systemic developments also affected Japan's financial regulatory structure in two areas during the 1980s, although in contradictory ways. During the first half of the decade, internationally active financial institutions (both Japanese and foreign) deftly exploited some of the regulatory idiosyncrasies which had begun to appear in the Japanese market in the 1970s. However, more significant in terms of indirect but long-term repercussions were the events of the second half of the decade. The artificial boom known as the 'bubble' took away the market incentive for pressing on with the structural reform of the finance system and economy more generally because of the myriad new business opportunities that it created for financial institutions operating in Japan.

Leading international financial institutions were not passive during the time that Yen-Dollar negotiations were taking place, but sought to take advantage of the newly politicised environment. At least three examples can be cited of successful market-led initiatives for regulatory change. First, in league with Nomura Securities, JP Morgan approached the MOF in June 1983 to request approval for a plan to establish a joint-venture trust banking company in Japan, an area which was known to be closed to both securities companies and foreign banks. As expected, the request was informally turned down, the Ministry fearing instability in the trust banking sector which it saw as too weak to sustain new competition. Morgan was thus able to turn to Washington and, in the midst of the Yen-Dollar negotiations, found the Treasury more than willing to put foreign access to trust banking in Japan on its agenda for deregulation. On hearing about the case, and recognising the symbolic nature of the issue, Nakasone publicly declared his support for licensing such joint ventures before being informed by the MOF that it would need two-to-three years for the FSRC to study the proposal in order to avoid potentially catastrophic market disruption.[65] However, in the highly charged environment, the MOF agreed to a compromise: it would license a very limited number of foreign banks to operate either on their own or in a joint-venture *with domestic trust banks* in the trust market, lift the prohibition on city banks undertaking trust business offshore and give securities firms and city banks greater latitude to provide investment advisory services.[66]

Second, Citibank announced in November 1983 that it wanted to purchase a stake in a UK stock brokerage which would effectively give it control over the firm's Tokyo branch, a clear violation of Article 65 of the Japanese Securities and Exchange Law which segregated the banking and securities sectors. After three months of internal debate, and again in light of the ongoing Yen-Dollar talks, the MOF licensed the deal on an 'exceptional basis'. Not wanting to be left behind, a number of Citi's competitors rushed to set up similar ventures, which the MOF found itself in no position to reject.

Third, Sumitomo Bank sought permission to purchase a small Swiss bank (Banca del Gottardo) in February 1984, attracted by its universal banking capabilities which would provide an indirect route into the European securities market. Again the MOF acquiesced in spite of reservations, whereupon Swiss and German banks seized on the opportunity to demand reciprocal access to Japan's securities market. They were initially rebuffed in line with Article 65, but after the Germany authorities responded by discriminating against Japanese institutions when liberalising participation in their bond market (foreign firms, but not the Japanese, were permitted to underwrite euro-deutschmark bond issues), and when the Swiss threatened similar sanctions, the MOF entered into a series of bilateral talks in 1985.[67] The MOF concluded negotiations agreeing to license certain foreign banks from these countries to open securities offices in Japan, as long as they did so indirectly (i.e. via overseas affiliates). Subsequently, many foreign banks took this route to establishing securities business in Tokyo.

In the latter part of the decade, the structural effects of the Yen-Dollar Agreement combined with the macroeconomic effects of the Plaza Accord to precipitate a speculative frenzy of domestic stock and property market investment which engulfed representatives from all sectors of the economy and spread to the international environment (Hashimoto 1995, pp. 183–238; Hayase 1997; McKinnon and Ohno 1997). The basic ingredients were provided by the volatile mixture of underlying economic and financial policies by which Japan's government chose to respond to the domestic and international developments already noted above.

After running up a very large deficit in the 1970s, successive Japanese administrations had adopted stringent fiscal policy to reduce the government's dependence on deficit-covering bonds. This coincided with the MOF's liberalisation of international capital controls in 1980 and the start of piecemeal liberalisation of domestic financial markets, soon formalised in the Yen-Dollar Agreement of 1984. As a result, private capital began to pour out of Japan, attracted particularly to the US where the first Reagan administration had adopted tight monetary and loose fiscal policies, pushing up the value of the dollar against the yen by nearly fifty percent between 1980 and 1985 (see Nakao 1995). This exacerbated the existing and already politically-sensitive trade imbalance and multilateral action to bring the value of the dollar back down followed, marked by the Plaza Accord. However, given the Nakasone administration's redoubled commitment (supported by the MOF) to reduce the government's outstanding deficit, Japan chose to follow the US and UK's lead in adopting monetary policy as its main tool of economic policy. The initial strategy was to effect a sharp increase in the money supply in order to reverse the yen's appreciation and rectify trade imbalances. But with no immediate effect, and under pressure from the government and MOF, the BOJ pushed harder on its monetary levers. Interest rates were cut (to 2.25%) following the Louvre Accord of February 1987 and Japan's money supply posted double-digit annual growth rates for almost the entire period from the beginning of 1987 until the end of 1990 (see Jackson 1994, fig. 2).[68]

With interest rates low and the money supply growing rapidly, both the corporate and household sectors found themselves with excess cash. Japanese firms used the funds to invest in plant and equipment, to acquire foreign businesses, and to purchase domestic and foreign financial assets and real estate. Individuals found themselves with fewer choices: they could either spend, place their savings in low-yield savings accounts with officially-controlled rates of interest, or invest in stocks and land where prices, and therefore returns, were not controlled. A period of rapid domestic economic expansion and phenomenal asset price inflation ensued.

The 'bubble's' formation was exaggerated by recent deregulation in the financial sector for which general prudential banking standards had yet not been tightened accordingly. Banks cast about in search of new borrowers as large manufacturers reduced their dependency by shifting increasingly to

The Case of Japan

Nikkei Index of Stock Prices (Left Index)
Residential Land Prices – Six Largest Cities (Right Index)

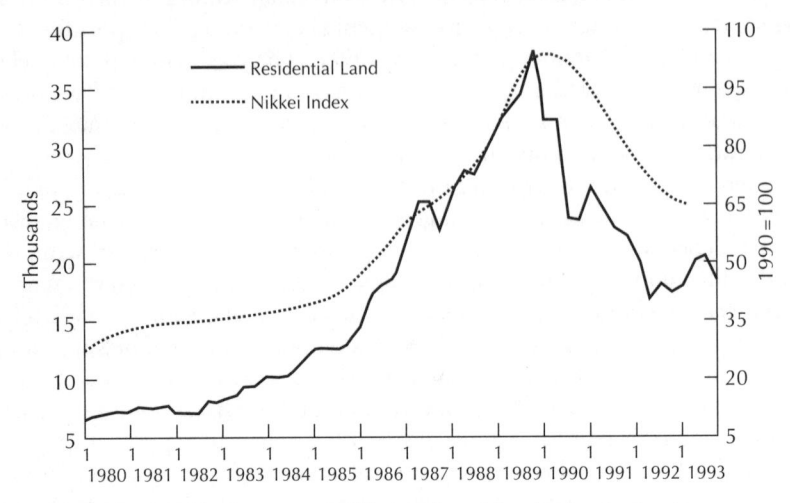

Figure 2.4: The Bubble Economy (Nikkei 225 and land price indices)
(*Source*: Jackson 1994, fig. 3)

retained earnings and direct credit (raised either at home or abroad). Much of the new lending was made at the luxury end of the market – for condominiums, hotels and golf courses – as banks softened credit standards in order to keep up with the spectacular rates of growth.[69] For landowners and shareholders, their inflated property and stock values proved good collateral for bank loans, which were in turn used to buy more land and stocks.[70] This coincided with the popularisation of many new financial products introduced under the Yen–Dollar Agreement, such as some derivatives.[71] The MOF had licensed derivatives for their hedging properties but they were used increasingly for blatant speculation, or 'financial engineering' (*zaitekku*) strategies, by which many large manufacturers sought to compensate declines in overseas revenues caused by the high yen.[72]

The bubble inflated the wealth of asset holders and investors/speculators, fuelling disparities in wealth among firms and individuals. These differences were not simply 'on paper'. The rises in land prices, in particular, excluded a whole segment of the population – mostly first-time buyers – from buying a home at all, and it was this that eventually sparked concern in the political arena (Sassen 1991). Belatedly realising what was happening, the BOJ began to ratchet up interest rates and slow the growth rate of the money supply in 1989.[73] While double-digit increases in the money supply had been the norm throughout Japan's high-growth period, it was now clear that they had not been compatible with the economy's lower potential growth rates of the

1980s. Four further rate increases followed in sharp succession, BOJ Governor Mineo Yasushi arguing that too much money was still being channelled into investments of 'nonproductive' and 'fictitious' value. The final hike in August 1990 left the ODR at six percent, versus the 2.5 percent level that had prevailed in 1987 and 1988, soon triggering the domestic stock market crash. The ensuing and seemingly bottomless 'triple decline' – in stock and bond prices, the value of the yen, and land and property prices – marked the end of the bubble economy and left the financial sector in a very fragile state as a significant proportion of its outstanding loans and/or investments turned sour.

When compared to the reforms of the 1970s, the amendments to Japan's financial regulatory regime made in the 1980s were of a much greater magnitude. Domestic developments were important in preparing the ground for reforms, but it was international developments that proved critical in an exact sense: US intervention decisively altered the balance of power among domestic coalitions regarding reform. The cooperative stance towards international monetary coordination which Japan's financial authorities took was also significant. It indirectly served to deepen their ideas about global financial regulatory norms.[74] Finally, systemic developments played a contradictory role, initially exploiting domestic and international events to prise further deregulation from the MOF, but later exaggerating the distortions of the bubble economy and thereby temporarily assuaging new demands for reform.

During the 1980s, it was the structural characteristics of Japanese financial regulation that changed most. The arbitrary suppression of interest rates was all but abolished, the rigid functional segmentation of financial institutions was further weakened, and rules and regulations were made more explicit. Hereby, the move away from a closed and bureaucratically controlled structure towards a fully international and market-determined one that had begun a decade earlier sped up considerably. Nevertheless, the system's administrative practices of regulation showed little sign of change. The MOF had managed to accommodate new developments in such a way that it still 'managed' deregulation in its conventional manner, and changes were undertaken in a familiarly reactive and cautious manner. Furthermore, because financial deregulation was proceeding much more dramatically elsewhere, the regulatory gap between Japan and its major competitors actually was greater by the end of the decade than it had been at the start.

Globalisation in the 1990s

Whereas international developments had the greatest effect in bringing about changes in Japan's traditional financial regulatory system in the 1980s, systemic developments contributed most strongly to reform in the 1990s.

They levied pressure through the domestic repercussions of the bubble economy, and via market forces which threatened increasingly to marginalise the Japanese financial markets.

(i) Domestic Developments: Scandals and Bureaucratic Complicity

On the domestic front, pressure for financial reform was generated by a profusion of scandals, almost all of which related in some way to the excesses of the late 1980s. To demonstrate how they affected Japan's financial regulatory regime, these events can be arranged into three categories: (i) scandals which led to a greater codification of financial regulation, (ii) scandals which narrowed the MOF's scope for administrative guidance, and (iii) scandals which undermined the convoy system.

Scandals which led to greater legal codification

Scandals resulted in a more explicit codification of financial regulation after several high-profile cases emerged involving insider trading and share-loss compensation payments. Two seminal insider trading scandals came to light during the mid-to-late 1980s (Tateho Chemical and Recruit Cosmos) and led to legislative changes which outlawed the practice in May 1988.[75] Prior to this time, insider trading was not banned specifically in law, and the practice was considered endemic in the country's stock markets (Kanazaki 1982). The MOF made a point of using the scandals as an opportunity to *show* that it was moving to bring Japan into line with international standards by modernising the securities market in preparation for the global trend towards disintermediation that was catching up with the country. Nevertheless, the actual substance of the legal revisions – in terms of resources for monitoring compliance and punitive sanctions mandated – fell well short of emerging international norms.[76]

Compensation payments made by securities companies to privileged clients for losses sustained in stock market trading were similarly prohibited in October 1991.[77] The practice was publicised first in December 1989 when the National Tax Agency (NTA) spotted that Daiwa, Yamaichi, and eighteen other securities companies had written off approximately ¥18 billion in such payments as 'business expenses'. The NTA ruled that these were non-tax-deductible 'entertainment expenses', and fined the brokerages accordingly. At the time Nomura and Nikkō denied that they were engaged in the practice, so considerable publicity followed a *Yomiuri Shinbun* article in June 1991 which exploded their claims. The MOF conducted a cursory investigation and announced that a total of ¥78 billion in such payments had been made between April 1991 and March 1997 (the statutory limitation for such investigations being five years). The Ministry had the Commercial Code amended to introduce harsher penalties for violations, particularly regarding the falsification of reports to regulatory authorities. The Ministry's Securities Bureau simultaneously reviewed its administrative ordinances (*shōrei*) and had several of them codified as TSE regulations.[78] As a result, the firms involved received unprecedented punishments by Japan's comparatively lax standards, and over the next few years the Securities and Exchanges Surveillance Commission (SESC – see below) brought six more cases to prosecution.[79]

However, a spate of new cases emerged in early 1997 by which Nomura, Dai-ichi Kangyō Bank (DKB), Daiwa Securities, Nikkō and Yamaichi were found to have persisted in compensating client losses. Prosecutors focused their attention on payments made to a single *sōkaiya*[80] (corporate racketeer) – Koike Ryûichi – although there were early indications that the scope of illegal activity was much wider.[81] Following high-profile investigations, which involved numerous televised raids on corporate offices and private residences, the firms involved were prosecuted and the MOF metered out more severe penalties.[82] Within six months, the Koike case had led to fifty-eight top-level corporate resignations, twenty arrests and one suicide; an investigation by the NTA was pending.[83] To deter further incidents and assuage public criticism that the penalties levied had been too lenient (see editorial sampler *JT* 24/8/97), politicians and bureaucrats deliberated revising the penalties for illegal securities trading and false reporting.[84] These were stiffened, ostensibly to take account of the impact of violations of social ethics, but the new penalties are still mild by international standards (*Nikkei* 15/4/97).[85] One legal expert explained that this relative laxity is almost inevitable because of the need to maintain a balance with other parts of the Commercial Code (interview with University of Tokyo law professor Kanda Hideki, 24/7/97). Early indications are that the new penalties are proving insufficient in deterring payoffs: recent surveys indicate consistently that the majority of corporate executives believe that relations with *sōkaiya* will continue for the foreseeable future because of the inherent difficulty of breaking such ties.[86]

Scandals which restricted the MOF's scope for administrative guidance

Scandals narrowed the MOF's scope for administrative guidance as a series of incidents illustrating bureaucratic incompetence and the abuse of power led to the Ministry being relieved of some of its regulatory functions. These highlight how adherence to traditional practices had made Japan's financial regulators highly susceptible to conflicts of interest. The three most important instances related to (i) the sloppy way in which the MOF initially dealt with the share-loss compensation scandal, (ii) its mishandling of the political and economic turmoil following Prime Minister Miyazawa's defeat in the 1993 general election, and (iii) evidence of corruption pervading almost all aspects of market supervision.

In the first instance, revelations of intransparency in regulation and the leniency in dealing with firms involved in the share-loss compensation scandal led to the MOF being stripped symbolically of some of its core regulatory functions. The ball was set in motion when the Fair Trade Commission (FTC) unexpectedly produced its own much more comprehensive assessment of the earlier share-loss compensation scandals in November 1991.[87] This revealed that between April 1987 and March 1991 the Big Four securities firms had actually paid out ¥172 billion to 231 clients (the Ministry's estimate was ¥78 billion), and that the securities firms had already received two written directives (*tsûtatsu*) from the MOF in December 1989 ordering them to cease compensating clients and close their *eigyō tokkin* accounts. The FTC report also substantiated a bitter and unusually public allegation by the then president of Nomura (Tabuchi Yoshihisa) that the practice of compensating losses had been informally approved by the MOF as a way to keep the Tokyo market buoyant during the bubble's aftermath.[88] Intense media criticism of the Ministry ensued, centring on the claim that it had become too close to the firms which it was meant to be monitoring.

In response, Prime Minister Kaifu Toshiki charged his standing third Provisional Council on Administrative Reform, led by businessman Suzuki Eiji, with the task of recommending financial regulatory changes. Suzuki made no secret of his own preference that Japan should set up a fully independent securities regulator modeled on the US Securities and Exchange Commission. The LDP's Finance Council also began debating the issue, and a solid majority there also seemed to favour this option (Vogel 1996, p. 187). This development threatened to deprive the MOF of its ability to orchestrate bargains by administrative guidance and maintain the system's essential balance. Thus, guided by a senior MOF bureaucrat with notoriously close ties to senior LDP politicians including former prime minister Takeshita (Ogawa Akira), the Ministry launched an all-out effort to stave off dismemberment.[89] It pursued a three-pronged strategy of bombarding the Provisional Council and Finance Council with extensive briefings on (i) the essential interconnectedness of financial regulation in an era of financial globalisation, (ii) the unsuitability of a Securities and Exchange Commission-type body in Japan's regulatory environment, and (iii) the fact that a separate new agency would contradict the spirit of the government's ongoing administrative reform drive.

The end result was political agreement on a much watered-down version of the US solution. A new securities regulator was established *within* the MOF, but its top three posts went to outsiders. A bill to make the necessary revisions to the Securities and Exchange Law was passed in the Diet in June 1992 with only minor revisions, and the Securities and Exchange Surveillance Commission (SESC) was launched the following month. Hereby, the LDP was able to give the impression of having responded to events but the substance of any changes was marginal (Keehn 1997).[90]

In the second instance, the insensitivity with which the MOF conducted itself during and after the political turmoil of 1993 led to the further curtailment of its discretionary powers in several areas of financial regulation. After the LDP's fall from thirty-eight years in power, the MOF, under the leadership of Vice Minister Saitō Jirō, made a critical miscalculation in opting to transfer its allegiance to Ozawa Ichiro in the belief that his progressivist party (Shinshintō) would retain political power for some time.[91] When the LDP resumed power in a new coalition government the following June, it found itself with both a rationale for punishing the MOF for its 'defection' and an environment which was becoming more conducive by the day to such action. The Ministry's standing in the public's eye had been falling for some time, and this situation had been exacerbated recently by the MOF's involvement in Prime Minister Hosokawa Morihiro's unpopular and rapidly aborted attempt to introduce a 'national welfare tax' in February 1994.[92]

Matters were brought to a head when the MOF put forward a plan to liquidate the country's bankrupt *jûsen*, the imminent default of which threatened to unsettle the financial system.[93] The plan, drawn up by the FSRC in September 1995, called for financial bailouts using public funds. When the media discovered that the MOF had intimate links to the *jûsen*, they jumped at the new opportunity to vilify the Ministry for its intransparent methods of regulation, economic mismanagement, and general arrogance in defending the scheme (see below). In view of the real dangers of financial instability, the LDP supported the MOF's plan and used it as the basis for two bills which were submitted to the Diet in the spring of 1996 and, after considerable shenanigans, passed in June.[94] These provided for an injection of ¥685 billion in public funds for the initial liquidation of the *jûsen*, and left the door open for further appropriations as necessary to cover one half of the huge secondary losses that were expected to result from uncollectable debts (commercial banks which founded the *jûsen* were expected to cover the other half). The press speculated that the plan represented the equivalent of requiring every man, woman and child in Japan to pay ¥10,000 – to which a *Yomiuri Shinbun* poll showed seventy-two percent of respondents opposed – and in Tokyo's gubernatorial elections, a former entertainer (Aoshima Yukio) was elected on a single platform of not using metropolitan funds for the bailouts. Amidst record profits boosted by ultralow interest rates, banks, too, drew fire for having been instrumental in founding the *jûsen* and influencing their day-to-day management decisions.[95]

Around the same time, the MOF was also involved in a major international scandal. Its action following a billion-dollar fraud case which came to light in September 1995 at the US subsidiary of Daiwa Bank drew attention to how far the Ministry's idiosyncratic style of regulation was out of line with global norms.[96] After being notified in early August by Daiwa's senior management of huge accounting irregularities at the firm's US subsidiary, the MOF advised that the incident be suppressed while it investigated whether the problem could be resolved quietly in order to minimise the negative repercussions for Daiwa and other internationally active Japanese banks. Eventually concluding that this would be impossible, the MOF belatedly notified US authorities – forty-one days later. This (in)action generated international outrage, and when it was subsequently defended by a senior MOF official, Finance Minister Takemura was forced to make a humiliating public apology to Treasury Secretary Rubin on behalf of the MOF and guarantee that such a thing would never be allowed to happen again.[97]

Hereby, the intensity of so-called 'MOF bashing' in media and political circles rose. The *Asahi Shinbun* was the first with its call to 'Break up the MOF' in an editorial (17/9/95), and others were quick to follow (see editorial sampler, *JT* 17/12/95). Anxious to get the *jûsen* bills passed, and seizing the opportunity to revenge itself on the MOF, political debate on breaking up the Ministry was set in motion by Prime Minister Hashimoto Ryûtaro in January 1996, following Murayama's resignation.[98] The new government adopted financial regulatory reform as a headline political initiative and stated its explicit aim of stripping the MOF of some of its powers to put an end to its traditional practices of financial regulation by administrative guidance and the convoy system. Following approximately a year of intense negotiations (see Appendix 1),[99] bills were submitted to the Diet proposing (i) the creation of an independent financial supervisory body, the Financial Supervisory Agency (FSA) and (ii) reform of the 1942 BOJ Law to give the central bank greater independence from the MOF. Both changes passed in June and went into effect the following year. The results were significant, although as with the earlier efforts to create a Japanese-style Securities and Exchange Commission, it was clear that the MOF had succeeded in substantially watering down the strength of the original proposals.

The MOF lost its remaining nominal control over financial supervision to the FSA, which absorbed the SESC and several parts of the Ministry's Banking and Securities Bureaus on June 22, 1998. Although housed in a Ministry annex and staffed mainly (ninety percent) by MOF employees, the FSA falls under the jurisdiction of the Cabinet Office, and is headed by a political appointee. Commentators have observed that its small number of employees gives cause for concern as to whether it will be able to fulfill its mandate for independently checking the affairs of financial institutions.[100] The MOF retained, moreover, its financial policymaking mandate. Many in the LDP had favoured expanding the FSA into a larger Finance Agency with financial policy and planning capacities, but the Ministry successfully defended itself on the basis that the integration of supervision and planning functions goes against the trend towards establishing regulatory firewalls in the US and Europe. In light of the scandals, some in the MOF's Budget Bureau and Minister's Secretariat had supported the idea of ditching altogether the Ministry's disgraced market-based divisions – the Banking and Securities Bureaus – for the sake of purity, so the outcome represented a compromise of opinions within the MOF, as well as with politicians (interview with Adachi Nobiru of the International Finance Bureau, 30/5/98).

The MOF also lost substantial influence over Japan's monetary policy. Against the background of having pressured the BOJ to maintain a loose monetary policy against its better judgment in the 1980s, the 1942 BOJ Law was revised to grant the central bank formal independence from the Ministry starting April 1998.[101] Hereby, the MOF was deprived of its two places on the Bank's Policy Board, which was entirely repopulated with cabinet appointees, although it secured the right to request that the BOJ delay implementation of a change in rates for short period (two weeks) should major disagreements over monetary policy arise.[102] It also maintained a modest degree of indirect control over the BOJ via the Bank's accountability to the Diet through the Finance Minister, his secretariat being made up exclusively of MOF staff. In comparative terms, the new BOJ Law has made the Bank more independent from the MOF, but less so politically than either the recently reformed Bank of England, the Bundesbank or, arguably, the US Federal Reserve.

Most importantly for the MOF, it managed to avoid amputation of its core budget-making role, a proposition that was favoured by the media and many in politics. Moves were made to explore the possibility of executing this ultimate sanction, and Hashimoto's Administrative Reform Council (ARC) came out in favour of the idea in late 1997.[103] However, after political deliberations on the Committee's proposal, the coalition government agreed in early 1998 to put the proposal on hold indefinitely. In theory, the Ministry was to be left in one piece so that it could manage the country's financial instability and the introduction of far-reaching reforms with minimal disruption. In reality, it looked like political horse-trading and other considerations underlay the proposal's subversion. A deal was apparently struck between the LDP and MOF shortly before the Big Bang announcement of November 1996, by which the LDP would protect the MOF in exchange for the Ministry's support and provision of major new policy initiatives (see section 2.3 below). Meanwhile, the need to strip the MOF of its budgetary function had been diminished almost by default. Hashimoto's administrative reform agreement meant that the MOF would automatically have much less power relative to the proposed new 'super ministries' – the new Economics Ministry, General Affairs Ministry, and Cabinet Office – which were set to emerge as the major bureaucratic power centres in the early years of the twenty-first century.[104] Purged thus of its 'diseased' supervisory and monetary policymaking functions, the Ministry could be left safely in tact for the time being.

Nevertheless, as a result of the political instability which followed the LDP's further loss of strength in the Upper House in July 1998, and Hashimoto's subsequent replacement by Obuchi Keizō, a resurgent opposition forced an unexpected revival of the issue of breaking up the MOF upon the LDP as the price for passing several critical financial stabilisation bills in the Diet.[105] Under the guise of holding the MOF responsible for Japan's current financial instability, politicians agreed to strip the MOF of its exclusive mandate for financial supervision by January 1, 2001. Hereafter, the MOF would have to share responsibility for supervision with an independent 'financial revitalisation' committee which was to be set up by the end of 1998 under a cabinet member who was also given responsibility for the FSA (*Nikkei* 27/9/98; 1/10/98). Hashimoto's resignation thus paved the way for the revival of the MOF issue as a political football. However, it is clear that considerable scope still exists for this latest agreement to be watered down in the familiar fashion prior to, as well as during, implementation.

In the third instance, evidence of corruption pervading the execution of financial regulation led to further curbs on the MOF's discretionary power through amendments to regulatory changes which were already in the pipeline, and via reformulations of existing internal codes of practice. This was a result of ministerial complicity, that was evident in three sets of scandals which emerged in the mid-1990s, (i) relating to the financial collapses which began in 1994, (ii) during the implementation of the *jûsen* resolution scheme of 1996, and (iii) as a result of investigations into the 1997 share-loss compensation schemes. These scandals indicated that regulatory conflicts of interest were endemic within Japan's financial supervisory structure, and not simply limited to a few incidents involving very large firms. However, their timing was such that they had more of an impact on the institutional practices of regulation, rather than on its codified structure.

First, with the financial collapses which began to emerge under the weight of huge amounts of bad loans in 1994 (see the subsection below), it became clear that the MOF had not supervised effectively the firms under its jurisdiction. When Anzen Credit collapsed, one third of its loans were revealed to have been made to a single borrower, Takahashi Harunori, who also had control of Anzen and another firm, Tokyo Kyōwa.[106] Forty percent of credit cooperatives were similarly shown to be run by executives who operated other businesses, and as a result of inherent conflicts of interest, almost all of them had loaned illegally large proportions of their assets to single clients (Hartcher 1998, p. 135). MOF supervision was again shown to have been lax when Hyōgo Bank collapsed in 1995 with twenty-five times more bad debts on its books than it had previously admitted to owning. Moreover, the general proliferation of criminal financial activity in the 1990s attested to regulatory failures. Among other things, these included the open involvement of leading domestic financial institutions with *yakuza* crime syndicates for the purpose of manipulating the stock market;[107] numerous cases of fraud for the purpose of funding speculation;[108] and proof of the pervasive reliance on dubious accounting practices.[109]

Second, with regard to the aforementioned *jûsen* (see also the following subsection), it emerged that the MOF had considerable involvement in this sector of the market where fully two-thirds of loans had turned sour (*NW* 29/4/96). MOF *amakudari* had been involved in the firms' establishment and management for more than twenty-five years.[110] This reflected poorly on the Ministry when a political investigation, which preceded the release of public funds for the *jûsen's* dissolution, found that supervision by MOF and BOJ had been 'nonfunctional' (Diet testimony, Lower House Budget Committee 16/2/96). It also looked bad when a number of *jûsen* executives and borrowers were arrested in April and May 1996 on charges of falsifying documents and obstructing land auctions.[111]

Similar scandals emerged in relation to other failed financial institutions, particularly credit cooperatives, where *amakudari* relations were again extensive. Media attention also fell on the group of bank employees known as *MOF-tan* whose sole job it was to attend their firm's relations with the Ministry, wining and dining officials in expensive restaurants, taking them golfing, and so on, in the hope of obtaining regulatory favours in the future (see Ōkura 1996). However, at this stage of events, only one or two cases involving bureaucratic complicity were ever prosecuted.[112] As a result, the Ministry responded in conjunction with LDP politicians by establishing a new internal code of ethics for bureaucrats which went into effect in December 1996.

Third, in conjunction with the share-loss compensation scandals of 1997, hard evidence was accumulated for the first time of the widespread practice of private firms wining and dining financial regulatory officials in return for regulatory favours and leaks of sensitive information.[113] In response, the National Police Agency launched a series of high-profile raids on both the MOF and BOJ in early 1998. Within six months, the probes had resulted in an alarming tally of arrests – five MOF officials, one BOJ official, and over sixty executives at Japanese financial institutions – as well as the suspension or resignation of ten senior bureaucrats and one cabinet minister, the disciplining of 210 regulatory staff, and six suicides.

These scandals emerged as four distinct events. The first involved a former director general of the MOF's Print Bureau. Isaka Takehiko was arrested in mid-January in his *amakudari* post as head of fundraising at the Japan Highway Public Corporation for taking bribes from ten financial institutions in return for leaking information about bond underwriting bids for the Corporation's regular public offerings.[114] The second involved two non-career MOF officials working in the Financial Inspector's Office. Head of the Office Miyagawa Kōichi and deputy chief Taniuchi Toshimi were arrested in late January for taking bribes from six city banks in return for giving tipoffs about upcoming spot inspections, classifying outstanding nonperforming loans leniently, and disclosing information about the financial affairs of other firms.[115] The domestic and international media had a fieldday with Miyagawa's case, thanks to his headline-grabbing penchant for entertainment at seedy *no-pan shabu shabu* restaurants (e.g. *Euromoney* 3/97). The third involved two career MOF officials in charge of regulating securities firms. Deputy director of the Securities Bureau's Coordination Division Sakakibara Takashi and senior inspector at the SESC Miyano Toshio were arrested in early March for taking bribes in return for regulatory favours which included classifying the cause of past share-loss compensations as 'accidents' (for which compensation payments are legal), and working for the early licensing of specific new financial products.[116] The fourth involved a BOJ official. Head of the Capital Markets Division Yoshizawa Yasuyuki was arrested in mid-March for taking bribes in return for leaking information about the Bank's highly market-sensitive *Tankan* quarterly economic survey, leniently assessing private collateral used for BOJ loans, and disclosing information about banks' new products to competitors.[117]

This deluge of shocking revelations was commonly attributed to the recent financial liberalisations which had increased competition between firms within the same and across different sectors (*JT* editorial sampler 15/2/98; 17/5/98). However, the timing and limited number of the scandals suggests that the series of events may have been more than coincidental. It was clear that in the wake of the *sōkaiya* payoff scandals, the Tokyo District Prosecutor's Office had been questioning various *MOF-tan* about excessive wining and dining of regulatory officials since late September 1997 (*Nikkei* 27/12/97). Yet it was not until just after a political deal had been struck between the LDP and its coalition partners (not to split up further the MOF) that they moved to take legal action against the Ministry. Any earlier move certainly would have jeopardised the coalition's agreement not to break up the Ministry further. The scandals also appeared to have provided cover for a humiliating reversal in government policy involving the suspension of a headline policy goal of fiscal reconstruction, and would have helped the LDP circumvent Ministerial resistance to this change. This receives support from the observation that many of the officials investigated seemed genuinely perplexed about the fuss that was made over what was held to be an established custom, particularly since numerous popular *exposé*-type books had alluded to such practices for years (e.g. Igarashi 1995; Ikuta 1994). Moreover, it was also curious that internal investigations which found such extensive evidence of wrongdoing – 112 staff at the MOF and ninety-eight at the BOJ warranted 'disciplining' – were wound up so speedily and without further arrests or dismissals.

Whatever the reasons, the result of the scandals was that internal codes of regulatory practice were tightened, transparency modestly improved, and new statutory codes of practice implemented. External reviews of MOF and BOJ procedures were initiated. In the case of the MOF, the review recommended that a permanent external monitoring body for the Ministry be established, that the MOF establish a regular 'liaison conference' at its own headquarters for exchanging information with private sector firms, that unannounced spot checks on firms be replaced with scheduled audits, that the practice of assigning young (under thirty) career employees to regional tax bureau chief positions be abolished, and that the makeup of financial inspection teams be routinely changed to prevent longstanding relationships developing between the regulators and regulated (*Nikkei* 8/5/98; 6/2/98). The latter recommended the establishment of a nonexecutive BOJ committee on legal compliance, but focused more heavily on integrating more recent public relations initiatives like salary reviews and the abolishment of the position of life-long honorary director and its associated perks for former governors. Finally, the ruling coalition drew up a new bill covering civil servants' ethics (based on a US law) which prohibited outright the acceptance of gifts and entertainment from those directly under a bureaucrat's supervision, and established a system of reporting other gifts of less than ¥5,000 to bureau chiefs and making public those of over ¥20,000. Significantly, no specific punishments were set for violators; they are to be dealt with under the existing National Civil Service Law (*Nikkei* 8/4/98).

Scandals which undermined the convoy system

Finally, scandals contributed directly to the weakening of the convoy system as the MOF's policy of forbearance eventually became unsustainable in the face of a lengthening recession and mounting levels of bad loans in the financial sector.

The 'scandalous' element in this equation involved the shattering of the MOF's reputation as the infallible guardian of the Japanese economy. Its staff's status as the 'elite of the elite' was undermined by involvement in bribery and other scandals noted above, but also by the Ministry's record of economic mismanagement. This became evident as it emerged that the MOF had resisted pressure from the BOJ to increase interest rates and forestall the bubble, and as it became clear that the MOF was subsequently adhering to a policy of forbearance in financial regulation to the detriment of the country's broader economic performance. The reason for persisting in covering up the extent of the bad-loan crisis in the financial sector was increasingly seen to be the Ministry's desire to obfuscate its own failures in macroeconomic management and financial supervision.

The Case of Japan

Signs of cracks in the convoy system first emerged in the early 1990s when a number of major banks approached the MOF for permission to liquidate affiliates that had accumulated unsustainable amounts of bad loans following the bubble's collapse. Sumitomo Bank asked to liquidate Hyōgo Bank in 1992, but the Ministry refused, indicating it would only sanction the dissolution if Sumitomo were to absorb the regional bank itself. When Sumitomo refused, the Ministry sent a former Banking Bureau chief to become Hyōgo's president in the hope that he could revive the firm. Sanwa and several other city banks also took the initiative in going to the MOF in 1992 for permission to wind up affiliated *jûsen*, but the MOF again refused, suggesting instead that they cut interest rates on their outstanding *jûsen* loans to aid the firms' restructuring efforts. It took about a year for it to become clear to the authorities that this policy of forbearance was not working. In late 1994, signs began to emerge which pointed to a change in official policy. BOJ governor Mineo Yasushi opined that it might be necessary and even desirable for some financial institutions to be allowed to fail (*Nikkei* 1/11/94), and under a new and much more progressive Banking Bureau chief, Nishimura Yoshimasa, the MOF reached the same conclusion and started to work on a clean-up scheme (interview with Adachi Nobiru of the International Finance Bureau, 27/6/97). The new tack was soon manifest as financial institutions began to collapse under the weight of accumulated bad loans in December 1994.

The first wave of failures to break over the Japanese financial system breached the convoy structure in December 1994. Within a year, five credit unions and one regional bank (Hyōgo) had collapsed, but administrative arm-twisting of financial affiliates and public loans from the BOJ had been sufficient to ensure that all of these failures were dealt with according more or less to traditional formulae. Aside from the shock caused by the unprecedented failures, the financial system incurred minimal disruption since all of the failed firms' ongoing obligations were taken on by new or existing intermediaries.[118]

While the convoy had been effectively regrouped, the action had all but exhausted the resources of the Deposit Insurance Corporation (DIC). New money would have to be found to deal with future failures which appeared all but inevitable. Significantly, a MOF Banking Bureau report issued in early June entitled *Reorganising the Japanese Financial System* (8/6/95) and set a five-year deadline for resolution of bad loans, called for better information disclosure, and hinted that the operations of some failed firms would have to be wound up. Led by sales of bank stocks, the Nikkei 225 Index fell heavily on this news, and so the FSRC's next report (27/9/95) merely hinted at the prospect but gave notice that the MOF would withdraw its blanket guarantee of all deposits after five years. Around the same time, Nishimura revealed in Diet testimony the scale of the bad loan problem to be almost double the figure which the MOF had thus far estimated publicly.[119]

- 12/94 *Tokyo Kyōwa Credit Union* and *Anzen Credit Union* announce bankruptcy. Their operations are taken over by *Tokyo Kyōdō Bank*, a specially created government-sponsored bank.

- 7/95 *Cosmo Credit Corp.* announces bankruptcy. Its operations are taken over by *Tokyo Kyōdō Bank*.

- 8/95 *Kizu Credit Union* announces bankruptcy. Its operations are taken over by the *Resolution and Collection Bank*, an organ created to replace *Tokyo Kyōdō Bank*.

- 8/95 *Hyōgo Bank*, a regional bank, announces bankruptcy, becoming the first bank to fail since the 1920s. Its operations are taken over by *Midori Bank*, a specially created private institution.

- 12/95 *Osaka Credit Union* announces bankruptcy. Its operations are taken over by *Tōkai Bank*, a city bank.

- 3/96 *Taiheiyō Bank*, a second-tier regional bank, announces its bankruptcy. Its operations are taken over by *Wakashio Bank*, a specially created private institution.

- 11/96 *Hanwa Bank*, a regional bank, is ordered by the MOF to close down operations because of excess bad loans. Its operations are taken over by a *Kii Yokin Kanri Bank*, a specially created private institution.

- 4/97 *Nissan Mutual Life Insurance Co.* is ordered to terminate business operations, becoming the first insurance company to fail in postwar Japan. Existing policy contracts are taken over by *Aoba Life Insurance Co.*, a specially created institution.

- 5/97 *Ogawa Securities Co.*, a third-tier brokerage, files for voluntary bankruptcy, becoming the first securities company to fail since the early postwar years.

- 10/97 *Kyōtō Kyōei Bank*, a regional bank, announces its bankruptcy. Its operations are taken over by *Kōfuku Bank*, another regional bank.

- 11/97 *Sanyo Securities Co.*, a second-tier securities firm files for bankruptcy under the Corporate Rehabilitation Law.

- 11/97 *Hokkaido Takushoku Bank*, a city bank, announces its bankruptcy. Its operations are to be taken over by *North Pacific Bank*, a regional bank.

- 11/97 *Yamaichi Securities.*, a Big Four securities firm, files for voluntary bankruptcy.

- 11/97 *Tokuyō Bank*, a regional bank, announces its bankruptcy. Its operations are taken over by *Seventy-seven Bank*, another regional bank.

- 11/97 *Eichigo Securities*, a third-tier securities firm, files for voluntary bankruptcy.

- 12/97 *Marusō Securities*, a second-tier securities firm, files for voluntary bankruptcy.

- 4/98 *Matsuhiko Securities*, a third-tier securities firm, files for voluntary bankruptcy.

Figure 2.5: Financial Failures in the 1990s
(*Source*: various *Nikkei* articles)

Nevertheless, external observers were insufficiently impressed with the Ministry's progress. In July, Treasury Secretary Rubin voiced US anxiety 'on-the-record' about the fragile state of Japan's financial system – something which the *Far Eastern Economic Review* interpreted as 'a sign that private talks are no longer enough' (*FEER*, 17/8/95). The IMF's 1995 International Capital Markets report was also critical of the way in which the bad loan crisis had been managed (August 1995). Hereby, the markets remained jittery throughout the summer in spite (or perhaps because) of limited moves taken to deal with the problem. Finance Minister Takemura Masayoshi's assurance that 'This [action] will put an end to a chain of announcements of liquidation programmes', and the MOF's promises that no bank with international obligations would be allowed to fail (*Nikkei* 21/8/95) had little effect on market sentiment. By the end of the year, the so-called 'Japan premium' (see Chapter 1 section 3.2.2) had risen to around 0.7 percent, up from 0.07 percent at the start of the year, amid increasingly bearish headlines such as *The Economist's* 'Something Nasty in the Woodshed: The Markets are having Nightmares about Japan's Financial System' (11/11/95).

The second wave of failures to break over the financial system came in 1996. Anticipated by almost a year of public negotiations, the *jûsen* resolution plan appropriated government money to fund the firms' liquidation on the basis that, in the future, the principle of self-responsibility would be upheld to preclude future recourse to the public purse. This stipulation was reinforced in speeches to the JFBA annual meeting in July 1996. Prime Minister Hashimoto instructed the bankers to write off their nonperforming loans quickly, Finance Minister Kubo Wataru stressed the need for 'comprehensive restructuring and the introduction of strict risk management', and BOJ governor Matsushita Mineo urged directors to come up with plans for thorough management improvement and better information disclosure (*Nikkei* 25/7/96).[120]

Consequently, the *jûsen* issue was perceived as a turning point in the history of financial regulation in Japan since it implied the promise of abandonment of the convoy system. Although accounting for less than twenty percent of all problem loans at the time, liquidating the *jûsen* signalled that henceforth private firms would be required to place new emphasis on the quality of bank capital and risk evaluation in both lending and borrowing activities (interview with Alicia Ogawa of Salomon Smith Barney, 17/6/98). And while it was obvious that favours were still being bestowed by the LDP on specific interest groups (the agricultural sector was the *jûsen's* largest lender), politicians managed to pin the majority of blame for the fiasco on the MOF. As former prime minister Miyazawa charged, 'If the *jûsen* mess had been properly addressed [in 1992], the bad debts would not have been so huge, and there probably would not have been any need to dip into taxpayer's money' (*Nikkei* 8/2/96).[121]

The third wave of failures to break over the financial system came unexpectedly in November 1997 and involved the collapses of large financial institutions, generating considerable confusion in the market. Ever since the Big Bang announcement a year earlier (see section 2.3), the demise of the convoy system had been repeatedly asserted by politicians and bureaucrats alike. But to stem the panic, new assurances were issued that none of the country's remaining top nineteen banks would be allowed to fail 'for the sake of systemic stability'. Accordingly, the LDP moved quickly to secure a ¥30 trillion public credit line to shore up the balance sheets of those banks as and when necessary.

Initially, only a small proportion of that money was used (see Chapter 4), but in light of continuing financial instability exaggerated by conflicting statements from leading politicians as to the future of the convoy system,[122] a new plan was drawn up by a government panel in June 1998 to resolve matters speedily. The plan was to involve recapitalisation using long-term public loans in exchange for promises to write off large amounts of bad loans and implement restructuring plans that could objectively be expected to lead to clear improvements in profitability. Essentially, the convoy system had been amended and shored up at the core, but allowed to atrophy at the periphery. The end-of-fiscal-2000 deadline for the termination of blanket government protection of all bank deposits was also reasserted, but eventually watered down and delayed for a year in 2000.

(ii) International Developments: US Revisionism and the Asian Crisis

The realm of international financial diplomacy was quieter in the 1990s than it had been in the 1980s. Nevertheless, two developments were significant in levying bilateral pressure for financial reform: the Clinton administration's 'revisionist' approach to Japan, and the Asian financial crisis of 1997. Both resulted in high levels of *gaiatsu* being applied in bilateral/multilateral arenas, but in neither case were successes unqualified.

The Clinton administration's new approach to Japan set the tone for the entire decade in US-Japan relations. In the early 1990s, the way for a change in bilateral relations was paved by a number of developments, including the end of Cold War, the perceived failures of the previous Bush administration's Japan policy, and the reversal in the competitive positions of Japanese and US financial institutions brought about by the collapse of Japan's bubble economy (see Chapter 3).[123] Following Clinton's election in 1992, the new administration took advantage of the mounting popularity of a revisionist view of Japan. Essentially, revisionist scholars stressed the endurance of differences rather than similarities between Japan and the US, and found many in Congress and industry receptive to their questioning of the effectiveness of market-opening measures which had formed the cornerstone of US trade policy towards Japan since the 1970s.[124] Clinton proceeded to recruit officials with unprecedented experience of Japan, for the purpose of dealing with the 'Japan problem' in a high-level manner that would deliver results.[125]

The critical ideology now driving US policy was that America should act aggressively to create a 'fairer' US-Japan relationship by strategically managing trade. As Robert Altman wrote in *Foreign Affairs*, their philosophy was not 'an attempt to reconstruct Japan in the US image' as most US administrations since the 1970s had sought, but rather 'to shift the debate away from the changing nature of the Japanese economic system' (Altman 1994, p. 5). In practice this meant that rather than pressing market-opening measures as a logical but indirect way to increase US exports, the Clinton team began to seek direct agreements on domestic market share quotas from Japanese officials. The new team believed that they knew how to target and exploit the hegemony of Japan's 'power elite' (Rothacher 1993) over the Japanese economy to America's advantage. As Asher explains:

> In effect, the Clinton administration wrote off the previous administration's goals of economic structural reform from day one, preferring the visible hand of the Japanese mandarins to the invisible hand of the market. Furthermore, it consciously adopted a tough negotiating style to minimise the Japanese negotiators' 'wiggle room' and demanded agreements based on verifiable indicators of progress and 'voluntary targets' for the industry-by-industry growth in US exports. In Altman's much-quoted words, the United States would 'wait until hell freezes over, if necessary' to get definite results from trade agreements with Japan (1997 p. 347).

Clinton's core initiative was the 'Framework for a New Economic Partnership between Japan and the United States' launched in mid-1993 and concluded in early 1995. In it the US put forward an agenda for addressing grievances in five principal areas: the Japanese government's procurement of medical and telecommunications technology, and the country's closed automotive, insurance, and fund management markets. Talks proceeded separately on each front. The deals reached in finance were generally more successful than those in other areas, particularly the strained auto negotiations between MITI Minister Hashimoto Ryûtaro and US Trade Representative (USTR) Mickey Kantor (e.g. Schoppa 1997, pp. 254–94; Nihon Keizai Shinbunsha 1995). Generally, the new US approach fostered acrimony on both sides. With their economy in the grip of a severe post-bubble recession, Japanese officials were not predisposed to radical reform, and in negotiations stood up aggressively to US demands for targets 'in the name of free trade'.[126] Commonly, deals were reached only at the eleventh hour and under the threat of sanctions.

Bilateral negotiations on opening Japan's ¥41 trillion insurance market began in July 1993. Discussions proceeded at deputy-level until the following February, when lack of progress led to them being upgraded to cabinet-level talks. Initial sticking points related to disputes over 'measuring' Japan's progress in deregulation, and an agreement was not reached until September 1994, two months behind the original schedule.[127] Ironically, it represented a decidedly managed (i.e. non-free market) compromise: the MOF agreed to defer its planned deregulation in the 'third sector' market, where US firms were strong, until the 'substantial' deregulation of Japan's primary life and nonlife markets which the MOF was planning had been achieved.[128] A commitment was also made to schedule regular consultations between the Treasury and MOF to monitor implementation of the accord and serve as a forum for addressing other bilateral financial issues.

Worried that Japan's imminent liberalisation of the insurance industry was about to break the 1994 agreement by opening its third sector to new subsidiaries of large domestic insurers before the life and nonlife sectors had been substantially deregulated, the US approached Japan with threats of trade sanctions in the summer of 1996. During negotiations, the MOF agreed to defer its plan to allow Japanese life insurers' nonlife subsidiaries into 'third sector' markets as soon as they were established from October 1996. A supplementary accord was eventually struck in December 1996, reportedly by telephone and thirty minutes before USTR Charlene Barshefsky's plane was about to leave Japan (*Nikkei* 15/12/96). In it (i) life insurers' nonlife subsidiaries would be permitted to enter the nonlife sector in January 1997, but the MOF promised to take measures to avoid 'radical change' in the third sector until 2001, (ii) the MOF agreed to substantially liberalise nonlife premiums by July 1998 (beginning with differentiated auto insurance from September 1997), and (iii) domestic subsidiaries would be allowed to sell cancer and medical policies by 2001. That is, deregulation of the life and nonlife sectors would be completed by the time the third sector was liberalised. Moreover, as a concession to make up for delayed liberalisation of the life and nonlife sectors, Tokyo agreed to eliminate restrictions on fixed premium rates on auto insurance beyond their existing ten-percent bands.[129] In conjunction with the accord, bills were also passed in June 1998 to reform the cartel-like industry rating organisations in the life and nonlife sectors, and the MOF agreed to speed up its procedure for approving new products. On almost all of these fronts, however, points of substantial disagreement remained.[130] Bilateral negotiations to resolve such points broke down in early June 1998, with the US side objecting to Japan's starting of a two-and-one half year clock counting down to third-sector deregulation before more substantial progress had been made on deregulating the country's primary markets.[131]

Negotiations on foreign access to Japan's ¥20 trillion pension fund market were settled more conclusively, despite having been expanded to encompass several issues thrown up by the implementation of the earlier Yen-Dollar Agreement. Chiefly, the additions were greater access for US firms to Japan's corporate bond underwriting and wholesale banking markets, items which were tabled ostensibly to speed up the conclusion of GATT's Uruguay Round. Framed in terms of reciprocity of access, the Japanese team found the US demands difficult to counter, and a comprehensive agreement was struck in January 1995 (*Nikkei* 11/1/95; 12/1/95).[132] By it, the US secured (i) access for foreign pension fund managers to Japan's Pension Welfare Service Public Corporation through *shiteitan* (active money-in-trust management), and access for foreign investment advisory firms to Japan's Employee's Pension Fund and other public and semipublic funds (e.g. NTT),[133] (ii) Japan's agreement to deregulate its investment trust management business, removing the barrier separating the investment trust from the investment advisory business, (iii) clarification of the category 'securities' to permit the introduction of several financial products that were common in other markets (e.g. exchangeable/strippable bonds, and dual currency bonds), (iv) a further relaxation of restrictions of euroyen products (specifically by issuing criteria), and (v) the wider licensing of derivative products. The Ministry also promised greater transparency in financial regulation by strict adherence to the new Administrative Procedures Law. The Japanese side agreed to US demands to assess progress in deregulation on the condition that this would not constitute numerical targets. The main losers were domestic trust banks and life insurers, who had a monopoly on public pension fund management. Acting Treasury Secretary Frank Newman concluded that the agreement represented the most comprehensive set of market opening actions in the Japanese financial sector in a decade.

Bilateral lobbying from other countries has been very low key in comparison to US initiatives. The only other significant actor is the EU, which held annual bilateral meetings with the MOF. These meetings, however, were limited to the presentation of a list of preferences drawn up to reflect the views of the European Business Council. The EU counsellor for economic and financial affairs explained that the EU, unlike the US, *never* gets involved in bilateral negotiations, but saves its gripes for arbitration in multilateral fora such as GATT and the WTO. Hence, it kept its wish lists limited to technical 'nuts-and-bolts' issues, and avoided larger macroeconomic reform issues. He stated simply that this was partly because they do not have the staff, and partly because of the difficulty of articulating a single EU voice, but insinuated that, historically, the EU have been happy to 'free-ride' on the back of US initiatives (interview with Ralph Wilkinson 10/11/97).[134]

The other important event in terms of international pressure being brought to bear for changes in financial regulation in Japan was the Asian financial crisis of 1997. Its wake brought to a head external calls for Japan to reform its domestic economic structure and implement tax cuts and large fiscal stimuli to get its economy back on track in order to be able to 'pull' the rest of Asia out of recession in a manner reminiscent of the failed locomotive strategy of the late 1970s. Such calls had been coming from the US since 1993, but they intensified dramatically in the shadow of the Asian crisis, with G–7 and regional states and international organisations such as the IMF, OECD and BIS joining in to create a chorus of *gaiatsu*.

Japan was largely able to avoid these petitions until the yen began to depreciate sharply in mid-June 1998, precipitated by new fears of domestic economic instability. However, in the midst of concern that further yen depreciation would force China to devalue the yuan, the Clinton administration agreed to participate in limited exchange market intervention to halt the yen's fall as it approached the 150-to-the-dollar level on June 17. Joint action was initiated after hurried negotiations between Hashimoto and the White House, and while both sides denied subsequently that any deal had been struck, most observers concluded that Japan gave the US verbal guarantees that it would undertake decisive action to resolve its bad loan crisis and implement tax cuts after the July 12 Upper House election (see section 2.3) in return.

What looked like a long-fought US victory was, in fact, a hollow one. It took the brink of a new regional crisis and a rare mixture of contextual political developments both, within and outside Japan, to precipitate a one-off bout of joint intervention, in return for which the reality of Japanese action remained nebulous.[135] More fundamentally, the ongoing uncertainty underlined the fact that the Clinton administration's new revisionist approach to Japan had failed to deliver any concrete results on its main target – the bilateral deficit. Because the MOF had made it clear repeatedly that tax and spending reforms were not a matter for common international negotiation, the US's singular focus on this area had served only to detract attention from the Bush administrations' pursuit of a structural solution to the deficit. Ignoring the tremendous post-bubble changes that were already appearing in the Japanese economy, Clinton's team blindly continued to act as if nothing had or ever would change in Japan. Thus, through a rigid and static view of 'Japan Inc.', it squandered numerous opportunities over six years to add to existing momentum for structural change within the system. Most significant in this respect was the support which Clinton denied to Hashimoto in maintaining the impetus behind his radical Big Bang initiative from September 1997 in the midst of the latter's flagging political support base and increasing opposition from domestic vested interest groups (see section 2.3 below and Chapter 4).

(iii) Global Systemic Developments: Declining Competitiveness

Systemic developments became the primary cause of financial regulatory changes in the 1990s, having been largely presaged by *gaiatsu* or obfuscated by the immense but superficial developments of the bubble economy during the 1980s. Two events marked formal responses by Japanese regulators to the perceived exigencies of financial globalisation: the Financial System Reform Act of 1992, and the Japanese-style 'Big Bang' announced in late 1996.

The Financial System Reform Act of 1992 was seven years in the making, largely because it was formulated according to the classic patterns of

Japanese policymaking. The MOF had realised in the early 1980s that the worldwide financial services industry was being transformed from within by the introduction of new process and product technologies (see Chapter 1), and that if Japan's markets were to retain their competitive position, they would have to respond by at least removing some of the rigid functional barriers separating different areas of the domestic banking and securities businesses. In particular, the Ministry's Banking Bureau was aware that the trend towards securitisation would disadvantage Japan's banking sector most, and so it moved first, instructing the FSRC to begin debating the direction of future regulatory changes in 1985 (Vogel 1996, pp. 180–9). Its first report on the matter in 1987 focused mainly on desegmentation within its own sector. It recommended that mutual banks (*sōgō ginkō*) be allowed to become commercial banks, a legislative change which occurred that same year, but it also touched on the issue of limited bank entry into the securities business to compensate for securitisation. This stirred its counterpart, the Securities Bureau, into action. Not wanting to be left out, it had its own deliberative commission, the Securities and Exchange Council (SEC), begin looking into the matter in 1988, while debate ran concurrently within the FSRC. In principle, both councils identified and discussed five scenarios for cross-entry between the banking and securities sectors: (i) piecemeal reform, (ii) a separate subsidiary structure, (iii) a multifunctional subsidiary structure, (iv) a holding company structure, and (i) a universal banking structure (see Vogel 1996, p. 182).

City banks had potentially the most to gain from radical reforms. They argued that universal banking would result in the greatest overall efficiency of the financial system, and therefore the greatest benefits for customers in terms of cost and convenience. By contrast, securities firms wished to preserve their monopoly as much as possible. They argued that a universal banking structure would give city banks undue influence in the financial system and would make them susceptible to conflicts of interest.[136] The FSRC report of May 1989 narrowed the realistic options to two: piecemeal reforms were clearly insufficient; universal banking was unrealistic because it would make city banks overly powerful and substantially disrupt the system's balance; and the holding companies option was also unattractive because it would require substantial revisions of antitrust law and therefore would invite considerable politicisation of the changes. Herein, Banking Bureau officials favoured the multifunctional subsidiary option, since it offered greater potential benefits to banks, but even this had several drawbacks. It would play into the hands of the long-term credit banks which had very little retail base, meaning that they would effectively become universal banks immediately, and would require more complex legal revisions.[137] For its part, the Securities Bureau insisted on either the piecemeal reform option or the separate subsidiary option. The BOJ came down in favour of the separate subsidiaries option because it was the closest way of ensuring that banking institutions did not carry the risks inherent in the securities business, and thus the makings of a deal were evident.

Both Councils submitted interim reports in June 1990 favouring the separate subsidiary option, although there was still considerable disagreement between the two on the conditions of cross-entry. The Securities Bureau wanted to ban banks from the lucrative securities underwriting business, while the Banking Bureau was concerned that this might undermine the very benefits which banks would seek from the new business. Almost a year later, both submitted their final reports, which were hailed as representing a 'comprehensive settlement', in May 1991. A deal had been struck on the basis of protecting the core business of each group in the short-term: banks would be allowed to underwrite bonds, but not sell stocks; banks and securities companies would be permitted to enter the trust business, but not the most profitable sectors of the market (loan trusts and pension trusts). Moreover, the MOF would maintain and possibly enhance its control in the short-term by directing the whole process.

The resulting LDP-sponsored package of bills was passed without incident as the Financial System Reform Act of June 1992, and enacted in April 1993. The changes involved revisions to both the Banking Law and Securities and Exchange Law. First, the mutual interpenetration of traditional business areas through the establishment of multiple majority-owned subsidiaries was to be permitted, initially in a way which would encompass just banks and securities companies, but later this was to be extended to include insurance companies, too. Second, financial industry restructuring would be made possible by two further clauses for cross-entry on an exceptional basis: (i) provision was made for long-term credit banks and the Bank of Tokyo to enable them to merge with other banks and acquire a large branch network without giving up their privilege of issuing bank debentures;[138] (ii) a clause was inserted to allow banks into the securities business without creating a separate subsidiary if they bought out an ailing securities firm;[139] and (iii) requirements were made for greater information disclosure.[140]

In terms of legal parity, the 1992 Reform Act suggested that convergence was once again taking place between the Japanese financial system and other core capitalist states'. And while conscious that the final deal was a result of too many compromises, the *Nikkei* described the changes as 'the most extensive revamping of Japan's financial system since the end of World War II'. JFBA chairman Wakai Tsuneo hailed the event as 'a significant initial step in the creation of a new financial system for the 21st century and one that could lead to the establishment of a system that is capable of being accepted internationally' (*Nikkei* 20/6/92). The bank branching restrictions of 1949 were lifted in May 1993 (*Nikkei* 21/5/93), and basic quantitative calculations suggested that differences in the cost of capital between Japan and the US, which had been falling since the early 1980s, were now negligible (Frankel 1993b).[141]

However, as the 1990s progressed, it became clear that though this 'parity' may have existed on paper in terms of structural equivalence, it certainly did not extend into regulatory practice. Just as the initial discussions on reform had been reactive and protracted, so too the pace of implementation was frustratingly slow. Foreign observers soon concluded that 'deregulation has proved to be more limited than planned' (Hall 1994, p. 99). To some extent this was disappointment due to misunderstanding and supposition rather than broken promises *per se*, as explicit comments made by MOF officials in advance of the changes made no secret of how they would be implemented.[142] However, it was evident that, in accordance with the convoy system, the Ministry was still unwilling to proceed with even some of the scheduled removals of barriers for fear of the disruption it might cause to weaker firms. When it came to granting new business licences, long-term credit banks and trust banks were favoured over the city banks and foreign firms in having their applications processed even though most firms applied at approximately the same time. This indicated that the goals of financial deregulation in Japan were diverging. Whereas desegmentation had been executed in other countries largely for global competitive reasons, the MOF was using it as a means to restore the balance of interests and power between market players, and hereby regroup the 'convoy', or at least core convoy members.

International participants in Japan's financial markets increasingly voiced two complaints during the first half of the 1990s: that the market was still overregulated, and that the MOF's system of regulation was still intransparent. In terms of overregulation, their objection was that Japanese regulators persisted in adhering to a rigid convoy system. The explanation given by the MOF for its comparatively tight regulation of the Japanese financial system was the need to protect market stability and the public from the potential dangers of new financial products. However, the fact that the MOF was so slow to establish the legality of even many straightforward products (e.g. asset-backed securities and forward rate agreements) suggested that this was only half of the story.[143] In essence, overregulation was being employed to protect industry stability by regulating competition and keeping out new entrants, both domestic and foreign. The MOF still defined many new financial instruments (e.g. swaps, CDs and commercial paper) according to arbitrary rather than objective criteria in order to keep them the preserve of either securities houses or banks. Similar considerations lay behind (i) its slowness in the granting of licences for new business activities in recently deregulated sectors, (ii) its snail-paced freeing of interest rates, (iii) foot-dragging in the opening of pension fund management to competition outside the trust banking and life insurance sectors, (iv) the continued exclusion of bank's securities subsidiaries from some areas of the securities business, and (v) the illogical separation of fund management and investment trust management which made the cost of new entry prohibitively high.

The foreigners' complaint of intransparency, by contrast, was an objection to the Ministry's persistence in relying upon an occluded form of administrative guidance as its main regulatory tool. To international participants, this rendered the Japanese market difficult to analyse and understand. Poor disclosure requirements and arcane accounting methods were commonly cited for disguising the health of market participants (especially banks) and making performance-related investment decisions difficult (e.g. in the investment trust management business).

These complaints combined with the publicity generated by the recent scandals. The *Nihon Keizai Shinbun* began to use the phrase 'financial socialism' (*kinyû shakaishugi*) when describing the convoy system, while *The Economist* and *Euromoney* regularly applied the more enigmatic adjective 'Byzantine' to Japan's model of financial regulation. Traditional methods of Japanese regulation were now being widely recognized as counterproductive and antirational; the markets' lack of transparency and overregulation meant that it was necessary to maintain other restrictions simply to preserve existing idiosyncrasies. Chief among these were restrictions on foreign exchange trading which were kept in place to prevent large scale arbitrage. Tokyo was now losing considerable business to London and New York, as well as Singapore and Hong Kong and was widely predicted to continue ceding ground in the future.[144] A Japan Center for International Finance survey identified other significant problems: (i) Japan's bond market required a smoother settlement processing system and more market-making to improve liquidity; (ii) its securities markets would have benefited from the abolition or at least reduction of the securities-transaction tax; and (iii) its derivatives markets needed to shift to international accounting standards and gain a clearer approval system for new products; other frequently cited complaints related to high operating costs, and the comparatively low diversity of financial and capital markets (*NW* 26/2/96).[145] An earlier feature article in *Euromoney* had summed up the same criticisms more bluntly, stating that despite almost a decade and a half of deregulation 'there is no satisfactory blueprint for the future of the Japanese financial system' (2/94, p. 33).

In response to the declining competitiveness of Tokyo as an international financial centre and Japanese financial institutions as international competitors (see Chapter 3), the MOF renewed its study of possible reforms during 1995 and 1996. Their plans were subsumed into just the sort of comprehensive blueprint for reform which critics had lamented did not exist: a so-called Japanese 'Big Bang' was announced in late 1996, modelled upon the UK's 1986 initiative, as the headline policy of the second Hashimoto administration. The plan's explicit aims were to make Japan's financial markets 'free, fair and global'; it had five core themes: (i) liberalising transaction fees; (ii) legalising financial holding companies to make way for 'one-stop' financial service companies; (iii) ending the tradition of convoy regulation and allowing less competitive firms to go out of business; (iv) lessening the rule of administrative guidance by increasing transparency through the introduction of a codified system of explicit rules; and (v) yen internationalisation.[146]

The plan seemed to represent a politically driven initiative which promised to put an end, finally, to Japan's particularistic regulatory regime by a stated implementation deadline of April 2001. That is, justified in terms of the rhetoric of financial globalisation as it was, it appeared that a fundamental turning point had been reached in the history of Japanese financial policymaking where the country's regulatory convergence was now being actively promoted. Nevertheless, as the history of regulatory reform in Japan as surveyed in this chapter might suggest otherwise, and as the case study in section 5.3 below confirms beyond doubt, this is not the case. Beneath the political rhetoric, the Big Bang plan evolved largely through traditional *shingikai* deliberations, and has thus far been executed following the all-too-familiar logic of administrative guidance and the convoy system.

In sum, the amendments to Japan's traditional regulatory regime made in the 1990s were again of a considerably greater magnitude than those made during the previous decade. Undertaken predominantly in reference to domestic developments resulting from the aftermath of the bubble economy and as a result of global market forces which increasingly threatened to marginalise Tokyo as an international financial centre, the changes all took place reactively and involved lengthy compromises and considerable costs in terms of economic efficiency. Formally, the regulatory changes brought the structure of Japan's postwar financial system more or less in line with global norms: functional segmentation was substantially diminished, the systems of rigid interest rate and commissions structures were abolished, and the MOF's discretionary control over the financial system was curtailed by the establishment of greater codification and transparency in regulation. Informally, however, the shadow of traditional administrative practices survived the changes with only a minimum of concessions being made to show that Japan was falling into line with contemporary global realities.

2.3 CASE STUDY: THE JAPANESE-STYLE 'BIG BANG'

On November 11, 1996, Hashimoto stunned the financial world by announcing that Japan would undertake its own even more radical version of the UK's highly successful Big Bang financial deregulation initiative. The announcement came without warning, and the plan was presented as the flagship policy of the new administration as a means to revitalise the Japanese financial system.[147] Once Hashimoto had repeatedly stressed his do-or-die commitment to the plan – famously asserting his willingness to 'burn himself to ashes' in order to overcome obstacles that the plan would be certain to encounter from vested interests (*Nikkei* 30/11/96) – the response from the financial community was overwhelmingly positive.[148] The *Nikkei* began running a special daily column dedicated to the Big Bang and the weekly *Economisto* described it as 'ambitious' and 'shocking', noting that traditional administrative policies had become 'outdated', and calling the new plan 'timely' or 'opportune' (7/4/97, p. 60). The *Far Eastern Economic Review* enthused that 'there *is* a difference this time ... Hashimoto's political will ... his timing ... [and] the Japanese bureaucracy's fall from grace' (26/12/96; 2/1/97); *The Economist* was equally optimistic; observing 'there now seems to be a consensus among politicians and bureaucrats that the Japanese financial system needs root-and-branch reform' (16/11/96).

(i) The Announcement

The Big Bang announcement was meticulously choreographed to ensure that it came across as a visionary top-down political initiative, representing a fundamental departure from Japan's past experiments with financial reform. As the headlines cited above indicate, it largely succeeded in this respect.

The domestic and international press were briefed by Finance Minister Mitsuzuka Hiroshi that at 3:30 p.m. on Nov 11 Prime Minister Hashimoto had summoned he and Justice Minister Matsuura Isao and presented them with a three-page, nine-point policy document entitled *Structural Reform of the Japanese Financial Market: Towards the Revival of the Tokyo Market by the Year 2001*. According to Mitsuzuka, Hashimoto had instructed them go back to their respective ministries and draw up a programme of radical financial deregulation based upon the document. In the same press conference, the document was then 'explained' by senior MOF staff, and copies were made available in both Japanese and English (a provisional translation) and subsequently posted on the Ministry's homepage.

The Big Bang proposal certainly appeared revolutionary, as its agenda set out in figure 2.6 suggests. The core idea outlined in Hashimoto's original document was to bring Japan's financial markets into line with global standards by making them 'free, fair and global'.[149] Its first line stated boldly 'Goal – An international market comparable with the New York and London markets by the year 2001', and under the rubric of 'free in principle, restrictions only as exceptions', the plan promised specific measures including (i) the removal of unnecessary barriers separating the banking, securities and insurance sectors, (ii) the liberalisation of various charges, commissions and premiums, (iii) the galvanising of disclosure rules, (iv) the establishment of new laws for introducing complex financial products such as derivatives, and (v) the reorganisation of corporate

Area	Substance of changes	Deliberative council	Target implementation
Supervision	Establishment of new Financial Inspection and Supervision Agency	Diet (1997 ordinary session)	July 1998
	revision of Bank of Japan Law Diet (1997 ordinary session)		April 1998
Banking	Revision of Foreign Exchange and Control Law	Committee on Foreign Exchange	April 1998
	abolishment of barriers separating city, long-term credit and trust banks	Financial System Research Council	fiscal 1997–98
	revision of rules governing banking, securities and trust subsidiaries	Financial System Research Council	from fiscal 1997
	financial holding companies	Financial System Research Council	from 1998
	revision of government-affiliated financial institutions	not designated	not specified
	revision of postal savings system	not designated	not specified
Securities	Liberalisation of brokerage commissions	Securities and Exchange Council	April 1998–March 2001
	Abolishment of restrictions on investment trust products	Securities and Exchange Council	by 2001
	Change to a system of registration for investment trust business	Securities and Exchange Council	by 2001
	Banks permitted to sell securities investment trusts over-the-counter	Securities and Exchange Council	around 1999
	Introduction of new system of pricing according to public demand	Securities and Exchange Council	Fiscal 1998
	Introduction of a stock lending system in the over-the-counter market	Securities and Exchange Council	fiscal 1998
	Abolishment of the prohibition on private investment trusts	Securities and Exchange Council	fiscal 1998
Accounting	Introduction of mark-to-market accounting	Business Accounting Council	from fiscal 1997
Pensions	Abolition of rules governing public and private pension contributions	MOF, MHW	from fiscal 1997
	Introduction of investment advisory business for private pensions	MOF, MHW	fiscal 1997
	Relaxation of fixed interest rates	MOF, MHW	from fiscal 997
	Introduction of fixed contribution system	MOF, MHW	fiscal 1999
Insurance	Liberalisation of premiums for non-life insurance	Insurance Council	fiscal 1997
	Banks permitted to sell life insurance products over-the-counter	Insurance Council	around fiscal 1999
	Expansion of mutual interpenetration within life and non-life sectors	MOF	fiscal 1999

Figure 2.6: Itinerary of the 'Japanese-style Big Bang' Proposal
(*Source*: amended from MRI 1997, p. 13)

accounting and taxation rules to bring Japan into line with emerging global standards.

The Japanese Big Bang plan was justified in terms of three related developments, all of which showed that it was a characteristically reactive initiative: (i) the hollowing out of the country's financial markets, (ii) the impending fiscal crisis associated with the country's rapidly aging population structure, and (iii) the declining competitiveness of the Japanese economy. The first point was evident from the plan's subtitle – *Revitalising the Tokyo Market by the Year 2001* – and from the fact that the high cost and low profitability of doing business in Japan was beginning to spur significant migration of foreign and domestic business to overseas markets.[150] The latter two points were evident in the following passage from the original document:

> In order for the Japanese economy to retain its vigour in the coming 'aging society', it is essential to secure the supply of funds to newly rising industries as well as to establish a place for efficient asset management. It is equally important to ensure that Japan provides a smooth supply of funds to the rest of the world ... Thus the Japanese financial market, which serves as the artery for the Japanese economy, needs to play its true role of optimal resource distribution, as the markets in New York and London do, so that Japanese individual savings of as much as ¥1,200 trillion can be fully utilised (MOF 1997).

It was explicitly recognised that such changes would require Japan's switch to global standards in regulation and henceforth its reliance on arbitration according to the invisible hand of the market rather than the visible hand of the mandarin.

(ii) Background

Led on by the government, the Japanese press traced the idea for the Big Bang back to the 1996 G–7 Summit in Lyon (June 26–29). Under the title of 'Making a Success of Globalisation for the Benefit of All', Western leaders conducted discussions on the premise of their financial markets already having been liberalised, and Hashimoto was reported to have left with an acute awareness of how far behind Japan was in terms of financial deregulation (*Nikkei Kinyû* 12/11/97). Two considerations would have made this especially portent.

The first was much evidence which attested to liberalised capital markets in the US and UK being responsible for the remarkable revitalisation and renewed competitiveness of these economies in the 1990s. By contrast, Japan's financial sector had acted as a considerable drag on its real economy in the 1990s (see Chapter 4).[151] Not only had progress in writing off bad debts been very slow, and the stock market remained depressed, but perhaps more conspicuous was the fact that Japan's enormous ¥1.2 quadrillion in personal savings was benefiting its economy little, there being few routes for channelling funds into future growth industries such as the hi-tech, high-risk and high return venture businesses of biotechnology and computer software. In this respect it was clear that the traditional bias in Japanese finance – the bank-intermediated supply of cheap funds to industry – needed to be augmented by developing the country's domestic stock and bond markets as the primary vehicle for new business funding and better asset management.

This observation confirmed an increasingly vocal consensus among domestic scholars that the Japanese financial system was experiencing 'institutional fatigue' (Nakamura 1996). As others put it, the country 'has to overcome one or two serious structural diseases ... [such as] the cancer of the blood circulation system – bad loans in the monetary system ... What we need is major surgery and Japan has not been ready to do this ... deregulation is the most important cure' (Shimada Haruo, *Nikkei* 2/1/97). As a professor of economics at Tokyo University, Nakakita Toru, pointed out:

> The postwar economic system geared to having Japan catch up with Western industrialized nations has run its course, and we now have to facilitate a new financial administration system that helps market mechanisms function ... Financial administration should now be focused on monitoring, not controlling, market activities (*Nikkei* 9/10/96).

The second realisation provoked at the Lyons Summit related to a change in the climate of opinion regarding European currency union when France and Germany reaffirmed their intention to launch the euro in 1999. For Japan, the euro's launch could constitute nothing other than a *de facto* demotion of the yen's role to that of a local currency, particularly if Hong Kong and Singapore continued to take the lead in standardising their capital markets according to developments in the US and Europe. As Ikeo Kazuhito, a scholar and key member of one of the Big Bang's working committees (see below) stressed retrospectively:

> What decided Big Bang was European currency integration ... If that happens, where does it leave Japan? The notion of 'Yen internationalisation' will become a non-starter. The launching of the euro will deliver a fatal blow to the yen. To preserve even the smallest role for the yen, all we can do is offer some sort of countermeasure, and that is Tokyo's Big Bang (*Tōyō Keizai* 7/5/97, p. 15).

However, looking at the sequence of domestic political developments leading up to the Big Bang announcement, it is clear that the idea had its genesis in events preceding the Lyons Summit of June 26–29. Earlier in the month (18/6/96), and with the end of his coalition government's term of office in sight, Hashimoto had announced his 'Vision for Administrative Reform' as the LDP's headline initiative on administrative and fiscal reform which was intended to preempt reformist initiatives by other parties and politicians.[152] Promising to cushion the public from the proposed two percent rise in consumption tax which was before the Diet, it called for a thorough review of public spending in light of the aging population and precarious state of state finances (establishing a target of keeping social security payments below fifty percent of GDP in the future) in order to maintain Japan's position as one of the world's business hubs (*Nikkei* 19/6/96).

The Vision drew on recent proposals that had been made by a number of ministerial advisory panels, and was followed by a new round of discussions on deregulation within the coalition government.[153] Particularly important were the ideas put forward at a cabinet debate on deregulation and budget policies on July 12 by EPA chief Tanaka Shûsei, a key member of New Party Sakigake, in preparation for the Economic White Paper for 1996.[154] Without prior briefing of his colleagues, Tanaka outlined his proposal for deregulation in six sectors of the economy – finance, telecommunications, employment, land and housing, and medical care and welfare. His ideas met with a cold reception from ministers who felt that their jurisdiction was being infringed upon, but Hashimoto instructed them to take the proposals back to their respective ministries and hold discussions on it in their relevant *shingikai* (*Nikkei* 13/7/96).[155] Subsequently, the EPA white paper submitted by Tanaka was adopted by the Cabinet at the end of the month (26/7/96). It stated that Japan now finds itself in a 'period of historical structural adjustment' and must ditch its rigid postwar economic system and accept the pain of reforms and risk taking as the only way to cope with changing global business conditions and 'mega-competition' in global markets. It also called for changes in traditional Japanese management practices – the main-bank system, *keiretsu* corporate groupings, cross-shareholdings, lifetime employment and seniority-based wages – saying that they were now robbing the nation of its capability to cope flexibly with the new global business environment, urged a review of the public sector's role in the economy, and advocated streamlining the social security system (*Nikkei* 27/7/96). Hereby, the press reported, 'Deregulation as an economic policy is now being driven by the strains on public finances, the forces of the global market and the spreading fears that high costs and low returns could trap Japan's economy in prolonged stagnation. Belatedly, perhaps, the nation's domestic politics has begun to respond to this clear danger' (*Nikkei* editorial 24/7/96).

The Economic Council (EC), an advisory council to the Prime Minister within the EPA, was also instructed to continue devising proposals for reforming the six areas. It played a key role in producing the Big Bang reform agenda. Working groups of three-to-four scholars were organised under the EC's Action Plan Committee headed by Minaguchi Kōichi (chairman of the Advisory Board of Nomura Research Institute) and Ikeo Kazuhito (a professor of economics at Keio University).[156] Discussions formally commenced on October 9, with three of the EC's six working groups (finance, telecommunications and employment) producing its seminal first report 'For Invigorating Japan's Financial System' a little over a week later (*Nikkei* 17/10/96). The report outlined the need for 'a Japanese version of the Big Bang' to reinvigorate Japan's financial markets by the end of fiscal 1999, and it was this is what effectively set the ball rolling for Hashimoto's flagship plan.[157]

Unsurprisingly, the EC report received a cold reception from the MOF, which countered that similar debates were already being undertaken there, and they would wait for those reports before commenting on the EC proposal. All the Ministry would say was that the direction of the reforms outlined in the EC report was basically the same as its own, but that it had some concern over the paper's detail. And so, not to be upstaged, the MOF sought to shun the EC's infringement on its jurisdiction by producing a more comprehensive report of its own (a 59 clause reform proposal *vis à vis* the EC's 30 clause proposal). Hereby, the MOF tried to usurp the initiative for Hashimoto's second cabinet's headline policy of a Japanese Big Bang, and the outspoken International Finance Bureau chief Sakakibara Eisuke was soon declaring that it was the MOF which had actually started the ball rolling (NKS 1997, p. 4).

Whereas the Big Bang was presented as a political initiative, Sakakibara's comments nonetheless raised suspicions that the MOF had played a major role in devising the plan. Earlier telltale signs had existed. These included the fact that the MOF had been remarkably well prepared to brief the press on Hashimoto's intentions concerning the Big Bang only hours after its supposed launch on November 11, and the fact that the Ministry seemed to be curiously supportive, excited even, by a plan which appeared to mandate a total shift in their approach to regulation. Nevertheless, when the proposition of MOF involvement was put to senior officials, they insisted that the plan was Hashimoto's initiative alone, and they were simply bound in their duty as civil servants to execute his instructions without grumbling (author's questions put to Head of Finance Minister's Secretariat Kuroda Haruhiko [13/11/96] and Director of Budget Bureau Kubota Isao [14/12/96] at graduate seminar series International Finance and Politics [University of Tokyo, Faculty of Law]).

Conflicting signals notwithstanding, it was obvious that Hashimoto's Big Bang plan capitalised upon a number of reform initiatives which the MOF had been working on for some time. As already noted (section 2.2. p. 111), the Banking Bureau had started to tentatively propose significant reforms in its regulatory approach in mid-1995 – particularly its implicit blanket guarantee of all banks – through concerns about the manageability of the escalating bad loan crisis. These discussions had continued since then, but had been kept low-key because the market's sharp negative reaction to them threatened to destabilise what was already a fragile situation.[158] Concurrently, the International Finance Bureau had begun to examine deregulating foreign exchange trading in mid-1995, for its part in order to stem Tokyo's decline as an international financial centre. A year later, its in-house *shingikai* the Committee on Foreign Exchange and Other Transactions (CFEOT), produced a widely publicised interim report in favour of completely deregulating foreign exchange trading: liberalising commissions, overhauling the authorisation system and extending participation to securities firms and nonbanks (*Nikkei* 18/6/96).[159] This resolution came as no great surprise because the aforementioned survey by the Japan Center for International Finance (page 109), a nonprofit foundation (*zaidan hōjin*) with extensive MOF *amakudari* ties, appeared to have been designed to persuade members of the dangers of deciding otherwise.[160] A month later, the Securities Bureau began to work on a new plan to reform Japan's securities market – to make it 'appropriate for the twenty-first century' – although the SEC's initiation of such discussions was deliberately not publicised at the time, according to Royama Shōichi, professor of international public policy at Ōsaka University and chairman of the SEC's General Council which conducted the discussions (*Look Japan* 4/97, p. 14).

One MOF official pointed out that while market developments had spurred these new initiatives, what made way for them was a change in the balance of opinions among top staff in favour of more radical deregulation following the Ministry's annual personnel change of June 1995.[161] This is confirmed by the fact that each of the new *shingikai* studies was initiated by a new bureau director-general, Nishimura Yoshimasa in the Banking Bureau, Sakakibara Eisuke in the International Finance Bureau, and Nagano Atsushi in the Securities Bureau. The change in the MOF's stance was borne out by the record of Sakakibara's own remarks. In his prior position as deputy-director general of the International Finance Bureau, Sakakibara began a 1994 interview with *Euromoney* by stating categorically 'We don't want Big Bang or shock therapy' (2/94, p. 36). But in his late 1996 briefing to explain the planned Big Bang he gushed:

> I would like to quote a statement by Edmund Burke, a very famous conservative philosopher, that sometimes in order to conserve what is good for the country you have to implement very radical reforms. That is what we are doing. We are going to implement very radical reforms ... We have been proceeding with deregulation in a sort of gradualist approach. In a sense I, as an outside philosopher, do not like shock therapy, but here, in this particular case, I think that shock therapy is necessary ... You say that our awareness has come belatedly, but better late than none [*sic*]; we are now thinking that this

is the last opportunity for us to revitalise the Tokyo market (cited in Hartcher 1998, p. 252).

The fact that the SEC's newest discussions on the deregulation initially were kept secret is enough to suggest that something unusual was taking place. But even before this was known, the possibility of a bargain having been struck between the MOF and Hashimoto did not pass by more astute observers (*Nikkei Weekly* 18/11/96; Lincoln 1997). And while there is no hard evidence to support this theory, the circumstantial evidence is compelling. In addition to the considerations already mentioned concerning Big Bang's press launch, there were three more intriguing 'coincidences'.

First was the fact that Hashimoto's Big Bang plan contained nothing new of substance that has since been shown to have been absent from the agendas of the various MOF *shingikai* which met from mid-1995 onwards to discuss the new shape of the financial system. That is, what Hashimoto appears to have done was taken up the various initiatives and packaged them with a market-friendly gloss for presentation to the world as a visionary political initiative. Second was a curious change of heart by one of Hashimoto's closest LDP allies, Katō Kōichi, involving his views on the MOF between 1995 and 1996. Katō reversed his position from being, along with party doyen Nonaka Hiromu, the LDP's most vocal proponent on breaking up the MOF for its betrayal of the party, to championing the MOF's cause in late 1996 against other members of the ruling coalition, both within and outside the LDP (see Appendix).[162] This dovetails with the notion that a deal existed and involved the LDP protecting the MOF from outright breakup in return for the MOF's support of Hashimoto, providing him with an all but ready-made policy initiative which would ensure Hashimoto's place in history as a visionary leader.

Third were the already noted and seemingly conflicting statements by MOF staff regarding the Ministry's role in the Big Bang plan. When questioned, an official in the International Finance Bureau repeated candidly that 'the idea of the Big Bang itself came from the prime minister', but, when pushed, conceded that 'one of the prime minister's personal secretaries is a person from the Ministry, and it is certainly possible that he would have talked to Ministry officials in the course of formulating the plan' (interview with Adachi Nobiru 30/5/97). This connection had already been made by at least one journalistic source, which credited Prime Ministerial Secretary Saka Atsurō with being at the centre of Hashimoto's Big Bang plan (NKS 1997, pp. 4–5).[163] Saka would have provided the perfect conduit for regular contact between the prime minister and senior MOF staff to broker a deal and ensure that things such as the SEC's deliberations were kept under wraps so as not to lessen the impact of Big Bang's eventual announcement.[164] Thus it would appear that while the idea for 'Big Bang' as the title of Japan's new financial reform initiative came from the prime minister (or more specifically, one of the prime minister's advisory councils), as the MOF claimed, the substance of the plan was crafted almost entirely by the Ministry.

(iii) Translating the Concept into Policy

Four days after Hashimoto's announcement of the Big Bang as a key policy objective, Finance Minister Mitsuzuka publicly instructed the MOF's three main financial sector advisory councils (the SEC, FSRC, CFEOT) and two others (the Insurance Council [IC] and Business Accounting Council [BAC]) to begin debate in order to flesh out Hashimoto's skeletal proposal as soon as possible. In a repeat of the earlier public relations move, it was also widely publicised that Hashimoto had personally summoned the five councils' leaders to underline the importance and urgency of the task (*Nikkei* 16/11/96). Similarly, he instructed the EC to continue its parallel discussions on the Big Bang, and announced that the Administrative Reform Council (ARC), which he himself headed, would include financial deregulation in its discussions. All the *shingikai* were instructed to make their discussions open and transparent to an unprecedented degree, by holding press conferences after each meeting and soliciting opinions from the public, both Japanese and foreign, via e-mail etc. To some extent, the purpose of this was to be seen to be circumventing the sort of immobilism and sectoral balancing of interests which had traditionally typified financial policymaking, by introducing parallel monitoring and raising the level of public interest and, thereby, accountability. But in retrospect, it seems that Hashimoto was also genuinely concerned about Big Bang being watered down in the process of implementation and the whole initiative backfiring upon him rather than the MOF.

Initial reports confirming and outlining the direction of Japan's Big Bank were all produced within six weeks of the November 11 announcement.[165] The locus of debate then shifted exclusively to the five MOF *shingikai* which, thanks to the extensive specialist knowledge they incorporated, were supposedly the only panels capable of formulating the detail of the reforms. But soon it was evident that traditional policymaking procedures were being followed to a tee, and thus a compromised outcome was likely. Sensing this, advocates of more radical reform bombarded the *shingikai* and public with a vast array of statistics and worked tirelessly to stir up a sense of impending crisis among the public.

In support of the government's own claims that its broader economic reform programme would generate 7.4 million new jobs in fifteen strategically important areas by 2010, numerous calculations were presented in reports by the EPA, MITI, and the OECD. The EPA released a report at the end of 1996 projecting that deregulation could produce favourable effects to consumers worth about ¥7.9 trillion and create a million new jobs annually (*Nikkei*, 26/11/96); another stated that deregulation undertaken between 1990 and 1996 had already yielded annual benefits to Japanese consumers and producers of ¥4.6 trillion (i.e. one percent of GNP – *Nikkei* 9/4/97). MITI's Industrial Structure Council produced a report (11/11/96) which predicted that 1.24 million jobs in manufacturing (i.e. about nine percent of the current work force) would be lost in the next five years and living standards would deteriorate between 2010 and 2025 if drastic reforms were not carried out (*Nikkei* 12/11/96; see also *Tōyō Keizai* 23/4/97). It also warned that Japan could encounter a current account deficit in 2000 (the first EPA report cited above said 2006). Another report estimated that Tokyo would lose twenty percent of its stock dealing as a result of Big Bang if tax costs were not lowered (*Nikkei Kinyû* 19/5/97), and another (21/5/97) that deregulation in five key sectors would generate ¥39 trillion in new investment and boost the economy by six percent (although it conceded that it might also cause substantial unemployment in sectors such as wholesaling and financial services – *Nikkei* 22/5/97). Yet another asserted that the financial industry's real annual growth rate could be 4.9 percent between 1997 and 2005 if sweeping deregulation were carried out, lifting real annual GDP by 0.3 percent annually and creating 220,000 new jobs; by contrast, if deregulation were not implemented, financial services output would decline by 0.5 percent annually and the economy would lose 250,000 jobs by 2005 (*Nikkei* 10/6/97).

Moreover, *gaiatsu* was solicited via the OECD which hailed Hashimoto's Big Bang plan in its first international symposium on regulatory reform, held in Tokyo (3/12/96) and cosponsored by the OECD, MITI, MOFA and Keidanren.[166] Criticising the level of Japan's public sector deficit as 'unsustainable', the OECD hypothesised that Japan had more to gain from deregulation than any other major industrial country. It forecasted that Japan's GDP would expand by 6.4 percent within ten years if comprehensive deregulation were to be carried out in the five key sectors identified originally by Hashimoto (*Nikkei* 24/12/96 – its final report was published in May 1997).

However, in spite of all the statistics, and regardless of the continual stream of events since the Big Bang announcement which contributed to maintaining the momentum of the pro-radical reform movement – bureaucratic scandals in the second half of 1996, the stock market slump and weak yen at the year-end, and the reemergence of share loss compensation scandals in 1997, and so on – debate in the MOF's *shingikai* continued as if in a vacuum. Comments made by its members in the press releases which followed their meetings showed that they were falling back towards a weakened version of the convoy system in spite of their unambiguous mandate to abolish it. On the one hand, this was justified in reference to the plan's guiding aim of creating a 'free, fair and global' financial market. As MOF *shingikai* member Ikeo stressed, 'the market must, of course, be free to be global, but making it free *and* fair is the difficult point' (*Nikkei* 26/5/97). And as his colleague at the EC Minaguchi explained, 'we must differentiate between the weak, who need protection, and those who lose in fair competition' (*Tōyō Keizai* 23/4/97). That is, the notion 'fair' became equated with a managed type of 'equal opportunity', rather than simply 'equality of opportunity' *per se*, as in all being treated equally under the law. Applied to the domestic financial sector, this created a rationale for protecting weaker institutions such as trust-, long-term-, and regional banks, and smaller securities and life insurance companies.

On the other hand, a managed type of 'fairness' was also justified in relation to external competition. An argument popularised by MOF officials demonstrated this beautifully. By positing the issue of regulatory change in terms of convergence upon an Anglo-American model, and stressing the positive aspects of a Japanese model *vis à vis* the negative aspects of the Anglo-American model, it was possible to stir up nationalist sentiment in favour of a traditionally 'Japanese' solution, in spite of Big Bang's originally stated aims. Sakakibara and others framed this in terms of the clever rhetorical analogy 'whither Wimbledon or J-League?' That is, the UK-style financial deregulation created, as with the highly respected tennis tournament, a world class competition in which most of the players and all of the winners tended to be foreigners. By contrast, J-League-style deregulation, it was suggested, could establish, as with the domestic soccer league, a national tournament based upon international rules and energised, but not dominated, by foreign talent. Hereby, Finance Minister Mitsuzuka was able to assure British Chancellor of the Exchequer Kenneth Clarke at a UK-Japan finance meeting in January 1997 that Japan would follow and implement orthodox international standards, at the same time as a traditionally Japanese compromise model was being hammered out in his Ministry's various *shingikai* (*Nikkei* 12/3/97).[167]

When the five MOF *shingikai* submitted their final reports in June 1997, it was certain that Big Bang would not live up to the expectations which its initial rhetorical presentation had generated. The timetable for desegmentation indicated that a 'managed' transition had been mapped out in such a way as to protect weaker sectors in order to maintain the system's traditional 'balance'. This much may have been inevitable, but the fact that the timetable for banks' entry into the various insurance markets had been set back at least beyond 2001 – in clear contravention of Hashimoto's originally stated target date for Big Bang's *completion* – was an unambiguous message that Japan was still pursuing compromise solutions to financial deregulation.[168]

It was also impossible to disguise the fact that differences of opinion on some sensitive issues had forced the omission of several important items from the preliminary reform schedule. The most notable items involved (i) reform of the nation's public financial sector, (ii) legal boundaries for establishing financial holding companies, and (iii) general tax- and commissions deregulation. These issues were resolved in subsequent political discussions between representatives of the ruling coalition parties, some taking more than six months to settle.[169]

Given the procedures for deliberation, compromised outcomes had always been likely. The press faulted the *shingikai* for failing to come up with a policy that would regulate all financial institutions in the same way, and one scholar summed up the general sentiment, concluding 'the reports remain focused on how to adjust the demands of various players in the financial industry, and I could not see any real attention being placed on users' needs' (Nakakita Tōru, *Nikkei* 20/6/97). In spite of Big Bang's aim to make Japan's three main financial sectors more integrated, the *shingikai* reports and political solutions were all drawn up by different panels, most having ties to a single sector and having a mandate of only recommending changes in that area. The fact that Hashimoto indicated his ARC would propose in its November 1997 report a complete scrapping of the *shingikai* system when the government is reorganised in 2000 was no coincidence (*Nikkei* 24/7/97).[170] But it never happened.

According to Kanda Hideki, a professor of commercial law at the University of Tokyo who was the central figure in drafting legislation for the MOF, the institutionally and temporally fragmented policymaking process meant that the necessary legal revisions for Big Bang would involve piecemeal amendments to existing legislation, rather than a wholesale revision of the financial regulatory framework (interview, 24/7/97). This contrasted sharply with the UK, where the Big Bang had been accompanied by a comprehensive package of new legislation, the Financial Services Reform Act of 1986. In Japan, revisions to the Foreign Exchange and Foreign Trade Control Law were passed on May 15, 1997, an early move to rule out any major backtracking over Big Bang, but the legal framework for most other reforms was not ready until the following year. Seeking to give the impression of wholesale change, the MOF submitted a government-sponsored package of twenty-two Big Bang bills to the Diet in March 1998 which they referred to as the Financial System Reform Law (*Nikkei* 26/2/98; 11/3/98). The bills promoted further market desegmentation and greater codification and transparency in regulation, and were passed without amendment before the ordinary Diet session ended in June. Their eight main points are summarised in figure 2.7.

While the Big Bang plan was tempered by Japan's formal policymaking process, it was also undermined considerably by direct bureaucratic and political intervention in the latter half of 1997. In conjunction with several unfortunate political developments, the economy faltered as a result of overzealous fiscal tightening (see Chapter 4), and this paved the way for a recourse to traditional patterns of crisis management which were widely interpreted as backtracking on the Big Bang.[171]

Financial Deregulation 'Japanese-Style'

Content of Reform	Date
• Securities industry participation possible on a registration basis	from 1/12/98
• Liberalisation of off-exchange stock transactions	from 1/12/98
• Liberalisation of over-the-counter sales of investment trusts	from 1/12/98
• Introduction of stricter penalties for insider trading	from 1/12/98
• Introduction of mandatory participation in policyholder/investor protection programmes for insurers/securities firms	from 1/12/98
• Financial accounts to be submitted on consolidated basis	from 1/4/99
• Brokerage commissions to be fully liberalised	by 31/3/00
• Extension of government guarantees on individual bank deposits extended to other sectors	until 31/3/00

Figure 2.7: Main Points of the 1998 Financial System Reform ('Big Bang') Law

The first signs of this emerged in October 1997, when the MOF hinted that it would delay its slated implementation of regulation by Prompt Corrective Action (PCA) for banks in fiscal 1998.[172] However, it was not until action was taken to shore up the financial system during the turmoil of November 1997, when several large financial institutions collapsed under the weight of poor management and accumulated bad loans, that observers began to realise *en masse* that Big Bang plan was being compromised. Thereafter, and within the space of nine months, action was taken (i) to shore up the balance sheets of Japan's major financial institutions, in order to counter the ensuing credit squeeze, (ii) to aid banks' disposal of bad loans, and (iii) to provide an institutional framework for managing future financial failures which would avoid serious knock-on effects for the real economy. Collectively, these actions constituted a *de facto* regrouping of the convoy, ostensibly for the sake of underwriting the stability of the financial system.

The first step involved a financial stabilisation package put together in December 1997 in the wake of Hokkaidō Takushoku Bank's failure and the soaring 'Japan premium'. Its centrepiece was a ¥30 trillion public credit line, ¥17 of which was earmarked for dealing with insolvent financial institutions by beefing up the Deposit Insurance Corporation (DIC), and ¥13 trillion of which was intended for recapitalising viable banks which found themselves with difficulty raising funds in the interbank market.[173] Reminiscent of the *jûsen* resolution scheme, the MOF prepared the way for the appropriation of public money by encouraging banks to increase their disclose in reporting bad loans and by promising stronger compliance checks (*Nikkei* 11/12/97).[174] And, to promote financial stability more generally, the blanket government guarantee of all individual bank deposits until 2001 was extended to the securities and insurance industries in the wake of the collapses of Yamaichi Securities and Nissan Mutual, again under a promise to introduce quantitative solvency benchmarks and PCA-type regulation (*Nikkei* 25/11/97).[175] Applications by banks for funds to shore up their balance sheets for the fiscal 1997 year-end were solicited in March, and twenty-one banks – including all nineteen major banks – were granted a total of ¥2.1 trillion.[176] Furthermore, to reassure the international markets about the credibility of the country's banks, Sakakibara promised that the MOF would not allow any more major Japanese financial institutions to go bankrupt (*Nikkei* 8/1/98), and Matsunaga Hikaru stated in his inaugural press conference 'I will carry out my duties as Finance Minister based on the position that the country's nineteen largest banks must not be allowed to fail' (*Nikkei* 1/2/98).

Initially, the collapses of several big financial institutions in November 1997 had been taken as evidence of how much Japan had changed in abandoning the convoy system. However, with news of the hastily assembled financial stabilisation package, such opinions were retracted: 'Japan Seen Softening "Big Bang" with Bailout Plan' read a Bloomberg Business News headline (10/12/97), while the *Far Eastern Economic Review* proclaimed that Hashimoto has 'announced a broad rollback of reform in an attempt to save weak banks' (8/1/98; see also *Nikkei* 13/12/97 and *JT* editorial sampler 30/11/97). Most telling, however, was a rare comment by Royama Shōichi, a professor of economics at Osaka University who had been centrally involved in the Big Bang plan as an advisor to the LDP's Financial System Stabilisation Panel. Royama told *The Economist* in early December 'I am very angry and very, very anxious' about the future of financial reform and the prospects for Big Bang (13/12/97).

The substance of these worries related to the fact that senior MOF officials had begun to speak out against free market forces (e.g. blaming Moody's for Yamaichi's collapse – *Economist* 13/12/97), and a group of LDP politicians critical of Hashimoto's leadership (inc. Hiranuma Takeo and Aso Tarō [former transport minister and EPA chief, respectively]) had approached cabinet secretary Muraoka Kanezō with a petition for Big Bang's timetable to be delayed to protect the financial system and domestic institutions (*Nikkei* 28/11/97). However, it should be pointed out that hereby, both the MOF and LDP were limiting themselves largely to seeking the postponement of parts of Big Bang in light of domestic economic exigencies, and not amendments to core elements of the plan.

The second step involved measures which were eventually incorporated in the April 1998 economic stimulus package and related to boosting the disposal of banks' bad loans. Based on an LDP study group's earlier recommendations, measures were introduced to revitalise the market in land and other collateral using tax breaks, private debt-collection agencies, and 'special purpose companies' (SPCs) to securitise assets.[177] In the meantime, banks were to benefit from temporarily 'modified' accounting rules to boost their capital ratios for fiscal 1997 book-closing. It was agreed in mid-March that stock and land holdings could be valued at the higher of market or historical prices as part of upcoming stimulus package (*Nikkei* 20/2/98).

The third step added the establishment of a public 'bridge-bank' plan, and incorporated the previous two in a 'Total Plan to Revitalise the Financial System' (*Nikkei* 29/5/98; 24/6/98). Through this coalition-sponsored enterprise, the FSA was given the power to sign insolvent financial institutions into bankruptcy, force their management to resign, temporarily nationalise banks and run the entity for a period of up to five years, during which other financial institutions would be able to scrutinise the quality of the failed firm's loan portfolio and decide if they wanted to take it over.[178] The RCB, currently cofunded by the DIC, BOJ and private banks, was also nationalised and given a lending function to act as a central holding company for the prospective bridge banks. Moreover, a failed bank's bad debts were to be taken over by the Cooperative Credit Purchasing Company (CCPC), the life of which was lengthened by three years, and its powers to subsequently prosecute inefficient management extended to cover banks (*Nikkei* 27/9/98; 1/10/98). The idea was that the CCPC would take over banks' 'category two' loans, and thereby remove the chance of a would-be purchaser getting cold feet at the prospect of getting a loan portfolio full of nasty surprises.[179]

This amounted to the establishment of a major means for injecting public funds into the banking system – directly, by nationalising failed banks, and indirectly, by subsidising healthy banks which take over failed the obligations of failed financial institution – as a means to insulate the fragile 'real' economy from the repercussions of financial instability. Specifically, however, it constituted the institutionalisation of a major *extension* of the state's role in the financial system, which was underlined by leaks in the Japanese press about MOF and BOJ contingency plans to lend domestic banks experiencing difficulty raising funds in the international markets as much as ¥10 trillion in state owned US Treasury Bills to use as collateral for international borrowing, and as much as $20–30 billion of the central bank's foreign exchange reserves.[180] Apparently, Japanese banks were to be given access to these funds at an interest rate of 0.05 percent in return for assurances that they would reduce their overseas assets and make public more information about their bad debts (*Nikkei* 27/9/98; 28/9/98).

(iv) Evaluation

Hereby, it was clear by the autumn of 1998 that, on its own terms, Japan's Big Bang could neither be acclaimed as an unqualified success nor scorned as an absolute failure. In line with its original aims, financial regulation was becoming considerably more transparent and explicitly codified,[181] desegmentation was proceeding largely apace, fixed cost structures such as commissions on securities and foreign exchange transactions were in the

The Case of Japan

final stages of liberalisation, and the formal structure of the country's financial system was falling much closer into line with international norms. Moreover, early quantitative indicators revealed in calendar 1997 a reversal of the hollowing out trend of the past seven years.[182] In short, there was no good reason to suppose that Japan's policymakers would not adhere in spirit to the 2001 deadline for most of the slated changes which the original Big Bang declaration promised.

Notwithstanding this, and contrary to earlier promises, the convoy system was conspicuously still in effect, bolstered even by the necessities of economic instability, and many of the proposed reforms had been watered down or otherwise amended during the policymaking process. To external observers, financial policymaking (and, therefore, the direction of future regulation) remained frustratingly intransparent and as idiosyncratic as ever (e.g. *Economist* 27/6/98). Traditional patterns and practices continued to be visible.

Regardless of its now seemingly misplaced faith in an Asian partnership to challenge Western market capitalism, the following statement to *The Economist* by Sakakibara in early 1997 has proved to be uncannily accurate as a portrait of the age-old logic which still undergirds financial reform in Japan:

> I, for one, have long defended the Japanese-style market economy, and my position remains unchanged. Job security, harmony within society, and co-habitation with nature should still be the cornerstone of the Japanese economy and society. However, we must adapt to the ever-increasing trend towards globalisation and quickly adjust our system in order to survive in this new environment. As we have done for the 130 years since the Meiji Restoration, we will quickly absorb what needs to be absorbed and become fully competitive with the Anglo-Saxon and other systems ... [T]he pivotal question facing Asia and Japan today is not an all-or-nothing choice between globalisation Western-style or receding into a pre-modern and backward tradition. Rather, the question is how Asian countries can help create a new global system along with the West. Many aspects of Western market capitalism need to be incorporated into the new system, and in this context reform – perhaps even revolution – needs to be implemented quickly. However, this does not imply that the traditional elements of the Asian economic structure – family and regional ties ... – need to be changed. Rather, the 'Asian Renaissance' may well create a new paradigm, one that is different from Western individualism or *laissez-faire* capitalism. In such a paradigm, it is likely that there will be an important role for Japan, because it is both part of Asia and a nation that has succeeded in modernising its system without fundamentally losing its culture and religion. In other words, the sun may well rise

again in the 21st century, with Japan not emulating the West but instead playing a leadership role in the effort to fuse modern Western capitalism with pre-modern but nonetheless well-developed Asian global commercialism (22/3/97, pp. 105–6; see also Sakakibara's comments in *FEER* 17/7/97 and Kojima 1997).[183]

In essence, then, Japan continued to hope to be able to deregulate on its own terms and create an alternative way forward in the sphere of financial management. Such attempts are doubly understandable in so far as radical deregulation could have engendered disastrous repercussions for an economy which was still in a weakened state after pretty well seven years of recession (see Chapter 4). Nevertheless, the signs to date that this strategy has been viable – in terms of the country's macroeconomic performance – are not particularly encouraging (see Chapter 4).

To observers eager to 'grasp' the significance of current changes in Japan, Big Bang has undoubtedly fallen short of what they were led to believe by Hashimoto's early pronouncements. For those in the financial services industry with a stake in deregulation, the compensations, nonetheless, are considerable. For example, most Western financial institutions operating in Tokyo report that new business is booming as a result of the deregulation under Big Bang which has taken place to date (see Chapter 3). But whether Big Bang is understood etymologically as either (i) an astronomical concept implying the cataclysmic *recreation* of the financial sector (the association most Japanese like to draw), or (ii) simply a *startling shock* (the association most Western observers stress), it stands in need of qualification. Proposals of alternative characterisations have included the 'Long Bang' (Alicia Ogawa, speaking at the Nikkei Forum *Japan's Big Bang*, 17/6/97) or a 'Series of Loud Pops' (*FEER* 29/7/97). More accurate, perhaps, is a 'string of damp firecrackers'. This highlights both the unpredictability of, and frequent disappointment at, eventual outcomes, yet warns that observers would be foolhardy to write off the plan's effectiveness in advance.

Conclusion

This chapter has traced the metamorphosis of Japan's financial regulatory regime over more than a century. It reviewed the emergence of Japan's postwar regulatory regime and traced developments from the late 1960s to the late 1990s that worked to undermine the integrity of the postwar regime.

Almost all of the developments, be they domestic, international or systemic, that have affected Japanese financial regulation in the postwar period can be linked to globalisation in its broad economic sense. But what is significant in recent years is the way in which the rhetoric of reform has incorporated a much greater emphasis of the intractability of global financial market forces. During the 1970s, the need for reform was justified

Pressure for change	1960s	1970s	1980s	1990s
Domestic developments	low	high	low	high
International developments	very low	low	very high	medium
Systemic developments	very low	low	medium	very high

Figure 2.8: Direct Causes of Financial Regulatory Change in Postwar Japan

in terms of structural changes in the domestic economy; during the 1980s, it was advocated in terms of the need to placate international expectations; but during the 1990s, it was asserted in terms of the necessity of bringing Japan into line with global financial standards for fear of exacerbating the country's marginalisation in international competition (figure 2.8).

But in spite of the Big Bang rhetoric, Japan's financial structure and regulatory philosophy continues to evolve within the context of its preexisting institutions, i.e. incrementally rather than radically. Due to the lengthy process of *ex ante* monitoring, which requires the establishment of a consensus before any action is taken, the implementation of proactive reform which seeks to anticipate future crises or specific opportunities remains elusive. Of course, this longstanding 'gradualist' approach to implementing reform (Endo 1996a) has an undeniable rationale – it does away with the need for *ex post* monitoring (e.g. recourse to the courts), and it produces stability – but this comes at the high cost of discouraging innovation (Kanda 1997, p. 315). The question, then, is how well such a framework can serve Japan in an era of heightened global competition where the degree of freedom allowed to firms and individuals to reap the rewards of innovation may well constitute the difference between national economic success or failure. To this end, the next two chapters examine recent trends in the competitiveness and institutional practices of Japanese financial institutions and the broader ramifications of financial globalisation for Japan's economy and society.

Chapter 3

'Awkward Convergence' in the Financial Sector

Introduction

This chapter examines the extent to which Japanese financial institutions are converging upon the institutional models and practices employed by leading firms in their industry. By charting the development and fortunes of Japanese financial institutions against a global backdrop, it becomes possible to piece together a picture of the payoffs arising from particular strategic actions and non-actions on their behalf.

Part one begins by mapping trends in the postwar internationalisation of Japan's financial sector, in terms of Japanese firms' overseas expansion and foreign firms' entry into Japan.[1] Part two turns to examine in more detail the factors which underlay the meteoric rise and subsequent fall of Japanese financial institutions on the global stage in the 1980s and 1990s. Part three examines how their strategies have evolved following the announcement of the Big Bang, and speculates about the future 'shape' of the Tokyo market.

3.1 THE INTERNATIONALISATION OF JAPAN'S FINANCIAL SECTOR

Chapters 1 and 2 have already introduced, albeit indirectly, many of the important players in the global and Japanese financial markets, so this section limits itself to providing an overview of their competitive interaction in the postwar period.[2] The internationalisation of the Japan's financial sector is approached as a two-way process involving (i) the external expansion of Japanese financial institutions, i.e. 'outward internationalisation' (*sotonaru kokusaika*), and (ii) the internal expansion of foreign financial institutions, i.e. 'inward internationalisation' (*uchinaru kokusaika*). This makes it possible to examine the rise to international prominence of Japanese financial institutions in the context of global systemic developments.

Japanese Financial Institutions at Home and Abroad

(i) Banks

One of the most remarkable characteristics of Japanese banks' *domestic* activity has been the stability of their operations throughout the postwar period, as shown in figures 3.1 and 3.2. Figure 3.1 demonstrates the empirical reality of the convoy system, which ensured that the number of domestically licensed banks in each subsector remained constant for almost half a century. The initial rise in the numbers of firms in the late-1940s to early 1950s was a result of the final pieces of financial infrastructure being put into place for Japan's postwar reconstruction, while the rise in firms' numbers after 1993 is entirely accounted for by double counting – a result of the deregulation of trust banking, which made it possible for banks in other subsectors to receive trust licenses.

Moreover, figure 3.2 shows how administrative restrictions employed by the MOF ensured that the number of bank branches expanded at a fairly constant rate, and in such a way that regional and second tier regional banks (Regional II) were 'compensated' for city banks' position to benefit disproportionately from the fruits of Japan's industrialisation and economic

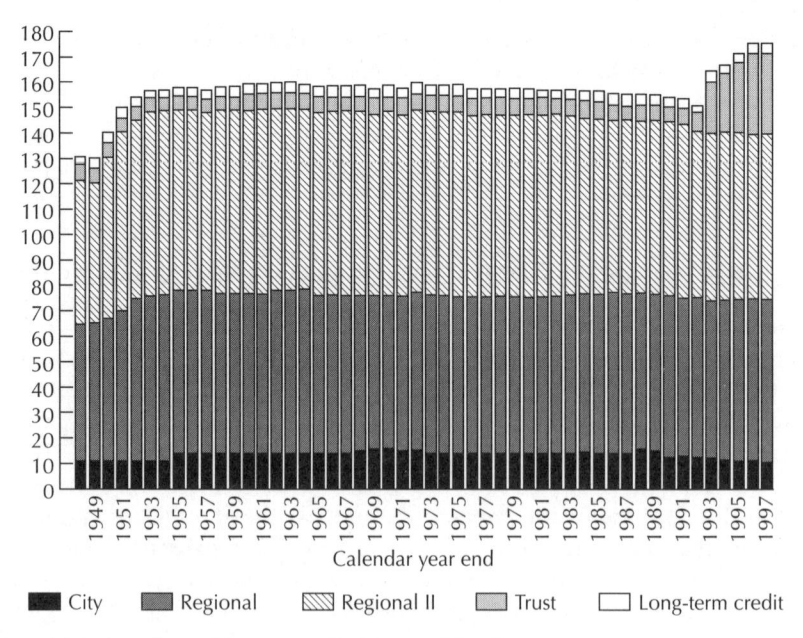

Figure 3.1: Number of Domestically Licensed Banks
(*Source:* BOJ *Keizai Tōkei Nenpō*)

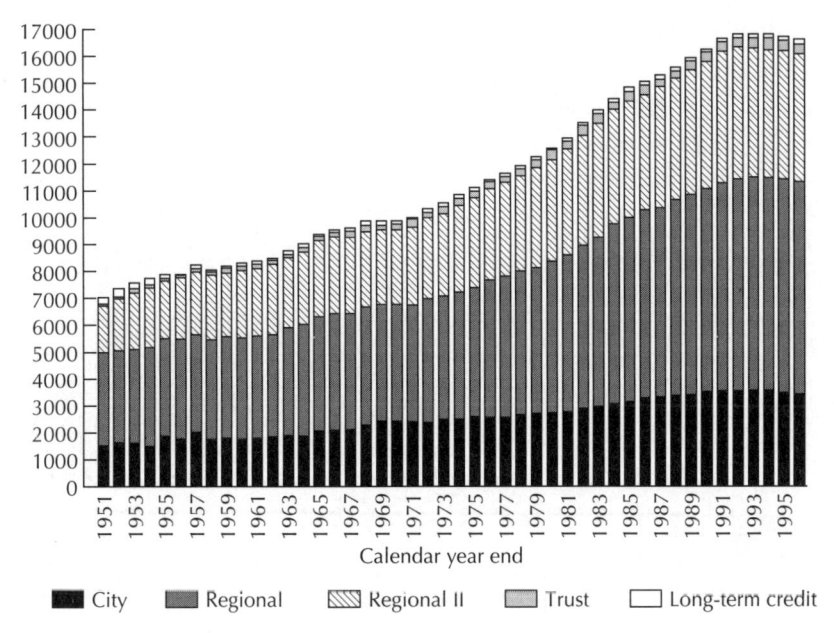

Figure 3.2: Japanese Banks' Domestic Offices
(*Source*: BOJ *Keizai Tōkei Nenpō*)

development. It is notable that neither graph bears much resemblance to the economy's fluctuating rates of growth.

By contrast, the overseas expansion of Japanese banks creates a markedly different impression – one dominated by an explosion of activity in the 1980s. Figure 3.3. shows that in terms of total levels of new activity, Japanese banks' postwar expansion began in the 1950s. This initially involved a small number of licensed foreign exchange banks expanding their network for procuring funds in order to finance the resumption of Japan's trade after WWII. By 1964, all of the major city, long-term credit and trust banks had received foreign exchange licenses, with the largest banks being the first to establish overseas offices in the early 1950s. In the 1960s, they began to expand their overseas presence in order to retain the business of large Japanese manufacturing clients who were starting to venture abroad, and it was at this time that many regional banks also began to apply for foreign exchange licenses. However, rapid expansion of overseas offices did not take off until the 1970s, when it was temporarily spurred by the lure of new opportunities in less-regulated financial centres (particularly the euromarkets), although new activity tailed off quickly as the domestic economy was hit by the oil crises. In the early 1980s, the deregulation of domestic foreign exchange controls paved the way for a fresh wave of expansion, centred upon the provision of loans to foreign borrowers and

The Case of Japan

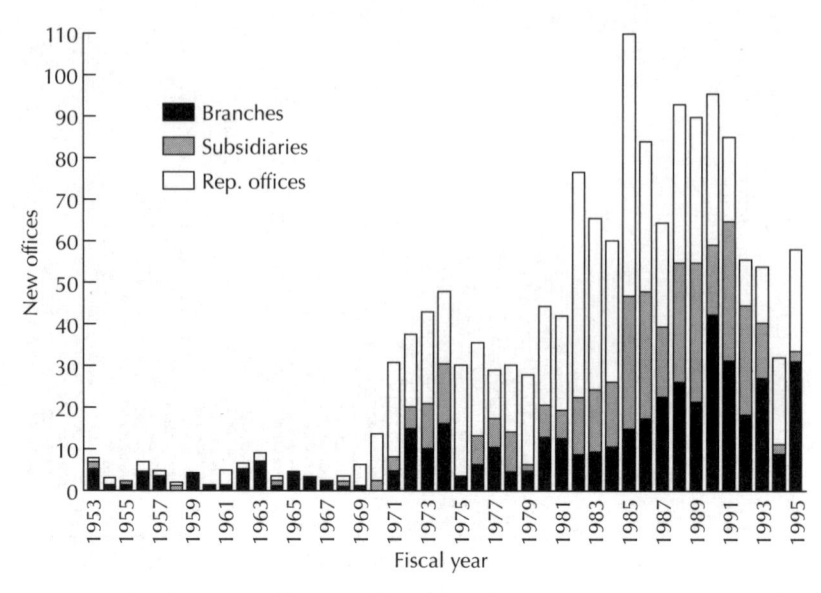

Figure 3.3: The Internationalisation of Japanese Banks
(*Source*: MOF *Kokusai Kinyûkyoku Nenpō*)

investment banking services to overseas Japanese corporations. This trend was greatly exaggerated during the middle and latter half of the decade by the high yen and stock market boom, during which time leading banks began to target more specialised markets in derivatives and M&A advisory services. The collapse of the bubble economy led to a sharp curtailment of such activity. Nevertheless, the soaring yen and boom in Asian interest encouraged a fresh bout of expansion in the mid-1990s, which was soon curtailed after the Asian crisis of 1998.

Breaking down the figures for Japanese banks' overseas expansion by type of office clarifies the picture. During the 1950s and 1960s, most banks venturing abroad opened branches or representative offices in order to expand internationally their banking services for existing Japanese clients. However, it was only in the 1970s that they began to upgrade some of these to the status of locally incorporated subsidiaries in order to undertake 'multinational banking' by competing directly for local business.[3] This applied particularly to city banks, which extended their overseas networks considerably at this time and began to market overseas loans and some investment banking services to non-Japanese clients. In the 1980s, much of the new expansion in branches and representative offices was accounted for by large numbers of medium-sized and, eventually, small regional banks.

By bank type, figure 3.4 shows how Japanese banks' overseas presence is still dominated by city banks, with the remainder of offices belonging

'Awkward Convergence' in the Financial Sector

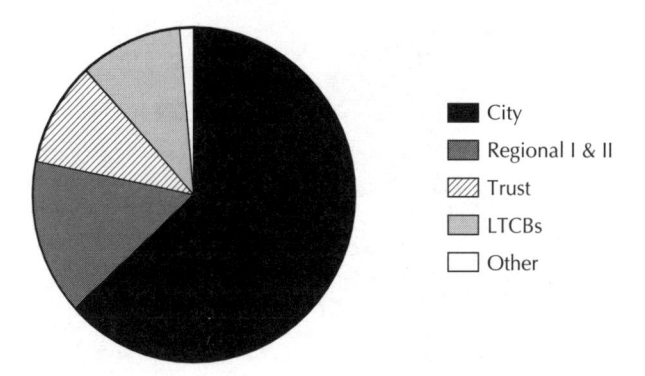

■ City
■ Regional I & II
▨ Trust
▢ LTCBs
☐ Other

Figure 3.4: Distribution of Japanese Banks' Overseas Offices
(*Source:* MOF *Kokusai Kinyûkyoku Nenpō*)

mostly to large regional banks, trust banks and long-term credit banks. Unsurprisingly, it is Japan's biggest banks that account for the majority of the country's overseas presence. As of the end of March 1998, of 347 banks which had foreign exchange licenses, sixty-nine had such operations, with Japan's nineteen biggest banks accounting for 364 out of 427 overseas offices – i.e. almost ninety percent (*Nikkei* 9/12/97).

Finally, by geographical distribution, most Japanese banks' overseas offices were in Asian countries as of 1995. This is a recent trend, and figure 3.5 is misleading in that it is skewed by the figures for newly opened representative offices. Japanese banks' presence in the US and Europe is actually more substantial, as a further breakdown of the figures demonstrates. In 1995, Japanese banks had 163 representative offices in Asia, *vis a vis* forty-four in North America and sixty-six in Europe; by contrast, they had only eighty-seven locally incorporated subsidiaries in Asia, *vis a vis* 103 in North America and 112 in Europe (MOF *Kokusai Kinyûkyoku Nenpō* 1996). With the exception of a small amount of retail business in California, all the rest of their overseas activity was in wholesale banking, i.e. providing services to corporate clients.

(ii) Securities Companies

Whereas the number of Japanese banks has remained remarkably steady since the early 1950s, figure 3.6 shows that the number of Japanese securities firms fell in the early postwar years, through early consolidation, and again following the securities crisis of the 1960s, through bankruptcies. Since the late-1960s, however, numbers have remained constant. In contrast to the gradual rise in banks' offices, the graph shows that the number of domestic offices maintained by securities firms has fluctuated considerably, with sharp rises in the mid 1960s and the late 1980s, both of which coincided with

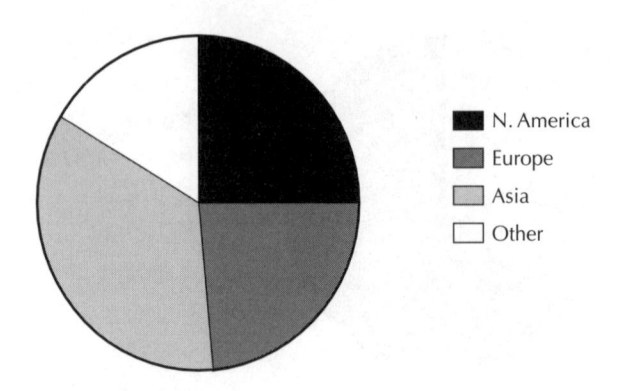

Figure 3.5: Distribution of Japanese Banks' Overseas Offices
(*Source*: MOF *Kokusai Kinyûkyoku Nenpō*)

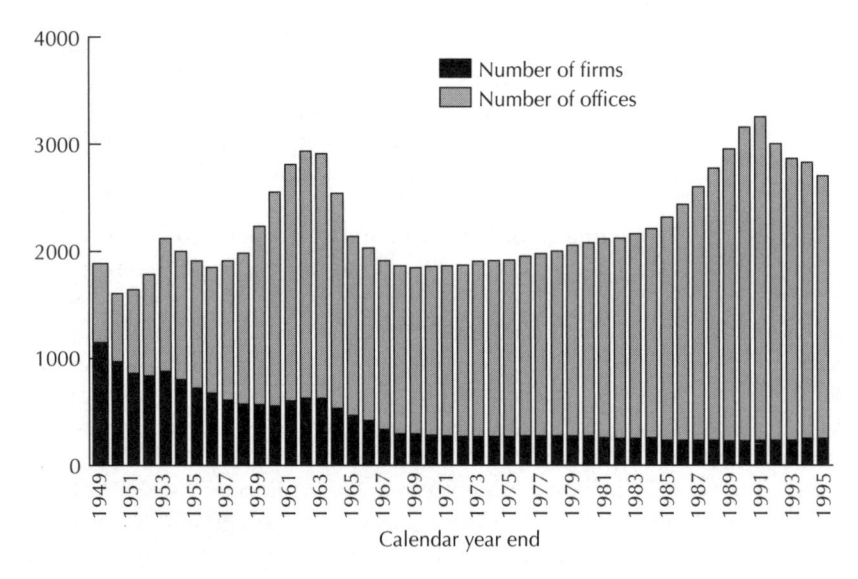

Figure 3.6: Domestically Licensed Securities Companies
(*Source*: MOF *Shōkenkyoku Nenpō*)

speculative stock market bubbles. It attests to the fact that while securities firms have been influenced by the convoy system, their activity has been less closely regulated than banks'. This is partly because the securities sector was never as central an element in the economic planners/regulators' agenda as was the banking sector, and partly because the MOF did not have the interests of various sub-sectors to balance, as it had in banking.[4]

In terms of their overseas expansion, Japanese securities firms resemble banks much more closely, with the caveat that their move abroad was much

'Awkward Convergence' in the Financial Sector

later and the numbers of offices involved much smaller (figure 3.7). Overseas expansion started gradually in the 1950s and 1960s, but took off at the end of the decade. The first firm to (re-)establish an overseas presence was Nomura (1953), followed by Nikkō (1955), Yamaichi (1956), and Daiwa (1964).[5] All these offices were in New York, but Nomura opened its first European office in London (1964), and then in Hong Kong (1967), and other firms followed. Initially, these offices served a dual purpose of providing information on the Japanese market to a small number of interested foreign investors and providing a base for the gathering of information on more sophisticated local market practices. Over time, the steady expansion of international networks as a means of increasing sales channels continued, but during the 1970s, the Big Four began to establish themselves as underwriters in the euromarkets. Even so, Japanese securities companies generally lagged behind their banking counterparts in terms of internationalisation until the early 1980s.

The catalyst for change was the amendment of the foreign exchange law in December 1980. This provided Japanese securities firms with a straightforward basis for two-way business: underwriting Japanese equity issues overseas and broking foreign equities to Japanese investors. Led by the Big Four, significant numbers of second-tier firms established overseas offices in the early 1980s; they were joined by third-tier firms, encouraged by the profitability of their domestic businesses and by the high yen in the latter part of the decade. Most of their business came from selling

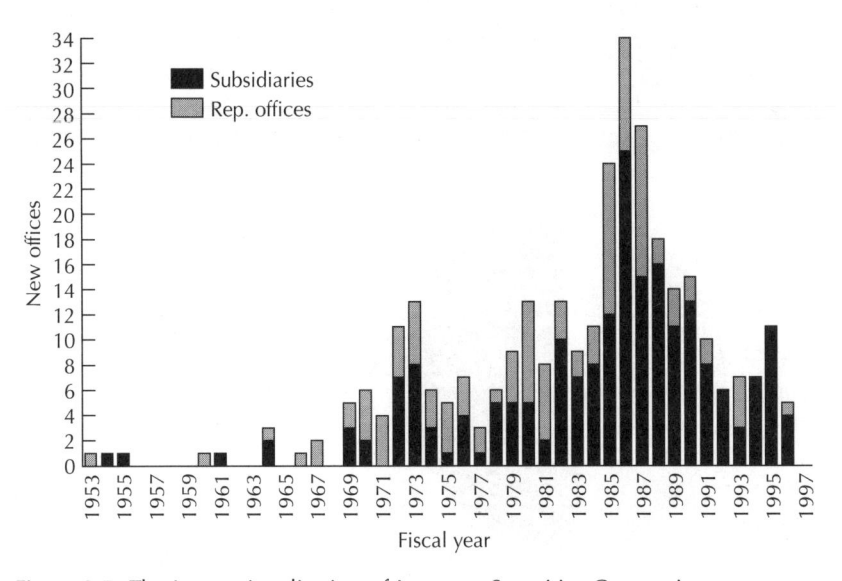

Figure 3.7: The Internationalisation of Japanese Securities Companies
(*Source:* MOF *Shōkenkyoku Nenpō*)

The Case of Japan

government bonds and, later, equities to Japanese investors, and from arranging international debt issues for Japanese firms. In the latter part of the decade, they began to list foreign firms on the TSE, and also to target advisory business such as M&A. As with their banking colleagues, the end of the bubble led to a sharp curtailment in activity in the early 1990s, but this was again cushioned in part by new opportunities in Asia in the mid-1990s.

By size of firm, figure 3.8 shows that in 1995 the overseas offices of Japanese securities firms were dominated by the Big Four, with second-tier firms accounting for most of the remainder. Of Japan's 220 securities firms, forty-one operated overseas, with roughly half of their offices belonging to Big Four firms. Ten second-tier firms accounted for a further thirty percent of offices, implying that, like the banking sector, Japan's securities sector is at least as oligopolistic overseas as at home (BOJ 1995, p. 350; Arora 1995, p. 126).

By geographical distribution, figure 3.9 shows that most overseas offices of Japanese securities firms were in Asia in 1995. As with the banks, this is misleading, being distorted by the high number of newly established representative offices. Securities firms had thirty-seven representative offices in Asia *vis à vis* three in North America and eleven in Europe, but had only forty-eight subsidiaries in Asia *vis à vis* seventeen in North America and seventy-two in Europe. The sequence of their expansion began in New York, with the move to Europe generally not occurring until the 1970s. Their now heavy concentration in Europe – the UK and Switzerland in particular – is accounted for by the volume of euromarket transactions in these centres and by the single European market. Establishment in Asia has been by country, with the Big Four opening offices in Hong Kong and Singapore in the late 1960s and early 1970s, and Seoul in the early 1980s. Their move into Taiwan was delayed by the collapse of Japan's bubble

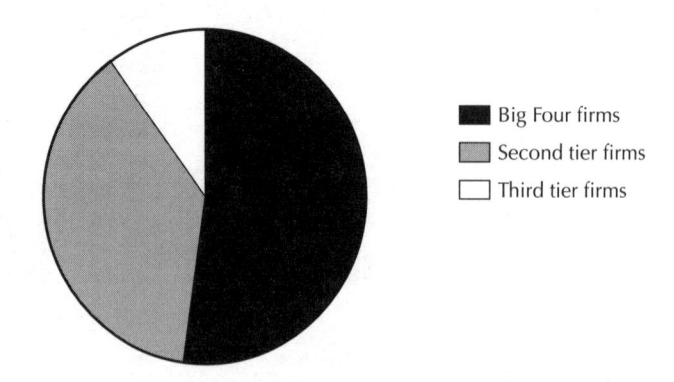

Figure 3.8: Distribution of Securities' Companies Overseas Offices
(*Source*: MOF *Shōkenkyoku Nenpō*)

'Awkward Convergence' in the Financial Sector

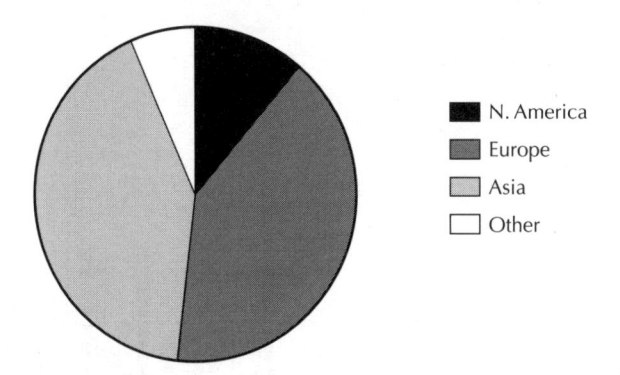

Figure 3.9: Distribution of Securities Companies' Overseas Offices
(*Source:* MOF *Shōkenkyoku Nenpō*)

economy and by legal wranglings but, by mid-1993, all of the Big Four had set up offices there after closing down units in Europe, the US and Australia. Apart from the Big Four, only a handful of firms have ventured into Asia beyond Hong Kong and, in some cases, Singapore.[6]

3.1.2 Foreign Financial Institutions in Japan

While a number of foreign financial institutions can trace the history of their operations in Japan back for more than a century, World War II meant that, as with Japanese financial institutions in the US and Europe, firms effectively restarted from scratch in the postwar period. Hence, figure 3.10 provides a picture of the entry and expansion of foreign financial institutions in Japan in terms of newly opened bank branches, bank representative offices, and securities companies offices.[7]

Foreign banks' expansion began immediately after the war, with a number of firms setting up during the Occupation to reestablish a presence in Japan. The earliest banks were the predecessors of large US and European firms such as Citibank (1946), Standard Chartered (1949), Bank of America (1950), ABN Amro (1950) and HSBC (1950). They were joined by Asian firms including International Commercial Bank of China (1950), Bank of India (1950) and Bangkok Bank (1955). Their second wave of expansion began in the 1960, and was in response to Japan's rapid economic growth. A third in the early 1970s, was spurred by the lucrative foreign monopoly on impact loans (see Chapter 2), and a fourth wave came in the early 1980s in response to domestic deregulation on the basis of reciprocal access agreements. A fifth wave in the mid-1980s was initiated by the lure of new business opportunities created by the Yen-Dollar Agreement, and a sixth was spurred by the bubble in the late 1980s. Finally, further deregulation in

The Case of Japan

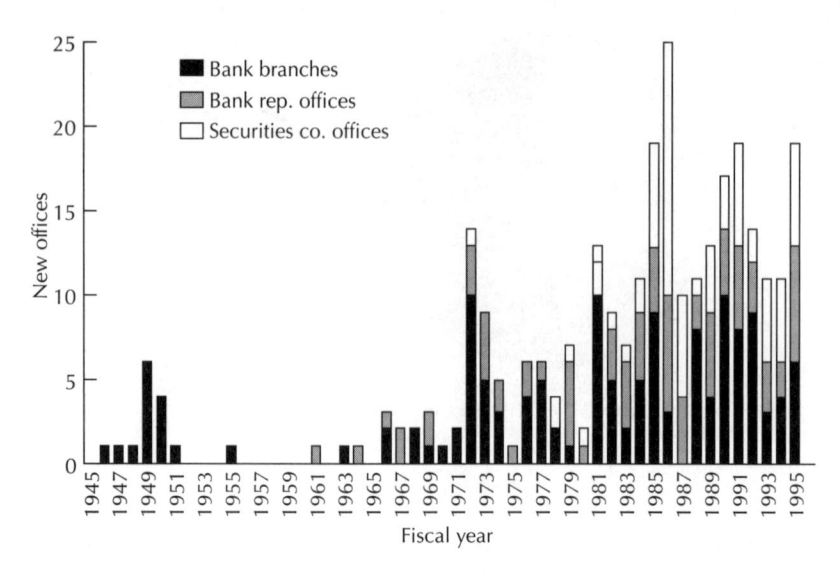

Figure 3.10: Foreign Financial Institutions' Expansion in Japan
(*Source:* MOF *Kokusai Kinyûkyoku Nenpō*)

the mid- to late-1990s has created a further wave of foreign expansion. As of July 1996, there were ninety-four foreign banks in Japan with 144 branches, and eighty-one foreign banks with 84 representative offices, making a total of 175 institutions with 228 offices (MOF *Kokusai Kinyûkyoku Nenpō* 1996).

By contrast, *foreign securities companies* did not enter the Japanese market until the 1970s. The first to do so was Merrill Lynch (1972), which was followed by Citicorp International Securities (1978) and Prudential Securities (1979). Even so, the majority of big-name brokerages held off until the mid-to late-1980s, when they could no longer resist the lure of Japan's rapidly inflating stock market, or until the 1990s, as new opportunities emerged with promises of deregulation. As of the end of June 1996, there were fifty-four foreign brokerages in Japan, having between them seventy branches (MOF *Kokusai Kinyûkyoku Nenpō* 1996).

By nationality of institution, figure 3.11 shows that in aggregate, almost half of foreign financial institutions operating in Japan in 1995 were European, with North American and Asian firms accounting for a little over twenty percent each. However, broken down into banks and securities firms, figures 3.12 and 3.13 show that the number of North American securities firms *vis à vis* Asian securities firms stands out thanks to the strong position held by Wall Street firms in their industry.

'Awkward Convergence' in the Financial Sector

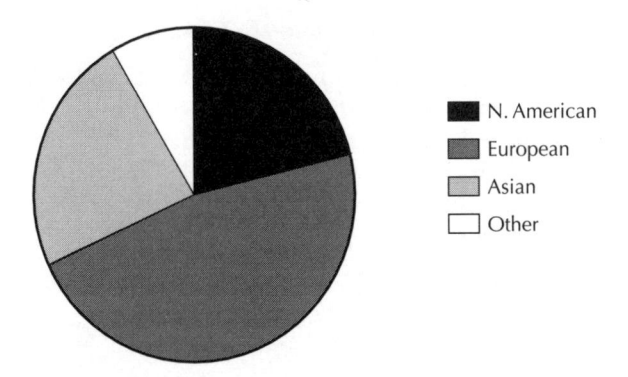

Figure 3.11: Foreign Financial Institutions in Japan (1995)

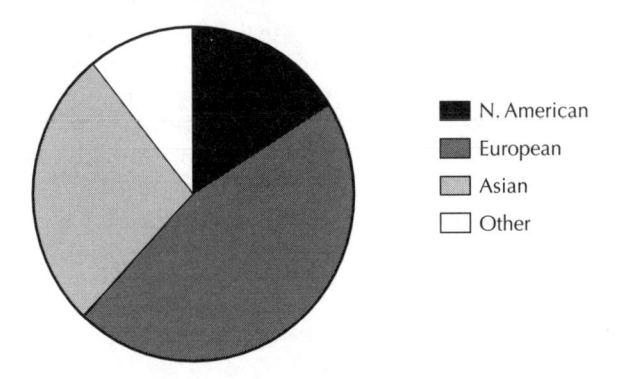

Figure 3.12: Foreign Banks in Japan (1995)

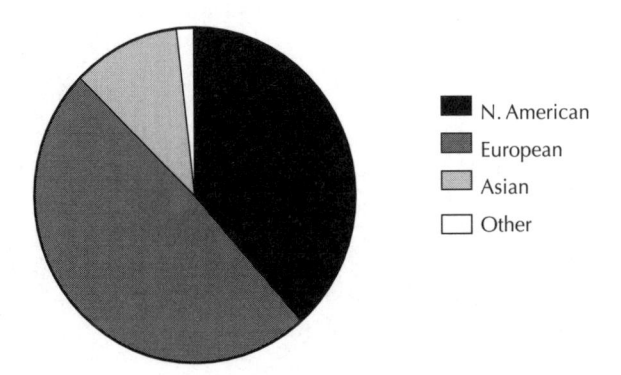

Figure 3.13: Foreign Securities Companies in Japan (1995)
(*Source*: MOF *Kokusai Kinyûkyoku Nenpō*)

The Case of Japan

3.1.3 'The Japanese are Coming!'

The outward expansion of Japanese firms and inward expansion of foreign firms noted above only hints at the tremendous influence which Japan's financial sector came to have on international capital markets in the 1980s. A clearer picture of this impact can be constructed by examining quantitative data relating to market share performance in key sectors of the international capital markets, and by sampling qualitative indicators of market sentiment concerning Japanese financial institutions' performance and prospects.

(i) Size

Size is a leading indicator of prominence in international finance because it is the most frequently cited comparative measure. At its crudest, size is measured by *assets*, and this provides a straightforward ranking of banks by market share – i.e. volume of loans extended. Since the BIS Capital Accord of 1988, however, it has become increasingly popular to measure size by *capital* which, as an indicator of resources available, provides a better measure of a firm's strength – i.e. its ability to withstand shocks.[8] In turn, since the mid-1990s, new ways of measuring size on the basis of capital have proliferated as some commentators have begun to question the validity of Tier One capital as an accurate comparative benchmark.[9] Figures 3.14 to 3.16 show that by all of these measures, Japanese banks emerged to dominate world rankings in the 1980s.

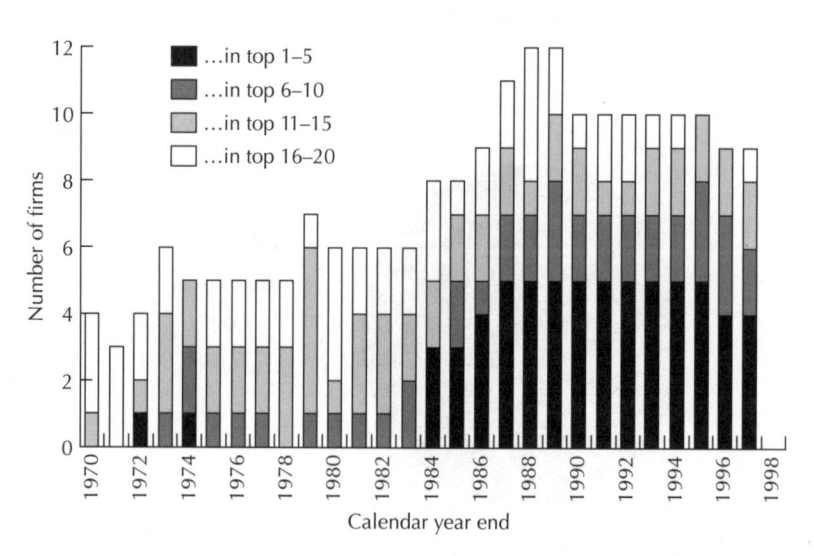

Figure 3.14: Japanese Banks in World Rankings by Assets
(*Source: Banker*)

'Awkward Convergence' in the Financial Sector

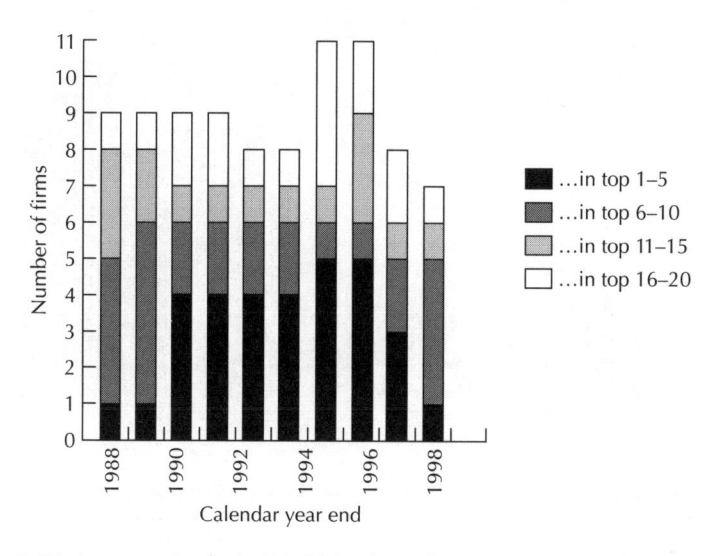

Figure 3.15: Japanese Banks in World Rankings by Tier One Capital
(*Source: Banker*)

	'Total Capital'				'Core Capital'	
	1993	1994	1995	1996	1996	1997
Number of Japanese banks in top 5	5	5	3	3	0	1
Number of Japanese banks in top 10	7	7	6	5	3	3
Number of Japanese banks in top 15	10	9	6	6	6	6
Number of Japanese banks in top 20	11	10	7	8	8	6

Figure 3.16: Japanese Banks in World Rankings by New Measures of Strength
(*Source: Institutional Investor*)

(ii) Share of key market sectors

Volume of transactions intermediated in leading international capital market sectors is another indicator of prominence. In banking, proportions of new international bank lending and ownership of international banking assets are the two common yardsticks reported by the BIS, while lead-manager tables for international syndicated loans provide a more accurate picture of firms' importance to international – as opposed to national – capital markets.[10] Figures 3.17 to 3.19 show that Japanese banks rose quickly to prominence, and in some cases dominance, on each of these fronts during the 1980s.[11]

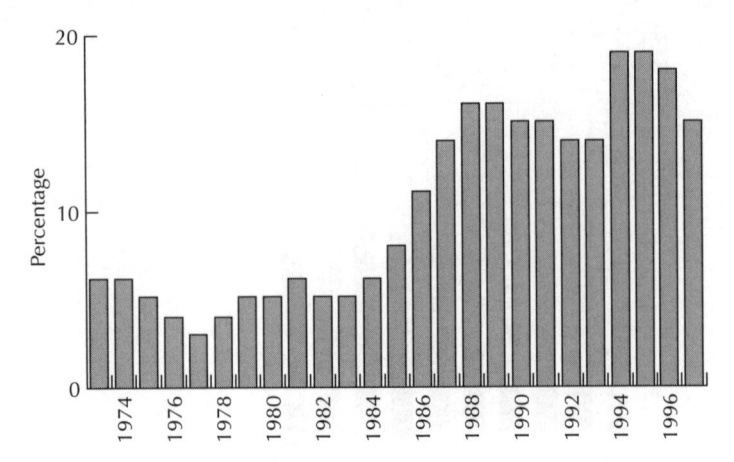

Figure 3.17: Proportion of New International Bank Lending by Japanese Banks
(*Source*: BIS)

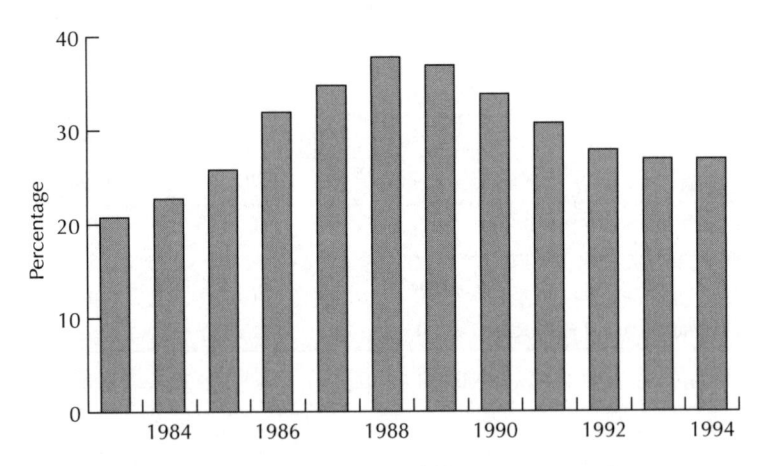

Figure 3.18: International Banking Assets Held by Japanese Banks
(*Source*: BIS)

In the international securities markets, Japanese brokerages similarly rose to dominate the eurodollar market, where the combined market share of Japan's Big Four rose to a high of forty-eight percent in 1989; they also played a major role in other sectors, as figures 3.20 to 3.22 show.

(iii) Market Perceptions

Finally, *Euromoney* articles from the 1980s which focus upon Japanese financial institutions and related market developments can be taken as a

'Awkward Convergence' in the Financial Sector

Year	No. of Jse banks in top 50	Share of market (%)
1983	2	3.0
1984	6	4.6
1985	6	4.7
1986	9	7.4
1987	10	6.8
1988	11	7.2
1989	12	9.4
1990	13	10.9
1991	11	8.9
1992	5	4.2
1993	7	3.1

Figure 3.19: Position of Japanese Banks as Lead Managers in International Syndicated Lending
(*Source: Euromoney*)

Year	Daiwa	Nikkō	Nomura	Yamaichi
1977	–	–	–	–
1978	–	–	12	–
1979	–	–	16	–
1980	10	–	20	18
1981	17	–	8	14
1982	18	–	13	–
1983	–	–	9	–
1984	13	18	7	–
1985	11	–	8	20
1986	5	10	2	12
1987	4	5	1	6
1988	4	6	1	5
1989	2	4	1	3
1990	4	7	1	11
1991	3	8	1	7
1992	11	10	2	–
1993	14	13	7	–

Figure 3.20: Position of Big Four Firms in Eurodollar Bond Issues
(Top Twenty Lead-managers/Bookrunners)
(*Source: Euromoney*)

The Case of Japan

Year	Daiwa	Nikkō	Nomura	Yamaichi	Market Share
1986	2	4	1	3	79%
1987	3	4	1	5	66%
1988	2	6	1	4	52%
1989	2	7	1	5	49%
1990	2	5	1	3	57%
1991	1	3	2	4	84%
1992	2	3	1	4	75%
1993	3	2	1	4	60%

Figure 3.21: Position of Big Four in Euroyen Bond Issues
(Top Twenty Lead-managers/Bookrunners)
(*Source*: Arora 1995, p. 177)

Year	Daiwa	Nikkō	Nomura	Yamaichi	Market Share
1986	2	3	1	4	60%
1987	4	2	1	3	85%
1988	3	4	1	2	95%
1989	4	2	1	3	93%
1990	2	3	1	4	90%

Figure 3.22: Position of Big Four in Issues of Eurobonds with Warrants
(Top Twenty Lead-managers/Bookrunners)
(*Source*: Arora 1995, p. 177)

proxy for market opinion concerning Japanese financial institutions.[12] They show that in the mid-1980s, most Western financiers woke up to the 'Japanese challenge', which was suddenly seen to constitute a threat to their customary dominance of international capital markets. The emergence of such sentiment was first reflected in an October 1985 article which, under the cover title 'The Japanese are Coming!' warned:

> By this time the world should be accustomed to assaults from the islands of Japan. First came the warplanes and the soldiers, then the automobiles and the video machines. Now the Japanese are in the very early stages of a fresh onslaught. Their banks and securities houses are preparing to invade the global capital markets in much the same manner as Honda and Sony have attacked and penetrated the world market for manufactured goods.
>
> The weapons to be used are already in place and the plans are drawn up. The tactics will be peculiarly Japanese: a mixture of stealth,

surprise, and self-sacrificing aggression. When they have finished, perhaps around 1990, the Japanese will control vast areas of the financial services business in Asia, Europe, and America.

As the quote implies, *Euromoney's* assessment of the 'challenge' placed considerable weight on considerations such as (i) the massive resources of Japanese firms, (ii) their aggressive and focused strategy, which had proved itself successful in other areas, and (iii) the complacency of Western firms, which persisted in spite of considerable inroads already made by Japanese financial institutions. These themes ran through the majority of subsequent articles which appeared during the latter half of the 1980s.

First, observers realised that the sheer size of Japanese financial institutions made them a force to be reckoned with. Japanese banks, led by DKB, owned thirty-eight percent of global assets in 1988, but the dollar-value of their holdings did not peak until 1990 ($2.12 trillion – *Euromoney* 6/96). By capital, IBJ became the largest bank in the world in 1987 ($86 billion), with the Bank of Yokohama, a *regional* bank, ranking thirtieth in the world 500. As for the country's securities firms, it was well known that Nomura had more customer assets in its custody – and thus largely under its control – than any bank in the world had deposits.[13] Nomura was also easily the world's largest financial institution by equity, and the most profitable, with colleagues such as Daiwa and Nikkō trailing not far behind. As *Euromoney* noted,

> There is no mistaking the essential point that Japanese securities houses have become a force in international finance that cannot be ignored ... Any of the Big Four could theoretically buy up all the clearing banks in London and then buy a major US money centre institution or two, without much strain on its financial underpinnings (7/88).

Moreover, hitherto unknown Japanese financial institutions became familiar names as they began to invest vast amounts of domestically-accumulated capital abroad: the chairman of Mitsui Mutual Life explained 'We can't lend any more money to domestic firms, so we have to look outside for investment opportunities' (Komiyama Toshio interview, *Euromoney* 3/87), while the chairman of Zenshinren Bank (the central bank for *shinkin* banks) noted with some embarrassment, 'Every year our members' assets rise, and it's now becoming more than a bit of a problem to find new areas for investment' (Obara Tetsugoro interview, *Euromoney* 7/88).

Second, observers commented on the aggressive strategies of Japanese firms, where their large resources were harnessed in the pursuit of competitive gains in a few narrowly targeted market sectors. When Nomura finally displaced CSFB from its long-term position atop the eurobond bookrunner rankings in 1987, CSFB's head of syndicate, Joan Beck, commented wearily 'We can't beat Nomura at their own game and have no intention of doing so' (*Euromoney* 7/88). More generally, it became clear that market attention was keenly focused upon what the Japanese were doing, in order that Western firms were tailoring their competitive strategies to avoid head-on competition wherever possible.

This siege mentality was accentuated by the fact that representatives of Japanese firms constantly spoke of their plans for expansion and entry into new markets. In 1985, Daiwa Securities had stated its ambition of becoming 'a world-class international bonds trader' like Salomon Brothers, IBJ its aim to secure a position in top five global banks 'in five years time', and Sumitomo its desire to be 'like Citibank' (*Euromoney* 10/85). A year later, Nomura and Daiwa obtained primary-dealer status for US Treasury bonds, and by the end of 1987 the former had already clawed its way into the top twenty of the forty-two primary dealers by market volume. Accordingly, the Big Four's New York staff had soared by an average of eighty percent in 1987, with Nomura predicting that, in spite of the October 1987 Black Monday crash, it expected to have 'several thousand' people in New York by 1991, up from under 400 at the start of 1987 (*Euromoney* 4/88). This appeared to underline the editorial observation several months previously that 'Three or four years ago, it would have taken a brave man to predict the rise to dominance of the Euromarkets by the Big Four. Now it should take a brave man to bet that they will not come to dominate dozens of other areas of financial activity as well' (10/87).

Japanese investor's appetite for US Treasury Bonds had become legendary, but there were increasing signs of diversification into new markets. By mid-1986, Japanese financial institutions were routinely bidding for between twenty and forty percent of all new US Treasury issues to feed overseas portfolios which, on average, consisted of eighty percent US Treasuries, ten percent eurobonds, one percent non-Japanese equities and ten percent 'other' (*Euromoney* 3/87). However, at the end of 1986, a shift towards US equities became discernible, and after Black Monday in October 1987 much more emphasis was placed on European, Canadian and Australian products (*Euromoney* 10/86; 4/88). Riding this trend, and simultaneously pursuing new business in areas such as municipal financing, mortgage-backed securities and M&A, Nomura president Tabuchi Yoshihisa declared his goal to achieve a fifty-fifty revenue split between domestic and foreign business by 1991. Considering the fact that his firm accounted for more than twenty percent of TSE trading volume (compared with US giant Merrill Lynch's seven percent share of NYSE's volume), this was an extremely ambitious undertaking (*Euromoney* 4/88; 12/88).

Third, and accordingly, commentators repeatedly observed that Western firms consistently underestimated the threat posed by the 'Japanese challenge'. There was never any doubt as to where Japanese financial institutions excelled and what their greatest sources of competitive advantage had been in their rise to prominence in the early 1980s. As *Euromoney* had noted in 1985, 'Japanese firms can offer a thoroughness and efficiency in the mundane details of financial transactions that many Western houses cannot match ... they have enormous domestic resources, a special knowledge of developing Asia, and the backing of the MOF' (10/85). However, on the basis of their low levels of experience in more advanced/complex financial products and analytical techniques, a Citibank executive spoke for many when he told the magazine 'I don't say they will never catch up, but it won't be for an age' (*Euromoney* 10/85).[14] Nevertheless, by the following year there were already signs of progress in rectifying many of these deficiencies. On the basis of this the magazine warned, 'The complacency of the [foreign] opposition will be one of the ingredients of Japanese success in the coming decade (10/86).

It was not just the fact that Japanese firms were moving up high-profile league tables in eurobond underwriting or international syndicated loans. They began to head-hunt experienced nonJapanese staff to boost their expertise in order to break into the unfamiliar markets – such as swaps and options, mortgage-backed securities, and M&A – upon which they had set their sights. In 1987, many specialists in international finance proclaimed Nomura's highly complex 'Heaven and Hell' multicurrency swap (devised for IBM by a young Japanese mathematician at the firm) 'Deal of the Year' (*Euromoney* 10/87). And in 1988, Sanyo Securities (Japan's seventh largest brokerage) opened a new dealing room in Tokyo – at 6,236 square meters, the world's largest unobstructed office space – with space for 500 dealers and 1,500 computer terminals running state-of-the-art systems, built at a cost of $5 billion (*Euromoney* 11/88).

The magazine also noted that 'Japanese banks and insurers have made a cottage industry out of investing in US securities houses'. Since Sumitomo Bank had purchased thirteen percent of Goldman Sachs in 1986, IBJ had bought primary bond dealer Aubrey G. Langston, Nippon Life had taken a thirteen percent stake in Shearson Lehman, and Yasuda Life now owned eighteen percent of PaineWebber (4/88). Five of the ten largest Californian banks were bought up by the Japanese (7/88), and general property investment by Japanese financial institutions was rising sharply. Another article warned,

> No corporation in the West will be safe from the coming wave of Japanese acquisitions. The shy, don't-want-to-be-hostile Japanese buyers of the 1980s will be succeeded in the 1990s by a new breed of aggressive purchasers. As for all those minority stakes the Japanese have accumulated – they're just preludes to outright control (8/89).

By this time, early rumours that the MOF was planning to nurture a 'Big Eight' or 'Big Ten' Japanese securities firms to compete on an equal footing with the top eight or ten New York or London firms in the international arena (e.g. *Euromoney* 7/86) were firmly entrenched. The Japan Offshore Market (JOM) which opened in December 1986 was interpreted as an attempt to usurp the euromarkets (*Euromoney* 10/87), and the BIS Capital Adequacy Accord's final formulation – an initiative supposedly intended to curtail Japanese banks' overseas expansion – was painted as a miscalculation on the part of lobbying Western bankers. Specifically, *Euromoney* argued that because Japanese banks would be permitted to use hidden reserves to boost capital, there would be no reason for them to abandon their predatory pricing tactics. In fact, likening the BIS guidelines to 'a large new weapon with which to cudgel their American and European counterparts', the magazine predicted 'The Japanese, contrary to every expectation and conventional wisdom, will be helped, not harmed, by the new regulations'. This was because, 'Through a series of manoeuvres, the Japanese will transform their appearance; the banks that seemed to have the poorest equity base in the world will suddenly emerge as the banks with the largest equity bases' (7/88).

This overview of the internationalisation of Japanese financial institutions shows that significant competitive interaction with foreign firms began only in the 1980s. The global standing of leading Japanese firms had climbed from low levels in the early 1970s to apparently very high levels at the end of the 1980s, as the opinions surveyed above indicate.[15] Appropriately, Nomura was designated as the firm which had single-handedly had the 'greatest impact on global capital markets in the 1980s' (*Euromoney* 10/89); more generally, the same thing appeared to hold true for Japanese financial institutions as a group. Thus, concluded Duser at the end of the decade in a book-length study of Japanese banks, 'It is believed that they will leave a lasting mark on future developments in international banking, comprising such aspects as investment attitudes, human resource management and international monetary arrangements' (1990, p. 3).

3.2 THE RISE AND FALL OF JAPANESE FIRMS AS GLOBAL COMPETITORS

To assess the extent to which the global prominence attained by Japanese financial institutions in the 1980s was a product of the generic driving forces associated with financial globalisation – i.e. of market deregulation and private competitive innovation (as identified in Chapter 1) – it is essential to examine the rise and fall of Japanese firms in terms of their strategic responses to new developments in their *field of action*.[16] While the bubble economy was, of course, the major factor in the equation, there were other important elements.

3.2.1 The Rise

(i) Environmental developments

The meteoric rise of Japanese financial institutions during the 1980s was made possible by the coincidence of a number of environmental developments which radically restructured their 'field of action' in the 1980s. The five most significant of these were (i) Japan's rapidly accelerating current account surpluses, (ii) the high yen in the latter part of the decade, (iii) the domestic stock market bubble (iv) the partial nature of domestic financial deregulation, and (v) other external developments.

The first three elements were push factors, causing Japanese financial institutions to become prominent in the international capital markets. First, with domestic savings well in excess of domestic investment, and with the country's current account surplus rising sharply to a cumulative total of over $350 billion in the latter part of the decade, Japanese financial institutions stood to gain a more prominent position internationally simply by virtue of their position as the natural intermediaries of a large proportion of the surplus. Analysing Japan's flow of funds figures for the 1980s, Nakao shows that Japanese banks were not in fact the major channel for the country's overall net capital outflows (1995, pp. 9–60; p. 119). Rather, it was securities companies that turned out to be the main beneficiaries, because Japanese investment abroad was biased towards securities purchases rather than foreign direct investment. At the end of 1981, Japan had net external assets of $11 billion; by the end of 1984, $74 billion; by the end of 1986, $130 billion, the point at which Japan overtook Britain as the world's largest creditor nation; and by 1988 the country had net foreign credits of $175 billion – a sixteen-fold increase in seven years.

Second, foreign exchange rate movements were, of course, a critical contributor to this situation. The strong yen (*endaka*) which emerged as a major trend after the Louvre Accord in 1987, spurred fresh waves of foreign securities investment by Japanese investors and foreign direct investment (FDI) by Japanese manufacturers. This heightened the prominence of Japanese banks in the international markets in their role of procuring foreign currency-denominated funds, since all such transactions had to be rooted through licensed foreign exchange banks. Moreover, Japanese banks became increasingly involved in seeking to exploit arbitrage opportunities, both on their own behalf and on behalf of domestic insurance companies and institutional investors, by borrowing in the weakening currency (Nakao 1995, pp. 61–78). Hence, at the same time as Japan was rapidly accumulating assets in its long-term capital account, it was accumulating large quantities of short-term liabilities: '[a]s a nation, Japan was borrowing short-term and lending long-term' (*ibid.*, p. 63). Consequently, Japanese financial institution's activity in the international financial system increased simultaneously on two fronts.

Third, Japan's domestic regime of cheap money and the resulting domestic stock market bubble of the late 1980s (figure 2.4) was an important factor in exaggerating the volume of funds available for investment (*kaneamari*) abroad as well as at home. The free-spending mentality which swept through all sectors of the domestic economy added considerably to FDI and portfolio investment outflows, particularly since foreign asset prices became increasingly cheap relative to domestic ones, which were inflated both by the bubble and yen appreciation.[17] Thus, Nakao notes, 'the boom in "capital exports" during the latter part of the 1980s was really just a reflection of the exceptional rise in Tokyo stock prices' (1995, p. 58). Here, again, Japanese financial institutions were the main intermediaries.

The fourth factor related to the significant opportunities for regulatory arbitrage opened between Japan and other core capitalist states which emerged in the 1980s. Essentially, this was a case of Japanese deregulation having proceeded far enough to permit considerable capital outflows, but not yet far enough to keep capital at home, because earlier or more radical deregulation abroad made foreign financial centres cheaper or deeper (i.e. more liquid) markets in which to conduct business. Developments which acted as important push factors were related mainly to the Yen-Dollar Agreement. They included the 1984 repeal of the thirty-percent withholding tax on foreign investment, the 1984 approval of euroyen loans, the 1986 raising to thirty percent the limit on overseas investments for insurance and trust fund money,[18] and the 1986 establishment of the Japan Offshore Market (JOM). Those that acted as significant pull factors included the continuing development of the euromarkets, the 1975 stock market deregulation in the US, and the 1986 Big Bang programme in the UK. The synergetic result was that much domestic financial activity relocated abroad. This was pronounced in the securities industry where the cost advantages and simpler procedures for issuing and trading bonds in the euromarkets led to a greater number of Japanese corporate issues being floated overseas than domestically in the late 1980s: foreign issues peaked in 1991 with sixty-eight per cent of Japanese corporate bond issues taking place abroad.[19] Japanese financial institutions, however, continued to underwrite the vast majority of these (Fuchita 1997, pp. 9–11). Accordingly, more than fifty percent of new instruments being sold in the euromarkets during the latter half of the 1980s were targeted exclusively at Japanese investors (*Euromoney* 8/87).

The situation in banking was equally distorted by regulations. Restrictions in the Japanese interbank market, restrictions in the JOM during the first few years of its operation after December 1986, and the BOJ's policy of 'window guidance' (which limited yen lending by the domestic but not overseas offices of Japanese financial institutions), all encouraged a 'round-tripping' of assets. Correspondingly, the international asset growth of Japanese banks was built, to a relatively large extent, on their own interoffice transactions.[20] This suggests that they, too, were not 'deeply-planted' in the local markets where they operated. Rather, as Takeda and Turner point out, 'their effective presence abroad remained much less than measures based on shares of international assets or liabilities would suggest' (1992, p. 85). Thus, *Euromoney* hypothesised,

> If the Japanese capital markets are re-arranged so that fees drop down to international levels, if certain types of instruments were approved, and if there was a move to a real shelf system, then there is no doubt that a huge amount of business which is now booked in London would flow back to Tokyo ... London is little more than an offshore booking centre used only because it circumvents a tiresome tangle of regulations which pushes up overall costs and imposes conditions with which issuers do not want to comply. Ask a Japanese corporation why it uses the euromarkets and the reply is invariably: 'It lowers costs and avoids strict MOF regulations' (11/89).

Hereby, short-term regulatory differences evidently were important factors in serving to exaggerate the rise of Japanese firms as global financial intermediaries. Statistics relating to the volume of foreign fund-raising in Japan's domestic financial markets bear this out. Contrary to what might be expected for a country in surplus, foreign shares listed in Tokyo accounted for a meagre 0.8 per cent of turnover in 1989 in contrast with New York's figure of over five per cent and London's figure of thirty per cent (Takeda and Turner 1992, p. 67). In short, the internationalisation of Japan's financial sector remained very much a one-way process even at the end of the 1980s.

A fifth feature of their environment was a number of external developments which acted as pull factors. The pursuit of Reaganomics in the US, and an extensive programme of privatisations in Europe, together created unique opportunities for Japanese financial institutions to expand their overseas activity, acting either for themselves or on behalf of cash-rich domestic clients. The former increased the yield spreads between JGBs and US TBs, and promised to compensate Japanese investors for much of the foreign exchange risk incurred; the latter created a host of relatively low-risk equity investment opportunities just at the point where Japanese investors were moving to diversify their foreign portfolios. Moreover, developments such as the Third World debt crisis and the US savings and loan fiasco hit their competitors, particularly US firms, either directly or by association, and resulted in the downgrading of many of their credit ratings. This gave Japanese firms an additional edge in raising funds cheaply in the international money markets, an advantage that came on top of others which they already enjoyed in being able to procure and supply capital cheaply as a result of unique features in their domestic environment (see below).

(ii) Strategic choices

While environmental push and pull factors structured the 'field of action' for Japanese financial institutions during the 1980s, strategic responses were the ultimate critical variables which determined the speed of, and momentum behind, their meteoric rise to international prominence. Actions taken by Japanese firms in the 1980s betray three crucial choices which were made by management. These were (i) the extension (and modification) of the market-share orientation which they relied upon for success in domestic competition; (ii) their exploitation of close ties with domestic clients, and (iii) their seizure of new opportunities to engage in activities from which they were prohibited at home.

First, Japanese financial institutions built their international strategies around the aggressive pursuit of market share, mimicking the route which their famed manufacturing clients had taken to success in international competition. In finance, this necessitated a willingness to extend loans and offer services at rates which would undercut the competition considerably. A number of factors contributed to their willingness to pursue this option. To a great extent, Japanese firms were ideologically predisposed to predatory pricing in so far as it involved a simple extension of the strategy on which they competed domestically, i.e. a quantitative focus on market-share and the deferment of immediate profitability in the hope of greater long-term gains. The cost of this exercise could be subsidised by drawing upon extraordinary (bubble-era) profits generated domestically, and by exploiting the competitive advantages in fund procurement and supply which gave them lower break-even margins than their overseas rivals.[21] The majority of Japanese firms were widely reputed to be losing money on many areas of their international business, but particularly on their euromarket underwriting activity. But although profit breakdowns between domestic and international business remained a closely guarded secret, Japanese firms at the time insisted that any losses were a necessary part of their 'start-up' costs, and that making money on international business was not important in the early years when they were building a strong presence in key market sectors (*Euromoney* 8/87; 7/88).

Second, Japanese financial institutions capitalised on long-term and close ties with their clients, effectively riding the wave of *their* internationalisation. Unlike truly global banks, the major part of Japanese banks' funding through their overseas offices flowed to Japanese residents or the overseas affiliates of Japanese corporations. One study of the US branches of Japanese banks concluded that about two-thirds of claims fell into this category (Terrell *et al.* 1990).[22] Similarly, Japanese securities companies rose to prominence in eurobond tables in the second half of the 1980s almost entirely as a result of (co-)lead-managing Japanese corporate issues, and their huge business in US TBs was almost entirely cultivated with domestic Japanese demand in mind (Takeda and Turner 1992, p. 81). By contrast, Japanese financial institutions abroad made little progress in serving non-Japanese clients (Dufey 1990; see also below).[23] It appears that Japanese firms actively encouraged existing domestic clients to pursue new financing and investment opportunities abroad, either to generate new business, or to substitute for the natural decline in their demand for funds over time. In the former case, clients were apt to take advantage of new investment outlets since they had been conditioned by Japanese brokers' long history of churning accounts for commissions at home; in the latter case, industry which now generated sufficient capital for its own investment needs in the form of retained income could easily be persuaded to continue borrowing cheaply to finance speculative *zaitech* activities overseas.

Third, Japanese financial institutions made the strategic choice to exploit new opportunities by engaging in business areas which they were prohibited from entering domestically. Thus, city banks became involved in trust banking, and all of the Big Four obtained banking licenses abroad. However, not wanting to be left behind, and flush with resources from their profitable domestic operations, many smaller banks and brokerages followed this lead without conducting feasibility studies. The logic was that 'all top global banks and brokers have extensive international networks and are active in a wide range of markets, *therefore* to become a top firm it is necessary to acquire these trappings'; rather than 'all top global banks and brokers ..., *because* they can operate competitively and profitably in many markets' (see, for example, *Euromoney* special supplement *Japanese Securities Companies: Hot on the Heels of the Big Four*, 8/87). Hereby, the Japanese entry into international markets was exaggerated by this ultimately unsustainable fad for an international presence.

3.2.2 The Fall

Shortly after the turn of the decade it became evident that the ground was shifting underneath Japan's financial institutions, radically altering their 'field of action'. Three developments stood out as particularly important in pressing them to curtail their expansion and contemplate restructuring: (i) the bursting of the domestic bubble, (ii) the Bank of International Settlements' (BIS) Capital Adequacy Directive, and (iii) further domestic deregulation.

First, and most significant, were the ramifications which followed the bursting of Japan's bubble economy in April 1990: an end of the regime of cheap money, the subsequent stock market crash, prolonged economic recession, and high levels of unperforming bank loans (see also Chapter 4). Japanese financial institutions were especially vulnerable to domestic downswings because of their high dependency on Japanese business, both at home and abroad. Their unenviable situation became reflected in downgraded credit ratings and in the so-called 'Japan premium'.[24]

Second, the domestic stock market fall presented a serious problem for Japanese bankers in light of the Bank of International Settlements (BIS) Capital Adequacy Directive of 1988 which recommended that all internationally active banks attain a minimum capital-to-assets ratio of eight percent by the end of fiscal 1992. Although Japanese banks had traditionally operated below this level, the MOF had secured a dispensation when signing up to the guidelines allowing forty-five percent of unrealised gains on stock holdings to be counted towards the eight percent figure.[25] Hereby, while the stock market remained buoyant, Japanese banks were able to meet this figure without difficulty, but, when it plunged, they faced a stark dilemma: issue new equity or cut back on lending. The former was not much of an option in a shell-shocked domestic market, and, although markets abroad were faring comparatively better, mounting questions about the fundamental competitiveness of Japanese financial institutions (see below) did not enamour prospective issuers to foreign investors.

Third, these developments coincided with a number of domestic regulatory reforms, some of which were already in the pipeline and some of which were spurred by recent developments, be they scandals or policies to beat the lengthening recession. The 1992 Financial Services Reform Act, the BOJ's 1993 abandonment of its 'window guidance' (*madoguchi shidō*) policy, and the 1994 deregulation of stock brokerage commissions on large trades (over ¥1 billion) all worked to encourage the repatriation of financial business which had migrated to less regulated centres.

Hereby, Japan's financial institutions were confronted with the need to reappraise their operations, and particularly those overseas. The two major sources of competitive advantage which they had ridden to prominence in the 1980s – cheap access to domestic funds and large volumes of portfolio investment flows from Japanese clients – had either been completely reversed or were diminishing rapidly. Moreover, new weaknesses were becoming apparent, many of which could be traced to peculiar national structures. Deprived of their familiar sources of competitive strength (i.e. profit), it was clear that the MOF's convoy system had shielded them from the need to accumulate the open competitive expertise and innovative skills which they would henceforth have to rely upon in international competition. In this new light, the *uncompetitiveness* of Japanese financial institutions was self-evident to all observers.

A reappraisal of market performance showed that the success of Japanese financial institutions had been concentrated almost exclusively in low margin, low-tech sectors of the international markets. To summarise the results of more than a decade of global financing surveys,[26] (i) in the euromarkets, Japanese banks and securities companies figured prominently during the 1980s as underwriters of euroyen bond issues, where they derived comparative advantages from the sector's strong 'currency-clientele effect' (CCE),[27] and in US-dollar issues, where pricing counts for everything; (ii) in international syndicated loans, Japanese banks figured high in terms of the total loans extended – again an issue of pricing (and access to capital) – but scored low on all sophisticated product tables; (iii) in derivatives, US firms led comfortably, Japanese banks figuring only as end-user intermediaries; (iv) in foreign exchange, US firms were also dominant, Japanese firms featuring only in yen-related business, again thanks to the CCE; (v) in mergers and acquisitions (M&A), European firms led, with Japanese firms' record limited to a small number of deals involving Japanese clients; (vi) in international equities, the Big Four played a prominent role between 1986 and 1988 as co-lead-managers for European privatisation programmes – again an issue of pricing – but their position in lead-management rolls – where expertise counts – was poor; and (vii) in international broking, Japanese securities firms enjoyed significant advantages in marketing yen-denominated issues where the CCE was high (and access to cash-rich domestic investors was important), but in yen warrants and derivatives – where the CCE is low – foreign brokers consistently performed better.

This quantitative survey is confirmed by qualitative assessments. *Euromoney*'s annual poll of professional opinion shows that Japanese firms' reputation for technical expertise and excellence in service has lagged considerably behind their high global presence.[28] In the overall rankings reproduced in figure 3.23, only a small number of Japanese firms even register on the scoreboard. In narrower categories not reproduced here,[29] Japanese firms figure prominently in yen-related sectors – where the CCE was high – and in raising capital via private placements, where their access to large domestic investors yielded a strong comparative advantage. But in other categories, such as 'most innovative firm', 'most improved firm', and in sophisticated product tables, not a single Japanese institution makes the list during the entire decade.[30]

Thus, in spite of what the initial overview in section 3.1 might suggest, it is clear that Japanese financial institutions had attained their position of dominance in highly visible market sectors by extending domestic competitive practices to their overseas operations under the highly artificial conditions of the time. This business model was anachronous to the new era of financial globalization and changes were absolutely unavoidable.

3.2.3 The Onset of Restructuring in Japanese Finance

Rationalisation was not new to the Japanese in the 1990s. Industry had restructured during the 1970s in response to the oil shocks, and in the late 1980s in response to the high yen. In finance, however, it was less

Year	Poll*	Capital Raising No. in best 10	Eurobonds No. in best 10	Euronotes No. in best 5	Euro-CP No. in best 5	Global equity No. in best 5	Syndicated loans No. in best 5	Derivatives No. in best 10
1988	U	1 Nomura [#10]	1 Nomura [#4]	0	0	–	0	–
	P	–	–	0	–	–	0	–
1989	U	0	2 Nomura [#4];	0	0	–	0	–
	P	–	– Daiwa Sec. [#10]	0	–	–	0	–
1990	U	1 Nomura [#8]	1 Nomura [#5]	0	0	–	0	–
	P	–	–	0	–	–	0	–
1991	U	2 IBJ [#3]	2 Nomura[#5]; IBJ [#9]	0	0	0	0	0
	P	– Nomura [#10]	1 Nomura [#2]	0	–	0	0	–
1992	U	2 Nomura [#6];	3 Daiwa Sec. [#6];	0	0	–	0	1 Sumitomo Bank [# 9]
		IBJ [#10]	Nomura[#7]; IBJ [#10]					
	P	–	1 Nomura [#6]	0	0	–	0	–
1993	U	0	0	0	0	0	0	1 Sumitomo Bank [#10]
	P	–	0	0	0	0	0	–
1994	U	0	1 Nomura [#8]	0	0	0	0	0
	P	–	0	0	0	0	0	–
1995	U	0	1 Nomura [#8]	0	0	0	0	0
	P	–	2 Nomura [#7];	0	0	0	0	–
1996	U	0	0 Daiwa Sec. [#10]	1 Nomura [#4]	0	0	0	0
	P	–	0	0	0	0	0	–
1997	U	1 (Nomura [#7])	0	0	0	0	0	0
	P	–	0	0	0	0	0	–

Figure 3.23: Position of Japanese Firms in Annual *Euromoney* Global Financing Polls
(Source: Euromoney September issues; *U = users' vote; P = peers' vote)

familiar.[31] The poor state of financial institutions' microeconomic fundamentals had long been obfuscated by continuous expansion, and the inflated profits conferred by the bubble had more than compensated for most managerial excesses and rising levels of general inefficiency. All this ended in a rude awakening with the bubble's collapse. Firms were forced to respond to a radically altered 'field of action', and seven new strategic trends emerged in their operations in the early- to mid-1990s. These were (i) a new cost-consciousness, (ii) the embrace of 'Western' technologies, (iii) strategic geographical diversification, (iv) product diversification, (v) synergetic mergers, (vi) localisation, and (vii) changes in human resource management.

First, while retrenchment has been imposed by exogenous trends, it took some time for Japanese firms to accept their loss of competitiveness *vis a vis* foreign firms and to start targeting efficiency gains according to 'normal' (i.e. bottom-line) criteria. Securities firms were the first to respond to the Nikkei's nearly forty percent decline (to around ¥24,000) during 1990 as profits plunged accordingly.[32] After a decade of unshackled expansion, rising personnel costs and overheads, the earliest casualties came in international operations, where foreign staff numbers were cut and capital repatriated.[33] The following year, rumours began to surface of domestic staff being 'encouraged' to quit by actions such as job transfers to rural offices where they would have no hope of career progression. New Japan Securities' actions were typical of the more overt actions taken. The firm announced that its capital investment programme in computerisation would be suspended, that non-sales staff would be redeployed on the sales side to boost business, and that it would scrap an existing plan to open ten new offices. Only Daiwa claimed still to be committed to overseas expansion, and most firms resorted to 'talking up' the Nikkei, with Nomura predicting that the index would recover and rise to between ¥45,000 and ¥50,000 by the end of fiscal 1990 (*Euromoney* 2/91).

In banking, a trend of significant cost-cutting emerged only after 1992. Again, this was initially visible in the overseas operations of leading firms, as many relocated to cheaper properties, cut expatriate staff numbers, and closed overseas offices (e.g. see *Banker* 9/96).[34] Soon, however, similar changes began to appear domestically, as a new emphasis on cutting operational costs swept through all sectors of the financial industry. Headcount at Japan's city banks fell by over ten percent (from a peak of around 155,000 at the end of fiscal 1993 to around 139,000 at the end of fiscal 1996). However, as figure 3.24 below shows, this understates the changes, as many firms affected much greater cuts.

The reductions hit middle and senior ranks hardest, with employees being either transferred to affiliated companies or encouraged to take early retirement (*Nikkei* 2/4/97).[35] Not captured in headline statistics were other significant changes: a sharp rise in the ratio of informal labour (part-time

The Case of Japan

Position	Company	Total staff (9/96)	Percentage Decrease (9/91–9/96)
1	Cosmo Securities	1,154	46.0
2	Dai-ichi Securities	1,520	42.6
3	Kokusai Securities	4,082	40.0
4	Sanyo Securities	2,982	40.0
5	Kankaku Securities	3,394	39.7
6	Okasan Securities	2,397	35.4
7	New Japan Securities	4,535	43.6
8	Tokyo Securities	1,963	32.2
9	Yamatane Securities	1,235	31.1
10	Wakō Securities	3,590	29.1
11	Daiwa Securities[†]	9,803	28.1
12	Nippon Trust & Banking	1,557	28.0
13	Midori Bank	2,528	23.3
14	Wakashio Bank	901	23.3
15	Nikkō Securities[†]	10,318	22.3
16	Yamaichi Securities[†]	9,828	21.6
17	Tokyo Sōwa Bank	2,793	19.6
18	Bank of Osaka	1,699	19.4
19	Sakura Bank*	19,564	16.0
20	Fukui Bank	2,152	15.7
24	Nomura Securities[†]	13,125	15.3
25	Asahi Bank*	13,588	14.4
27	Bank of Tokyo-Mitsubishi*	20,104	13.6
28	Chuo Trust & Banking	3,260	13.5
30	Yasuda Trust & Banking	4,265	13.1
32	Hokkaido Takushoku Bank*	5,672	12.8
38	Sumitomo Bank*	16,249	9.4
40	Daiwa Bank*	9,151	9.1
43	Tōyō Trust & Banking	4,531	8.7
44	Mitsubishi Trust & Banking	5,361	8.4
48	Sumitomo Trust & Banking	5,727	7.9
49	Dai-ichi Kangyō Bank*	18,477	7.3
59	Mitsui Trust Bank	5,251	5.5
73	Fuji Bank*	15,733	3.8
79	Nippon Credit Bank	2,932	2.6
88	Tōkai Bank	11,941	2.3
90	Sanwa Bank*	14,543	1.5
			Percentage Increase
111	Industrial Bank of Japan	5,325	0.6
135	Long Term Credit Bank	4,384	4.2

Figure 3.24: Personnel Cuts by Major Japanese Financial Institutions (9/91–9/96)
* city bank; [†] Big Four securities company
(*Source: Nikkei* 5/5/97)

and temporary staff) to full-time staff, more outsourcing of work, and a widening gap between core and non-core staff in terms of contractual provisions and renumeration (Tanaka 1997a; Makino 1997).[36] Bonuses – the most flexible part of renumeration – fell in line with corporate misfortunes, and many banks (including all of the city banks) switched from calculating them as a proportion of each employee's salary to calculating them as a proportion of the firms' semiannual results.[37] Many smaller banks and at least one major bank went so far as to cut monthly salaries,[38] and others indirectly followed their lead by introducing new methods of calculating salaries which effectively discriminated against non-core employees. Accordingly, bank workers' unions began to express concern, yet seemed resigned to the inevitability of many changes.[39]

Second, and related, was a new embrace of 'Western learning' (*yōgaku*) which was evident in the belated adoption by Japanese firms of management and operational technologies which had long been employed by their competitors. Most dramatic was the revelation that until the 1990s, even major city banks had had no internal credit rating systems for approving and monitoring loans. This meant that it had been impossible for them to calculate, even approximately, their market-, interest rate- or foreign exchange-risk exposure at any point in time. Following their sustainment of massive losses through domestic loans which turned sour when the bubble burst, computer-based risk management systems began to be purchased from leading American and European firms, with city and large regional banks leading their counterparts (NW 20/5/96).[40]

Third, Japanese financial institutions shifted from a pattern of overseas expansion which displayed strong 'herding' tendencies (Arora 1995) to one which was calculated strategically. As a result of the prevalent but mistaken belief that every first-rate bank must have substantial overseas business interests, Japanese firms had overextended themselves in many areas.[41] This, combined with the realisation that their domestic market was 'over-banked',[42] attested to a need for more carefully planned geographical diversification. Emerging markets were selected as their best option because, as *Euromoney* pointed out, 'While Western corporates ... see Japanese firms as second-tier players, for Asian and eastern European borrowers, Nomura and the others, with their access to the large Japanese investor base, look at least as prestigious as large US or European investment banks' (1/96). Accordingly, Japanese government policy encouraged their expansion in Asia, with MITI agreeing to provide insurance against political risk for loans made to the region (a guarantee which extended to foreign-owned banks in Japan). As a result, Japanese banks quickly captured the lion's share of Asian infrastructure project financing, and with private capital flows into the area increasing at an average annual rate of $10 billion, BIS figures showed that at the end of 1996, Japanese firms had roughly forty percent of this market, *vis à vis* forty and ten percent for European and US firms respectively

(*Euromoney* 9/95; *Banker* 9/95, 5/96; *NW* 10/6/96; *Nikkei* 6/1/97).[43] Accordingly, when it came, the Asian crisis hit them hard.

Fourth, in conjunction with the relaxation of domestic regulatory restrictions such as those separating the banking and securities industries (see Chapter 2), Japanese firms broadened their revenue bases through product diversification. Securitization became a major domestic growth area for banks; by April 1995, they had come to underwrite around twenty-five percent of all new bond issues through newly established securities subsidiaries, and a year later they had overtaken all but the Big Four securities firms, holding the next ten places in domestic bond underwriting tables (*NW* 15/1/96; 13/5/96; *Nikkei* 21/4/97).[44] Venture capital emerged as another important new business area for banks.[45] As for securities firms, the Big Four increased their propriety trading operations, in part to compensate for declines in their brokerage business.[46] International private banking (IPB) emerged as a profitable business area for subsidiaries of both banks and securities companies.[47]

Fifth, the Financial Services Reform Act of June 1992 included two little-noted provisions which paved the way for a new type of synergetic merger between Japanese firms. The first was a clause allowing banks to enter the securities business without creating a separate subsidiary *if* they bought out an ailing securities firm. The second allowed the long-term credit banks and the Bank of Tokyo to merge with other banks without losing their privileges to issue bank debentures. Hereby, Daiwa Bank took control of Cosmo Securities in August 1993; Mitsubishi Bank took over Nippon Trust Bank in October 1994; and the Bank of Tokyo, under the leadership of former senior MOF official Toyoo Gyohten, merged on an equal footing with Mitsubishi Bank in April 1996. Of the three, the last was especially significant in that it marked a change in the traditional pattern of financial mergers in Japan. Mergers and acquisitions (M&A) deals need approval from the MOF and this has been given traditionally for defensive rather than strategic reasons: Dai-ichi and Nippon Kangyō Banks coming together as Dai-ichi Kangyō Bank (DKB) in 1973, Mitsui and Taiyō Kōbe Banks creating Sakura Bank in 1990, and Kyōwa and Saitama Banks forming Asahi Bank in 1991 were all cases of bigger banks taking over smaller ones. They did not produce significant cost savings or synergetic effects. Hence, when announced in March 1995, it was generally expected that the Bank of Tokyo-Mitsubishi (BOT-M) deal would create a super-vehicle for taking over troubled domestic institutions – 'the world's largest vacuum cleaner' as *The Banker* called it in a headline reference (10/95). In fact, this supposition could hardly have been more wrong. Rather than helping to shore-up domestic banking, the BOT-M has unabashedly sought to position itself among the ranks of the global elite, cutting approximately 1000 staff and forty overseas offices from its combined total during its first year of operations (NW, 19/2/96; 1/4/96). Ever since, the Japanese financial press began to speculate about similar mega-mergers, the most eligible candidates having been seen as IBJ, Nomura Securities, Sumitomo Bank and Daiwa Bank (e.g. *Economisto* 23/3/96).

Sixth, Japanese firms took unprecedented steps towards decentralisation and localisation in the early 1990s.[48] Long criticised for their reluctance to appoint foreigners to senior management positions, many firms began to increase foreign directorial appointments in overseas offices. Nomura made its first real step towards localisation in the US by hiring an American (Max Chapman) to co-lead its operation there in October 1989, and then hired a local to run its Singapore operation in 1995 (*Tōyō Keizai* 12/3/97, pp. 103–4). Sakura Bank hired a former Midland Bank executive to build up their syndicated loan business in Europe (*Economist* 1/8/96), and Sumitomo Bank went so far as to start holding its directors' meetings in London in English rather than Japanese, ostensibly to give more weight to the opinions of non-Japanese and make the lines of communication with the bank's headquarters in Tokyo more open (*Nikkei* 29/1/97).[49] As Makihara Minoru (president of Mitsubishi Corp.) pointed out, Japanese firms began to feel they needed more foreigners in management positions 'to help inject new creativity and change outmoded ways of thinking' (interview in *Nikkei* 2/4/97).

Seventh, and closely related, considerable other evidence emerged of Japanese firms abandoning their traditional human resource management (HRM) practices in the 1990s. The issue, according to *The Banker,* was that Japanese corporate culture had proved itself unsuited to the business of global banking: 'No Japanese bank can expect to rank along the truly globalised banking institutions of the future without first undergoing a fundamental change in management culture' (9/96, p. 75). A *Euromoney* survey of foreign fund managers' perceptions of Japanese financial institutions shed light on such perceptions, which were common in the industry (2/94). It found that most respondents expressed frustration about management practices at Japanese financial institutions. Japanese firms were seen to be slow, inflexible, and insufficiently innovative, with communication difficulties and even doubts about their levels of commitment to foreign clients being cited as causes for additional concern. Significantly, city banks like DKB, Sakura, and Sumitomo had already began experimenting with hybrid forms of HRM a few years earlier, and many were by this time in the process of abolishing traditionally 'Japanese' practices such as job rotation, seniority pay and lifetime employment for core staff in favour of short-term contracts with much higher performance-linked renumeration. Accordingly, books and articles hailing an end to the era of the group-oriented generalist and the beginning of the era of the individual with specialist skills in finance began to proliferate in 1995 and 1996 (see the review article in *Kinyû Bijinesu* 10/96, pp. 27–8 for an overview of this literature).[50]

Nevertheless, for all their restructuring efforts, the uncompetitiveness of Japanese firms continued to be widely asserted by foreign and Japanese

Year	Overall No. in top 25	Underwriting No. in top 25	Trading No. in top 25	Advisory No. in top 25
1994	1 [Nomura # 20]	3 [Nomura # 11; Daiwa Sec. # 14; IBJ # 19]	0	0
1995	2 [Nomura # 19; IBJ # 20]	3 [Nomura # 16; Daiwa Sec. # 19; IBJ #20]	0	0
1996	1 [Nomura # 16]	1 [Nomura # 11]	1 [Nomura #19]	0
1997	1 [Nomura # 19]	2 [Nomura # 13; Nikkō # 19]	1 [Nomura #19]	0

Figure 3.25: Japanese Firms' Rankings in Polls of Professional Opinion
(*Source: Euromoney*, various December & January issues)

specialists alike. Commonly portrayed as lagging their Western counterparts by between five and ten years,[51] Okabe Shinji of Moody's calculated that Japanese banks were the world's least profitable even *without* their bad loans (having return on assets [ROA] averages of around 0.5 percent compared to US banks at 2.5 percent – *Economist* 9/3/96). Similarly, the magazine *Shûkan Tōyō Keizai* published a comparison of Japan's leading bank (BOT-M) with a top US firm (Citicorp), which cast doubt on whether Japanese firms could survive on an equal footing in fully competitive international market (*Tōyō Keizai* 7/5/97, pp. 21–3).[52]

Stripped of the massive volumes of bubble-era business to intermediate, *Euromoney*'s *Poll of Polls* annual survey showed that Japanese firms no longer figured prominently in global financing league tables.[53]

Accordingly, the magazine observed that, in contrast to their apparent domination in the 1980s, Japanese financial institutions in the 1990s

> ... are nowhere in privatisation ... their derivatives experience is negligible ... They don't touch M&A (apart from a handful of Japan-related deals). In equities, they have a steady business in selling Japanese equities to Western institutions, and a tiny business in selling US and European equities in Japan – but nothing else (1/97).

Moreover, with attention in the industry increasingly shifting towards return on equity as the ultimate measure of corporate performance – since profit and asset growth became increasingly recognised as a means of increasing shareholder value rather than being an end in themselves – *Euromoney* published a table ranking the top fifty global banks (by market capitalisation) according to total shareholder return (TSR) over the period 1993 to 1998.[54] The results were summed up in an accompanying article, which commented: 'Overall, banks in recent years have achieved returns that CEOs of other companies would die for. The single exception is

Japanese banks, which have the unenviable distinction of consistently destroying value' (7/98). The six Japanese firms listed had filled the last six places, and were the only ones to record negative TSR values.[55]

3.3 BIG BANG: PAVING THE WAY FOR INSTITUTIONAL CONVERGENCE?

No secret was made of the fact that one of the Big Bang's main aims was to raise the efficiency of Japanese financial institutions by increasing levels of competition in the domestic market via deregulation. In the press conference accompanying the announcement on November 11, 1996, Sakakibara explained:

> We recognise that the Tokyo market has lagged behind New York and London and maybe Frankfurt, *we recognise that Japanese financial institutions have lagged behind... We would now like to provide the opportunity for Japanese financial institutions to catch up with their counterparts in Europe and the US.* We recognise that one of the reasons for the regeneration of the American economy is financial deregulation (cited in Hartcher 1998, p. 252, my emphasis).

As elsewhere, financial deregulation in Japan was bound to favour the country's biggest and potentially most efficient financial institutions. Specifically, liberalising transaction fees would increase the market share of the most competitive firms; legalising holding companies would enable large, cash-rich firms to exploit economies of scale more effectively; allowing uncompetitive firms to fail would concentrate more power in the hands of a few; and yen internationalisation would compensate internationally active Japanese firms which have been disadvantaged by the Japan premium.[56] Thus, stripped of its rhetorical veneer of establishing consumer sovereignty (see Chapter 4), Big Bang was at heart a strategy to restore national competitiveness by levelling the international playing field for top Japanese firms in the hope of transforming them into 'national champions'. The dilemma for the MOF was how to achieve this whilst minimising collateral damage to small and less competitive domestic firms and avoiding playing into the hands of preying foreigners. They chose to pursue a 'third way' in deregulation, the compromised solution which was set out in Chapter 2. In this context, the following case study examines the competitive responses which Japanese financial institutions made to Big Bang.

3.3.1 The New Scramble to Restructure

Japanese financial institutions scrambled to intensify their restructuring efforts in 1997 and 1998. Within six months of Hashimoto's announcement, most firms had established Big Bang-related policy committees, and thirty regional banks had gone as far as to co-commission Mitsubishi Research Institute to conduct a six-month study on the issue on their behalf (*Nikkei Kinyû* 3/3/97). The strategies embarked upon can be summed up under four headings: (i) a heightened emphasis on cost-cutting and efficiency; (ii) the introduction of new products and management technologies; (iii) strategic retrenchment; and (iv) cooperative tie-ups.

First, Big Bang added urgency to firms' ongoing drive to reduce costs and increase efficiency. Personnel costs continued to be targeted as an area of potential cost savings, both in terms of employee reduction and the restructuring of renumeration (figure 3.26; see also subsection [ii] below). Data indicates that securities firms have reduced staff by thirty-five percent since the bubble burst, but banks less so, many perceiving a need to hold staff for future expansion into new business areas (again, see below); insurers have moved less quickly still, sheltered from banks' direct participation in 'their' business sector until at least 2001.[57] The numbers also show that employees in the financial sector saw their lowest salary hikes – both in terms of amount and percentage – since the Ministry of Labour (MOL) began collecting statistics in 1969 (*Nikkei* 10/12/97).

Curtailing overseas operations was the other area of significant potential cost saving. Here, too, it is clear that Japanese financial institutions embarked upon a fresh wave of international retrenchment in order to cut fixed costs and develop a more strategic focus (see subsection p. 249 below).

Second, Big Bang caused Japanese firms to increase the pace at which they introduced new and innovative financial products, services and management technologies into their domestic operations. Faced with market desegmentation, product deregulation, and the anticipation of increased competition, Japanese firms seized upon the fact that there was still considerable scope for them to mimic the actions of more advanced foreign competitors in a sort of 'catch up' strategy.

At the retail end of the market, newly debuted products/services include longer service hours,[58] 24-hour automated teller machines (ATMs),[59] telephone/internet access to financial services,[60] general securities accounts (GSAs),[61] 'wrap' accounts,[62] foreign-currency-denominated accounts,[63] small-lot investment funds,[64] over-the-counter (OTC) investment trusts,[65] discount brokerage services,[66] sub-divisible nonlife insurance policies,[67] and portable electronic money.[68] At the wholesale end of the market, they include credit derivatives,[69] asset-backed securities,[70] the off-exchange trading of listed securities,[71] unlisted stock/venture capital funds,[72] remote banking,[73] and multilateral netting services.[74]

Firms also began introducing new internal management practices and/or technologies, many of which were pioneered in foreign markets. The upgrading of internal risk management systems was an area of ongoing innovation,[75] as was the switch to performance-based renumeration. Interestingly, the latter now appears to be driven more by the need to

'Awkward Convergence' in the Financial Sector

Date announced	Company	Comment
4/97	Bank of Tokyo-Mitsubishi	To cut staff by 1,000 following recent merger, mostly from managerial ranks.
4/97	Industrial Bank of Japan	To implement performance-based staff remuneration; establish a 6-year a specialist personnel development programme for fast-track recruits (consisting of 1 year in a major office then 5 in a particular division); and increase of local staff proportions at overseas offices, especially for senior posts.
4/97	Nomura, Daiwa, Nikkō & Yamaichi Securities	To cut staff bonuses for fiscal 1996 to zero due to poor business conditions; for Nomura, this was the first time in four years; for others, the first time in two years.
5/97	Yasuda Trust and Banking	To cut staff from 4,716 to 4,000 in three years through natural attrition.
9/97	Bank of Tokyo-Mitsubishi	To cut staff by 12% (2,300) by 2001.
10/97	Fukutoku Bank & Bank of Naniwa	To cut combined staff from 2,430 to 2,000 through natural attrition following merger.
11/97	Yamaichi Securities	To cut staff by one-third (i.e. 2,500) by 2001.
12/97	Sumitomo Bank	To cut staff from almost 16,000 to 14,500 by 2001.
1/98	Long Term Credit Bank	To introduce new wage system for 1,600 employees and new retirement system to cut retirement payments.
1/98	Tokyo Securities	To reduce staff from 1,639 to 1,250 by end of fiscal 1999.
1/98	Dai-ichi Securities	To cut staff by 30% to under 1,000 by end of fiscal 1998.
1/98	Taiheiyō Securities	To cut staff by 30%.
1/98	Cosmo Securities	To cut staff by 30%.
2/98	Yasuda Trust	Commences negotiations with labour union, seeking to cut salaries by an average of 10%; this is first salary cut proposed by a 'healthy' bank for ordinary employees.
2/98	Kankaku Securities	To cut staff by one-third from 3,100.
3/98	Dai-ichi Kangyō Bank	To cut staff by 10% (i.e. 2,000) by 2001, salaries by 3% (10% for directors) and bonuses by 20%.
3/98	Bank of Tokyo-Mitsubishi	To cut staff by 1,500 to 19,000, management salaries by 5%, bonuses, and executive pay by 30%.
4/98	Yasuda Fire & Marine	To introduce annual salary system for its 2,200 managerial-level staff, whereby goals are set in conjunction with peers, and attainment is rewarded with higher salaries. The practice of honouring employees with large retirement payoffs for many years of service is to be abolished.
5/98	Major 19 banks	To cut new hirings from 8,345 to 7,500; 14 of 19 to cut new recruitment, Sanwa by 300; Fuji and Daiwa plan to hire more, BOT-M same, and Asahi and Chuo undecided; Several firms will stop hiring graduates for clerical work.

Figure 3.26: Examples of Recent Personnel-Cost-Reduction Initiatives

Date announced	Company	Comment
5/98	Midori Bank	To cut staff by 500.
7/98	Daiwa Securities	To cut 370 staff in New York, London, and Hong Kong.
8/98	Sumitomo Bank	To introduce 3 new wage scales 10/98, 1 for financial specialists and 2 for career-tract employees (see text).
8/98	Long Term Credit Bank	To cut staff by 20% (700) by 4/98 and reduce monthly salaries of board members to ¥800,000 for rest of fiscal year, cummulatively cutting personnel costs by 30%.
9/98	Mitsui Trust & Banking	To cut workforce by 10% to 5,000 by April 2000.
9/98	Daiwa Securities	To cut 800 of its 1,800 overseas staff by April 1999.

Figure 3.26: Examples of Recent Personnel-Cost-Reduction Initiatives (*continued*)

maintain employee morale and hang on to valuable staff rather than by that of containing the high fixed costs associated with seniority pay and lifetime employment.[76] One senior foreign banker observed that luring good people away from Japanese firms was 'as easy as shooting fish in a barrel' because they continue to pay their junior and mid-level staff so poorly in comparison with leading Western firms (interview with Keith Percy, 4/6/98). Accordingly, several leading Japanese firms have also begun to offer specialist training and in-house qualification programmes to boost their attractiveness to existing staff and potential recruits.[77] Others abandoned tradition entirely: at Nomura Asset Management, forty percent of staff were hired mid-career from outside companies (*FT* 30/10/97), while Sumitomo Bank took the unusual step of inviting an outsider (Kubota Tatsuo, chairman of Citibank [Japan]) to sit on its board as a nonexecutive director (*Nikkei* 17/3/98).

Japanese financial institutions also began embarking upon programmes of internal restructuring to increase their allocative efficiency and strategic focus (figure 3.27, see also [iii] below). Amalgamating administrative departments has been a particularly popular move, a typical example being Fuji Bank, which announced plans to reorganise its internal structure into the following six new divisions to encourage specialisation and increase efficiency: (i) large companies, (ii) foreign firms, (iii) small/medium-sized firms, (iv) individuals, (v) investment banking and dealing, and (vi) settlements and new instruments (*Nikkei* 6/1/98).

Finally, in their newfound eagerness to please the markets, firms started to implement investor-friendly management policies, such as the adoption of US standards in information disclosure and accounting.[78] Both the JFBA and LIAJ (see glossary) announced plans to adopt US Securities and Exchange Commission disclosure rules (see *Nikkei* 14/1/98 and 7/4/98

'Awkward Convergence' in the Financial Sector

Date announced	Company	Comment
2/97	Sanwa Bank	To cut 8 of 41 departments in head office reorganisation.
4/97	Industrial Bank of Japan	To restructure general administration, merging general affairs, management, and accounting departments.
4/97	Nomura Securities	To merge previously separate division, Nomura Research Institute, into securities division to create synergies and make its output more commercially oriented; to increase young directorial appointments and abolish fifteen of firm's forty-five directorships; to aid information flows and de-bureaucratise the firm, by flattening corporate structure by reducing the overall number of ranks and senior positions, effecting a shift from its present 'pyramid shape' to a 'paperweight shape'.
4/97	Mitsui Trust & Banking	To split itself into 8 divisions with intention of managing them as separate profit centres from fiscal 1999.
8/97	Nomura Securities	To restructure overseas operations, switching from regional structure to single global structure.
9/97	Nippon Credit Bank	To create 'internal company' structure as part of overhaul.
9/97	Sanwa Bank	To introduce 'expert programme' 4/98, whereby core staff have salaries tied to performance; performance-based bonus can be from 0 to 200% of salary; fixed-term employment contracts of 3 to 5 years.
9/97	Sakura Bank	To upgrade status of investment banking division and reorganise others in 'in house' company structure.
11/97	Yamaichi Securities	To restructure in three divisions, with much greater emphasis on performance-based pay.
12/97	Fuji Bank	To form holding company to restructure Fûyō group; to reorganise 7 divisions into 6 'in house' business units.
1/98	Sakura Bank	To form holding company to restructure Mitsui group.
2/98	Long-term Credit Bank	To trim board of directors from 28 to 8 members, abolish position of 'advisor' and half number of 'councellor' positions as part of move to leaner management structure.
5/98	Daiwa Securities	To relocate headquarters for overseas operations to London.
7/98	Daiwa Securities	To form holding company by 4/99 to restructure operations in conjunction with Sumitomo Bank tie-up.
8/98	Daiwa Securities	To implement 'Western-type' pay systems, and executive boards in three new subsidiaries to be established 4/99, in order to aid competitiveness and facilitate prompt decisionmaking. President Hara promises 'It will be a European-American style investment bank' run on Anglo-Saxon lines (*FEER* 6/8/98).
9/98	Dai-ichi Kangyō Bank	To review its retail, wholesale, international and market businesses with a view to spinning off noncore operations and replacing several branches with limited-service ATM-based electronic banking terminals.

Figure 3.27: Examples of Recent Internal Restructuring Initiatives

respectively).[79] A few firms sought NYSE listings in order to raise their global profiles and underline the fact that they have nothing to hide under the stricter disclosure rules,[80] while others have adopted explicit medium- and long-term targets for return on equity considerably above their historical averages.[81] Moreover, in response to the proliferation of financial industry scandals, industry umbrella organisations also took steps to increase industry transparency, drawing up ethics charters, and collectively seeking agreements to abolish the practice of wining and dining civil servants (see *Nikkei* 30/4/97).

Third, the Big Bang spurred an unparalleled wave of strategic retrenchment in the activities of Japanese financial institutions. Reductions in staff numbers, branch networks, asset portfolios and capital bases have all been incorporated in new medium- or long-term corporate business plans which brim with familiar euphemisms, such as '*gōrika*' (rationalisation), '*surimu-ka*' (slimming), and '*daunsaijingu*' (downsizing).

There was also an intensified drive for geographical retrenchment, both internationally and domestically, as figure 3.28 shows. In November 1997, fifteen of the country's nineteen major banks announced closures or plans to merge overseas offices when they released half-year earnings results, and one regional bank (Hokkuriku Bank) sought to put a positive spin on its retreat by proclaiming that it was 'coming home' (*Nikkei* 9/12/97).

Japanese financial institutions also pursued retrenchment in other areas, announcing capital and asset reduction programmes,[82] share buybacks,[83] the unwinding of cross-shareholdings,[84] and the refusal of financial support for troubled affiliates.[85] Representing significant breaks with tradition, many of these developments are unprecedented.

Fourth, Big Bang precipitated a proliferation of cooperative tie-ups as firms began to prepare for a new era of heightened competition. As figures 3.29 and 3.30 show, the most popular type of tie-up over the last eighteen months has been the cooperative agreement. Often akin to representative – or correspondent banking relationships, cooperative agreements simply function to expand the distribution capacity of firms with limited branch networks. The clearest example of this is the many domestic (and a few foreign) financial institutions which have sought tie-ups with the Post Office to gain access to its ATM network, which spans nearly 25,000 branches nationwide.[86] However, most cooperative agreements involving investment trusts are intended also to serve an alternative strategic purpose.[87] For the Japanese party, the attraction of handling foreign investment trusts is usually to gain expertise and staff training in new product areas; for the foreign party, to increase end-user familiarity with their products.

Joint ventures are a way of exploiting comparative advantage structures in a more institutionalised way. In three major cases of foreign-Japanese tie-ups, the common denominator has been the foreign firm bailing out the

'Awkward Convergence' in the Financial Sector

Date announced	Company	Comment
5/97	Hokkaido Takkushoku Bank	To shut 13 of 20 overseas offices and scale down remaining 7 by 9/97 to cut annual overseas operating expenses from ¥4.3 billion to ¥0.3 billion prior to eventual closure.
5/97	Tokio Marine & Fire Insurance	To sell one of its 8 US subsidiaries to UK's Commercial Union.
5/97	Yasuda Trust & Banking	To cut assets from ¥8.6 trillion to ¥6.6 trillion over next 3 years and integrate overseas branches.
6/97	Daiwa Bank	To shut Australian subsidiary.
6/97	Yamaichi Securities	To pull out of futures and options trading in London.
7/97	Tōkai Bank	To shut US subsidiary.
7/97	Dai-ichi Securities	To shut Swiss subsidiary.
10/97	Fukutoku Bank & Bank of Naniwa	To close 30 domestic branches within three years following merger to save ¥4 billion annually.
11/97	Ashikaga Bank	To withdraw from international operations.
11/97	Yamaichi Securities	To slim down international operations in drastic restructuring programme.
11/97	Fuji Bank	To sell Hong Kong affiliate.
11/97	Long Term Credit Bank	To sell US affiliate, Greenwich Capital.
12/97	Hokkuriku Bank	To withdraw from international operations, closing offices in New York, London and Hong Kong.
12/97	Yasuda Trust & Banking	To withdraw from overseas operations and sell Tokyo head office following absorption into Fûyō group holding company, led by Fuji Bank.
12/97	Sumitomo Trust & Banking	To cut 10 domestic and overseas branches by 2001.
12/97	Sanwa Bank	To cut half of its approximately 100 overseas branches by 2001.
12/97	Sumitomo Bank	To sell California subsidiary; to cut domestic branches from 348 to 300 by 2001.
12/97	Fuji Bank	To sell California affiliate, Heller Financial.
12/97	Takagi Securities	To liquidate Hong Kong affiliate and close 3 domestic branches.
1/98	Sakura Bank	To amalgamate overseas branches, and close all unprofitable offices following absorption into Mitsui group holding company.
1/98	Sumitomo Marine and Fire Insurance	To trim domestic operations in restructuring programme.
1/98	Tokyo Securities	To withdraw from overseas operations by end of fiscal 1999 (closing New York, Hong Kong and London subsidiaries), 4 of 45 domestic branches, and affiliated research institute.

Figure 3.28: Examples of Recent Strategic Retrenchment Initiatives

Date announced	Company	Comment
1/98	Dai-ichi Securities	To withdraw from overseas operations and close several domestic branches.
2/98	Kankaku Securities	To withdraw from overseas operations by end of fiscal 1997.
3/98	Dai-ichi Kangyō Bank	To cut 30% of overseas branches and 10% of domestic branches.
3/98	Bank of Tokyo-Mitsubishi	To cut at least 40 domestic branches.
3/98	Sakura Bank	To cut 20 of 86 overseas branches.
3/98	Sanwa Bank	To cut 60 domestic branches.
3/98	Sumitomo Bank	To sell California affiliate and 14 US branches.
4/98	Bank of Yokohama	To withdraw from overseas operations in 1998 (closing New York, London, Hong Kong, and Singapore branches and affiliates).
5/98	Midori Bank	To close 50 domestic branches.
6/98	Sanwa Bank	To cut 11 overseas branches.
6/98	Nippon Credit Bank	To pull out of foreign exchange business.
6/98	Nikkō Securities	To close 20 overseas branches in 1998.
6/98	Long Term Credit Bank	To withdraw from overseas operations.
7/98	Mitsui Trust & Banking	To close Swiss subsidiary.
7/98	Nippon Shinpan	Japan's largest consumer credit firm to liquidate US, UK and Hong Kong subsidiaries.
7/98	Dai-ichi Kangyō Bank	To close Milan and Madrid offices; to review future of Paris office.
7/98	Daiwa Securities	To close marginal branches in Europe, including Budapest, Madrid, Milan and Warsaw.
8/98	Long Term Credit Bank	To end all overseas activity, sell domestic headquarters building in Tokyo and welfare facilities as part of 'comprehensive' restructuring package.
9/98	Daiwa Securities	To close 12 of its 30 overseas offices, including Amsterdam, Bombay, Bangkok, Chicago, Kuala Lumpur, Toronto, and Zurich.

Figure 3.28: Examples of Recent Strategic Retrenchment Initiatives (*continued*)

Japanese firm in return for access to the latter's client base. The idea behind the short-lived Bankers Trust-Nippon Credit Bank venture was to provide a way for NCB to withdraw from international operations while enhancing its technical proficiency and product range without losing large corporate clients or spending money (*Banker* 5/97); the ill-fated Swiss Bank-LTCB and much better Travellers-Nikkō ventures both aimed to shore up the

'Awkward Convergence' in the Financial Sector

Date announced	Parties	Type of tie-up	Comment
4/97	Citibank & Post Office	Cooperative agreement (CA)	Citibank card holders to get access to funds via Post Office's ATM network.
4/97	Bankers Trust & Nippon Credit Bank	Joint venture (JV)	Cross share holding equity investment of ¥1–2 billion is first foreign-Japanese tie-up in finance, and is expected to provide way to introduce new technology; establishment of joint venture, International Cash Management Services will also provide NCB with access to BT's international network once its overseas offices are closed.
4/97	Goldman Sachs & IBJ, Kokusai, & Daiwa Securities	CA	Investment trust marketing and sales tie-up.
6/97	Barclays Bank & Hokkaido Takushoku Bank	CA	Cooperation on securitisation and new product development for Japanese market; HTB to use Barclay's international network once its overseas offices are closed.
7/97	Swiss Bank & Long Term Credit Bank	JV	Establishing new investment bank in 50:50 venture to subsume SBC Warburg (Japan) and LTCB Securities, to launch LTCB UBS Brinston Co. 6/98.
7/97	Smith Barney & Nikkō Securities	CA & JV	Cooperation to develop and sell 'wrap' accounts; will form joint management consultancy by end of year.
8/97	Goldman Sachs & Kokusai, Nikkō, and Daiwa Securities	CA	Marketing link for Goldman Sachs Asset Management to sell mutual funds through these firms' retail outlets.
9/97	Citibank & Sumitomo Trust & Banking	CA	Tie-up to sell investment trusts to individual investors; funds collected will be co-managed and entrusted to between ten and twenty major foreign fund managers.
10/97	Goldman Sachs & Yasuda Trust	CA	Cooperation on real estate-backed bad loan purchase and securitisation.
10/97	Putnam Investments & Sakura, DKB and Sanwa	CA	Marketing link for Putnam to sell investment trusts through these firm's retail outlets (Putnam already has ties with six Japanese brokerages and Nippon Life).
11/97	Investco Asset Management & LTCB	CA	Marketing link for Investco to sell investment trusts through LTCB's retail outlets.
11/97	American International Group & Mitsubishi Trust	CA	Marketing link for AIG to sell investment trusts through Mitsubishi Trust's retail outlets.

Figure 3.29: Examples of Recent Foreign Firm-Japanese Firm Tie-ups in Response to Big Bang

The Case of Japan

Date announced	Parties	Type of tie-up	Comment
12/97	GE Capital & Kōei Credit	Acquisition (A)	GE Capital to purchase Kōei as way into consumer finance market.
12/97	IBM & Daiwa Bank	CA & JV	Ten-year outsourcing contract for IBM to operate Daiwa's information systems; Joint venture to develop and sell new information systems to regional banks.
12/97	Fidelity Investments & Sanwa Bank	CA	Agreement to cooperate on investment trust sales and marketing.
1/98	Brown Brothers Harriman & Daiwa Bank	CA	Two-year agreement for BBH to provide foreign equities research and staff training; Daiwa will invest ¥1.8 trillion of its ¥9.6 trillion in trust assets abroad.
2/98	GE Capital & Tōhō Life Insurance	JV	*De facto* takeover by Capital, which is putting ninety percent of funds into the venture to acquire Tōhō's 10,000 marketing staff, contacts and existing contracts; new firm to be called GE Capital Edison Life Insurance.
3/98	Capital Group Companies & Dai-ichi Mutual Life	CA	Investment trust marketing and sales tie-up.
3/98	Dresdner Bank & Meiji Life Insurance	JV	Merger of investment advisory subsidiaries, Dresdner RCM Global Investors Japan and Meisei Capital Management, to form Meiji Dresdner Asset Management, exploiting Meiji's pensions pool and Dresdner's financial expertise.
3/98	Jardine Flemming & Fuji Bank, Yasuda Fire & Marine Insurance, Marubeni, and others	JV	JF Investment Trust and Advisory to establish new securities firm in conjunction with twelve Fūyō *keiretsu* companies, to sell investment trusts through Fūyō's distribution network.
3/98	Fidelity Investments & Asahi Bank	CA	Fidelity to sell investment trusts through five Asahi branches in Tokyo from December.
3/98	Merrill Lynch & Sanwa	CA	Merrill to sell investment trusts through several Sanwa branches from December.
4/98	Unum Corp & DKB, Chiyoda Mutual Life Insurance	CA	Unum (a US life insurer) to sell policies through DKB and Chiyoda's branch network.
4/98	American International Group & Aoba Life	A	AIG plans first outright foreign buyout of Japanese life insurer.

Figure 3.29: Examples of Recent Foreign Firm-Japanese Firm Tie-ups in Response to Big Bang (*continued*)

'Awkward Convergence' in the Financial Sector

Date announced	Parties	Type of tie-up	Comment
4/98	United Asset Management & Tokio Fire & Marine Insurance	CA	Five-year tie-up to give UAM (a US holding firm of more than fifty investment firms) access to Tokio's distribution network.
4/98	Goldman Sachs & Daiwa Securities	CA	Parties will jointly develop new investment fund called Daiwa Giga Fund.
4/98	American Express & Post Office	CA	Amex applies to Post Office for use of its ATM network.
5/98	Societé Générale & Yamaichi Asset Man't	A	Soc Gen to take over Yamaichi's asset management arm.
5/98	Goldman Sachs & Fuji, Asahi, and Sumitomo Banks	CA	Three separate collaborative agreements to co-develop and sell investment trusts.
5/98	Hong Kong Shanghai Corp. & Chūō Trust	CA	Distribution agreement for HSBC-managed investment trusts; HSBC to provide training for Chūō's staff in return.
5/98	Associated First Capital & DIC Finance	A	Assoc. First Capital, a financial services subsidiary of Ford Motors, to buy DIC, a financial services subsidiary of Daiei.
6/98	Salomon Smith Barney & Nikkō Securities	JV & Capital injection (CI)	Joint venture will create Japan's second largest brokerage (capitalised at ¥150 billion, and having 1,500 employees); SSB's parent, Travellers Group to take 25% equity stake in Nikkō; will target Travellers' and Nikkō's institutional clients.
6/98	Chase Manhattan & Daiwa Bank	CA	Distribution agreement for Chase investment trusts.
7/98	American Express & Credit Saisson	CA	Credit card tie-up.
7/98	Prudential & Mitsui Trust	JV	Establishment of investment trust alliance, Prudential Mitsui Trust Investments.
7/98	GE Capital & Lake Co.	A	GE to buy Japan's fifth largest consumer credit firm.
7/98	Bank of Yokohama & Fidelity Investments, Morgan Stanley Asset Mgmt, and Schroeder Invest't Trust Mgmt	CA	Investment trust distribution tie-ups.

Figure 3.29: Examples of Recent Foreign Firm–Japanese Firm Tie-ups in Response to Big Bang (*continued*)

The Case of Japan

Date announced	Parties	Type of tie-up	Comment
7/98	GE Capital & Ryōshin Leasing	A	GE to buy 80% stake in Mitsubishi group company from Mitsubishi Corp. and Mitsubishi Trust & Banking.
8/98	Fuji Bank & Credit Suisse Invest't Trust Mgmt, Schroeder Invest't Trust Mgmt	CA	Investment trust distribution tie-ups.
8/98	Tokio Marine & Fire & Coller Capital	JV	Establishment of investment cooperative with a UK pension fund manager and other Japanese partners.
8/98	Fuji Bank & MasterCard Int'l	CA	Fuji to join MasterCard's Maestro international credit card settlement system from 7/99.
8/98	Fuji Bank & Lord, Abbett	JV	Fuji to sell 25% stake in its European investment advisory subsidiary to a leading US asset management firm.
9/98	Merrill Lynch & Post Office	CA	Merrill to be first foreign broker to gain access to Post Office ATM network.
9/98	AMBAC Assurance & Mitsui Fire & Marine and Yasuda Fire and Marine Insurance	CA	US reinsurance firm to tie up with Japanese insurers to sell financial guarentee insurance to Japanese insurers and investors.
9/98	Charles Schwabb & Sony Corp.	CA	To cooperate in research on the possibility of establishing a discount brokerage and investment trust joint venture.
9/98	HSBC & Yasuda Fire & Marine Insurance	CA	To sell corporate fire, equiptment and shutdown insurance policies in Japan.
9/98	JP Morgan & Dai-ichi Kangyō Bank	JV	To set up investment trust company together, marking first capital tie-up between a foreign financial institution and a Japanese city bank.

Figure 3.29: Examples of Recent Foreign Firm-Japanese Firm Tie-ups in Response to Big Bang (*continued*)
(*Source*: various *Nikkei* articles)

'Awkward Convergence' in the Financial Sector

Date announced	Parties	Type of tie-up	Comment
1/97	Nomura Investment Trust & Nomura Investment Advisory	Merger (M)	Nomura Securities affiliates to merge to pursue investment trust business.
3/97	Asahi Investment & Kankaku Securities	M	Both are Dai-ichi Kangyō Bank (DKB) affiliates.
4/97	Yasuda and Nippon Trust Banks & Hiroshima and Daiwa Banks	Cooperative agreement (CA)	Representative banking arrangements to provide trust banks with greater product distribution capacity.
9/97	Sanwa Capital Management & Sanwa Investment Trusts	M	Two Sanwa affiliates to merge in December to take advantage of deregulation in the over-the-counter investment trust market.
10/97	Fukutoku Bank & Bank of Naniwa	M	Two Osaka banks to merge under MOF supervision; will receive funds from Deposit Insurance Corporation to aid the marriage.
10/97	Kōfuku Bank & Kyōtō Kyōtei Bank	A (acquisition)	Kōfuku to take over Kyōtō Kyōtei's operations following its failure.
11/97	Daiwa Securities & Nichiei, World, Chūō, Kankaku, Dai-ichi, and Wakō Securities	CA	Distribution venture for Daiwa's dollar-denominated Mega Fund; this is first time for Japanese broker to offer its products to other corporate groups (e.g. Nichiei and World are Nomura group companies, Chūō is Yamaichi group).
11/97	North Pacific Bank & Hokkaido Takushoku Bank, Chūō Trust & Banking	A	NPB to take over HTB's regional business, CTB to take over its business in Honshu following HTB's collapse.
11/97	Seventy-seven Bank & Tokuyō Bank	A	Seventy-seven to take over Tokuyō's operations following its failure.
12/97	Fuji Bank & Yasuda Trust, Yasuda Fire & Marine Insurance, etc.	Holding company (HC)	Fuyō *keiretsu* companies announce restructuring plans one day after holding company bill is enacted; this is first major financial group to announce that it will form a holding company; Fuji and Yasuda Trust announce plans to integrate US custody operations 7/98.

Figure 3.30: Examples of Recent Japanese Firm-Japanese Firm Tie-ups in Response to Big Bang

The Case of Japan

Date announced	Parties	Type of tie-up	Comment
1/98	Chiba Bank & Chūō Securities	CA	Chiba makes substantial equity investment in Chūō to tie-up on investment trusts.
1/98	Sakura Bank & Mitsui Trust, Mitsui Mutual Life Insurance, and Sakura Securities	HC	Mitsui *keiretsu* companies announce restructuring plan to establish holding company, with group companies engaged in asset management, securities, and trust bank operations teaming up to enhance competitiveness.
1/98	Kyōei Life Insurance & Dai-ichi Mutual Life Insurance	CA	Marketing tie-up for investment trusts.
2/98	Sanwa Bank & Yamaichi Asset Management	CA	Marketing and product development tie-up for investment trusts.
3/98	Nissay Investment Trust Management & Nissay Asset Management	M	Nippon Life Insurance investment firms merge.
5/98	Kaisei, Nippon, and Yamaka Securities	M	Nikkō Securities affiliates merge and will concentrate on selling to individual investors.
5/98	Nomura Securities & Industrial Bank of Japan	Joint venture (JV)	Nomura and IBJ to set up three joint ventures, two in asset management and one in derivatives 'to compete head to head with foreign institutions'; Daiwa Bank (a Nomura affiliate) and Nippon Life and Meiji Life (IBJ affiliates) asked to invest in the new joint ventures.
5/98	Dai-ichi Kangyō Bank & Kankaku Securities	Acquisition (A)	DKB injects ¥30 billion into troubled affiliate, boosting stake from 4.9% to 37%; recent change in Anti-monopoly Law paves way for first time a bank takes securities firm with more assets than liabilities under its wing; increases stake to 54% 9/98.
5/98	Softbank & Yahoo (Japan) and Morningstar (Japan)	JV	Establish new brokerage to sell stocks investment trusts over the internet.
6/98	Dainana Securities & Ryokō	M	Affiliates of former Bank of Tokyo and Mitsubishi Bank to merge 4/99.

Figure 3.30: Examples of Recent Japanese Firm-Japanese Firm Tie-ups in Response to Big Bang (*continued*)

'Awkward Convergence' in the Financial Sector

Date announced	Parties	Type of tie-up	Comment
6/98	Sumitomo Trust & Long Term Credit Bank	M	Sumitomo Trust to effectively take over the failing LTCB.
7/98	Daiei Group & Sanwa, Sumitomo, Fuji, and Tōkai Banks	CA	Credit card tie-up to allow bank card holders to pay for goods in Daiei supermarkets and Lawson convenience stores.
7/98	Sumitomo Bank & Japan Research Institute	CA	Sumitomo and JRI to develop a multilateral netting service to corporate clients, using Sumitomo's client base and banking skills and JDI's information systems.
7/98	Bank of Yokohama & Nomura Securities, and Nikkō Securities	CA	Investment trust development and distribution tie-ups.
7/98	Sumitomo Bank & Daiwa Securities	JV	To establish three ventures: (i) Daiwa SB Capital Markets to subsume Sumitomo Daiwa Securities Capital Securities and concentrate on investment banking; (ii) SBCM Daiwa Securities Financial Products to deal in derivatives, and (iii) Dicam SB Asset Management to target Japan's growing personal asset market.
7/98	Tōkai Maruman & Naigai Securities	M	Tōkai effectively to buy out the former Yamaichi affiliate to boost its presence in Naigai Securities Kansai, Chūbu and Kantō regions, becoming Japan's eighth largest brokerage.
7/98	Daiwa Securities	HC	Daiwa to restructure itself into a holding company 4/98 in line with Sumitomo Bank joint venture.
8/98	Tokio Marine & Fire & Bank of Tokyo-Mitsubishi, Mitsubishi Trust, Shizuoka Bank and Nikkō Securities	JV	Establishment of investment cooperative with 10 partners, including a UK firm.
9/98	Secom Co. & Tōyō Fire & Marine Insurance	A	Secom to acquire 34% of Tōyō stock and subsequently co-develop insurance products.

Figure 3.30: Examples of Recent Japanese Firm-Japanese Firm Tie-ups in Response to Big Bang (*continued*)

Date announced	Parties	Type of tie-up	Comment
9/98	Bank of Tokyo-Mitsubishi & Mitsubishi Trust & Banking, Meiji Life Insurance and Tokio Marine & Fire Insurance	JV	Four Mitsubishi group companies to set up two jointly owned investment trust ventures and cooperate in developing and selling insurance products.
9/98	Meikō Securities & National Securities	M	Two second-tier brokerages, one Ōsaka-based, one Tokyo-based, to merge in preparation for Big Bang.
9/98	Tokyo Marine & Fire & Lawson Inc.	CA	Nationwide convenience store to sell nonlife products.
9/98	Softbank Corp. & Osawa Securities	A	Softbank to purchase the second-tier brokerage to gain TSE seat, a small number of branches and staff for electronic trading joing venture with US firm E-Trade.
9/98	Asahi Bank & Tōkai Bank	HC	Two smaller city banks, one Nagoya-based, one Tokyo-based, to establish a strategic alliance in order to survive Big Bang.

Figure 3.30: Examples of Recent Japanese Firm-Japanese Firm Tie-ups in Response to Big Bang (*continued*)

'Awkward Convergence' in the Financial Sector

Japanese parties' capital base and boost their technical prowess while using the corporate culture of the Western party to promote dramatic restructuring.[88] Joint ventures between Japanese firms have been different. Those like the Softbank, Morningstar and Yahoo venture are conventional, in that they involve the sharing of expertise and pooling of risk. Others, such as a Nomura-IBJ venture was interpreted by many commentators at the time as a prelude towards permanent cooperation in a fully fledged merger (e.g. *Nikkei* 14/5/98).[89]

Mergers and acquisitions represent long-term responses to the new competitive environment. All recent cases of foreign financial institutions taking over Japanese firms have involved acquisitions for the sake of access to retail client bases. However, most of the high-profile Japanese-Japanese mergers are aimed either at exploiting economies of scale following deregulation (e.g. those involving investment trust and advisory affiliates) or at promoting efficiency as a purely defensive strategy (e.g. those involving the integration of regional competitors or affiliates). To the latter category, but not captured in figure 3.30, also belong the proliferation of lower-level mergers within the ranks of *shinkin* banks, credit associations, agricultural cooperatives, and so on.[90]

The formation of holding companies may also technically fall under the term 'merger'. By facilitating the centralisation of corporate accounting functions, financial holding companies should allow more efficient risk, resource, and tax management as separate units can be managed as individual profit centres. Hereby, they are seen as a potentially important option for major Japanese firms seeking to regain competitiveness *vis à vis* their Western counterparts.[91] However, relatively few holding companies have been announced to date. Although formally legalised in June 1997, they were not due to be taxed on a consolidated basis until fiscal 1999. The easing of divestiture requirements should also increase their attractiveness in time.

3.3.2 Deconstructing the 'Normalisation' of JFIs

All of the developments above concur with the logic of financial globalisation and can be interpreted as evidence of 'normalisation'. However, a careful reading of developments challenges this interpretation by revealing the skin-deep nature of many of the changes. This subsection completes – and complicates – the picture by citing considerable evidence of nonconvergence in the recent restructuring efforts of many leading Japanese financial institutions.

(i) All-out cost cutting and the prioritising of profitability?

In spite of much anecdotal evidence of Japanese financial institutions' renewed drive to cut costs, several considerations cast doubt on how high a priority is actually being given to improving efficiency. Aside from the employees of bankrupt financial institutions, there have been no cases of mass redundancies, and more coercive moves to 'encourage' early retirement have met with little success.[92] It is generally agreed that Japanese financial institutions suffer from overstaffing, but to date almost all moves to remedy this problem have involved nothing more than reduction by natural attrition.

To a great extent, the much trumpeted new wage systems are proving to be superficial in that they either apply only to a very small number of employees, or the proportion of total wages made up by performance-related bonuses is extremely limited.[93] Moreover, the way in which they are introduced can often render them meaningless. For example, a senior managing director of Sanwa's International Department explained that their 'experts programme' only incorporates forty to fifty of the firm's nearly 15,000 staff, and 'if they don't like it or are not performing they can go back to the ordinary [employment] course' (*Euromoney* 2/98). As the magazine concludes from its recent survey of Tokyo financial analysts,

> The careers of the vast majority of Japanese bankers – 99.9% is a low estimate – are still governed by the seniority principle. An employee's bonus is guaranteed and his rank and pay is virtually identical to other employees of the same age. A new graduate will be brought in at a salary of ¥3 million a year and look to become a general manager when he is 44 and earn between ¥12 million and ¥20 million. If he doesn't make it into senior management and is transferred to a subsidiary his pay will decrease by some 30%. The whole structure remains conducive to risk averse behaviour (2/94).

Thus, it is unsurprising that Japanese financial institutions' record on cost-cutting lags far behind the very trends to which they are seeking to respond. Goldman Sachs estimated that while Japanese securities companies' revenues had fallen by sixty percent in the last five years, their cost bases had only declined by one third, and this gap appeared set to widen because brokerage commissions – the mainstay of most brokers' revenue – were forecast to fall by another thirty percent during the following three years (*FT* 14/11/97).

In the banking industry, the story is similar, as shown by firms' records on bad debt. The outlook here, too, is ominous, since many top executives give every indication that they will abandon their current efforts to prioritise profitability and bottom-line criteria as soon as their bad debt problems have been brought under control. Comments made in interviews with *Euromoney* by the chairmen of two top banks underline this point. BOT-M's Takagaki Tasuku noted that their ongoing restructuring efforts were intended to make the firm 'more profitable so we can clear our bad debts more substantially'; IBJ's Kurosawa Yoh concurs, 'We, too, need a certain profit in order to clear up bad loans', and goes on 'But once we get back to a reasonable figure [for bad loans], then we'll be in a normal situation and will ask for reasonable profit'. He elaborates, 'Profit is very important. Our profit is too small. But profit is not 100% the purpose of IBJ. Our philosophy is to serve clients and Japanese industry. There must be profit, but profit must be reasonable. If we make too much profit, we are eating the profits of our clients ... *We don't intend to maximise our profits'* (2/98, my emphasis).[94] Clearly, many senior bank executives had yet to accept the transition to a fully market-oriented financial system which Big Bang was ostensibly meant to bring about.

(ii) Consumer/investor-friendly products and managerial changes?

Second, while it is undeniable that Japanese firms increased the pace at which they introduced new, differentiated products and management technologies, here also there was evidence that firms remained reluctant to engage in open competition. Many newly introduced products appeared to be of dubious competitive worth, intended merely to differentiate firms from their competitors on a nonprice or core-service basis.[95] Others, such as 24-hour ATMs, were being introduced at an extremely slow pace, with customers still being charged for using them outside of 'normal' business hours.[96] Thus, it seemed that industry bodies such as the JFBA were still aiming to restrict competition with the consent of their members, in spite of the fact that they trumpeted considerable progress in lifting restrictions on competition (see interview with JFBA director Kagomiya Noriyasu *JT* 7/2/98).[97] This claim of reluctant competitive engagement came as no surprise to those familiar with developments in the insurance industry, where domestic and foreign members were forced to leave industry rating organisations if they wish to market discounted policies (e.g. Orix Life – see *Nikkei* 29/8/97; and American Home Insurance and Zurich Insurance – see *Nikkei* 25/9/97; 12/5/98).

Japanese firms' adoption of what were generally thought of as up-to-date managerial norms and practices also has been limited. For example, the idea of slimming down firms' corporate boards – which in Japan were seen as massively bloated and ill-suited to the task of strategic decisionmaking – was resisted by some of the largest banks. When questioned about slimming down his firm's board of sixty-nine directors, Chairman Takagaki of BOT-M countered: 'If we decide suddenly [to slim down our management structure] and say you are now dismissed from the board, are we now saying your recognition is dismissed? These are very experienced and highly qualified staff, you know' (*Euromoney* 2/98).[98] The problem was a fundamental one concerning the way in which careers at Japanese banks are structured. Privileged positions on the board and, lower down, in the personnel and corporate planning departments, meant that there was no internal incentive to change. Management had no stock options, and were not directly or financially renumerated for their contribution to the firm's performance. Instead, when executives retired, in addition to receiving a 'golden handshake', it was common for firms to continue to provide them with a car, driver, office and secretary, and they would expect to be asked to advise on future senior appointments. Such a structure did not prove much of a hindrance in a stable, highly regulated and incrementally changing financial system, but it appeared ill-suited to the demands of a new globalising environment. As one long-term foreign employee at a large Japanese bank commented, 'Japanese banks' function has been, and still is, as far as I can see, that of a gentlemen's club, not a money-making institution; there has been no change of late' (interview with Alex Wellsteed of DKB 24/7/98).

Even the actions of supposedly more progressive firms, which *appear* to be making market-oriented changes, give cause for concern. In April 1997, both IBJ and Nomura Securities embarked upon major programmes of organisational and personnel reform explicitly aimed at rebuilding their internal infrastructure 'based on a Western investment banking model' (*Nikkei Kinyû* 17/4/97; 24/4/97; 25/4/97; 30/4/97). Nomura, in particular, made much of the fact that its new president (Ujiie Junichi) was educated in the US, and that it would appoint an American to sit on its executive board. But David Atkinson, an economist at Goldman Sachs, stated dismissively 'All this stuff – management is younger, the new president was educated in the US – it's all rubbish. I was educated in the West and I wouldn't run it any differently.' The point he makes is that Japanese financial institutions will never be forced to make major changes in the way they run their businesses so long as they remain majority-owned by their affiliates and customers (*Euromoney* 2/98). As for IBJ, its chairman Kurosawa told *Euromoney* with undisguised pride that 'on principle' his firm never rehired people who left it, regardless of their potential skills or the contribution they might be able to make. More generally, managers IBJ feels to have become too 'Westernised' were derisively referred to *batâ kusai*, literally 'stinking of butter', which is a perjorative historical reference to the high fat content of Western food.[99]

The revelations of systemic corruption which came to light in wining and dining and other scandals at leading Japanese firms (noted in Chapter 2) remain, for analysts, a salutary reminder to treat with extreme caution the apparent 'normalisation' of the way in which Japanese firms do business in the post-Bubble era. As the head of risk management at Citibank pointed out,

> It's not that US or European firms by nature are cleaner than Japanese firms, but simply that we no longer have the option of carrying on like that. It's a regulatory problem of incentives and sanctions, but it's

playing out right now in the harsh way in which we have to look at and assess their businesses and actions. Of course, we'd like to be charitable and believe what they say, but we can't because our clients' money, and our reputation, is at stake' (interview with Bo Hammerich, 11/8/98).

(iii) Strategic retrenchment?

Third, in the area of strategic retrenchment and repositioning there was more evidence of the partial nature of Japanese firms' convergence. Most analysts recognised that the number-one problem in Japanese finance was, and is, overcapacity (e.g. Alicia Ogawa, Nikkei Forum on *Japan's Big Bang* 17/6/97). Nevertheless, rather than shrinking their assets, many troubled firms sought, perversely, to expand their capital bases in order to maintain their BIS ratios. Large banks including Nippon Credit Bank and Yasuda Trust pursued this option, and managed to arrange for affiliates to purchase the stock in a depressed domestic stock market.[100] Others, such as Nissan Mutual failed to cajole other life insurers into bailing it out prior to its collapse. Nevertheless, just as it is the myriad of firms which were not selling their cross-shareholdings in the new environment, rather than the one or two that were, that is salutary, so also it was the many examples of firms which had recently bailed out their affiliates with financial support, rather than the few which had refused support, that was more representative. One example of this was Nomura Securities' initial agreement to purchase new Sanyō Securities stock on the basis of the latter implementing a nine-year restructuring plan (*Nikkei* 27/9/97), a promise which incidentally came to nothing after nine life insurers turned down pleas for their purchase of subordinated Sanyō debt, leaving the company no option but to file for bankruptcy in November 1997.[101]

More generally, most recent examples of radical retrenchment in Japanese finance were reluctant and reactive rather than strategic and progressive. Amidst tumbling share prices and ratings downgrades, NCB and HTB both announced that they would pull out of international business and sharply curtail their domestic operations (*Nikkei* 29/3/97; 30/3/97; *Nikkei Kinyû* 7/4/97); the following summer LTCB's repeated their moves under similar circumstances (*Nikkei* 21/6/98). For a while, such actions were sufficient to see these firms through, but Yamaichi's attempt to do likewise in early November 1997 came too late, and the firm collapsed very quickly (*Nikkei* 7/11/97).

Similarly reactive was firms' entry into new markets, a move which was often presented as entirely contingent upon the action competitors took. This was the case for firms seeking tie-ups with the Post Office, as mentioned earlier. Another example related to *shinkin* banks, whose leaders stated that their entry into the investment trust market would depend solely upon whether regional banks sought to enter that market (interview with National Association for Shinkin Banks managing director Sahara Shōzō, *JT* 20/4/98). Here again it appeared that, given the chance, many Japanese firms would prefer to pursue a quiet life rather than to seek competitive gains by reforming themselves and innovating in a deregulated environment. In the case of the *shinkin* banks, their very public announcement of intent seemed intended as a threat to the MOF: *shinkin* bankers candidly admitted that they had no experience or expertise in dealing with risk-related financial products in the hope that regulators would dissuade regional banks from entering the market and so protect the financial system's overall balance and stability.

These examples lead to the related observation that, to a very great extent, recent strategic retrenchment in Japanese finance may have been driven by the market but it was still orchestrated by the MOF. Since early February 1997, when rumours that NCB was in serious trouble began circulating, regulators assured the markets that major banks which were 'seen to be taking all-out efforts to restructure would not be allowed to fail' – i.e. they would receive official help in order to prevent systemic instability (*Nikkei* 11/2/97).[102] Nevertheless, the Ministry has repeatedly indicated its desire to promote consolidation at all levels in the financial industry in the longer term through the application of PCA in domestic regulation.[103] The problem was that in the meantime a situation of moral hazard was created in so far as firms were encouraged to wait to pursue strategic retrenchment until the markets compelled them to because of an implicit government guarantee. Furthermore, if for no other reason than the fact that the Ministry (and FSA) had limited resources available for bank inspections, they were not in an ideal position to advise on strategic private sector decisions. As a result, Fuji Bank Research Institute warned that the Japanese financial system could only be expected to retain its overcapacity for the medium-term, drawing the inescapable implication that the future of even potentially viable firms' survival was being compromised by the reduced opportunities for reaping the rewards of innovation (*Nikkei* 20/6/97).

Related to this was the fact that banks were extremely slow to embark upon asset reduction programmes in spite of overwhelming evidence that this was necessary. In 1992, Mitsubishi Bank released calculations that every 1,000 point fall in the Nikkei 225 Index cut banks' BIS ratios by an average of 0.15 to 0.2 percent (which implied that the subsequent drop would have cost banks a four to five percent cut in their ratios). Yet in spite of rumours of banks cutting credit as much as possible, the official line remained that they would not cut loans to corporate borrowers. Takashima Akihide, assistant general manager at Sakura Bank's planning group expressed this by insisting 'Clients are our precious property ... If we ignore customer demand, we will, without exception, have to pay for it five or ten years down the road' (*Nikkei* 29/6/92). However, it was only since financial instability surfaced in November 1997 that banks began to curtail lending to borrowers considered bad risks. Analysts agree that as a result of the policy of forbearance, egged on by an MOF eager to avert a credit crunch, banks' portfolios of bad loans swelled by a factor of three to four *during* the recession, i.e. banks' stocks of bad loans were largely the result of recession-era excesses, not bubble-era ones (interview with Ken Okamura, 5/8/98). As late as 1998 observers still had doubts about banks tightening lending policies as the government sought to obtain guarantees from them that they would keep lending to small- and medium-sized borrowers of dubious credibility in return for fresh injections of state capital to forestall a deterioration in BIS ratios (interview with Ken Okamura, 5/8/98, and Russell Jones, 11/18/98). North Pacific Bank, for example, promised the MOF that it would continue to lend to troubled borrowers following its acquisition of HTB's regional business, its president asserting 'If we don't accept more [problem loans], that will mean big trouble for Hokkaido' (*FEER* 6/8/98).

(iv) Competitive tie-ups?

Fourth, the proliferation of recent tie-ups both with foreign partners and between domestic firms also warrants qualification. In the wake of the Big Bang announcement, many mergers had been anticipated as firms prepared themselves for a new era of heightened competition (e.g. *Nikkei Kinyû* 3/3/97); however most of the tie-ups to date represent calculated amendments to existing strategies rather than radically new ventures established on an open and purely free-market footing.

Most of the foreign-Japanese tie-ups announced involve short-term, non-exclusive cooperative agreements. Among the few major deals involving joint ventures, what was notable was that foreign firms became increasingly more cautious in their approach to Japanese firms. Initially, leading foreign firms appeared to have sold themselves short by establishing ventures with second-rate Japanese firms, e.g. SBC in their deal with LTCB, which has turned into a headache as LTCB collapsed (interview with anonymous SBC Warburg employee 31/3/98; *Nikkei* 11/8/98; *FT* 13/8/98). The Travellers-Nikkō venture was different in that the deal was evidently structured to give Travellers the chance to sniff out any problems in advance of committing itself wholeheartedly.[104] Indeed, the fact that Travellers made the largest ever investment in a Japanese financial institution, yet chose *not* take one over lock, stock and barrel, hinted at what has become almost a general principle in such ventures:

> The rule of thumb, for the legion of foreign firms trying to elbow their way into the Japanese markets, has been simple: take care what you

buy, because you don't know what nastiness might be hidden inside. The result has been a series of rather clumsy joint ventures in which foreigners, keen to take advantage of financial deregulation, hope to gain access to Japanese firms' clients without acquiring their problems (*Economist* 6/6/98).

More broadly, it was clear that the interests of Japanese and foreign institutions were destined to be incompatible so as long as the former saw their *raison d'être* as something other than maximising profit, i.e. as long as they identify themselves as *Japanese* financial institutions, rather than as financial institutions that happen to be Japanese. In the words of a senior manager at Salomon Smith Barney in Tokyo, 'The danger, of course, is of divided loyalties and *conflicting goals*' (interview with Alicia Ogawa, 17/6/98).

On a practical level, too, many of the ventures and cooperative agreements between Japanese and foreign firms seemed destined for trouble precisely because of their short-term nature. Both parties were betting on different outcomes in so far as foreign firms hoped that local distribution would acquaint Japanese customers with them and their products, Japanese firms hoped that the tie-ups would give them a chance to learn new skills. As the Dresdner-Meiji Life joint venture to manage Japanese pension funds illustrates, Dresdner said that it will not seek to poach clients but it will welcome those who decide to make the switch (*FEER* 2/4/98).[105]

Japanese-Japanese tie-ups were hindered in some similar ways, as the obstacle of divided loyalties affects domestic firms, too. Mergers or joint ventures between companies from different *keiretsu* groups remained quite rare, and those which did take place either involved firms from groups which did not compete directly or firms in dire straits (e.g. various firms' investment trust and advisory affiliates and Sumitomo Trust-LTCB, respectively). Moreover, intransparency in the affairs of Japanese financial institutions was more than just a trap for the unwitting foreign firm. The HTB-Hokkaido Bank merger floundered on hidden obstacles – in this case, undisclosed bad loans – which were only discovered by the latter after the merger had been announced. Subsequent mergers, such as the Sumitomo Trust-LTCB deal, fell apart for just this reason. Furthermore, the fact that many Japanese financial institutions remained overcapitalised and had poor balance sheets made them generally unattractive as acquisition targets. As *Euromoney* commented wryly in explaining why the much touted (e.g. *Nikkei* 4/4/97) consolidation of small and medium-sized securities companies had not materialised, 'Other than Kokusai, the second tier [brokers] are all ugly sisters' (10/97).[106]

Finally, in spite of Big Bang, the aggressive pursuit of M&A activity in Japan has remained constrained by social norms which act as a brake on the pace of subsequent rationalisation. As noted in Chapter 2, Japan's regulatory authorities sought to guide the restructuring process under deregulation by tempering the pace of consolidation according to their political and bureaucratic estimates of what the economy and society would, or should, bear. Hereby, the legalisation of financial holding companies was seen by analysts as a less aggressive and more 'Japanese' substitute for (often hostile) acquisitions in strengthening strategic ties across different businesses (*Banker* 9/97). This explains why recent mergers between many Japanese financial institutions have not involved a great cultural shift.

For the above reasons, and in spite of the unprecedented wave of restructuring in Japanese finance since the Big Bang's announcement, there remained good reasons to be skeptical about the degree to which Japanese financial institutions were converging on emergent global standards. As Morgan Stanley's financial sector analyst in Tokyo, Betsy Daniels, pointed out concerning the idea of the 'normalisation' among Japanese financial institutions, 'We don't have irrational exuberance ... we have irrational optimism' (*Euromoney* 2/98). Others concur, with James Fiorello, bank analyst at ING Baring Securities (Japan), commenting 'I have still not seen enough evidence from management I've met at Japanese banks that they will behave in a more proactive way in the future' (*Euromoney* 2/98). Instead, it seemed that many Japanese financial institutions were simply learning what it is that they needed to say to temporarily catch news headlines.

3.3.3 Outlook

The reality of an era of heightened competition will ultimately test the rhetoric of restructuring in Japanese finance. However, it is possible already to discern the contours of the post-Big Bang Japanese financial system. This last subsection seeks to define the emerging environment in terms of the strategy and potential fortunes of distinctive groups of competing Japanese financial institutions.

(i) Generalists and specialists

As a result of deregulation, Japanese firms are or will be able to pursue business in almost any area of finance. Thus, rather than being differentiated by function, as has traditionally been the case, the emerging difference will be between general service providers and specialists. Only the largest institutions are in a position to even contemplate pursuing 'full-line' ambitions, and most appear intent to specialise in one way or another; the remainder have no choice but to pursue strategies targeted at particular regional or product markets. As figure 3.31 shows, this development is confirmed by indications of long-term strategic goals articulated by several prominent firms. Of course, firms within each sector and subsector are responding differently, but a number of general trends can be discerned. Hit

Date announced	Company	Comment
2/97	Industrial Bank of Japan	To focus on wholesale banking market.
3/97	Nomura Securities	Aims to be a top-ten global securities company, but will pursue a domestic retail investor-based strategy.
4/97	Hokkaido Takushoku Bank	To abandon its city bank status and become a 'super-regional bank'.
4/97	Sumitomo Bank	Aims to strengthen position in global custody market, targeting more fee-based business, and becoming a 'full line' service provider to foreign institutional investors attracted by Japan's Big Bang.
8/97	Nomura Securities	New president Ujiie Junichi states emphatically 'We don't want to be a financial supermarket'.
2/98	Daiwa Securities	To concentrate on retail sales to individuals.
4/98	Daiwa Bank	To refocus on lending to smaller firms and individuals.
4/98	Sakura Bank	To refocus overseas activity on lending to Japanese clients abroad, rather than to local European/US firms.
5/98	Nomura/IBJ	Joint ventures to focus on serving Japanese clients.
5/98	Kankaku Securities	Aims to focus on retail sales.
5/98	DKB Securities	Aims to focus on wholesale business.
5/98	Daiwa Securities	To give up full-line operations, scaling down international operations.
6/98	Nikkō Securities	To concentrate on retail sales of securities to individual investors.
9/98	Dai-ichi Kangyō Bank	Aims to become Japan's number-one domestic retail bank, and maintain a position in wholesale banking.
9/98	Daiwa Securities	Aims to focus on Japanese market
9/98	Asahi & Tōkai Banks	Aims to become like NationsBank of the US, focusing upon retail banking and bringing regional banks and other financial services firms together under holding-company structure.

Figure 3.31: Examples of Recent Specialisation Initiatives

hard in the international markets by the Japan premium,[107] and under the MOF's imminent shift to regulation by prompt corrective action (PCA – see Chapter 2), Japanese banks have been forced to cut down their involvement in high-volume, low-margin US and European lending. Many have chosen either to target exclusively domestic business, to restrict their international activity to serving only Japanese clients, or to position themselves for international business much more carefully. Sanwa Bank, for example, remains committed to developing its Asian business in spite of the recent regional crisis;[108] Sakura Bank and Nippon Credit Bank seized upon opportunities to capitalise on their colleagues' retreat from international activity in one way or another;[109] and others are concentrating on specific wholesale and/or retail strategies which target small firms or consumers.[110]

For securities companies, commissions deregulation and the promise of new competition have led many to boost their activities in markets where Western firms derive much of the profits, e.g. proprietary trading, investment banking, and fund management. They, too, are focussing more narrowly upon specific client groups, such as domestic retail investors, where GSAs and CMAs are expected to provide a means to counter the new offensives of banks and foreign firms into what was traditionally securities firms' (and, in some cases trust banks and insurers') exclusive territory.

For their part, foreign financial institutions will largely concentrate on boosting their existing and new operations in investment banking and wholesale financial services.[111] Securitized products,[112] derivatives,[113] and investment trusts[114] together with M&A advisory are the main areas where foreign firms foresee growth, and have already established a considerable bulwark in Japan.[115] Hereby, even the likes of HSBC, which initially announced that it would not change its Japan strategy as a result of Big Bang (*Nikkei* 9/9/97), have begun belatedly to expand Tokyo operations (*Nikkei* 26/5/98). Moreover, a notable exception to the general rule of foreigners sticking to wholesale financial service provision is the handful of major global institutions pursuing retail ambitions in Japan. Citibank,[116] Merrill Lynch,[117] Fidelity Investments,[118] and a small but growing number of insurers, including American Home Insurance,[119] Zurich Insurance,[120] American Life,[121] and Axa-UAP[122] are betting that they can attract customers by exploiting globally recognised brands, superior product/service provision and discount pricing.

As a result of deregulation, domestic financial institutions are also facing new competition from nonfinancial companies. General trading firms such as Nisshō Iwai,[123] Marubeni,[124] and Itōchû,[125] and other major firms like Sony,[126] Softbank[127] and Secom[128] are targeting niche markets where they can exploit existing corporate networks and/or their widely recognised names to sell financial products to wholesale and retail investors.

(ii) Winners and losers

LTCB Research estimated that during the five years of fiscal 1996 to 2001 inclusive, money in Japan invested in bank deposits would fall substantially from ¥448 to ¥350 trillion; postal deposits would fall marginally from ¥213 to ¥210 trillion; while that invested in insurance would rise from ¥253 to ¥294 trillion, and that in securities would more than double, from ¥232 to ¥546 trillion (*Nikkei* 25/9/97). In light of firms' emerging strategies to cope with these market dynamics and new competition noted above, picking winners and losers from the Big Bang on the back of these projections becomes a relatively straightforward exercise.

In general, firms in the banking sector were thought to have more to gain than most in the securities or insurance sectors due to the chance for them to diversify their earnings base from interest-related to fee-based income, in line with global financial trends, and thanks to the advantages which their unrivalled branch networks and large capital bases confer. On one hand, their distribution capacity is a major source of competitive advantage (figure 3.32):

Of course, competitors would be able to overcome their disadvantage to some extent through cooperative arrangements, such as access to postal ATMs and product distribution agreements. However, these were generally considered unlikely to be able to compensate for long-established relationships of trust which most banks have with their customers.

On the other hand, the ban on holding companies should make it possible for major city banks to exploit synergies by establishing new businesses and bringing affiliates together under one roof. Trust and long-term credit banks are seeing their profitable monopolies dismantled by deregulation, but leading firms in each area would still have considerable resources in the form of large corporate client bases and technical expertise which should make them valuable as potential partners in joint ventures or targets for acquisition. Similarly, healthy regional banks would be able to exploit their hand in negotiations with a range of potential partners. Smaller and/or weaker banks, however, seem to have much to fear from increased competition. They have neither the balance sheet strength nor the expertise to do much more than sandbag their existing niches with pleas for state protection and/or look for salvation through cooperative tie-ups and mergers.[129]

For securities companies, on top of their loss of considerable straight corporate bond business to banks' newly established securities subsidiaries since 1995 (*Nikkei* 20/3/97), ongoing commissions deregulation is forecast

Institutional category	Number	Branches	Average
City Banks	10	3,381	338
Regional Banks	64	7,885	123
Regional Banks II	65	4,497	69
Trust Banks	7	363	52
Long-term Credit Banks	3	67	22
Foreign Banks*	94	145	2
Securities Companies	232	2,411	10
Post Office	1	24,638	24,638

Figure 3.32: Domestic Retail Sales Potential (1996)
* indicates 1995 figure
(*Source*: BOJ)

to further squeeze revenues.[130] Small and medium-sized brokers are being hit hardest because of a lack of sales volume and the JSDA has already voiced concern about the fact that the gap between leading and lagging firms grew sharply in the past year or so (*Nikkei* 19/5/98). Notwithstanding this, analysts also note that if banks make a serious commitment to developing the more risky investment trust business at retail level, most personal assets now in deposit accounts could be moved into investment trusts by the banks themselves.[131] As Miharu Aizawa of Salomon Brothers (Japan) explains, this is because regional banks command deep trust among the local populace (*Nikkei* 1/1/98). With the exception of a few second tier firms and the remaining Big Four firms, the outlook is not bright.

For insurers, the future looks almost as dark. Japan is already over-insured by conventional standards, and deregulation is likely to accelerate the haemorrhage of money which began flowing out from small and medium-sized firms in 1996 in search of higher returns promised by trust banks and foreign fund managers (e.g. *Economist* 23/8/97).[132] To date the country's top insurers have not been affected, but they, too, are likely to see some loss of business to foreign firms in the short term and to banks' insurance subsidiaries in the long term, after the barriers between the two sectors are dismantled in the early years of the Twenty-first Century.[133] Nevertheless, Standard and Poors pointed out that those firms which make considerable progress in diversifying sales networks and introducing innovative products will certainly see their relative positions strengthened (*Nikkei* 24/6/97). Many nonlife insurers have already begun transferring significant numbers of staff to affiliated investment advisory units (*Nikkei* 12/8/98).

As a group, foreign financial institutions are all but guaranteed to be the biggest winners from Big Bang. Their unparalleled sophistication and narrow focus on profitability mean that they are well placed to take advantage of deregulation in almost all areas of the financial sector. In the past year, moreover, they have enjoyed windfall gains as a result of the so-called 'flight to quality' when many of their domestic competitors were hit by rumours of instability and scandals.[134] For the first time ever, foreign firms had a larger share of stock transactions than the Big Four in August of 1997, with Morgan Stanley having a larger share of the Tokyo market than in New York in October (*Nikkei* 28/12/97).[135] Elsewhere, the dire financial position of many Japanese firms has forced them to begin to abandon traditional practices and relationships in favour of greater reliance on foreign expertise. Japanese financial institutions, for example, have reportedly begun to off load property-backed bad loans on foreign firms at 'fire sale' prices for the latter to repackage and sell as securitised assets (e.g. *Nikkei* 27/2/98).[136] Meanwhile, leading nonfinancials like Sony also have begun to realise the advantages of doing business with more professional foreign financial institutions.[137]

(iii) Global competitors?

As a result of winners strengthening their positions, and losers disappearing from the market altogether, most analysts were betting on substantial consolidation in the Japanese financial services sector (figure 3.33). In particular, the leading survivors of Big Bang are likely to be city banks, albeit in consolidated form. Independent firms like Nomura should also emerge strengthened, but most others will limp on for the time being, either to be subsumed into holding companies or confined to local business. As a recent Moodys report predicted accurately, 'We expect the Japanese banking system to enter the next century in a debilitated state, burdened by chronically poor asset quality and low underlying profitability' (*Nikkei* 14/2/98).

For the handful of Japanese financial institutions that emerge 'victorious' from Big Bang, the key question is can they become globally competitive? A number of considerations suggest that in the short- to medium-term, they will be able to continue to capitalise upon existing advantages which should partially compensate for the lead that Western firms have. First and

Analyst/affiliation	Prediction	Reference
Moodys Investor Services	Top 6 banks will gain substantially from Big Bang as they alone will be in position to swallow up securities companies and trust banks in the same *keiretsu* when financial holding companies legalised.	*Nikkei Kinyu*, 27/1/97
Betsy Daniels (Morgan Stanley)	Big Bang will result in survival of 7 or 8 large general financial institutions.	*Toyo Keizai* 7/5/97
Mitake Keiichi (Yamaichi Securities)	Only 5 or 6 Japanese banks and similar number of brokerages will be operating offshore in a few years.	*Euromoney* 10/97
Jesper Koll (JP Morgan)	1 in 3 Japanese financial institutions will eventually go bust, merge or be bought as result of Big Bang.	*FEER* 4/12/97
Fitch IBCA	Japanese banks likely to integrate into ten universal banks over next decade through mergers.	*Nikkei* 6/12/97
Jesper Koll (JP Morgan)	25% to 30% of Japanese financial institutions will not exist in their current form in 2001.	*Euromoney* 2/98
Steven Church (Analytica)	There will be six *keiretsu* banks left, plus independent outfits like Nomura and IBJ.	*Euromoney* 2/98
Ken Okamura (Dresdner KB)	As many as many as half second-tier securities firms could disappear through mergers or bankruptcies.	*The Journal* 3/98
David Atkinson (Goldman Sachs)	Half of Japan's 19 major banks, and three-fifths of the 130 regional lenders could go bust.	*Asiaweek* 1/5/98

Figure 3.33: Examples of Analysts' Predictions for Financial Sector Consolidation

foremost, Japanese financial institutions are in the enviable position of being the natural mediators of their country's massive ¥1.2 quadrillion in personal savings. In the context of a rapidly aging society and declining long-term rates of economic growth, the proportion of these funds handled by leading institutions is likely to increase substantially (see section 4.3 in the next chapter).[138] Second, *keiretsu* links will continue to provide a valuable source of business, stability and opportunity. And third, their position as intermediators of the bulk of Japan's massive Asian aid, trade and investment flows should also provide them with opportunities for building relationships and establishing an enduring presence in what should be again, in the early years of the new century, the world's fastest growing region.

Nevertheless, leading Japanese financial institutions still face considerable barriers in their quest for global competitiveness. Most fundamentally, there is the question as to whether the lead gained by US and European firms is assailable. Testifying before a House of Representatives Committee in his official capacity as head of MOF's Banking Bureau, Yamaguchi Kimio voiced doubts about whether Japanese banks could survive at all in a deregulated market, since they trail so far behind Western firms in financial technologies (*Nikkei* 9/4/97).[139] Notwithstanding this, Japanese competitors appear to be hindered by a national culture which makes it relatively more difficult for them to succeed in the global financial services industry than Americans, Europeans and, to a lesser extent, even Hong Kong-, Singapore- or Taiwan-Chinese. This is more than just a case of their historical tendency to rely upon rigid, hierarchical relations which stifle flexibility and creativity. Unlike manufacturing, finance is an inherently social business, where the ability to interact smoothly on the basis of commonalities such as language and values is critical. Thus, to the extent that Japanese firms are unwilling or unable to recruit, integrate, and promote to senior positions significant numbers of foreign staff, they will remain as reliant upon domestic business as they are today.[140] Hereby, the fortunes of leading Japanese financial institutions appear to be intrinsically tied to the long-term vitality of the Japanese economy.

Conclusion

In the wake of their meteoric rise, and equally rapid fall, on the international stage, there has been much evidence of accelerated convergence in the Japanese financial services sector in the 1990s, especially following the Big Bang's announcement. Still, many of these changes can be challenged as partial, superficial, and insufficient. As a result, the outlook for the sector as a whole is one of increasing specialisation and polarisation. Signs of this already happening are proliferating, and herein it is clear that financial globalisation is currently changing the face of Japan's financial sector in a familiar manner. As analysts are unlikely to be taken in repeatedly by superficial steps in the direction of normalisation, major firms that continue to seek to avoid falling into line are certain to face marginalisation.

Ultimately, the responsibility for Japanese financial institutions' poor recent performance lies with their management. However, in so far as the actions of Japan's financial regulatory authorities shaped much of the immediate environment against which corporate strategies were formulated, the state also bears responsibility. David Asher's (1996a) description of Japan's *awkward convergence* with the world of democratic capitalism' (my emphasis) captures the way in which firms' attempts to transform themselves according to global industry norms have progressed within the restrictions imposed by a domestic regulatory framework. While the Big Bang promised to accelerate firms' normalisation by removing regulatory barriers which hitherto provided incentives for them to resist convergence, the reality is that regulators remain loathe to cede to the market the ultimate control to determine outcomes. This suggests that only firms which are truly forward- and outward-looking are likely to take full account of the structural forces of globalisation when weighing up the incentives of whether or not to abandon traditional practices. The majority are likely to react only to opportunities and constraints in their immediate environment, and therefore will find their fortunes tied up with those of other areas of the economy which are resisting change. To this end, and to evaluate the costs and benefits of the country's awkward convergence in financial services, the next chapter turns to examine the broader effects of financial globalisation on the Japanese economy and society.

Chapter 4
Societal Implications of a 'Gradualist' Approach

Introduction

As noted in the Introduction to this book, the fundamental question which lies at the heart of Political Economy is *cui bono*? This chapter seeks to address the question as it relates to Japan by mapping the societal implications of the state's gradualist approach to financial globalisation and its financial institutions limited convergence. Part one examines the macroeconomic effects of Japan's particularistic policy responses to financial globalisation in a comparative setting, and goes on to focus upon the macroeconomic costs of nonconvergence. Part two looks at the microeconomic repercussions of gradualism in terms of the distribution of costs accruing from policy-induced macroeconomic distortions for the corporate and household sectors. Finally, Part three investigates the likely societal implications of Big Bang, plotting the programme's likely beneficiaries against the political rhetoric with which it has been promoted.

4.1 THE MACROECONOMIC EFFECTS OF GRADUALISM

Japan's macroeconomic performance has been affected strongly in recent years by financial globalisation. The seminal events of the last two decades – the Bubble Economy and the so-called Heisei Recession – are both linked to financial globalisation: the Bubble because it developed out of inappropriate policy responses to international and global structural developments, and the Recession because it resulted from inappropriate policy responses to domestic and global structural developments. Consequently, financial globalisation has effected the lives of those in all sectors of society.

Overview of Japan's Macroeconomic Performance in the 1980s and 1990s

As established in Chapter 1, financial globalisation affects a country's macroeconomic performance indirectly, via the competitive responses of its government and corporations (particularly financial institutions) which act as conduits for its influence and may, if they are at the forefront of developments, also act as its main agents. Fate and history, of course, endow each country with different resources (including institutional structures) which affect their responses, so it must be conceded that every country's performance under financial globalisation will be constrained and path-dependent to some extent. Yet, where global structural changes are largely exogenous, inaction on the part of states and firms may count as much as action in determining outcomes – a point established repeatedly in Chapters 2 and 3.

(i) Headline international comparisons

While financial globalisation can be traced back to the late 1960s, and arguably earlier, it was only in the 1980s that it began to have a major impact on developed economies such as the US, the UK, Germany and Japan. Headline measures of real gross domestic product (GDP) growth rates, stock market performance, and unemployment statistics provide a rough indication of Japan's macroeconomic performance alongside its main competitors during this period.

First, trends in economic growth show that Japan's performance was broadly in line with its major industrialised competitors in the 1980s, albeit with slightly higher growth in the latter half of the decade. However, in the 1990s, Japan fell out of sync with its competitors. Japan's downturn in growth at the beginning of the decade was slower and less pronounced, yet it has not followed the same cyclical recovery trend which its competitors mapped out in the 1990s.

Second, long-term stock market data are a complementary indicator of the relative performance of each country's economy. They confirm that Japan's market moved broadly in line with its competitors until the early 1990s, after which point, the country has generally languished in recession while its competitors all rebounded strongly.

Third, unemployment figures show that Japanese rates have remained far below its competitors' throughout the 1980s and 1990s. Common trends are evident, although differences in the degree of fluctuation are startling. All four countries moved broadly in line in the 1980s, but in the 1990s differences are again confirmed as having become more pronounced. Germany's trajectory appears to be following the Anglo-American example, with Japan alone in tracing a consistently rising trend.

These three sets of headline figures allude to the structural transformation in the world economy associated with economic globalisation, as set out in Chapter 1. That is, they provide apparent support for the often alleged trade-off between governments either 'biting the bullet' and promoting painful economic restructuring in the short-term in order to

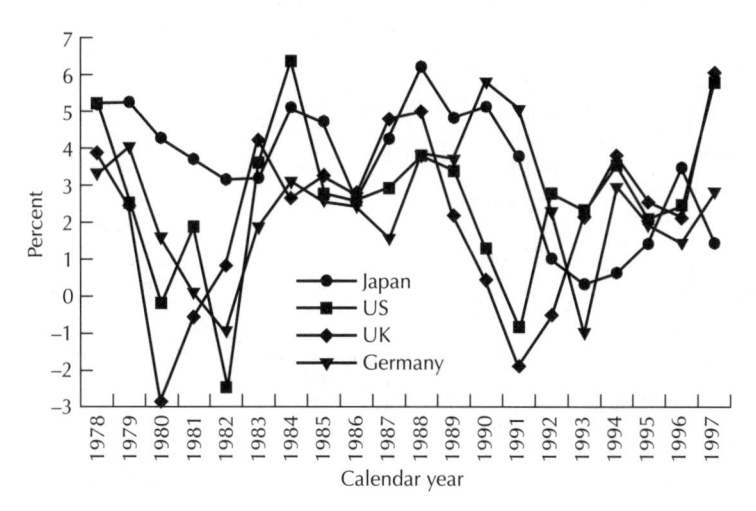

Figure 4.1: Comparative Rates of Economic Growth (nominal GDP)
(*Source*: BOJ Kokusai Hikaku Tōkei)

place their economies on a path for future growth, or putting off the socioeconomic and political disruption associated with restructuring to the detriment of their economies' long-term performance. Still, before drawing such a conclusion, it is necessary to note both the inherent dangers of extrapolating recent trends and the fact that specific factors affecting individual countries must also be taken into account when investigating comparative anomalies and divergent trends. For example, that both the US and UK relied heavily on monetarist supply-side economics throughout the 1980s accounts for much of the similarity in their records, while German reunification in 1991 explains the sudden rise in unemployment there after 1992. In Japan's case, the Bubble Economy is, of course, a major distorting factor, as is the prolonged Heisei Recession which followed it.

The speculative bubble, which developed in Japan's stock and property markets in the late 1980s, spilled over to affect all other areas of the economy between 1987 and 1991. Essentially, this was the first major expression of the implications of enduring structural asymmetries between the Japanese economy and the international economy in an era of globalisation.

As explained in Chapter 2, persistent trade imbalances and exchange rate misalignments between Japan and the US became too large to ignore in the 1970s. Convinced that the crux of the problem lay in structural asymmetries within the Japanese economy, the US pushed for Japan to take unilateral steps to amend specific areas of its economy through

The Case of Japan

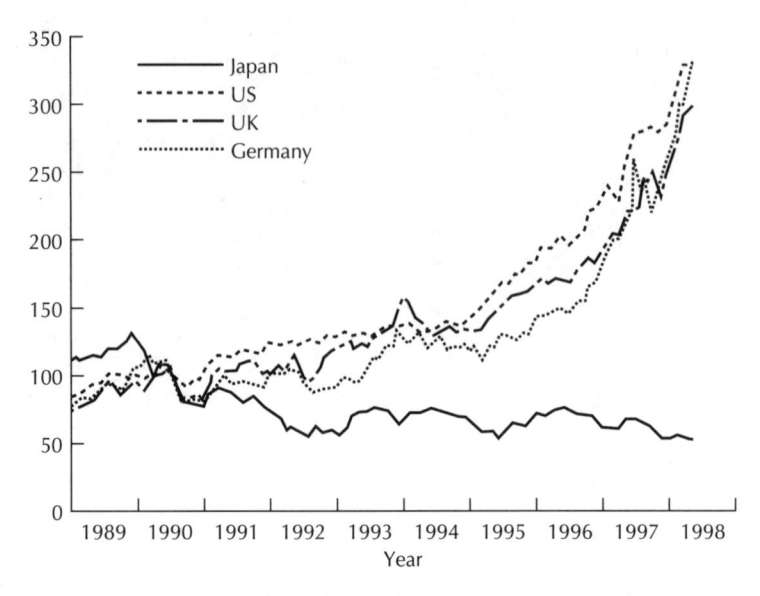

Figure 4.2: Comparative Stock Market Performance (1990 = 100)
(*Source*: BOJ Kokusai Hikaku Tōkei)

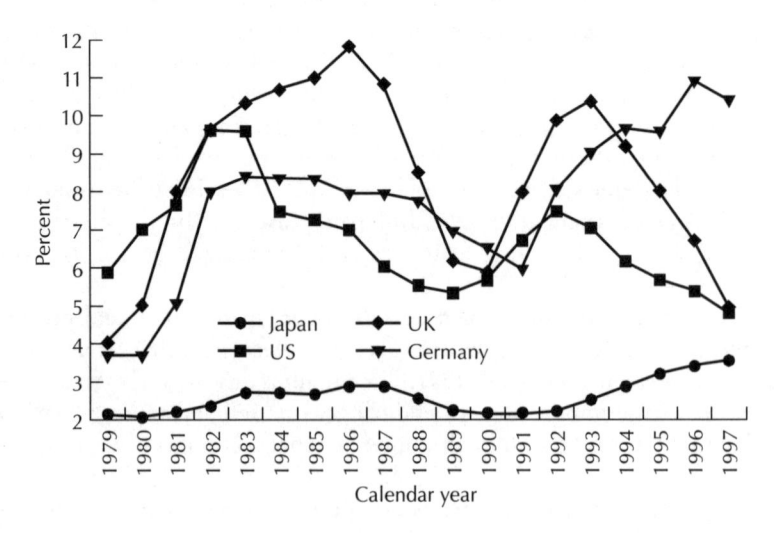

Figure 4.3: Comparative Rates of Unemployment (seasonally adjusted)
(*Source*: BOJ Kokusai Hikaku Tōkei)

changes in domestic regulation and government policy. Most significant in the area of regulatory changes were (i) the lifting of foreign exchange controls in 1980, and (ii) the Yen-Dollar Agreement of 1984, under which a piecemeal timetable for financial market liberalisation was established. In the area of economic policy, (iii) the stimulation of domestic demand was undertaken, with the government relying heavily on loose monetary policy to more than compensate for its fiscal rectitude as successive administrations sought simultaneously to reduce the country's reliance on deficit-covering bonds. The fact that all of this happened at a time when financial globalisation was making viable a host of new investment vehicles and strategies (e.g. *zaitech*), and providing unprecedented access to overseas markets which were also in the process of deregulating, raised the stakes dramatically in terms of what would be the implications of any miscalculations. As it happened, the artificial stimulation of domestic demand in the context of inefficient and relatively rigid domestic asset markets proved highly volatile.

Like any asset bubble, Japan's distorted macroeconomic performance figures by boosting economic growth temporarily and lining the economy up for a period of correction which would inevitably prove more difficult because of the inertia which certain distortions had provided for. The correction came in the form of the Heisei Recession, which lasted for most of the decade.[1]

The Recession has endured far beyond the short, sharp corrections experienced by Japan's competitors, although this appears to have been offset partially by the fact that positive rates of economic growth have been sustained throughout most of the period. This has been achieved by considerable and ongoing efforts on the part of the government to provide for a 'soft landing' by averting the costs which would inevitably be borne disproportionately by certain sectors of the economy. Large fiscal and monetary injections have been made to prop up the economy while institutional frameworks to encourage banks to write off quickly their large inventories of bad loans – something which would exaggerate levels of corporate and individual bankruptcies – and to encourage corporations to restructure their operations – which would sharply increase unemployment rates – have generally been notable by their absence. Nevertheless, the consensus among economists (Japanese and foreign) and international organisations is almost universally critical: short-term pain has been averted only at considerable cost in terms of the economy's longer-term viability.

The Bubble was destined to be a temporary affair, almost by definition. Not so the Recession, which constitutes a suboptimal state of equilibrium. For this reason – that is, because the consequences of economic structural misalignment were only felt fully in the 1990s – the Recession is by far the more important of the two events. In fact, this is doubly so since the

The Case of Japan

Japanese state has managed inadvertently to hold up Japan's economic structural convergence by purposefully working to allay its negative effects.

A Closer Look at the Heisei Recession

Closer analysis of the Heisei Recession shows that Japan's macroeconomic situation in the 1990s is more serious than the comparative statistics cited above suggest.

The official government statistics cited above record no negative annual GDP growth in the period 1990–1997 and thereby give the impression that the country was not in recession at all.[2] This obfuscates reality for at least three reasons: (i) quarterly (rather than annual) statistics show clear periods of negative growth, (ii) a vast array of indicators confirm that Japan's corporate and household sectors are experiencing recessionary conditions, and (iii) the Japanese government has pumped vast sums of money into the economy throughout the period with apparently negligible effects on long-term economic growth.

(i) Breaking down the annual GDP and Unemployment figures

In spite of the fact Japan's annual real growth figures for fiscal 1997 recorded the first year of recession since 1974, quarterly figures for real economic growth cited in figure 4.4 show periods of real economic decline throughout the 1990s.[3] What is more, room remains to doubt even the EPA's quarterly real growth data, as many private-sector economists feel

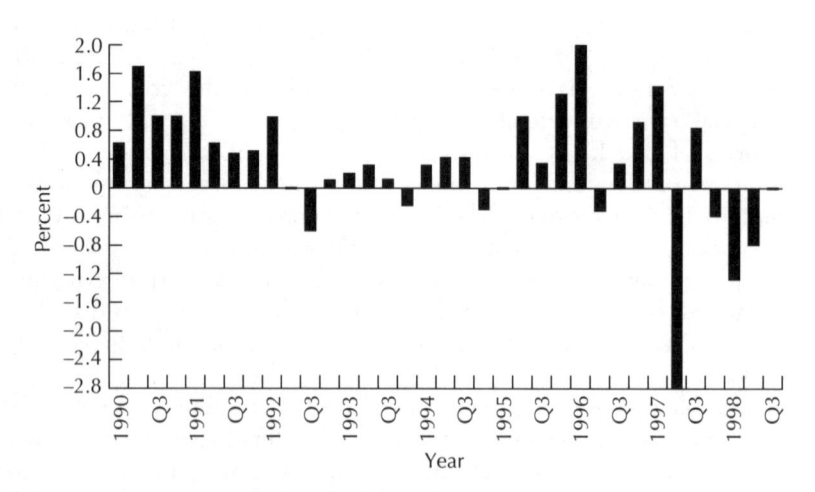

Figure 4.4: Real Economic Growth (seasonally adjusted)
(*Source*: BOJ Keizai Tōkei Geppō)

that these figures are often manipulated to give an overly optimistic impression of the state of the economy.[4]

Similarly, there are good grounds for questioning Japan's supposedly low unemployment figures, even if the rising trend stressed in section 4.1.1 is clear from the government data. Numerous private sector estimates suggest that were the statistics calculated as they are in the US, for example, Japan's rates would more or less double.[5] Others argue that Japan's huge army of underemployed workers should also be accounted for in the statistics.[6] Doing either would imply a figure close to German rates, rather than the current figure which is very close to US and UK levels, and doing both would imply a figure approaching southern European levels of fifteen-to-twenty percent.[7]

(ii) Leading economic indicators

A whole range of economic indicators – quantitative statistics and qualitative measures relating to firms (e.g. production, inventory, operating profits and bankruptcies) and households (wages and salaries, jobs/applicants, department store and passenger car sales) – give a clear picture of the state of the economy as experienced by those living and working in it.

The BOJ's *Tankan* quarterly economic survey constitutes the most representative overview of business sentiment.[8] Figure 4.5 shows that recessionary conditions have been experienced continually since the second quarter of 1992.

To this, one can add corporate bankruptcy statistics. Figure 4.6 shows that these more than doubled in numerical terms, and more than quadrupled

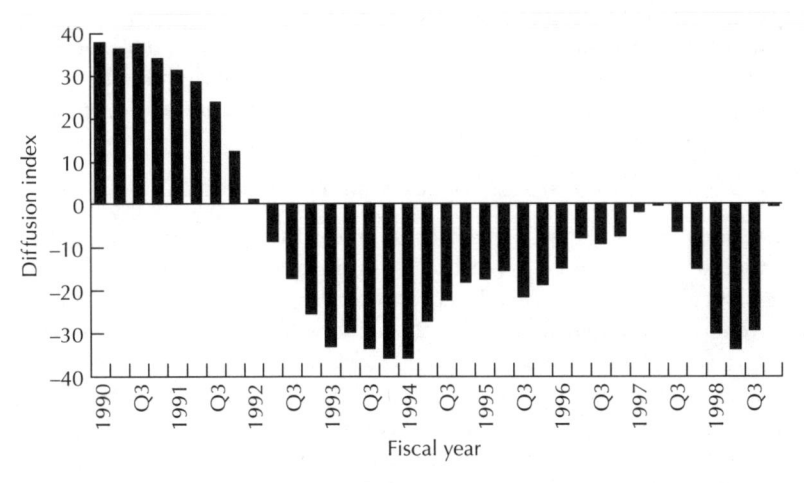

Figure 4.5: Overall Business Conditions (from 'Favourable' to 'Unfavourable')
(*Source:* BOJ Keizai *Tōkei Geppō*)

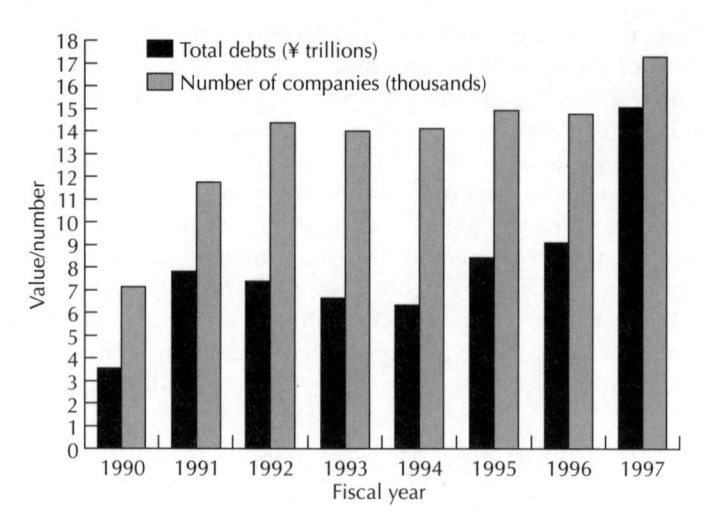

Figure 4.6: Corporate Bankruptcies (firms with debts over ¥100 million)
(*Source*: Teikoku Data Bank)

in value terms over the past seven years. Moreover, while the rising trend in bankruptcies for firms with debts in excess of ¥10 million shows no sign of abating, indicators cited below in an alternative context (figure 4.19) make it likely that as very small firms (i.e. those capitalised at under ¥10 million) have been hardest hit by the recession, the true picture for corporate bankruptcies is considerably worse than figure 4.6 suggests.[9]

Turning to household indicators, figure 4.7 shows that personal consumption also dropped dramatically and is yet to recover.[10]

Chris Calderwood, an economist at BZW in Tokyo, famously likened the official GDP data to a 'bad toupee' of 'sleek brown figures sitting on top of the grey head of the rest of the economic data' (*Euromoney* 9/96, p. 208).

(iii) The scale of government intervention

The seriousness of Japan's macroeconomic situation is underlined by the fact that what economic growth the country recorded during the Heisei Recession was achieved solely as a result of large and repeated injections of government spending. Appendix 2 sets out the history of the myriad stimulus and reform packages which the state has announced since 1992.[11] However, the measures implemented thus far have not achieved their ultimate goal; they succeeded merely in allaying a full-scale recession for much of the decade. Many critics allege that this is because the *scale* of fiscal injections has been overstated, and that the government must spend more if it is to reinvigorate the Japanese economy.

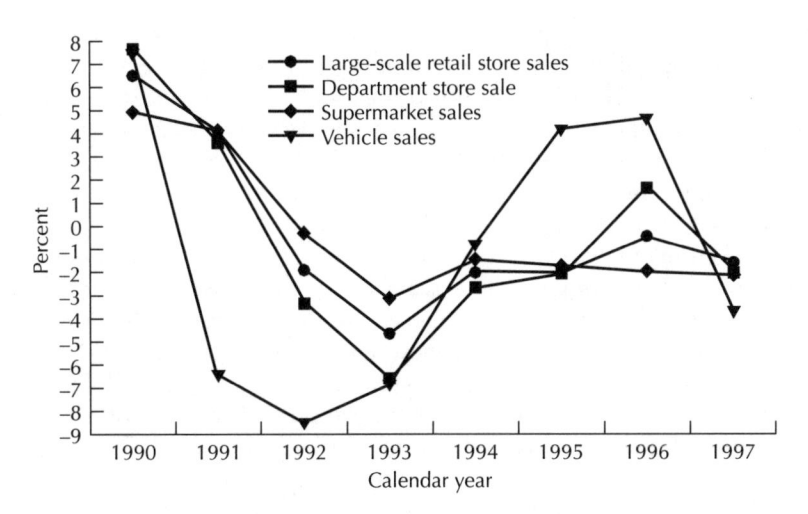

Societal Implications of a 'Gradualist' Approach

Figure 4.7: Year-on-year Changes in Personal Consumption
(*Source*: BOJ Keizai Tōkei Nenpō)

Trade officials and representatives of the US and other foreign governments which run large trade deficits with Japan, spendthrift Japanese politicians, and commentators of various persuasions have argued that successive Japanese governments have yet to implement sufficient fiscal stimuli to pull the economy out of recession. Their arguments centre upon several (or a mixture) of the following five propositions: (i) that the governments' stimulus packages contain on balance little new spending because many of the public works projects are simply advanced ahead of schedule; (ii) that the MOF perennially negates any fiscal stimulus by trimming down the eventual size of the stimulus package from that which the government announces and by offsetting increased spending on public works projects with reduced budget allocations to local and prefectural governments; (iii) that the EPA consistently overestimate economic growth forecasts, which are used for budgetary purposes, in order to reduce the country's reliance on deficit-covering bonds, regardless of voters' desires as expressed through the policies adopted by elected politicians; (iv) that Japanese accounting standards are recondite, and that the government can afford to spend more on pump-priming the economy without damaging its fiscal position, and (v) that it does not matter how much the government spends to prop up the economy because, as long as inflation remains low, it will all be redeemable after the economy recovers.

The first claim holds some truth in so far as front-loading public works projects already in the pipeline have accounted for a large part of many of the respective stimulus packages (see Appendix 2). However, this does not

The Case of Japan

mean that little new government spending has emerged. Levels of government spending related to economic stimulus measures have grown considerably, both in absolute terms and as a proportion of the government's annual budget. Figure 4.8 shows how annual public works spending was more than double 1990 levels in some years as a result of new pump-priming measures.

The basis for this allegation, at least for poorly informed critics, tends to rest on an elementary misunderstanding about national budgetary procedures. Many commentators seem to have equated the value of new economic stimulus packages announced by the government with entirely new spending. However, the Japanese government, like any other, has a degree of discretion in allocating its current budget, and will fund any stimulus package by reallocating existing funds wherever possible. As it must obtain legislative approval for any entirely new funds it intends to spend, observers wanting to argue about year-on-year spending changes must focus instead upon supplementary and regular national budget figures passed in the Diet. As figure 4.9 shows, significant increases in spending have occurred in line with the proliferation of economic stimulus packages, although, as one would expect, they do not amount to anything like the face-value of the stimulus packages announced.[12] For any who still insist that the figures are paltry, a single example puts things in perspective. In 1993, Japan's GDP, ¥475 trillion at 1990 prices, posted 0.4% real year-on-year

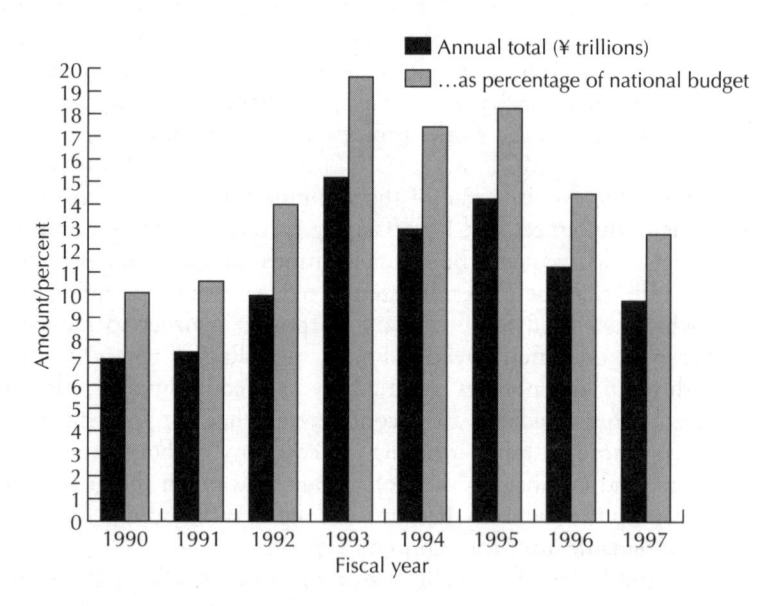

Figure 4.8: Public Works Spending
(*Source*: BOJ Keizai Tōkei Nenpō)

Societal Implications of a 'Gradualist' Approach

Fiscal Year	Stimulus Packages	Reform Packages	Supp. Budgets	Initial Budget (¥ trillions)	Supp. Budgets (¥ trillions)	Total (¥ trillions)
'91	0	0	0	70.35	–	70.35
'92	2	1	1	72.22	2.99	75.21
'93	3	0	3	72.36	5.09	77.45
'94	0	2	2	73.08	1.69	74.77
'95	3	1	3	70.99	9.06	80.05
'96	1	4	1	75.11	2.67	77.78
'97	1	2	1	77.39	1.14	78.53
'98	3	?	2	77.67	10.33	88.00

Figure 4.9: Major Economic Stimulus Measures During the Heisei Recession
(*Source*: compiled from BOJ *Geppō* and various *Nikkei* articles)

growth, a rise of ¥2.1 trillion. This implies that the government's ¥5.09 trillion in supplementary budgets accounted for a boost in GDP growth of more than one percent that year, saving it from recording negative growth of more than minus 0.6 percent, quite apart from any multiplier effects which they would also have engendered.[13] This demonstrates that government spending has been propping up the economy throughout the period.

The second claim – that the MOF negates the effects of new public works spending by restricting local government outlays – appears to have more substance in that a breakdown of the expenditure budget for the government's general account indicates that public works spending increased by far the most of any items that rose, while local finance expenses were the most significant area of cuts. Local government expenses shrunk both in relative and absolute terms between 1990 and 1995, from twenty-three percent of the government's total budget (¥15.9 trillion) to sixteen percent of the budget (¥12.3 trillion). However, while plotting the figures does indicate a very rough inverse correlation, it is by no means perfect (figure 4.10). Moreover, even if the correlation were approximate, what is more significant is that if the decline in local finance expenses were subtracted from the increase in public works spending, the overall increase in spending would still be large, e.g. amounting to ¥31.6 trillion, or about 6 percent of GDP, for the period 1991 to 1994.

As to the third claim – that growth forecasts are deliberately overestimated to allow the government's deficit to be trimmed more than would otherwise be possible – the record does show that the EPA have consistently overestimated GDP growth throughout the Recession. However, as figure 4.11 shows, this phenomenon is by no means peculiar to official Japanese forecasts.

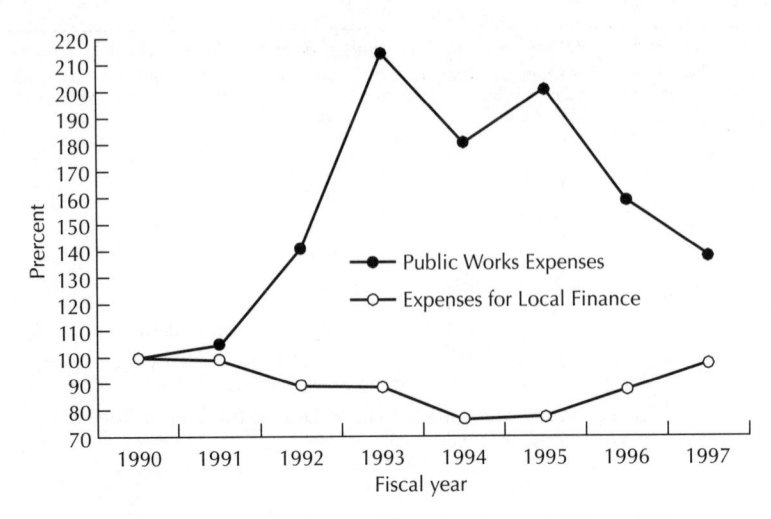

Figure 4.10: Changes in Selected General Budget Items (1900 = 100)
(*Source*: BOJ Keizai Tōkei Nenpō)

Year	Actual	Japanese government	Error	Private sector consensus*	Error
1991	+3.4	+3.8	+0.4	+5.9	+1.5
1992	+2.9	+3.5	+0.4	+3.1	+0.2
1993	+0.4	+3.3	+3.1	−0.3	−0.7
1994	+0.5	+2.4	+1.9	0	−0.5
1995	+0.7	+2.8	+2.1	+1.2	+0.5
1996	+2.4	+2.5	+0.1	+2.4	0
1997	−0.7	+1.9	+2.6	+2.0	+2.7
1998	−2.7	+1.9	+4.6	−1.4	+1.3

Figure 4.11: Real GDP Growth Forecasts Versus Actual Results (percentages)
* figures taken from *The Economist* poll of GDP forecasts
(*Source*: BOJ Keizai Tōkei Nenpō; Economist, June issues)

Furthermore, treasuries and finance ministries in all countries are notably reluctant to let government deficits increase because their job necessitates their becoming proponents of good housekeeping. So whether or not the MOF has been working covertly to reduce the deficit, figure 4.12 suggests that any attempts to hold down the government deficit have failed spectacularly.

The fourth claim – that Japanese accounting practices render a false impression of the country's government deficit much larger than it would be

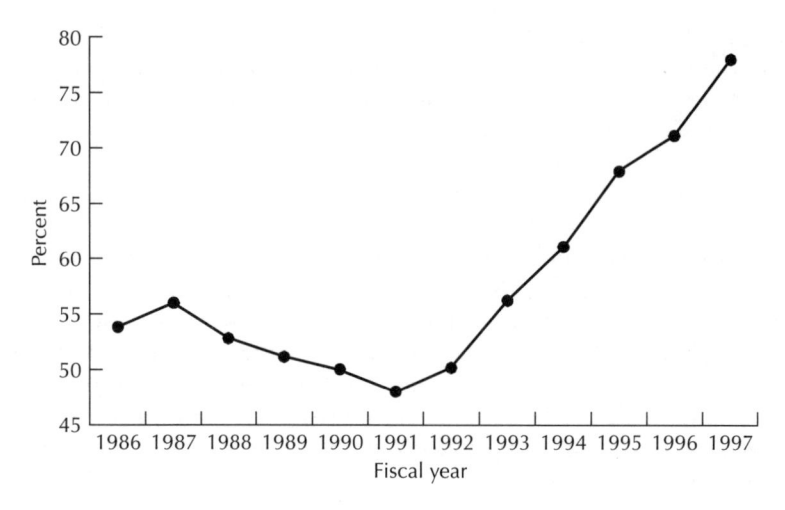

Societal Implications of a 'Gradualist' Approach

Figure 4.12: Outstanding Government Debt (ratio to GDP)
(*Source:* BOJ Keizai *Tōkei Nenpō*)

by conventional measures – is frequently alluded to by foreign critics. Thus, *Times* economist Anatole Kaletsky, for example, argues that because a large proportion of Japan's government debt is owned by the MOF's Trust Fund Bureau, the country's *net* government debt was only about sixteen percent of GDP in 1997, much less than the US's forty-nine percent figure, or that of any other G–7 country (26/9/97).[14] Such a claim actually cuts just as well in the other direction. MIT economist Rudi Dornbusch, by contrast, points out that the government's unfunded pensions liabilities should be included as part of Japan's national debt, as they tend to be elsewhere, something which would push its gross debt up to over 200 percent of GDP (*FEER* 26/2/98).[15] Essentially, there is no consensus on this point; by selectively including additional considerations the statistics can be rendered so elastic as to support almost any line of argument.

The related and final claim – that fiscal responsibility need not matter for Japan at the moment – seems to be a product of unreformed Keynesian logic. However, the argument does have substance in relation to the fact that the Japanese government's debt financing costs are comparatively low (see section 6.2. p. 305 below). And with its debt maturing in an average of five years, the deficit is arguably not a huge problem so long as the bull market in low-yielding JGBs of the last few years continues. But this cannot go on for ever, and the general international consensus of orthodox economic thought clearly and explicitly rejects the notion that size of debt is unimportant. This is seen, for example, in the fact that one of the main eligibility criteria for EU states wishing to join the European Monetary

Union (EMU) project is that member states achieve a government deficit-to-GDP ratio of less than three percent in order to protect the integrity of the new currency. Following recent recommendations by the MOF's Fiscal Structure Council, Japanese authorities officially have realised the importance of this figure in that the government adopted the same target, albeit by fiscal 2005 rather than fiscal 1998. As figure 4.13 shows, the country's recent record demonstrates a drastic deterioration from the best to the worst in its group of closest competitors. As a direct consequence of this, Moody's placed the government's AAA debt status under review in April 1998, and warned of an imminent ratings downgrade three months later (*Nikkei* 4/4/98; 24/7/98). Government officials protested that this move, which could affect their cost of funding, was unjustified in terms of the country's trade position and personal savings resources, but many agree that Moody's is right to be concerned about the Japanese government's spiralling deficit.[16]

Together, the above considerations demonstrate that claims of the Recession's endurance being a simple result of insufficient government spending are tenuous. Whereas most economists agree that the Japanese economy had the potential to grow autonomously at real rates of three to four percent per year throughout the 1990s (e.g. NRI's Suzuki Yoshio [1996]; OECD *Economic Outlook* [12/97]), the country has spent the past seven years mortgaging its future in the process of maintaining often barely positive annual growth rates. Moreover, the near-term outlook for Japan at the time of writing was far more of the same. The OECD forecasted in December 1997 that Japan's economy would shrink by 0.3 percent in real terms (*ibid*) in 1998, but revised its estimate to positive growth of 1.5 to

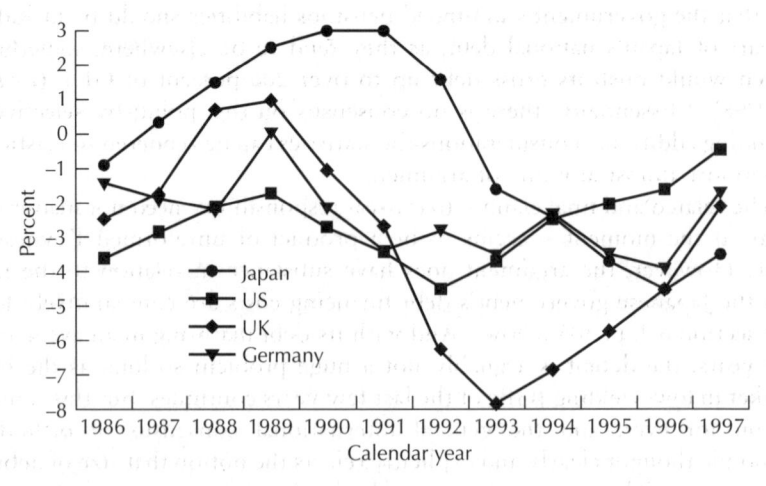

Figure 4.13: Central Government Fiscal Balances (ratio to GDP)
(*Source:* BOJ Kokusai Hikaku Tōkei)

two percent in light of the government's largest ever fiscal stimulus of ¥16 trillion, announced in April 1998 (*Nikkei* 27/5/98).

Policy Responses to the Recession

Successive Japanese governments have relied upon a tried-and-tested recession-busting formula, centred upon fiscal stimulus, to buck the Heisei Recession. But as the previous subsections indicate, their strategy has proved ineffective.

(i) A familiar formula

Any toolkit for macroeconomic management consists of four types of policy instruments: (i) monetary policy, which involves manipulating liquidity by direct or indirect means – i.e. by open market operations or by altering interest rates; (ii) broad fiscal policy, which involves altering the levels and/or makeup of government spending and taxation; (iii) direct intervention, which is mainly used as a tool for crisis management; and (iv) regulatory amendments, which may target any area of the economy in order to induce or retard structural changes. In Japan's case, successive administrations have responded to the Recession by relying upon a loosely identifiable formula, centred upon economic stimuli, effected through loose monetary and fiscal policies, and supplemented by periodic direct intervention executed to prop up the country's stock, property, and currency markets at points of imminent crisis. Regulatory reform initiatives have been touted with increasing regularity, yet have not delivered anything in terms of growth to date.

In monetary policy, the BOJ has pursued a loose but non-inflationary monetary policy throughout the Recession (Cargill *et al.* 1997, pp. 57–9; 91–116). The Bubble was deflated by monetary tightening which took the form of raising interest rates, but after inflationary pressures had been checked and the economy stalled, the BOJ progressively cut rates by increasing liquidity in line with the exigencies of unfolding developments. Some criticised the Bank for excessive monetary tightening and for being slow to ease rates, but its actions were entirely consistent with a general conservative bent and justified by the monetary overhang left by the Bubble. In practical terms, Japan's scope for further significant monetary stimuli to extricate the economy from recession was largely exhausted after the Official Discount Rate was cut to an all-time historic low of 0.5 percent in September 1995, opening up a large gap between Japan and its competitors.[17]

Fiscal policy over the period of the Recession has been extremely loose, as established in the previous subsection. A significant exception to this rule, however, was most of fiscal 1997. With economic recovery apparently

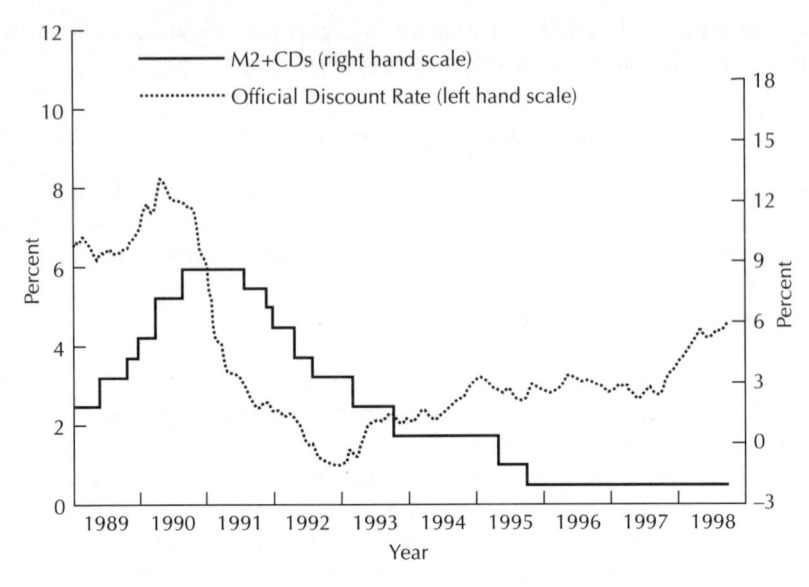

Figure 4.14: Official Discount Rate and Money Supply
(*Source*: BOJ Keizai Tōkei Geppō)

gaining momentum, the Diet passed legislation which would set the stage for fiscal reconstruction. This was one of Prime Minister Hashimoto's personal ambitions, but it soon became clear that the action was premature and over-zealous as the economy nose-dived in late 1997.[18] In response, a new package of pump-priming measures and temporary tax cuts was hastily drawn up in December 1997 and January 1998 (see Appendix 2) and again that autumn. As a result, government spending to kick-start the economy picked up where it had left off, with the allocation of new funds following a long-established pattern of targeting public works projects. Taxation changes have continued to play only a supplementary role, a means to provide relief for hard-hit and politically sensitive sectors of the economy (e.g. banking, small- and medium-sized enterprises) and/or to stimulate consumer demand which plunged following the consumption tax hike of April 1997. Here, the government has done almost everything possible by way of fiscal policy to stimulate the economy without altering established spending and taxation structures in anything other than temporary or marginal ways.

By way of direct intervention, the government launched a series of measures to prop up the stock market (and, to a lesser extent, the property market) in order to shore up the corporate sector in mid-1992. In what has become known derisively as price keeping operations, or 'PKOs',[19] public money was used periodically to purchase stocks, and administrative guidance exploited to dissuade domestic institutional investors (particularly banks and insurers) from selling/issuing stocks, and to provide firms with temporary relief from full disclosure by suspending normal accounting and loss-liquidation rules on equity holdings (see section 4.2). To mitigate the Recession's effects on small businesses, the most vulnerable have received extensive state help in the form of low-interest loans, credit guarantees, and tax breaks (see Appendix 2).

Finally, in terms of regulatory changes, an increasing number of high-profile reform packages and deregulatory measures have been announced as the Recession has worn on, and to make up for the increasing ineffectiveness of other measures. Initially it appeared that some of the changes would bring about substantive, radical changes to Japan's economic structure.[20] Over time, however, the majority of politicians have shown that they have no stomach for the disruption which such changes would engender.[21] This was particularly clear in the case of Prime Minister Hashimoto's radical deregulatory solutions to Japan's economic woes, which ran out of steam at the end of 1997 against a background of domestic economic and financial weakness and severe regional instability. He was forced to water down plans for administrative, fiscal and financial reform and to acquiesce in calls for his government to resort to a traditional reliance upon fiscal stimuli (see Appendix 2).

Thus, as early as the fall of 1998, it was evident that Japan had made very little progress in addressing its ailing macroeconomic performance despite six years of trying. The danger of the economy falling into a deflationary spiral was as evident as it had been in late 1992 or 1995,[22] yet Japan's policy responses were almost indistinguishable (Appendix 2). Optimists pinned their hopes upon new efforts to rid the banking system of its bad loans, large amounts of new spending and tax cuts scheduled for 1999.[23] However, pessimists were right to point out that on neither front were the omens for recovery good. The LDP's bridge-bank plan announced in early July proved unworkable in its initial form, and the recently weakened government and strengthened opposition were still at odds over trying to establish a viable framework for dealing with the inevitable proliferation of financial failures. Recent 'total' and 'comprehensive' plans have proved to be failures, and without meaningful structural changes, which would necessarily take several years to implement, there appeared little reason to believe that the Japanese economy could set itself upon the path towards self-sustaining recovery.

(ii) Why no change?

The obvious answer as to why the familiar three-step formula employed by the Japanese government – loosen monetary policy, deliver a sharp fiscal stimulus, and shore up crisis areas with direct intervention – has not worked in the Heisei recession is that global structural developments have emasculated these tried-and-tested solutions. But before accepting this, it is necessary to assess briefly the main alternative hypotheses for how Japan might realistically buck the recession.

The first of three alternative proposals is that Japan has not yet achieved the right policy balance to effectively combat the Recession. Thus, many domestic and foreign critics suggest large monetary and fiscal stimuli, major direct intervention in the financial sector (e.g. forcing nationalisation upon major failing banks), and a real commitment to meaningful structural reforms, starting with the immediate and full disclosure of financial information.[24] The second is that Japan only need persist with the tried-and-tested formula, which still works, and everything will return to normal. Hereby, some domestic and foreign critics submit that the only real problem with the government's response to the Recession was that fiscal reconstruction was initiated too soon – it killed the economy just as it was getting back onto its feet.[25] A third proposition is that the government should simply inflate its problems away by printing money. *Ergo*, a number of (mostly) foreign economists hold that the root of Japan's problems is a temporary reluctance on the part of firms and consumers to spend.[26]

Prototypically, the first alternative recession-busting strategy should be seen as substantively indistinguishable from the global structural change hypothesis, in that it calls for fundamental changes in the way in which the Japanese government should respond to the Recession. The second can be dismissed in light of evidence presented above (see also section 4.2 below) which suggests that real growth figures indicating that the Recession was ending in 1997 were an aberration; that is, there had been no significant improvement in the economy's autonomous performance apart from the effects of large injections of public money. The third must also be dismissed as impractical – it assumes the economy has no fundamental structural impediments to address, would require a massive increase in the money supply to be effective[27] – and would violate the BOJ's new-found sovereignty (see Chapter 2). More fundamentally, and as with the previous alternative, it also would do nothing to address Japan's microeconomic structural problems which are understood to be the fundamental root cause of its current problems. Hereby, we can accept the global structural change hypothesis, and the issue becomes one of asking why successive Japanese governments have been unable to break free of their reliance upon their traditional formula in spite of the fact that it is proving ineffective. Clearly, the issue more than that of blindness to global structural changes, as the prevalence of recent debate about the need for structural reform demonstrates.[28] Instead, reasons can be explored in terms mutually-reinforcing circumstantial, pragmatic, and systemic considerations.

First, circumstantial factors certainly have played a part in determining the progress made by leading advocates of alternative or supplementary policy responses to the recession. Several prime ministers in the 1990s were staunchly pro-reform, but individual factors such as each leader's scope for, and selection of, discretionary projects have been important. For example, the priority which prime minister Hosokawa Morihiro (8/93–5/94) gave to political reform meant that he was unable to make progress with his chosen economic deregulation initiatives before becoming embroiled in a campaign-financing scandal and being forced to resign. Alternatively, Murayama Tomiichi's (6/94–1/96) lack of personal power meant that he had to balance interests in a precarious coalition government, and thus did not have the requisite opportunities or resources to promote his government's economic structural reform agenda. Even Hashimoto (1/95–8/98), who came to power as a popular and powerful LDP lawmaker, and dedicated his political career to the pursuit of a five-pronged reform policy, did not see the fulfilment of his objective. The fact that he made significant progress with it before losing considerable public support over his misjudged appointment of the previously convicted Satō Koko to his cabinet suggests that public opinion was essential to the progress of his agenda. Yet while many commentators have claimed that Hashimoto's lack of a strong factional support base within the LDP made his ability to pursue this agenda highly susceptible to swings in public opinion and (thus) economic downturns, others have pointed out that he only made good progress with the planning stages of his agenda, and it was when he came to begin the much more difficult and contentious implementation stage that he ran into difficulties and was forced to back down on several fronts.[29] What is clear from this is that the structure of Japan's political system has a strong in-built conservative bias which makes digression from established policy responses to recurrent issues such as economic downswings intrinsically problematic. Such an assertion receives indirect and direct support in the course of an evaluation of the remaining two factors below.

Strategic choices made by other potentially important pro-reform advocates in the policymaking arena have also been instrumental. Domestically, major business lobby groups such as Keidanren and Keizai Dōyûkai have tended to vacillate in their support for pro-reform forces in government.[30] At least as significant has been the US government's poor level of support for, and wavering stance in regard to, structural change in Japan (Chapter 2, section 2.2). In Hashimoto's case, this appears to have contributed significantly to the demise of his ability to sustain the momentum behind an alternative policy response to the Recession.[31]

Second, it is also clear that there remains a strong pragmatic rationale underlying reliance upon traditional policy strategy. In spite of well-founded objections to the formula,[32] there are good reasons for increasing public works spending dramatically in times of recession. These include the fact that the economic multiplier effect for this form of spending is still much higher than for any other (e.g. tax cuts), a claim backed up by both public and private research.[33] They also include the unique possibility that public works spending allows the government to target problem areas of the economy where workers have been displaced by industrial restructuring. The construction sector is sufficiently large and flexible to absorb easily large numbers of workers from unrelated industries. Hereby, approximately one million workers were absorbed by the sector between 1990 and 1997, increasing its workforce by sixteen percent and offsetting almost entirely the 1.08 million jobs shed by the manufacturing sector (*Nikkei* 3/5/98).[34] Moreover, even if they do not provide incentives to address the country's fundamental structural problems, regular injections of public works spending have proved successful so far in keeping Japan out of a potentially disastrous deflationary spiral.

Third, systemic factors are also highly significant, since the nature of Japan's core political, social and economic structures creates additional incentives for policymakers to adhere to the *status quo*. In terms of political structure, institutionalised patterns of decisionmaking, such as the *shingikai* system of policymaking (Schwartz 1998), entail a strong conservative bias and a proclivity towards incremental change, as Chapter 2 documented in regard to financial reform. Furthermore, it can be argued that such tendencies are backed up by socio-cultural norms which place a relatively high value upon social cohesion and stability *vis à vis* outright allocative efficiency, although it is conceded that much of the bedrock evidence relating to 'theories of Japanese uniqueness' (*nihonjin-ron*) is selective and highly anecdotal (Mouer and Sugimoto 1981).

It is also evident that Japan's particularistic economic structure has become akin to an ever-more-finely balanced house of cards which ill-timed or roughly executed structural reforms risk undermining with disastrous consequences. One way to demonstrate this is in reference to the *keiretsu* system, which binds corporate affiliates together by networks of stable cross-shareholdings. It is now well known that such a system can provide a source of comparative advantage in reducing firms' transactions costs as a result of the trust built up through long-term relational contracting (e.g. Fruin 1994; Kester 1996). However, less commonly perceived is the fact that such a proposition rests upon a fundamental but implicit assumption of relative economic stability. In a prolonged recession where fears of deflation exist, *keiretsu* relations can become a drag on competitiveness as they tie the fates of potentially competitive firms to those of uncompetitive firms. Stronger firms feel a duty to support related but weaker ones, and when they get to the point where this becomes unsustainable as their own position is also in danger, they are forced to either sever ties or go down with their colleagues. Either way, the repercussions are likely to be much more destabilising for the economy as a whole because hidden pressures which have been building up gradually are released suddenly, and because to the obscure nature of the process destroys the confidence of other participants.

In this way, the impact of a large corporate bankruptcy tends to have exaggerated effects upon the economy, both locally and nationally.[35]

This sheds light upon successive governments' tendency to intervene and provide short-term solutions to any problems which threaten to damage the economy's short-term performance, even if the action would seem to be detrimental to the economy's long-term prospects. Into this category fall the state's intervention to prop up the stock market towards the end of accounting periods when firms calculate their results (March 31 and September 30), its suspension (and nonrigorous checking) of normal accounting standards which encourages (or allows) firms to 'dress up' their books (*funshoku kessan*), and its repeated provision of 'temporary' tax-breaks for strategically important sectors such as banking.[36] The logic runs as follows.

Cross-shareholding relations are a well-known feature of Japan's stock market and are said to be responsible for the relatively high price-earning ratios (PER) of stocks. They represent a source of hidden wealth in so far as corporate accounting standards have generally recorded equity holdings at book- (i.e. historical-) rather than market-value and many firms have not traded large parts of their equity portfolios for years. However, when stock prices decline sufficiently, hidden reserves become hidden losses if the blocks of shares are not sold and repurchased or if accounting rules are not changed. For most firms, the critical level is generally perceived to be between ¥13,000 and ¥15,000 for the Nikkei 225. Thus, towards the end of an accounting period, levels in or below this range tend to cause panic. Of course, should firms begin to liquidate major holdings to avoid becoming embroiled in the trap, the act of selling stocks is likely to drive down prices further both for them and others. While this is disturbing enough for ordinary firms, it is even more critical for banks. Additionally, they now count forty-five percent of their equity holdings as part of their capital base, implying that changes in the market value of their share portfolios affect their solvency directly as well as indirectly.[37] Moreover, exposure is compounded in that they also feel the effects of falling stock prices on their borrowers' solvency as bad debt start to rise.

Other considerations can be cited which attest to the delicate nature of Japan's socio-economic structure. Douglas Ostrom (1997) has argued that Japan's lack of substantial social safety nets renders the consequences of any social disruption which would be engendered by substantive structural reforms in a time of recession all but unthinkable. Noting that unemployment benefits are provided for nine weeks or less, he estimates that radical deregulation of the financial services, trucking, and distribution sectors would put 4.6 million people out of work, pushing the official unemployment rate up to 6.7 percent from its current 3.5 percent (see also *Economist* 18/4/98). Hence, in spite of the fact that Japan's existing economic structure is becoming anachronistic to its new global structural environment, there are important reasons for the government's continued pursuit of superficially 'irrational' policy responses to the Recession. Its hope is that by initiating economic recovery Japan will be able to muddle through its present difficulties and institutional change can then be managed in a controlled manner. The paradox, however, is that to the extent that the economy picks up, the incentives for carrying out disruptive reforms are weakened. Japan's record to date, moreover, suggests that its government will be unlikely to take a lead in promoting painful restructuring as, for example, the Thatcher administration did in the UK during the 1980s.

(iii) The rising macroeconomic costs of forbearance

While it is impossible to estimate the opportunity cost of policy forbearance throughout the Recession – both because there is as yet no end in sight and due to the difficulties of calculating 'what ifs' – it is clear that the government (and most economists) vastly underestimated these costs in so far as they consistently misjudged the Recession's depth and duration.

Initially, the Heisei Recession was seen as merely a cyclical contraction in the economy, a short-term but inevitable correction in the wake of the Bubble. In fact, in 1992 Finance Minister Hata Tsutomu told the IMF Interim Committee 'We do not see any problems with our banking sector or financial system, because the basic strength of our economy has not changed' (*Nikkei* 29/4/92). However, as time dragged on, the consensus view began to reinterpret the Recession as a period of structural change or 'normalisation' during which Japan was falling into line with new global realities. Public officials and private sector economists alike were encouraged that Japan would soon recover by signs that a host of meaningful reforms were in the pipeline (see BOJ *Annual Reviews* 1994 to 1996). As of late 1998, however, the consensus was that, even if the latest pump-priming measures and financial system revitalisation initiatives work effectively, Japan was destined to continue operate at suboptimal growth rates for the foreseeable future.[38] The reason was that few believed policymakers would be willing or able to implement meaningful structural reforms in a way which would revive Japan's fundamental economic performance for at least the next five years (conversations with various economists and strategists in Tokyo, June to September 1998).[39]

Hereby, the Heisei Recession had become by far Japan's longest and severest of the postwar period, more than twice as long as that following the second oil crisis of 1978. Successive governments' policy responses have averted crisis but in the process inadvertently prolonged and deepened the Recession. Indeed, persistent reliance upon a traditional formula has induced distortions in the economy which promise to affect its future as well as current performance. It is obvious that the costs of the spiralling government deficit will have to be paid in the future, that overreliance on public works spending has bloated the construction sector to unsustainable proportions, and that abstruse government intervention in the stock market and banking sector has damaged investor sentiment.[40] However, it is also evident that state-induced macroeconomic asymmetries entail a redistribution of costs and benefits which simultaneously affect all sectors of the economy.

4.2 THE MICROECONOMIC EFFECTS OF GRADUALISM

This section examines how government policy-induced distortions have affected Japan's corporate and household sectors at the local level, then goes on to examine more generally how each sector is changing under financial globalisation in the 1990s.

Local Implications of Macroeconomic Policy-induced Distortions

Japan's particularistic policy responses to the Heisei Recession have engendered significant distortions in the country's stock market, in the value of the yen, and in the level of domestic interest rates. These policy-induced asymmetries have worked to favour certain sectors of society at the expense of others.

(i) Stock market distortions

Directly, it is clear that a number of sectors benefited from the state's resort to PKOs. Foremost were the private trust banks and securities firms through which the stock investments were made, in so far as their business and commissions income was boosted by large injections of government funds.[41] Other major beneficiaries were weaker listed firms, in that the act of propping the market up kept them solvent and reduced the chances of their stock falling prey to waves of panic selling.[42]

Indirectly, most shareholders gained in having the value of their portfolios underwritten by an implicit state guarantee. Major Japanese shareholders tend to be long-term in their investment strategy, by nature of the cross-shareholding tradition and by virtue of the large, concentrated domestic portfolios which banks and pension funds necessarily hold as a result of their low levels of international portfolio diversification. Thus, they are able to react only slowly to market movements and have difficulties liquidating large positions when the market plunges.

By contrast, liquid and value-oriented shareholders were generally disadvantaged by Japan's resort to PKOs. The imposition of a price floor mitigated the chance to pick up bargains and/or to exploit superior skills in fundamental and technical analysis at the expense of the greater majority of less astute shareholders. Hence, foreign institutional investors (and a handful of leading Japanese firms) have been deprived of significant profit-making opportunities during the Recession (interviews with Jarret Wait and Alan Marrantz, 18/8/98).

It is sometimes alleged that the public, whose money was used to fund PKOs, has been the main bearer of the costs. In the long term there may be some truth in such a claim, but such an argument is unsustainable when applied to the short-term. As a result of other asymmetries induced by longstanding financial regulatory structures (Chapter 2), returns on postal savings and insurance have continued to compare favourably with private sector alternatives throughout the Recession.[43] Moreover, since the funds for PKOs do not come from mandatory tax or savings contributions, postal customers who oppose the idea of their funds being used to this end are ultimately free to take their savings elsewhere. In sum, PKOs worked to protect the majority at the expense of the few, and hereby contributed to maintaining levels of equality among participants in the economy.

(ii) Exchange rate distortions

The effects of the government's PKOs combined with the BOJ's early post-Bubble contraction of liquidity to induce a sharp appreciation in the value of the yen. For most of the period from August 1993 to June 1996 the yen remained below ¥100 to the dollar, creating what Asher (1997) has called the 'yen bubble' in reference to its lack of basis in economic fundamentals. This policy-induced macroeconomic distortion engendered various domestic repercussions, not all of which were perceived by analysts at the time.

For a natural resource-poor economy like Japan's, the dominant wisdom was that increases in the national currency's value will disadvantage the corporate sector, which derives a large proportion of its business from exports, but benefit the household sector, by boosting the purchasing power of the national currency.[44] As it happened, however, large manufacturers were able to exploit both modern corporate financing techniques (*zaitech*) and power asymmetries in *keiretsu* relations in order to avoid or pass on to their suppliers and subcontractors many of the effects of yen appreciation. Consumers, meanwhile, found Japan's myriad economic structural impediments prevented them from enjoying the natural benefits of yen appreciation.

The 'ultrahigh yen' (*chō-endaka*) presented Japan's large manufacturers with a new dilemma. They had coped with the currency's long-term appreciation by progressively shifting production overseas and cutting domestic costs, yet this new development was unprecedented in its scale and severity. Thanks to forward contracts, most large firms were able to hedge short-term currency changes, and thus the sharp appreciation had relatively little effect on their immediate earnings. However, it was the concern that the yen might remain at around ¥100 to the dollar that prompted a fresh wave of restructuring which was notable for its ruthless exploitation of dependent subcontractors and suppliers.

By taking a more selective approach to domestic suppliers, and increasing levels of overseas procurement and production, a ripple effect was sent through the *keiretsu* system. By 1995 auto manufacturers were pushing their component makers and subcontractors to cut costs by around thirty percent, having already cut their own staff bonuses and overtime, laid off part-time workers, and seconded many workers to affiliates (Ikeda 1998).[45] In this way, Toyota was able to maintain its number one position for profitability among major Japanese companies for the seventh consecutive year in fiscal 1994 (*Nikkei* 3/6/95).[46]

In the electronics industry, the hollowing out continued, with Aiwa producing seventy percent of its goods overseas in 1995. Hitachi designated 22,749 of its domestic workforce 'surplus' in 1993–4. Of these, 16,799 were dispatched temporarily to affiliates (*shukkō*), 3,931 were transferred permanently to affiliates (*tenkin*), 1,240 received incentives to change companies (*tenseki ōen*), leaving only 799 (i.e. 3.5 percent) in direct redundancies (Nishinarita 1998, p. 214). Section 4.2.2 provides a review of performance results by industry type, firm size and sector, but it is clear that the ultrahigh yen provided large manufacturers with a tangible reason to push rationalisation on their employees and suppliers and, as a result, they themselves have become considerably more competitive.

Small manufacturers, of course, appear less sensitive to exchange rate movements because they depend more heavily on domestic business. However, a Japan Small Business Corporation survey conducted during March and April in 1995 reported that ninety percent of small firms felt that their business had been damaged by recent yen appreciation. Half of the respondents explained that their poor performance reflected pressure from larger business partners to cut costs, while a further third said that it was because orders from parent companies had declined (*Nikkei* 26/5/95). Domestic industry was bearing the brunt of adjustment pressure, and not just in the form of increased price competition from cheaper imports. MITI officials underlined this in mid-1995 by noting that even businesses which are often considered not to be affected by yen appreciation, because they mainly do business in the domestic market and because yen appreciation lowers the prices of their raw materials and energy consumption (e.g. cement and steel), tend to be affected indirectly because many of their customers, seeing their own bottom lines squeezed, push their suppliers for lower costs or turn to lower-priced foreign products.

For consumers in a high-cost economy like Japan's, domestic currency appreciation was expected to bring down both the prices of goods, through greater import competition, and energy bills. Apparently confirming this, an EPA survey, which noted that the strengthening yen had handed a ¥40,000 saving to a typical family of four via lower prices during the calendar 1993, was taken up and publicised by then Finance Minister Hashimoto Ryûtarō (*Nikkei* 3/6/95). However, a comparative survey by Fuji Research Institute conducted the following year noted that a one percent rise in the yen only pushed consumer prices down by 0.1 percent, whereas in Germany a one percent rise in the deutsche mark reduced consumer prices by an average of 0.5 percent. The difference was attributed to the structure of the Japanese economy, and particularly to the distribution system, which absorbed most of the savings itself (*Nikkei* 6/10/95). What accounted for a large part of the EPA's findings was the fact that large-scale 'price destruction' (*kakaku hakai*) in the form of twenty-to-forty percent discounts for beverages and foodstuffs, clothing, and consumer durables had been spurred by a phenomenal growth in discount stores. But this was more a result of limited deregulation and consumers having become thrifty due to the enduring Recession. Similarly, in June 1995 MITI announced that about ¥14 would be cut off the average monthly electricity bill from July because the nation's ten electric power companies were expected to gain about ¥300 billion a year from the appreciating yen. However, officials at the Agency of Natural Resources and energy said that MITI's calculation was misleading because, while the impending rate cut was based on an exchange rate of ¥99 to the dollar and a crude oil price of $17 per barrel, MITI's profit projection figure was calculated at an exchange rate of ¥85 to the dollar and an oil price of $17 per barrel (*Nikkei* 3/6/95). Despite the political rhetoric, the link between yen appreciation and lower consumer prices was in no way straightforward.

(iii) Interest rate distortions

The Japanese government's inability to affect meaningful structural economic constitutes the root cause of the Heisei Recession's endurance. To counter persistent deflationary pressures, the BOJ has needed to keep interest rates at a very low level, 0.5 percent from September 1995. This action has favoured certain sectors of the economy at the expense of others.

The banking sector is most commonly alleged to have been the major beneficiary of ultralow interest rates, and this is true in so far as interest payments on deposits represent commercial banks' single largest cost (see figure 4.15). The BOJ denies cutting rates specifically to help the banking sector, but since it claimed at the time that lower rates would promote reform in the corporate sector by boosting profitability in order to enable firms to bear the costs of adjustment, the banking sector was always set to gain most. In fact, banks gained even more in the short term because when interest rates fall the value of their substantial bond holdings rise, and while lower interest rates are reflected immediately on the liability side of their balance sheets (e.g. deposit rates paid), adjustment takes place more slowly on the asset side since the average maturity of assets (e.g. loans and mortgages) tends to be longer. Over time, however, these temporary profits are ameliorated by adjustment.

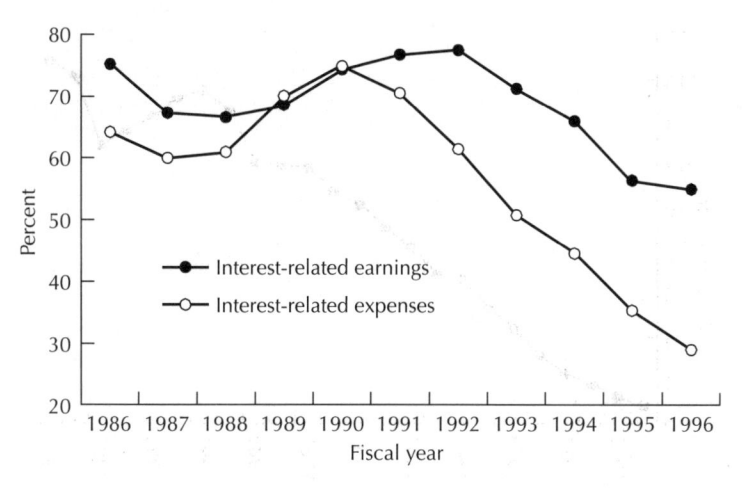

Societal Implications of a 'Gradualist' Approach

Figure 4.15: Banks' Interest-related Earnings and Expenses (as a percentage of income)
(*Source*: BOJ Keizai Tōkei Nenpō)

Less widely recognised is the fact that the government was a major beneficiary of persistently low interest rates, in so far as it was heavily indebted yet can float large quantities of public bonds cheaply. With the yield on ten-year JGBs falling consistently since mid-1990 to historic lows of below one percent in August 1998, the Japanese government has been able to borrow more cheaply than any other state in recorded history since late 1997 (*Economist* 21/2/98). Figure 4.16 shows how, in spite of the massive increase in the total level of outstanding government debt in the 1990s (see section 6.1), actual debt servicing costs fell for several years and remain at relatively low levels thanks to ultralow interest rates and a depressed stock market.

Other beneficiaries were the corporate sector, in so far as firms are in deficit with the banking sector and/or they desire new credit,[47] the wholesale/retail sector, because low interest rates stimulate consumption, and mortgage holders/house buyers, since their supposedly cost of borrowing is reduced.

The main losers from low interest rates were ordinary depositors. This is because the household sector has more financial assets than liabilities, and the majority of these are held in the form of bank/postal deposits (see section 4.2.3) so net interest income is reduced by lower interest rates. Because the elderly rely upon this form of income more heavily than most, they tend to be particularly hard hit. Individual (and corporate) investors in insurance, pension, and trust funds also have been negatively affected to the extent that their policies are invested in yen-denominated bonds and money

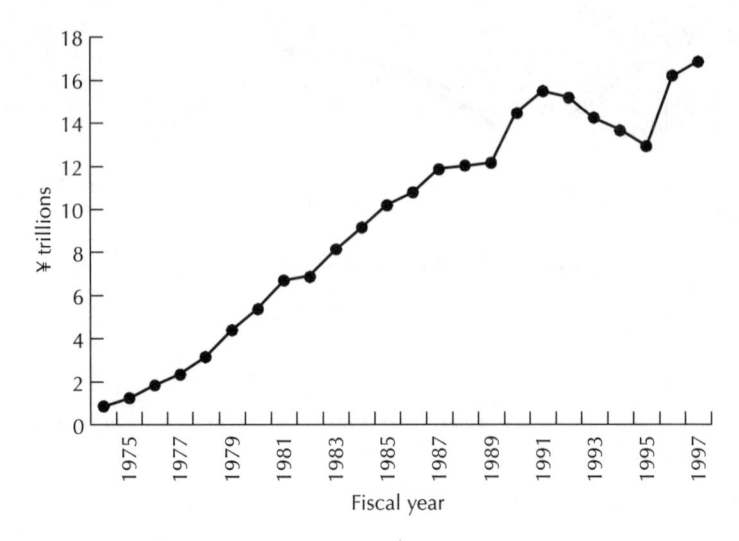

Figure 4.16: Annual Government Debt Servicing Expenses
(*Source*: BOJ Keizai Tōkei Nenpō)

market products. Hereby, the EPA announced that the household sector's net income from financial assets and property hit a seventeen-year low of ¥15.6 trillion in fiscal 1996, down ¥2.1 trillion from the previous year. Noting that the financial sector's net income from these things hit an all-time high of ¥23.4 trillion in fiscal 1996, it concluded that banks had received the lion's share of benefits from the BOJ's easy monetary policy to the detriment of ordinary depositors (*Nikkei* 16/12/97).[48]

Corporate Sector Developments in the 1990s

Bearing in mind the short-term winners and losers noted above, it is important to turn to the longer-term implications for the corporate sector of the state's gradualist approach to financial globalisation. This can be done by examining terms of the corporate sector's recent performance record, its changing financing patterns, and the state of its ongoing restructuring efforts.

(i) Performance

Corporate performance can be measured in a multitude of ways, but this subsection relies upon two complementary indicators which, over time, provide a representative overview: profitability data by type of industry, firm size, and sector (taken from the MOF's *Hōjin Kigyō Tōkei*), and key subjective surveys of business conditions for manufacturers and nonmanufacturers and principal firms and small firms (taken from the BOJ's *Tankan*).[49]

By type of industry, figure 4.17 shows that manufacturers' profitability fell rapidly during the first three years of the recession. A drop-off in domestic demand, which translated into costly excess capacity and increasing inventory, was exacerbated by falling export demand as a result of significant yen appreciation beginning in early 1993. However, rationalisation and balance sheet adjustment turned the tide in fiscal 1994, and thereafter profitability was steadily boosted by increasing export demand as the yen began a steady depreciation which lasted from mid-1995 until the end of 1996. Nonmanufacturers' profitability mapped out a slower decline. This sector had much less stock inventory and excess capacity to adjust for, little direct exposure to exchange rate movements, and substantial support in the form of new public investment in the face of weakened private expenditure. Yet even with the sharp edge having been taken off balance sheets adjustment pressures, the sector has remained highly vulnerable to declines in personal consumption in the face of still weak consumer confidence, as profit figures for fiscal 1996 and 1997 demonstrate.

By subjective experience, figure 4.18 confirms that manufacturers have been much more sensitive to the Recession, both in terms of feeling its effects earlier as well as more deeply than nonmanufacturers.

By firm size, larger firms were hit earlier and more heavily by the Recession, as one might expect, with small firms (i.e. ¥10 to ¥100 million in capital) being shielded somewhat by government spending measures to

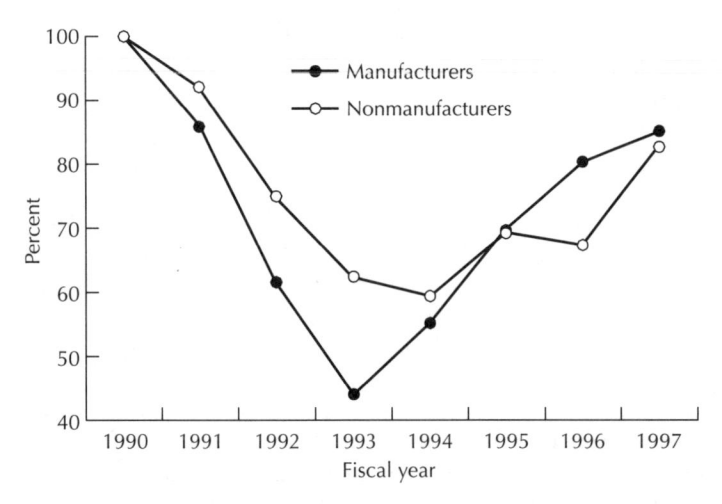

Figure 4.17: Changes in Profits for Manufacturers Versus Nonmanufacturers (1990 = 100)
(*Source*: MOF Hōjin Kigyō Tōkei)

The Case of Japan

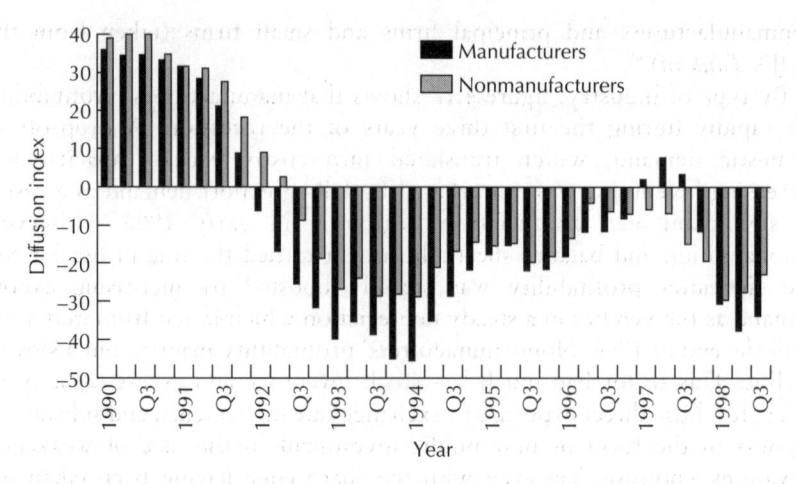

Figure 4.18: Sectoral Business Conditions (from 'Favourable' to 'Unfavourable')
(*Source*: BOJ Keizai Tōkei Geppō)

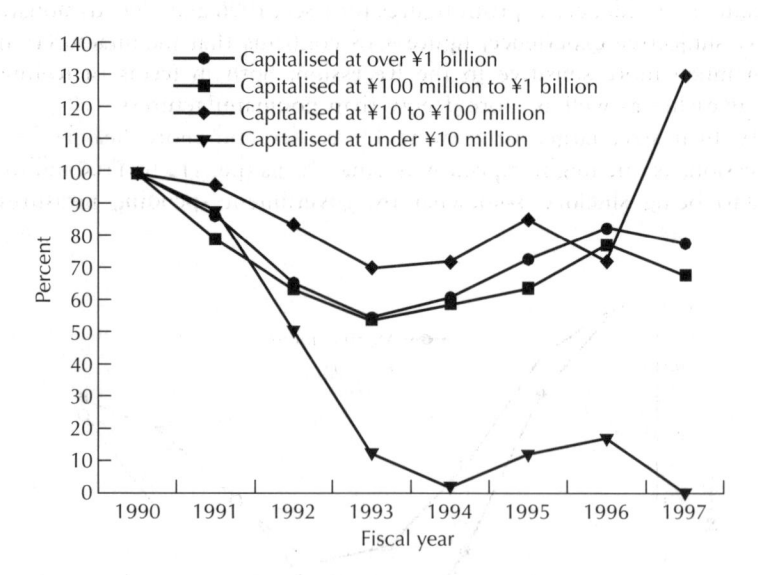

Figure 4.19: Changes in Annual Profits by Firm Size (1990 = 100)
(*Source*: MOF Hōjin Kigyō Tōkei)

compensate for falling domestic demand. However, very small firms (i.e. those with under ¥10 million in capital), which fall outside many government and private statistics (e.g. the BOJ's *Tankan* and Teikoku Data Bank's corporate bankruptcy records – see figure 4.6 above), were hit tremendously hard by comparison. This appears to be a result of the fact that they are too small to benefit from the government's various actions to alleviate the effects of the Recession, and have faced the full force of falling private demand from the personal and small business sectors.

Accordingly, surveys by the People's Finance Corporation, which regularly polls approximately 6,600 firms with under 30 employees, reaffirm that very small firms have been hardest hit by the stagnant economy. They also show that firms in predominantly rural areas have been hardest hit by the Recession: those in Hokkaido and Tōhoku had fared particularly badly, with those in Fukuōka and Kyûshû having fared relatively better – the result of strong regional trade links – at least until the Asian currency crisis curtailed foreign demand in late 1997 (*Nikkei* 22/1/98).

By subjective experience, figure 4.20 highlights another interesting point of variation.

For manufacturers, principal firms were initially hit harder than small firms, but as the Recession drew on small firms began to feel the its effects more deeply. This development again reflects successful restructuring efforts by principal manufacturers, and the fact that large firms have been able, over time, to pass on the pinch to subcontractors and suppliers. Additionally, and in contrast to their smaller and nonmanufacturing counterparts, large manufacturers did not, on the whole, take on new debt to finance speculative investments during the Bubble. Consequently, they were able to adjust their balance sheets unimpeded by the burdens of additional debt.

For nonmanufacturers, figure 4.21 shows that it was larger firms that were hit hardest throughout the Recession, at least until the middle of 1996. This reflects the fact that small firms, which account for the majority of

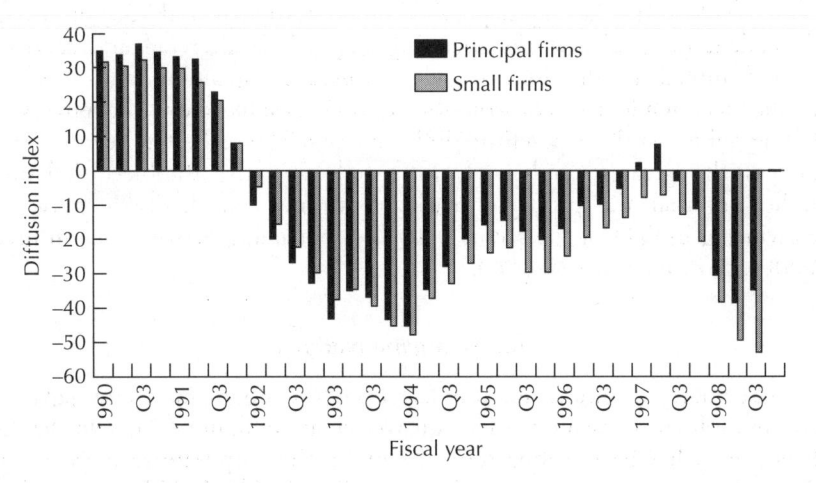

Figure 4.20: Manufacturers' Business Conditions (from 'Favourable' to 'Unfavourable')
(*Source*: BOJ Keizai Tōkei Geppō)

The Case of Japan

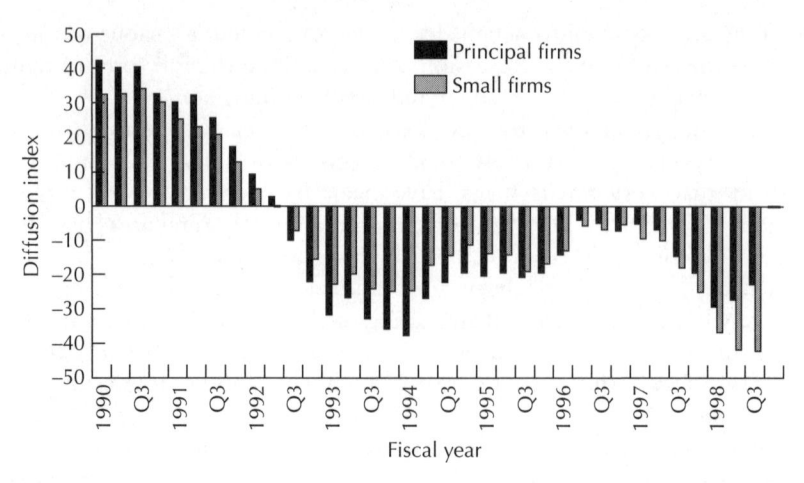

Figure 4.21: Nonmanufacturers' Business Conditions (from 'Favourable' to 'Unfavourable'
(*Source*: BOJ Keizai Tōkei Geppō)

employment in Japan, have benefited most from the governments' various initiatives to prop up the domestic economy, but that fiscal consolidation and the increasing ineffectiveness of such intervention over time has resulted in a period of correction on the basis of increasing inequalities in economic fundamentals following more substantial rationalisation by larger firms.

By sector, figure 4.22 shows that manufacturers which are very dependent on exports (e.g. electronics and transport), were hit heavily but rebounded strongly, reflecting yen movements and successful rationalisation. Nonmanufacturers heavily dependent on domestic demand but not heavily dependent on public works spending (e.g. wholesale/retail and services) posted mixed results in line with consumer spending and business confidence, while the construction sector's results show the effects of falling public works expenditure in later years. The real estate sector stands out as the greatest underperformer, reflecting the Bubble's deflation. Indicators that the property market bottomed out in 1996 were not convincing in light of the sector's steadily worsening performance in fiscal 1998 (e.g. *Economisto* 25/8/98).

(ii) Financing patterns

As elsewhere, disintermediation has been the dominant trend Japanese corporate finance during the past quarter century (figure 4.23). On the one hand, there has been a long-term decline in the corporate sector's overall demand for indirect financing, which was disturbed by Bubble but has since been exaggerated by the Recession; on the other, there has been a general

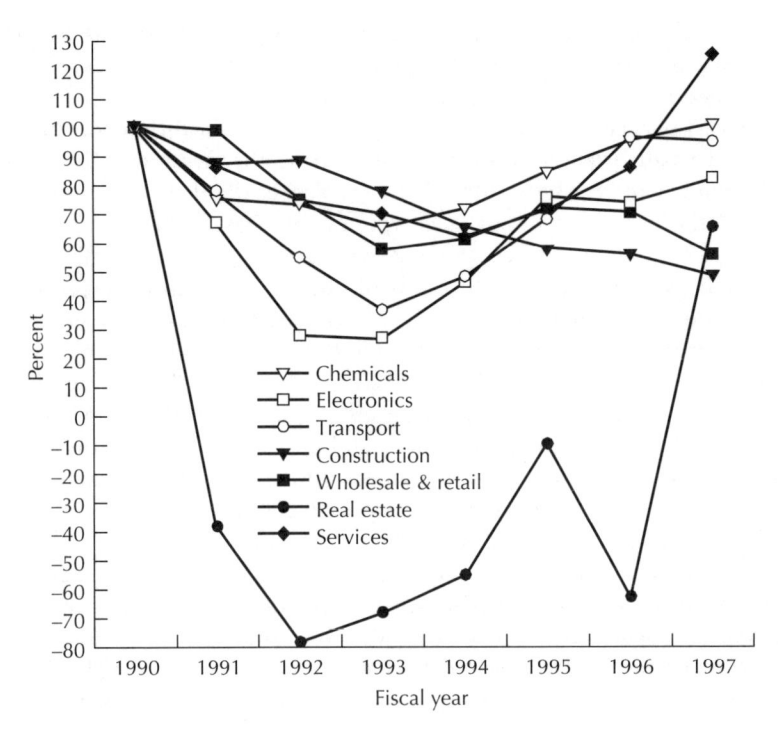

Societal Implications of a 'Gradualist' Approach

Figure 4.22: Year-on-year Changes in Annual Profits for Selected Sectors
(*Source*: MOF Hōjin Kigyō Tōkei)

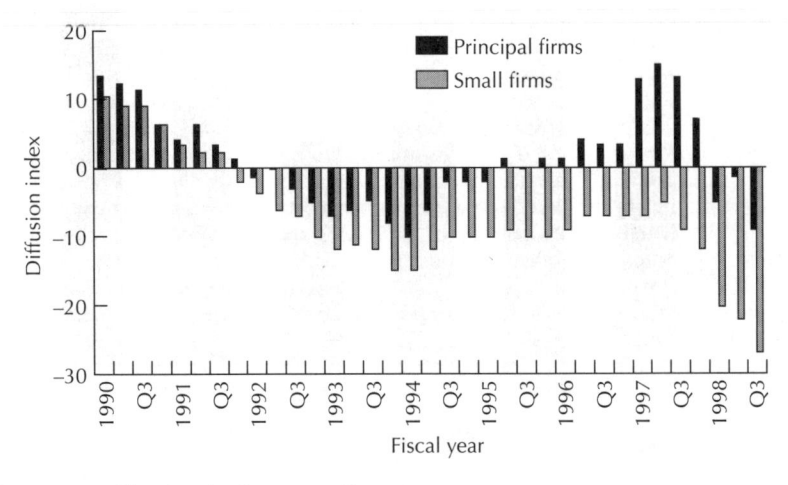

Figure 4.23: Changes in Corporate Finance
(*Source*: BOJ Keizai Tōkei Nenpō)

The Case of Japan

move towards greater reliance on direct financing, although this trend has been concealed in recent years by the Recession's substantial depression of business conditions and the domestic stock market.

In terms of access to funds, figure 4.24 shows that the differences between large and small firms grew substantially during the Recession. Small firms have found it increasingly difficult to get access to adequate funding as a result of the increasing importance which banks have begun to place upon borrower creditability since 1992. It was at this point that falling stock prices and swelling bad debts forced banks to increase their loan spreads and curtail lending in order to meet BIS capital adequacy standards. Generally, large companies were less affected, having more retained earnings to rely upon and being able to fall back on issuing bonds or borrowing abroad. From 1994, moreover, rationalisation efforts at larger firms began to pay dividends and their funding difficulties all but disappeared. By contrast, the funding position of small firms remained difficult, and deteriorated rapidly from 1997, when larger firms also began to experience a new credit crunch. Against a background of deteriorating domestic and regional economic conditions, and with the looming spectre of a newly competitive financial environment promised by Big Bang, banks began to curtail the extension of new loans to less creditworthy borrowers regardless of size.

In the summer of 1997, early reports began to emerge of firms having had more or less routine loan requests turned down by their banks, but it was

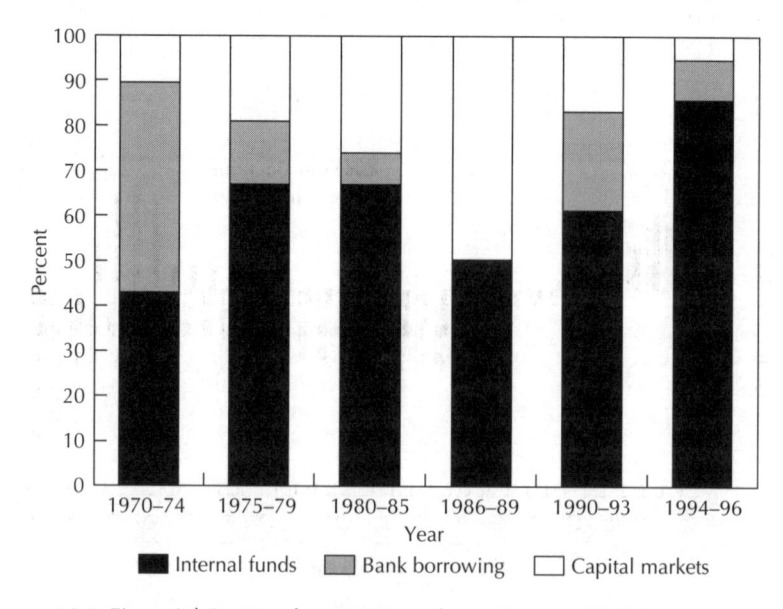

Figure 4.24: Financial Position by Firm Size (from 'Easy' to 'Tight')
(*Source*: BOJ Keizai Tōkei Geppō)

only in the wake of the domestic financial turmoil of November that the issue became a political one.⁵⁰ That autumn, BOJ figures confirmed that despite record-low interest rates, lending by Japanese commercial banks had fallen sharply from the previous year, while loans by foreign banks operating in Japan had increased by more than twenty percent (*Nikkei* 19/8/97; 4/11/97). Teikoku Data Bank figures released in December showed that of the 169 companies with liabilities of over ¥10 million that had gone bankrupt in first eleven months of 1997, the majority occurred since the summer: thirty-three percent of the failures were put down to banks refusing fresh loan requests, twenty-nine percent to banks' imposition of stricter balance sheet screening, and fifteen percent to bank requests for existing borrowers to provide additional collateral. Small firms had been hit especially hard, with twenty-one percent of the failures being capitalised at under ¥10 million and a further sixty-six percent being capitalised at ¥10–50 million (*Nikkei* 16/12/97).

Following the collapse of Toshoku (a medium-sized trading company listed on the first section of the TSE), which filed for bankruptcy after banks refused to provide it with new loans in December, the government took action to induce private banks to increase their lending and to boost public financial institutions' financing role for small and medium-sized firms.⁵¹ This eventually helped alleviate the credit crunch, but at the cost of further delaying the economy's structural adjustment. Still, the fact that small firms access to credit remains relatively tight may suggest that banks have, nonetheless, begun to start pricing credit risks more appropriately.

(iii) Institutional changes

Financial globalisation has contributed to institutional changes in the corporate sector where the governments' formulaic policy responses to the Recession have not altogether mitigated new competitive pressures. As financial globalisation has gradually introduced new and more effective means of financial control and evaluation (e.g. credit rating systems), and as leading Japanese firms have been exposed to such pressures abroad, the market has begun to push firms to improve their competitive performance as measured against standardised quantitative criteria. Hereby, pressures have been steadily building for Japanese firms to reevaluate traditional patterns of organisation and corporate governance. Institutional change can be noted on all three of the following axes: (i) firms' relationships with each other, (ii) with their employees, and (iii) with their owners.

a) firms' relations with each other

As already noted in section 4.1, a core characteristic of the Japanese model of corporate organisation is cross-shareholding, in which firms are linked to fellow *keiretsu* partners which often include one (or more) 'main bank(s)'.[52] In recent years, significant changes can be observed which qualify as amendments to, rather than signs of the imminent demise of, such embedded institutional structures.

In terms of firms cross-shareholding relations with each other, there has been a general decline in the extent of the practice in the 1990s. Asher noted that the proportion of so-called 'free floating' (not cross-held) shares on the TSE had risen to thirty-eight percent by the end of fiscal 1995, up ten percent from their lowest levels in 1988 (1996, p. 229). Most of this seems attributable to peripheral attrition. As a 1995 FTC survey of Japan's 74 largest companies (62 responded) found, nearly eighty percent of those polled believed that the cross-shareholding system would not disappear any time soon. However, sixty-eight percent confirmed that they had become more selective about which shares they hold (*Nikkei* 22/12/95).[53] Recent work by Nakata (1998) though, shows that there has been no perceptible long-term weakening in cross-shareholding among the main nonfinancial shareholders of Japan's six largest *keiretsu*. Firms have simply been reappraising their long-term portfolios in order to weed out nonessential stocks.

In terms of firms' relations with their main banks, recent changes have also been largely peripheral, although there was some evidence of genuine change on the part of large corporations in line with disintermediation. Research by Teikoku Data Bank, which looked at banks' holdings of major corporations' stock, found that overall levels had remained remarkably stable between fiscal 1991 and 1996. However, it did note some variation according to type of bank, showing that banks under greater competitive pressures had cut shareholdings marginally, and vice versa.[54] Looking at the relationship from the opposite side, a study by Nippon Life Institute showed a general decline in corporations' holdings of bank stocks. It noted that whereas 33.3 percent of all outstanding bank shares were held by long-term stable shareholders in fiscal 1987, cross-shareholding accounted for only 28.2 percent of bank shares in fiscal 1996. Of this, nonbanks holdings of bank shares had fallen from 31.3 percent to 26.5 percent, while cross shareholdings between banks had only fallen from two percent to 1.8 percent.[55]

b) firms' relations with their employees

By causing firms to focus on quantitative measures of profitability and efficiency, the Recession also has led many to reappraise their propagation of traditional 'Japanese' employment practices.

As the Recession dampened demand, payrolls at most Japanese firms rose substantially as a proportion of pretax profits, in spite of cuts in overtime pay and bonuses. From an average of 68.6 percent of value added in 1991, they rose to 73.8 percent in 1993, before settling back to around the seventy-three percent level in 1995 where they have remained ever since – a level far higher than their foreign competitors (MOF *Hōjin Kigyō Tōkei*), while the country's real exchange rate, a measure of export competitiveness reflecting shifts in the unit cost of labour, rose sharply. This meant that firms were beginning to experience significant employment adjustment pressures. Although Japanese firms are permitted to lay off workers only if they can show they are losing money, their major constraint has been social rather than legal/technical. Thus, work force rationalisation has generally proceeded indirectly, i.e. through reliance on natural attrition, reductions in new hiring, and induced early retirement/semi-retirement, and via peripherally-introduced changes in existing employment structures.

Big business has long realised that, used on a large scale, practices such as lifetime employment and seniority-based wages produced unwieldy and expensive fixed cost structures, and that job rotation could be detrimental to fostering specialist skills among employees. The Recession provided them with an opportunity to slim down these structures, some of which – lifetime employment, for example – had only ever applied to core employees. Hence, big business organisations such as Keidanren, Keizai Dōyûkai and Nikkeiren began proactively promoting revisions to these institutionalised practices in the early 1990s. Their aim was both to coordinate action for public relations purposes, and to have legal restrictions amended to provide them with greater flexibility in employment matters.

One prominent aspect of this strategy related to making greater use of temporary staff. Temps allow companies to keep their fixed costs down, particularly since they do not have to pay them bonuses, retirement allowances or health and pension contributions (the latter of which are covered by their agencies). Historically, over ninety-five percent of registered temps have been female, but the numbers of male temps has been increasing steadily since 1995, when legislative changes increased the categories of work for which temping agencies were allowed to dispatch workers.[56] MOL figures showed that there were 460,000 registered temps in fiscal 1995, up 7.4 percent on the previous year, with an increasing proportion working in white-collar jobs. As figure 4.25 shows, the number of companies employing temps has risen in recent years, and a recent Nikkeiren survey of 486 leading companies found that over seventy percent predicted their reliance on temps would increase in the next three-to-five years. In fact, only 9.9 percent said that they expected Japan's traditional lifetime employment system to continue to be viable in the global economy of the future.

Another aspect is the move towards flatter and more decentralised organisational structures, also led by large corporations. Okubayashi (1998) documents how corporate restructuring during the Heisei Recession began to touch white-collar workers in middle- and executive-management positions. He notes that firms' administrative divisions were being slimmed

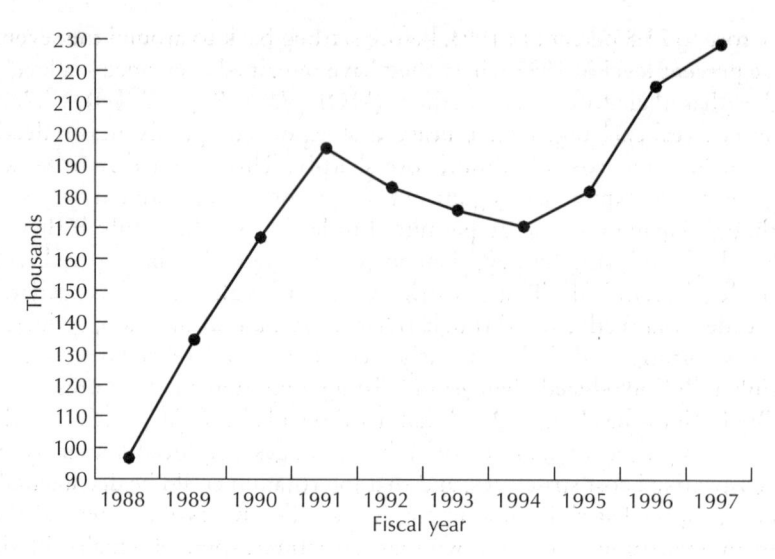

Figure 4.25: Companies Hiring Temporary Workers
(*Source*: MCA Shûgyō Kōzō Kihon Chōsa)

down because the maintenance of traditional personnel practices (i.e. promotion by seniority) in a new era of lower growth made many firms top-heavy.[57] In April 1998, for example, Matsushita began to give all of its staff the chance to opt for higher monthly salaries in return for giving up retirement benefits – a so-called 'full salary payment plan' – as a way of reducing its ballooning fixed cost structure (*Nikkei* 19/6/97; 26/3/98).[58]

Accordingly, firms also started moving away from a rigid collective style of personnel management to a mixed, flexible system which could better tap and develop individual enthusiasm and ability (Dirks 1997; Watanabe 1998). On the whole, such changes are being introduced from the bottom-up (i.e. through amended contracts for new recruits), but many firms are now taking the initiative to renegotiate contracts for existing employees. Hereby, regular surveys of corporate employment practices show that firm's reliance on performance-based pay has increased dramatically in recent years. In the 1980s, approximately ten percent of Japanese firms used performance-based pay, but by 1996 this figure had more than doubled to almost twenty-two percent.[59] Moreover, as the results of an extensive EPA survey reproduced in figure 4.26 show, ninety-one percent of the 2,117 listed companies polled in 1998 intend to rely upon some form of performance-related pay system within five years, up from forty-three percent who actually did at the end of fiscal 1997 (*Nikkei* 4/5/98).

In short, Japanese firms are responding to their new business environment in the 1990s by moving towards a more universalistic, global model for

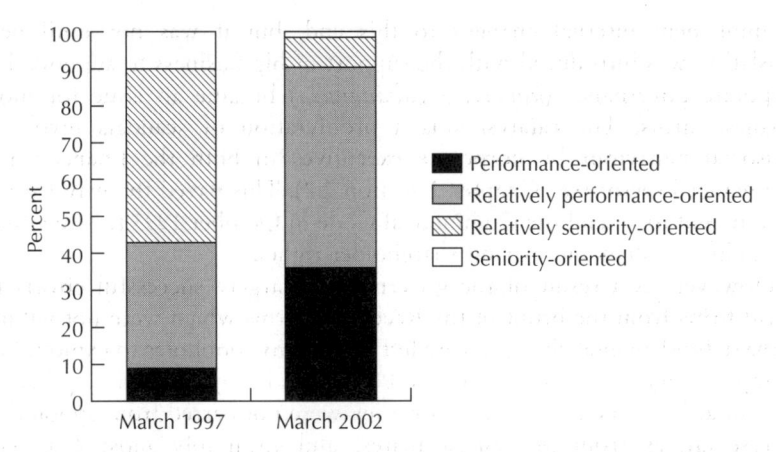

Figure 4.26: Employment Contracts at Listed Firms
(*Source:* EPA)

employee relations. However, due to enduring social (and legal) constraints, and as in the banking sector, this evolution is expected to continue to be marked by peripatetic rather than radical moves.

c) firms' relations with their owners

Finally, financial globalisation has promoted amendments to traditional corporate governance practices through its state-mediated effects on Japan's domestic financial system and general business environment.

With the Bubble's end, global market developments caught up especially quickly with listed Japanese firms, exerting pressure for firms to improve performance according to orthodox (i.e. financially quantifiable) criteria. On the one hand, the sudden slowdown in growth meant that capital gains could no longer be assumed, and investors became increasingly sensitive to poor performance. On the other, the diffusion of new financial products and evaluation technologies, such as professionally managed investment trusts and credit ratings, combined with the increasing presence of foreign institutional investors such as CalPERS, served to promote more sophisticated investor behaviour.[60] Leading and internationally-oriented firms were best placed to make the transition.

In an early and influential article, Sony chairman Morita Akio (1992) criticised traditional Japanese management practices based on low margins, low wages and large-scale output. He proposed, instead, that firms should shift their focus to criteria such as profitability, shareholder returns, and better reporting, in order to reduce excess competition, improve living standards, and increase transparency. Several more progressive firms began to implement internal changes to this end, but it was not until new legislation was introduced with the support of big business to support that corporate governance (*kōporeito gabânanusu*) became an issue for most Japanese firms. The catalyst was a proliferation of scandals involving antisocial behaviour by corporate executives in both the financial and nonfinancial sector (see Chapter 2 section 2.2). This paved the way for the government to amend the Commercial Code in October 1993 to strengthen the auditor system and expand shareholder rights.

However, as a result of the government's largely successful efforts to shield firms from the brunt of the Recession, firms which were not willing to make fundamental changes were left with many loopholes to exploit. For example, while all firms with over ¥500 million in capital were required to appoint at least one external auditor, they were not barred from appointing representatives from *keiretsu* affiliates, and invariably most did. The proliferation of newly mandated in-house auditor positions also could be used, and was, as another conduit for retiring executives who had failed to win appointment to the firm's board of directors. Hereby, Nakata (1998) demonstrates that rather than working to promote nonexecutive functions in corporate leadership as intended, Japanese business proceeded largely to circumvent the legal changes, with an expanded corporate hierarchy of executive directors continuing to rubber-stamp strategic decisions made on a group-wide basis at monthly *keiretsu* presidents' club meetings.[61]

Quantitative and qualitative indicators confirmed that very few changes of real substance had taken place during the Recession. The generic measure of return on equity (ROE) showed that in 1997 Japanese firms continued to perform dismally by international standards – at an average of four percent, compared with twenty percent for US firms (*FT* 6/5/98) – and there was no noticeable decline in the number or type of corporate scandals which weak governance mechanisms were facilitating. Hereby, at the behest of big business, the government agreed to legalise stock options (*sutokku opushon*) in May 1997, and ease the rules on share buybacks from March 1998 in order to boost the sector's flagging performance.[62] The LDP's Judicial Affairs Subcommittee on the Commercial Code also its resumed research with a view to toughening the October 1993 legislation, its chairman Ōta Seiichi noting that Japan's traditional systems of corporate governance appeared to be experiencing something akin to 'metal fatigue'(*Nikkei* 24/6/97).[63]

In the year to May 1998, approximately seventy companies announced share option schemes (*FT* 6/5/98), and by the end of August more than 1,000 firms had changed company rules to allow share buybacks. However, what looked like radical changes were greeted by analysts with measured skepticism. While leading firms like Sony and Toyota have made real progress implementing internal reforms,[64] the majority of firms were apparently more intent on being *seen* to be implementing progressive reforms than actually doing so (interviews with Okamura Ken at Dresdner Kleinwort Benson [Japan], 5/8/98; and Simon Fraser at Fidelity Investments [Japan], 19/8/98). Most stock options were seen as too small to induce managers to pursue unpopular restructuring, and the majority of the 270 share-buyback schemes were small, left unimplemented, or merely announced at the end of the financial year in order to boost share prices.[65]

As a result of this general lack of significant reform, the performance of Japan's corporate sector has continued to decline throughout the Recession. In May 1998, a MITI report based on analysis of labour costs, capitalisation, technical innovation and regulations in thirty major economic sectors showed that US-Japan productivity gap widening, with Japan now leading in only four sectors – autos, construction, chemicals, and finance (!) – versus the US's lead in thirteen, a gap which was explicitly attributed to insufficient restructuring by Japanese firms (*Nikkei* 13/5/98). Meanwhile, Stephen Hay of Goldman Sachs calculated that US industrial firms (S&P Industrials Index) have generated average return above cost of capital of about 4.5 percent since 1990, while their Japanese nonfinancial counterparts (Nikkei 300 Index) have failed consistently to achieve returns above their cost of capital. In fact, over the past seven years, the latter have made cumulative losses totaling ¥21 trillion by investing in projects which generated negative returns. Net ROE figures for TSE Tier One nonfinancial companies have recently fallen to 3.5 percent, versus twenty-seven percent for similar firms in the US and an average of 14.5 percent in Europe (*FT 6/5/98*).

Having downgraded the credit ratings of twelve major Japanese firms in the first three months of 1998, Moodys said in a report that all Japanese firms must amend their management practices if they were to avoid further declines in ratings (*Nikkei* 21/5/98). It was clear that neither Japan's financial system, nor its corporate institutional structure, its tax and legal frameworks, or social environment had yet created sufficient incentives for anything more than a few firms to give priority to maximising profits. Most continued to overinvest because (i) the financial and tax systems encouraged them to do so,[66] (ii) cross-shareholdings removed the threat of hostile takeovers as a means to effect corporate governance, (iii) the government's various measures to 'help' the corporate sector survive the Recession provided a multitude of ways for errant firms to avoid implementing painful but fundamentally necessary reforms, and (iv) social norms have not yet permitted more progressive firms to make mass layoffs prior to bankruptcy. To be sure, examples of recent changes can be cited on most of these fronts, but the issue is one of whether these have been sufficiently widespread and radical.[67] In view of the recent and ongoing trends surveyed here, it seems that the polarisation of Japan's corporate sector – between a small number of globally competitive firms and a much larger number of irredeemably uncompetitive firms – will inevitably accelerate.

Household Sector Developments in the 1990s

A more general overview of the effects of the Japanese government's gradualist approach to financial globalisation on the household sector can be gained by looking at trends in income and consumption, employment and personal bankruptcy, and savings and investment.

(i) Income and consumption

As a result of the Recession, average real household fell significantly between 1993 and 1995 and have remained marginally negative since (figure 4.27).

Annual survey figures compiled by the Ministry of Health and Welfare (MHW) showed that housewives became aware of this the following year, with 1994 constituting the first *perceived* year-on-year decline in household incomes since the MHW began conducting such surveys in 1961. The following year, the MHW survey recorded that 46.5 percent of households felt that they were 'hard up', the largest proportion in ten years, and sixteen percent felt 'very hard up'. Only 4.6 percent said they were 'comfortable' or 'quite comfortable' living on their income (*Nikkei* 29/6/97).

Other statistics, however, prove that average 'worker household' (i.e. families with one or more working member) incomes have continued to grow throughout the Recession, albeit at significantly reduced rates. However, figure 4.28 also shows that worker households' consumption growth rates, which are influenced by psychological factors, fell steadily and

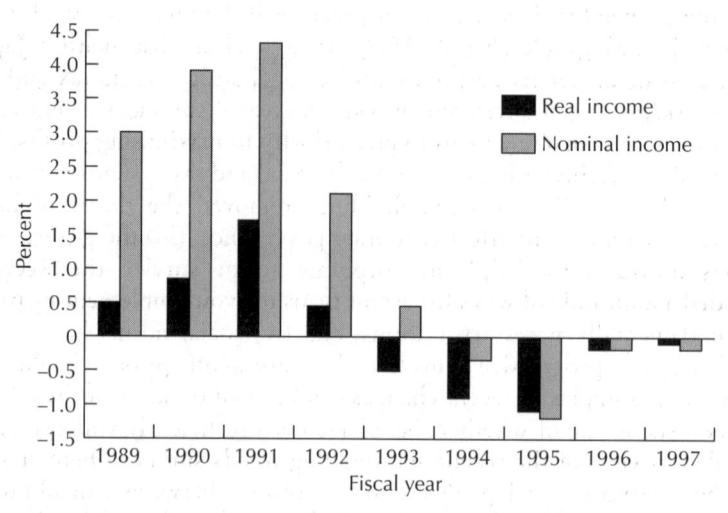

Figure 4.27: Year-on-year Changes in Household Income
(*Source:* BOJ Keizai Tōkei Nenpō)

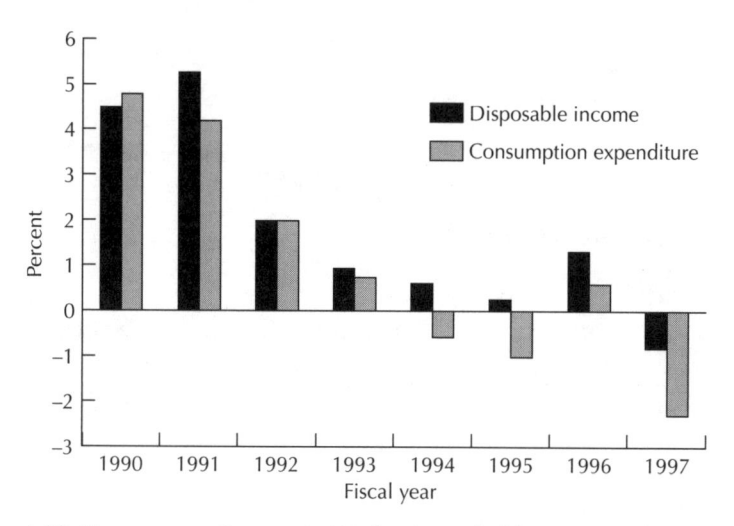

Societal Implications of a 'Gradualist' Approach

Figure 4.28: Year-on-year Changes in Worker Household Income and Expenditure
(*Source:* BOJ Keizai Tōkei Nenpō)

turned negative in 1994. They returned to growth briefly in 1996, but have since resumed their downtrend.

The latest annual survey of public attitudes concerning the future conducted by the Prime Minister's Office suggest that consumer's propensity to consume is likely to deteriorate further from its all-time current low level of seventy-two percent (down from 75.3 in 1990 – BOJ *Keizai Tōkei Nenpō* 1998). It found seventy-two percent of respondents pessimistic about the future, up sixteen percent from 1997, with only thirteen percent expecting a bright future. Of the vast majority expecting their own situations to deteriorate further, seventy-two percent cited the poor state of the economy and fifty-nine percent cited the government's swelling deficit as significant reasons for pessimism (*Nikkei* 3/5/98). Hereby, while it is evident that the Recession has hit non-working households considerably harder than worker households, household income and consumption patterns also indicate that most Japanese have little confidence in the effectiveness of their government's broader macroeconomic strategy.

(ii) Employment and personal bankruptcy

Recent trends in unemployment and personal bankruptcy show that there is real substance underlying the personal sector's pessimism. As figure 4.29 shows, Japan's headline unemployment rate has risen to more than four percent, while the ratio of job offers to job applicants, which fell beneath the 1:1 level in late 1992, reached an all-time low of 0.55 in June 1998. Most

The Case of Japan

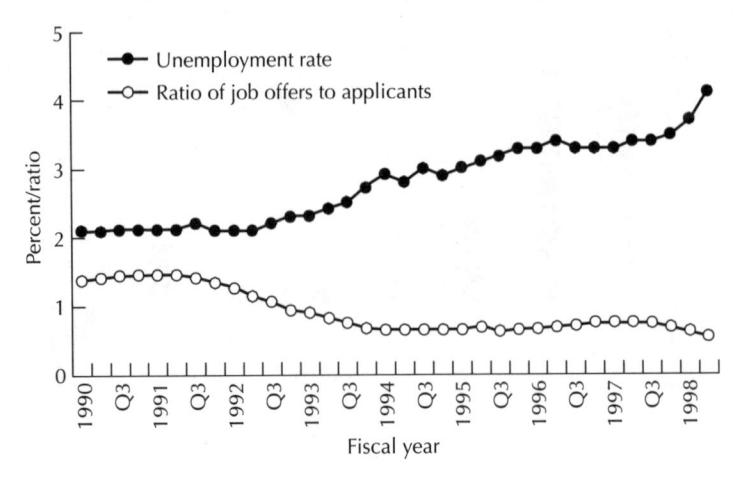

Figure 4.29: Key Unemployment Indices
(*Source:* BOJ Keizai Tōkei Geppō)

private sector economists were expecting Japanese unemployment to exceed five percent by the end of 1998, and some predict rates in excess of ten percent in three-to-five years time.[68]

Breaking down the statistics yields two further observations. First, by age group, both younger (i.e. twenty-five to thirty-four year-olds) and older workers (i.e. over sixty-fives) have been particularly hard hit, with the middle-aged (i.e. forty-five to fifty-fives) also recording rates persistently above average (figure 4.30).[69] And here the young and old are thought to be substantially under-represented in official statistics because many of their members do not apply for compensation out of procedural ignorance, anticipation that they will be able to find a job soon, and social stigma.

Second, there has been a general rise in the proportion of involuntarily versus voluntarily unemployed persons from 1992, as one would expect in a Recession. However, breaking down the proportions shows that a consistently large proportion of employees are resigning on a voluntary basis to look for new work (figure 4.31). This can be explained partially as a manifestation of workers being indirectly 'encouraged' to leave struggling firms before they are forcibly pushed, and partially as a result of institutional changes in the labour market (see below).

An important indicator of institutional change is changing employee attitudes to traditional labour market structures such as seniority pay and lifetime (or, at least, long-term) employment (Nihon Keizai Chōsa Kyōgikai 1997). Recent surveys have found that approximately three-quarters of employees are skeptical about the wisdom of Japanese firms continuing with seniority wages and broadly approve of a shift to performance-based

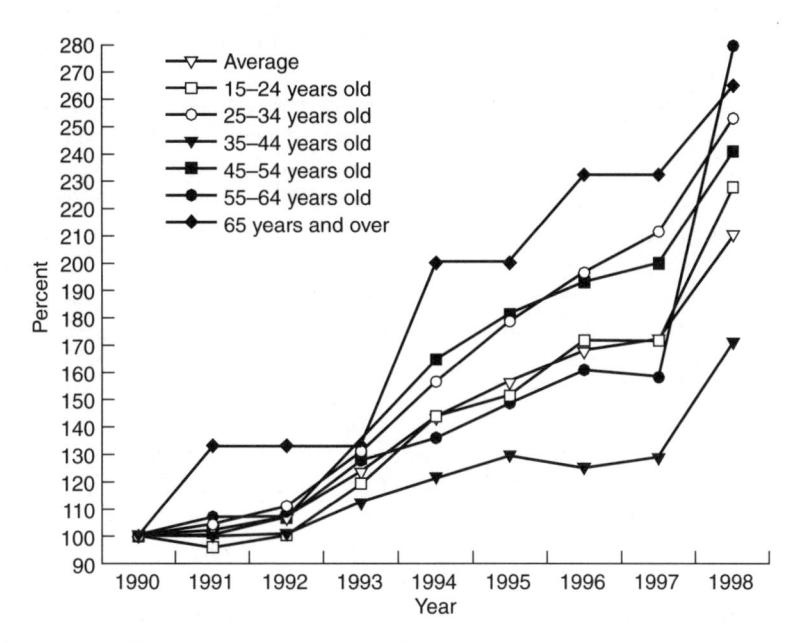

Societal Implications of a 'Gradualist' Approach

Figure 4.30: Changes in Unemployment by Age Group (1990 = 100)
(*Source*: MCA Rōdōryoku Chōsa)

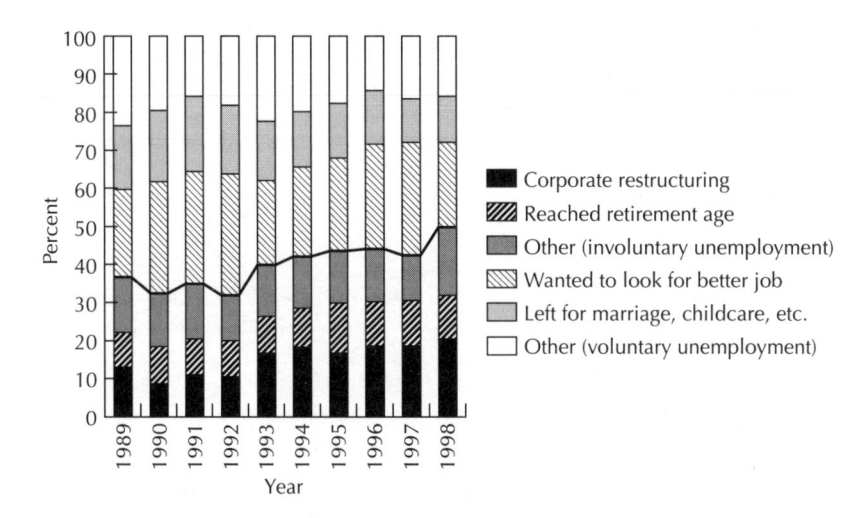

Figure 4.31: Unemployed Persons by Reason for Redundancy
(*Source*: MCA Rōdōryoku Chōsa)

compensation.[70] Accordingly, an increasing number are beginning to prepare themselves for such changes by studying at home, enrolling in evening classes.[71]

Related, too, is the trend towards more short-term and/or part-time work, which figure 4.32 demonstrates. Temping agencies report that a large proportion of their employees quit their previous jobs voluntarily in search for more freedom and autonomy to develop their careers. They also note that the fastest growing group of recruits in their industry are single men in their twenties (*JT* 24/9/97).

While increasing levels of polarisation in Japan's household sector are hinted at in recent incomes and unemployment statistics, they are emphasised most starkly by personal bankruptcy data. Figure 4.33 shows that personal bankruptcies rose in from just over 10,000 in 1990, to exceed 50,000 in 1996 for the first time ever. Based on an extrapolation of the figures for the first half of 1998, applications to the Supreme Court were expected to be close to 100,000, nearly ten times 1990 levels (*Nikkei* 15/7/98).

Within the above figures, two categories of personal bankruptcy stand out as new and, therefore, particularly notable. The first are those related to credit cards, which rose substantially in the early 1990s and affect mainly young people. The second are those related to mortgage defaults, many of which involved 'step-up' mortgages (in which repayments are increased every five years in line with presumed rises in the debtors' income) which were sold by non-bank lenders in the late 1980s.[72] A temporary hot-line service set up by the Judicial Scriveners Association in Ōsaka found that it takes an average of four years for people to become

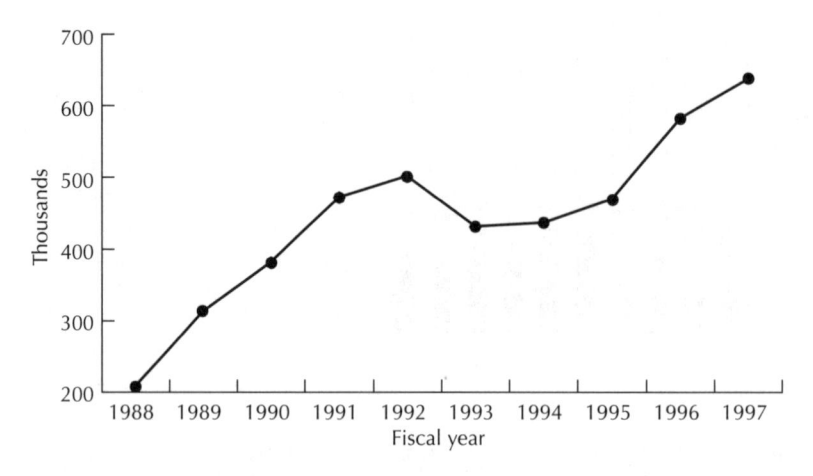

Figure 4.32: Temporary Staff Registered with Agencies
(*Source*: MCA Shûgyō Kōzō Kihon Chōsa)

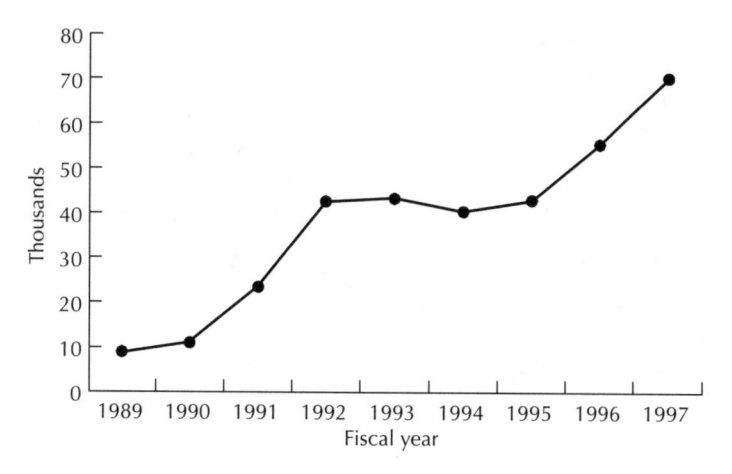

Societal Implications of a 'Gradualist' Approach

Figure 4.33: Personal Bankruptcies
(*Source*: Supreme Court Shihō Tōkei Nenpō)

ensnared in a vicious circle of debt. Many of their calls came from blue-collar workers who had seen reductions in their bonuses and overtime from the Recession and had turned to consumer finance companies to cover their mortgage repayments as falling house prices left them with negative equity.[73] The number of suicides which can be directly related to economic problems has also increased by a factor of three so far duing the Recession (*Nikkei* 12/6/98).[74]

(iii) Household saving and investment

The changes in income and employment noted above have had a direct impact on the savings and investment behaviour of Japanese households. To demonstrate this, it is useful to begin by putting contemporary trends in historical perspective. The country's stock of personal financial assets grew rapidly in the postwar period, surpassing 100 percent of GDP in 1970 and 200 percent in 1986, and amounted to ¥1,239 trillion at the end of fiscal 1997 (*Nikkei* 2/7/98).

The year-on-year growth in personal assets has mapped out a falling trend over time, reflecting slowing GDP growth rates and rises in consumers' propensity to consume. Yet while it is natural for a maturing economy with an aging population to experience a falling savings rate, figure 4.35 shows how the effects of the Recession have interfered with this process in Japan.[75]

Comparing national trends in the allocation of personal financial assets sheds light on the ways in which Japan moved increasingly out of line with global trends in the 1990s. Figures 4.36 to 4.38 show that Japanese

The Case of Japan

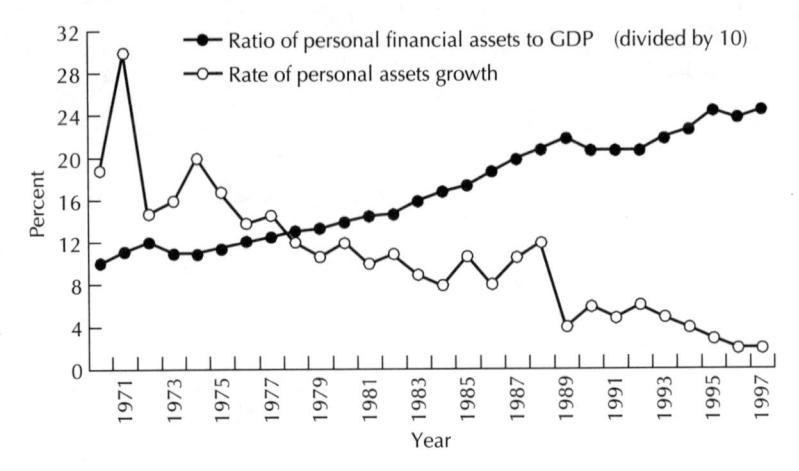

Figure 4.34: Personal Financial Asset Growth and Ratio to GDP
(*Source: Kinyû Jyânaru* 10/97, p. 79)

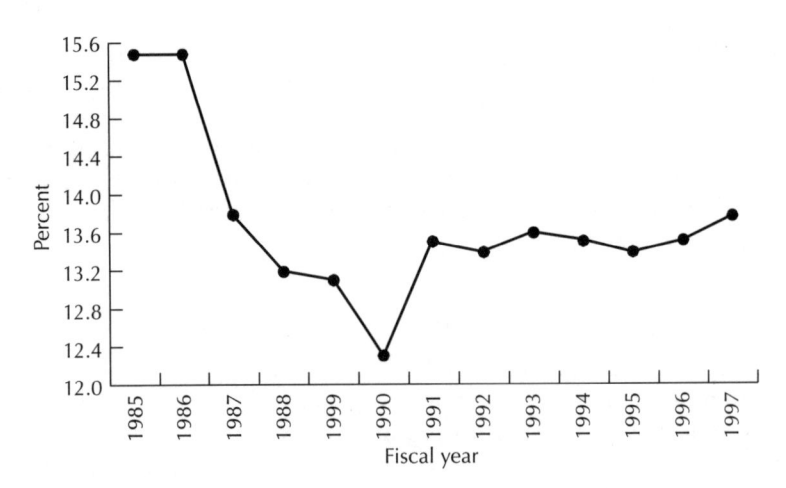

Figure 4.35: Average Household Savings Rate
(*Source:* BOJ Kokusai Hikaku Tōkei)

households are unique in their continually high allocation of savings to bank deposits, and in their declining interest in securities investment.

The reason for Japanese households' high and increasing preference for low-risk assets, in opposition to the dominant global trend towards higher-risk assets, is attributable to (i) the narrow choice of investment opportunities, and, (ii) the effects of the Bubble and subsequent Recession upon investor confidence. Moreover, with the slightly higher rates of interest on deposits paid, and with increasing anxiety concerning potential private

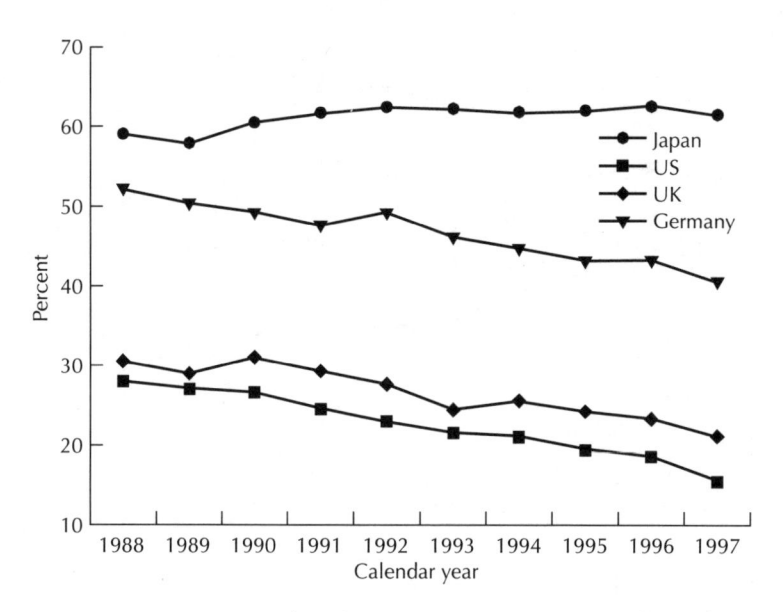

Societal Implications of a 'Gradualist' Approach

Figure 4.36: Currency and Bank Deposits as a Percentage of Personal Assets

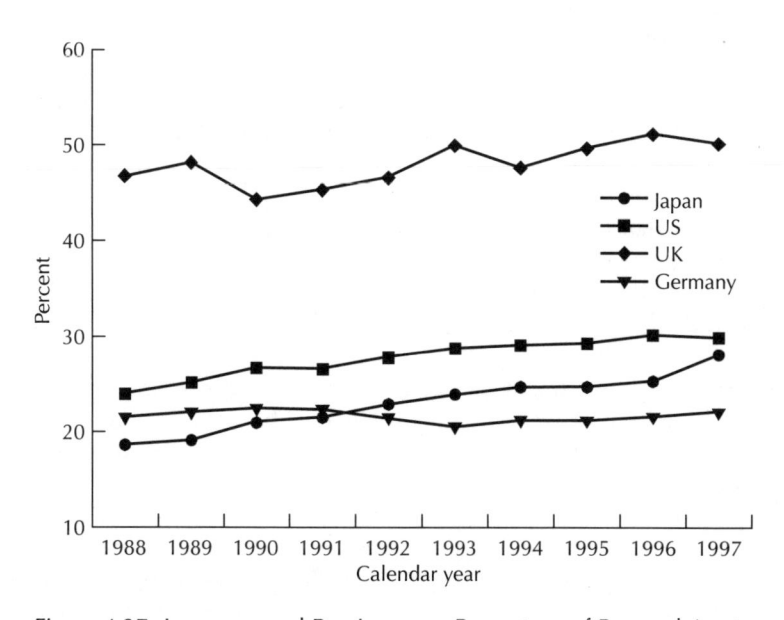

Figure 4.37: Insurance and Pensions as a Percentage of Personal Assets

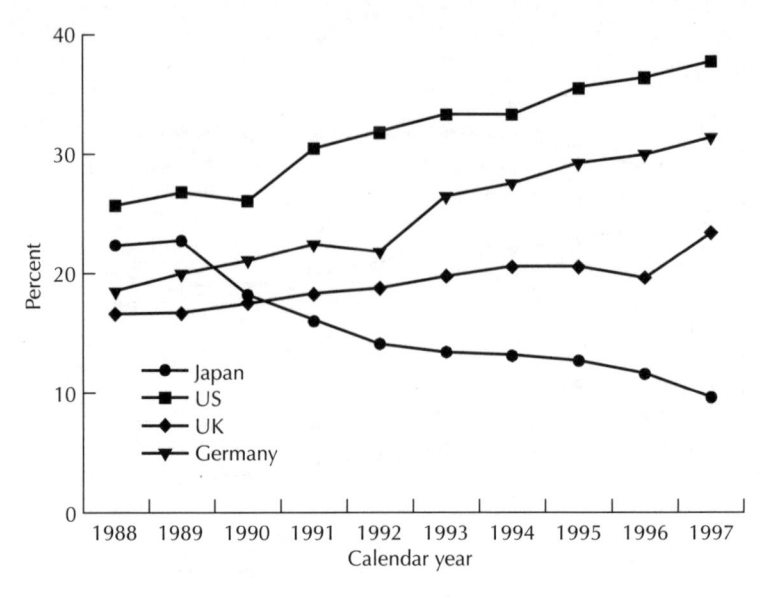

Figure 4.38: Securities Holdings as a Percentage of Personal Assets
(*Source*: BOJ Kokusai Hikaku Tōkei)

sector bank failures, it was almost inevitable that the Post Office was the major beneficiary of this trend.

In terms of future trends, a comparative 1997 Ministry of Posts and Telecommunications (MPT) survey of 2,200 adults in Japan and the US (reply rates of 69.1% and 68.5% respectively) conducted shortly after the Big Bang was announced found evidence that these differences in investment behaviour of showed no signs of abating in the near future. Figure 4.40 shows that while a similar proportion of Japanese and American households recognised that financial liberalisation would make their investment decisions more complex, the former were much more pessimistic and agnostic than the latter about what financial liberalisation would mean for them.

In terms of future investment decisions, figures 4.41 and 4.42 show the differences to have been equally large, with Japanese households adamantly intending to prioritise safety and, hereby, bank deposits, insurance products and pensions.

Two central aims of Big Bang were to reinvigorate the country's stock market and to provide better returns on Japan's massive stock of personal assets.[76] At present, the overwhelming effects of the Recession appear to be mitigating such changes, but as Chapter 2 (section 2.3) indicated, Big Bang was formulated as a long-term policy to bring the structure of the Japanese economy into line with global norms.

Societal Implications of a 'Gradualist' Approach

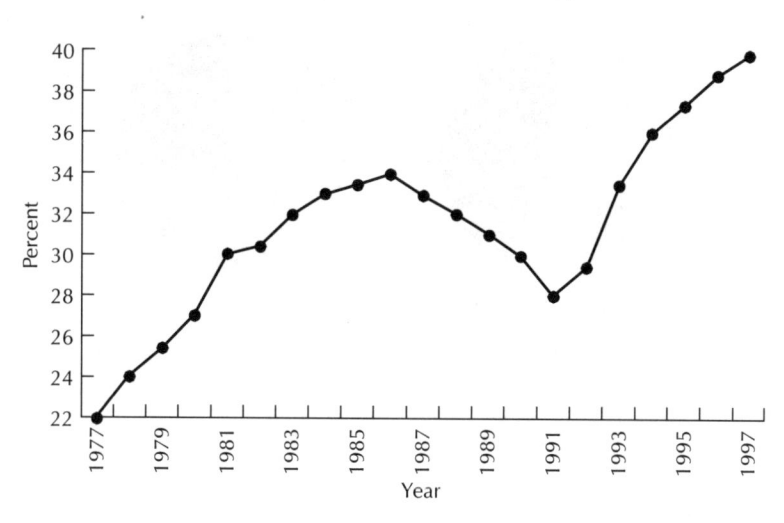

Figure 4.39: Balance of Postal Deposits to Total Cash and Bank Deposits
(*Source:* NKS 1997, p. 74)

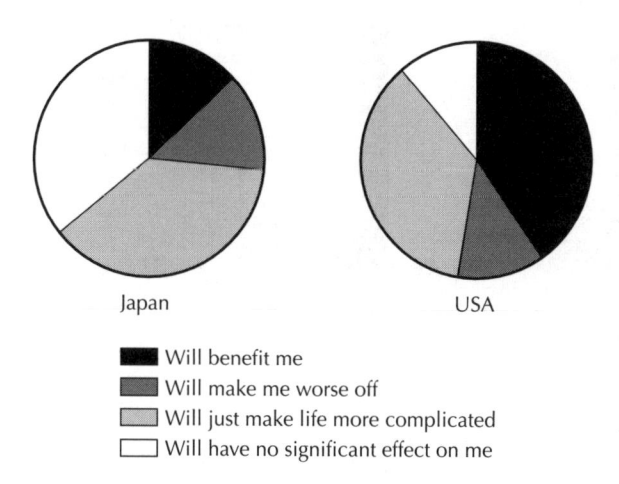

■ Will benefit me
■ Will make me worse off
▨ Will just make life more complicated
□ Will have no significant effect on me

Figure 4.40: What Do You Expect from Financial Liberalisation?
(*Source:* MPT)

4.3 CASE STUDY: THE SOCIETAL IMPLICATIONS OF BIG BANG

In the Big Bang, Japan's policymakers promised financial service users a new environment of expanded choice, lower costs and greater convenience. The issue was presented as one of maturity and self-responsibility: i.e. the government recognised that its overly protective and restrictive approach to financial regulation has become outdated, and that individuals should be

The Case of Japan

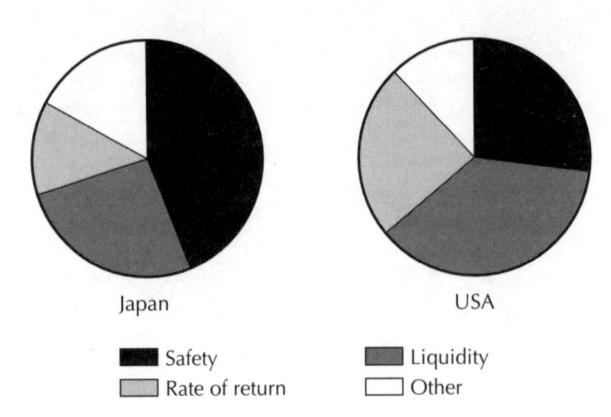

Figure 4.41: Which Characteristic will you Prioritise when Investing?

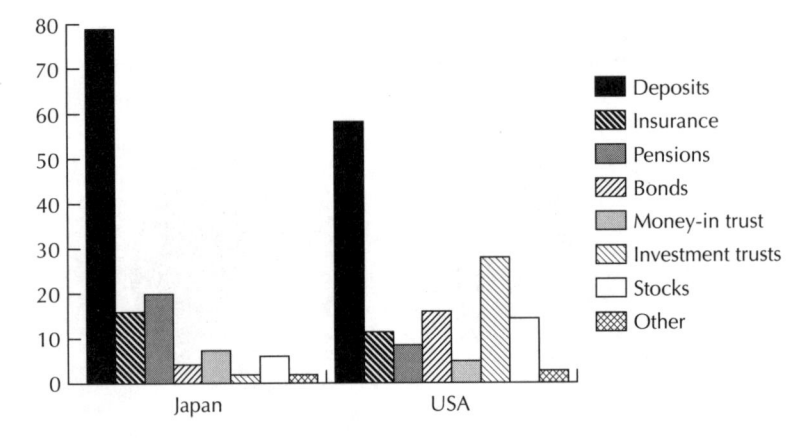

Figure 4.42: Which Products do you Intend to Invest in?
(*Source:* MPT)

allowed to make their own choices and freely reap the benefits/consequences of their actions. Protection had been made synonymous with discrimination, and deregulation with emancipation.

This section proceeds with a systematic analysis of the distribution of benefits which can be expected from new financial products and services associated with Big Bang, and concludes by drawing together these findings as general societal implications.[77]

A Survey of Twenty-five Key New Products and Services

Of the myriad new financial products and services which Big Bang is likely to usher in either directly, through deregulation, or indirectly, via increased competition, twenty-five examples can be selected as a representative core of new changes associated with Big Bang.[78] This subsection briefly describes each and comments upon their likely consequences for corporates and households.

1. Foreign exchange deregulation

As the centrepiece of Big Bang, Japan's foreign exchange business was fully deregulated in one sweep in April 1998. Hitherto, the over-the-counter cost of conducting a foreign exchange transactions was relatively high – about three yen per one US dollar, or 2.5 percent if $1 equals ¥120.[79] However, with commissions liberalisation, heightened competition between banks was expected to lead to lower charges and better services for small- and large-lot transactions. The parts of society which should benefit particularly from this are firms engaged in the export or import business, individuals who travel, shop, and/or send money abroad frequently (e.g. the parents of students studying abroad), and the wealthy, for whom overseas investment will be an increasingly attractive option (see below).

The other notable aspect of foreign exchange deregulation concerns user convenience. Much was made of the fact that the business would be opened to non-banks, and hence foreign exchange transactions would become possible at virtually any convenience store or other retail establishment. Following a handful of feasibility studies, Bic Camera (a discount electronics store chain) and the AM–PM convenience store franchise are the only notable new entrants, although the latter is currently only selling fixed quantities of US dollars. It seems that the cost of acquiring the necessary expertise, the large up-front investment in settlement systems technology, and security concerns about accepting fake bills proved to be insurmountable barriers to the majority of potential entrants (*Nikkei Manê* 12/97; *Nikkei* 2/4/98). As a result, user convenience was expected to be increased only marginally.

2. General Securities Accounts

General Securities Accounts (GSAs), known in the US as Cash Management Accounts (CMAs), were partially legalised in Japan in October 1997. They are deposit accounts operated by securities companies, which function in exactly the same way as ordinary bank accounts but pay a floating and potentially much higher rate of interest. Funds collected are invested in bond and money market products of varying liquidity, such that the depositor's principal investment can be guaranteed. Checks can be drawn or bills payed from the account so long as an outstanding balance above a set level is maintained. By February 1998, all of the Big Four (now Big Three) had launched GSAs.[80] Initially, none could have salaries paid directly into them, but they did pay higher rates of return than deposit accounts, and analysts predicted that rates of return would be bid up further with competition from new entrants. In contrast to bank accounts, no transactions (*furikomi*) charges are levied for paying pills or transferring money, but commissions are charged on each new investment made. It was expected to be late 1998 before GSAs would provide a good substitute for bank accounts, partly because securities firms were still in the process of establishing payment system tie-ups with various banks, the Post Office, and credit card companies (see Chapter 3).[81]

Analysts believe that GSAs will suit investors who wish to conduct regular low-risk, low-return investment transactions. But, while most Japanese fit this simple profile, relatively stringent qualification requirements relating to savings and/or income levels were expected to limit such benefits to wealthier segments of the population (*Nikkei Manê* 12/97).

3. Hi-tech deposit accounts

To compensate for a possible loss in business to securities firms offering close substitutes for deposit accounts such as GSAs, banks have been allowed to offer innovative hi-tech deposit accounts. They have been able to take advantage of the MOF's administrative deregulation of derivatives used in products targeted at individual investors (see below) to market deposit accounts which invest in high-risk, high-return products.[82] For example, Sakura Bank introduced a Hybrid Fixed-term Foreign Currency Deposit Account, which used options to hedge foreign exchange risk; Aomori Bank set up a popular Lucky Zone Account, which invested in US financial products and had promised a higher rate of interest if the yen-dollar rate stayed between ¥113 and ¥128 to the dollar between November 1997 and mid-February 1998 (– it did not); and the Bank of Tokyo-Mitsubishi launched its Premier and Safe Accounts, both of which used options to hedge interest rate risk. Other variations, such as deposit accounts using equity swaps to link their interest rates to stock market indices such as the Nikkei 225, were expected to debut soon. Nevertheless, as with GSAs, it was only the wealthier sectors of society which will be in a position to benefit from such innovations because of substantial income/savings and minimum deposit requirements (*Nikkei Manê* 12/97).[83]

4. Overseas accounts

Yen-denominated overseas bank accounts were legalised in April 1998. Hitherto, Japanese citizens could only hold overseas bank accounts denominated in foreign currencies if they proved to the MOF that they had more than ¥200 million to invest abroad. The change in the law was expected to benefit individual investors in so far as such accounts would provide access to higher returns on assets and tax/capital gains exemption from Japanese law.[84]

For investors who go through domestic institutions, the reality was that minimum deposits of several million yen would continue to be necessary.[85] Theoretically, ordinary citizens could open an overseas account with a foreign institution directly by telephone, fax, or email. Nevertheless, practical barriers such as having to conduct the application and transactions procedures in a foreign language and general unfamiliarity with foreign retail banking practices appeared likely to preclude the average Japanese citizen from making much of this (*Nikkei Manê* 12/97).

5. Small-lot investment funds

Investment funds provide a comparatively safe way of investing in securities because of their risk-pooling functions. They come in a variety of forms, most guaranteeing the principal investment, and return on average four percent per year by using derivatives to hedge high-risk investments. To date, most funds had been targeted at institutional investors, but this was changing under Big Bang. By late 1997, minimum investment lots had fallen to ¥5 million and were expected to fall eventually to around ¥100,000. So-called 'spot-type funds', which run for a comparatively short period (i.e. five years) already had become popular with individual investors and were drawing savings away from fixed deposits until the financial instability of late 1997 put a temporary cap on their expansion.[86] Hereby, savvy and reasonably wealthy investors were expected to be able to substantially increase their return on assets by exploiting such products (*Nikkei Manê* 12/97).

6. Derivatives

Big Bang is slated to effect the complete liberalisation of derivatives, and this should lead to a proliferation of new investment vehicles since derivatives are a central element of many hi-tech financial instruments. In July 1998, over-the-counter sales of derivatives on a whole range of products – including stocks, bonds, interest rates, currencies and stock indices – were legalised. In time, this was expected to increase investment options by allowing products to be customised to customer needs. However, a crucial proviso was that the customised attachment of derivatives would add hugely to the cost of products, particularly if they were intended cover more than one contingency. Individual investors would need to be at least as well informed about the possibilities of future market developments as professional investors to make good use of them. As this was unlikely, the development was unlikely to be of much significance in itself. The corporate sector, however, was much more likely to benefit in so far specific contingencies which affect their business could be insured against more easily (*Nikkei Manê* 12/97).

7. Individual stock options

Sales of options on the top twenty stocks sold on the TSE and OSE began in July 1997, and were expected to be expanded to cover about 200 stocks in the near future. Hitherto, options sold in Japan were only available on the Nikkei 225 and Topix Indices, but were so expensive that they were only bought by institutional investors. Individual stock options, however, should prove much cheaper, and provide investors interested in pursuing high-risk strategies with an opportunity to make large speculative gains. Nevertheless, because they are extremely difficult to price, individual investors interested in long-term investment gains would be unlikely to find that such products make a big contribution to their portfolios (*Nikkei Manê* 12/97).

8. 'Wrap-around' Accounts

So called wrap-around accounts were pioneered by securities companies in the US after stock investment trusts were liberalised in 1975, and proved immensely popular during the 1980s. Essentially deposit accounts geared for securities investment, wrap accounts combine personal brokerage and portfolio management services with access to professional advice and research. Account holders select the type of investment strategy which they want to pursue, and then hand everything over to an investment manager, making strategic adjustments only periodically. For their part, brokers make a service charge (typically one-to-two percent of assets invested) which covers all transaction fees, and hereby the incentive for brokers to 'churn' clients' accounts for extra commissions is eliminated because the management fee is tied to the performance of the client's portfolio. The closest equivalent to wrap accounts in Japan has been trust banking services, which were the preserve of the corporate sector and very rich (i.e. individuals with more than ¥1–2 billion to invest).[87]

In the US there are two main types of wrap accounts: investment trust accounts and investment advice accounts.[88] In Japan, the first type was liberalised in April 1998, and the second will be liberalised from April 1999. Nikko Securities began such services in 1998 for customers with a minimum of ¥3–5 million to invest, and Yamaichi had indicated that it would start with a minimum requirement of only ¥1 million. Generally, analysts believed that those wishing to open investment advisor-type accounts would need to make an initial financial commitment of at least ¥10–20 million. Nevertheless, wrap accounts were expected to be popular with people who wish actively to manage a large pool of savings and those with high salaries who want to invest aggressively for several years prior to retirement (*Nikkei Manê* 12/97; Nikkei 24/7/98).

9. Private banking

Initially popularised by the Swiss, private banking services are personalised cash management and trust banking-type services marketed to wealthy individuals. As such services entail large margins, more and more financial institutions in Japan have been launching such services, with the result that private banking is moving down the income scale. The emerging consensus on minimum personal assets necessary for the service to be profitable was around ¥100 million, and some 600,000 Japanese currently fit this profile. Sumitomo Bank began marketing private banking services to its 6,000 customers with more than ¥100 million in financial assets or ¥300 million in real estate, and Sakura to individuals with more than ¥50 million in financial assets; Asahi Bank chose to target individual business owners and executives; and Daiwa Bank was pursuing telephone and internet-based route into the industry. Following the lead of Citibank, Fuji and Sumitomo both began issuing international cash cards to private banking clients in November 1997.[89] The implication was that for those with substantial sums to invest, the services available were improving dramatically (*Nikkei Manê* 12/97; *FEER* 30/4/98; *Nikkei* 21/8/98; 7/9/98).

10. Discount brokerage services

With brokerage commissions set to be fully liberalised in 1999, intense price competition was expected to transform the lower end of Japan's securities industry. The proliferation of 'discount houses', which offer execution only services (i.e. no access to in-house advice or research) was a notable feature of markets like the US, where more than 100 discount houses such as Charles Schwab have risen rapidly to occupy more than ten percent of the entire market – some offering commissions fees fifty percent lower than those of full-service brokerages like Merrill Lynch. Firms operating over the internet have begun offering to execute single transactions for as little as $10, so if it usually costs ¥10,000 to execute a single ¥1 million trade, savings of up to ninety percent have become possible. In Japan, one domestic brokerage announced that it would cut commissions by up to fifty percent,[90] others were in the process of launching discount operations,[91] some of which are internet-based;[92] and new competition was expected from non-financial firms (see number 23 below).

As a result, transactions costs were tumbling for individual investors active in the securities market. However, for less well informed small investors who still wished to have access to full-services, it was likely that commissions could even go back up somewhat as a result of liberalisation, as they did in the US and UK (*Nikkei Manê* 12/97; Nikkei 4/2/98;). Commissions on larger trades (i.e. over ¥1 billion) were liberalised in 1994, and those on medium-sized trades (i.e. ¥50 million to ¥1 billion) were liberalised in April 1998. As a result, commissions for full-service brokerage have fallen by up to forty percent. The major beneficiary of this development (outside of the financial sector) has been the corporate sector in so far as firms have excess funds to invest in the stock market.

11. Electronic money

The term 'electronic money', or 'e-money', refers new ways of storing and transferring money digitally, using either networked computer systems or 'electronic purse' -type devices which may vary from prepaid telephone-type cards loaded with financial credits to 'smart' integrated circuit (IC) cards which can be used to transfer money to similar cards away from expensive computer hardware. Various competing e-money trials have been underway in Japan since January 1998, including debit and IC cards and virtual (i.e. internet-based) schemes.[93]

While it would be dangerous to underestimate the long-term impact of such inventions, analysts note that as with credit cards, applicants for all but the most simple IC cards are likely to have to meet certain asset/earnings and credit history requirements, and network operators will levy registration/user fees. Substantial investments in new computer hardware may also be necessary for those who wish to re-charge IC cards remotely (e.g. via the internet) or conduct transactions with other individuals. This suggests that while electronic money at its most basic could be open to everyone, its more advanced forms would incorporate formal and informal barriers which exclude certain sectors of the population from participation on the basis of wealth and technological grasp. For their part, high transaction and hardware investment costs initially deterred many potential retail users, with most preferring to wait for one or two formats to emerge as dominant before allocating limited counter space to more than a couple of systems (*Nikkei Manê* 12/97; *Nikkei* 2/9/98; 17/7/98; 30/7/98).[94]

12. Unlisted stock and venture capital investment funds

The Japan Securities Dealers Association (JSDA) lifted its ban on the public sale of unlisted securities in July 1997 in an effort to stimulate the development of a venture capital market in Japan. Elsewhere, it is common for unlisted stocks to be issued by new start-up companies, yet due to their notorious volatility, they had been banned in Japan in an effort to protect individual investors who might be attracted by the potentially high returns offered but be incapable of evaluating the risks of prospective investment.[95] However, large financial institutions can fulfil an analysis and risk pooling function in offering professionally managed venture capital investment funds, many of which specialise in a specific market sector (e.g. biotechnology), to individual investors. As of the beginning of 1998, all of the Big Three securities companies, as well as several smaller ones and a few specialist start-up brokerages, had begun marketing such funds.

For informed investors who are interested in purchasing relatively risky but potentially high return products, unlisted stock funds would constitute an attractive option. The minimum necessary investment from individuals is similar to that of investment trusts (see number 14), but since intermediaries will certainly not guarantee the investor's principal investment, such funds are viewed appropriate only as one part of a large, well-diversified portfolio. Of course, for new businesses in hi-tech sectors, such funds should prove beneficial as sources of funding to the extent that they are popular with investors (*Nikkei Manê* 12/97).

13. Deregulation of specific injury and illness insurance sales

Hitherto, only small and medium-sized domestic nonlife insurers were allowed to sell specific injury and illness insurance policies (e.g. cancer insurance); large domestic and foreign insurers could only cover these with general medical insurance policies (see Chapter 2, section 2.2 p. 133). However, this area was to be liberalised as a 'third-sector' issue from 2001, and should eventually lead to lower costs and more closely tailored insurance policies for individual and corporate consumers (*Nikkei Manê* 12/97).

14. Over-the-counter investment trusts

Known as mutual funds in the US, investment trusts (ITs) come in three basic types: stock ITs, bond ITs, and mixed ITs. They had been the exclusive preserve of securities companies and, more recently, trust banks. However, starting from December 1997, IT sales by ordinary banks were partially liberalised as the first major step towards their complete deregulation. Specifically, over-the-counter sales of ITs *through* ordinary banks were legalised, and from December 1998 banks were able to market their own versions of the products. This move was seen to be one of the most significant of Big Bang as the proportion of personal assets currently invested in ITs was relatively low: i.e. 2.7 percent as of fiscal 1997, in contrast to 6.3 percent in the US. It is rare for ITs to guarantee the principal sum invested, nor do they promise a specific rate of return on investment. Thus, in anticipation of wide take-up by the general public, new consumer-protection legislation was passed in November 1997 mandating that vendors provide clients with written as well as verbal explanations of their products. The main concern among regulators was that customers may not be able to distinguish these funds, which do not guarantee the principal, from bank deposits, which do. A simple five-stage risk-return rating system is already widely used (RR1 representing a supposedly low risk, low return profile, and RR5 a high risk, high return profile), but government officials and financial planners were eager to stress the importance for consumers to take responsibility for their investment decisions in conducting their own research prior to purchase (see number 25 below).

In December 1997, four large banks (Sanwa, Fuji, Sumitomo, and LTCB) and two regional banks (Chiba and Yokohama) began IT sales on a trial basis at a limited number of branches in or close to Tokyo. However, all major banks have since introduced or were about to launch direct IT sales, many in conjunction with other domestic or foreign firms (see Chapter 3 section 3.3.1 [iv]).[96] With minimum investment lots of around ¥10 million, it seemed that a relatively large proportion of the population was likely to gain from IT deregulation, although it was the wealthier and best informed who were likely to benefit most. The corporate sector was also likely to benefit substantially in the long run from an the increasing volume of domestic savings flowing into the stock market.[97] (*Nikkei Manê* 12/97; *Nikkei* 23/3/97; 16/4/98; 13/7/98; 17/8/98).

15. Bank sales of straight corporate bonds

Ordinary bank-intermediated financing of industry in Japan had been limited to short-term financing (under three years), with longer-term financing (three-to-ten years) the exclusive preserve of the long-term credit banks. However, with the legalisation of financial holding companies in fiscal 1999, ordinary banks are to gain access to the long-term sector of the market, and the full removal of remaining barriers between ordinary and long-term credit banks is expected to follow shortly thereafter. In itself, this development will have no direct ramifications for individual savers/investors, but it may indirectly benefit them as more competition within the banking industry feeds through to better customer services and higher deposit rates. However, for the corporate sector, the increase in competition will have some impact in pushing up the cost of long-term borrowing (*Nikkei Manê* 12/97).

16. Foreign currency-denominated accounts and other products

As a result of Japan's continuing environment of ultra-low interest rates, foreign currency-denominated deposit accounts (which bear deposit rates akin to those prevailing in the country of currency) and other foreign financial assets (which invariably afford higher returns because they must compete for funds against banks with higher deposit rates) appear to represent highly attractive investment opportunities. Following a recent surge in popularity for Citibank's foreign currency deposit accounts, the Bank of Tokyo-Mitsubishi launched a similar service at its head office in November 1997, help its customers open dollar accounts at its subsidiary in California. Other Japanese banks were in the process of arranging tie-ups with foreign banks to offer such services, and some were seeking to go a step further by linking such accounts to foreign investment products such as mutual funds.[98] In this regard, Kikuchi Takashi (financial sector analyst at LTCB) said that he expected between three to five percent of yen deposits to go overseas in the next three years, up from the current level of 0.4 percent (*JT* 1/1/98).

Here again, the potential benefits are greatest for those with most to invest, since various minimum income/asset qualification criteria apply to each product/service. On the whole, financial institutions apparently agree that it is not worth their effort to manage the international exposure of funds for small-lot individual investors – i.e. those with less than ¥100 million to invest (*Nikkei Manê* 12/97; *Nikkei* 4/2/98; 1/8/98).

17. Sub-divisible insurance policies

Historically, there was little variation in insurance premiums in Japan since rates were fixed by a central industry body. Essentially, this meant that low risk policyholders subsidised high-risk holders in almost all sectors of the market, but most obviously in the fields of household and car insurance. That is, home owners in typhoon-prone Okinawa paid similar damage insurance rates to those in under-populated rural Hokkaido, while middle-aged drivers in rural areas paid similar car insurance premiums to young drivers in urban areas. However, in June 1996, the MOF introduced a plus or minus ten percent band of flexibility for premiums, and following the US-Japan Insurance Talks of December 1996, agreement was reached on further undermining the universal premium structures for car insurance (from September 1997) and household insurance (from July 1998 – see also Chapter 2 section 2.2).[99] Car insurance premiums have been allowed to rise for eighteen year-olds by a factor of three over forty year-olds, and household insurance premiums are expected to fall in some areas by up to twenty-five percent for the average ¥100,000 premium. To date, only a few insurers have cut premiums significantly, but there are some signs of imminent change.[100]

Though some policies will go up in price, but most are expected to fall; all will become more complex. Representatives of Japanese insurers had argued that major social costs would be incurred as higher premiums for young drivers would lead to more uninsured vehicles on the road, but this does not appear to be happening. Deregulation in the non-life sector, moreover, is expected to produce knock-on effects for the life sector, and some minor changes were already slated for introduction in April 1999 (e.g. pay-as-you-go medical insurance policies which are heavily discounted for those who accept coverage for a smaller proportion of the total bill for treatment). Similar changes are afoot in the corporate insurance market, with major nonlife insurers poised to begin sales in autumn 1998 of damage insurance carrying flood damage waivers, which should lower premiums by two-to-five percent, and typhoon damage waivers, which should lower premiums by ten-to-fifteen percent (*Nikkei Manê* 12/97; *Nikkei* 16/8/98).

18. Shops accepting foreign currency

MacDonald's restaurants in Okinawa and boutiques in the New Kansai International Airport already accepted payment in US dollars, but from April 1998 it became technically possible for all retail establishments in Japan to accept payment in foreign currencies. In the runup to Big Bang, commentators made much of the novelty of this, but with the exception of the one or two convenience store chains which were likely accept small payments (i.e. up to $10) in US dollar bills (change to be given in yen), analysts expect few changes. In short, this may mean a marginal increase in convenience for returning overseas travellers, who will be able to get rid of surplus small denomination bills, but since the exchange rates provided were unlikely to be competitive, there will be few knock-on effects (*Nikkei Manê* 12/97).

19. Securitised financial products

Big Bang is paving the way for a greater securitization of assets in Japanese finance. Over time, analysts expect the securitization of bad loans backed by land, as well as car loans and mortgages to increase the liquidity of capital in the market and, thereby, enhance flexibility for corporate borrowers and investors. However, as individual investors do not have the capability (in terms of size or access to information) to participate directly in this market, they are likely to experience no immediate ramifications from the changes (*Nikkei Manê* 12/97).

20. Off-exchange trading of listed securities

The trading of large quantities of well-known listed securities off-exchange was liberalised in late 1998. The change promised large institutional investors advantages in terms of cost and speed over transactions routed through one of Japan's eight stock exchanges. Analysts believed that as information disclosure rules were strengthened in fiscal 1999 with the introduction of US-style accounting rules, the size of this market could increase substantially. However, most of the benefits would accrue to blue-chip borrowers and large corporate investors, with individuals benefiting only from spinoffs such as the development of internet trading systems (*Nikkei Manê* 12/97).

21. Corporate and private investment trusts

The MOF's general restriction limiting private group participation in investment trusts to no more than fifty persons was to be scrapped by the end of fiscal 1998 and was expected to provide a substantial boost to Japan's IT market in the form of corporately pooled funds. In the US it has been these types of ITs – so-called corporate mutual funds – as opposed to the type already in existence in Japan – contract ITs – that have provided most of the growth in the industry. Major firms such as Sony were already gearing up for this change, and there were signs of Japanese policymakers seeking to introduce tax-exempt 401(K)-type defined-contribution schemes to supplement current state *kōsei nenkin kikin* and *tekikaku* defined-payment schemes, over the coming years. Of course, such changes would indirectly benefit the household sector as much as the corporate sector, but in terms of concrete changes currently in the pipeline, it would be large corporations with independent pension schemes that become the main beneficiaries (*Nikkei Manê* 12/97; *Nikkei* 19/6/98).

22. 24-hour automatic teller machines (ATMs) and electronic banking

Commonly, banks in Japan have charged customers for the use of ATMs outside of banking hours, and most machines were not accessible between the hours of nine p.m. and seven a.m. or between Saturday afternoon and Monday morning. Moreover, although it was possible to conduct simple banking transactions via ATMs (e.g. paying cash into an account and transferring money electronically) typically these services were unavailable outside normal banking hours. As a result of increased competition under Big Bang, however, the country's banking environment has begun to change.[101] In May 1997, Tokyo Sōwa Bank (a regional bank) became the first Japanese bank to introduce 24-hour ATMs, and led by Sumitomo and Sanwa, city banks began to follow suit in 1998 (see Chapter 3 section 3.3.1). Telephone-banking services also started to appear in mid-1997, and now all major banks are in the process of launching telephone and PC-based banking services.[102] These are significant developments which are likely to benefit most of the population in one way or another, and similar improvements in services are beginning to emerge targeted at corporate customers, e.g. examples of remote payment/settlement systems (*Nikkei Manê* 12/97; *JT* 20/8/98).

23. Non-financial firms' entry into the financial services industry

As a result of deregulation associated with Big Bang, the MOF opened the financial services industry to nonfinancial firms by replacing the prior licensing requirement with a registration system. New entrants to date suggest that there are two major reasons for entry: in-sourcing functions to cut costs and the exploitation of established corporate brand-names. In the former category, major conglomerates such as Itōchû and Nisshō Iwai have established financial subsidiaries and/or tie-ups with domestic or foreign financial institutions in non-life insurance and securities trading. Here, their diversified structure and international network can provide them with a firm footing for competing in certain niche sectors with established financial institutions, but their operations are being initially focused on in-house needs. In the latter category, firms like Sony and Softbank have sought to capitalise upon their reputations for quality and innovation in selling to household and corporate investors.[103] While such developments are making a moderate impact on the nonfinancial corporate landscape, individual investors should benefit only to the extent that increased competition bids down prices/commissions and bids up general service levels (*Nikkei Manê* 12/97; *Nikkei* 31/7/98).

24. Investment clubs

In the US, investment clubs have a history of more than fifty years, with the National Association of Investment Clubs boasting a membership of 12,400 clubs (comprised of over 265,000 individual participants) which post average annual returns on investment of approximately twelve percent – a figure which compares favourably with professionally managed funds.[104] Following an initiative sponsored by JSDA in May 1996, the MOF gave the go-ahead for the establishment of investment clubs in Japan in July 1996.[105] At the end of 1997, about thirty such clubs had been established, and their numbers were expected to grow as a result of new interest in stock investments generated by Big Bang. Nevertheless, investment clubs are unlikely to have a significant impact upon the market. Due to the restricted scale of their operations,[106] and the fact that the recent proliferation of 'virtual' trading opportunities has provided an alternative outlets for interested parties,[107] such clubs are expected to perform a largely social role for a small number of dedicated investors (*Nikkei Manê* 12/97; *Nikkei* 22/4/97; 30/5/98).

25. Investment advisory and evaluation services

As is clear from the above survey, a proliferation of new products under Big Bang is creating a new era of increased financial complexity for Japanese corporations and households alike. The level of risk which investors in either sector can take in the pursuit of potentially larger profits or losses has risen commensurately. Large corporate investors and very wealthy individuals have access to many sources of professional research, but there is a limit to the information which smaller investors can access and absorb. These people are coming increasingly to rely upon three sources of advice to navigate their way through their new world: financial planners, credit rating agencies, and personal interest publications.

Financial planners have already seen a rise in demand for their services, particularly from individuals in upper-middle income brackets who do not have a firm grasp of, or interest in, current opportunities and appropriate investment strategies.[108] Credit rating agencies, which supposedly provide simple, easy to understand information on the current and future business outlook for stock and bond-issuing corporations and governments, saw the importance accorded to their ratings heighten dramatically since 1997 as investors increasingly rely upon them as a general guide to the *health* of potential investment opportunities. Here, though, there is good cause for concern as it is clear that many investors do not have a clear grasp of what the ratings actually imply. Some mistake them for a guide to *good* investment opportunities,[109] while others appear to react excessively to news of a downgrade, regardless of the type of rating change or accompanying rationale.[110] Finally, consumer finance publications anticipated a massive boom in business since they provide a concentrated and timely source of information for individual investors. As is typical for the print-media industry in Japan, the sheer volume of such publications (books and magazines) is immense. However, as this author's own research has found, the range in quality is broad, with the best necessitating a good grasp of the basics of personal finance before they would be of clear use (*Nikkei Manê* 12/97; *Nikkei* 31/8/98).

Societal Implications

Figure 4.43 provides a summary of the findings from the above survey of the benefits associated with each of the twenty-five key new products and services debuting under the Big Bang. By assigning simple values to the estimated impact of each change, a rough estimate of the relative inter-sectoral effects of Big Bang can be gauged. This suggests that the impact of Big Bang will be relatively evenly spread, with the corporate sector benefiting to a marginally greater extent.

At least as important, however, is the intra-sectoral distribution of benefits from Big Bang. The above discussion has noted already how formal and informal barriers of access to some products exclude large sections of the population on the basis of wealth, awareness/interest and technical grasp. In the corporate sector, moreover, stock-exchange listed firms and those with larger cash management needs are set to benefit disproportionately from the increasing proportion of personal assets flowing into the stock market and in terms of opportunities to make use of new products and services. Figure 4.44, which shows this in stylised form, highlights how most benefits are likely to accrue to the upper parts of each sector.

Large listed firms and very wealthy individuals are not likely to see their positions enhanced as much as their nearest smaller/less wealthy counterparts because their size and wealth has long given them access to such products and services in international markets even prior to domestic deregulation. Unlisted firms, which are generally small, and comparatively

The Case of Japan

	New product/service	Debut date	Intermediary	Corporate impact	Household impact
1.	Foreign exchange deregulation	4/98	Banks, retailers & travel agencies	3	2
2.	General securities accounts	10/97	Securities firms	1	2
3.	High-tech deposit accounts	Ongoing	Banks	1	2
4.	Overseas bank accounts	4/98	Foreign banks	1	1
5.	Small-lot investment funds	4/98	Banks & manufacturers	1	2
6.	Derivatives	Unspecified	Banks	2	1
7.	Individual stock options	7/97	Securities firms	1	1
8.	Wrap-around accounts	4/98	Securities firms	1	2
9.	Private banking	Ongoing	Banks & securities firms	1	2
10.	Discount brokerage services	Fiscal '98–'99	Securities firms	2	3
11.	Electronic money	Ongoing	Anyone	2	2
12.	Unlisted stocks & venture funds	7/97	Securities & investment firms	2	2
13.	Specific illness/injury insurance	Fiscal 2001	Life & non-life insurers	2	2
14.	OTC investment trusts	12/97; 12/98	Banks	3	3
15.	Straight corporate bond sales	Fiscal '99	Banks	3	1
16.	Foreign currency accounts	Ongoing	Banks, securities & investment firms	2	2
17.	Sub-divisible insurance policies	7/98; 9/99	Non-life insurers	3	3
18.	Shops accepting foreign currency	4/98	Retailers	1	1
19.	Securitised financial products	6/97	Banks, securities firms	2	1
20.	Off-exchange trading for listed stocks	Fall '98	Securities firms	2	1
21.	Corporate & private investment trusts	Fiscal '98	Banks, securities & investment firms	3	1
22.	24-hour ATMs & electronic banking	Ongoing	Banks, securities firms & insurers	3	3
23.	Miscellaneous financial services	Unspecified	Nonfinancial firms	2	1
24.	Investment clubs	7/96	Securities firms	1	1
25.	Advisory and evaluation services	Ongoing	Anyone	2	3
	Total			47	45

Figure 4.43: Impact of New Financial Products and Services by Sector (from 1 = low to 3 = high)

Societal Implications of a 'Gradualist' Approach

	Corporate Sector				Household Sector			
Benefit	Large listed	Med. listed	Small listed	Unlisted	Very rich	Upper-middle	Middle	Lower
More choice	2	3	2	1	2	3	2	1
Lower costs/prices	3	3	2	1	3	3	2	1
Better returns	3	3	2	1	3	3	2	1
Better service	2	3	3	2	2	3	3	2
Total	10	12	9	5	10	12	9	5

Figure 4.44: Distribution of Benefits from Big Bang (from 1 = low to 3 = high)

poor households are unlikely to experience many net benefits as a result of their low levels of participation in the financial system. Hereby, levels of polarisation are set to rise considerably as a result of Big Bang. It is these *relative* losses that will constitute the biggest societal cost.

Conclusion

Japan's macroeconomic performance in the 1990s has been sacrificed by the government's unconventional policy responses to financial globalisation. Its policy of attempting to shore up existing structures with traditional formulae has not worked, and the notion of 'not writing off Japan yet because it still has an abundance of personal financial assets and high quality human resources' (e.g. Ezra Vogel, *JT* 24/8/98) is losing its purchase.

In the corporate sector, manufacturing firms have been hit hardest by the Recession, but have also made best progress in restructuring to regain competitiveness. Non-manufacturing firms were sheltered to a much greater extent by the governments' 'emergency measures'; it is no coincidence that they have made less progress in restructuring. By size, very small firms, which tend to fall outside most statistical surveys, slipped through the government's safety net, which functioned mainly to delay, rather than aid, the competitive adjustment of small and medium-sized firms. Very large firms, which derived comparatively little benefit from the government's measures, were compelled to make rapid adjustments and, for the most part, were able to do so. Hereby, qualified evidence was found of longer-term institutional changes taking place in the corporate sector.

Within the household sector, government policy served again to alleviate the short-term effects of the Recession for the majority. A growing minority of the unemployed and the aged, however, received little protection. In the longer term, it appears that the household sector will still have to pay a substantial price for the government's policy choices throughout the Recession and the country's corresponding decline in competitiveness; this fact is not lost on most Japanese. Household savings and investment patterns attest to this in demonstrating how distortions in the financial sector have contributed to undermine confidence and the efficient functioning of the domestic economy. The express purpose of Big Bang was to rectifying the situation, but survey data indicate that the majority of households are not yet ready to change their established patterns of savings behaviour.

Finally, the study of twenty-five new financial products and services which are currently being introduced into Japan found considerable evidence that this new wave of financial deregulation will exaggerate Japan's currently low levels of social inequality by providing opportunities for increasing relative material well-being largely on the basis of existing levels of wealth and participation in the financial markets. This need not imply that Big Bang will be bad for Japan, since the alternative to pressing ahead with such reforms would be accelerating levels of relative, if not absolute, decline.

To the extent that Big Bang proceeds as planned, it will spur Japan's convergence on emerging global norms (see Chapter 1) as it redefines the role of the state in society. By giving financial institutions much freer reign to market new products, the government is backing away from its traditional role as the arbiter of 'distributive justice' and assuming a more modest role as the underwriter of 'economic justice'. As a result, the corporate sector will gradually find itself increasingly judged according to free-market (bottom-line) criteria, and consumers will come to terms with the new risks that they have to bear in return for new opportunities to exploit. Hereby, individualism will be no longer discouraged but actively promoted, and risk no longer centralised and nationalised but devolved and privatised. Thus, Japan's future should be seen to rest as much upon its citizen's embrace of these changes as upon the state's commitment to encouraging such a transition.

Part Three

Lessons for Global Theorists and 'Japanologists'

Conclusion

This book set out to test a sophisticated version of the financial globalisation thesis using recent developments in Japan as a case study. It began by adopting and defending a pluralist theoretical approach in order to capture as much as possible of the complex totality of the phenomena. Drawing upon a wide a range of established scholarship related explicitly or implicitly to globalisation, Chapter 1 proceeded to build up a nuanced version of the financial globalisation thesis. The result appeared both internally coherent and empirically sustainable, and thus represented a suitable prototype against which to evaluate the case of Japan.

Part Two of the book then surveyed related developments in Japan's regulatory, financial and social spheres, drawing upon a range of primary and secondary sources. The overall impression generated was that Japan is now at an advanced stage of formally abandoning many now idiosyncratic practices, and is converging on a market-oriented model which constitutes the emerging global standard. Nevertheless, it is clear that substantial differences remain which reflect strongly the legacy of preexisting institutions. Chapter 2 showed this in terms of policymakers promoting formal regulatory parity with leading developed states under Big Bang, yet simultaneously manipulating the administration of regulation in traditional ways to create a 'third way' forward. Nevertheless, Chapter 3 documented the implications of this in the financial sector, where most restructuring efforts currently undertaken by Japanese financial institutions are being judged by the market as less than adequate. Similarly, Chapter 4 investigated the broader societal effects of this Japanese approach, noting the growing macro- and microeconomic costs associated with trying to shore up Japan's existing system.

In the process of these explorations, Part One uncovered many reasons behind the impasse commonly reached in the globalisation debate, and Part Two highlighted particular institutional, ideological and practical rationales underlying Japan's record of qualified convergence. But separately understanding financial globalisation and making sense of contemporary developments in Japan's financial system is not enough. It is important to bring these two components together synergetically in order to say, first, what the Japanese experience tells us about financial globalisation and, second, what a nuanced version of the financial globalisation thesis reveals about Japan's current situation.

(i) What Does Japan Tell Us about Financial Globalisation?

Due to its legacy of heightened institutional differences, Japan sheds new light on the concept of financial globalisation. First and foremost, the case of Japan confirms the significance of financial globalisation as *the* major structural force now reshaping the Japanese financial system and engendering profound and far-reaching consequences which reverberate throughout the country's economic, political and social spheres. Herein, this book's empirical research attests resoundingly to the relevance of globalisation as a framework for describing and analysing contemporary changes in the world economy which affect states, firms and individuals regardless of their position in relation to the East/West civilisational divide. That is, globalisation is shown to be globally relevant, even if the concept originated in the West.

More specifically, Chapters 2 to 4 found evidence of the growing salience of global financial and knowledge structures, identified in Chapter 1, within Japanese society. On the domestic level, this is evident throughout society, in the growing gap between leading and lagging financial institutions, and in the polarisation of the corporate and household sectors of the economy that is being fed, at least partly, by developments in the financial sector. On the international level, it is apparent from the lead that frontrunning Western states and firms have extended over their Japanese counterparts as a result of the advantage which the former have had in establishing global benchmarks for financial deregulation/reregulation and innovation.

Second, a case study of Japan, nevertheless, exposes the limits of even what is currently considered to be a nuanced version of the concept of financial globalisation. It documented the way in which both the Japanese state and Japanese financial institutions have managed to avoid, and continue to do so to a great extent, capitulation to the forces of convergence associated with globalisation, whilst simultaneously retaining some degree of international competitiveness. In neither 'normalising' nor being totally marginalised, they demonstrate not only the fact that globalisation is not yet an all powerful force – which was something that a nuanced version of the globalisation book already acknowledged – but also that states and firms do not necessarily face an all-or-nothing choice between convergence or nonconvergence. This point may appear obvious, but is commonly misconceived.

For the sake of representational clarity, the convergence/nonconvergence debate tends to be portrayed as a choice between A or B, with more nuanced versions of the globalisation book positing the existence of a continuum between these two extremes. That is, states and firms locate at some point on the line and are rewarded by a particular payoff according to their actions relative to those of others. This is an extreme example of pseudoscientific reductionism which distorts reality in several ways.

One problem is the notion's implicit *ceteris paribus* assumption. The unidimensional picture emasculates the very issue of globalisation which it purports to represent – i.e. structural change. In reality, the whole background against which such a continuum rests would need to be moving, as institutional and technological development proceed constantly and unpredictably (but not randomly), and as all manner of social, political and economic happenings constantly affect the environment within which states and firms strive to approach the optimal institutional structure for their environment at any particular point in the future. As this case study shows, one of the difficulties of evaluating convergence/nonconvergence is the difficulty of judging whether gradual regulatory and institutional changes which appear to be in the direction of 'normalisation' constitute actual convergence, i.e. in *relative* terms.

Another problem, which is related to the first, is that imperfect information will inevitably hinder both states' and financial institutions' moves in the direction of convergence upon a more efficient institutional model as well as the markets' subsequent evaluation of any such moves. For this reason, choices made in reality proceed more on the basis of trial and error than by prior selection of some point on an imaginary continuum. A third problem, related to the second, is that of institutional fit. Institutional fit is likely to preclude not only radical changes in the short-term but will also complicate the viability of pick-and-mix approaches to engineering institutional change more generally. This was clear from the Japanese case, where both the state and private financial institutions came across as more than just 'unwilling' to converge fully on a universal (i.e. Western) model.

A final problem is that transactions costs clearly exist, will differ according to issues of institutional fit, and are likely to preclude movement towards an 'optimal' model for each state/firm beyond a certain point. Transaction costs will differ individually and corporately, and depend upon a myriad of contingencies at any particular point in time. Hence, while it is teleologically possible to posit a notion of convergence upon a single institutional model, the abilities of individual firms to identify and approach such a point will always differ in practice. Even in the long run, the notion of absolute convergence must, therefore, remain fictitious.

Similarly, as the abilities of individual states and firms to pursue convergence are imperfect and differ, so too do the capacities of individual commentators and the market to assess convergence. It is an elementary point that as convergence proceeds, it highlights existing differences in new ways in that it brings them into sharper contrast. Furthermore, at this point, states and firms often find it viable to reassert their differences in new ways according to strategies of competitive differentiation. This is why, for the time being at least, Japanese national institutional traits are taken to be in little danger of extinction. Financial globalisation, while extending and strengthening the regime of market rationality, can only be antithetical to diversity among core states and firms up to a particular point, although that point is indeterminate in advance. This is not to denigrate the usefulness of convergence as a descriptive or analytical device, nor to point out a specific flaw in more nuanced versions of globalisation theory – it should be recalled that in Chapter 1, the notion of *significant* convergence was stressed, rather than *absolute* convergence. If anything, this realisation emphasises a point which tends not to be made explicit in the literature, with the consequence that it is easily misconstrued by less than fastidious critics.

Accordingly, reiterating what is commonly interpreted as a structuralist observation about the continuing significance of institutions and highlighting the elementary flaws of scientific rationalism in no way confirms the incommensurability of diversity (Lasch 1995). The idea that all nonconformist state and corporate responses to globalisation will be able to continue coexisting in a harmonious state may be 'politically correct' and attractive to certain intellectual positions, but it is jejeune and wishful thinking. This book's case study of Japan has shown this beyond reasonable doubt by painstakingly documenting exactly how and why both the Japanese state and Japanese financial institutions are being compelled to 'normalise' in response to contemporary structural developments in the global financial sector.

Notwithstanding this, the Japanese example stresses that moves in the direction of convergence need not be absolute. In order to be considered successful any such moves must only suffice to convince the markets that they are significant steps in the right direction so as to attract/retain analysts' interest and, more importantly, investors money. Hereby, while it may not be possible to say even retrospectively whether the actions which a particular state or financial institution undertook in response to financial globalisation were *optimal*, given its particular circumstances and constraints, what is clear is whether the action taken was *satisfactory*, by the minimum criteria for adequacy, which is at least protecting that state/firm's current absolute position. Beyond this, scope remains for balancing interests and privileging certain outcomes according to local predispositions, although this will often engender a tradeoff in terms of relative performance.

In this context of 'satisfying' rather than optimising, the importance of political or corporate entrepreneurship becomes apparent. Informational asymmetries mean that the way in which change is marketed can be at least as important as the actual substance of any changes made. Hashimoto's stage management of organising and presenting Japan's Big Bang to the international financial community demonstrated his instinctive grasp of a strategy which the MOF had exploited masterfully for years. In promising radical change, and backing this up with apparently impressive legislative and administrative changes, Hashimoto bought time from the market for Japan. But while in this case, the substance of change has fallen sufficiently short for analysts to form a consensus, there is clearly a margin of leeway within which states and firms can benefit beyond the extent of changes actually made, and vice versa. This fact, that managing convergence is more of an art than a science, is another element which was missing from the theoretical literature.

In one other area the Japanese experience did not fit neatly with the major tenets of the financial globalisation thesis. Japan's example provides little support for the idea of power leaking downwards and upwards to new heightened degrees, since the locus of important decisions still seems to be intensely concentrated at the level of the state by virtue of nothing more than its central position in society. As for the notion of power leaking downward, a striking impression is of the great extent to which Japanese financial institutions continue to depend upon the protection of the state. Where national financial institutions are globally competitive, financial deregulation strengthens their hand at the expense of the state, but where they are not competitive, deregulation, conversely, strengthens the position of the state as a potential source of shelter.

There is also little evidence of power increasingly leaking upward in so far as the participation in international fora having brought Japan closer into line with global regulatory norms. Any evidence which did exist was episodic and related mainly to superficial legal amendments. In this respect, it seems that an acutely nationalist ideology, fortified by the nation's proud economic achievements of the postwar period, has provided an enduring sense of 'Japaneseness' which has thus far precluded the development of preferential transnational epistemic identities. Hereby, the Japanese case underlines the fact that particular national institutional and ideological structures can mitigate the development of some of globalisation's supposedly central symptoms.

Third, the case of Japan highlights some of the problems of empirical research applied to 'big' theoretical constructs such as globalisation. Most notable of these is the danger of falling into an arbitrary or predetermined interpretation of the data on the basis of a poorly defined or carelessly executed research agenda. It is clear that there is enormous scope for selectively appropriating and randomly interpreting the evidence relating to globalisation thanks to the sheer volume, diversity and elasticity of the data. Hence, the importance of an approach which makes use of as wide a variety of local and international sources as possible – from comparative and historical scholarship to journalism, and from qualitative professional opinion to quantitative economic data – and is cautious about extrapolating the conclusions drawn from its findings.

Using the 'dirty' complexity of reality to test the 'clean' abstraction of theory in this way is a necessarily laborious process. However, such an analysis – and representation – are essential to understanding the dynamics of large/contested issues in order to contribute to the scholarly enterprise in which theory should conform to reality which it purports to explain.

(ii) What Does Financial Globalisation Tell Us about Japan?

A sophisticated version of the financial globalisation thesis provides an unparalleled aid for understanding economic developments in contemporary Japan. First, it throws invaluable light upon Japan's current economic imbroglio. An awareness of the progression of globalisation as *the* major structural force fundamentally changing today's environment in which national economies and firms interact reveals why trying simply to buttress the country's existing economic structure and continue with a strategy of forbearance is inappropriate. By showing that much of the rise of Japanese financial institutions to global dominance in the 1980s was a mirage, and by documenting the rising economic costs of inefficiencies in the financial system – a structure which not only lies at the heart of the economy, but also represents a microcosm of Japan's problems more generally (from inefficient resource allocation to chronic overcapacity, and from intransparency to systemic corruption) – this book demonstrated the absurdity of claims which hold that the 'Japanese system' is fundamentally sound as it stands.[1] The slowdown in growth in the 1990s was more than a cyclical downturn, a manifestation of one or two problems in the political or financial system, or a result of the economy having outgrown its 'developmentalist' model (Murakami 1996). It related fundamentally to the fact that the Japanese model has become anachronous to its new global setting.

It follows that Japan must pursue domestic structural change more effectively, reforming key economic institutions such as the financial system and labour markets to promote better resource allocation and economic flexibility. The Big Bang and various administrative reforms pursued by Hashimoto are important steps in this direction, but have not yet effected sufficiently radical and rapid change to redress Japan's current problems. These reforms are in danger of being judged by the market as amounting to 'too little too late' as a result of the system's strong bent towards conservativism and compromise.

Of course, if Japanese citizens choose to prioritise the maintenance of social stability and the country's supposedly low levels of inequality by favouring this sort of gradualist approach, this is their perogative.[2] However, as the mounting costs of such a strategy become increasingly apparent, it is inevitable that newer and greater strategic amendments will become necessary. What is not clear at this moment is the size of the crisis which it will take to dislodge the present *status quo* or the degree of change which a new approach will incorporate.

Second, and related in so far as it underlies parts of the policy debate, is the fact that recognising how the structural forces associated with globalisation are affecting the Japanese state and Japanese financial institutions provides insight into the current representation of 'revisionist' versus 'traditional' approaches to Japanese studies. This is essentially a debate about Japanese uniqueness which has been elevated to the status of a benchmark dichotomy against which many believe it is possible to locate all recent social science-related work which deals with Japan (e.g. Williams 1996; Katz 1998; see also Chapter 2 section 2.2). The major problem with this schematic is its unacknowledged static representation, which a globalisation perspective reveals. This is best demonstrated in reference to a review article by Yamamura (1997), who explicitly links the revisionist debate to the issue of convergence, but skews the former because of his misunderstanding of the latter.

In his survey of contemporary opinion regarding Japanese politics and economics, Yamamura re-asserts that 'revisionist' approaches stress the social embeddedness of many uniquely Japanese institutions and the persistence of difference – 'formal and informal institutions exert strong homeostatic pressures making change "path dependent"' (p. 296) – while 'traditionalist' work emphasises the effect of market forces and modernisation in bringing about convergence by raising the costs of noncompliance (p. 295). Predictably, he 'finds' the revisionist camp to be colonised by area-studies specialists (mostly political scientists and sociologists) and the traditionalist camp to be dominated by neoliberal economists, although he is careful to point out that '[f]ew in Japan or elsewhere hold either view [i.e. convergence or nonconvergence] without qualification' (p. 295). He then places himself 'somewhere between the mid-point of the two genotype views and the nonconvergence view' (p. 325), i.e.

```
                                         Yamamura
                                               |
_____
convergence                                    nonconvergence
```

He justifies this by explaining that convergence entails a 'trade-off between efficiency and equity ... because any changes made in institutions to increase efficiency also affect the distribution of income, typically in favour of the holders of capital' (p. 328), due to imperfections in the trickle-down mechanism (p. 329). He goes on to explain,

> What about national preferences? Some economies choose to be far more competition-oriented than others for complex reasons of politics, history, and culture, while other economies opt, also for

complex reasons, to place more emphasis on equity today than on efficiency and equity in the unspecified future. Except neoclassical economists who still believe that institutions do not matter at all, most of us are for respecting national preferences. If the Japanese wish to overwork, so be it (p. 330).

Herein, we return to the very same problem encountered above in regard to common perceptions about convergence. Yamamura's alluring live-and-let-live attitude – which, incidentally, does not extend to neoclassical economists (see also his pot-shots on page 325) – is widely shared by area studies specialists (e.g. Streeten 1996), but this belies the fact that it offers no practical insight because it fails to address Japan's present impasse, which is largely the result of globalisation. That is, the existence of ongoing and increasingly fast-paced global structural change means that Japan does not face the option of making a one-time choice to locate at some point on this continuum. Yamamura's belief that Japan can chose a particular trade-off between efficiency and 'equality' fails to grasp that the costs of any such choice which does not at least ensure the ongoing viability of the Japanese system are rapidly becoming unsustainable. To the extent that he fails to recognise this dynamic condition, he warps Japan's current dilemma, because choosing to stand still will mean falling behind increasingly quickly, and not just relatively but absolutely, too.

What this says is that 'revisionists' must take on board some of the insights of 'traditionalists'. Neoclassical economists have long been berated for not taking sufficient account of the insights of area studies specialists, but Japan's current situation shows how the pendulum has now begun to swing in the other direction. Area studies specialists can forever seek refuge in micro data which will always 'prove' the endurance of difference and the limits of 'universal' macro laws, but the pointlessness of repeating this exercise unreflectively is now apparent. Globalisation provides an opportunity by which Japan specialists can take on board and benefit from the insights of others. This is a point which is relevant to all institutional theorists, be they political scientists or sociologists. It just appears more transparent in the case of Japanese studies because of the more explicit nature of the country's historical differences.

Third, and consequently, an awareness of the significance of globalisation as *the* major structural economic change of the late Twentieth Century necessitates that a global perspective should imbue all other contemporary social science-based Japan debates. This is not to propose that globalisation must overshadow all other areas of study. Rather, it is to observe that globalisation is the moving but often unacknowledged background against which other debates take place. Thus, as a critical component of Japan's contemporary architecture, globalisation must be embraced as central to many fields, for example, Japanese international relations, business studies, and welfare – all of which are linked in some way to the issue of national competitiveness. Since the background against which developments in each of these areas unfolds in the future will not be an approximately linear function of the past, the inherent sustainability of unique Japanese institutional structures cannot be assumed. As Chapter Two showed, the complex nature of financial policymaking is not amenable to unitary or ahistorical explanation.[3] Each change must be assessed individually – in its unique domestic social, political and bureaucratic context, bearing in mind emerging structural or systemic forces as well as external (international) ones.

This insight is relevant not only to Japan specialists, but should also be borne in mind by those who intend to use contemporary Japan for comparative purposes. In the past, it has been possible to ignore the impact global structural developments on narrowly defined issue-areas. Now it is not. This makes scholarship today all more difficult and complex, but the ramifications of ignoring this are infinitely more serious in that they threaten to render any scholarly 'findings' irrelevant or, worse, misleading.

(iii) Areas for Further Study

Finally, in terms of potentially fruitful areas for further study suggested by the findings of this book, three stand out as particularly important and/or interesting. The most obvious is the continued documentation and analysis of the political and economic situation in Japan. Only the events of the coming months and the next few years under the Big Bang will tell how accurate the analysis and conclusions drawn above have been. This will be of some interest in so far as deducing the extent to which this author's perspective has been skewed inadvertently by the events and prevailing consensus of opinion at the time of writing. More generally, however, it will contribute to our understanding of the convergence debate by confirming or giving cause for the modification of many of our rudimentary perceptions of the impact of financial globalisation in and on Japan.

Second, this book has made it clear that we still know very little about issues of institutional fit and change. With the rise in pressures for convergence now being felt strongly in Japan and elsewhere, this is obviously an area of enormous practical as well as theoretical significance. The above-proposed ongoing documentation of developments in Japan is one avenue which promises to shed more light on the limits of the Japanese system in this respect. Specifically, the next few years will provide ample opportunity for identifying the types of shock required to dislodge particular socially embedded institutions, determining whether and how easily such changes can be legislatively led, and analysing the way which in which newly adopted institutional structures are adapted and become embedded in an unfamiliar environment. Another avenue is to scour the broad range of existing case studies of financial deregulation in the hope of divining patterns and potential parallels concerning the way in which transitions from traditional to new institutional structures have been managed in the past and with what side-effects. A major object of this exercise would be to find out more about the options open to non-Anglo-American states seeking to work with, rather than against, the grain of the market.

Third, an extensive up-to-date research project comparing the experiences of Japan and various European states in financial deregulation would offer considerable insights into the extent to which the Japanese response to financial globalisation has proceeded in a distinctive and extraordinary manner. The common comparison made with leading Anglo-American states is natural in so far as it is these economies that tend to be more progressive in terms of pushing forward the boundaries of deregulation and financial innovation. However, such a comparison is not always apt in so far as it elevates the leaders' actions to the status of norms, and this automatically gives the (false) impression that the actions of laggards are outliers from a universal trend. The gradualist response to financial globalisation pursued by Japanese policymakers would appear to have clear parallels in, for example, the *dirigiste* record of the French state and the conservative nationalism of the German government.

Epilogue
Entering the Twenty-first Century: Beyond the Big Bang

Philip Cerny, Glenn Hook and James Malcolm

INTRODUCTION

As this book argues, the gradual transformation of the Japanese political economy in the face of financial globalization has exerted a profound influence on the nature of the economy as a whole as well on the specific role and function of Japanese financial institutions, especially banks. The bank-led model of development pursued by Japan has been under threat as a result of globalization as it not only erodes the very cohesion of the state-bank-industry nexus at the heart of its capacity to act as a cartel, but also provides an alternative source of capital and transnational systemic organization (Pempel 1998a and 1998b; Kusano 1999). At one level, the challenge stems from the sheer volume of highly mobile international capital that is available today, dwarfing the capacities of domestically biased bank-led systems to provide cheap, liquid capital for investment in general.

At a second level, however, the challenge comes from the fundamental transformation in the structure of the financial system itself. For capital to be made available, both foreign market actors and internationally linked domestic market actors must be confident that their money will gain a market rate of return and that the financial instruments they have bought can be sold again at market prices. Thus, whereas the former refers to the process of marketization, the latter refers to liquidity. In addition, investment must be seen to flow into uses that are determined by the markets, not by state planners, 'relationship' bankers, or oligopolistic industrialists. This is particularly important at a time of rapid technological change. In the current Third Industrial Revolution, the focus on volatile and rapidly changing high technology industries involves at heart a redirection of investment. That process of redirection is away from older industries and towards newer, more flexible, 'post-Fordist' industries.

THE 'TRIPLE ECONOMY'

At the beginning of the twenty-first century Japan is undergoing such a process. It has been characterized in a number of ways: first, as the emergence of a 'dual economy' (Katz 1998). In this case, the vision is of a structural divide between the internationally competitive export sector and the backward, protected sector. Second, as evidence of a 'split economy' (*FT* 10/2/00, 24/2/00). Here the split is seen to exist between the old economy, including both of the above, and the new economy, such as high tech industries. Third, a *three-way split* or 'triple economy' (Cerny 2001). What this tripartite division implies is the rapid transformation of the economy to include the market-financed high-tech sector. Thus, the 'triple economy' of today is composed of the internationally competitive export sector, made up of household names like Sony. The protected sector made up of the banks as well as agriculture, distribution, construction and a range of other uncompetitive industries. And, third, the high-tech sector illustrated by Softbank, the internet investment group, and other companies able to exploit the advantage of new technology. Let us examine each in turn.

The internationally competitive export sector has for some years grown steadily more independent of its bureaucratic sponsors. The reason is straightforward: it no longer needs their capital. On the one hand, the companies in this sector are in a position to finance many of their investment needs from retained profits and have been more willing to direct these investments to relocated production facilities in East Asia and further afield. On the other, their very competitiveness, increasing profitability and internationalization mean that they already have easy access to international capital, without the constraints of bureaucratic 'administrative guidance' (Shindō 1992). They have 'grown up', and treating them as infant industries according to the traditional bank-led model of development is not just counterproductive but patently irrelevant.

The protected sector, meanwhile, has grown increasingly dependent on traditional domestic channels of support. Restructuring vast swathes of subsectors and firms would lead to extreme consequences for production and employment. Japan has been going through a crisis of demand for some years, with consumption levels stagnating despite regular attempts by the government to reflate the economy; retrenchment in the protected sector would hit demand hard. The balance shifted in favour of retrenchment in structural reform following signs of an emerging banking crisis, which led to the major bankruptcies of 1998. The change of prime ministers from Hashimoto Ryūarō to Obuchi Keizō in July 1998 signalled the reverse of previous policy. From then on the LDP government, as well as future coalition governments, have relied on regular reflationary packages and a very loose monetary policy. The measures adopted have included the implementation of fiscal stimulus packages in November 1998 and November 1999, worth ¥18 trillion each, with another package expected in November 2000. Significantly, both of these packages contained several trillions in spending which would impact directly on GDP, ¥7 trillion in the former case and ¥5 trillion in the latter. The two packages called for supplementary budgets of ¥5.7 and ¥6.5 trillion respectively. At the same time, in an attempt to boost spending, the government in March 1999 introduced three bills featuring an unprecedented ¥9.4 trillion in tax cuts, including ¥3 trillion in permanent income tax cuts. This was followed by the agreement between the LDP and the Komei Party to push through the Diet a ¥700 billion scheme of distributing ¥20,000 shopping vouchers to families with children. Finally, the government has adopted a number of measures to tackle the credit crunch. In October 1998 it adopted a two-year, ¥20 trillion public credit guarantee scheme to halt bankruptcies among small firms. The scheme was extended for a year and topped up to ¥30 trillion in November 1999. The BOJ also implemented a zero rate policy in February 1999, though it successfully resisted pressure from the MOF and LDP for it to increase its underwriting of national debt.

These measures, in essence, have shifted more risk from the private sector to the public. With unemployment rates at a very high level by traditional Japanese standards, having reached a postwar high of 4.9 percent in February and March, and a high of 5.2 percent for males in March 1999, the government became increasingly sensitive due to the risks of political fallout. Prime Minister Mori Yoshirō proposed in May 2000 to introduce emergency measures if the overall rate of unemployment topped five percent, but it didn't, and the LDP-led coalition escaped with a loss of 'only' 42 seats in the June 2000 general election.

In this context, the roles of both the state and private sector are increasingly problematic. The state is split between the political imperatives of maintaining the protected sector (both financial and industrial), on one hand, and the economic as well as political imperative to restructure that sector and to develop an internationally linked, marketized financial system on the other. Evidence of schizophrenic reactions to this dilemma abound. As seen earlier in this book, the 1996 Big Bang programme initiated under Hashimoto has for the most part been legislated for, but different parts of it have been variously either pursued more aggressively or neglected and postponed, depending on the shifting balance of influence among and within political coalitions and factions, bureaucratic agencies, and competing private firms and sectoral interests. State actors, having initiated the programme in order to try to control the process of financial deregulation and liberalization (Vogel, 1996), are increasingly being whipsawed by accelerating trends in the financial markets and the Third Industrial Revolution themselves. Some of those trends have resulted from *gaiatsu*, but greater weight should be given to internal pressures, or *naiatsu* (Kusano

1999). *Naiatsu* has been generated by both endogenous causes such as sclerosis in the protected sector and cross-cutting, globalizing pressures, especially from those sectors most entangled in international markets and from internationally exposed and market-oriented domestic elites in both business and government.

A number of points are salient. First, within the political system and the bureaucracy, differences between more internationalist and more domesticist bureaucrats, especially within the MOF and the LDP, have grown in recent years; at the same time, BOJ officials seem to be increasingly supportive of restructuring. Second, the political calculations which led Hashimoto to initiate the Big Bang reforms have hardly disappeared: Japan, if it is to prosper, needs to respond effectively to financial globalization. Third, inter-agency and intra-agency disputes have increased in severity as particular regulatory functions have been spun off through organs such as the Financial Reconstruction Commission (FRC) and FSA. This was reflected, for instance, in the recent change of direction at the former when the director implied publicly that a soft landing might be arranged for smaller regional banks in trouble. The new FRC Chief, Ochi Michio, seems less willing to take radical action and more willing to let the public auditors to take a soft line in their scrutiny of banks' capital adequacy ratios. Finally, political pressure from new constituencies has been growing. This has included both individual and institutional savers and lenders such as mutual funds and pension funds seeking to invest at international market rates. Other pressures come from urban voters who resent the transfer of government funding to agriculture, rural construction and other protected sectors. The LDP is also split between those who see further liberalization as inevitable and those who seek to backtrack on reform for electoral purposes. With the results of the June 2000 election showing the LDP has been punished by urban rather than rural voters, the intra-party battles between progressive and reactionary forces are set to continue.

The main pressures for change, however, have come from multiple actors in the private sector. These include foreign firms and investors seeking to enter or expand within the Japanese market; domestic firms and investors seeking to exit the vicious circle of the protected sector; new entrepreneurs seeking to expand venture capital activities, especially in new technology sectors such as the internet; companies seeking to import practices such as hostile takeovers; old firms restructuring and downsizing in the face of international competition, whether in industrial sectors like the automobile industry (Nissan) or through bank megamergers; young consumers turning to fashionable high-tech products sold at newstores where sales are often not captured in official statistics, and other actors generating pressures for change. Two kinds of reforms are generally crucial in such a context (Cerny 1993). The first is the decompartmentalization of financial markets themselves. Japan's main regulatory barrier has been the prohibition of commercial banks from dealing in securities and of securities firms and investment banks from engaging in commercial banking activities, that is, taking deposits from the public. Banks have sought to catch up and to compete with securities firms. While the latter have taken the lead in innovation, the former's greater capitalization and financial strength gives them the competitive edge. Indeed, while banks remain the main sources of capital even in financial market economies, it is their increasing need to enter into and compete within wider financial markets which has led to a marketization and securitization of banks themselves.

Entrenched barriers between different types of institutions operating in compartmentalized markets formed a fundamental building block of the traditional cartellized system in Japan (Brown 1999). The Big Bang began lowering these compartmental barriers, as in allowing different firms to merge into federalized holding companies made up of partially or wholly owned subsidiaries operating in different market sectors. Japanese financial services firms are currently in the throes of profound structural changes allowing them to engage in new forms of arbitrage fundamental to competitiveness in the globalizing financial marketplace. In this way, Japan has seen in the last few years the emergence of a new range of powerful firms seeking to exploit the opportunities being thrown up by financial globalization.

With different markets opened up to arbitrage, the second key structural reform is to enable market actors to fully compete on price and quality of service across those markets. The first stage was to deregulate interest rates. A combination of the bad loans crisis, financial innovation, the lack of compartmentalization in global financial markets, and the rapid pace of change in Japanese securities markets has led to greater support for such deregulation. The deregulation of brokerage commissions in securities markets is also taking place. The most important financial innovations in recent decades have been in securities markets, and freedom of market actors to negotiate commissions in an increasing range of market sectors serves to undermine cartel-like price fixing in the financial services sector. Following the liberalization of brokerage commissions in October 1999, Japanese financial markets have been hit by a veritable avalanche of change. At the core of this process is a rapid and far-reaching process of marketization, propelled by both new sources of the supply of capital, which has served to undermine the cartellized bank-led monopoly from without at the same time as it has been collapsing from within, and mushrooming new varieties of demand.

The first visible sign of change was the swath of bank failures and mergers taking place in Japan in the late 1990s. Certainly, the government has not been willing to see key financial institutions go under and has adopted a variety of measures in order to restore confidence and prevent a large-scale crisis in the financial system. In December 1998, for instance, it moved to nationalize Nippon Credit Bank, despite the Bank's opposition. Then, in February 1999, the Diet passed a ¥60 billion financial stabilization fund in order to boost the assets of unstable banks and other financial institutions, protect depositors in case of failures, and fund the reconstruction of failed banks. Despite these measures, a number of second tier regional banks have filed for bankruptcy in the last couple of years. The shake up amongst major banks can also be seen in the spate of mergers starting with the March 1999 tie-up between Mitsui Trust and Chuo Trust. This was followed in August by that of the Industrial Bank of Japan, Fuji Bank, and Daiichi Kangyo Bank which will be reorganized as Mizuho Holdings in Spring 2002 (and will then become the world's largest bank by assets). A smaller merger was announced in October 1999 between Tokai Bank and Asahi Bank; then, later in the same month, Sumitomo Bank and Sakura Bank announced they were to merge in Spring 2002 making it the world's second largest bank by assets, Universal Financial of Japan. While the announcements of these mergers indicate an increasing awareness on the part of the staid and stuffy of the Japanese banking world that their competitive position is under threat from financial globalization, melding different institutional cultures and traditions brings with it a range of complex problems that must be resolved if these new Japanese financial power houses are to make a mark globally; indeed, the final form of individual merger proposals is still fluid (for example, Asahi has recently threatened to pull out of its scheme).

Another manifestation of these changes, mainly since the mid-1990s, has been the increasingly visible entry of foreign financial firms into Japan. Reflecting this, foreign direct investment into Japan topped one trillion yen for the first time ever in the 1998 fiscal year, and jumped to a record 1.3 trillion yen between April and September 1999, nearly equalling the full-year record set in the year to March 1999. Large investments have been made in the automotive, financial services and telecommunications sectors. This surge was partly due to the liquidity crunch in the traditional financial sector, but it also reflects the restructuring strategies of Japanese firms as companies reshuffle their assets, the *keiretsu* system begins to unravel and the banking sector restructures. Foreign investors and firms are now increasingly welcomed by a growing range of market actors and the business media. Rapid growth, albeit from a very low base, has been seen in the venture capital industry in Japan, a sector which virtually did not exist a few years ago, as well as the investment trust and mutual funds sector. In cultural terms, too, foreign firms are becoming fashionable as employers of high-flying Japanese graduates, once the province of the bureaucracy or the top Japanese institutions. In a survey of 1999 graduates, Merrill Lynch was rated the eighth 'most promising' company in Japan, up from 425th the previous year, and ahead of all Japanese banks; it was also rated the 115th 'place I most want to work', up from 474th the year before, behind top

Japanese banks like Tokyo Mitsubishi, but ahead of most other Japanese brokers and smaller banks (*FT*, 19/11/99).

Furthermore, new forms of demand seem to be emerging at a rapid rate. As in other countries, the new effervescence of Japanese markets has been to a large extent driven by the development of new technology and industrial sectors. For instance, Japan, after an initial lag of several years, now has the most densely penetrated mobile phone market in the world, with the young and frivolous as well as the old and serious counting these mini gadgets as an essential part of their everyday life. It is also leading in the use of the internet by mobile phone with DoCoMo, the market leader, hardly able to keep up with demand, which has been a record-breaking 400,000 new subscribers per month since the service's launch in February 1999 (*Far Eastern Economic Review* 8/6/00). Japanese subscribers are just as likely to access their email and surf the net while riding the train, waiting for the bus or sitting in a coffee shop. The market for desk and portable computers is suffering as a result. Even venerable firms like Sony are planning major restructurings in order to focus more on internet-related activities (*Far Eastern Economic Review* 22/6/00). In contrast to the Tokyo Stock Exchange of old, dominated by internal *keiretsu* trades, 29 percent of total equity purchases in 1999 were by individual investors. As a consequence, the brokerage industry itself is being profoundly shaken up, with the survival of many existing firms an issue. This is especially so for the smaller firms unable to compensate for lower margins on commission income through larger volumes of business, and the new megabanks are rushing to consolidate and restructure their brokerage subsidiaries (*Nikkei Weekly* 2000: 27/3/00). New financial startups, especially online trading firms, have been growing rapidly, putting increasing competitive pressure on existing financial firms. Of course, the on-line brokerage industry is still in its infancy and the initial success these firms have experienced may not continue, with shake outs to be expected as customers compare the quality and price of services, whether on line or not. That being said, 'dot.com fever' in Japan should be seen as an indicator of deep structural change in the financial system and other sectors that will have long-term implications. Mergers and acquisitions activity have also risen strongly, as *keiretsu* restructure and spin off less profitable activities and firms with high cash flows but relatively low market value and weak management are thought to be bargains in a more marketized environment (*Nikkei Weekly* 14/2/00); even hostile takeovers, once ruled out, are on the agenda, if as yet in an embryonic form. Non-financial firms are starting to make major inroads into the financial sector too. Current plans include those by Ito-Yokado, owner of the huge Japanese chain of Seven-Eleven convenience stores, to become a bank in order to utilize its 24-hour ATM network in a country where until very recently ATMs have only been open during normal banking hours; indeed, Seven-Eleven already provides a service where internet consumers can order their goods online in the stores and return to pick them up there too, a useful innovation in a country where much consumer resistance remains to pure mail order purchasing. And Softbank is the leading suitor for taking over the operations of the failed (and nationalized) Nippon Credit Bank.

Other changes in the system include the establishment of a new exchange for young companies, the Tokyo Stock Exchange (TSE)-sponsored 'Mothers' market (Market for High Growth and Emerging Stocks). While initial take up has been low, with most issues having traded at below initial float value for some time, the exchange illustrates the opening up of new opportunities for companies locked out of the bigger stock exchanges. The launch in 2000 of NASDAQ Japan, a joint venture between Softbank and the National Association of Securities Dealers of the US, can be expected to fare somewhat better. Compared with 'Mothers', it has much stricter listing requirements in order to facilitate cross-listing with NASDAQ US and the latter's planned European venture (now associated with the proposed merger of the London Stock Exchange and the Deutsche Börse), with the intention of creating a globally integrated exchange for high technology shares. Meanwhile, MOF's Financial System Council has recently come out in support of transforming the TSE from a membership organization into a publicly held company, a reform similar to changes being carried out or considered by other major exchanges across the world. Marketization of the Japanese financial markets themselves is proceeding apace. This can be seen, for instance, in the proliferation of electronic bond fora, as pioneered by in the interdealer market by MTS Japan. These will serve to increase liquidity and bring down transaction costs, and as such they are manifestations of financial globalization.

CONCLUSION

Although these private sector-led changes have been enabled by bureaucratic shifts and the Big Bang programme, pressures for them have not come from the Japanese state but from external market developments and technological change. They are not dependent for their momentum on the state nor, indeed, on the rapid or comprehensive conclusion of the entire Big Bang programme as originally envisaged. In other words, the combination of market decompartmentalization and price competition within the financial services industry, along with rapid technological change and the reorientation of investors' funds, cannot be understood without reference to financial globalization. The changes now taking place in Japan can only accelerate further as funds shift from traditional uses to new uses, as the restructuring of the banking system itself proceeds and the new megabanks and holding companies become more market-driven and profit-oriented, as individual investors search for higher rates of return, and as the government eventually runs out of funding for further reflationary packages. Japan's bank-led model of development can no longer resist the restructuring imposed on it by the global financial marketplace. Thus, financial globalization will remain the watchword for understanding the ongoing restructuring of the Japanese financial system in the twenty-first century.

Notes

INTRODUCTION

1. The title of the summit's declaration was 'Making a Success of Globalization for the Benefit of All'. Globalisation also has become a topic for discussion at the Trilateral Commission (e.g. its March 1997 meeting in Tokyo), the World Economic Forum (e.g. its February 1998 meeting in Davos). Other recent examples include a major conference called 'International Solidarity and Globalization' in October 1997 sponsored by Sweden to bring together G–7 as well as Asian, Latin American and African participants. The United Nations Conference on Trade and Development (UNCTAD) also has a division with the term in its title: the 'Globalization and Development Strategies Division'.
2. A word search of the *Amazon.com* internet book shop in April 1998 revealed that it has in stock 279 different items with the word 'globalization' in the title, most of them published in the last two years.
3. *The Economist* ran a series of six two-page articles recently under the heading 'School's Brief' to try to investigate and explain globalisation (18/10/97 to 22/11/97). Other recent popular works claiming explore the phenomenon are Goldsmith (1994); Mander and Goldsmith (1997), whose book was on the US bestseller list for twenty-seven weeks); Martin and Schumann (1997), two journalists from *Der Spiegel* whose book was translated into more than twenty languages after more than 250,000 copies were sold in Germany; and Gray (1997).
4. *Euromoney* acknowledged this as the 'worst global financial crisis since the 1930s' (2/98). The ramifications for the real economies concerned are tremendous. For example, the Indonesian rupia lost eighty percent of its value against the dollar, wiping out the evidence of twenty years of growth by reducing average per capita income from $1,130 per year to $340. As a direct result, the country's unemployment figure swelled by six million by the end of 1997 alone, sparking fears of social unrest which, with the help of the military, the government managed to 'contain' to rioting in several rural areas. In Thailand, the crisis brought down the government, and in South Korea, where food prices soared by fifty percent, the jobs of twelve percent of the work force were expected to be lost.
5. See Williams (1996) for more on the general relevance of Japan to Western social science.
6. For example, although Coleman recognises that he should include Japan in his five country study, he explains that he does not because of the language barrier (1996, p. x).

Notes

7 Helleiner (1993; 1994) predicted that Japan's power and voice in the international arena would grow substantially, and that this would lead to (i) a more equitable and better functioning international financial system than existed under US hegemony, (ii) a more active and managerialist approach to the international financial system, and (iii) an acceleration of a trend towards regionalisation in international finance.

8 For example, Cox, Gill and van der Pijl (1992) develop an impressive fractional analysis of capitalist interests, but this is incapable of analysing competitive dynamics between leading and lagging firms and between different industrial sectors. More generally with regard to this type of approach, Jones warns:

> the reflective features of the Gramscian approach to global hegemony rest upon strongly rationalistic foundations; a complication that raises serious questions about the sustainability of purely 'reflective' approaches. The danger of such rationalistic perspectives is that the persuasiveness of the internal argument dominates, and ultimately displaces, the complexities and curiosities of the empirical world that is nominally being examined. The meta-theoretical character of holistic [i.e. neo-Marxist] theories both promotes such a tendency and preserves them from subsequent challenges in the realm of empirical experience (1995, p. 196).

9 Heterodox IPE draws explicitly on literature from three disciplines: (i) international political economy/international relations (particularly, critical theory, world-systems theory and neo-Gramscian Marxism), (ii) new institutional economics (particularly, the theory of international production, economic sociology, evolutionary economics, American institutionalism, French regulation theory, Schumpeterian economics, and historicist Marxist political economy), and (iii) development studies (area studies, historical sociology, economic and political geography, and cultural studies). NPE draws on a good deal of the same work but frames its sources differently, identifying four relevant literatures: (i) international political economy (particularly the work of Wallerstein; Cox; and Strange), (ii) state theory (particularly the work of Poulantzas and Jessop; Giddens; Cerny; and Lash and Urry), (iii) government-industry relations (particularly the work of Cerny; Smith, Wilks and Wright; and Esping-Andersen), and (iv) public choice (particularly the work of Shand, Garretson, Dunleavy, Ward, Dowding, and Olson). Another explicit cross-disciplinary synbook, this time arising from human geography, is Thrift (1994) who draws on six literatures: (i) international political economy, (ii) economic sociology, (iii) cultural studies, (iv) reflexive modernisation, (v) ethnomethodological sociology/psychology, and (vi) new institutional economics.

10 See Berger and Dore 1996 for a general overview of this debate.

CHAPTER 1

1 Specifically, Perraton et al. recognise, 'conceptions of globalisation underlying current debates are inadequate and their analysis of empirical evidence consequently misleading' (1997, p. 257). They go on to spell out a foundational understanding of globalisation, but fail to acknowledge, even in a footnote, their considerable debt to a substantial body of theoretical work on globalisation which obviously informs their work (see also their other article Goldblatt et al. 1997). Consequently, in her endeavour to take to task what she asserts is the 'orthodox' accounts of economic globalisation, Weiss can dismiss their efforts in

Notes

a footnote as merely 'an argument which is more open-ended than conventional accounts' (1997, fn. 2).

2 For example, see the special issue of *New Political Economy* on globalisation and the politics of resistance edited by Gills (1997). Herein, Douglas' categorisation of Strange's work as an example of those who believe globalisation to be an entirely external and autonomous process (1997, p. 168) is a particularly glaring case of misrepresentation.

3 Gills lists the 'litany of sins' of globalisation discourse as: its economism; its economic reductionism; its technological determinism; its political cynicism, defeatism and immobilism; its de-socialisation of the subject and re-socialisation of risk; its teleological sub-text of inexorable global 'logic' driven exhaustively by capital accumulation and the market; its ritual exclusion of factors, causes or goals other than capital accumulation and the market from priority of values to be pursued by social action' (1997, p. 12).

4 On the classical debates in international relations, see Smith (1995b).

5 Beck is careful to note that a wealth disadvantage will often lead to a risk disadvantage, but he stresses that whereas in the past, risk had been a latent side-effect from which the rich and powerful could insulate themselves, now it returns to its sources in a 'boomerang effect' to touch also those who produce it.

6 Perhaps most notably, the question of whether or not globalisation is a new and distinct phenomenon is left unresolved.

7 Many skeptics and some adherents of the concept of globalisation emphasise continuity in the present era of capitalism. See, for example, Marshall (1996), Hirst and Thompson (1996), Frank and Gills (1993), Arrighi (1994), Amin (1996), and Palan and Abbot (1996, pp. 15–20).

8 As Amin and Palan caution, 'The very 'fact' of globalisation is under considerable dispute. Only in part can we assert empirically that yesterday's world was less intensively or extensively integrated than today's world' (1996, p. 213).

9 This is not to deny that it is possible to show that by some measures the world economy may appear quantitatively less integrated today than a hundred years ago.

10 With its roots in the French Regulation School's theorisation of different historical forms of capitalism (see Amin 1994), the concept of post-Fordism has been adopted by scholars in fields, notably Olson, Porter, and Williamson in New Institutional Economics (NIE).

11 Management tools developed by groups such as the Boston Consulting Group (BCG) are highly characteristic. Most famously, the 'BCG Matrix' gained universal acceptance as an orthodox formula for corporate product portfolio management. The Matrix is a simple device which enables a company to locate its range of products on a four square grid by plotting each product's market share against that market's growth rate. According to which quadrant a product falls into, it is rated as a 'question mark', 'star', 'cash cow' or 'dog' and the Matrix prescribes clear strategic action, respectively 'building' (heavy investment), 'holding', 'milking' and 'divesting'. For a general review of the management consultancy business, see the *Economist* special survey (22/3/97).

12 An AMEX Bank Review article is representative of the simple way in which the two apparently contradictory trends of the 1980s and 1990s can be reconciled. It begins, '[i]t is now *de rigeur* to dismiss the 1980s as the decade of excesses – and few trends were more 'hyped' than globalisation. In short, the rumours of the 'death' of global finance in the more sombre 1990s are as exaggerated as the global hype was overdone in the 1980s' (2/93).

13 Perraton *et al.* (1997) show that foreign trade flows and patterns of FDI, which are highly concentrated and take place overwhelmingly between advanced states,

are generally now more extensive and more enmeshed with national markets and production than ever before. They also argue that, while TNCs have not become totally 'footloose', While TNCs have replaced MNCs in common parlance today, empirical studies show that there are few if any truly transnational corporations in the sense of firms with significant foreign ownership and top management. See also Thrift (1994) and Budd (1995).
14 Mills posited a strong link between the economic and governing elites, suggesting that 'not violence, but credit may be a rather ultimate seat of control within modern societies' (cited in Soref and Zeitlin, 1987, p. 56); Lindblom took up and considerably refined the idea that the business sector benefits from structural power in modern capitalist societies. For a concise overview of these traditions, see Smith (1995b) and Evans (1995).
15 For a fuller explanation of the ways in which capital 'disciplines' labour and the state, both nationally and internationally, through behavioural and structural power, see Gill and Law (1988, pp. 83–102).
16 Short selling refers to the practice of selling something which one does not have on the expectation that its price will fall and it can be bought up at a profit before delivery is made.
17 See also Kelsey's (1995) New Zealand study and Moses (1994). A dissenting view is Garrett and Lange (1991), who argue that despite the constraining effects of international financial integration on macroeconomic policies, national economic policies have in fact remained partisan to such influences over the 1980s.
18 A considerable amount of other work approaching the issue from different angles supports the same conclusion. For example, Pringle (1992) uses the notion of a 'bankers bargain' to show that the financial sector is demanding more than ever from states. His work is supported by other chapters in the same volume, for example Epstein and Schor (1992). Popular literature such as Grieder (1997) also addresses the issue and draws broadly similar conclusions.
19 The conventional view among economists is that in the long run, the effects of a state's monetary and fiscal initiatives on aggregate economic performance tend to be neutral. Specifically, Rational Expectations Theory suggests that there is in fact no permanent negative slope to the Phillips Curve, i.e. that there is no fundamental inverse relation between inflation and unemployment.
20 The Mundell-Flemming condition, first put forward in the early 1960s, indicates that a country can realistically pursue at most two of the following three goals: (i) a fixed exchange rate, (ii) autonomy in monetary policy, and (iii) capital mobility – what have become known popularly as the 'unholy trinity' (e.g. Cohen 1993). For a brief exposition and references, see Frieden (1991, pp. 430–3).
21 Some work has been done investigating these limits, for example, by Goodman (1992) relating to central bank independence, and by Tavlas (1993) on optimum currency areas (cited in Cohen 1996, pp. 283–5).
22 Economic sociology, sometimes defined as 'the structural analysis of business', traces its genealogy from Political Economy and Organisational Sociology and emerged as a coherent sub-discipline during the 1980s (see Granovetter 1990). Extensive collections of both theoretical and empirical studies are edited by Mizruchi and Schwartz (1987) and Zukin and DiMaggio (1990).
23 Economic Sociologists tend to divide themselves into 'financial control theorists' and 'social class theorists': the former assert the existence of a key resource dependence-induced hierarchy among institutions (i.e. that control over the financial structure confers a structurally privileged position on financial institutions); the latter, that all corporations remain the tools of a dominant capitalist class whose interests both embody and transcend those of any

particular organisation. These two positions are commonly set up in juxtaposition to one another but can actually be seen to be complementary, as the ensuing discussion in the text demonstrates. This suggests that in reality 'social class theorists' might better be labelled 'social class *faction* theorists' because their emphasis tends to be focused on theorising a much narrower zone of corporatist/elitist unity.
24 See Sheard (1994) for a similar study of bank executives on corporate boards in Japan.
25 In Foucault's work, the relationship between knowledge and power is understood in terms of 'discursive formation': knowledge is discursively and textually constructed in the context of predominating politico-economic and socio-cultural conditions as certain ideas and practices become institutionalised over time in the actions of individuals, even though their implications may be only partially understood by those they encompass (1972, p. 31–40). An example of this is Galbraith's (1992) characterisation of life in contemporary Western societies having come to constitute a 'culture of contentment' in which most of us have come to be exemplars of a commodified and normalised society *par excellence*. Foucault (1980) suggested that in modern societies, many new knowledge structures have emerged to overlap with, cut across, and fragment traditional forms of authority such as the state. He defined this in terms of numerous competing 'circuits of power' which interact at various levels and in increasingly complex ways. He argued that in such an environment certain technical devices, or 'intellectual technologies', such as record-keeping can work to render a realm knowable and therefore controllable. Hereby, rather than being a series of ideas which exist in a political vacuum, knowledge is shown to constitute a powerful means for shaping social organisation.
26 Other examples are work by Boyes-Watson (1995), a sociologist who investigates record-keeping as a 'technology of power', and Goss (1995), a geographer who critically assesses the implications of the 'revolution' in marketing research and the uses of geo-demographic systems. More generally, see the journals *Accounting, Organisations and Society*, and *Critical Perspectives on Accounting* for other work in this vein.
27 See also Strange (1990), who dubs this group the 'business civilisation', and Thrift (1994) and Hirst and Thompson (1995) who use the terms 'transnational business class' and 'club class'.
28 For a survey of historical trends in the size and roll of the public sector in advanced capitalist states in juxtaposition to the rhetoric of globalisation and small government, see the *Economist* survey 'The Future of the Nation State' (20/9/97).
29 More generally he argues that it is a fallacy to liken states to corporations because even in a globalising economy states do not compete for markets in the zero-sum fashion in which corporations are assumed to compete.
30 Baum (1996) provides a concise overview of Polanyi's work.
31 Whether or not national models of political economy are converging under globalisation is an emotive issue. Berger (1996) provides an introduction to some of the key work in the field and outlines many of the debates key themes. The convergence debate mirrors the economic globalisation debate in that much of the intransigence appears to be a result of imprecise definitions and supposition. But, whereas it is relatively straightforward to give the economic globalisation debate a point of orientation, no such mechanism is at hand in the convergence debate. Section 1.3, nevertheless, takes up the issue of convergence in the somewhat more concrete context of developments in the financial sector.

32 The period of British hegemony which followed Napoleon's defeat at Waterloo in 1815 provided the stable economic and politico-legal environment which made way for a systematic development of extensive international financial relations to finance trade and development by pooling risks. This is not to deny that the roots of modern international finance can be traced back to the mid-Fifteenth Century, when the Catholic church's prohibition on usury in European states broke down during the Renaissance and allowed international banking networks to spread slowly from Italy northwards. Moreover, international equity financing was pioneered in the Seventeenth and Eighteenth Centuries, both to finance state military campaigns and merchant ventures related to colonialism, exploration and trade, but the instability caused by civil war in France and the Revolutionary War in the US, and the damage caused to London by the 'South Sea Bubble', meant that the extensive development of international financial relations did not take place until the 'Golden Era' of 1815 to 1914. See De Cecco (1974), Strange (1988), and Hayes and Hubbard (1990).

33 Political scientists periodically rediscover the 'paradox' that, in practice, deregulation commonly involves reregulation (e.g. Vogel 1996). This observation should be evident to all but the most casual observer. However, it is the *type* of regulation that changes – from direct intervention in a certain sector or market to the maintenance of a 'level playing field'. The term 'reregulation' is sometimes advocated as an alternative to 'deregulation' (e.g. Cerny), but this gives no indication of qualitative change. As was made clear in section 1.1, this book understands deregulation as a form of reconfiguration in state-market relations which does not imply the withdrawal of the state *per se* from a particular area of the economy.

34 Although the postwar liberalisation of capital movements was first raised in Europe as one of the formal objectives of the 1957 Treaty of Rome, the issue received little attention in the 1960s and 1970s in spite of Germany's early accession (Helleiner 1994, p. 157).

35 In 1984, Bank of England Governor Robin Leigh-Pemberton stated 'Change in the United States has already gone further, leading and requiring change here' (cited in Helleiner 1994, pp. 151–2).

36 For example, Reinicke calculates that between 1960 and 1985 communication costs and data processing costs declined annually by fifteen and twenty-five percent, respectively (1995, pp. 50–2).

37 The original system is Euroclear. Instead of bonds being physically transferred, as had previously been the case, investors registered with Euroclear had transactions cleared by bookkeeping entry and funds transfer only, their bonds never physically leaving the system's base in Brussels. Euroclear was hugely successful, proving more efficient and less expensive than the previous physical delivery system based in New York and, in 1970, it was joined by a computer-based competitor called Cedel. Nationally, various computer-networked interbank clearing and settlement systems now compete and supplement each other: for example, in the US, Fedwire, Chips (Clearinghouse Interbank Payments System) and Bankwire; in Japan, the BOJ-Net, *gaitame*, and *zengin*. See Earle and Fried (1992).

38 NASDAQ was actually the first 'pure' computer market, not the eurodollar market which, although being the first 'stateless market', was initially at least a telephone market. Other similar screen-based trading systems now exist such as Instinet, a Reuters system giving twenty-four hour access to the NYSE, and Cores, giving access to the Tokyo Stock Exchange (TSE). In 1992, NASDAQ

International was launched to link with London's Stock Exchange Automated Quotation system (SEAQ).
39 Globex was developed by the Chicago Mercantile Exchange (CME) in conjunction with Reuters in 1986. The system incorporates more than half of the worlds financial futures and options business by providing investor access to the markets of the CME, the Chicago Board of Trade (CBOT), Marché à Terme des Instruments Financiers (MATIF) in Paris, and the Singapore International Monetary Exchange (SIMEX) (Melamed 1992, p. 31). More recent but less extensive networks include Aurora at the CBOT, Elos at the Amex Commodities Corporation, Soffex at the Swiss Options and Financial Futures Exchange, Tiffe at the Tokyo International Financial Futures Exchange, and Fox which gives access to both the London Futures and Options Exchange and New Zealand Futures Exchange.
40 Several systems already exist for small orders, e.g. Posit, Was and Spaworks (Kurtzman 1993, p. 37).
41 In the mid-1990s, Reuters had over 400,000 active networked terminals worldwide. Competing services included services included Bloomberg Business News (BBN), with 90,000 terminals; Telerate, with 85,000 terminals; and ADP, with 68,000. The most recent development in this vein is the proliferation of internet-based services. McGraw-Hill (publishers of *Business Week*) and Dow Jones Inc. (publishers of the *Wall Street Journal* and *Barrons*) both provide major online financial information services, as do Moody's Investor Services and Standard and Poors among others. Reuters replaced its Dealing system with Money 2000, a historical database and analysis system capable of displaying graphics as well as text, before launching a 3000 version of the system in April 1996, developed at a cost of more than $100 billion and capable of providing more sophisticated stock and bond price analysis (*Banker* 6/98).
42 The eurodollar market had its origins in dollar deposits transferred to Europe in the immediate postwar years by Communist Bloc states seeking to avoid possible sequestration by the US (Wachtel 1986).
43 The FRN market was established in 1970 and made an important contribution to financial globalisation. Being fixed against benchmarks such as US Treasury Bills or the London Interbank Offer Rate (LIBOR), FRNs worked to bring about a convergence of market interest rates internationally (Hamilton 1986, p. 65). The euromedium-term note (EMTN) market was established in 1986 and grew extremely rapidly. It represents the predominant means for issuing international debt in the 1990s, and had over $500 billion in outstanding issues at the end of fiscal 1995 (Johnson 1994, p. 119; *Euromoney* 5/96, pp. 94–6).
44 NIFs and RUFs allow short-term borrowers in the eurocurrency markets to issue euronotes with maturities of less than one year without having to arrange a separate issue every time they borrow.
45 Straight bonds are redeemable over a set period at the face value of the bond but have a coupon attached and so pay a set rate of interest prior to redemption. A convertible bond can be converted into ordinary or preference shares in a company at a fixed date and price. A warrant confers the right to subscribe for ordinary shares in a company on a fixed date and usually at a fixed price.
46 PEPs and 401(k)s were both government initiatives and so demonstrate how financial product innovation is not limited to the private sector. Introduced in the UK under the Finance Act of 1987, the former offer tax benefits to small-lot (i.e. up to £6,000 [£3,000 for single company]) investors in UK-quoted companies. Stock selections may be managed or self-selected; reinvested dividends are free of income tax, and capital gains tax is not incurred if the

investment is held for a complete calendar year. In June 1997, there were nearly seven million PEP accounts in the UK, up from just under three million in December 1994. Over the same period, funds invested rose to £32 billion, up from £12 billion (*Banker* 9/97). Named after section 401(K) of the Internal Revenue Code, which was inserted in 1978 to permit employees of designated companies to set aside tax-deferred funds, the latter is a savings plan which seeks to encourage Americans to put aside money for retirement. 401(K) plans differ according to employer, but generally give employees the choice of investing their savings in mutual funds, guaranteed investment contracts and, in some cases, stocks.

47 In a narrow descriptive sense, the term securitisation describes the pooling of loans that bring in regular repayments and interest – mortgages, leases and car loans, for example – in units that can be sold off as income-bearing bonds or even as self-liquidating assets in which shares can be sold. In a broader theoretical sense, it is significant as the process that has come to dominate mature financial markets: the conversion of more and more borrowing into paper that can be bought and sold in a secondary market (Hamilton 1986, p. 64). Securitisation tends to be a cheaper means of raising credit for large, well-known and credit-worthy private and public borrowers, and, where primary and secondary markets are broad and deep, it also provides investors with a more flexible and profitable investment instrument than straight bank deposits. Three events are commonly cited as having contributed to its rise in recent years: (i) the instability created by the oil shocks in the 1970s, which prompted multinationals and governments to borrow heavily in the euromarkets, (ii) the Third World debt crisis of the early 1980s, which encouraged many banks to reduce their loan portfolios and expand their fee-based business, and (iii) 1998 the imposition of stricter capital adequacy standards by the Bank of International Settlements (BIS) regime, which again encouraged banks to reduce loans and expand their off-balance sheet activities (e.g. OECD 1995). Intimately linked to the latter, the growth of asset-backed securities (ABS) has rocketed since 1988, with worldwide issues rising from below $50 billion to almost $500 billion in 1997. ABS involve the pooling and transformation of various financial assets with similar streams of revenue over a fixed period into immediately tradable commodities. Pioneered in, and still heavily biased towards, the US market, everything from New York parking fines to the royalties earned by a few famous pop stars has been securitised in recent years, although the vast majority of ABSs are still made up of mortgages and credit card loans (*Economist* 9/5/98).

48 There are three main types of derivatives: futures, options and swaps. Futures contracts are standardised forward agreements to buy a fixed quantity of a currency, commodity or security at a set point in time. The initial outlay is not the nominal value of the contract but a proportion, known as the margin, typically 10 percent. By this simple means a currency speculator, for example, can secure tremendous leverage in the market, gaining $10 million of currency exposure for every $1 million he commits. Options contracts secure the right, but not the obligation, to enter into a given transaction. As a result, they can be used as insurance since the price paid is analogous to an insurance premium. A call option is the right to buy at an agreed price, a put option, the right to sell. Swaps relate to either currencies or interest rates. In the case of the former, a borrower may find it cheaper to raise money in one currency and swap this with a counter-party than to raise funds directly in the currency he wants. In the case of the latter, two interest payments, often one fixed, the other floating, are exchanged. It is quite common for both types to be combined. Combinations of derivative

products can also be assembled, such as a 'swoption', which is an option to enter into a swap.
49 An *Economist* survey (10/2/96) on derivatives and corporate risk management cites a number of recent academic studies and provides a comprehensive review of the main debates currently being addressed by practitioners. It also includes a list of derivatives losses to speculative abuse, the largest of which include $1.4 billion by Showa Shell Sekiyu in 1993, $1.5 billion by Kashima Oil in 1994, $1.7 billion by Orange County in 1994, and $1.4 billion by Barings in 1995. For a more general discussion, see Roberts (1995, pp. 20–44; 230–56).
50 The London International Financial Futures Exchange (LIFFE) was established in 1982, Marché à Terme des Instruments Financiers (MATIF) in 1986, and Deutsche Terminbörse (DTB) in 1990.
51 A significant to contribution to CAPM was the Sharpe-Lintner-Black model (named after William Sharpe, John Lintner and Fisher Black), and an important addendum to Black-Scholes was the Merton-Scholes (named after Robert Merton and Myron Scholes) option pricing model. The latter two economists received Nobel prizes in October 1997 for their contribution to this field.
52 This 20,000 foot trading space was the first purpose-built exchange designed for the use of computers. In 1984, the CBOE moved again, to a space more than double the size, which then constituted the world's largest trading floor.
53 The recent creation of 'credit derivatives' may represent a fourth milestone in the history of derivatives. Credit derivatives allow banks to manage more effectively the credit limits imposed upon them by local and international regulators. As a recent feature article in the financial press enthused, '[t]he potential uses are so widespread that some market participants argue that credit derivatives could eventually outstrip all other derivative products in size and importance' (*Euromoney* 4/96, p. 28). Official statistics are so far unavailable, but an IMF document cited industry estimates of $40 trillion in outstanding transactions at the end of calendar 1996 (Folkerts-Landau *et al.* 1997, p. 158).
54 Aside from the hyperbole which is often inherent in popular writings, Waters asserts misleadingly in his authoritative introduction to globalisation that 'financial markets have dedifferentiated'and that in this sphere globalisation is 'largely accomplished' (1995, p. 88; p. 94).
55 In the BIS's categorisation, 'international bank loans' includes all international banking business, i.e. business in both domestic and foreign currencies done with nonresidents, and business in foreign currencies done with residents. The Bank no longer uses euromarket data because new markets have blurred the previously clear-cut boundaries between domestic and international financial activity. International securities business is similarly defined, but the data is divided into two categories: (i) international bond issues, which include eurobonds and foreign bonds but exclude debt-rescheduling bonds and ecu-denominated bonds (because they are marketed in the EU as domestic bonds), and (ii) euronote facilities, which includes euro-commercial paper, other short-term paper, and EMTNs. For more on measuring the volume of international financial activity, see *The BIS Statistics on International Banking and Financial Market Activity* (8/95).
56 Although the BIS has collected derivatives statistics since 1988, OTC and exchange-traded figures were not comparably calculated until 1990. Foreign exchange trading is only surveyed triennially.
57 In the currency markets, domestic interest rates and euromarket rates are the closest, and studies show that US monetary policy, in particular, tends to influence world rates via the the eurodollar market (Gibson 1996, pp. 247–53;

see also Fukao and Hanazaki 1986). Specifically, there is considerable evidence that 'covered interest parity' (CIP) holds across major economies (Gagnon and Unferth 1995). In this context, 'covered' refers to situations where forward contracts are used to remove foreign exchange risk from the equation. For a discussion of how to measure interest rate parity relations, and a general survey of the field, see Gibson (1996, pp. 50–84; 235–58).

58 For a critical review of efficient markets theory see, for example, Henwood (1996, pp. 161–70).

59 Specifically, governments have often lowered interest rates in the runup to a general election to stimulate short-term economic growth. Where this leads to inflation, investors see the real value of their holdings fall.

60 The Concordat was prepared in 1975, following the Herstatt and Franklin National banking collapses, but not made public until 1981. It represented a first step in the direction of an internationally accepted approach to banking supervision by asserting joint supervisory responsibility for internationally active banks for the host and parent authorities. The Concordat was revised in 1983 in the wake of the Banko Ambrosiano scandal, and again in 1991 following the collapse of BCCI. The Accord, which came into effect from April 1992, was a G–10 initiative. It established minimum capital adequacy standards – eight percent of assets – for internationally active banks. It was updated in September 1996, and amended in April 1998. All of the BIS documents can be downloaded from the organisation's internet site (*http://www.bis.org/*).

61 A prime example is the establishment of insider trading rules, which were based on US norms and imposed the costs of convergence upon non-US firms and regulators. However, Underhill notes that since the establishment of the European Union, the bias of power within IOSCO has changed in favour of European firms (Underhill 1995).

62 Essentially, a realisation is dawning among central bankers that risk management is internal to banks, and not something which can be imposed effectively from outside. A recent G–30 report (7/97) made proposals for greater self-regulation through risk-management systems and improved disclosure. Such moves have been supported by the Institute for International Finance, a Washington-based group of international banks with 282 members in 56 countries, which recently called for an overhaul of the 'simplistic' Basle ratios. Many leading US banks have more sophisticated ways of modelling and managing risk, and believe that they are penalised by the crudeness of the current BIS framework (*FT* 20/11/97).

63 In regard to banking activity, the classic fear is that unregulated competition may lead to the mispricing of risk such that 'bad' money eventually drives out good, and the integrity of the financial system is undermined. Known as Gresham's Law, this is explained in Strange (1988, pp. 93–8). However, in the case of the BIS Capital Accord, there is considerable speculation that the moves may have been motivated by a desire on the part of US and European regulators to curtail the expansion of Japanese banks which, for institutional and domestic political reasons, historically operated on very low capital adequacy reserves (see chapters two and three).

64 Global custody refers to the comprehensive cash and portfolio management services offered by the investment banking arms of large retail banks. They provide risk management and tax minimisation strategies for large corporate clients and institutional investors.

65 The Citigroup deal, announced in early April 1998, was the largest merger in history at the time. It created a conglomerate with a market capitalisation of $155 billion – larger than the Mexican stock market – and assets of $700 billion –

Notes

comparable to the net assets employed in a medium-sized country like Argentina – employing 161,700 staff and serving 100 million customers in 100 countries (*FT* 7/4/98).

66 For example, the UBS-SBC mega-merger announced in December 1997 – which brought together two firms with combined assets of more than $600 billion – was designed to benefit from economies of scale by being able to cut duplication. The firm planned to cut 13,000 overlapping jobs worldwide over its first three-to-four years.

67 In the insurance industry, synergies in distribution and technology were claimed as the reason for a number of high-profile mergers and acquisitions across the life/nonlife barrier in the early 1990s. However, it seems that people tend not to buy life and nonlife policies from the same company, computer systems do not dovetail, and the different risk profiles mean that companies have to manage their life and nonlife funds separately. Thus, insurers are under pressure to specialise in either life or property coverage, as a recent trend towards de-mergers has shown. Examples include Chubb, which spun off its life business in 1997, and Prudential, which got out of property insurance. Giants still straddling both fields include Axa-UAP and Royal and Sun Alliance (*Economist* 4/4/98).

68 It appears that after a decade of looking upstream for growth most leading investment banks have realised that future growth is only available downstream. The wholesale end of the market is now highly concentrated, but the retail end of the market is still fragmented. Following a model pioneered by Merrill Lynch, and in the wake of legislative changes in the US domestic market in December 1996, many US brokerages scrambled to build up their retail broking operations by soliciting tie-ups with commercial banks (see *Banker* 4/98).

69 For example, one analyst calculates that the average internet bank site costs a couple of thousand dollars to build, compared with $1.5 million for the bricks-and-mortar version (*Banker* 9/97).

70 For a general overview of recent trends, see *Survey of Technology in Finance: Turning Digits into Dollars* (*Economist* 26/10/96).

71 As one prominent investment banker noted, 'organisations hit a technology barrier which eventually prompts a decision to buy in, rather than create their own systems' (*Banker* 5/96). JP Morgan sell their Credit Manager software for approximately $25,000 per year (*Euromoney* 12/97).

72 Sainsbury's Bank, a joint venture with the Bank of Scotland, and Tesco Personal Finance, a joint venture with the Royal Bank of Scotland, both attracted over half a million savers within their first year of business. A similar venture by Safeway has been launched. Merrill Lynch estimates that both Sainsbury's and Tesco have the potential to capture more customers than Barclays Bank and Safeway more than National Westminster Bank (*Economist* 28/3/98).

73 In December 1996, the Federal Reserve Board raised the proportion of revenues that a bank subsidiary can earn from underwriting and dealing in securities from ten percent to twenty-five percent. The result is that 'there are now no serious obstacles to US banks – or foreign banks with US operations – entering into securities activities' (*Banker* 4/98).

74 At present, bank holding companies in the US are still prohibited from insurance underwriting, but the law is expected to be revised during 1998.

75 With aging population structures in much of the West, the life insurance business is considered a growth industry, and steady streams of income and payout make short-term risk-management much less important than in the nonlife insurance sector.

76 For example, see Wellons (1987). More generally, see Pauly and Reich (1996).

77 Norway, in particular, has been slow to follow, at least partly because its economy is supported by extraordinary revenues from North Sea oil.
78 On institutional investors and the reproduction of neoliberalism more generally, see Harmes (1998).
79 For conglomerates, the trend has been towards holding company structures, whereby each division can be managed at arms length on the basis of simple financial criteria.
80 Stock options draw on developments in Principal-Agent Theory to discourage shirking and self-interested behaviour by management by linking their renumeration directly to the firm's stock price performance. Stock options have been controversial because at times they have been used to encourage management to take unpopular decisions, such as laying off large numbers of employees.
81 For example, in the US market, the mutual fund industry grew from around $600 billion in 1990 to over $4 trillion in 1997, *vis à vis* bank deposits which remained little altered at around $2.2 trillion (*Banker* 4/98).
82 Specialist media coverage of the financial industry proliferated from the late 1960s onwards, and general media coverage in the 1970s. For example, the first edition of the magazine *Euromoney* appeared in 1969, and in 1971 America's NBC was the first TV network to start broadcasting regular financial news. CNN followed with Moneyline in 1980. See also Hayes and Hubbard, who provide a chronology of media developments specifically related to the euromarkets (1990, p. 57).
83 A common hypothetical example relates to an employee, A, who invests part of his wages in a private pension scheme in order to ensure a comfortable retirement. As part of its efforts to ensure optimal returns on its investments, the pension fund, which invests in the corporate stock of A's company, pushes that company's management to improve profitability, with a result that ironically A's job is deemed superfluous and cut. On the more general irrationality and contradictions of developed financial markets, see Henwood (1997).

CHAPTER 2

1 Examples of such work include Frankel (1984; 1993) on capital market reform; Horne (1985; 1988), Rosenbluth (1989), and Mabuchi (1993; 1995) on financial policymaking, Arora (1995) on Japanese financial institutions in Europe, and Nakao (1995) and Iwami (1995) on external capital flows. Comparative case studies of regulatory reform include Pauly (1988), Sobel (1994),Vogel (1994; 1996) and Lawrence (1996).
2 Consciously or otherwise, this 'quest' is promoted by Japanese and non-Japanese scholars alike. It is most explicit in the literature pertaining to 'theories of Japanese uniqueness (*nihonjinron*) – see Mouer and Sugimoto (1981) for a critique. Traces of it are also evident throughout Gibney (1998), which includes contributions by eminent Japanese and Western scholars and practitioners, and is tellingly entitled *Unlocking the Bureaucrats' Kingdom: Deregulation and the Japanese Economy*. A classic example relating to finance is Sakakibara (1993).
3 Subsequently, legal foundations for a separate category of trust banks (*shintaku ginkō*) were established in 1900.
4 The French system served as the model for these institutions, which received most of their state funding from the postal savings system.
5 These were Mitsubishi Bank, Mitsui Bank, Sumitomo Bank and Yasuda Bank (see Ōsono 1992).

6 For example, in 1921 Finance Minister Takahashi Korekiyo had first recommended the amalgamation of small regional banks to strengthen the banking system, and in 1924 the MOF outlined its first plans for consolidation within the banking sector (Horne 1985, p. 26).

7 By 1945, the four accounted for almost fifty percent of 'ordinary' deposits and seventy percent of all loans (Tsutsui 1988, p. 13).

8 Apart from the addition of two new bureaus (the Securities Bureau and the Customs and Tariff Bureau), the subsuming of the Repairs and Assets Bureau into the Finance Bureau, and the renaming of the Exchange Bureau as the International Finance Bureau, the structure of the MOF remained unchanged. Of the 210,000 Japanese purged from public life, 2,000 were civil servants, but only nine of these were from the MOF (Sakakibara and Noguchi 1977, p. 17).

9 SCAP did transfer some monetary powers from the MOF to the BOJ's Policy Committee, but supervisory responsibility remained with the MOF, leaving the wartime chain of command unbroken. As the BOJ was not granted legal independence from the government, MOF control over the governor was simply replaced in law by MOF control over the Bank's Policy Committee.

10 The Official Discount Rate was set by the BOJ, but strongly influenced by the MOF. Controls on deposit rates are generally thought to have been effective, but controls on lending rates were undermined somewhat by a practice whereby banks came to demand extra collateral from borrowers in the form of compensating balances (*kōsoku yokin*) in the 1950s and 1960s (Hamada and Horiuchi 1987, p. 237).

11 Among others, Zysman has pointed out more generally that this characteristic applies to countries like France as well as Japan (1983, pp. 324–51).

12 Made up of representatives from the largest banks and securities companies, the Bond Issue Committee effectively rationed capital market credit by (i) imposing stringent requirements regarding the size and financial soundness of prospective issuing firms, (ii) setting artificially low issue rates, and (iii) broadly managing the timing and size of issues in conjunction with macroeconomic conditions. Public offerings were made only by major corporations as a substitute for loans during periods of tight monetary policy. This exacerbated the marginal role of the capital market because whenever money was tight firms relied more heavily on direct financing, depressing stock prices and destabilising the market. It was also a prime cause of the 1965 securities market crisis which worked to decrease further corporate reliance on direct domestic financing (for more on this, see Gotō 1980, pp. 118–40). The Committee also made direct financing available to public corporations on remarkably favourable if sometimes arbitrary terms. For example, new NTT bonds (the first debt securities to be traded on the market after the war) were allocated only to new subscribers for telephones. Moreover, until 1966 no secondary market in government bonds existed, and this made it possible to maintain artificially high prices (Hamada and Horiuchi 1987, p. 233, 236).

13 A persistent complaint from the financial industry is that securities regulators have assumed that investors do not have sufficient knowledge and know-how necessary for making use of publicly-disclosed corporate information in their investment decisions (Endo 1996, pp. 11–13). Nevertheless, it should also be noted that this blanket restriction served the interests of many incumbent firms in the industry by freeing firms from the need to compete through innovation.

14 The strict segmentation of financial institutions in Japan is a 'principle' attributed to the infamous Matsukata Masayoshi, Finance Minister for a decade just before the turn of the century. Based on the concept of economies of scale, it was first implemented during the Taisho Era (1912–26 – Teranishi 1993, p. 165).

Notes

15 For a comprehensive survey of administrative guidance more generally, including its history, effectiveness, problems and prospects, see the book-length study by Shindō (1995).
16 Thousands of ministerial injunctions are issued each year. While it is difficult to generalise about their efficacy as a form of bureaucratic control, it is commonly held that firms adhere to administrative guidance for fear of subsequent discrimination by the regulator: for example, the holding up of a licence application's processing or its subordination to a rival firm's request.
17 A considerable volume of popular literature has appeared on this subject in the mid-1990s. See for example Ōkura (1996).
18 *Amakudari* (literally, 'descent from heaven') refers to the practice of senior bureaucrats retiring to lucrative posts in the private sector, often to firms which were under their previous regulatory jurisdiction. The practice is unique to Japan in so far as the movement is a unilinear and sequential one, unlike in the US where there is often movement in both directions. For more discussion see Inoki (1995) and Nakano (1998).
19 The most important of the umbrella organisations are the Japan Federation of Bankers' Associations (JFBA), the Japan Securities Dealers' Association (JSDA), and the Life Insurance Association of Japan (LIAJ). Nevertheless, such fora exist for every subsector of the financial system, e.g. the City Bank Roundtable, the Federation of Regional Bankers' Association, the Federation of Mutual Bankers' Association, the Second Tier Regional Bankers' Association, the Trust Companies Association of Japan, the Marine and Fire Insurance Association of Japan (MFIAJ), the Investment Trusts Association of Japan (ITAJ), the Japan Securities Investment Advisers Association (JSIAA), the National Association of Shinkin Banks (NASB), and the National Central Society for Credit Cooperatives (NCSCC).
20 Much popular literature and some more scholarly work portrays the MOF in this light, e.g. Kawakita (1989), Kishi (1993), Fingleton (1995), Ōkura (1996) and Hartcher (1998). Scholarly work has repeatedly debunked this myth. In addition to the examples cited in the text above, Rosenbluth shows how in the case of ceilings on compensating deposits, for example, banks repeatedly failed to meet MOF guidelines without being subject to sanctions (1989, p. 41), and Haley's study of MITI sounds a note of caution regarding administrative guidance more generally. The latter points out that it should be treated of as a generally 'weak' means of enforcing government policy because, absent from formal controls and sanctions, it may leave considerable room for manoeuvre and manipulation on the part of those being regulated (1986, p. 22).
21 See Stockwin *et al.* (1988) for more on immobilism in Japanese politics.
22 The convoy system is attributed to Finance Minister Takahashi Korekiyo, who first recommended the amalgamation of many small regional banks in order to strengthen the foundations of the banking system by preventing excess competition and promoting sound management.
23 The 1967 report of the Financial System Research Council (FSRC) concluded that, while the banking sector's overall structure was appropriate, there was a pressing need for amalgamation among the least efficient firms. A year later the Law Concerning Amalgamation and Conversion of Financial Institutions was passed which again paved the way for mergers among similar financial institutions. Over a six-year period ninety-five mergers took place; nearly all involved small credit cooperatives and credit associations. The formation of Dai-ichi Kangyo Bank (DKB) in 1971 and Taiyo Kobe Bank in 1973 were two notable exceptions.

24 A *Yomiuri Shinbun* poll showed that by 1979, fifty-three out of seventy-one mutual banks employed a total of sixty-three former MOF officers, with twelve of the eighteen troubled firms having ex-MOF men in the position of president (18/6/79). Moreover, for every five career MOF officials in 1980, there was one retired in a financial institution (Horne 1988, pp. 187–9). The promotion structure of the Japanese bureaucracy encourages this movement as most career officers have to 'retire' between the ages of fifty and fifty-five. For MOF officials, the other popular destinations for second careers are public financial institutions, semigovernmental bodies, and the Diet (as LDP politicians).
25 Examples from the banking and securities industries, where such disputes were most intense, include the introduction of commercial paper, mortgage trusts and securitized loans (Schaede 1990; Kanda 1997, pp. 306–9; Rosenbluth 1989, pp. 100–5). See also section 2.2 above.
26 See Schwartz (1993) for a general overview of Japan's approximately 220 *shingikai*.
27 Of course, this tripartite separation of forces is a reification; the lines delineating one sphere from another should be considered porous, so it has been necessary to assign developments to one sphere or other on the basis of dominant rather than absolute characteristics.
28 The share of deposits held by banks declined from 68.8 percent in 1970 to 54.5 percent in 1979. Over the same period, the share of postal deposits rose from 19.0 percent to 32.6 percent (Horne 1988, pp. 179–83).
29 The Banking Bureau's Financial System Research Council (FSRC) debated between 1968 and 1970 the possible licensing of a number of new products, including short-term money market products, *gensaki* (repurchase agreements), and certificates of deposit (CDs – a short-term method of gathering surplus funds from the corporate sector). The argument for introducing short-term money markets was that they could make the Japanese financial system overall more efficient by making greater use of fund surpluses in some areas of the financial sector and shortages elsewhere, and could help restore some balance between institutions in sectors where business was declining and those in sectors where it was flourishing. The argument against introducing them was that they would undermine existing functional barriers and lead to a diminution of regulatory control.
30 That is, some deregulation in Japan's short-term money markets took place in the late 1960s, and a *gensaki* market was established in 1970 in response to changing business needs, but progress in potentially much more significant areas such as CDs was nonexistent.
31 Between 1970 and 1975 the government deficit averaged one-third the size of the corporate deficit; in the second half of the decade, the government deficit rose by 100 percent, while the corporate deficit shrunk by fifty percent (Cargill and Royama 1992, pp. 335–41).
32 In some years more than ninety percent of new legislation had been drafted by bureaucrats and, after closed-door LDP committee meetings, rubber-stamped by the Diet, but as much as twenty-five to fifty percent was commonly being written by Diet members themselves by the early 1980s. Agreement on party policy within the LDP traditionally had been achieved through interfactional bargaining behind closed doors, but was steadily brought under the control of the party's Policy Affairs Research Council (PARC) and its specialised divisions (*bukai*). These divisions became the focus of lobbying by interest groups, and their 'policy cliques/tribes' (*zoku giin*) came to play a much more central role in

policymaking (Inoguchi and Iwai 1987). As a result, the Ministry's authoritative assertions about what could and could not be done in fiscal policy matters no longer carried such weight. Many politicians had ten or twenty years of hands-on experience in financial policymaking in contrast to the nonelected officials who were frequently rotated among different sections of the MOF. A 1986 *Mainichi Shinbun* survey of bureaucrats in eighteen ministries found broad support for the notion of bureaucratic power having fallen significantly since the 1960s. Over sixty percent agreed that Japan's postwar prosperity was a result of their leadership, but only twenty percent claimed that the Japanese economy was still led by bureaucrats (Higashi and Lauter 1990, p. 89).

33 Since the time when the first postwar deficit-financing government bonds were issued in 1965, a designated group of banks had consistently absorbed about sixty percent of all issues. The burden that this placed upon the banks was minimal, because the BOJ would customarily repurchase the bonds before maturity as part of its open market operations to manage Japan's money supply, and the MOF often conferred less tangible privileges upon its syndicated firms.

34 The ban on reselling JGBs during their first year of acquisition was lifted in 1977, and in the subsequent Banking Act revision (1981), banks were granted the rights to trade bonds on behalf of customers and to deal on their own account in order to profit from price fluctuations. Secondary bond trading rocketed from less than five percent in 1977 to sixty-two percent at the end of 1982.

35 Japan's nominal participation in the international financial community began when it joined the IMF in 1952. It subsequently joined the OECD's Development Assistance Committee in 1960, and two years later, following a European tour by Prime Minister Ikeda Hayao, pledged money to become one of the founding members of the IMF's General Agreements to Borrow. Hereafter, Japan made serious efforts to enter the inner circle of the world's elite economies, although the small size of its gold reserves initially affected its status in international monetary discussions. By joining the OECD as a full member in 1964 and acceding to Article 8 status of the IMF Charter in 1964, Japan committed itself to the liberalisation of international capital transactions in five stages from 1967. The change of status at the IMF brought with it an immediate invitation to join the Fund's key international finance discussion group, Working Party Three (WP3), and an invitation to join the Bank of International Settlements (BIS) soon followed. In this way, the late 1960s marked the end of the Japanese economy's period of international isolation, and from here on, domestic regulatory policy would necessarily be subject to international scrutiny for the effects it had on other countries.

36 The agreement was for the yen to appreciate by just under seventeen percent, although Gyohten reveals that then Finance Minister Mizuta Mikio had a mandate to go as high as twenty percent. Even this, however, was greeted in the Japanese press as a defeat, the public not really understanding the issues involved (1992, p. 96).

37 Negotiations took place between July 1972 and June 1974 under the auspices of the Committee of Twenty (C–20) which was initiated by the US in 1972 to lay the groundwork for a new monetary system following the Smithsonian Agreement. Its secretariat was led by Jeremy Morse of the Bank of England, Robert Solomon of the Federal Reserve and Suzuki Hideo, Japan's representative at the IMF. The C–20 consisted of representatives from the G–10 as well as regional representatives from other countries, and its core finance ministers group survived as the Interim Committee of the IMF.

38 After considerable bureaucratic infighting between the MOF and MITI, the Diet passed a new version of the Foreign Exchange and Trade Control Law in 1979, effective from 1980.
39 The 'locomotive' experiment was an idea put forward by US economist Lawrence Klein, first at a Brookings Institution conference in 1976 and then to Congress. It called for Japan (and Germany) to expand domestic demand by deficit spending to 'pull' the rest of the world out of recession, and was pushed strongly in international fora such as the Trilateral Commission, the BIS and the IMF.
40 Until the mid-1950s, the MOF had maintained a strict noncompetition understanding between domestic banks and the few foreign banks which were licensed to operate in Japan. Foreign banks were given a virtual monopoly on trade financing and foreign currency-related business, but were prohibited from pursuing purely domestic business, including retail deposits. But starting in 1955, this system began to be undermined as the Bank of Tokyo, and then other leading domestic banks, were permitted to expand gradually overseas to facilitate trade and support the activities of their major clients (see chapter five). In return, a few more foreign banks were permitted to enter Japan on an exceptional basis and some were given leave to pursue small amounts of yen-related domestic business. Nevertheless, with segmentation and restrictions on access continuing to limit competition among lenders quite effectively, and with double-digit GDP growth rates, profitability within the banking sector was all-but-guaranteed and few tensions arose during the 1960s.
41 Moreover, large domestic manufacturers began lobbying in the wake of the first oil shock for greater access to overseas capital markets where the costs of borrowing were cheaper for top-tier corporate names; their wish was granted in 1975 so as not to disadvantage them *vis à vis* their multinational colleagues. However, their parallel call for liberalisation of the domestic corporate bond market carried much less weight in view of the relatively new and flourishing *gensaki* (repurchase agreement) market which had recently made it possible to shift some of their domestic fundraising from indirect to direct financing.
42 Other firms began lobbying their home governments to take action on their behalf (see section 2.2.2 [ii] above).
43 During the 1970s, applications for banking licenses in Japan from Canadian, Australian, Indonesian and Texan banks were all denied by the MOF on the grounds of Japanese firms being denied foreign banking licenses there.
44 The Three Bureaus Agreement was struck between the Banking, Securities, and International Finance Bureaus of the MOF. It was eventually relaxed in the spring of 1993 after the Financial System Reform Act was passed in June 1992 (see section 2.2.3 [iii]).
45 The Advisory Friends Group was one such means, comprising an informal circle of Nakasone's long-time friends, including bankers, businessmen and former officials who provided consistent support for allowing the yen to appreciate and the liberalising of Japan's capital markets. Prominent among the group was Koyama Goro, a senior banker at Mitsui Trust and Banking, and Hosomi Takashi, former Vice Minister for International Affairs at the MOF. Another was the infamous Maekawa Committee. Fostering aspirations for a higher national profile abroad, Nakasone's reform policies appealed to the large and as yet untapped affluent urban middle class. Though well integrated within 'corporate Japan', this segment of the population was underrepresented in the political process. It recognised increasing threats to its economic welfare posed by protectionism abroad and, more generally, the failure of the Japanese economy to

keep pace with international developments (see Muramatsu and Krauss 1987). Nakasone's strategy helped the LDP to a record victory in the 1986 general election, which enabled him to gain an unusual one-year extension in his term as party leader and, therefore, prime minister.

46 These were (i) the Administrative Reform Promotion Council, set up in July 1983 to monitor the implementation of measures recommended in the five reports which Suzuki's Research Council had produced; (ii) the Committee on External Economic Relations (the Okita Committee), set up in March 1985 to formulate specific reform measures which could be used to fend off criticism regarding trade imbalances at the April 1985 OECD meeting in Paris; and (iii) the Maekawa Commission, set up in November 1985 to examine trade friction in preparation for the May 1986 Tokyo Summit and, more generally, to identify policy options for the 'harmonisation of Japan's economic relations with other countries'.

47 The three proposals relating to finance were: (i) the government should promote greater liberalisation and internationalisation of the nation's financial markets; (ii) it should work for the realisation and stabilisation of the yen-dollar exchange rate at an appropriate level; and (iii) it should review the preferential tax treatment of savings. The other three were: (i) the government should strive for economic growth; (ii) it should promote basic transformations in the nation's trade and industrial structure; and (iii) it should actively contribute to the well-being of the world community through international cooperation (Higashi and Lauter 1990, p. 125).

48 In April 1978, senior officials from the Federal Reserve Bank of San Francisco informally took up complaints from American bankers with the MOF during a regular visit to Tokyo. The following month, a delegation from the Financial Institutions Division of the EEC Commission met formally with senior officials from the MOF, BOJ and the Ministry of Foreign Affairs (MOFA).

49 Evidence cited included restrictions on foreign firms issuing CDs and debentures, on branching, and on the acquisition of domestic financial institutions.

50 For example, foreign banks were allowed into the consumer finance field and into the *gensaki* (repo.) market in 1979.

51 Herein, the US approach to the 'Japan problem' moved from the macroeconomic to microeconomic level, and in this respect the Committee can be seen as the first forum on 'structural impediments' (see Schoppa 1997).

52 That is, Japan's closed regulatory structure insulated low Japanese interest rates from the rest of the international financial system, encouraged large capital outflows seeking higher rates of return abroad, and thus further depressed the value of the yen. This argument was made most explicitly in the Solomon-Murchinson report of 1983, the underlying logic of which has been questioned by some scholars (e.g. Frankel 1984).

53 The FSRC's April 1983 report recommended the incremental liberalisation of interest rates on large unit deposits, recognising the need to create a short-term market to refinance the huge quantities of government bonds that would begin reaching maturity in 1985.

54 The ideological orientation of the US team has been widely commented upon because it had a major impact on both the direction and tone of the discussions. Treasury Secretary Donald Regan had previously been the CEO at Merrill Lynch and, impatient with what he saw as too much theoretical hairsplitting, stated from the outset that he was only interested in concrete results 'as reflected by the markets'. His team was made up of ardent monetarists, including Beryl

Sprinkel who, as Undersecretary for Monetary Affairs, had frequently criticised the Federal Reserve for loose monetary policy (Moran 1994, pp. 108–112; see also Frankel 1984).

55 At the time of the first Committee report, the MOF published a document of its own outlining its new thinking (MOF 1984). This was followed a year later by a report which set out the various steps necessary to internationalise the yen (MOF 1985). A final report was published in 1987 outlining the latest plans for deregulation and internationalisation. The Yen-Dollar Committee was dissolved in 1988.

56 This last category involved abolishing the 'real demand law' in 1984 (a control designed to prevent currency volatility due to speculation by ensuring that forward contracts were always related to actual underlying transactions), and a rule that required all foreign-exchange transactions be routed through a foreign-exchange broker.

57 The Temporary Interest Rate Adjustment Law of 1947 was designed specifically to eliminate 'destructive' interest rate competition and contribute to price stability. Its effectiveness was eroded during the 1970s by the introduction of numerous amendments and exemptions, but in the 1980s still provided a basis for *de facto* loan rate ceilings and floors to be effected through administrative guidance in both the private and public banking sectors.

58 Particularly significant was the case of trust banking. US law gave Japanese banks in the US the *right* to participate in trust banking, although they had not done so out of deference to administrative guidance from the MOF. US firms demanded the same right, fully intending to take it up (see Pauly 1988, pp. 86–9).

59 Conspicuously absent, however, was the (straight) corporate bond market which remained relatively underdeveloped, although the 'with-warrants' segment of the market flourished during the latter half of the 1980s. The reasons for this were the inflexibility (compared to the eurobond or corporate debenture market) of eligibility criteria and issuing terms and onerous reporting requirements maintained by the BOJ, as well as the absence of a centralised settlement system.

60 The most sensitive case was that of interest rates. As part of the Agreement, the MOF agreed in principle to work towards their deregulation, but only set a tentative schedule after an agreement had been secured with the Post Office in April 1984, and the FSRC debated the issue in 1985. The MOF began by deregulating rates on large-lot deposits, which were more sensitive to differential rates of return and, therefore, more susceptible to capital flight. The gradualist schedule provided plenty of warning to smaller banks to prepare for the changes. In 1990, Deputy Assistant Treasury Secretary David Mulford protested what he saw as Japanese foot-dragging, and demanded the complete deregulation of all remaining deposit rates within a year. The process was completed in October 1994 (Vogel 1996, pp. 176–80, which includes a detailed table of various interest rate liberalisations on p. 179).

61 Under the first Reagan administration the value of the dollar strengthened, buoyed by high US interest rates and capital inflows from Japanese investors. Publicly, the Reagan administration welcomed the change after the weak dollar of the Carter era, asserting (in line with their early monetarist orientation) that it was a sign of international confidence in their policies. Treasury Secretary Regan rejected outright an early French-led proposal for coordinated exchange-market intervention in April 1984 based on the conclusions of the Jurgensen report, an early study on multilateral action which became the basis for later interventions. However, as the dollar continued to rise, the Federal Reserve eventually lost its nerve and cut interest rates in the autumn of 1984. The results were negligible,

Notes

and it was only further rises at the beginning of 1985, precipitating the promise of an unprecedented rate of one pound for one dollar and leading Prime Minister Thatcher to approach the President Reagan for help in intervening to support the pound, that provoked a reappraisal of US policy.

62 This was reflected in personnel changes which took place when the second Reagan administration began. Chief of Staff James Baker switched jobs with Regan at the Treasury, taking with him his assistant Richard Darman who replaced Beryl Sprinkel as Undersecretary for Monetary Affairs. Sprinkel was moved out of the direct policymaking chain to chair the Council of Economic Advisors. The new Treasury team, and Darman in particular, were receptive to the ideas of Fred Bergsten's new Institute for International Economics in Washington and Bob Roosa among others. A vague allusion to the idea of an international monetary conference came in Reagan's State of the Union address in late January of 1985. This was made more overt by George Schultz in a speech at Princeton University in April. Volcker notes that he perceived in Baker a sense of interest in the idea of longer-term international monetary reform, an area where a Treasury secretary could potentially make a lasting impact (Volcker and Gyohten 1992, p. 241; see also Funabashi 1987).

63 Interestingly, the objective was not formulated in terms of dollar *depreciation* in order that the US would not be made to look as if its power was waning.

64 The Plaza Accord made public the existence of the G–5 for the first time. As a result, Canada and Italy demanded to be included and the G–5 was formally superseded by the G–7. The Louvre Accord was made public at the May 1987 G–7 summit in Venice and based on intervention guidelines agreed to at the Tokyo Summit of May 1986. The Tokyo Summit was also notable for the announcement of the Baker-Miyazawa initiative (secured the previous summer at secret meetings in San Francisco) by which the US had agreed to stop 'talking down' the dollar in exchange for Japan's implementation of a ¥3 trillion domestic demand-stimulation package in new government spending and tax cuts.

65 Japan's trust banks were not simply opposed to domestic securities firms and foreign banks encroaching on their market. A greater worry was that through the partially open door would later come domestic banks. For their part, city banks were worried that the door would remain only partially open, and their main domestic rivals (the securities firms) would steal a march on them.

66 By the March 1985 deadline, nine foreign banks had applied for trust banking licences. To avoid an embarrassing protest, it was announced in July that all nine applications had been successful.

67 Another seminal event was the application in late 1984 by Japan's Big Four securities firms to the British authorities for permission to engage in banking in London. Made with the support of the MOF's Securities Bureau, the application was initially rejected on technical grounds which only partially veiled the underlying reason – reciprocity. The MOF responded with a moratorium on new British securities companies entering the Japanese market.

68 The money supply is defined here as M3: that is, M1 (currency in circulation plus money in deposit accounts) plus all other private sector bank deposits and certificates of deposit. With the yen approaching the 200 level, the BOJ implemented the first of five cuts in its official discount rate (ODR) under pressure from the government to alleviate the burden which the high yen was having on domestic producers. The Bank also came under international pressure at BIS and G–5/7 meetings to loosen monetary policy for the sake of reducing Japan's trade surplus. In the Baker-Miyazawa Initiative cited earlier, the MOF implemented major fiscal stimuli for similar reasons.

Notes

69 Accordingly, the assets of domestic Japanese banks increased by over 450 percent between 1980 and 1990.
70 Many banks lent money up to ninety percent of the inflated values of depositor assets. According to Salomon Brothers, twenty to twenty-five per cent of total city bank lending went into the property market (*Banker* 1/92).
71 Futures derivative products which could be used for speculative investments proliferated in the late 1980s. A government bond market in them opened in 1985, a NIKKEI index market in them in 1987 (based in Osaka), and a wide range of others including euroyen and eurodollar interest rate futures opened in 1989.
72 Financial engineering describes the fund management activities which arise out of the treasury functions of currency, futures and options dealing which *all* transnational corporations undertake to manage financial risk in today's volatile macroeconomic environment. For example, in 1987 Nissan converted a substantial operating loss into a small overall profit thanks to *zaitekku*. Toyota posted profits of ¥180 billion of which 160 billion came from trading financial assets, while the year's top ten electrical goods exporters derived an average of forty-nine percent of their total profits from money management activities (Eccleston 1989 quoted in Leyshon 1994, p. 133).
73 Some commentators argue that the delayed response of Japan's monetary authorities was understandable because the process of prior liberalisation had made the usual financial indicators difficult to read for Japan's monetary authorities (Takeda and Turner 1992, p. 95); others have argued that excessive financial deregulation was one of the causes of the bubble (see Kaizuka and Harada 1993).
74 As Paul Volcker asserts, 'Put plainly, coordination commits a government to take actions on the basis of international consultation that are different from those it might otherwise have taken, often in conjunction with decisions other countries are making that *they* might not otherwise have made' (Volcker and Gyohten 1992, p. 145, italics in original).
75 Tateho's management and bankers had dumped large amounts of stock in the market shortly before a public announcement about the company's imminent bankruptcy. Recruit Cosmos was floated on the over-the-counter market in 1986 after which its share price rose sharply. Between 1987 and 1988, it came to light that favours had been solicited from leading public figures – particularly LDP politicians – with offers to buy shares in Recruit Cosmos at discount prices prior to its flotation (Rothacher 1993, pp. 108–118).
76 Moran relates these events, but suggests that the MOF implemented the changes reactively, i.e. under the compelling weight of public opinion and international investor sentiment (1992, pp. 112–8). However, even on his own evidence, this is a misinterpretation. Moran cites the TSE's own investigation of the Recruit case as evidence that insider trading was not, of itself, an issue for Japanese regulators – the TSE concluded that no offences had been committed under existing regulations and its president stated emphatically that 'the transfer of shares to influential people, including politicians, represented no legal issue' (cited in Moran 1991, pp. 116). He goes on to argue that the speed with which the MOF drafted legislative changes is evidence of their sudden awakening to the modern realities of global investment – the Ministry's Securities and Exchange Council (SEC) set up a panel of legal and financial experts in October 1987 to examine the issue, and its report the following March provided the basis for straightforward amendments to the Securities and Exchange Law which would bring Japan into line with international standards. He concludes that, having seen the light of

reason, the Ministry exploited public outrage to push more radical legislative amendments through the Diet than would otherwise have been possible. The problems with this hypobook are (i) that it ignores the fact that the MOF had already struck two agreements covering insider trading with the US Securities and Exchange Commission shortly before the scandals surfaced – i.e.the scandals did not a cause 'sudden awakening to reason', and (ii) that Japan's new legislation was hardly 'in line with international standards' – its maximum penalties for transgressions being extremely lax (up to six months in prison and a fine of ¥500,000). He also neglects to point out (iii) that the legislation was not used subsequently to rigorously prosecute suspects in either of the two cases cited, and (iv) that the MOF did not then (and still does not – see discussion of Securities and Exchanges Surveillance Commission below) have the administrative resources to make full use of the legislation. Finally, (v) recent events (as narrated in the text above) demonstrate repeatedly that equality of codification between Japan and other states does not equate even approximately with equality of administrative practice. In short, Moran's interpretation of this event appears to have been driven unwittingly by his book of convergence. A more careful examination complicates rather than refutes this picture.

77 The rationale behind this practice was that it provided a basis for securities firms to compete for business in a market where price competition was banned because commissions were fixed. Effectively, brokers had found an alternative means to give their best clients commission discounts which, if commissions had been deregulated in Japan, would have happened automatically; i.e. large clients would be paying lower commissions and smaller clients higher ones, as deregulation in both New York and London showed. Nevertheless, discounts secured via this form of tacit competition were not equivalent to those secured through free competition because they exposed brokers to unlimited liabilities in a falling market, and thus violated prudential banking principles.

78 Compensating clients for trading losses had been illegal since the Commercial Code was amended in 1982, but legal revisions to the Securities and Exchange Law in 1991 made it an offence to *solicit* business with such promises. Henceforth, brokers were banned by the TSE from operating money-in-trust (*eigyō tokkin*) accounts which had been the major conduit for loss compensation payments.

79 Nomura was ordered to suspend its equity sales and propriety trading operations at its head office and eighty-one of its 153 branches for between four and six weeks, something which analysts estimate cost the firm approximately $36 million in lost revenue. The other cases included Chiyoda Securities, which was ordered to suspend operations for two months in March 1996, and Naitō Securities and Ark Securities, which were fined ¥500,000 and ¥7.6 million, respectively, in July 1997.

80 *Sōkaiya*, also called *tokushu kabunushi* (literally, 'special shareholders'), extort money by buying up a block of shares in a certain company to gain access to its annual shareholders' meeting and threatening to disrupt it by asking awkward or potentially embarrassing questions. To minimise the threat of disruption, listed companies tend to hold their shareholders' meetings on the same day in the knowledge that *sōkaiya* can only be in one place at one time.*Sōkaiya* also produce 'research' publications, to which firms are 'encouraged' to subscribe at exorbitant rates under similar threats. National Police Agency figures show that the number of known *sōkaiya* fell to 900 in 1997, with 650 operating as individuals and the remaining 250 operating as members of thirty groups (*Nikkei* 27/6/97; see also *Japan Quarterly* 8 [July–September 1997], pp. 15–21).

81 During the course of early investigations into loss-compensation at Nomura, it was reported that the brokerage was still operating discretionary 'VIP accounts' on behalf of approximately 10,000 politicians, bureaucrats and businessmen (*Nikkei* 29/3/97). A MOF *shōrei* had been issued in 1991 for firms to close down these dubious accounts, but the 1997 investigation into this aspect of the case was apparently dropped by public prosecutors for political reasons. One might speculate that journalists were complicit in the matter in return for access to information about the high-profile Koike case, a possibility which Alex Harney, a Tokyo correspondent for the *Financial Times*, agreed was likely in light of the closed *kishakai* ('press club') system (interview 9/6/98 – for more on Japan's media and the *kishakai*, see Feldman 1993; Pharr and Krauss 1996). Prosecutors did, however, pursue two other *sōkaiya* scandals which received much less press coverage, one involving payments to Terubo Tei by Asahi Bank and Hitachi group companies, the other involving Ikeda Kagehiko who threatened to kill a Daiwa Securities employee unless his demands for loss compensation were met (*Nikkei* 25/2/98; 25/10/97).

82 Nomura's case had been under investigation since February 1993 following a tip-off to the SESC by a disgruntled former employee. The Ministry ordered Nomura to suspend proprietary trading and public bond underwriting for twenty-one weeks, close its head office for 17 weeks, and cease all transactions for a week (*Nikkei* 31/7/97). It was also fined ¥100 million each by the TSE and JSDA, but these organisations did not go as far as to suspend the firm's membership for a maximum-possible six months (*Nikkei* 9/8/97). The MOF fined DKB the maximum ¥500,000 for false reporting, forbade it to open any new offices or operate in new business areas at home or abroad for one year, prohibited it from extending new loans (except mortgages) domestically, and banned it from bidding for public bond underwriting contracts for twenty-one weeks (*Nikkei* 6/8/97). Daiwa received a four-month suspension from proprietary trading (*Nikkei* 19/12/97). ¥200 million of the ¥355 million which it had paid Koike had been to prevent him from discussing the bank's ¥10 billion in financial assistance to one of the failed jûsen (*Nikkei* 24/3/98). Nikkō received a ten-week suspension from proprietary trading, and Yamaichi, which had guaranteed Koike an annual yield of ten percent on his investments, collapsed before its penalty was handed out (*Nikkei* 19/12/97).

83 By the end of 1997, the number of arrests had swollen to thirty-three: Koike, three Nomura officials (including a former president), eleven DKB officials (including a former chairman), seven Yamaichi officials (including a former president), four Nikkō officials (including a former vice-president), six Daiwa officials (including a former vice president). Koike pleaded guilty to accepting ¥12.4 billion in illicit payments from these firms between 1992 and 1997, although Nomura's ties to Koike were traced back to the early 1970s (*Nikkei* 1/12/97).

84 The MOF, the Ministry of Construction (MOC), MITI and the National Public Safety Commission began examining the issue in July 1997 (*Nikkei* 6/9/97). The LDP's Executive Council subsequently took up the matter, and its recommendations served as the basis for the coalition government's final proposals.

85 Some LDP lawmakers criticised the amendments at the time of their proposal, saying that the penalties should be stiffer (*Nikkei* 8/10/97). A package of bills which included seventeen amendments to the Securities and Exchange Law, Banking Law, Insurance Law, and Commercial Code was passed in December 1997. The changes prohibit *sōkaiya* from demanding (not just receiving, as previously had been the case) any kind of profit from companies. Violators face up to three years in prison and a fine of ¥3 million, up from six months and

¥300,000. Threatening corporate executives is now punishable by a fine of up to ¥5 million and five years imprisonment; corporate executives making payoffs face up to ten years and ¥10 million, compared to the previous maximum of seven years and ¥3 million; financial institutions that hide crimes such as payments to *sōkaiya* face a maximum fine of ¥200 million and one year in prison for executives, up from ¥500,000 and no term of imprisonment; and the maximum fine for ignoring a government order to halt operations was raised from ¥1 million to ¥300 million (*Nikkei* 24/12/97). These penalties still appear lenient when compared, for example, to the US, where authorities fined Daiwa Bank (USA) $340 million for failure to report promptly its insider trading scandal (see below).

86 In a survey of 4,400 major companies (response rate twenty-five percent) by an institute affiliated with the electricians' union, Denki Rengō Research and Information Center, sixty percent of firms reported that they would not be able to sever their ties with *sōkaiya* over the next ten years (*Nikkei* 26/3/98). Another survey of 1,927 listed companies found that sixty-four percent of respondents believed that the practice would continue (*Nikkei* 1/11/97).

87 The FTC involved itself with the issue on the basis that brokers which had not compensated clients had been put at a competitive disadvantage. This was the first time that the FTC had investigated the securities industry since its establishment in 1947, but it seems that its director (Yamada Akio) may have selected this opportunity to help his organisation put an end to its reputation as a toothless regulator and its supposed subordinate standing *vis à vis* the MOF (Wood 1988, pp. 169–74).

88 One popular 'theory' as to why the MOF condemned the practice when it did is that by doing so the 'guilty' brokerage houses would no longer be held liable for their clients' losses. By June 1991 the stock market had fallen forty-two percent from its 1989 high, but most clients who were promised compensation had only been reimbursed up to March 1990. The Ministry's 'disciplining' of the securities companies therefore saved them billions of yen in further compensation payments (Keehn 1997, p. 324). Another 'theory' relates to dynamics within the National Tax Agency, since the affair coincided with the appointment of a new head (Kadotani Masahiko) in June 1991, who took a much more zealous approach to his job (see Wood [1988, pp. 119–123; 164–9] who confirms this with interviews). The latter explanation is more probable, since the former cannot account for Tabuchi's outburst.

89 Ogawa was a tax specialist who played an important role in getting Takeshita's sales tax proposal introduced in 1989. For his successful efforts in defending the powers of the MOF's Securities Bureau in 1991 he was appointed as its director-general (Kishi 1993, pp. 100–1).

90 Although the number of staff involved in securities industry regulation increased, the SESC's resource capability paled into insignificance when compared to other international bodies. It was initially envisaged that the SESC would be launched with 200 workers, in contrast to the US Securities and Exchange Commission which has around 3,000. However, as of 1997 it had only ninety-one staff. It had filed eleven complaints with prosecutors since 1992, five of these in 1997 (*Nikkei* 2/10/97).

91 The MOF had shared an unofficial pact with the LDP ever since they battled over how to restore order to the financial system in 1967–68, following which the MOF agreed broadly to support the LDP in exchange for the LDP's protection from general political interference. Their mistake was in not opting for political neutrality following the general election in the summer of 1993 (Mabuchi 1997, pp. 30–4).

Notes

92 A major cause of Japan's ballooning public sector deficit in the 1990s was prolonged low economic growth combined with numerous 'pump-priming' spending packages which failed to jump-start the economy (see Appendix, Chapter 4). Hosokawa announced the plan for a new tax – which would raise the consumption tax from three to seven percent – at a hastily convened midnight press conference. His coalition partners killed the politically volatile proposal in less than twenty-four hours. Nevertheless, it was the MOF which suffered most for the incident. An opinion survey in the *Nikkei* confirms this by showing that most people believed it had been behind Hosokawa's initiative (4/94 – cited in Mabuchi 1997, pp. 5–6). For more on the MOF's objectives in budgetary politics, see Campbell (1977) and Kato (1994).

93 Between them, the seven firms had ¥6.4 trillion in bad debts, accumulated through reckless lending and speculation during the bubble.

94 It was alleged in the media that the LDP sponsored the *jûsen* bills in order to reduce by an equivalent amount the losses that would have been borne by agricultural financial institutions, the largest funding source of the *jûsen* and, representing farmers, a powerful political interest group. The main opposition party (Shinshintō) sought to make political capital out of its opposition of the scheme, and resorted to political spoiling tactics including a 'sit-in' in the Diet which succeeded only in delaying other business.

95 Once the bills had been passed, public debate continued but shifted to focus on whether the commercial banks that founded the *jûsen*, and the agricultural cooperatives which lent most heavily to the *jûsen*, should shoulder a greater share of the costs of their liquidation, and thereby reduce the burden borne by tax payers. One proposal was to set up a fund from which interest payments would be returned to the government. Initially, the banks claimed this would be impossible, arguing that, while they themselves had no objection to the idea, shouldering extra costs would encourage shareholder lawsuits. Their stance softened dramatically after public opinion turned against them. The decisive event was a skirmish between Chief Cabinet Secretary Kajiyama Seiroku and JFBA chairman Hashimoto Shunsaku. Kajiyama juxtaposed record banking industry profits with the low burden being borne by related banks and pointed out that the public should not be footing the bill. In his defence of the banks, Hashimoto argued that their profits were merely incidental because Japan's interest rates were directed solely by the BOJ and that the link between high profits and a share of the burden was spurious. In return, Kajiyama berated the banks in general, and Hashimoto in particular, for their arrogance. Soon after, and anxious to avoid any further damage to their images because of possible withdrawals of deposits, the banks agreed to shoulder half of the burden 'in the interests of maintaining stability in the financial system' (*Nikkei* 8/6/96).

96 A rogue trader at Daiwa's New York branch, Iguchi Toshihide, had fraudulently covered up losses from over 12 years of unauthorised trading in US Treasury Bonds, for which the bank eventually sustained $1.1 billion in losses. The US Securities and Exchange Commission fined the bank $340 million for negligence and failure to give prompt notification – the largest fine ever for a financial institution – and ordered it to close its US operations.

97 The fallout from the suppression of information concerning Daiwa's losses by Nishimura Yoshimasa, head of the Banking Bureau, was made worse when the decision was later defended by Sakakibara Eisuke, head of the International Finance Bureau, who implied that no impropriety occurred.

98 The vindictive rationale was articulated most clearly by Minister for Home Affairs Nonaka Hiromu, who stated at an informal cabinet meeting that he held

Saitō Jirō personally responsible for Hosokawa's failed attempt to introduce a new consumption tax and requested the support of his colleagues in demanding Saitō's resignation (*Nikkei* 15/3/95). Both Saitō and the MOF resisted strongly, but eventually acquiesced one month before he was due to retire. Ironically, the MOF's whole personnel rotation in 1996 was moved forward one month in order to shield Saitō from embarrassment and deprive the LDP of a symbolic victory.

99 These events are catalogued in detail in an appendix because they have yet to be treated fully in either Japanese or English.

100 The US version of the FSA has over 9,000 officials, whereas the FSA was launched with less than one twentieth that number, although Okumura Hirohiko of Gakushûin Univerity argues that the size of the Japanese economy suggests that the FSA should have approximately half as many staff as its US equivalent (*Nikkei* 19/6/98; *NW* 23/6/97).

101 The BOJ's subordinate relationship with the MOF was another issue which had been raised periodically, and two abortive attempts to create a more independent central bank were made earlier (see Kawakita 1996).

102 This postponement, however, is subject to ascent by majority vote of the Policy Board.

103 The ARC also debated the proposed privatisation of the MOF's Mint and Printing Bureau, and called for the transfer of the National Tax Agency to the proposed General Affairs Ministry.

104 An Administrative Reform Bill to reduce Japan's twenty-two ministries and agencies to one Cabinet Office and twelve ministries in 2000 was passed by the Diet in June 1998.

105 In the Upper House election of July 12, the LDP needed to win nine more seats to regain a majority, but lost substantial ground by conceding a further fifteen. Hashimoto's successor was chosen in an LDP balot on July 21, and Obuchi succeeded Hashimoto on July 30 (*Nikkei* 14/7/98; 22/7/98; 31/7/98).

106 A subsequent probe of these two firm's operations showed that the Tokyo Metropolitan Government had warned the MOF that they had been exceeding the twenty percent limit on lendings to a single depositor for some time. They were also found to have paid illegal dividends to their members by embellishing their accounts. The issue was sensitive for Prime Minister Murayama Tomiichi, who was supported by a labour group which held huge savings accounts with both firms (*Nikkei* 22/2/95).

107 Traditionally, middlemen formed a buffer between financial institutions and the *yakuza*, but during the 1980s gangsters sought direct involvement in domestic stock and property market speculation for which they required the services of financial institutions. Notable cases which took place between 1989 and 1990 and were brought to trial after 1991 included (i) Nomura financing and aiding Ishii Susumu, former head of the Japan's second largest *yakuza* group (Inagawa-kai), to corner the shares of Tokyû Corporation; (ii) Nikkō aiding and financing him to do the same to Honshû Paper shares; and (iii) Sumitomo Bank aiding Itō Suemitsu, a front man for Ho Yong Chung (an Ōsaka-based Korean businessman with *yakuza* connections), to gain a place on the director's board of Itōman, a prominent Osaka trading company, and then use the firm's main-bank relations with Sumitomo as a means of borrowing cash elsewhere for massive property speculation which ended in bad debts of more than ¥500 billion.

108 Again emerging in 1991, Japan's two biggest ever bank fraud cases tarnished the images of Japan's two most conservative and traditional banks: Fuji Bank

uncovered ¥260 billion of CDs which had been forged internally over a four-year period and only came to light when some of the borrowers defaulted on interest payments; then IBJ discovered that it had made ¥240 billion in dubious loans to a sixty-one-year-old spinster owner of two Ōsaka restaurants, Onoue Nui, who became notorious as the TSE's biggest individual speculator of the late 1980s, but was eventually responsible for the collapses of two local credit unions, Tōyō Shinyō Kinko and Kizu Credit Union. She was convicted of breech of trust and fraud to the tune of ¥274 billion in March 1998 and given a twelve year prison sentence. Similar cases were announced by Tōkai Bank, Kyōwa Saitama Bank, Hanwa Bank, Eichigo Securities and Daiwa Securities, among others.

109 Japanese firms routinely 'doctor' their accounts as the financial year-end approaches by selling assets to affiliated firms with different financial year-ends. The mutually agreed price bears no relation to market value, but an agreement commonly exists to repurchase the asset at that price plus some margin for the service. The practice became widely publicised when a number of these so-called *tobashi* (literally, 'free', as in 'let fly') deals were reneged upon as the recession deepened. The resulting court cases drew public attention to the MOF's lax attitude to this ethically dubious practice. In February 1992, Cosmo Securities suffered a ¥36 billion loss on such a deal with Skylark, a restaurant chain, with whom the repurchase agreement fell through; Yamatane Securities lost ¥19.5 billion on a similar trade; and in March, Daiwa Securities announced that it would pay ¥73.5 billion to settle lawsuits brought by five companies, all concerning *tobashi*. Around the same time, NHK aired an investigative journalism TV programme tracing a 'land *tobashi*' deal gone wrong struck between Mitsui Trust Bank and property developer Azabu Building. *Tobashi* were the main cause of Yamaichi Securities' dramatic collapse in December 1997, the firm having ¥160 billion in off-the-books debts to ten related firms.

110 The *jûsen* were created in the early 1970s by the MOF in conjunction with city banks with the purpose of expanding home ownership. MOF *amakudari* Niwayama Keiichiro in Small Business Finance Corp. and Sanwa Bank founded the first *jûsen* (Nippon Housing Loan Co.) in 1971, and within six months three more had been established. However, during the 1980s *jûsen* expanded beyond small borrowers and housing loans, partly because of competition from a public financial institution, the Housing Loan Corporation. At the time of their dissolution, ¥9.2 trillion of the outstanding ¥11.4 trillion lent by the *jûsen* had gone to corporations instead of individuals. Banks, moreover, had used their affiliated *jûsen* as a conduit for dubious clients and illegal lending, especially after 1990 when the MOF instructed banks to curtail their lending to the real estate sector. Hence one newspaper assigned to the *jûsen* the epithet of 'financial garbage cans' (*NW* 22/1/96). In 1996, at least fourteen former MOF officials held the title of chairman, managing director or president at *jûsen*.

111 Five businessmen were initially arrested on suspicion of hiding assets to prevent their seizure and sale by the Housing Loan Administration Corporation (HLAC), which was set up in July 1997 to recover *jûsen* assets. More arrests were subsequently made, and by March 1998 the HLAC had issued notices to eleven banks that it intended to sue over the introduction of problem borrowers to the *jûsen* (*Nikkei* 29/4/98).

112 For a brief resume of these scandals, see *Euromoney* (12/95). Tokyo Customs House Chief Taya Hiroaki was found to have taken free international trips on the private jet of credit cooperative boss Takahashi Harunori, and subsequently

was removed from his post. Shortly thereafter, and again in conjunction with Takahashi, the deputy budget director of the MOF, Nakajima Yoshio, was found to have received ¥120 million from dubious business acquaintances, which he then failed to report to tax authorities. He claimed the gifts were *tanimachi* (the gifts *sumō* wrestlers receive from their patrons). Nakajima resigned from the MOF pending disciplinary action, and was prosecuted for accepting more than ¥50 million in 'cash donations' and ¥100 million in low-interest loans while at the MOF from 'businessmen and acquaintances' (*Nikkei* 8/9/95; 29/9/95; 2/2/96). He avoided indictment by the NTA (which is under the MOF's jurisdiction) on tax evasion charges, and Finance Minister Matsunaga eventually withdrew an earlier pledge to call for a new investigation if Nakajima was cleared (*Nikkei* 14/2/98). Prior to Nakajima, the only MOF official to be arrested in the postwar period was Fukuda Takeo in 1954, in conjunction with the Yamashita Steamship bribery scandal. He escaped the charges and went on to become prime minister of Japan in 1976.

113 This connection between the loss-compensation scandals and bureaucratic corruption was made public when it was announced that MOF official Miyagawa Kōichi had deleted part of a 1994 in-house report on the problem loans which Dai-ichi Kangyō Bank's (DKB) had extended to *sōkaiya* Koike Ryûichi (*Nikkei* 29/1/98).

114 Four Nomura executives and one Industrial Bank of Japan (IBJ) executive were arrested for entertaining Isaka to the tune of several million yen in golf outings and restaurants in Tokyo and several European cities between 1994 and 1996 (*Nikkei* 7/2/97). Isaka was eventually charged with taking ¥7.2 million from seven financial institutions, the others being Nikkō Securities, Daiwa Securities, Fuji Bank, Sakura Bank and Long Term Credit Bank (*Nikkei* 1/7/98).

115 The two were initially arrested for taking ¥9.2 million from Asahi Bank, Sanwa Bank, Hokkaido Takushoku Bank and Dai-ichi Kangyō Bank between 1992 and 1997. They were subsequently charged with taking an additional ¥3.8 million from Sumitomo Bank and Bank of Tokyo-Mitsubishi (BOT-M – *Nikkei* 28/1/98; 18/2/98). Miyagawa was sentenced to two-and-a-half years' imprisonment, suspended for three years, and fined ¥8.11 million for taking bribes (*Nikkei* 25/9/98).

116 The two were arrested for taking ¥8.9 million from Sumitomo Bank and all of the Big Four brokerages between 1993 and 1997 (*Nikkei* 7/3/98; 29/5/98).

117 Yoshizawa was initially arrested for taking ¥4.3 million from IBJ and Sanwa Bank, but was later suspected of having taken a further ¥7 million from other firms, including Sumitomo Bank, Sakura Bank, and BOT-M (*Nikkei* 12/3/98; 12/6/98).

118 Hyōgo Bank failed six months after the Kōbe earthquake with ¥790 billion in unrecoverable debts – five times its capital – but its obligations were taken over by a new institution – Midori Bank – funded by the Deposit Insurance Corporation (DIC), the government and a consortium of thirty local banks. Moreover, an MOF *amakudari*, Akine Minoru, was appointed as managing director of the new bank.

119 By extending the definition of bad loans to encompass those on which interest rates had been lowered below the ODR, the Ministry's estimate rose from ¥12.5 trillion to ¥22.5 trillion. Within six months it was clear that this had been a tactical move in preparation for the recourse to public funds, as had been the necessary for solving the US Savings and Loan crisis in 1991.

120 This rhetoric was given substance by the fact that two weeks later Matsushita announced that the BOJ had instructed several major Japanese banks to

improve their overseas operations after checks in the wake of the Daiwa scandal had uncovered weaknesses in their management systems (*Nikkei* 8/8/96).
121 By the time the *jûsen* were liquidated, their bad debts had rocketed: Nippon Housing Loan's, for example, rose by seventy-eight percent since 1992 (from ¥450 billion to ¥800 billion – *Nikkei* 15/2/96).
122 For example, a large group of more than thirty politicians, scores of bureaucrats, and more than a dozen chief executives of major Japanese companies went to the US on a recent mission to 'explain' the latest stimulus package and 'talk up' the economy. Several of the group expressed deep misgivings about pursuing survival-of-the-fittest policies to solve the banking crisis (*Washington Post* article reprinted in *JT* 11/5/98).
123 Schoppa argues that the end of the Cold War enabled the US to delink the economic and geostrategic components of its Japan policy (1997, p. 293). He fails to mention other complementary considerations, such as the fact that the Achilles heel of Bush's Japan policy was that, targeting structural reform, it did not deliver quick results when measured against swelling annual bilateral trade imbalances. Moreover, the fall in competitiveness of Japanese financial institutions meant that there was a natural drop in demands from US firms to 'level' the playing field with structural reform initiatives.
124 The 'revisionists', as *Business Week* dubbed them in a widely publicised cover story (7/8/89), consisted of a group of veteran Japan specialists – former Berkeley professor Chalmers Johnson, head of the Economic Strategy Institute in Washington, Clyde Prestowitz, and journalists James Fallows and Karel van Wolfren. They all had in common the fact that they stressed the persistence of difference, not similarity, between the ideological, behavioural and structural foundations of Japanese and American capitalism, essentially advocating that the US learn from Japan and make dramatic changes to its own internal and external policies by adopting Japanese-style industrial policies at home and mercantilism abroad. Hence they predicted the failure of the Bush administration's Structural Impediments Initiative (SII), advocating instead the establishment of a results-oriented policy of quantitative market share targets which would force the Japanese to deliver or face retaliatory sanctions.
125 Council of Economic Affairs Chairwoman Laura Tyson, Undersecretary of Commerce Jeffrey Garten, Labour Secretary Robert Reich, White House Special Assistant Ira Magaziner, and Treasury Undersecretary for International Affairs Lawrence Summers had all written about the Japanese economic challenge and appeared eager to draft a truly strategic trade and industrial policy under the aegis of a new National Economic Council (NEC). Deputy Treasury Secretary Roger Altman, Commerce Department Secretary Ron Brown, and the NEC's Chairman Robert Rubin and Senior Special Assistant Bo Cutter (the point man on Japanese trade policy in the White House) also had dealt with the Japanese in their respective business careers and shared the revisionists' skepticism about dealing with Japan in a conventional fashion (Asher 1997, p. 346).
126 Schoppa suggests that Japan's willingness to rebuff US *gaiatsu* in the 1990s was buoyed by the December 1993 multilateral agreement on dispute resolution mechanisms for the soon-to-be-established WTO, and by changes in domestic politics, particularly the new election system established in 1994 (1997, pp. 286–8).
127 The US approach in insurance built upon a May 1993 American Chamber of Commerce in Japan (ACCJ) report that claimed US access to Japan's nonlife

market was limited on the basis that the sector was *keiretsu*-dominated. Negotiations began in September that year, and were concluded one year later.
128 In Japan, 'third sector' officially refers to the market for new insurance products which fall between the life and nonlife sectors; in practice most third sector items are nonlife products which falloutside of the nonlife sector's historical remit, e.g. personal accident, sickness or travel insurance. The sector comprises only five percent of Japan's total insurance market, but represents a mainstay of foreign firms' earnings.
129 Interestingly, the head of the Insurance Council Mitsushima Kazuya openly asserted his displeasure of his Council having being sidestepped by MOF in the negotiations, hinting that the timetable agreed to would be difficult for the industry to meet (*Nikkei* 21/12/96).
130 In mid-1998, Barshefsky was protesting three alleged Japanese breaches of the 1996 agreement: (i) that a Japanese firm (INA Himawari Life) was engaging in third sector business, (ii) that the MOF had not kept to the agreement to approve all new products within two months of application, and (iii) that Tokio Marine and Fire Insurance Company was marketing an illegal cancer policy. Japanese government spokesmen insist that there has been no breach of the agreement. In the first instance, they point out that INA Himawari Life is ninety percent owned by a US firm (CIGNA Corporation), and in the second case, they point out that approval of new products within two months has been impossible where applicants have submitted applications backed up with insufficient documentation; to date there had been no direct response to the third claim (*Nikkei* 10/6/98; 11/6/98; 12/6/98; 13/6/98).
131 The US side claims that domestic firms still control over ninety-seven percent of Japan's primary market (*Nikkei* 3/7/98).
132 The US delegation was led by Lawrence Summers; the Japanese team was led by by Chino Takado, Vice Finance Minister for International Affairs. In defence of the *status quo*, the Japanese side could do little more than point to the existence of outstanding interstate banking regulations in the US.
133 Under the agreement, Japan would allow investment advisors to manage public pension funds through 'limited partnerships' in which the trust banks and insurers holding the funds will invest.
134 The EU Delegation of the European Commission has a tiny staff of fifty-two in Tokyo, only twelve of whom are EU diplomats.
135 For the US, contextual political considerations were at least as important in agreeing to participate in joint intervention. In light of an upcoming and controversial trip to China, Clinton's advisors wished to make his trip as smooth as possible to maximise his chances of the trip being seen as a success. China was becoming hypercritical of the falling yen, and its threat to devalue the yuan and spark a new wave of regional devaluations and financial instability would have damaged US relations with China and its similarly controversial recent Asia policy more generally. In Japan, Hashimoto promised that radical action on cleaning up the banking sector bad loan problem would follow the July 12 Upper House elections, but the LDP lost ground making it impossible for the Obuchi to deliver on his predecessor's pledge to take decisive action on the country's banking crisis. A domestic political accord on Japan's promised financial stabilisation bills was eventually secured in late September. It involved the LDP's capitulation to opposition parties over the issue of how to deal with major financial failures such as the Long Term Credit Bank, and most analysts agreed that it was unlikely to translate into 'decisive action' (*Economist* 19/9/98; *Nikkei* 27/9/98; 1/10/98; see also Chapter 4).

Notes

136 Reflecting the Banking Bureau's more progressive stance, all of the subsequent FSRC reports were all entitled 'On the New Financial System' (*Atarashii Kinyû Seido ni tsuite*); by contrast, the Securities Bureau's more defensive stance was reflected in the fact that all the Securities and Exchange Commission reports included the phrase *kihon mondai* ['basic/fundamental problems/issues'] in the titles of all their reports.

137 Interestingly, for fear of losing out to the long-term credit banks, and particularly the IBJ, many city banks favoured the more conservative separate subsidiaries option.

138 Debentures are the most common form of long-term corporate loans, and may also be issued in the form of stock. In line with this provision, the Bank of Tokyo announced its equal-footing merger with Mitsubishi Bank in March 1995.

139 This second clause was particularly ingenious because it provided an incentive both for large banks to take on the costly task of saving a troubled securities firm, as well as posing a credible threat that could push the Big Four securities firms to do the same, simply to keep the banks out. In line with this clause, Daiwa Bank took over Cosmo Securities in August 1993.

140 The guidelines promised in the June legislation were subsequently issued by the MOF in December 1992.

141 See McKenzie (1992) for a survey of other measures of the degree of global integration.

142 For example, senior MOF officials made statements to the effect that it would be important to guarantee the fair treatment of all sectors. Some observers took this to mean equal access and were surprised when weaker institutions and those in declining sectors gained priority in having licences approved. Rather, it was 'fair' in the sense of imposing a handicap on a faster runner to even the race. More obvious statements were also made: that the Ministry would try to prevent the confusion that might occur if all banks set up brokerages at the same time, and that major banks should stick to underwriting and not use the opportunity for their own fundraising purposes (*Nikkei* 20/6/92).

143 Another example of recalcitrance to come to terms fully with new product developments was the BOJ's practice of not differentiating between hedged and unhedged exposure for outstanding swap positions. This, and some of the other cautious licensing decisions, can be attributed to the legacy of the speculative frenzy exploiting newly approved *zaitekku* products during the bubble.

144 Among others, JP Morgan, Lehman Brothers, Bank of Montreal, and HSBC all moved their foreign exchange operations in whole or part out of Tokyo in the early 1990s.

145 The survey of 145 foreign banks and brokers 'Opinions and Strategies of Foreign Financial Institutions Regarding the Tokyo Money and Capital Markets' was published in December 1995. None of the firms surveyed thought that MOF was doing enough to deregulate, and all saw the Tokyo market's further decline as inevitable.

146 See Nihon Keizai Shinbunsha (1997), Imai (1997) and Fuchita (1997) for a comprehensive exposition of what the Big Bang plan entails.

147 The Big Bang was the headline policy initiative of the new Hashimoto administration reform's efforts in five areas (administrative, economic structural, financial, fiscal, and social security) to which a sixth (education) was added in December 1996.

148 Within a month of the announcement, there were signs of a dramatic reversal in foreign financial institution's gradual withdrawal from Tokyo which had begun

seven years previously. The market was buzzing with announcements of new expansion by several firms, including Deutsche Morgan Grenfel, Société Générale, BNP Securities, and HSBC (*FT* 10/12/96).

149 'Free' was defined as 'liberalising regulation such that Japan's financial markets work according to free market principles', 'fair' as 'transparent and trustworthy' and 'global' as 'progressive to the point of regulation anticipating rather than lagging changes in the global financial services industry'.

150 See *Nikkei* 6/5/97 for figures of foreign firms delisting from the TSE in fiscal 1996. During the same period, high transaction commissions had spurred the first significant signs of withdrawal by Japanese institutional investors when, in April 1996, the Pension Welfare Service Public Corporation demanded sharply discounted trading commissions (0.01 percent rather than Japan's normal 0.35 percent) from the UK arm of a major Japanese brokerage for trading Japanese stocks on the LSE. This pension corporation was the first to operate fund stocks on overseas stock markets, and its relative performance was further boosted by the continuation of ultralow interest rates in Japan. It diverted overseas an estimated ¥600 billion from stock trading in Japan (*Nikkei* 24/8/96). More generally, communications costs were estimated to be approximately four times higher in Tokyo than Singapore (*Tōyō Keizai* 23/6/97, p. 77).

151 According to the World Economic Forum's global competitiveness ratings, Japan ranked thirteenth in 1996 and fourteenth in 1997, the US being third and fourth and the UK being fifteenth and seventh, respectively (*Nikkei* 23/5/97). Moreover, commenting on the statistic that since 1992, America's GDP had expanded cumulatively by twenty-two percent but Japan's by only six percent, Minister for International Trade and Industry Satō Shinji stated 'it is clear that the current Japanese economic system, which supported the half-century of economic development following World War Two, has reached its limit' (*Economist* 11/1/97).

152 Since the previous election, the fear of losing the reform initiative was no longer hypothetical. First, there were ongoing efforts by Sakigake's Hatoyama Yukio and others to regroup pro-reform dissidents into a new party in the runup to the general election. Second, on 1 August 1996, a nonpartisan lawmakers' study group, headed by Hosokawa Morihiro (Shinshintō), EPA chief Tanaka Shunsei (Sakigake) and former MPT Koizumi Junichi (LDP) submitted a document – 'Urgent Proposals for Administrative Reforms: Vol. 1' – which made eight suggestions for a ten-year programme of privatisation of government businesses and special corporations, etc. apparently trying to steal the political initiative ahead of possible realignments in the runup to the election [Tanaka had served as a close aid to Hosokawa when he was Prime Minister] (*Nikkei* 2/8/96). Third, Hosokawa soon afterwards published a set of radical administrative and financial reform plans 6/8/96 to Shinshintō's executive board, requesting that they be adopted as policy (*Nikkei* 7/8/96). Moreover, by the run-up to the October 1996 general election, the across-the-board political consensus had transformed even the protectionist agenda of the SDP.

153 Most notably, the subcommittee of the Fiscal System Council, under Honma Masaaki (professor of economics at Osaka University), had released a report 31/5/96, proposing no sanctuary for spending cuts and calling for overhauling the public works system to restore the nation's finances (*Nikkei* 1/6/96).

154 MOF official Adachi Nobiru pointed out that the EPA has had close links with the MOF's Budget Bureau since consumption tax was introduced in 1989 (interview 30/5/97).

Notes

155 Tanaka had spent two weeks prior to the cabinet meeting 'doing the rounds' (*nemawashi*) to solicit private support for his proposals. In his meetings with Keizai Dōyûkai and other business leaders at a Tokyo hotel (1/7/96), and then at a management seminar organised by the Japan Center for Socio-economic Development in Karuizawa (9/7/96), Tanaka framed the defence of his predictably well received arguments for deregulation in terms of Japan lagging its competitors, the globalisation of the Japanese economy, and the need to create flexible labour markets. These meetings received considerable press coverage, and Hashimoto would have certainly been consulted by Tanaka prior to his *nemawashi* tour.

156 Crucially, unlike other government advisory panels, the EC did not hold consultations with other ministries before making its recommendations. Moreover, on Hashimoto's express instructions, the group made all its material available to the press, including individual reports, drafts and counter arguments by individual ministries in order to avoid usurpation by vested political interests.

157 Minaguchi and Ikeo were first to use the term Big Bang in conjunction with Japanese financial reforms. Their report made proposals under three headings – (i) the realisation of wideranging competition, (ii) the liberalisation of assets trading, and (iii) the revision of system of rules and supervision – from which Hashimoto's Big Bang plan was directly derived (NKS 1997, pp. 1–3 [see especially the chart outlining their plan's content on p. 2]).

158 The MOF first announced that poorly performing banks would be allowed to fail from 2001 as part of its new bad loan write-off strategy, but the Nikkei 225 plunged 2.6 percent on the news (*Nikkei* 10/6/95).

159 The panel also urged the MOF to begin an extensive study of electronic money and its systematic introduction. The report stated that debate on all the relevant legal amendments would begin in the autumn.

160 The Japan Center for International Finance was headed by Ōba Tomomitsu, an MOF *amakudari* with strong ongoing ties to the International Finance Bureau, who had risen to the exalted rank of Vice Minister for International Affairs.

161 A senior MOF official on sabbatical at the University of Tokyo pointed out that the MOF's change of heart regarding deregulation followed liberal progressives like Nagano Atsushi and Nishimura Yoshimasa taking over as bureau chiefs from notable conservatives such as Hidaka Sōhei at the Securities Bureau (interview with Adachi Nobiru 30/5/97; 27/6/97).

162 As chairman of the LDP's Policy Research Council, Katō summoned the head of the Finance Minister's secretariat, Komura Takeshi, in February 1995, and berated him for the MOF's lack of progress in implementing a 1993 government directive that the Ministry cut down its proportion of recruits from the University of Tokyo to a maximum of fifty percent within five years. In 1994 eighty-six percent of new recruits were from the University of Tokyo, and in 1995 the proportion was ninety percent. By 1997 the proportion had dropped to seventy percent, which could possibly be construed as cooperation (Hartcher 1998, p. 13). Katō is not a natural supporter of the MOF, as evidenced by his support of the Post Office against privatisation in late 1997 (see Appendix).

163 One MOF official explained that although only one of five seconded prime ministerial secretaries, Saka is the oldest and therefore Hashimoto's most senior secretary, although not the closest to Hashimoto – 'that would be Komura-san from the Ministry of Health and Welfare'. Saka had also served as secretary to Hashimoto when the latter was finance minister in the early 1990s (interview with Adachi Nobiru 27/6/97).

164 The NKS book suggests that Saka was important in informing Hashimoto's broader reform plans, but not in brokering a deal *with* the MOF *per se*. Driven by its thesis that the MOF continues to be the 'root of all evil' in the Japanese financial system, the book argued only that Saka was instrumental in persuading Hashimoto of the need for prioritising financial reform above administrative reform, and hereby ensuring its own survival as a organ necessary for overseeing Big Bang's implementation. The series of events recounted above imply that Hashimoto was not a naive victim of the MOF's manoeuvrings, but rather that he was fully party to a deal in which he extracted a 'pound of flesh' in the form of securing all credit for the Ministry's forward-looking financial reform initiatives.

165 A revised draft of the EC's earlier report (13/11/96) maintained the basic points and original schedule for completion (March 2000), which the MOF had criticised for its proposed timetable being too tight; the ARC's report (5/12/96) touched on five areas of financial deregulation related to Big Bang (*Nikkei* 14/11/96; 6/12/96). The SEC's General Council under Royama was able to produce a report on its first official meeting to discuss Big Bang (29/11/96), having already met nine times since July; the CFEOT produced its preliminary report on Big Bang (16/12/96), as per its interim report on June 1996, outlining its aim to achieve the complete deregulation of its sector; and the FSRC's Financial Institutions Activisation Committee under Kaizuka Keimei (Chûō University) produced an outline strategy for the banking sector from scratch (26/12/96).

166 The idea of holding such a symposium to draft guidelines for deregulation in each member country was originally proposed by Hashimoto at an OECD ministerial meeting in 1995 which he was attending as Japan's Minister for International Trade and Industry. Government officials readily acknowledged in advance of the symposium that a prime reason for holding it in Tokyo was to increase public awareness of the need for deregulation in Japan (*Nikkei* 7/8/96).

167 Other interpretations of the J-League metaphor are possible. Ikuyo Yushiro, Vice President of Smith Barney (Tokyo) warned that, if the overly cautious approach to deregulation continues, the Japanese market will end up like J-League, with star players being snapped up by foreign teams (i.e. firms), leaving Japanese teams (firms) to sit on the spectator benches in international competitions (*Nikkei Kinyû* 26/5/97).

168 In the insurance sector, it was decided that securities firms would be given prior access, and banks would only be allowed into certain parts of the industry (over-the-counter sales of fire and credit-life insurance) from 2001, with no deadline for full access mentioned.

169 First, public sector financial reform was taken up by various party and ministry panels, and by the ARC. The LDP panel on administrative reform, under Satō Koko, agreed to merge the Export-Import Bank of Japan and Overseas Economic Cooperation Fund and abolish the Japan Development Bank, establishing a new organ to take over its vital functions; however, it dropped an earlier plan to privatise the Central Bank for Commercial and Industrial Cooperatives (*Nikkei* 12/7/97). More importantly, the ARC proposed privatising the postal insurance system and transferring the postal savings and postal services to a new body under the jurisdiction of a new General Affairs Ministry, with the aim of their eventual privatisations (*Nikkei* 22/8/97). Under strong opposition from the Post Office, this latter proposal was turned down by the ruling coalition (see section 2.2.3).

Second, the general ban on holding companies was lifted in January 1998, after a bill to revise the Antimonopoly Law was passed in the Diet in June 1997 (*Nikkei* 2/1/98; 12/6/97). It was framed in terms of giving impetus to the international competitiveness of Japanese firms and revitalising the economy by encouraging venture businesses. Specific conditions for establishing financial holding companies were agreed upon eventually by the ruling coalition, and passed in the Diet in early December 1997 for implementation in March 1998. They will be able to acquire an equity stake of up to fifty percent in nonfinancial companies so long as as this investment does not represent more than five percent of their combined asset holdings (*Nikkei* 1/10/97; 6/12/97).

Third, although the Tax Commission began studying tax issues related to financial deregulation since May 1996 for implementation in fiscal 1998, the LDP's Research Commission on the Tax System ruled that the securities trading tax should continue until fiscal 1999, but that greater capital gains taxes would be needed to make up the shortfall in revenue (*NW* 23/9/97). This represented a clear compromise between ministers who had wanted liberalisation earlier because of the imminent liberalisation of foreign exchange trading (from April 1998), and the SESC and JSDA, who had called for complete liberalisation by April 2002 to protect smaller firms (*Nikkei* 2/8/97). Following coalition meetings, the government announced that Japan's various securities transaction taxes would be halved from April 1998, and abolished entirely from April 1999 (*Nikkei* 10/1/98). It was also considering scrapping the withholding tax from April 1999 to boost the international role of the yen (*Nikkei* 14/4/98).

170 This observation contradicts the assertion by Yashiro Naohiro of Sophia University that the open *shingikai* system has proved very effective in overcoming vested interests and giving a much needed stimulus to reform (*Tōyō Keizai* 23/4/97, p. 17).

171 Events which were unfortunate for Hashimoto during the second half of 1997 were (i) the stalling of progress with his headline administrative reform agenda, (ii) his aborted appointment of convicted bribe-taker Satō Koko to head of the Management and Coordination Agency, which cost Hashimoto a fifty percent fall in his public popularity rating, and (iv) his embarrassing policy reversal over fiscal reform (see Chapter 4).

172 PCA was to be the keystone of the Ministry's new transparent and nondiscretionary framework for bank regulation. Basic guidelines for PCA were agreed upon by the MOF's FSRC at the end of September 1996, and were based upon the Second BIS Capital Adequacy Guidelines. The MOF notified all banks that four new benchmark standards to gauge the healthiness of their operations (particularly to monitor bad loans) would be put in place immediately as a transitional measure, and that banks failing to meet the new standards would be required to submit an action programme for improving their operations within thirty days. Failure to improve operations would lead, ultimately, to an order to suspend operations. The capital-assets benchmarks were eight percent for internationally active banks and four percent for domestic banks, measured by self-assessments to be checked by external auditors (*Nikkei* 1/10/96). The MOF actually announced the suspension of PCA's introduction in December (*Nikkei* 24/12/97).

173 This financial stabilisation package was put together under the direction of an LDP task force made up of former prime ministers Nakasone, Miyazawa and Kono Yōhei, and businessmen, which first convened in late November (*Nikkei* 27/12/97). The ¥30 trillion plan was put forward by Kajiyama Seiroku, and consisted of ¥10 trillion in government bonds and ¥20 trillion in government

guarantees. The entire package was approved in the Diet in mid-February (*Nikkei* 17/2/98).

174 Greater bad loan disclosure was to be mandated by the introduction of US Securities and Exchange Commission standards, under which all loans on which interest payments are three months or more in arrears are classified as bad, as opposed to the six-month criteria hitherto common in Japan. The bad loans disclosed by Japan's top nineteen banks in their fiscal 1997 earnings reports came to ¥22 trillion by this new definition, but would have amounted to only ¥14 trillion by the previous definition (*Nikkei* 20/6/98). The DIC was also to get stronger investigative powers to determine management responsibility, file complaints with prosecutors, and impose fines of up to ¥500,000; at present it only has a mandate to do these things with respect to *jûsen*. Legal amendments submitted to ordinary 1997 Diet session also made the RCB capable of taking over failed financial institutions; previously its mandate was limited to dealing with failed credit cooperatives.

175 The MOF promised to introduce a solvency yardstick for securities firms and insurers from fiscal 1998. Securities firms would have to keep capital adequacy ratios above 120 percent, and those whose margins fall under 100 percent for three consecutive months firms will be banned from trading. Public disclosure of margins every quarter will thus be made mandatory (*Nikkei* 3/2/98). For insurance companies, formal instructions to improve management would be issued by the Ministry if a firm's solvency margin falls below 200 percent and suspension order issued if it falls below zero (*Nikkei* 10/3/98).

176 The funds were available for the purchase of either preferred stock or subordinated debentures. Initially, qualifying criteria were set which included the possibility of a rumour-driven share price collapse and subsequent run on bank deposits. To disqualify no-hopers, another criteria was that firms must not have been in deficit for the past three years or have paid out no dividends for three years. However, the reluctance of weak banks to apply for the funds for fear of signalling their precarious situation to the market meant that stronger banks were also encouraged to apply for funds to shield the weak. Hence, Japan's nine city banks all applied for an identical sum of ¥100 billion, while each of the others applied for between ¥50 billion and ¥300 billion (*Nikkei* 29/2/98; 6/3/98;10/3/98).

177 More specifically, (i) the NTA announced that it would broaden the criteria for tax-free write-offs of nonperforming loans to include not just affiliates but business-partner companies that have accepted lender's officials as board members, and companies to which lenders have extended debt forgiveness in the form of lower interest rates (*Nikkei* 4/6/98); (ii) the LDP agreed on bills to lift the ban on specialised debt collection agencies and make it easier for banks to auction collateralised problem loans, both of which were submitted to an extraordinary summer 1998 Diet session and were expected to boost turnover in the property market (*Nikkei* 2/6/98); and (iii) the LDP agreed on a new bad loan task force to mediate between borrowers and lenders in order to help financial institutions writeoff bad loans (*Nikkei* 20/5/98).

178 The Total Plan drew heavily on the US's two-pronged Resolution Trust Corporation and Federal Deposit Insurance Corporation solution to the saving-and-loan crisis of the 1980s. Formally, the time limit for Japan's bridge banks was set at two years, with three one-year extensions theoretically possible (*Nikkei* 3/7/98).

179 This was supposedly a major reason for other major banks or brokerages refusing to take over Hokkaidō Takushoku Bank's operations in late 1997 (interview with Jeffrey Young, economist at Salomon Smith Barney, 24/6/98).

180 The Japanese state holds roughly $300 billion T-bills in foreign exchange reserves.
181 Most notable was the MOF's new framework of PCA which, although delayed in implementation by one year, promised to reduce the Ministry's scope for reliance on administrative guidance considerably (see Footnote 172 above). Hence, the MOF announced in June 1998 that it was abolishing 382 of its 400 extra-legal *tsûtatsu* (notifications) and 234 of its less authoritative *jimu renraku* (administrative communiqués), because they were 'excessively minute' and many items covered were now codified, e.g. the requirement for periodic reporting is now covered by Article 24 of Bank Law, which will also be beefed to specify punishments for noncompliance (*Nikkei* 9/6/98).
182 Japan recorded a net investment fund inflow (¥2.4 trillion) in calendar 1997 for first time in fifteen years (*Nikkei* 13/2/98).
183 In spite of his reputation for outspokenness, Sakakibara was promoted to the MOF's number two position of Vice Finance Minister for International Affairs in July 1997, indicating that his philosophy and comments are generally in line with those of the Ministry.

CHAPTER 3

1 Japanese insurers are left out of the Chapter's discussion until section 3.3. This is because they did not compete directly with foreign firms or other financial institutions until at least the mid-1990s.
2 On the pre-WWII history of Japanese banking, see Tamaki (1995).
3 Often, the term 'international banking' is used to refer to the cross-border extension of national banking, whereby a bank intermediates credit between deposits in its home country and borrowers overseas. 'Multinational banking' goes a stage further, referring to a banks' overseas office intermediating credit between overseas lenders and overseas borrowers (Duser 1990, p. 13).
4 With regard to the latter point, it should be noted that, unlike in banking, the distinction between different securities firms (i.e. tier one [the 'Big Four'], tier two, and tier three) is defined on the basis of size, not function. Hence, firms will automatically fall from tier one to tier two status if their capitalisation shrinks sufficiently, and vice versa. This implies that the boundaries are porous and informal, and serve only a descriptive roll. Hence, it is not necessary to subdivide figure 3.6 into the three tier classification in the same way that figure 3.1 must subdivided for banks.
5 Nomura has established the first overseas office of any Japanese securities firm in 1927 in New York.
6 Outside these three central zones – North America, Europe and Asia – Japan's securities firms are notable by their absence, with only the Big Four in Australia, Nomura and Daiwa in Brazil (Sao Paulo), and the Big Four and three others in Bahrain.
7 The distinction between foreign banks and securities firms is made on the basis of their classification in their home market/registered jurisdiction, and does not correspond to the business in which they are engaged in Japan. Hence, they can be best be viewed in aggregate on the same diagram.
8 Tier One capital thus became the most widely used benchmark for routine international comparisons.
9 The main problem with Tier One capital measures is that the figures needed to calculate it are often not included in companies' annual reports or disclosed individually by the BIS. *Institutional Investor* magazine's index of 'total capital'

was intended as a more market-oriented gauge of banks' true cushion against financial shock, while its subsequent 'core capital' index was intended to 'level the playing field' by using a more universal measure – shareholder equity/ shareholder funds – as a benchmark comparison. These measures were first published in 1995 and 1997, respectively (see various August issues).

10 Because of their very large size, syndicated loans are commonly conducted in the international markets, and are thus a better proxy for international prominence than other bank lending statistics, which are more likely to reflect a large proportion of domestic activity.

11 Due to changes after 1990 and 1993 in the way *Euromoney* publishes its global ranking tables, it has not been possible to provide completely up-to-date versions of figures 3.19 to 3.22. This does not, however, detract from the argument set out in the text, which seeks to demonstrate the meteoric rise of Japanese financial institutions in international markets during the mid-to-late 1980s. Sections 3.2 and 3.3 concentrate on their relative decline in the 1990s.

12 *Euromoney* is arguably *the* leading publication covering international financial issues, a distant second place being occupied by *The Banker*, which incorporates a wider variety of news but covers it in less detailed. Both of these periodicals are published in London and, hence, suffer much less from the overt North American bias which dominates rival publications such as *Institutional Investor* and *US Banker*. Although recognising *Euromoney's* inherent Western (and possibly European – see footnote 28 below) bias, this book has relied heavily on this particular source in the absense of any better alternative – Japanese publications, for example, being much more locally focused. Nevertheless, to supplement information and keep a check on the balance of opinion expressed in *Euromoney*, *The Banker* and, to a lesser extent, *Institutional Investor* have also been used periodically as proxies for professional opinion expressed in the largely Western-dominated international financial markets.

13 As *Euromoney* noted, 'in the past five years, [Nomura's] assets have grown more than ¥31 trillion, up some 106 percent' (8/87).

14 Another area of frequent criticism related to the observation that Japanese securities firms' research reports were little more than thinly disguised sales promotion tools, although this was directed more at the level of sophistication of Japanese investors.

15 Of ten tiers of international banks which Bachan (1976) identified in 1974, US firms ranked highest and Japanese firms lowest; by 1976, Japanese firms ranked five of seven.

16 A firm's *field of action* is taken to be its sphere of activity, either real or potential, as created by exogenous and endogenous developments or actions.

17 Between 1981 and 1985, over seventy percent of manufacturers' funds went into fixed investment; this figure dropped steadily and by 1989 it had dropped to below fifty per cent, with financial assets accounting for over forty per cent of manufacturers' funds invested. The personal sector's level of indebtedness also rose to US levels, surpassed only by levels in the UK. In Japan, personal indebtedness rose from seventy per cent of disposable income in 1985 to ninety-six per cent in 1990; the figures for US being from eighty per cent to ninety-seven per cent and, for the UK, from seventy-seven per cent to 107 per cent (Takeda and Turner 1992, p. 50, 56).

18 Since the early 1970s, the MOF had imposed a ten percent limit on funds which could be invested overseas (up from zero in 1970).

19 The Japanese government eventually passed legislation (March 1995) deregulating domestic corporate bond issues, which took effect from January 1996, and

foreign issues fell rapidly to seventeen per cent during the first half of that year (Fuchita 1997, p. 11).

20 In the six years to 1987, Japanese banks almost doubled their loan assets at overseas branches, going from ¥19.4 trillion to ¥40.6 trillion. By 1986 they were the world's biggest lenders, according to BIS (9/12/97). Fifty per cent of these funds were secured through interbank borrowing compared with an average of thirty-five percent for banks of other nationalities (Takeda and Turner 1992, p. 85).

21 For securities firms, extraordinary profits were largely the result of artificially high fixed commission rates. During the early years of the bubble, even, the Japanese brokerage industry as a whole recorded enormous year-on-year gains in profitability, rising from an already high base of thirty-two percent in 1983–4, to fifty-three percent in 1984–5, and eighty-six percent in 1985–6 (*Euromoney* 4/87). For banks, lower funding costs were the result of (i) lower capital reserve requirements which were tacitly supported by the BOJ, (ii) the established practice of not having to pay such high dividends to shareholders, and (iii) semi-regulated and ultra-low domestic interest rates which were held down artificially, at least until 1989. This gave them an estimated advantage of 100–125 basis points over foreign firms when raising funds domestically (*Euromoney* 4/87).

22 Looked at from another perspective, Arora cites MITI figures which show that Japanese firms abroad rely on Japanese banks for an unusually high proportion of their funding needs – over fifty per cent in the late 1980s (1995, p. 186).

23 The only significant exception to this trend was in selling Japanese equities to foreign portfolio managers.

24 The Japan premium is a credit risk premium imposed by the international capital markets on Japanese banks' borrowing in the interbank market (commonly measured in terms of basis points on three-month eurodollar loans *vis à vis* the rate which US and European firms are charged). It is supposed to reflect the lack of transparency and assumed weakness of their domestic operations, and first emerged in the spring of 1992 after the Nikkei 225 Index fell dramatically. Hereafter, it gradually declined only to reemerge suddenly in July 1995 in the wake of Cosmo Credit Association's failure, which sparked fears of proliferating financial bankruptcies. It was fed by the Daiwa Bank (USA) scandal that September and reached almost forty basic points (i.e. 0.4 percent) later that month, since when it has emerged periodically in times of instability, such as Hanwa Bank's failure in December 1996 and the stock market's fall in January 1997 (see Fuchita 1997, pp. 9–14). Following the collapses of Hokkaido Takushoku Bank and Yamaichi Securities in November 1997, the Japan premium reached a record of nearly 120 basis points in December 1997 (Endo 1998, p. 24).

25 For a full discussion, see *Kokusai Kinyû* 15/12/92.

26 *Euromoney* survey results are published as *Annual Financing Report* (March supplement), *Global Financing Guide* (September issues), and periodically in the form of various articles. The results are not amenable to straightforward tabulation, since bases, scoring systems, and content vary from year to year.

27 The CCE favours firms intermediating business in their home currency. The performance of Japanese banks in yen-related issues is particularly impressive when one considers that they were prohibited by the MOF from lead managing Japanese corporate issues abroad under the Three Bureaus Agreement (1974–1993 – see Chapter 2) which was intended to reserve the business for Japan's securities companies by prohibiting Japanese banks from lead-managing yen-denominated debt issues by Japanese companies in foreign markets.

28 For the past decade, *Euromoney* has asked more than 200 users and market professionals – defined as 'chief financial executives, executives at corporates, sovereigns, banks and supranational organizations active in the international capital markets') – which institutions have provided them with the best service. It should be noted, however, that there is a substantial geographical bias to these polls. Typically, twenty-five percent of respondents are based in the UK, sixteen percent in Germany, eleven percent in Scandinavia, and twenty-one percent elsewhere in Europe, fifteen percent in North America, nine percent in Asia, two percent in South America, and one percent in Africa (see *Global Financing Guide*, September issues).

29 The reason for this is that, as above, consistent year-on-year comparisons are not possible, and many categories are too narrow/technical to allow for concise performance summaries.

30 Unfortunately, universally comparable measures of competitiveness such as profitability and productivity are not illuminating, because both capital and revenue figures for Japanese firms were distorted massively by the bubble and its collapse. For example, it is difficult to make sense of return on equity figures, by which Japanese city banks scored extremely poorly *vis à vis* US firms during the late 1980s, when the Big Four did almost twice as well as leading US firms. Nevertheless, by productivity, Japan's seven biggest banks and the Big Four compare well when measured by the criteria of 'revenue generated per unit of non-interests expense' over the period 1985–9 – something which is commonly attributed to the lower levels of salaries in Japanese firms (for a more detailed discussion, see Arora 1995, pp. 197–202).

31 During the 1980s, Japanese banks had embarked upon limited rationalisation efforts in order to respond to the demands of having a much greater part of their business overseas. Thus, Mitsui Bank (now Sakura) initiated an overhaul of its operations in 1986, which involving an organisation regrouping of activities, while Mitsubishi Bank created a new merchant banking division in response to its move into investment banking. Others such as Nippon Credit Bank, for example, announced a restructuring plan with the aim of targeting business from Western companies expanding into the Japanese market (*Euromoney* 4/87).

32 During the first half of fiscal 1990, profits fell fifty-five percent at Nomura, sixty percent at Daiwa, and seventy-four percent at both Nikkō and Yamaichi (*Euromoney* 2/91).

33 Nikkō's head of international strategy, told *Euromoney* in early 1991: 'Overseas, it will not be necessary to keep all our present employees ... We will be checking the performance and capacity of all our staff, and if we find they are not producing, we will have to show a tough face' (interview with Kanazaki Yasuo, 2/91).

34 Most dramatically, Sumitomo Bank, after becoming embroiled in a US treasury bond trading scandal and being banned from operating in the US for two years, announced that it would half its international assets. Between 1993 and 1996 it had cut ¥20 billion in costs, partly by reducing its staff by 1,300 and and by closing thirty branches (*Euromoney* 9/96).

35 Sakura Bank, for example, introduced both a voluntary retirement programme for over forty-five year-olds, its so-called 'New Career Choice System' which offered a pay-off of one to two years salary, and a six-month leave program at eighty percent pay to encourage employees to find new jobs elsewhere. The Bank of Tokyo-Mitsubishi, meanwhile, cut pension incentives for employees to stay with the firm beyond twenty years (Makino 1997, pp. 138–9).

36 Makino emphasises that the long-standing male-female discrimination in Japanese banking has extended to divide core and non-core *male* staff, bringing about unprecedented divisions in the white-collar work force.
37 Thus at Dai-ichi Kangyō Bank (DKB), for example, bonuses have been zero for the four year period fiscal 1993 to 1996 (*Nikkei Kinyû* 9/3/97).
38 The Long Term Credit Bank of Japan was the first major bank to introduce an actual wage cutting plan in January 1996, reducing the monthly salaries of its non-core staff by up to 20 percent (Makino 1997, pp. 157–8)
39 Makino notes that many of these changes were described by the City Bank Workers Union as 'understandable' austerity measures given the poor state of corporate affairs in the 1990s (1997, p. 160).
40 These systems rely on allocating credit ratings to loans from which the firms' risk exposure can be calculated according to a multitude of scenarios.
41 A comparative survey of Japanese banks abroad and foreign banks in Japan, carried out by the MOF, confirms this, asserting 'a simple case of Japanese banks having overdone it'. Only in Taiwan did Japanese banks appear to be under-represented (*Nikkei Kinyû* 27/3/97).
42 A serious problem is the weakness of revenue in Japan's banking industry, stemming from the fact that it is 'overbanked'. As of fiscal 1995, outstanding loans accounted for 148 percent of GDP in Japan compared to thirty-eight percent in the US (comparative figures for ROE, which are low, reflect this – see *Economist* 31/8/96 for details).
43 The magazine *Project and Trade Finance*, which broke these figures down by firm, ranked Sumitomo Bank first, Sakura Bank third, and Sanwa Bank fourth, with the Bank of Tokyo-Mitsubishi, the Industrial Bank of Japan (IBJ) and Fuji Bank all following in the top ten (survey results cited in *Nikkei Kinyû* 14/2/97). By contrast, their figures for the global syndicated project financing market showed that Japanese banks no longer figured prominently. Sumitomo, the top Japanese firm, ranked eleventh, followed by Sakura in twentieth place.
44 Banks were first allowed to set up securities subsidiaries in 1993. In 1995, the Big Four retained fifty-six percent of the market between them.
45 Fuji Bank, for example, set up a unit to screen new businesses for venture capital in January 1995, and then launched a special R&D start-up fund in October 1996; Sakura followed suit soon after and Sanwa was reported to be planning similar moves (*Nikkei* 21/3/97).
46 Their New York offices were particularly hard hit by Japanese investors' loss of appetite for US Treasury Bills.
47 Citibank was the first to establish a private banking operation in Japan in 1987. It enjoyed spectacular growth between 1993 and 1996. Nomura Trust and Banking and Asahi Bank set up their operations in January and February 1996, respectively, and a recent research report published by Sakura Research Institute suggests that IPB in Japan is likely to become highly competitive after bank holding companies are legalised, possibly before the century's end (*NW* 6/5/96).
48 In Japanese, the term *dochakucha* (a word used by farmers to describe the process of adaptation to local soil conditions) was used to describe firms' policy of 'global localisation' in adapting to the new environment through the delegation of authority and the targeting of more local business.
49 At this time, Sumitomo had 5,200 staff overseas, 460 of which are Japanese. Moreover, because thirty-three of the fifty-five directors at the London meetings were non-Japanese, this suggests that firms' degree of localisation was high by the historical standards of Japanese financial institutions abroad. Sumitomo was reportedly considering extending the practice to its Hong Kong operation.

50 The BOT-M provides a radical example of the sort of HRM changes that seem likely to emerge as the industry norm. Management exploited the launching of the new bank as an opportunity for changing salary, retirement, welfare and working conditions under the auspices of creating a globally-competitive bank with strong management. Seniority pay has been completely abolished, replaced by a new renumeration structure of thirty-seven grades which gives a complex tabular formulation for more than 200 pay levels for ordinary employees. Almost inevitably, many employees discovered that their salaries had fallen under the new system, but management were simply able to respond by pointing out that pay levels were now formulated more accurately and reflected each employee's contribution to the firm! (Tanaka 1997a, pp. 181–4; 188). Sakura Bank launched a similar system in July 1996, its so-called 'Human Resource Value System' (for details, see Makino 1997, pp. 150–2; 156–7).

51 Ikushiro Yushiro, an analyst at Smith Barney (Japan) asserts that in terms of risk and cost management technologies, information strength and product development capabilities, Japanese banks are about five years behind European/US banks (*Tōyō Keizai* 7/5/97, p. 23); A *Kinyû Bijinesu* editorial is less generous: 'Japanese banks are about ten years behind the Americans' (1/97, p. 27). Ten years seems to be most quoted figure by the *Asahi* and *Nikkei* newspapers.

52 While in asset size the BOT-M (¥80 trillion) is over twice as large as Citicorp (¥34 trillion), measures of profitability, efficiency and safety favour Citicorp heavily: ROA figures of 0.05 percent (BOT-M) versus 1.40 percent (Citicorp); ROE figures of 1.22 percent (BOT-M) versus 18.95 percent (Citicorp); bad loans being over ten times bigger for BOT-M; profit of international business being much higher for Citicorp; and the proportion of business coming from stable fee-based services being much greater for Citicorp.

53 In the 1990s, *Poll of Polls* had largely replaced their regular publication of league tables in the 1980s in *Annual Financing Report* and *Global Financing Guide*.

54 According to *Euromoney*, TSR is 'a measure which reflects the market's view of future performance in delivering value' (7/98).

55 It should be noted that the poor Japanese performance was attributed to more than just domestic economic conditions. The top bank in the survey was from Spain, and other positions were not dominated by US firms. The article concluded, 'The tough implication here is that equity should be returned to shareholders if high-spread opportunities cannot be identified. Equity should not be conserved merely to prove 'strength'. Clearly, companies' individual strategies will differ. But as the league table shows, *value can be optimised in widely varying circumstances* – and that is what shareholders demand today' (7/98, my emphasis).

56 Internationally active Japanese banks suffer from a funding constraint in that most of their overseas liabilities are denominated in dollars. With the partial exception of the Bank of Tokyo-Mitsubishi, which owns two retail banks in California (and therefore has direct access to dollar funding), Japanese banks must exchange yen or borrow in other currencies in the interbank market to conduct their activities. Yen internationalisation will make the yen exchange rate less dependent on domestic economic conditions, and therefore Japanese firms less vulnerable in the process.

57 Brokerages cut their total workforce by thirty-five percent since the bubble burst, and now have total of 108,072 staff, down from 166,965 in September 1991. While the cuts were exaggerated in 1997 by the collapses of Sanyo (2,600) and Yamaichi (7,500), the JSDA says it is still necessary to cut 'superfluous flesh', and that the sector's workforce will inevitably fall below 100,000 (*Nikkei* 25/2/98).

58 Sakura Bank announced plans in October 1997 to open some of its branches for limited services on weekends and national holidays, becoming the first major bank to do so (*Nikkei* 15/10/97).
59 24-hour ATM services were first offered in Japan by a small regional lender, Tokyo Sōwa Bank, in May 1997. Sumitomo Bank was the first city bank to offer the service in February 1998 and Sanwa Bank followed in July. Meanwhile, other city banks have been busy upgrading their ATM facilities, replacing machines and introducing longer service hours (*Nikkei* 28/9/97). Daido Mutual Life Insurance announced in February 1998 that it planned to be the first insurer to offer 24-hour ATM services (*Nikkei* 12/2/98).
60 Sanwa and Sumitomo Banks were the first to start telephone banking, in June 1997, with DKB planning to begin that August, and Fuji from April 1998 (*Nikkei* 30/7/97), and BOT-M was scheduled to provide account holders with email access to check their bank balances from August 1998. Led by Nomura and Daiwa, securities firms began to offer internet-based trading services in April 1996 (see section 4.3 in next chapter).
61 Akin to US cash management accounts (CMAs), GSAs were legalised in Japan in October 1997, since when all the major securities firms have launched their own versions of the accounts which function like bank accounts (see section 4.3 in next chapter).
62 Wrap accounts are deposit accounts geared for either the active or passive securities investor. They were legalised in April 1998, since when several large brokerages and trust banks have launched their own versions (see section 4.3 in next chapter).
63 Foreign currency accounts were legalised in April 1998, since when most city banks have launched their own versions (see section 4.3 in next chapter).
64 Small-lot investment funds began to be offered by a few brokerages and trust banks after liberalisation in April 1998 (see section 4.3 in next chapter).
65 OTC investment trusts began to be sold in leading city and regional banks following partial deregulation in December 1997 (see section 4.3 in next chapter).
66 Anticipating the completion of commissions deregulation in 1999, several brokers have announced that they will launch discount brokerage services, with Matsui Securities, for example, promising that it would cut commissions rates by fifty percent (see also section 4.3 in next chapter).
67 Following partial industry deregulation in July 1998, all major insurers will begin selling disaster insurance tailored to the needs of individual customers from September (*Nikkei* 17/8/98; see also section 4.3 in next chapter).
68 BOT-M announced in July 1997 that it would be the first bank to launch its own e-cash system in April 1998 (*Nikkei* 16/7/97).
69 Fuji Bank was the first Japanese bank to market credit derivatives (*Nikkei Kinyû* 26/3/97).
70 Based on the US model, a securitised loan market was opened in April 1997 to help the banking sector rid itself of bad loans and pave way for securitisation more generally. Securitised assets are expected to become a major new business area in Japan. Following their partial deregulation in fiscal 1997, the government and the MOF plans full deregulation in fiscal 1999 (*Nikkei Kinyû* 2/4/97).
71 This became possible after the JSDA lifted regulations banning off-exchange trading of unlisted securities in July 1997 (see section 4.3 in next chapter).
72 See section 4.3 in next chapter.
73 Sumitomo Bank has announced plans to link its in-house computer network to firms' LANs to make remote/PC banking possible; similarly, Sanwa Bank has

signed an agreement with NTT to offer a unique remote client-client payment system over the internet (*Nikkei* 19/7/98).
74. Sumitomo has announced plans to offer corporate clients multilateral netting services in conjunction with Japan Research Institute, the first Japanese bank to offer such a product (*Nikkei* 10/7/98).
75. For example, Yokohama Bank announced that it would shift from a five-tier to a ten-tier grading system from fiscal 1998 as part of their 'Innovation 21' medium-term plan to strengthen risk management (*Nikkei Kinyû* 11/4/97).
76. For example, New Japan Securities introduced a system of ten worker grades with eight scales each, which was applied to all employees with over four years experience from April 1998; Kankaku Securities introduced its scheme from July 1998, which applies to all staff and can result in maximum difference of ¥8 million annually among managers (*Nikkei* 9/5/98).
77. Daiwa Securities was to introduce its own four-stage qualification programme into management to increase the level of professionalisation of its staff(*Nikkei Kinyû* 17/4/97). A Nikkei Research survey, the third of its kind since 1995, found clear evidence that firms are placing greater emphasis on offering better customer service, more highly trained staff and better products (*Nikkei Kinyû* 21/2/97).
78. The shift is one to mark-to-market (rather than historical cost-based) accounting, which was to be introduced from fiscal 1998. Significantly, this would also enable leading Japanese financial institutions to participate in short-term, high credit exposure transactions (e.g. derivatives-based arbitrage trading) with foreign firms on an equal footing (*Nikkei Kinyû* 7/4/97).
79. In this respect, BOT-M has gone furthest, announcing in August 1998 that it will apply US Securities and Exchange Commission standards to its bad loan portfolio from October 1998, implying that 'unrecoverable' Category Four loans will be completely written-off, all loans for which interest payments have been restructured will appear as Category Three loans (i.e. those with 'questionable' prospects for recovery), and Category Two loans (i.e. those at risk of going bad) will be subdivided into two categories according to their prospects for recovery. Analysts believe other banks are likely to follow BOT-M's lead, and that the JFBA may adopt the method as a unified standard (*Nikkei* 21/8/98).
80. Tōkai Bank is the latest to seek NYSE listing. Meanwhile, Sumitomo Bank made public its fiscal 1997 earnings data in an unprecedented move to appeal to investors by increasing transparency (*Nikkei* 23/7/98).
81. For example, BOT-M announced its would aim for eight percent ROE by end of fiscal 2000 (*FEER* 25/9/97), while Fuji Bank said it would seek seven percent ROE in three years and eight percent in five (*Nikkei* 1/1/98).
82. National Securities announced that it had reduced its capital to ¥10 billion, from ¥19 billion, to write off accumulated losses (*Nikkei* 19/8/98). Meanwhile, in the first half of fiscal 1997, Fuji Bank slashed its loan book by ¥3 trillion, and Sanwa and Sumitomo were rumoured to be doing likewise (*Economist* 13/9/97).
83. Shizuoka Bank, one of the largest and most progressive regional banks, became the first to announce a share buyback initiative to boost ROE by taking advantage of June 1997 legal revisions (see chapter four – *Nikkei* 20/11/97). Fuji Bank was also rumoured to be mulling the idea (*Nikkei* 1/1/98).
84. The Bank of Yokohama, Japan's biggest regional bank, became the first financial institution to announced that it was considering selling most of its domestic stock holdings, particularly financial stocks, to improve the firm's financial position. It said it had already notified the banks concerned (*Nikkei* 8/11/97). Nomura Securities followed soon after, telling the *Financial Times* virtually the same story (*FT* 10/2/98). Daiwa Bank then announced it would take the same route (*Nikkei*

4/4/98). Similarly, when their financial 1997 accounts were released, the shareholder lists of Japan's eight leading city banks plus the LTCB and IBJ showed that Nippon Life Insurance had sold 34 million shares in these firms that year, including 6.46 million in Sumitomo Bank alone. Meiji Life was also notable for having sold large quantities of Tōkai Bank and IBJ stock (*Nikkei* 5/7/98).

85 Revelations about main-banks refusing financial support to affiliates have risen dramatically since the Big Bang was announced. For example, in November 1997 Sakura Bank publicly relinquished its lender-of-last-resort role to Tokushoku, a food trading company, which subsequently collapsed with ¥140 billion in debts. Six months later, Nippon Life announced that it would suspend new subordinated lending to all financial institution amid a surge in contract cancellations and worries over being sued by policyholders if the loans subsequently turned sour (*Nikkei* 7/6/98).

86 As of the end of April 1998, the Post Office had received applications from seventy-seven private financial institutions, including two foreign firms (Citibank and Amex), for access to its ATM network, and plans to begin hooking up applicants from January 1999 (*Nikkei* 8/5/98). The Post Office first met with a group of fifteen banks (including Citibank) in May 1997 in a series of research committee meetings to discuss the idea of establishing a public-private banking network.

87 It should be noted that for the Post Office, the rationale for pursuing cooperative tie-ups is more than simply distributional; agreeing to sign agreements with its most vocal critics is a way for it to weaken the private sector coalition in favour of curtailing its deposit-taking and insurance business. Daiwa Bank was the first city bank to pursue ties with the Post Office, and the remaining eight soon followed out of a sense of compulsion (*Nikkei* 26/3/98); Sumitomo Life was the first insurer to approach the Post Office, but thus far only Nippon Life and Dai-ichi Mutual have reluctantly followed (*Nikkei* 15/5/98).

88 In the Swiss Bank-LTCB venture, it was asserted at the start that the new firms would operate in English, salaries would be based on performance evaluations, and monitoring would be '360 degree' – i.e. by superiors, colleagues, and subordinates (*Nikkei* 17/11/97). Nevertheless, as a result of continued fears about LTCB's solvency, Swiss Bank agreed to take a larger stake in the joint venture, announcing in September 1998 that it would increase its ownership to 100 percent 'as soon as possible' (*Nikkei* 24/9/98). With regard to the latter example, the *Far Eastern Economic Review* commented perceptively, 'Travellers' biggest contribution is an excuse. Instead of implementing painful reforms himself, such as merit-based pay, Kaneko [Masashi – Nikkō's president] can tell his employees that he is being forced to do so by foreigners' (11/6/98).

89 Nomura originally stated its intention of uniting its group companies in a holding company structure sometime after April 1998 (*Nikkei Kinyû* 6/2/97). IBJ, too, has voiced its interest in bringing together its banking, securities and investment advisory services in a holding company structure by offering a complete range of wholesale banking services (*Nikkei Kinyû* 12/2/97).

90 Realising that their survival is at stake, these institutions' national associations have begun actively promoting consolidation among their members. The National Mutual Insurance Federation for Agricultural Cooperatives is to merge all prefectural bodies by 2001 in preparation for the Big Bang. Agricultural cooperatives run three types of businesses – farm product sales, banking, and insurance – and decided in 1991 to streamline their operations, but until recently such moves were delayed by opposition from local groups (*Nikkei* 22/7/97; see also *Nikkei* 3/4/97 and the latest MOF statistics).

Notes

91 As head of the Daiwa Institute of Research Yoshikawa Mitsuru notes, 'If [financial holding companies] work as envisaged, they will provide a vehicle for finance returning to its original function [of establishing and controlling *zaibatsu*-type corporate groupings]' (*Nikkei* 15/3/97). See also *Nikkei* 4/2/97 for an interview with a spokesman from Sakura Bank framed in these terms.

92 For example, after Nikkō Securities announced in February 1998 that it would 'reassign' 1,500 female clerks (almost half of its female staff of 3,400) to work as temporary staff at affiliates in order to cut its medium-term personnel costs, labour union trouble and legal difficulties forced the firm to cancel the plan in May. A spokesman for the company explained that the move simply had been attempted 'too early' (*Nikkei* 21/2/98; 13/5/98).

93 An apparent exception to this general rule is the recently announced pay structure revisions at Sumitomo Bank. Staff who retire and are rehired as 'financial specialists' will see their pay ceiling raised to four times the current level, and a floor introduced at eighty percent of the current level. Career-track employees, however, will see their pay ceiling raised to double their current level, and a floor set at ninety-five to ninety-eight percent of the current level. Western analysts still object to any notion of a pay ceiling. They say that to pass judgment on Sumitomo's new pay scale it will be necessary to find out just what pay variations actually translate into in practice (interview with Alicia Ogawa, former financial sector analyst at Salomon Smith Barney [now head of Asian Research there], 18/6/98).

94 Comments in the same article made by Elizabeth Daniels, a bank analyst at Morgan Stanley, confirm this attitude among top Japanese bankers. She recounts how one banker asked her why Western analysts are so focused on lending margins and profitability, saying 'Don't you realize we're doing Japan a service by lending at a good, affordable price to those who need it?'. Similarly, Jason James, head of equity research at James Capel (Tokyo) agrees, 'One can't help having the suspicion that if they got out of their bad-debt problem they'd go back to where they were before' (interview 10/3/98).

95 For example, Japan's first drive-through ATMs were opened by a regional bank in Hokkaido in July 1997 (*Nikkei Kinyû* 24/4/97), and BOT-M now boasts the world's fastest ATM machine, from which ¥50,000 can be withdrawn in nine seconds (*Nikkei Kinyû* 28/3/97). Tokio Marine and Fire has announced that it will introduce new car accident insurance policies to cover drivers even when they are not driving, and will charge customers a twenty-percent-over-average premium for the service (*Nikkei* 16/7/98). Nippon Shinpan, Japan's largest consumer credit firm, debuted its 'NICOS print card' in June 1998, a credit card which boasts its users' photograph, while another firm, Sumitomo Credit Service, introduced a credit card in April 1997 entitling its owner to free membership of the company's 'club to help parenting' (*Nikkei* 2/7/98). More recently, Tōkai Bank announced plans to allow dollar account holders to withdraw dollars from ATMs at 109 of its 236 branches, although it refused to provide analysts with estimates of how much offering this service would cost the firm (*Nikkei* 15/8/97).

96 In spite of the fact that free 24-hour ATMs are a standard banking service in the rest of the developed world, and even some parts of the developing world (e.g. Thailand), large Japanese banks until recently claimed that the reason that they did not provide 24-hour ATM services was (i) that it would be a terrible loss of face if someone were to find one empty, and so they would have to man them with technicians 24-hours a day, and/or (ii) that the cost of new computer systems necessary to operate the systems would make them prohibitively expensive. Sumitomo Bank began operating 24-hour ATMs at only ten of its city branches, and Sanwa Bank geared up for the service by initially extending its

Notes

ATM hours to 11 p.m. at around twenty-five city branches. Other major banks are yet to commit themselves to 24-hour banking beyond expressing their vague intention to follow. Incidentally, Citibank began to offer free 24-hour ATM services at its twenty branches in Japan in 1994.

97 Kagomiya cites as his example the JFBA's 'recent' lifting of restrictions on commercial radio and TV advertising. In fact, the JFBA lifted its bans on these things on 21/3/90 and 2/1/91, respectively. It also began to extend cash dispenser hours around the same time (on Saturdays [from 2 p.m. until 5 p.m.] on 19/4/90, and on Sundays on 14/1/91), yet seven-to-eight years later has still to approve the full deregulation of 24-hour services or even regular hours service at ATMs on weekends.

98 BOTM, nevertheless, announced its 'intention' to slim down its board to between forty and fifty directors 'in the future' (*Nikkei* 18/3/98).

99 Sumitomo Bank, by contrast, recently hired Kubota Tatsuo, former head of Citibank's private banking division to revitalise the bank's retail banking operations (*FEER* 3/9/98).

100 At the end of March 1997, NCB announced that it would seek to raise ¥300 billion of new capital from major life insurers to write off its bad loans, and pledged to cut its assets by ¥10 trillion (*Nikkei* 27/3/97; *Nikkei Kinyû* 28/3/97). At the end of that year, Fuji Bank and Yasuda Fire & Marine Insurance agreed to purchase ¥100 billion in new Yasuda Trust stock, although the latter agreed to cut its loan portfolio by fifty percent as part of the deal (*Nikkei* 5/12/97). More recently, Fuji Bank itself, and Sakura Bank, have both appealed to their respective *keiretsu* affiliates to participate in a plan to boost their capital bases by ¥200 billion to ¥300 billion each in order to strengthen rapidly deteriorating balance sheets (*Nikkei* 1/9/98; *FT* 14/9/98).

101 Other examples include IBJ's agreement to support New Japan Securities by extending ¥20 billion in subordinated loans, Sakura's extension of ¥4 billion to Yamatane Securities (*Nikkei* 10/12/97), and five major life insurers' consideration of a request from North Pacific Bank to purchase ¥40 billion in subordinated debt to boost its capital base following its absorption of HTB's regional business (*Nikkei* 13/8/98).

102 This announcement was first made by the Minister of Finance on February 10, 1997, then reiterated by the Governor of the BOJ (*Nikkei* 11/2/97; 15/2/97).

103 In November 1997, MOF officials indicated that they planned to reduce to the number of Japanese banks operating abroad to between fifteen and twenty institutions by barring those who do not meet the eight percent BIS capital to assets ratio(*Nikkei* 17/11/97). Currently about eighty banks operate overseas, and about half of these previously had been thought capable of continuing to do so (*Nikkei Kinyû* 27/3/97). More recently, the deputy director of MOF's Banking Bureau, Nakai Sei, has gone on record as predicting that only two to four Japanese banks will ultimately prove to be internationally competitive: 'The rest will return to regional status' while maintaining a small international presence (*FEER* 4/12/97).

104 Travellers' direct equity investment was ¥84 billion, plus ¥136 billion in convertible bonds, meaning that it can decide in future whether or not it wants to increase its equity stake in Nikkō.

105 Japanese life insurers are known to be desperate for foreign expertise because with interest rates having fallen sharply and equity market prices remaining lackluster, they are bleeding red ink from over-generous policies they wrote in the 1980s.

106 Kokusai Securities's biggest shareholder is Nomura, and its large capitalisation still makes it unattractive.

Notes

107 For example, Merrill Lynch calculates that a one percent Japan premium for three months wipes ¥10 billion off major banks' profits (*Nikkei* 2/12/97).

108 While cutting branches in the US, Sanwa was still planning expansion in Asia. The bank opened offices in Taipei and Manila in 1997, and was planning to open in Beijing and Ho Chi Minh in 1998.

109 Sakura Bank was offering to provide specialist foreign exchange services on behalf of smaller regional firms (*Nikkei* 3/4/97); NCB plans to sell consultancy services to non-affiliated firms hoping to withdraw from overseas business as part of their restructuring plans (*Nikkei* 14/8/98).

110 Wholesale cash management services and retail investment trust sales are two major areas of new banking business development.

111 For example, Goldman Sachs Investment Trust Management, which began in June 1996, intended to increase its staff from 600 to 700; ING Barings planned 'substantial' expansion of its current staff of 200 (*Nikkei* 13/11/97); JP Morgan planned to boost its staff from 500 to 800 by 2001 (*Tōyō Keizai* 7/5/97, p. 40); and Commerzbank planned to increase its staff from below 80 to over 200 by end of fiscal 1998 (*Nikkei* 18/10/97).

112 Goldman Sachs, Merrill Lynch, Morgan Stanley, Bankers Trust, Lehman Brothers, and others had all set up property arms to package and resell problem loans purchased from Japanese banks.

113 Credit Swiss Financial Products, a world-renowned risk management specialist, announced that it would open its first overseas branch in Tokyo, starting April 1998, largely eyeing future Japanese demand for credit derivatives (*Nikkei* 21/7/97). This marked the first case of a specialist licence being granted to a foreign bank, and was understood as a precursor to things to come (*Nikkei* 9/4/97; *Nikkei Kinyû* 15/4/97).

114 As of September 1997, there were sixteen Japan-based foreign investment trust companies, up fourfold from five years ago. These numbers are still growing, with major firms like Merrill Lynch International Capital Management and Fidelity Investments both having entered the business by the end of that fiscal year, and Chase Manhattan to enter the business by the end of fiscal 1998.

115 In investment trusts, for example, foreign firms were expected to capture ten percent of the market by the end of August 1998, up from 0.1 percent in 1990. By product, six of the top ten investment trusts (by assets) were foreign ones, with foreign firms occupying the top four spots. Goldman Sachs Asset Management was the largest foreign fund operator in July 1998, with over ¥1.2 trillion under management, followed by Alliance Capital (¥740 billion) and Credit Suisse Investment Advisory (¥380 billion) (*Nikkei* 13/8/98; 8/8/98).

116 Citibank began ordinary retail banking operations in Japan in 1994.

117 Merrill Lynch is the only non-Japanese group to be engaged in fully-fledged retail brokerage activities following its purchase of fifty retail outlets and 2,000 staff from the failed Yamaichi Securities. It planned to begin operations in July 1998 (*Nikkei* 13/2/98). The firm established a small retail sales business in Japan in the late 1980s, but closed down the unprofitable venture in 1993. Now Merrill chairman Winthrop Smith says his firm aims to join Big Three, to revive Japan's Big Four securities companies.

118 Fidelity began operations in Japan in April 1998 and expects to make the country its largest non-US market, soliciting business largely through direct sales. Fidelity has also acquired a discount broking license, and there is speculation that Charles Schwab will follow it into the Japanese market (interview with Bill Wilder, *JT* 12/11/97; interview with Simon Fraser of Fidelity Investments 19/8/98).

119 In September 1997 American Home Insurance became the first firm to sell differentiated rate auto insurance in Japan (*Nikkei* 25/9/97).
120 In January 1998, Zurich Insurance became the second firm to sell differentiated insurance (*Nikkei* 12/5/98).
121 In March 1998, American Life became the only foreign insurer to have branches in all of Japan's forty-seven prefectures (*Nikkei* 11/3/98).
122 Axa-UAP announced in August 1998 its plans to enter Japan's non-life market, and was considering a direct marketing-based strategy (*Nikkei* 14/8/98).
123 In April 1998, Nisshō Iwai became first nonfinancial company to enter the securities business in Japan (*Nikkei* 22/5/98).
124 Marubeni announced plans in May 1998 to market four investment trust funds to individuals, to sell asset-backed securities, and to enter the brokerage business by purchasing a small broker in 1998 (*Nikkei* 22/5/98).
125 Itōchû jointly established Global Cosmos Insurance with a consultancy firm in April 1998 to market policies to small and medium-sized businesses, acting as an agent for thirty insurance firms (*Nikkei* 22/5/98).
126 In July 1998, Sony announced plans to enter the nonlife insurance market in late 1999 using direct marketing (*Nikkei* 2/7/98).
127 Softbank plans to enter the securities business via the internet, in association with Yahoo Japan, having recently begun an investment trust sales business in cooperation with Morningstar (*Nikkei* 16/5/98).
128 Secom recently announced that it would buy a 33.4% stake in Tōyō Fire & Marine, making it Japan's first general contractor to 'acquire' an insurer (*Nikkei* 18/7/98; 19/8/98).
129 Hereby, representatives of banking subsectors set to lose out from deregulation under Big Bang have consistently sought to delay its pace. For example, Trust Bankers' Association chairman Nakano Tōyōshi and National Association of Shinkin Banks chairman Katō Keikichi have both protested that reform under Big Bang is happening 'too quickly' (*Nikkei Kinyû* 25/4/97; *Nikkei* 22/5/97). By contrast, larger banks have consistently sought to speed its pace, as shown by the comments of JFBA chairmen such as Hashimoto Toru (*Nikkei* 8/5/97). Accordingly, Fuji Bank Research Institute released a major report to bolster pro-reform sentiment, showing that protection has led to excessive competition which threatens all banks' profitability. It argues that the MOF should use PCA to shut down weak firms and boost profitability elsewhere, a move which will facilitate the writing off of bad loans to the benefit of the whole economy. It also also blames government agencies such as the Housing Loan Cooperation Agency (HLCA) for providing low-interest loans which undercut banks' profitability (*Nikkei* 20/6/97).
130 Moody's claims that most brokers cannot cope with changes, as fifty percent of revenues may eventually disappear through deregulation (*Nikkei* 29/4/98).
131 Hence, Moody's estimated that brokers could see their share of investment trust market fall from ninety percent to under fifty percent due to new competition (*Nikkei* 11/7/98).
132 A case in point is Japan's ¥170 trillion pension market. Deregulation in 1996, which relaxed the so-called five-three-three-two rule (i.e. no more than half of pension fund money could be invested in cash, thirty percent in stocks and bonds, and twenty percent in property) made it easier for better performing fund managers to shine. As Japanese life insurers cut their guaranteed returns from 4.5 percent to 2.5 percent, Nenpuku, a public fund managing ¥19 trillion withdrew ¥5 trillion from the life insurers, and redistributed it to trust banks and foreign firms. At the end of that fiscal year, InterSec Research figures

showed that trust banks now managed more pensions than life insurers (¥75.6 trillion versus ¥52.8 trillion, and total funds under management of ¥205 versus ¥189 trillion). Foreigners, too, increased their share of Japanese pension assets under management from 16% to 21% in fiscal 1996, with the number of Japanese firms giving money to foreign fund managers having risen from 120 to 261. Analysts estimate that, in general, foreigners secure twice as high returns (i.e. fifteen-to-twenty percent) through greater exposure to foreign equities. They are also less likely to feel compelled to invest in the stocks of poorly performing domestic firms which allocate them the funds in the first place (*Economist* 23/8/97).

133 Cancellations on insurance contracts at Japan's forty-four life insurers rose twenty-one percent over the quarter when rumours began to circulate about Nissan Mutual and other firms being in trouble. However, industry leader Nippon Life, and three other firms saw no perceptible decline in their business (*Nikkei* 28/8/97).

134 In the space of one year, Citibank saw its level of personal deposits rise forty-five percent (*Nikkei* 16/8/97).

135 The twenty-one foreign brokers expanded their share of all stock transactions to thirty-three percent in August, vis à vis twenty-five percent for the Big Four (*Nikkei* 24/8/97). Consequently, the fifty-seven foreign brokers in Japan saw their combined profits grow threefold in fiscal 1997 (*Nikkei* 21/5/98).

136 BOT-M estimates that Japanese banks have sold nearly ¥4 trillion in bad debts to foreign banks in the past year, with firms like Goldman Sachs, Loanstar Opportunity Fund, Secured Capital and Merrill Lynch being the main purchasers. The main sellers to date have been Sakura, BOT-M, IBJ, Fuji, Sumitomo and Daiwa, and the trend was anticipated to continue accelerating over the coming year (*FT* 19/8/98).

137 In late 1997, Sony appointed Salomon Brothers to lead-manage a bond placement, the first time it had ever selected a non-Japanese broker (*Nikkei* 27/9/97). Several months later, Sony shunned Japanese life insurers from its team of contracted pension fund managers, to rely exclusively upon foreign firms and domestic trust banks (*Nikkei* 27/2/98). Another example involved eight foreign banks providing a 'commitment line' (i.e. a pre-negotiated credit facility) to NEC, a service which would conventionally have been performed by the firm's main bank(s) (*Nikkei* 17/3/98). Other major Japanese firms recently turning to foreign financial institutions include Toshiba, Mitsubishi Electric, Misawa Homes, Ōji Paper, Orix, and Dainippon Ink & Chemicals (*Nikkei* 21/8/98).

138 As *The Banker* (9/95) pointed out, Tokyo is still by far largest financial centre in terms of fund management opportunities as measured by institutional equity holdings.

139 This appeared, as the *Nikkei* commented, to be a surprising statement for a top MOF bureaucrat to make in public. However, it makes sense when interpreted as part of the Ministry's plan to protect the industry and 'manage' deregulation (see Chapter 2).

140 With the partial exception of Nomura, almost all foreign economists and analysts in Tokyo speak derisively about the *quality* of the local competition (various interviews 6–8/9/98).

CHAPTER 4

1 In accordance with the Economic Planning Agency's (EPA) criteria, the Japanese government officially acknowledged the Recession as having lasted until the end

Notes

of 1993 (i.e. three years). But, for reasons that shall become clearer in the next subsection, many believe that more than four years on from this point in time Japan is yet to emerge from the Heisei Recession.
2 An official announcement in Japan about whether the economy is in recession is determined by a panel of scholars and usually comes one-to-two years after a recession actually sets in – i.e. usually after it is over. The EPA has been criticised for concealing the opinions of some of its panel members who believe that the economy is in recession (*Nikkei* 3/3/98). It conceded recently that 'the economy remains stagnant' and that 'the situation is more serious than before' (*Nikkei* 11/4/98), yet as of September 1998 it had still avoided using the word 'recession' (*keiki kōtai*).
3 Real economic growth for fiscal 1997 was minus 0.7 percent *vis à vis* minus 0.4 percent in fiscal 1974, which had been Japan's worst postwar figure since the EPA began collecting statistics in 1955.
4 It is a common allegation that the EPA makes inadequate adjustment for leap years compared to authorities in the US and Germany, e.g. leading officials to overestimate the first quarter figure for 1996 by up to 0.5 percent of GDP, and that it has undefined leeway to adjust private consumption data.
5 Most notably, US monthly rates are calculated on the basis of persons actively seeking work during the previous four weeks, whereas Japan includes only those not working but actively seeking work in the last week of each month. Furthermore, Japan's statistics define as *employed* 'All persons who worked as unpaid family members for at least one hour during the survey week' (MCA). Hereby, *The Economist* suggests that Japan's 'true' rate of unemployment is around seven percent (6/6/98). *The Financial Times* obtained a September 1995 internal Japanese MCA study showing that Japan's estimated true unemployment rate was actually nine percent, at the time a full percentage point higher than the adjusted figure for the US (see *FT Japan Industrial Survey* 25/9/95), and now supposedly much higher.
6 Dai-ichi Mutual Life Insurance calculates Japan's latent unemployment rate was above ten percent at the end of March 1998. Based on BOJ and other data, DMLI reckons that 4,345,000 Japanese (6.6 percent of the workforce) were engaged in redundant jobs. It calculates that the ratio of corporate labour costs to sales has risen by twenty-five percent since 1991, and estimates that reducing this ratio to earlier levels would require 6,706,000 redundancies, pushing rate up the country's unemployment rate to 13.5 percent (*Nikkei* 10/8/98).
7 In April 1998 Japan's official unemployment rate had fallen to the same as the US's, which reached a twenty-eight year low of 4.3 percent. And in May, the rate of male unemployment in Japan (4.2 percent) surpassed that in the US (4.0 percent).
8 The *Tankan* is a survey of approximately 10,000 large and small businesses in all sectors of the economy. The diffusion index method employed in the *Tankan* involves subtracting the percentage of those giving negative answers from those giving positive answers.
9 It should be noted that Teikoku Data Bank's figures used in figure 4.6 do not include bankruptcies such as Yamaichi Securities, which was liquidated voluntarily. Corporate bankruptcies increased by thirty percent in the first half 1998, i.e. 10,173 firms with ¥6.93 trillion in debts (*Nikkei* 15/7/98).
10 The sharp rise in 1996 figures reflects the impact of spending ahead of the consumption tax hike at the beginning of fiscal 1997.
11 Hereby, Japan is exceptional among the OECD states for pursuing major fiscal expansion since 1992, where it has continuously devoted a much larger share of

GDP – an average of seven percent versus under three percent for the US and most European states (*FEER* 30/4/98) – to public works projects.
12. It should come as no surprise that the government tries to 'talk up' any stimulus measures at the time of announcement because a key goal of any stimulus package is to quell observers' skepticism in the hope of restoring their confidence in the economy.
13. Of course, this assumes unreasonably that all of the money was spent during the same year; in reality a three-to-six month time lag is usual. The EPA's own figures indicate that the average multiplier for public works spending is 1.32 during the first year of a project's implementation.
14. JP Morgan economists calculated the governments net debt to have been approximately eighteen percent of GDP, although they put the gross debt level at eighty-seven percent of GDP in 1997 (*FT* 7/4/98).
15. Using similar logic, Asher and Smith (1998) estimate the true size of the government's gross deficit to be 150 percent of GDP, which still places Japan in a worse fiscal state than Italy.
16. In response to Moodys April rating outlook change for Japan, the MOF announced that its affiliate, the Japan Center for International Finance, would conduct a study of seven major ratings agencies' performance, and release the results in the autumn (*Nikkei* 23/4/98). For a review of the economics of this debate, see *Economist* 1/8/98.
17. At that time, comparable rates in the US, the UK and Germany were 5.25 percent, 6.75 percent, and 3.5 percent respectively. The BOJ, however, did retain some 'wiggle room' to losen monetary policy further, (i) by absorbing larger quantities of outstanding government bonds from the market (which it has been doing consistently since December 1997), (ii) by guiding overnight interest rates lower than the ODR (which it did in Septermber 1998, aiming for a level of 0.25 percent), and (iii) by reducing domestic banks' reserve requirements for their mandatory deposits with the central bank (which, thus far, has only been talked about – *Nikkei* 19/3/98; 10/9/98).
18. With the aim of curtailing the fiscal deficit to no more than three percent of GDP by the end of fiscal 2003, the second Hashimoto administration brought about a ¥9 trillion increase in the public burden in fiscal 1997 by not renewing special income and residential tax breaks, allowing an increase in the consumption tax from three to five percent and introducing revisions to the health insurance scheme to reduce the state's share of coverage.
19. PKO is a common acronym used in conjunction with the participation of Japan's self-defense forces in United Nations activities. In this case, however, the PKO refers to 'price-keeping-' as opposed to 'peace-keeping operations'.
20. Most notable here have been deregulation programmes targeting the financial, telecommunications, and retail sectors. As elsewhere, the progress of reform in both of these fields has been marked by gradualism and a considerable lag between rhetoric and reality, as this book has shown in the case of finance. For more on telecommunications deregulation, see Vogel (1997, pp. 137–66).
21. For a wide variety of short empirical papers by leading Japanese and non-Japanese academics, bureaucrats and politicians on the problems of recent deregulation initiatives in Japan, see Gibney (1998). For more extensive studies of the problems entailed by deregulation in Japan, see Miwa (1997) and Suzuki (1995).
22. On the basis of recent economic data, EPA chief Sakaiya Taichi noted that although Japan was not yet in a deflationary spiral, it was 'at the entrance of one' (*Nikkei* 9/9/98).

Notes

23 The government has pledged to implement nearly ¥7 trillion in tax cuts – ¥4 trillion of which were to be income tax cuts – and ¥12.5 trillion public works spending in fiscal 1999. Technically, the money for these programmes will come from a second supplementary budget for 1998 in November and from the regular budget for fiscal 1999, both of which the MOF combined in an unusual fifteen-month budget (*Nikkei* 11/8/98; 1/9/98).

24 This proposition has been at the heart of recent US *gaiatsu*, spurred on by the spiralling trade deficit, and is commonly voiced in the international financial press, which has an interest in maximising short-term growth in Japan. It was forcefully expressed by Larry Summers (deputy secretary to the US Treasury) at the February 1998 G–7 Summit in London, who berated Japan for its hitherto 'virtual' economic policy, and by the *Financial Times* which called for an end to 'the Japanese policy striptease in which one small expansionary package follows another to the floor' (27/2/98).

25 Proponents necessarily refuse to admit that the Japanese economy has any fundamental structural problems which would hinder its performance in a globalising economy. For an economically-based assertion of this position, see Posen (1998).

26 Krugman has proposed in two widely cited papers (1988a; 1988b) that the way for Japan to escape recession is for the BOJ to 'credibly promise to be irresponsible' by promising to make inflation occur.

27 An article in *The Economist* (25/7/98) evaluated Krugman's proposal in terms of monetary economics and draws this conclusion.

28 A cursory glance at any Japanese business magazine or serious newspaper shows that such issues were widely discussed by politicians, bureaucrats, businessmen, academics and social commentators. Chapter 2 proved this in reference to financial policymaking; see also Tago *et al.* (1997) with regard to the debate on Japan's convergence on various emerging global standards.

29 It should be noted that it is common for such reform initiatives to be killed off indirectly by agreement to reexamine the issues in several years time, as happened to Hashimoto's plan to privatise parts of the Post Office.

30 Big business became overtly critical of the Hashimoto administration's efforts to maintain their structural economic reform agenda whilst simultaneously formulating emergency measures to deal with the effects of the recession and domestic credit crunch. Between April and July 1998, Keizai Dōyûkai chairman Ushio Jirō was vociferous in his criticism of Hashimoto's leadership, and called for the latter's resignation on more than one occasion (*Nikkei* 21/4/98; 12/7/98).

31 Driven by their overwhelming aim to see Japan play a greater role as an immediate locomotive to pull Asia out of crisis (and therefore relieve the burden on the US, and its spiralling trade deficit), the Clinton administration appeared to have largely (but not wholeheartedly) opted to push for short-term improvements in the Japanese economy since late 1997, encouraging recourse to the traditional formula, and inevitably weakening Hashimoto's, then Obuchi's, domestic political position in the process.

32 Critics note (i) that Japan spends more on public works than its competitors – approximately six percent of GDP per year compared to two-to-three percent for other G–7 countries; (ii) that the system is costly, inefficient and obtuse, as shown by the bid-rigging (*dango*) system and figures which indicate private construction costs have fallen twenty-eight percent since the Bubble but public projects costs having fallen by only five percent; (iii) that the country's scope for continuing to implement such projects is increasingly limited, as almost all the nation's rivers are now encased in concrete and many half-finished roads in the

countryside appear to lead nowhere; and (iv) that it works to entrench vested interests and retard economic structural change. See Sumita (1997), who argues that bureaucratic abuses are at the heart of Japan's problems, and Kitaoka (1998), who argues that the LDP's pork-barrel politics are at root of country's inability to restructure.

33 Japan lags behind the West considerably in terms of basic public amenities such as sewers, parks, waste-disposal facilities, expressways, water storage facilities, and air and sea ports. The Ministry of Construction maintains that private and public construction costs are lower in Japan than the US or UK, and the EPA's estimates are for an initial-year multiplier effect of 1.32 for public works spending versus 0.45 for tax cuts, and a three-year multiplier of 2.13 versus 1.26 (*Nikkei* 1/3/98). Fuji Research Institute backs up the gist of the government's figures by estimating that an additional ¥1 trillion in public works spending boosts Japan's GDP by an average of ¥806 billion, while ¥1 trillion in tax cuts boosts GDP by only ¥275 billion (*Nikkei* 24/3/98).

34 The result is, however, a chronically bloated construction sector, accounting for over fourteen percent of GDP, employing more than ten percent of the working population, and heavily dependent of the state's public works budget. Fuji Research Institute predicted that 700,000 jobs would necessarily be lost during the next three years as a result of the Hashimoto administration's fiscal reconstruction programme, pushing up unemployment by 0.7 percent. However, as a result of the government's spring 1998 fiscal stimulus package (which was to target Hokkaido, Kyûshû, southern Kantō and Kinki regions – areas of high unemployment), the institute estimates that its earlier prediction would be delayed by a year (*Nikkei* 3/5/98; 3/6/98).

35 For example, when the regional nonbank Nishiki Finance finally declared bankruptcy in fiscal 1995, its failure led to the collapse of 588 affiliated companies (*Nikkei* 16/4/96).

36 In mid-1992, the stock market fell below half the value of its all-time Bubble high and, with no apparent floor in sight, the government moved to implement PKOs to maintain the Nikkei 225 above the ¥15,000 level. In addition to the government deferring slated public offerings (e.g. of NTT shares) and the MOF requesting financial institutions to refrain from selling shares in return for them waiving normal reporting requirements, ¥2.8 trillion of indirect stock market support was provided in the form of fund injections from the postal savings, postal insurance and national pension schemes, and a relaxation of the ban on loan trusts (*kashitsuke shintaku*) investing in the securities market. Similar action was taken to prop up the stock market in the springs of 1995 and 1998 (*Nikkei* 7/3/98).

37 Banks are particularly exposed to stock market movements because of their ¥180 trillion equity portfolio, forty-five percent of which counts towards their BIS ratios. Analysts reckoned that this portfolio would lose ¥3.86 trillion were the Nikkei 225 to finish fiscal 1997 at 14,000. Goldman Sachs estimated that if this happened, and the yen was at ¥135 to the dollar – neither of which, in fact, happened – the nineteen major banks would have each, on average, seen their tier-one capital ratios touch the four percent minimum acceptable level for them to engage in international business (*Euromoney* 2/98). At the end of the half of fiscal 1998, analysts reckoned that the Nikkei 225's closure at ¥13,406 had resulted in the country's top 19 banks sustaining unrealised losses of around ¥3.83 trillion (*Nikkei* 1/10/98).

38 Hereby, the BOJ's latest *Annual Review* (1997) dropped all mention of structural reform, which had dominated their previous two reports as reasons for optimism concerning the country's economic outlook. Rather, the 1997 report focusses

extensively upon the short-term effects of pump-priming spending upon Japan's macroeconomic data.
39 Conversations with Jeffrey Young (chief economist at Salomon Smith Barney [Tokyo]) 24/6/98, Russell Jones (chief economist at Lehman Brothers [Tokyo]) 11/8/98; Larry Duke (chief economist at Citibank [Tokyo]) 5/8/98; Okamura Ken (strategist at Dresdner Kleinwort Benson [Tokyo]), Darrel Whitten (senior strategist at ABN-Amro [Tokyo]) 6/8/98, and Okuda Yasushi (economist at JP Morgan [Tokyo]) 3/9/98.
40 For more on the damaging macroeconomic effects of PKOs, see Asher (1997) who links them directly to the 'yen bubble', a period between August 1993 and June 1996 when the yen remained below the ¥100-to-the-dollar level for much of the time.
41 Apparently, some of these firms profited beyond this, too. In late 1992, rumours surfaced of several trust banks and securities companies conspiring to falsify accounts in order to defraud the Trust Fund Bureau over the investments, yet eager not to draw attention to the practice of using PKOs for fear of stirring up public criticism of the recondite practice, the MOF dismissed the issue, which was never resolved (*Nikkei* 7/10/92).
42 While Asher estimated that the government had, in effect, been buying up about two percent of all Japan's quoted shares every year at an annual cost of about $65 billion (1996, p. 221), this author was unable to verify his estimate and instead found some grounds for doubting that the actual amount of money set aside to bolster the stock market actually did so. Rather than being given set quotas for investment in equities, bonds, etc., trust fund managers were given the money for a five-year period upon the condition that they would achieve an average five percent annual return by September 1997. Initially, at least, there was no sign of this money pouring into the stock market, as, ironically, it appeared that most fund managers had chosen to hold the money in cash until the market picked up (*Economist* 10/10/92).
43 In 1998, ordinary postal deposits paid a rate of interest of 0.5 percent, versus an average of 0.25 percent for bank deposits. Postal time deposits and life insurance policies pay a fixed premium which the state is obliged to honour regardless of the actual returns which it secures upon its investments. However, there were signs that the returns promised thus far are likely to be lowered substantially for new policies as a result of the state's declining average return on investment. For example, in 1990 and 1991, the Post Office offered a fixed rate of interest of 6.33 percent on ten-year fixed deposits, but said recently that it would be unfeasible to continue offering such high rates for policyholders who wish to roll over their investments policies maturing at the turn of the century (*Nikkei* 24/7/98).
44 In 1992, Nikkō Research Institute estimated that every ¥10 increase in the value of the yen against the dollar that was sustained for over three months would lead to an average five percent decline in the profits of all Japanese corporations, and a fifteen percent decline in manufacturers earnings in particular. Around the same time, James Capel estimated that for every ten percent appreciation in the value of the yen, the domestic consumer price index would fall by 1.5 percent during the first year, and a further 1.5 percent during the following two years (*Economist* 10/10/92; 27/11/92).
45 These trends have continued since Ikeda's published research was conducted. Japan's four largest auto manufacturers cut 4,300 jobs in 1997, with Toyota responsible for 1,800. Most job cuts related to those on short-term contracts, rather than Toyota's 60,000 regular employees, but the firm noted that 1,500

extra jobs could go by autumn 1998 if domestic sales did not pick up (*Nikkei* 25/4/98), which appears to have been the case (*Nikkei* 25/9/98).

46 Toyota claimed that a ¥1 change in the value of the dollar could affect its profits either way by about ¥10 billion a year. But through fresh waves of rationalisation and FDI in the early 1990s, the firm was able to reassure analysts in early 1995 that its operations had been made competitive up to a level of ¥100 to the dollar. And as the rate moved above this level, they were also quick to point out that their profitability that year would not be affected because of forward contracts which they had in place to cover results for that financial year.

47 For the (nonfinancial) corporate sector as a whole, interest and discounting expenses as a proportion of total value added fell from 14.3 percent in 1991 to 7.1 percent in 1996 (MOF *Hōjin Kigyō Tōkei*).

48 Hereby, many social critics and even some LDP politicians (led by acting Secretary General Nonaka Hiromu) began calling for Japan's discount rate to be raised in order to benefit citizens/voters in early 1998 (e.g. *Nikkei* 14/4/98). The government and BOJ both discussed the issue but resisted on the grounds that such action ran counter to orthodox economic logic and was likely to exacerbate the recession rather than ease it.

49 The BOJ defines as 'principal firms' those with 300 to 999 employees, and as 'small firms' those with fifty to 299 employees (manufacturers), or twenty to 299 employees (nonmanufacturers). It should also be noted that all figures cited in the charts below for the third quarter of 1998 were firms' estimates.

50 In one week in mid-November, more than half of the branches of the Japan Chamber of Commerce and Industry received complaints about banks refusing supposedly standard loan applications (*Nikkei* 20/11/97). A survey of small and medium sized firms in the Kantō region confirmed that they were experiencing a sharp 'credit crunch', and, noting his region's high concentration of small firms which rely upon exports to Asia, Ōsaka Chamber of Commerce and Industry chairman Ōnishi Masafumi formally approached BOJ vice-governor Fukui Toshihiko to request the expansion of loans from government-affiliated financial institutions. The BOJ responded that it was monitoring the situation and would ensure that firms meeting the necessary criteria would receive the funds they needed (*Nikkei* 28/11/97).

51 To induce private banks to lend, (i) the MOF suspended their slated April 1998 implementation of the Prompt Corrective Action framework for bank regulation (*Nikkei* 20/12/97), (ii) Prime Minister Hashimoto summoned representatives of the country's top commercial banks to express his concerns and urge them not to hold back on making new loans to small and medium-sized firms, and (iii) public funds were appropriated to boost banks' capital bases and distributed to stable banks and unstable banks alike with the understanding that the former would directly increase their lending as a result (*Nikkei* 26/5/98).

52 A firm's 'main bank' is commonly its largest lender but, by definition, its lender of last resort. For more on Japan's main bank system, see Aoki and Patrick (1994), Scher (1997) and Sheard (1997).

53 The firms surveyed had an average of 116 subsidiaries in which they held more than fifty percent of the shares, and fifty-nine affiliates in which they held between twenty and fifty percent.

54 Its analysis, which focused on the top-ten shareholders of various firms noted rises for city banks, up 0.5 percent from 1991, but drops for trust banks (0.2 percent) and long-term credit banks (1.6 percent – *Nikkei* 17/7/97). Research by Suzuki (1997) also showed little change, particularly with regard to the top six city banks' corporate shareholdings.

55 The NLI study broadly confirmed the Teikoku and Suzuki findings noted above in its observation that the proportion of nonfinancial company shares owned by banks had risen slightly, from 9.8 to 10.1 percent during the period (*Nikkei* 24/10/97).
56 To cope with excess *demand* for labour, legislation concerning dispatched workers – the Law for Securing the Proper Operation of Worker Dispatching Undertakings and Improved Working Conditions for Dispatched Workers – was passed in 1985 and took effect the following year. This legalised the operation of private placement services for sixteen occupations, including software development, financial management, office filing and secretarial work, and machinery and engineering design. In late 1995, the act was revised ostensibly to promote greater flexibility of the labour market, but effectively to cope with excess *supply* of labour. A further eleven categories of businesses were added, while temping for any occupation to substitute for workers taking leave of absence for personal reasons (e.g. maternity and looking after sick relatives) was also legalised (*Nikkei* 1/3/96).
57 Many other authors have noted the 1990s trend towards flatter corporate structures. See, for example, Maekawa (1993) and Nakata (1998).
58 Similarly, Nissho Iwai introduced a new system of meritocratic retirement payoffs, where points are awarded against level of skill necessary for each promotion (*Look Japan* 9/97). Mitsubishi started early retirement system a decade ago: anyone over 48 could apply and receive a topped-up pension if they left (*Economist* 18/7/98).
59 Annual Institute for Labour Administration surveys conducted since 1981 found that 21.8 percent of Japanese firms used performance-based pay in 1996, up 6.5 percent on the previous year. Forty-three percent of firms had introduced schemes to induce early retirement, by giving higher retirement pay to those who quit before the mandatory age of sixty, up from thirty-eight percent in 1995. It surveyed 2,829 major firms, receiving replies from 307 (*Nikkei* 19/1/97).
60 CalPERS, the California Public Employees' Retirement System, had approximately $5 billion of its $128 billion portfolio invested in Japan. It has been particularly vocal in pushing for better investor returns and greater transparency. In March 1998 it drew up a list of corporate governance principles for Japanese firms, translated them and began to distribute them (*Nikkei* 19/3/98).
61 In the US and the UK, more than half of board members usually come from outside the company, and outside directors head (i) the audit board, (ii) the committee which nominates the chairman and the president, and (iii) the committee which determines executive pay and bonuses. In Germany, labour union representatives sit on the audit board. In Japan, the board almost always follows the president's will, and, recognising this, a US government advisory panel linked with the Structural Impediments Initiative (SII) called for greater use of independent auditors in Japanese firms almost a decade ago.
62 In January 1998, the LDP supported a Keidanren-sponsored share-buyback plan to amend the Commercial Code by making it possible for firms to use capital reserves as long as reserves and profit equal more than one quarter of capital in order to prop up stock market (*Nikkei* 30/1/98).
63 Ōta said his group, which began reevaluating the issue in May 1997, would consider raising the number of outside auditors mandated by law, causing firms to establish a separate, nonexecutive board of directors, and bringing information disclosure and transparency rules up to par with generally accepted international standards. Other groups are also examining the issue. In April 1997, the MOF proposed that a system of 'auditing auditors' be introduced to prevent collusion between certified public accountants (CPAs) and their client companies,

mirroring the system of 'peer review' which exists in the US. For its part, Keidanren agreed at its 1997 annual summer forum to promote stronger checks on management by hiring more auditors. Keidanren also established a special committee on corporate governance under Katada Tetsuya of Komatsu, a large company which held its first meeting on the issue in August 1997. In advance of this, Hashimoto Tōru of Fuji Bank, then chairman of JFBA, had proposed that more than half of company auditors be appointed from outside (*Nikkei* 27/7/97). To date, no formal recommendations for legal amendments to the October 1993 legislation have been submitted to the government for debate.

64 Sony reduced its number of its board directors from thirty-eight to ten (including three outside directors) in June 1997. The firm is also broke itself into ten operating companies and began using US-style cash flow models to rate divisional performance. It had jumped the stock options gun in 1995, using equity warrants to grant directors option-like incentives (*Forbes* 8/9/97). Toyota repurchased 27 million of its own shares in fiscal 1997 at a cost of ¥93 billion (*Nikkei* 19/3/98).

65 Analysts at Goldman Sachs estimated that if all of the announced share buybacks schemes were honoured, average TSE returns on equity would increase by a minimal 0.5 percent (*Nikkei* 29/8/98).

66 While having dropped during the Recession, business investment in Japan was still running at around 16.5 percent of GDP in Japan, compared to ten percent for the US (*Economist* 11/4/98). One frequently cited reason for this is that, unlike most other OECD states, Japan allows its firms to apply accelerated depreciation when accounting for investment costs, which encourages overinvestment as a tax shield.

67 One significant change not mentioned in the above text is the fact that US-style accounting practices will be applied in some areas from April 2000, forcing corporations to divulge the extent to which their corporate pension funds are underfunded – a figure which Daiwa Institute of Research estimates at a whopping ¥60 trillion (*Nikkei* 11/8/98). Nevertheless, there is no expectation of other accounting rules which encourage unprofitable activity for the sake of tax sheltering being tightened. For example, companies earning less that ¥8 million annually receive large tax breaks, and sixty-five percent of firms fall in this bracket. Subsidiaries, moreover, are left off companies' books unless they are over fifty-percent owned, creating a major conduit for hiding skeletons (*FT* 22/12/97; *Economist* 11/4/98).

68 Independent economist Nakamae Tadashi (formerly of DIR) believed Japan's unemployment rate would reach seven percent by end of 1999 (*Economist* 21/3/98), while Kagami Nobumitsu, a professor or economics at Sophia University, expected it to rise to ten percent within three to five years (*FT* 3/6/98).

69 N.B. The 1998 statistics used in figure 4.30 are *actual* figures for June 1998, used as a proxy for the annual average, which will not be available until January 1999.

70 A 1998 survey by Japan Management Association found that seventy percent of employees at large companies basically approved of a shift to ability-based pay, while a similar study by Keidanren affiliate Japan Institute for Social and Economic Research found seventy-six percent of employees believed seniority-based pay was unsustainable (*Nikkei* 4/6//98).

71 The aforementioned Keidanren survey of 996 major firms found forty-eight percent of employees had begun such preparations, while a Pasona Inc. survey of 2,600 middle managers found twenty-five percent of those polled were studying independently to improve their career prospects.

72 The Housing Loan Guarantee Corp. compiles statistics on the number of housing loans in arrears. Their figures show a dramatic rise in fiscal 1996–9,644

cases, up 1,200 from the previous year – which they attributed to the worsening employment situation and to 'step-up' mortgages (*Nikkei* 5/10/97).
73 Consumer finance companies usually lend up to ¥500,000. Their unmanned ATMs, which were introduced in 1993 (2,678 machines were in operation nationwide by the end of 1996), have often been identified by critics as a source of the sharp rise in personal bankruptcies. However, data tabulated by five leading companies showed more failures from people who applied for loans in person than by unmanned machine. Data also showed that the state of the economy was at least as much of a factor as aggressive marketing by the firms. Nevertheless, the companies agreed to reconsider catchy advertising and impose self restraint by closing ATMs on holidays when other screening procedures were not in place. They also agreed to make it a policy to refuse loans to those with outstanding loans from four or more other companies. However, with only forty percent of such firms belonging to an industry organisation, the prospects for deterring compulsive borrowers appear poor (*JT* 14/12/96; 3/3/97).
74 The National Police Agency noted that nationwide suicides totalled 24,391 in 1997, 14.6 percent of which were attributed to the economic slump.
75 Italy was the only major industrialised country with a higher savings rate – about fifteen percent in 1996. Comparable rates for the US, UK and Germany were five percent, eight percent, and twelve percent.
76 Annual returns on personal assets in Japan have averaged a meagre 2.5 percent over the past fifteen years (*FT* 26/3/98).
77 Surprisingly, none of the now extensive literature on Big Bang has attempted to tackle this task. Of the few authors who have claimed to examine the impact of Big Bang on ordinary savers and investors, most make only general observations based one or two (not necessarily representative) examples to make a particular point (e.g. Furukawa 1997; Matsumoto 1997).
78 This survey is based loosely on an analysis of the consumer implications of these same twenty-five products and services published in personal finance magazine *Nikkei Mane* (12/97).
79 Several banks began to lower their exchange transactions charges in the run up to April 1998. Hokkaido Takushoku Bank, for example, launched a ¥2 per $1 service in October 1997; others began offering 'free' overseas money transfer services, although this was a misnomer in that the receiver was had pay a transaction fee on receipt of the money.
80 Following TV advertising campaigns which had been underway since the summer of 1997, Daiwa Securities and Yamaichi Securities launched GSAs in October 1997 under names like 'lifestyle account' (*seikatsu koza*). These invested in domestic and overseas Money Reserve Funds (MRFs), which are public bond funds (e.g. *chûkoku* funds) of between ¥100,000 and ¥5 million, and they initially paid interest rates of 0.276 percent (Daiwa) and 0.32 percent (Yamaichi), *vis à vis* average rates of 0.1 percent on ordinary bank accounts and 0.7 percent on Money Market Funds (MMFs) which represent their closest comparison, although GSAs are considerably safer and more liquid than straight MMFs. Nikko launched its GSA in December 1997 and Nomura followed in January 1998.
81 The Big Three brokerages reached a basic agreement in December 1997 to connect their computerised networks of ATMs to those of the Post Office (*Nikkei* 5/12/97).
82 Hitherto, the MOF had insisted that individuals not be exposed to the risks of derivatives, and they could only be used explicitly in products marketed to corporate clients.

Notes

83 The Sakura account mentioned above required a minimum deposit of ¥12 million, and the Bank of Tokyo-Mitsubishi accounts, which only pay interest rates slightly above average, required deposits of ¥3 million and ¥6 million respectively and an initial deposit period of three months.
84 In Japan, both tax withheld on interest and capital gains tax are twenty percent. By contrast, non-resident assets held in the UK, for example, are tax-free, while those in Canada and the US are exempt from capital gains taxes. Nevertheless, to keep an eye on large scale tax evasion and money laundering, the MOF will require financial institutions to report all overseas transactions of over ¥2 million.
85 Citibank's International Personal Bank Account, for example, was only available to Citibank's domestic Japanese bank account holders who already had at least $12,000 to invest in the US.
86 The Bank of Tokyo-Mitsubishi launched its BFT Series of four funds in August 1997 (some of which guarantee less than 100 percent of the principal in return for potentially higher returns), and announced that 70 percent of subscriptions had come from individuals; a securities firm, Nippon Unicom, began marketing its unique Columbus Discovery Fund in October, which had a very short life (one year) and offered individual investors the choice of having their funds professionally managed or making their own investment decisions; while another firm launched eight high-risk, high-return funds over the internet in June 1997, and claimed that (as of its October data) that the best was returning 16.93 percent and the worst 9.1 percent.
87 An exception to this rule was the struggling Yasuda Trust, which began marketing personal trust services to individuals with more than ¥100 million to invest.
88 At Smith Barney, the minimum investment for each was $10,000 and $50,000.
89 Citibank pioneered the provision of private banking services in Japan twelve years ago, and advertises in Japanese press solely addressing those with more than ¥100 million in financial assets. It had about 4,000 such accounts in mid-1998.
90 For example, Matsui Securities, a mid-sized Tokyo-based brokerage, was set to halve transaction commissions from April 1998 on deals worth ¥50–180 million (to ¥272,500), and will halve them for all transactions in 1999.
91 Fidelity Investments (Japan) was planning to launch discount brokerage services, as were the Big Three domestic brokerages and several others via smaller affiliates.
92 In the US, about ten percent of small-lot trading was conducted over the internet, with Charles Schwab's E-trade system (launched in February 1996) offering single transaction executions for as little as $15 (against an average transaction fee of around $300). Daiwa Securities and Nomura began to offer limited trading services via the internet in April 1996, and by mid-1998 they covered about 300 stocks, or thirty percent of their total coverage, over the internet.
93 E-money trials included a scheme launched by the Ministry of Posts and Telecommunications, JR East, Daiei, and others which began operating in January 1998 with 70,000 IC cards issued; one involving the Bank of Tokyo-Mitsubishi, Sumitomo Bank and Visa Cash which began operations in Tokyo in June 1998 and aims to issue approximately 100,000 cards which function as both IC and credit cards; one operated by NEC and IBM Japan, which began with 20,000 participants in July 1998; one involving Mitsubishi Shōji, Toyota, Nippon Sekiyû, and Family Mart, which launched a national network of 1 million debut card holders during the summer of 1998; the Shibuya Smartcard Society, which involved seven credit card companies and nine banks (including Visa International) issuing 130,000 e-money cards and began operations in September 1998; a cashless shopping trial in Kyōto involving 600 stores, the Post Office and Sanwa

Bank, which also began in September, and a project involving the BOJ, Post Office and NTT, which was set to debut in January 1999 in a nationwide trial involving 10,000 participants and 1,000 small retail stores.

94 To date, the Shibuya e-money trial is notable for its limited acceptance by retailers, both large and small, who are reluctant to pay the required six-percent of each transaction to the card consortium. Special terminals must also be purchased at a cost of ¥150,000 per unit. However, transactions costs for the Post Office's nationwide trial, which will begin in January 1999, are expected to be as low as one percent.

95 The majority of new business start-ups are liquidated quite quickly, but for those that succeed, the potential return on initial investment can be several hundred fold. Japan had a booming market in unlisted stocks during the 1950s but the market dried up under pressure from the MOF to reduce market volatility.

96 Fuji Bank, for example, was to launch its so-called Fuji All Stars series of fourteen different ITs as a result of its tie-ups with five foreign and three Japanese firms.

97 In the short-term, an increasing proportion of IT investments in Japan appear to be flowing into overseas products.

98 IBJ Securities and New Japan launched joint dollar-denominated investment trusts for individual investors in late February 1998, while Nikko marketed Japan's first ECU-denominated money market fund in July 1998.

99 The issue of deregulating telephone/internet sales of insurance policies was still under bilateral discussion at the time of writing.

100 To date, only American Home Insurance Association has started heavily discounting policies (offering up to a thirty percent discount on their existing policy for drivers between the ages of twenty-five and sixty-five). In September, the company became the first of its kind to offer mail order sales in Japan of differentiated rate (according to driver and vehicle risk profiles) auto insurance. It calculated that fifty-seven percent of all drivers in Japan would be able to save fifteen percent or more in premiums, and in some cases thirty percent or more, in this way. Other companies offered discounts within the minus ten percent band, but most were foreign companies, the sole exception being Mitsui Fire and Marine Insurance. Yasuda Fire and Marine Insurance began to discount premiums by about 4.5 percent in January 1998, and planned to raise this to ten percent by October 1998. Daihyaku Mutual Life Insurance and American Life Insurance began also selling nonsmoker insurance policies, with premiums thirty percent lower than normal, while Tōhō Mutual Life introduced a health insurance policy incorporating reduced premiums for policyholders of above average fitness.

101 Citibank introduced 24-hour ATMs for its relatively small number of domestic account holders in 1993, but (under pressure from the MOF) Japanese banks failed to follow suit, stating that it would be costly and that there was no real demand for such services from customers anyway.

102 Sumitomo Bank was the early pioneer of internet banking (i.e. access to bank account balances, simple transactions, etc. via e-mail), with the Bank of Tokyo-Mitsubishi having started its services in August 1998. Japan's electronic banking market received a major boost in July 1998 when Microsoft launched a Japanese version of its popular Money software programme. At present, most banks are waiving registration and/or user fees in an attempt to attract customers as there is also current battle to determine which of several non-compatible systems will emerge as the national standard.

103 Sony was building up its non-life insurance arm to sell to corporate clients; Softbank had announced its intention to offer a wide range of personal audit, tax, discount brokerage and casualty insurance products via links with US and Japanese firms over the internet.
104 One club, run by a group of housewives known as the Beardstown Ladies, became synonymous with the phenomenon. By investing $25 each per month in a portfolio of twenty blue-chip stocks, the Ladies generated a return on investment of 23.4 percent over a ten-year period, and their fund now has more than $80,000 in assets. Their story is outlined in a bestselling book which sold more than half a million copies.
105 The MOF specified that (i) clubs must be formed according to civil law and register a specific number of designated members, (ii) members must make investment decisions collectively (i.e. a small group must not make decisions by proxy), and (iii) no professional management fees are allowed to be paid to any members of the club. In addition, the JSDA's supplementary guidelines state that each investment clubs (i) has between two and twenty members, non of whom are professionals in the securities industry, (ii) meet at least ten times per year, (iii) agree in advance upon fixed sums for each member to invest each month, and (iv) invest only in over-the-counter stocks, convertible bonds, warrants, bonds, and investment trusts.
106 Strict rules still guide the activities of investment clubs, and most mandate that their members pool only ¥10,000 each per month for investment.
107 Nomura launched its Virtual Stock Investment Club in autumn 1996 and had 14,000 registered 'players' as of April 1998; Daiwa modelled its Investor Club scheme on an interactive American Investor Club programme; and Nikko began Internet Stock Investment Simulation Game in September 1997, the latter two both claiming around 9,000 players a piece.
108 The financial planning profession emerged in the US during the 1970s, but the Japan Financial Planners Association (JFPA) was only established in 1987. Its membership, which grew at an average rate of 1,000 per year for much of the 1990s, added 5,000 new members in 1997, taking its total roster to 19,000 as of January 1998. Over seventy percent were employees of financial institutions (mostly sales staff at insurance companies), the remainder being licensed tax accountants for insurance agencies, and auditors; full-time financial planners made up a marginal percentage. Independent financial planners typically charge ¥10,000–15,000 per hour for their services.
109 Kubota Isao, director general of the Minister's Secretariat of the National Land Agency, wrote that ratings indicate whether the agencies 'recommend those corporations as candidates for investment', and went on to state explicitly 'Naturally, A indicates a strong recommendation' (*JT* 26/1/98).
110 For example, there are at least four types or rating published for financial institutions, relating to financial strength, long-term deposit, senior debt, and short-term credit. Moody's Takemoto Kazumi admits that many Japanese depositors have begun to react excessively to ratings changes, particularly in withdrawing savings from financial institutions where their deposits were fully insured by the state anyway (*JT* 29/1/98).

CONCLUSION

1 Notable proponents of this view include old 'Japan hands' such as Chalmers Johnson, who apparently believes Japan is still on course to be the next global hegemon and argues that the current disarray is nothing more than a

bureaucratically manufactured smokescreen, and Ezra Vogel, who holds that in light of Japan's massive pool of savings and well-educated workforce it would be premature to write off the 'Japanese challenge' altogether (see *JT* 24/8/98). They also include prominent social commentators in the West, such as Will Hutton, who believes that the Japanese system should not be deregulated but rather shored up internally as a way for the country to regain the vitality which it had in the 1960s and 1970s (*Daily Yomiuri* 4/2/98).

2 It should be noted that the assertion of Japan being a highly egalitarian society is contested. While measurements of income distribution based on Gini coefficients show a much higher degree of equality exists in Japan than in most Western societies, wage differentials by corporate size and gender show considerably lower levels of equality than exists in Western states. See, for example, Keizai Kikakuchō Keizai Kenkyûjo (1998), Koike (1991), and Morita (1997).

3 Example of this type of generalisation include (i) Moran, who concludes his study (which focused heavily on the Yen-Dollar Agreement) with the bold assertion 'there is a key state actor in the Japanese financial services revolution, but it is the American rather than the Japanese state'; (ii) Horne, who focuses more on prior developments and concludes that the influence of external actors on the Japanese financial policymaking process is small (1985, p. 22); (iii) Vogel, who concludes his analysis of the 1992 Financial System Reform Act stating 'only in Japan have regulators been so thoroughly in charge of the 'deregulation' process' (1994, 220); (iv) Leyshon (1994), who argues that change in Japan is increasingly driven by growing volumes of disintermediated credit (i.e. the market); (v) Rosenbluth (1989), who asserts that regulatory reform is driven largely by financial institutions themselves; (vi) Lawrence (1996), who places greatest emphasis on the threat of exit by institutional investors; and (vii) Enkyo (1996), who stresses corporate technological and structural innovation.

Appendix 1
Moves to Break up the Ministry of Finance (1/94–9/98)

19/1/94   BOJ Governor Mineo Yasushi declares his belief in the need for reform of the 1942 BOJ Law.

23/12/95   Having sensed trouble, MOF releases preemptive report outlining plans for internal reform, including the merging of its Banking and Securities Bureaus. In the accompanying press conference Vice Minister Ogawa Tadashi argues that all aspects of the economy which deal with money should stay within the Ministry's jurisdiction (i) 'for the sake of efficiency' and (ii) in order to allow Japan to present a unified front in international fora such as the G–7.

18/1/96   Prime Minister Hashimoto announces that his new coalition government will establish a project team under Itō Shigeru (SDPJ) to study the idea of stripping the MOF of some of its powers. The committee is to produce a definitive report by September in order to be able to submit actual reform bills to the Diet in early 1997.

4/6/96   Itō's committee releases preliminary report establishing its goals of (i) bringing an end to administrative guidance and the convoy system, and (ii) replacing them with greater reliance on market discipline, stronger disclosure rules, and more rigorous inspections in order to bring Japan into line with international norms. Press conference comments from committee members indicate they may settle for simple reorganisation of the MOF along the lines of its own report (12/95) worry commentators. In particular, Itō confirms that Japan needs a stronger and more independent central bank, but calls for a separate committee to be established to investigate the issue. However, he says that 'The Ministry cannot stay the way it has been. It has to change in a way that is clearly visible to all'.

Appendix 1

3/7/96   Responding to intense media criticism of the MOF over the *jûsen* bills, Finance Minister Kubo Wataru (SDPJ) announces that he has ordered the Ministry's internal project team to intensify its parallel studies on 'shifting Japanese finance from a convoy system to a rule-driven one'.

13/6/96   Coalition agrees on 30/9/96 deadline for plan to reform Japan's financial regulatory structure in order that bills can be submitted to the ordinary 1997 Diet session.

19/6/96   MOF announces restrictions on senior bureaucrats retiring to jobs in private sector financial institutions as a part of its bid to clean up its image. This is particularly in response to revelations of top MOF *amakudari* involvement in bankrupt *jûsen* and credit cooperatives.

10/7/96   Hashimoto announces the appointment of a seven-member private advisory body, the Advisory Group on the Central Bank, headed by Torii Yasuhiko (president of Keio University).

7/8/96   LDP turns down draft proposal by Itō's committee on the basis that he has not followed the correct procedures to have it endorsed as the basis for coalition policy. Itō threatens to resign, but LDP Secretary General Katō Kōichi steps in to reaffirm common goals, criticising the MOF for influencing the political debate through intense lobbying and waging a campaign of disinformation. No details of the draft proposal are released.

31/7/96   After the first meeting of the Advisory Group, Torii tells a press conference that he sees no reason for reform thus far.

18/9/96   MOF releases its report, which agrees that future financial regulation should become more transparent and geared towards protecting depositors and investors rather than financial institutions. No concrete measures for its own institutional reform are included.

25/9/96   Coalition announces agreement on a blueprint for MOF reform, asserting their intention to create a new financial watchdog under Article 3 of the National Administrative Organisation Law, like the FTC whose members are appointed by the prime minister, rather than under Article 9 of the Law, which would classify it as an internal body of the MOF. Senior MOF officials such as Ogawa express displeasure, stating 'Administrators must shoulder the responsibility of decisions made in the areas under their jurisdiction, and the 'majority rules' nature of an independent agency does not meet this need'. He also charges that the proposed body would have to set up new regional offices and hire personnel, and that this will run counter to Prime Minister Hashimoto's consecutive agenda for administrative reform.

29/10/96   Following a general election, in which the LDP fails to win a majority of seats in the Lower House, Prime Minister Hashimoto announces a new all-LDP government. The future of the coalition's previous blueprint for MOF reform is immediately in doubt as the LDP is notoriously divided on the matter.

11/11/96   Finance Minister Mitsuzuka Hiroshi states that he 'hopes' to follow the coalitions previous call for the new regulatory body to be independent. Four days later he reaffirms both and Prime Minister Hashimoto's commitment to this end.

12/11/96   Having met a total of ten times, with its stance in favour of central bank reform hardening each time, the Advisory Group submits its final report to the Prime Minister. Calling for 'comprehensive reform' of the BOJ Law 'in order to secure the trust of the global financial markets', the report calls for the Bank to be given greater independence from the MOF in return for greater accountability to the Diet. Nevertheless, some commentators express disappointment that the report was not more radical.

17/11/96   LDP Secretary General Katō Kōichi now begins to champion the MOF's cause. He speaks out against the coalition plan in a TV debate, arguing that the new agency should be formed under Article 9. The MOF's two parliamentary vice ministers (new political appointees) urge more debate on the matter, one having declared himself in favour the coalition's plan and the other against.

19/11//96 Under Tachi Ryūichiro (professor emeritus of Tokyo University), the FSRC is instructed to debate revisions and draft a new BOJ Law on the basis of the Advisory Group report.

25/12/96   Following further committee discussions and missed deadlines, an agreement on stripping the MOF of its supervision and inspection functions is reached. Opinions on the new body have been divided broadly along party lines, the SDPJ and New Party Sakigake having consistently advocated more radical changes than the LDP, although some LDP members (including Hashimoto) favoured substantial changes. The crux of debate came down to two questions: (i) whether the MOF would be stripped of both its supervisory and its inspection powers, or just the latter; and (ii) what degree of autonomy would the new body would be given, as determined by its legal status. The committee recommends that the MOF be stripped of its supervision and inspection functions, which are to be transferred to a newly created Financial Supervision Agency (FSA). The MOF's Banking and Securities Bureaus are also to be amalgamated. The FSA is to be formed under Article 3, overseen on a need-for-discussion basis by a non-permanent cabinet consultative forum, and headed by a political appointee of the prime minister who would have full control over personnel matters. Nevertheless, almost all of the FSA's initial staff will come from the MOF employees and be eligible to return there at a later date. At the earliest, the FSA was to be launched in April 1998. For its part, the MOF would retain its authority over financial administration, financial policymaking and international finance. It would also keep its powers to step in and liquidate bankrupt financial institutions in extraordinary circumstances.

24/1/97   SDP and Sakigake propose government panel headed by PM be established to deal with future financial crises in attempt to get the LDP to agree to separate all financial markets administrative functions from MOF and transfer them to FSA. LDP has maintained that some be left with MOF so it can deal with financial crises. Deadline for agreement was originally set for 3/12/97.

6/2/97   Following a month of FSRC hearings on the FSA proposal and two months on the BOJ Law reform proposal, the MOF submits two draft financial reform bills to the government. The FSA bill maintains the basic shape of the government's earlier proposal; the BOJ bill now becomes clear. It proposes to delete a clause in the 1942 BOJ Law stating 'The Bank shall be supervised by the Finance Minister' and a corresponding clause in the law establishing the MOF. Where previously the MOF had two seats on the BOJ's Policy Board, the Ministry will no longer be represented, and neither will the government under normal circumstances; a remodelled Policy Board will incorporate independent financial and economic experts instead of financial industry insiders. The Finance Minister will, however, retain control over the BOJ's administrative budget, but henceforth will have to give a reason for rejecting any request. The government will also have to show good cause for the dismissal of any Policy Board member, with disagreements over monetary policy constituting insufficient grounds for such action. Finally,

Moves to Break up the Ministry of Finance (1/94–9/98)

new reporting requirements will mandate that the BOJ's governor make periodic reports to the Diet (as with the US' Federal Reserve) while the Policy Board will have to publish the minutes of its meetings after a time lag (as does the Bank of England). BOJ governor Matsushita declared qualified approval of the proposed changes.

11/3/97 Government submits both bills to Diet in little altered form.

16/4/97 The Administrative Reform Committee (ARC), a separate advisory panel to the prime minister headed by Hashimoto himself, indicated that, in the process of its proposals for reforming the structure of government, it is considering calling for the MOF's budget-forming mandate to be transferred to the Cabinet, and proposing the privatisation of its Mint and Printing Bureaus. The significance of this is that it would symbolically deprive the Ministry of its greatest source of power. The ARC's subcommittee charged with investigating the issue is headed by Satō Kōji and Fujita Toshiyasu (professors of law at Kyōtō and Tōhoku Universities respectively).

17/4/97 Vice Minister Ogawa speaks out in defence of his Ministry at a press conference, arguing the need for both fiscal and financial policymaking to be under one roof, and calling attention to the fact that this is the case in other major industrialised nations.

29/5/97 FSA bill passed in Lower House despite being opposed by Shinshintō, the DCP and JCP.

11/6/97 New BOJ Law passed in Diet.

16/7/97 FSA bill passed in Upper House.

22/8/97 After an intense four-day series of interim meetings, the ARC agrees to a compromise plan for restructuring the MOF. Its September report will call for the National Tax Agency to be split off from the MOF and transferred to a new General Affairs Ministry, but will support the Ministry's retention of its responsibility for fiscal and financial matters. Throughout the meetings, MOF lobbied hard for this outcome (ostensibly, for the sake of keeping the nation's currency stable). Commentators agreed that a major reason for leaving the MOF with the majority of its powers in tact was the fact in the context of the ARCs broader plans for ministerial reform the MOF's relative power is set to fall considerably anyway. The coalition agreed to produce a final report by November in order that a reform bill could be submitted to the Diet the following spring.

Appendix 1

27/8/97   Government announces FSA to start 7/98. Will start with 424 staff, 373 of which will come from MOF, plus 51 new inspectors. Will be headed by director general with same rank as MOF's vice minister. Secretariat staff of 62 will handle general affairs. Will have 186 staff working on inspections, 68 of which will be inspectors. SESC will get 15 more staff, bringing its total to 106 within the FSA. Financial Intelligence unit will also be set up within FSA to monitor money laundering. Decision to establish FSA came after financial failures and public criticism of MOF. FSA will have to consult with MOF on matters of financial stability which affect the whole system.

29/8/97   MOF plans to reorganise Banking, Securities and International Finance Bureaus into a Finance Bureau and an International Bureau 7/98 in line with new FSA. Three *shingikai*, Insurance Council, SEC and FSRC will become one in the new body. 77% of SESC, Banking, Securities and FM's Secretariat staff will move to new FSA. MOF will retain control of financial markets planning and legal frameworks. New proposed bureaus will have 124 and 134 staff respectively.

3/9/97   ARC issues interim report on administrative reform. Suggests MOF should retain fiscal and financial functions, but proposes that the issue of separating National Tax Administration from MOF should be discussed.

3/12/97   Coalition fails to resolve differences on MOF reform, shelved its decision until mid-January. LDP insists on MOF retaining some administrative functions to deal with possibility of more financial failures. SDP, Sakigake want all such functions, including international finance ones shifted to FSA.

3/12/97   ARC final report says Conference on Economic and Fiscal policy should be created within the Cabinet Office, and the task of drawing up the budget should be transferred from MOF.

20/1/98   Coalition agrees that MOF will keep its administrative powers over the financial sector 'for the time being' to avoid disrupting the fragile economy and to deal with financial failures. It will keep international financial functions in order to respond to Asian crisis. Sakigake had been insisting on separation, but compromised on an LDP promise that it would eventually happen. It demanded that a clear timetable be set for stripping the MOF of its monetary functions. The parties agreed on a proposal for upgrading the FSA into a financial agency with a cabinet minister at its head. LDP insisted on leaving financial

Moves to Break up the Ministry of Finance (1/94–9/98)

	risk management and planning with MOF to deal with failures but to transfer all other market administrative functions to the FSA. LDP called for coalition to establish a financial security conference under the PM and within his Office.
12/2/98	ARC draft proposes Treasury Ministry to take over budget functions, and Financial Agency to be established to take over from FSA.
1/4/98	New BOJ Law takes effect.
20/5/98	FM Matsunaga announces that recently disciplined officials will not work in FSA.
21/5/98	New FSA chief named as Hino Masaharu, head of Nagoya High Public Prosecutor's Office.
26/5/98	Cabinet announces FSA to be launched 22/6/98 with staff of 403, 80% from MOF.
22/6/98	FSA launched and MOF's market-based divisions restructured.
18/9/98	Democratic and Heiwa Kaikaku Parties reignite the debate on splitting up the MOF, demanding the removal of its financial planning functions as part of a political agreement with Prime Minister Obuchi's LDP over a comprehensive plan to restore health to the financial system.
26/9/98	LDP agrees to principle of seperating MOF's fiscal and financial policymaking functions as part of political deal to pass four key financial stabilisation bills.
30/9/98	LDP and opposition parties agree to set up an independent financial supervisory agency in two stages – from January 2001, and by January 2003 – based around the FSA but under an independent financial resuscitation committee to be established by the year-end and headed by a cabinet minister.

(*Source*: various *Nikkei* articles)

Appendix 2
Economic Stimulus Measures (1/91–9/98)

1/7/91 BOJ cuts Official Discount Rate by 0.5% to 5.5%.

4/11/91 BOJ cuts Official Discount Rate by 0.5% to 5.0%.

30/12/91 BOJ cuts Official Discount Rate by 0.5% to 4.5%.

16/3/92 Nikkei 225 index falls below 20,000.

31/3/92 Government announces economic stimulus package, Japan's first pump-priming measures since 1987. It includes:
- front-loading ¥5 trillion of public works projects for fiscal 1992
- low-interest loans from public financial institutions for small businesses, and for others investing in capital equipment
- relaxation of bond-issue limits to stimulate the bond market
- adoption of five-day working week to boost consumption.

1/4/92 BOJ cuts Official Discount Rate by 0.75% to 3.75%.

10/4/97 Diet passes ¥72.22 trillion budget for fiscal 1992.

21/4/92 Nikkei 225 falls below 17,000.

27/4/92 Government announces plans for ¥6–7 trillion economic stimulus package.

27/6/92 BOJ cuts Official Discount Rate by 0.5% to 3.25%.

10/7/92 Government announces plan to cut total average annual working hours over next five years to 1,800 to stimulate household consumption.

11/8/92 Nikkei 225 falls below 15,000.

18/8/92 Finance Minister Hata calls on banks and corporations to stop selling stocks and allows firms to defer reporting stock losses until the end of the financial year.

Economic Stimulus Measures (1/91–9/98)

28/8/92 Government announces ¥10.7 trillion economic stimulus package. This includes
- ¥8.6 trillion of new public works projects
- ¥2.1 trillion in aid to small businesses
- ¥1.2 trillion of postal savings funds to be used to prop up the stock market
- relaxation of ban on loan trusts investing in corporate stocks
- relaxation of ban on firms purchasing their own stock

28/8/92 Nikkei 225 rises above 18,000.

22/9/92 Yen strengthens to ¥122 to the dollar, the highest rate since 1988.

10/12/92 Diet passes ¥2.99 trillion supplementary budget for 1992.

12/1/93 Government announces tax reform measures for fiscal 1993. These include:
- ¥32 billion in annual income tax cuts
- revision of special measures for corporate tax relief
- reinstitution of preferential tax treatment of residential property sales

3/2/93 BOJ cuts Official Discount Rate by 0.75% to 2.5%.

8/2/93 MOF issues unprecedented notice to banks to start lending to small businesses.

21/2/93 Yen strengthens beyond ¥117 to the dollar.

4/3/93 Diet passes ¥72.36 trillion budget for fiscal 1993.

4/3/93 LDP promises to 'study' income tax cut to boost the economy.

7/3/93 Nikkei 225 Index rises sharply amid rumours that government is conducting unofficial 'price-keeping operations' to boost the stock market using ¥7 trillion of postal savings and insurance funds.

13/4/93 Government announces ¥13.2 trillion stimulus package of New Comprehensive Economic Measures. This includes:
- ¥10.6 trillion of new public works projects
- ¥1.9 trillion of loans and aid to small- and medium-sized businesses
- ¥700 billion in business incentives to spur capital investment and employment
- ¥150 billion of tax incentives for home buyers

18/6/93 Diet passes ¥2.19 trillion supplementary budget for fiscal 1993.

Appendix 2

30/6/93	MOF announces that tax revenues for fiscal 1992 fell short of budget estimates by ¥3.19 trillion, the first revenue shortfall in eleven years.
1/8/93	Yen strengthens beyond ¥105 to the dollar.
8/7/93	Japan rejects calls at G-7 for further economic stimulus measures.
1/8/93	Yen strengthens to touch ¥100 to the dollar during trading.
16/9/93	Government announces ¥6.2 trillion stimulus package of New Package of Economic Measures. This includes • ¥1.8 in new public works projects • ¥2.9 trillion of low-interest housing loans • ¥1 trillion of loans to aid small- and medium-sized businesses • various deregulation measures (elimination of 94 regulations on housing, passports, and credit cards)
20/9/93	BOJ cuts Official Discount Rate by 0.75% to 1.75%.
19/11/93	Tax Commission recommends the government lower its dependence on income tax revenues and raise its dependence on consumption tax revenues.
28/11/93	Nikkei 225 Index falls below 16,000.
15/12/93	Diet passes ¥709 billion second supplementary budget for fiscal 1993.
29/1/93	Nikkei 225 rises above 20,000 on news of passage of Hosokawa's political reform bill and anticipation of fresh economic stimulus package.
8/2/94	Government announces ¥15.25 trillion stimulus package of Comprehensive Economic Measures. This includes: • ¥7.2 trillion of new public works projects • ¥5.47 trillion in one-time income and residential tax cuts • ¥1.57 trillion of aid for small- and medium-sized businesses, for others investing in capital equipment, and for employment support • ¥230 billion of assistance for agriculture
12/2/94	US-Japan Framework talks end in failure over issue of objective targets for reducing Japan's trade deficit.
15/2/94	Yen surges to ¥101 to the dollar during trading after Hosokawa government announces a relatively austere budget proposal for fiscal 1994 which displays no signs of breaking with tradition in fund allocations.

Economic Stimulus Measures (1/91–9/98)

23/2/94	Diet passes ¥2.19 trillion third supplementary budget for fiscal 1993.
24/2/94	MOF, MITI and the Small and Medium Enterprise Agency announce one-year measure to ease loan conditions for small firms.
20/5/94	Government announces one-year freeze on public services charges (i.e. domestic telephone charges, public building rents, highway tolls, etc.).
21/6/94	Yen strengthens above ¥100 to the dollar.
26/6/94	Diet passes ¥73.08 trillion budget for fiscal 1994.
4/10/94	Government announces tax reform plans for fiscal 1995. These include: • ¥3.45 trillion special reduction in income and residential taxes • review of special measures for small- and medium-sized firms • an increase in the consumption tax
7/10/94	Government announces ¥630 trillion 10-year Public Investment Programme to raise standards of living and improve welfare.
17/11/94	Government announces deferral of slated change to make full pensions payable from age 65 rather than from age 60.
17/11/94	Economic Planning Agency announces the ongoing recession, which started in April 1991, bottomed out in October 1993.
25/11/94	Diet passes tax reform bills. These include: • ¥2 trillion in permanent cuts in income tax from fiscal 1995 in place of existing special tax breaks • 2% hike in consumption tax to 5% from fiscal 1997 • ¥3.5 trillion in tax exemptions for small businesses from new consumption tax
13/12/94	Tokyo Kyōwa Credit Union and Anzen Credit Union file for bankruptcy. Their operations are taken over by Tokyo Kyōdō Bank, a specially created government-sponsored organ.
20/12/94	Diet passes ¥673 billion supplementary budget for fiscal 1994.
25/12/94	Government announces further administrative reform and deregulation initiatives relating to special public corporations and decentralisation.
17/1/95	Great Hanshin Earthquake.
28/2/95	Diet passes ¥1.02 trillion second supplementary budget for fiscal 1994.

Appendix 2

8/3/95	Yen strengthens to hit ¥88 to the dollar during trading.
17/3/95	Diet passes tax reform bills for fiscal 1995. These include: • rationalisation of the various special tax measures in place • review of property and housing taxes
20/3/95	Sarin nerve gas attacks on Tokyo subway.
22/3/95	Diet passes ¥70.99 trillion budget for fiscal 1995.
31/3/95	Government announces five-year deregulation plan. Measures include: • deregulation of domestic telephone charges for corporations • simplification of procedures for importing foreign foods and cosmetics • diversification of insurance sales channels • easing of the system of biannual car inspections • deregulation of districts for taxi firms
31/3/95	MOF releases plans to deregulate cross-border financial transactions.
10/4/95	Yen strengthens to ¥80 to the dollar. Prime Minister Murayama instructs his cabinet colleagues to work out an economic stimulus package in response.
14/4/95	Government announces a package of Emergency Measures for Yen Appreciation and the Economy. This includes: • front-loading parts of government's ten-year public works plan • measures to aid small- and medium-sized businesses • front-loading various existing deregulation and structural reform initiatives • promotion of the yen as an international reserve currency • import promotion measures • measures to encourage financial institutions to write-off bad loans within five years
14/4/95	BOJ cuts Official Discount Rate by 0.75% to 1%.
19/4/95	Yen strengthens to all-time high of ¥79.95 to the dollar during trading due to lack of progress in trade talks with the US.
19/5/95	Diet passes ¥2.73 trillion supplementary budget for fiscal 1995.
7/6/95	Diet passes amendment of Insurance Business Law to allow life- and non-life firms to enter each other's business areas.
8/6/95	MOF releases plans for financial system reform to promote transparency and encourage banks to write off bad loans.

Economic Stimulus Measures (1/91–9/98)

9/6/95	Nikkei 225 falls below 15,000 level for first time since August 1992.
27/6/95	Government announces Measures for Implementing and Supplementing the Emergency Measures for Yen Appreciation and the Economy (above). These include: • front loading ¥2.4 trillion of public works for fiscal 1995 • Extension of ¥2 trillion of special income tax reductions through fiscal 1996 • various measures (e.g. tax breaks) to stimulate property and stock markets • more deregulation and structural reform initiatives
25/7/95	Cosmo Credit Corp. files for bankruptcy.
2/8/95	MOF announces measures to promote overseas investment and lending to bring down the high yen.
11/8/95	Kizu Credit Union files for bankruptcy. Its operations are taken over by the Resolution and Collection bank, an organ created to replace Tokyo Kyodo Bank.
13/8/95	Hyōgō Bank, a regional bank, announces bankruptcy, becoming the first bank to fail in postwar Japan.
15/8/95	Yen weakens beyond ¥95 to the dollar.
8/9/95	BOJ cuts Official Discount Rate by 0.5% to 0.5%, an all-time low.
8/9/95	Yen weakens beyond ¥100 to the dollar for first time in eight months.
20/9/95	Government announces ¥14.22 trillion stimulus package of Economic Measures toward Steady Economic Recovery. This includes: • ¥4.63 trillion of new public works projects • ¥3.23 trillion to stimulate the property market • ¥1.1 trillion to help farmers adjust to deregulation in agricultural • ¥910 billion to improve educational and technological infrastructure • new measures (e.g. tax breaks) to stimulate property and stock markets
5/10/95	Deregulation Subcommittee adds 6 new items to government's 27/6/95 package.
18/10/95	Diet passes ¥5.33 trillion second supplementary budget for fiscal 1995.

Appendix 2

15/12/95   MOF releases plans to deregulate the securities market.

19/12/95   Government announces plans for dissolving *jûsen*.

8/2/96   MOF releases plans for deregulation of international financial transactions. Measures include:
- liberalisation of yen interest rate swaps
- liberalisation of overseas currency-denominated deposit and trust accounts
- simpler administrative procedures for international transactions and settlements

12/1/96   Government announces tax reform plans for fiscal 1996. They include special reductions in income and residential tax, and reforms of tax on land and securities.

16/2/96   Diet passes ¥1 trillion third supplementary budget for fiscal 1995.

29/3/96   Government revises five-year deregulation plan of 31/3/95, shortening its timetable for implementation to three years, i.e. by end of fiscal 1997.

23/4/96   Nikkei 225 closes above 22,000 for the first time in four years.

10/5/96   Diet passes ¥75.11 trillion budget for fiscal 1996.

18/6/96   Diet passes *jûsen* resolution bills.

3/7/96   Yen weakens beyond ¥110 to the dollar.

11/11/96   Government announces Big Bang financial system reform initiative.

16/12/96   Government announces Economic Structural Reform Programme. 500 immediate measures include:
- promotion of specific new growth industries
- creation of internationally attractive business environment
- restraining of government spending to strengthen economic viability

19/12/96   Government announces specific targets for fiscal reconstruction. Measures include:
- restraining the growth of expenditures below the rate of economic growth
- national and local government deficit reduction targets
- balancing the national budget deficit and breaking dependence on deficit bonds

17/12/96   Government announces Economic Structural Reform Plan. Measures include:

- promotion of new industries
- creation of an internationally attractive business environment
- reduction of the public burden to maintain Japan's economic vitality

20/12/96   Nikkei 225 falls below 22,000.

25/12/96   Government announces new four-year administrative reform programme. Measures include:
- reorganisation of central government ministries and agencies
- promotion of transparency in administrative regulation
- promotion of deregulation

27/12/96   Yen weakens beyond ¥115 to the dollar for first time since April 1993 on weak Japanese macroeconomic data.

10/1/97   Government announces tax reform plans for fiscal 1997. Measures include:
- review of tax on land and housing
- consolidation of special tax measures
- reform of tax on Japanese distilled liquors

[termination of one-year special income tax reduction and rise in consumption tax]

10/1/97   Nikkei 225 Index falls below 18,000.

29/1/97   Yen weakens beyond ¥120 to the dollar on strong US macroeconomic data.

28/3/97   Diet passes ¥77.39 trillion budget for fiscal 1997.

28/3/97   Government announces Second Revision to the Deregulation Action Plan of 31/3/95. 890 new items are added to its agenda, encompassing fields such as land/housing, information/technology, distribution/transport, agriculture, legal affairs, and finance. Specific Measures include:
- abolishing restrictions on foreign exchange trading
- easing restrictions on banks' securities and trust subsidiaries

7/4/97   Yen weakens beyond ¥125 to the dollar, a fifty-month high, buoyed by expectations of higher interest rates in the US.

25/4/97   Finance Minister Mitsuzuka orders Nissan Mutual Life Insurance Co. to halt trading, making it the first insurance company to fail in postwar Japan.

?/5/97   Ogawa Securities, a third-tier brokerage, announces bankruptcy, becoming the first brokerage to fail in postwar Japan.

12/5/97   Yen strengthens beyond ¥120 to the dollar.

Appendix 2

16/5/97	Diet passes bill to amend the Foreign Exchange and Trade Control Law.
21/5/97	Yen strengthens beyond ¥115 to the dollar on expectations of lower interest rates in the US.
3/6/97	Government announces fiscal consolidation measures. These include: • cutting the fiscal deficit-to-GDP ratio to below 3% by fiscal 2005 • balancing expenditures (apart from debt-servicing costs) and tax receipts to break its reliance on deficit-covering bonds by 2005 • restraining the growth of general expenditures below the economic growth rate
11/6/97	Diet passes bill to amend the Anti-monopoly Law to legalise holding companies.
31/7/97	MOF announces broad timetable and content of its Big Bang package of financial deregulation measures.
8/8/97	Yen weakens beyond ¥115 to the dollar.
1/9/97	Nikkei falls below 18,000.
24/9/97	Government announces measures to streamline public financial institutions.
3/11/97	Sanyo Securities, a second-tier brokerage, files for bankruptcy.
18/11/97	Hokkaido Takushoku Bank, a city bank, files for bankruptcy.
18/11/97	Government announces economic stimulus package in preparation for the twenty-first century. Measures include: • structural reform focussed on deregulation • steps to activate land transactions to stimulate the property market • steps to ease financing conditions for small firms
24/11/97	Yamaichi Securities, a Big Four brokerage, files for voluntary bankruptcy.
26/11/97	Finance Minister Mitsuzuka and BOJ Governor Matsushita issue a joint statement to avert panic in wake of major financial collapses, repeating the government's intention to protect all depositors.
5/12/97	Diet passes two bills legalising financial holding companies and easing procedures for bank mergers.

Economic Stimulus Measures (1/91–9/98)

9/12/97	Yen weakens beyond ¥130 to the dollar for the first time since May 1992.
17/12/97	Government announces emergency ¥2 trillion special cut in income and residential taxes to stimulate household demand.
17/12/97	Bank of Japan sells approximately $1.5 billion to prop up the value of the yen, pushing its value up from ¥133 to ¥127 to the dollar, and boosting the Nikkei 225 more than 1,000 points to 16,541.
20/12/97	Diet passes ¥1.14 trillion supplementary budget for fiscal 1997.
22/12/97	Nikkei 225 falls below 15,000 for first time in 29 months.
24/12/97	MOF announces one year delay in implementation of Prompt Corrective Action to alleviate the credit crunch.
23/12/98	Prime Minister Hashimoto announces ¥2 trillion in special income tax cuts to be included in the new year's budget.
9/1/98	Finance Minister Mitsuzuka resigns following the securement of a political deal to enable ¥13 trillion in public funds to be used to shore up the capital bases of weak large banks. Two days later, Matsunaga Hiroshi is appointed in Mitsuzuka's stead.
17/2/98	Diet passes bill allowing ¥30 trillion injection of public funds to boost the Deposit Insurance Corp., ¥13 trillion of which is earmarked for shoring up commercial bank balance sheets.
13/3/98	Cabinet approves use of ¥2 trillion of the ¥13 trillion fund to shore up the capital bases of 21 major commercial banks.
16/3/98	¥1.4 trillion in public funds allocated to boost capital of 17 major banks ahead of fiscal year end.
19/3/98	Government adds 500 new steps as part of 1998–2000 economic deregulation programme.
3/4/98	Moodys lowers outlook from 'stable' to 'negative' for Japan's AAA credit rating on JGBs and long-term foreign debt.
3/4/98	Yen weakens beyond ¥135 to the dollar for first time in more than 6 years
9/4/98	MOF and BOJ intervene in currency markets, selling an estimated $10 billion to support the yen.
20/4/98	Government announces [approximately] ¥10 trillion economic stimulus package, including the front-loading of more than eighty percent of public works projects for fiscal 1998 into April to September period.

Appendix 2

24/4/98   Government announces Comprehensive Economic Package of ¥16.65 trillion, the largest ever to be implemented. It includes:
- front-loading of 80% of fiscal 1998 projects into first six months of fiscal year
- ¥4 trillion in income and residential tax cuts
- ¥7.5 trillion in public works spending, including ¥1 trillion on telecommunications infrastructure
- ¥2 trillion in measures to help small business
- ¥2 trillion in measures to boost land markets
- injection of ¥4 billion in postal savings funds to prop up stock market

24/4/98   Hashimoto's Conference on Fiscal Reform panel gives go-ahead to revision of Fiscal Structural Reform Law to pave way for above fiscal stimuli. Implementation from fiscal 1999 of 2% spending cap on welfare-related expenses is suspended until 2001.

26/5/98   Yen weakens beyond ¥137 to the dollar for first time since 28/8/91 on comments by Treasury Secretary Rubin that US will tolerate a weaker yen.

29/5/98   EPA announces Japan's unemployment rate rose to 4.1% in April, a postwar record and the first time the figure had topped the 4% mark.

5/6/98   Package of four major Big Bang laws enacted by Diet, liberalising Foreign Exchange law, liberalising brokerage commissions by end of 1999, abolishing restrictions on cross-entry between banking and securities business by 2001, and legalising Special Purpose Companies to speed bad debt disposal.

5/6/98   Diet approves revisions to Fiscal Structural Reform Law of 12/97, postponing target for fiscal consolidation by 2 years to fiscal 2005.

8/6/98   Yen weakens beyond ¥140 to the dollar to a seven-year low. In response, senior Japanese officials pledge decisive action to stem its fall.

12/6/98   EPA data show economy shrank by annualised 5.3% during last three months of fiscal 1997, bringing the year's growth to −0.7%., the worst figure in the postwar period (surpassing the −0.5% figure for fiscal 1974).

15/6/98   Yen weakens beyond ¥145 to the dollar, dragging Nikkei 225 below 15,000 for first time in five months.

Economic Stimulus Measures (1/91–9/98)

17/6/98	Japan and US intervene in currency markets to prop up the value of the yen, selling approximately $2 billion to send the yen below ¥135 to the dollar.
2/7/98	LDP announces Total Plan For Financial Revitalisation, featuring creation of government-run bridge banks.
12/7/98	LDP suffers large election setback in Upper House. Prime Minister Hashimoto promises to step down to take responsibility.
23/7/98	Moodys announces it has placed some Japanese government debt on review for a possible downgrade.
24/7/98	LDP elects Obuchi Keizō as next leader, a candidate who promised to compile a supplementary 1998 budget of ¥10 trillion in new spending.
29/7/98	LDP submits six bridge-bank bills to the Diet.
29/7/98	Former Prime Minister Miyazawa Kiichi accepts post as Finance Minister to head up Obuchi's 'economic reconstruction Cabinet'.
5/8/98	LDP agrees that Obuchi's promised spending increases will include income tax cuts of ¥4 trillion, and corporate tax cuts in excess of ¥2 trillion
11/8/98	Yen weakens beyond ¥147 to the dollar, marking an eight year low.
28/8/98	Nikkei 225 falls to 13,889 in interday trading, marking the Index's lowest level since 1986, as the government's bridge bank plan is bogged down in Diet debate and economic instability abroad dampens investor sentiment.
21/9/98	Nikkei 225 falls to 13,500-level on turmoil surrounding extent of government's capitulation to opposition demands that it abandon its LTCB bailout plan.

(Source: various Nikkei articles)

Bibliography

BOOKS AND ARTICLES

Akdogan, Haluk (1995) *The Integration of International Capital Markets*, Aldershot: Edward Elgar.
Albert, Michel (1993) *Capitalism Against Capitalism* [trans. Haviland, Paul], London: Whurr Publishers.
Altman, Roger C. (1994) 'Why Pressure Tokyo?', *Foreign Affairs* 73:3 (May/June), pp. 2-6.
Amin, Samir (1996) 'The Challenge of Globalization', *Review of International Political Economy* 3:2 (summer), pp. 216-59.
Amin, Ash (1994) 'Post-Fordism: Models, Fantasies and Phantoms of Transition', in Amin, Ash (ed.) *Post Fordism: A Reader*, Oxford: Blackwell.
Amin, Ash and Palan, Ronen (1996) 'Editorial: The Need to Historicize IPE', *Review of International Political Economy* 3:2 (summer), pp. 209-15.
Amoore, Louise; Dodgson, Richard; Gills, Barry K.; Langley, Paul; Marshall, Don; and Watson, Iain (1997) 'Overturning "Globalisation": Resisting the Teleological, Reclaiming the "Political"', *New Political Economy* 2:1, pp. 179-95.
Aoki, Masahiko and Patrick, Hugh T. (eds.) (1994) *The Japanese Main Bank System: Its Relevance for Developing Countries*, Oxford: Oxford University Press.
Arora, Dayanand (1995) *Japanese Financial Institutions in Europe*, Amsterdam: Elseiver.
Arrighi, Giovanni (1994) *The Long Twentieth Century*, London: Verso.
Asher, David (1997) 'A US-Japan Alliance for the Next Century', *Orbis* 41:3 (summer), pp. 343-74.
Asher, David (1996a) 'What Became of the "Japanese Miracle"?', *Orbis* 40:2 (spring), pp. 215-234.
Asher, David (1996b) 'En Babburu no Haikei' [Background to the Yen Bubble], in Gibney, Frank (ed.) *Kanryōtachi no Taikoku* [The Bureaucrats' Kingdom], Tokyo: Kodansha.
Asher, David and Smithers, Andrew (1998) 'Japan's Challenges for the 21st Century: Debt, Deflation, Default, Demography and Deregulation', *SAIS Policy Forum Series* (March).
Baum, Gregory (1996) *Karl Polanyi: On Ethics and Economics*, Montreal: McGill-Queen's University Press.
Beck, Ulrich (1992) *Risk Society*, London: Sage.

Bibliography

Bell, Daniel (1976) *The Coming of Post-Industrial Society*, New York; Basic Books.
Berger, Suzanne (1996) 'Introduction', in Berger, Suzanne and Dore, Ronald (eds.) *National Diversity and Global Capitalism*, Ithaca: Cornell University Press.
Berger, Suzanne and Dore, Ronald (eds.) (1996) *National Diversity and Global Capitalism*, Ithaca: Cornell University Press.
Bernard, Mitchell (1997) 'Globalisation, the State, and Financial Reform in the East Asian NICs: The Cases of Korea and Taiwan', in Underhill, Geoffrey R.D. (ed.) *The New World Order in International Finance*, London: Macmillan.
Bernard, Mitchell (1994) 'Post-Fordism, Transnational Production, and the Changing Global Political Economy', in Stubbs, Richard and Underhill, Geoffrey R.D. (eds.) *Political Economy and the Changing Global Order*, London: Macmillan.
Bhagwati, Jagdish (1998) 'The Capital Myth: The Difference Between Trade in Widgets and Dollars', *Foreign Affairs* 77:3 (May/June), pp. 7–12.
Bosworth, Barry P. (1993) *Saving and Investment in the Global Economy*, Washington DC: Brookings Institution.
Boyer, Robert (1997) 'Markets: History, Theory, and Policy', in Boyer, Robert and Hollingsworth, J. Rogers (eds.) *Contemporary Capitalism: The Embeddedness of Institutions*, Cambridge: Cambridge University Press.
Boyer, Robert (1996a) 'The Convergence Debate Revisited: Globalization but Still the Century of Nations?', in Berger, Suzanne and Dore, Ronald (eds.) *National Diversity and Global Capitalism*, Ithaca: Cornell University Press.
Boyer, Robert (1996b) 'State and Market: A New Engagement for the Twenty-first Century', in Boyer, Robert and Drache, Daniel (eds.) *States Against Markets: The Limits of Globalization*, London: Routledge.
Boyes-Watson, C. (1995) 'Recordkeeping as a Technology of Power', *British Journal of Sociology* 39, pp. 1–32.
Brown, J.R. Jr. (1999) *The Ministry of Finance: Bureaucratic Practices and the Transformation of the Japanese Economy*, Westport, CT and London: Quorum Books.
Budd, Leslie (1995) 'Globalisation, Territory and Strategic Alliances in Different Financial Centres', *Urban Studies* 32:2, pp. 345–60.
Bull, Headley (1977) *The Anarchical Society: A Study of Order in World Politics*, London: Macmillan.
Calder, Kent E. (1997) 'Assault on the Bankers' Kingdom: Politics, Markets, and the Liberalization of Japanese Industrial Finance', in Loriaux, Michael; Woo-Cumings, Meredith; Calder, Kent E.; Maxfield, Sylvia; and Perez, Sofia A. *Capital Ungoverned: Liberalizing Finance in Interventionist States*, Ithaca: Cornell University Press.
Calder, Kent E. (1993) *Strategic Capitalism: Private Business and Public Purpose in Japanese Industrial Finance*, New Jersey: Princeton University Press.
Calder, Kent E. (1988) 'Japanese Foreign and Economic Policy Formation: Explaining the Reactive State', *World Politics* 40:4, pp. 517–41.
Campbell, John Creighton (1977) *Contemporary Japanese Budget Politics*, Berkeley: University of California Press.
Cargill, Thomas F., Hutchinson, M. and Ito, Takatoshi (1997) *The Political Economy of Japanese Monetary Policy*, Cambridge, MA: MIT Press.
Cargill, Thomas F., and Royama, Shoichi (1992) 'The Evolution of Japanese Banking and Finance', in Kaufman, George G. (ed.) *Banking Structures in Major Countries*, Boston: Kluwer Academic Publishers.
Castells, Manuel (1989) *The Information City: Information Technology, Economic Restructuring, and the Urban Regional Process*, Oxford: Basil Blackwell.

Bibliography

Cerny, Philip G. (2001) 'Financial globalization and the unravelling of the Japanese model' in G. D. Hook and H. Hasegawa (eds) *Japan Goes Global: the Political Economy of Japanese Globalization*, London: Routledge.

Cerny, Philip G. (2000). 'Restructuring the political arena: globalization and the paradoxes of the competition state', in R.D. Germain, (ed.) *Globalization and Its Critics: Perspectives from Political Economy*, London: Macmillan.

Cerny, Philip G. (1997) 'Paradoxes of the Competition State: The Dynamics of Political Globalization', *Government and Opposition* 32:2 (spring), pp. 251–74.

Cerny, Philip G. (1995) 'Globalization and the Changing Logic of Collective Action', *International Organization* 49:4, pp. 595–625.

Cerny, Philip G. (1993) 'The Political Economy of International Finance', in Cerny, Philip G. (ed.) *Finance and World Politics: Markets, Regimes and States in a Post-hegemonic Era*, Aldershot: Edward Elgar.

Cerny, Philip G. (1990) *The Changing Architecture of Politics: Structure, Agency, and the Future of the State*, London: Sage Publications.

Cerny, Philip G. (1989) 'The Little Bang in Paris: Financial Market Deregulation in a Dirigiste System', *European Journal of Policy Research* 17, pp. 169–92.

Chandler, Alfred (1977) *The Visible Hand: The Managerial Revolution in American Business*, Cambridge, MA: Belknap Press.

Cohen, Benjamin J. (1996) 'Phoenix Risen: The Resurrection of Global Finance', *World Politics* 48:4, pp. 268–96.

Coleman, William D. (1996) *Financial Services, Globalization and Domestic Policy Change: A Comparison of North America and the European Union*, London: Macmillan.

Corbridge, Stuart; Thrift, Nigel; and Martin, Ron (eds.) (1994) *Money, Power and Space*, Oxford: Blackwell.

Cox, Robert W. (1995) 'Critical Political Economy', in Hettne, Bjorn (ed.) *International Political Economy: Understanding Global Disorder*, London: Zed Books.

Cox, Robert W. (1992a) 'Global Perestroika' in Miliband, Ralph and Pantich, Leo (eds.) *New World Order? Socialist Register 1992*, London: Merlin Press.

Cox, Robert W. (1992b) 'Towards a Post-hegemonic Conceptualisation of World Order: Reflections on the Relevance of Ibn Khaldun', in Rosenau, James N. and Czempiel, Ernst-Otto (eds.) *Governance Without Government: Order and Change in World Politics*, Cambridge: Cambridge University Press.

Cox, Robert W. (1981) 'Social Forces, States and World Orders: Beyond International Relations Theory', *Millennium* 10:2 (summer), pp. 126–55.

Deane, Marjorie and Pringle, Robert (1994) *The Central Banks*, New York: Viking Penguin.

Danemark, Robert A. and O'Brien, Robert (1997) 'Contesting the Canon: International Political Economy at UK and US Universities', *Review of International Political Economy* 4:1 (spring), pp. 214–38.

De Cecco, Marcello (1974) *Money and Empire: The International Gold Standard*, Oxford: Blackwell.

Dirks, Daniel (1997) 'Employment Trends in Japanese Firms', in German Institute for Japanese Studies (ed.) *The Japanese Employment System in Transition: Five Perspectives*, Tokyo: Deutsches Institut für Japanstudien.

Dodd, Nigel (1994) *The Sociology of Money: Economics, Reason and Contemporary Reality*, Cambridge: Polity Press.

Douglas, Ian R. (1997) 'Globalisation and the End of the State?', *New Political Economy* 2:1, pp. 165–178.

Bibliography

Dufey, Gunter (1990) 'The Role of Japanese Financial Institutions Abroad', in Goodheart, Charles and Sujita, George (eds.) *Japanese Financial Growth*, London: Macmillan.

Drucker, Peter F. (1993) *Post-Capitalist Society*, New York: Harper Business.

Durkheim, Emile (1984)*The Division of Labour in Society* [originally published 1895], Basingstoke: Macmillan.

Duser, J. Thorsten (1990) *International Strategies of Japanese Banks: The European Perspective*, London, Macmillan.

Earle, Dennis M. and Fried, Jane F. (1990) 'Twenty-four Hour Trading, Clearance, and Settlement: The Role of Banks', in Edwards, Franklin R. and Patrick, Hugh T. (eds.) *Regulating International Financial Markets: Issues and Policies*, Boston: Kluwer Academic Publishers.

Edwards, Franklin R. and Patrick, Hugh T. (1992) Introduction', in Edwards, Franklin R. and Patrick, Hugh T. (eds.) *Regulating International Financial Markets: Issues and Policies*, Boston: Kluwer Academic Publishers.

Endo, Yukihiko (1998) 'Can the 'Big Bang' Cure the Ills of Japan's Financial System?', *NRI Quarterly* (summer), pp. 20–37.

Endo, Yukihiko (1996a) 'Historical Development of the Japanese Financial System', in Hayakawa, Shigenobu (ed.) *Japanese Financial Markets*, Cambridge, UK: Gresham Books.

Endo, Yukihiko (1996b) 'Looking Towards the Twenty-first Century', in Hayakawa, Shigenobu (ed.) *Japanese Financial Markets*, Cambridge, UK: Gresham Books.

Enkyo, Soichi (1996) 'Financial Liberalisation and Structural Changes in Japan's Financial System', in Nakamura, Kiyoshi (ed.) *Going Global: Structural Reforms in Japan's Economic and Business Systems*, Tokyo: Japan Times Books.

Epstein, Gerald A. (1996) 'International Capital Mobility and the Scope for National Economic Management', in Boyer, Robert and Drache, Daniel (eds.) *States Against Markets: The Limits of Globalization*, London: Routledge.

Epstein, Gerald A. and Schor, Juliet B. (1992) 'Structural Determinants and Economic Effects of Capital Controls in OECD Countries', in Banuri, Tariq and Schor, Juliet B. (eds.) *Financial Openness and National Autonomy: Opportunities and Constraints*, Oxford: Clarendon Press.

Esping-Andersen, Gøsta (1996) 'After the Golden Age? Welfare State Dilemmas in a Global Economy', in Esping-Andersen, G. (ed.) *Welfare States in Transition: National Adaptations in Global Economies*, London: Sage.

Evans, Mark (1995) 'Elitism', in Marsh, David and Stoker, Gerry (eds.) *Theory and Methods in Political Science*, London: Macmillan.

Feldman, Ofer (1993) *Politics and the News Media in Japan*, Ann Arbor: University of Michigan Press.

Feldstein, Martin and Horioka, Charles (1980) 'Domestic Saving and International Capital Flows', *Economic Journal* 90 (June), pp. 314–29.

Fingleton, Eamonn (1995) 'Japan's Invisible Leviathan', *Foreign Affairs* (March/April), pp. 69–85.

Folkerts-Landau, David; Malkinson, Donald J.; and Schinaci, Garry J. (1997) *International Capital Markets: Developments, Prospects, and Key Policy Issues*, Washington: IMF (November).

Foucault, Michel (1980) *Power/Knowledge: Selected Interviews and Other Writings 1972–1977*, Gordon, Colin (ed.) New York: Pantheon Books.

Foucault, Michel (1972) *The Archaeology of Knowledge*, (trans. Sheridan-Smith, A.M.), New York: Pantheon.

Frank, Robert and Cook, Peter (1995) *The Winner-Take-All Society*, New York: Simon and Schuster.

Frank, Andre Gundar and Gills, Barry (1993) *The World System: Five Hundred Years or Five Thousand?*, London: Routledge.

Frankel, Jeffrey A. (1993a) *On Exchange Rates*, Cambridge, MA: MIT Press.

Frankel, Jeffrey A. (1993b) 'The Evolution of the Japanese Financial System and the Cost of Capital', in Walter, Ingo and Hiraki, Takato (eds.) *Restructuring Japan's Financial Markets*, New York: New York University Press.

Frankel, Jeffrey A. (1984) 'The Yen/Dollar Agreement: Liberalising Japanese Capital Markets', *Policy Analyses in International Economics* No. 9, Washington DC: Institute for International Economics.

Frieden, Jeffry A. (1991) 'Invested Interests: The Politics of National Economic Policies in a World of Global Finance', *International Organization* 45:4 (autumn), pp. 425–51.

Frieden, Jeffry A. (1987) *Banking on the World: The Politics of American International Finance*, New York: Harper and Row.

Fruin, W. Mark (1994) *The Japanese Enterprise System: Corporate Strategies and Cooperative Structures*, Oxford: Clarendon Press.

Fuchita, Yasuyuki (1997) *Shōken Biggu Ban: Nihon Shijō Daikaikaku e no Kōsō* [The Securities Big Bang: Ideas for Major Reform of the Japanese Market], Tokyo: Nihon Keizai Shinbunsha.

Fukao, Mitsuhiro and Hanazaki, Masaharu (1986) 'Internationalisation of Financial Markets: Some Implications for Macroeconomic Policy and for the Allocation of Capital', *OECD Economic Studies* 8 (spring), pp. 35–92.

Furukawa, Tetsuo (1997) *Daidokoro kara Nozoita Biggu Ban* [Big Bang as Seen from the Kitchen], Tokyo: Goma Shōbō.

Gagnon, Joseph E. and Unferth, Mark D. (1995) 'Is There a World Real Interest Rate?', *Journal of International Money and Finance* 14:6, pp. 845–55.

Galbraith, John Kenneth (1992) *The Culture of Contentment*, New York: Houghton Mifflin.

Gamble, Andrew (1997) 'The New Medievalism', paper presented at the Regionalism Seminar, Kobe Institute, Japan, (March 13–14).

Gamble, Andrew (1995) 'The New Political Economy', *Political Studies* XLIII (September), pp. 516–530.

Garrett, Geoffrey (1995) 'Capital Mobility, Trade, and the Domestic Politics of Economic Policy', *International Organization* 49:4, pp. 657–87.

Garrett, Geoffrey and Lange, Peter (1991) 'Political Responses to Interdependence: What's "Left" for the Left?', *International Organization* 45:4, pp. 539–64.

Germain, Randall D. (1997) *The International Organization of Credit: States and Global Finance in the World Economy*, Cambridge: Cambridge University Press.

Ghosh, Atish R. (1995) 'International Capital Mobility Amongst Major Industrialised Countries: Too Little or Too Much?', *Economic Journal* 105, pp. 107–28.

Gibney, Frank B. (*ed.*) (1998) *Unlocking the Bureaucrats' Kingdom: Deregulation and the Japanese Economy*, Washington DC: Brookings Institute.

Gibson, Heather D. (1996) *International Finance: Exchange Rates and Financial Flows in the International System*, London: Longman.

Giddens, Anthony (1990) *The Consequences of Modernity*, Cambridge: Polity Press.

Gill, Stephen (1995a) 'Globalisation, Market Civilisation, and Disciplinary Neoliberalism', *Millennium* (autumn) 24:3, pp. 399–423.

Gill, Stephen (1995b) 'Global Structural Change and Multilateralism', in Gill, Stephen (ed.) *Globalization, Democratization and Multilateralism*, Tokyo: United Nations University Press.

Bibliography

Gill, S. (1992) 'The Emerging World Order and European Challenge', in Miliband, Ralph and Pantich, Leo (eds.) *New World Order? Socialist Register 1992*, London: Merlin Press.
Gill, Stephen (1990) *American Hegemony and the Trilateral Commission*, Cambridge: Cambridge University Press.
Gill, Stephen; Cox, Robert; and van der Pijl, Kees (1992) 'Structural Changes and Globalising Elites: Political Economy Perspectives in the Emerging World Order', paper presented at the International Conference on Changing World Order and the UN System, Yokohama, Japan (March).
Gill, Stephen and Law, David (1988) *The Global Political Economy: Perspectives, Problems and Policies*, Hemel Hempstead: Harvester Wheatsheaf.
Gills, Barry K. (1997) 'Editorial: "Globalisation" and the "Politics of Resistance"', *New Political Economy* 2:1, pp. 11–16.
Goldblatt, David; Held, David, McGrew, Anthony, and Perraton, Jonathan (1997) 'Economic Globalization and the Nation-State: Shifting Balances of Power', *Alternatives* 22, pp. 269–85.
Goldsmith, James (1994) *The Trap*, London: Carrol and Graf.
Goodman, John B. and Pauly, Louis W. (1993) 'The Obsolescence of Capital Controls? Economic Management in an Age of Global Markets', *World Politics* 46:1, pp. 50–82.
Goodman, J. B. (1992) *Monetary Sovereignty: The Politics of Central Banking in Western Europe*, Ithaca: Cornell University Press.
Goss, Jon (1995) '"We Know Who You Are and We Know Where You Live": The Instrumental Rationality of Geodemographic Systems', *Economic Geography* 71:2, pp. 171–98.
Gotō, Shinichi (1980) *Nihon Kinyû Seido Hattatsushi* [], Tokyo: Kyōikusha Rekishi Shinsho.
Gough, Ian (1996) 'Social Welfare and Competitiveness', *New Political Economy* 1:2, pp. 209–32.
Gramm, Wendy L. (1992) 'Automation of the Financial Markets: Implications for Clearance, Settlement, and Payment Procedures', in Edwards, Fraklin R. and Patrick, Hugh T. (eds.) *Regulating International Financial Markets: Issues and Policies*, Boston: Kluwer Academic Publishers.
Granovetter, Mark (1990) 'The Old and New Economic Sociology: A History and an Agenda', in Friedland, Roger and Robertson, A.F. (eds.) *Beyond the Marketplace: Rethinking Economy and Society*, New York: Aldine de Gruyer.
Gray, John (1997) *False Dawn: The Delusions of Global Capitalism*, London: Granta.
Grieder, William (1997) *One World Ready or Not: The Manic Logic of Global Capitalism*, New York: Simon and Schuster.
Haas, Peter (1992) 'Introduction: Epistemic Communities and International Policy Coordination', *International Organization* 46:1, pp. 1–35.
Haley, John O. (1986) 'Administrative Guidance vs. Formal Regulation: Resolving the Paradox of Industrial Policy', in Saxenhouse, Gary and Yamamura, Kozo (eds.) *Law and Politics of the Japanese Economy: American and Japanese Perspectives*, Seattle: University of Washington Press.
Hall, Maximilian (1994) 'Financial Reform in Japan', *Journal of International Banking Law* 3, pp. 90–100.
Hall, Maximilian (1993) *Banking Regulation and Supervision: A Comparative Study of the UK, USA and Japan*, Aldershot: Edward Elgar.
Hamada, Koichi and Horiuchi, Akiyoshi (1987) 'The Political Economy of the Financial Market', in Yamamura, Kozo and Yasuba, Yasukichi (eds) *The Political*

Bibliography

Economy of Japan Volume 1: The Domestic Transformation, Stanford: Stanford University Press.

Hamilton, Adrian (1986) *The Financial Revolution: The Big Bang Worldwide*, London: Viking.

Harmes, Adam (1998) 'Institutional Investors and the Reproduction of Neoliberalism', *Review of International Political Economy* 5:1 (spring), pp. 92–121.

Hartcher, Peter (1998) *The Ministry: How Japan's Most Powerful Institution Endangers World Markets*, Boston: Harvard Business School Press.

Harvey, David (1989) *The Condition of Postmodernity*, Oxford: Blackwell.

Hashimoto Jurō (1995) *Sengo no Nihon Keizai* [The Postwar Japanese Economy], Tokyo: Iwanami Shinsho.

Hayakawa, Shigenobu (ed.) (1996) *Japanese Financial Markets*, Cambridge, UK: Gresham Books.

Hayao, Kenji (1993) *The Japanese Prime Minister and Public Policy*, Pittsburgh: University of Pittsburgh Press.

Hayase, Yasuyuki (1997) 'Babburu no Kyoren to Nihon-han Biggu Ban' [Lessons on the Bubble Economy and the Japanese-style Big Bang], *Sakura Sōgō Kenkyûjo Chōsa Hōkoku 1*.

Hayes, Samuel L. and Hubbard, Philip M. (1990) *Investment Banking: A Tale of Three Cities*, Boston: Harvard Business School.

Helleiner, Eric (1994) *States and the Reemergence of Global Finance: From Bretton Woods to the 1990s*, Ithaca: Cornell University Press.

Helleiner, Eric (1993) 'Japan's Financial Rise', in Cerny, Phillip G. (ed.) *Finance and World Politics*, Aldershot: Edward Elgar, pp. 207–28.

Henderson, Cullum (1998) *Asia Falling: Making Sense of the Asian Crisis and its Aftermath*, New York: McGraw-Hill.

Henderson, David (1992) 'International Economic Integration: Progress, prospects and Implications', *International Affairs* 68:4, pp. 633–53.

Henwood, Doug (1997) *Wall Street: How it Works and for Whom*, London: Verso.

Higashi, Chikara and Lauter, G. Peter (1990) *The Internationalisation of the Japanese Economy*, Boston: Kluwer Academic Publishers.

Hirst, Paul (1997) 'The Global Economy – Myths and Realities', *International Affairs* 73:3 (July), pp. 409–26.

Hirst, Paul and Thompson, Graeme (1996) *Globalization in Question: The International Economy and the Possibilities for Governance*, London: Polity Press.

Holt-Dwyer, Jennifer (1997) 'The Dynamics of Financial Market Reform in Japan 1975–1995', in Underhill, Geoffrey R. D. (ed.) *The New World Order in International Finance*, London: Macmillan.

Horne, James (1988) 'Politics and the Japanese Financial System', in Stockwin, J. A. A.; Rix, Alan; George, Aurelia; Horne, James; Ito, Daiichi; and Collick, Martin(eds) *Dynamic and Immobilist Politics in Japan*, London: Macmillan.

Horne, James (1985) *Japan's Financial Markets: Conflict and Consensus in Policymaking*, Sydney: George Allen and Unwin.

Igarashi, Fumihi (1995) *Ōkurashō Kaitairon: Nihon o Ikasu Chō-erîtotachi no 'Tsumi' to 'Batsu'* [The Theory of Breaking up the MOF: The 'Crimes' and 'Punishments' of the Ultraelite who Run Japan], Tokyo: Tōyō Keizai Shinbunsha.

Ikeda, Masayoshi (1998) 'Globalisation's Impact upon the Subcontracting System', in Hasegawa, Harukiyo and Hook, Glenn (eds) *Japanese Business Management: Restructuring for Low Growth and Globalization*, London: Routledge.

Ikeo, Kazuhito (1997) 'Kankyō Henka ni Teigōshita Kinyû Shisutemu no Kōchiku' [The Structure of the Financial System which has Resisted Changing with the Times], *Nihon Kisha Kurabu Kaihō* (June 17), pp. 1–11.

Bibliography

Ikuta, Tadahide (1994) *Ōkurashō 'Dokusai': Seiji no Jyakutaika de Masumasu Tsuyomaru Kanryō Pawâ* [The MOF 'Dictatorship':The Increasing Strength of Bureaucratic Power which Undermines Politics], Tokyo: OS Shuppan.

Imai Kiyoshi (1997) *Nihonhan Biggu Ban* [The Japanese-style Big Bang], Tokyo: Tōyō Keizai Shinbunsha.

Inoguchi, Takashi and Iwai, Tomoaki (1987) *Zoku-giin no Kenkyû* [A Study of 'Policy Tribe' Parliamentarians], Tokyo: Nihon Keizai Shinbunsha.

Inoki, Takenori (1995) 'Japanese Bureaucrats at Retirement: The Mobility of Human Resources from Central Government to Public Corporations', in Hyung-Ki, Muramatsu, Pempel and Yamamura (eds.) *The Japanese Civil Service and Economic Development: Catalysts of Change*, Oxford: Clarendon Press.

Ito, Osamu (1995) *Nihongata Kinyû no Rekishiteki Kōzō* [The Historical Structure of Japan's Financial System], Tokyo: Tokyo University Press.

Iwami, Toru (1995) *Japan in the International Financial System*, London: Macmillan.

Jackson, James K. (1994) *Nihon Keizai: Babburu kara Hōkai made* [Japan's Economy: From Bubble to Burst], Washington: Library of Congress Research Report.

Jessop, Bob (1994) 'Post -Fordism and the State', in Amin, Ash (ed.) *Post-Fordism: A Reader*, Oxford: Basil Blackwell.

Jessop, Bob (1993) 'Towards a Schumpeterian Workfare State? Preliminary Remarks on Post-Fordist Political Economy', *Studies in Political Economy* 40 (spring), pp. 7–39.

Johnson, R.B. (1994) *The Economics of the Euro-market: History, Theory and Policy*, London: Macmillan.

Johnson, Chalmers (1982) *MITI and the Japanese Miracle: The Growth of Industrial Policy 1925–1975*, Stanford: Stanford University Press.

Jones, R.J. Barry, (1995) *Globalisation and Interdependence in the International Political Economy: Rhetoric and Reality*, London: Pinter.

Julius, Deanne (1997) 'Globalization and Stakeholder Conflicts: A Corporate Perspective', *International Affairs* 73:3 (July), pp. 453–68.

Kaizuka, Kenmei and Harada, Yutaka (eds.) (1993) *90-nendai no Kinyû Seisaku* [Financial Policy in the 1990s], Tokyo: Nihon Hyōronsha.

Kakurai, Yasuo (1995) '"Kisei Kanwa" no Haikei o Saguru' [Searching the Background of 'Deregulation'], in Kakurai (ed.) *'Kisei Kanwa' de Nihon wa Dō Naru?* (How will Japan Change through 'Deregulation'?), Tokyo: Shinnihon Shuppansha.

Kanazaki, Katsuro (1982) 'Developments in Insider Trading in Japan', *Journal of Comparative Law and Securities Regulation* 4, pp. 391–4.

Kanda, Hideki (1997) 'Finance Bureaucracy and Regulation of Financial Markets in Japan', in Baum, Harald (ed.) *Japan: Economic Success and Legal System*, Berlin: Walter de Gruyter.

Kapstein, Ethan B. (1994) *Governing the Global Economy: International Finance and the State*, Cambridge, MA: Harvard University Press.

Kato, Junko (1994) *The Problem of Bureaucratic Rationality: Tax Politics in Japan*, Princeton: Princeton University Press.

Katz, Richard (1998) *Japan – The System that Soured: The Rise and Fall of the Japanese Economic Miracle*, New York: ME Sharp.

Kawakita Takao (1996) *Nihon Ginkō: Nani ga Towareteiru no ka?* [The Bank of Japan: What's All the Fuss About?], Tokyo: Iwanami Shoten.

Kawakita, Takao (1989) *Ōkurashō: Kanryō Kikō no Chōten* [MOF: The Pinnacle of Japan's Bureaucracy], Tokyo: Kodansha.

Keehn, E. B. (1997) 'Virtual Reality in Japan's Regulatory Agencies', in Baum, Harald (ed.) *Japan: Economic Success and Legal System*, Berlin: Walter de Gruyter.

Bibliography

Keizai Kikakuchō Keizai Kenkyûjo (1998) *Nihon no Shotoku Kakusa: Kokusai Hikaru no Shiten kara* [Japan's Income Gap: A Comparative International Perspective], Tokyo Ōkurashō Insatsu Kyoku.

Kelsey, Jane (1995) *The New Zealand Experiment: A World Model for Structural Adjustment*, Aukland: Aukland University Press.

Kester, W. Carl (1996) 'American and Japanese Corporate Governance: Convergence to Best Practice?', in Berger, Suzanne and Dore, Ronald (eds.) *National Diversity and Global Capitalism*, Ithaca: Cornell University Press.

Kirkpatrick, Jeane J. (1979) 'Politics and the New Class', in Bruce-Briggs, B. (ed.) *The New Class*, New Brunswick: Transaction Books.

Kishi, Nihide (1993) *Ōkurashō o Ugokasu Otokotachi* [The Men who Move the MOF], Tokyo: Tōyō Keizai Shinbunsha.

Kitaoka, Shinichi (1998) '"Han-Ozawa" kara "Han-Jimin" e: Ittō Yûisei wa Fukkatsu shinai' [From 'Anti-Ozawa' to 'Anti-LDP': The One-Party-Dominance System will not Revive], *Chûō Kōron* 4 (April), pp. 36–47.

Koike, Kazuo (1991) *Shigoto no Keizaigaku* [The Economics of Work], Tokyo: Tokyo Keizai Shinpōsha.

Kojima Tomotaka (1997) *1998-nen Gaikawase Jyûka to Biggu Ban: Kinyû Shisutemu Jiko Kaikaku e no Chōsen* [The 1998 Liberalisation of Foreign Exchange and the Big Bang: The Challenge of Reforming the Financial System from Within], Tokyo: Seihon.

Krasner, Stephen D. (1994) 'International Political Economy: Abiding Discord', *Review of International Political Economy* 1:1 (spring), pp. 13–19.

Krugman, Paul (1998b) 'Further Notes on Japan's Liquidity Trap', http://www.web.mit.edu/Krugman/www/.

Krugman, Paul (1998a) 'Japan's Trap', http://www.web.mit.edu/Krugman/www/.

Krugman, Paul (1996) *Pop Internationalism*, Cambridge, MA: MIT Press.

Krugman, Paul (1995) *Development, Geography, and Economic Thought*, Cambridge, MA: MIT Press.

Krugman, Paul and Lawrence, Robert (1994) 'Trade, Jobs and Wages', *Scientific American* 270:4, (April), pp. 107–121.

Kurtzman, J. (1993) *The Death of Money: How the Electronic Economy has Destabilized the World's Markets*, New York: Simon and Schuster.

Kurzer, Paulette (1993) *Business and Banking: Political Change and Economic Integration in Western Europe*, Ithaca: Cornell University Press.

Kusano, A. (1999) 'Deregulation in Japan and the role of *naiatsu* (Domestic pressure)', *Social Science Journal Japan* 2:1 (April): 65–84.

Lasch, Christopher (1995) *The Revolt of the Elites and the Betrayal of Democracy*, New York: Norton.

Lash, Scott and Urry, John (1994) *Economies of Signs and Space*, London: Sage.

Laurence, Henry (1996) 'Regulatory Competition and the Politics of Financial Market Reform in Britain and Japan', *Governance* 9:3, pp. 311–341.

Lederman, Jess and Klein, Robert A. (1995) (eds.) *Virtual Trading: How Any Trader with a PC Can Use the Power of Neural Nets and Expert Systems to Boost Trading Profits*, Chicago: Probus.

Leyshon, Andrew (1994) 'Under Pressure: Finance, Geo-economic Competition and the Rise and Fall of Japan's Postwar Growth Economy', in Corbridge, S., Thrift, N. and Martin, R. (eds) *Money, Power and Space*, Oxford: Blackwell.

Lincoln, Edward J. (1998) 'Japan's Financial Mess', *Foreign Affairs* 77:3 (May/June), pp. 57–66.

Lincoln, Edward J. (1997) 'Big Bang or Big Whimper? An American Perspective', http://www.gwjapan.com/nrca.

Lindblom, Charles E. (1977) *Politics and Markets*, New York: Basic Books.
Mabuchi, Masaru (1997) *Ōkurashō wa Naze Oitsumerareta no ka? Seikan Kankei no Henbō* [Why has the Ministry of Finance been Hunted Down? The Transformation of Relations between Politicians and Bureaucrats], Tokyo: Chūō Kōronsha.
Mabuchi, Masaru (1995) 'Financing Japanese Industry: The Interplay between the Financial and Industrial Bureaucracies', in Hyung-Ki, Maramatsu, Pempel and Yamamura (eds.) *The Japanese Civil Service and Economic Development: Catalysts of Change*, Oxford: Clarendon Press.
Mabuchi, Masaru (1993) 'Deregulation and Legalisation of Financial Policy', in Allinson, Gary and Sone, Yasunori (eds) *Political Dynamics in Contemporary Japan*, Ithaca: Cornell University Press.
Maekawa, Yukikazu (1993) *Gendai Kigyō Kenkyû no Kiso* [Fundamentals of Research on the Modern Corporation], Tokyo: Moriyama Shōten.
Makino, Tomio (1997) 'Ginkō ni okeru Risutora: "Gōrika"' [Restructuring in Banking: 'Rationalisation'], in Yamada, Hiroshi and Noda, Masaho (eds.) *Gendai Nihon no Kinyû: Hatan no Kōzō to Kaikaku no Hōkō* [Contemporary Japanese Finance: Structural Failure and the Direction of Reform], Tokyo: Shin Nihon Shuppansha.
Mander, Jerry and Goldsmith, Edward (eds.) (1997) *The Case Against the Global Economy: And for a Turn to the Local*, San Francisco: Sierra Club Books.
Marshall, Don D. (1996) 'Understanding Late-Twentieth-Century Capitalism: Reassessing the Globalization Theme', *Government and Opposition* 31:2, pp. 193–215.
Marston, Richard (1995) *International Financial Integration: A Study of Interest Rate Differentials between major Industrial Countries*, Cambridge: Cambridge University Press.
Martin, Hans-Peter and Schumann, Harald (1997) [trans. Camillar, Patrick] *The Global Trap: Globalization and the Assault on Democracy and Prosperity*, London: Zed Books.
Martin, Ron (1994) 'Stateless Monies, Global Financial Integration and National Economic Autonomy: The End of Geography?', in Corbridge, Stuart; Martin, Ron; and Thrift, Nigel (eds.) *Money, Power and Space*, Oxford: Blackwell.
Marx, Karl (1977) *Selected Writings*, Oxford: Oxford University Press.
Matsumoto Susumu (1997) *Kinyû Biggu Ban o Ikinozoku Hinto: Kashikoi Kurashikata, Okane no Tsukaikaka* [Hints for Surviving the Financial Big Bang: Smart Ways to Live and Spend Your Money], Tokyo: PHP Kenkyûjo.
Matsuoka, Mikihiro and Rose, Brian (1994) *The DIR Guide to the Japanese Economy*, Tokyo: Daiwa Institute of Research.
Maxfield, Sylvia (1990) *Governing Capital: International Finance and Mexican Politics*, Ithaca: Cornell University Press.
McGrew, Anthony G. (1992) 'Conceptualizing Global Politics', in McGrew Anthony G. and Lewis, Paul G. (eds.) *Global Politics: Globalization and the Nation State*, Cambridge: Polity Press.
McKinnon, Ronnald I. and Ohno, Kenichi (1997) *Dollar and Yen: Resolving Economic Conflict Between the United States and Japan*, Cambridge MA: MIT Press.
Melamed, Leo (1992) 'The Telecommunications and Information Revolution: Implications for Financial Markets, Trading Systems, and Regulation', in Edwards, Franklin R. and Patrick, Hugh T. (eds.) *Regulating International Financial Markets: Issues and Policies*, Boston: Kluwer Academic Publishers.

Mills, C. Wright (1942) *The Power Elite*, Oxford: Oxford University Press.
Mitsubishi Sōgōkenkyûjo (MRI) (1997) *Nihon-han Biggu Ban no Shōgeki* [The Shock of the Japanese-style Big Bang], Tokyo: Kindai Sêrususha.
Miwa, Yoshirō (1997) *Kisei Kanwa wa Akumu desu ka?* [Is Deregulation a Nightmare?], Tokyo: Tōyō Keizai Shinhōsha.
Mizruchi, Mark S. and Schwartz, Michael (eds.) (1987) *Intercorporate Relations: The Structural Analysis of Business*, Cambridge: Cambridge University Press.
Mizuguchi, Hiroshi (1993) 'Political Reform: Much Ado about Nothing', *Japan Quarterly* 40, pp. 48–62.
Montagna, Paul (1990) 'Accounting Rationality and Financial Legitimation', in Zukin, Sharon and DiMaggio, Paul (eds.) *Structures of Capital: The Social Organization of the Economy*, Cambridge: Cambridge University Press.
Moran, Michael (1991) *The Politics of the Financial Services Revolution: The USA, UK and Japan*, London: Macmillan.
Morita, Nariya (1997) *Shihonshugi to Seisabetsu: Jendâ to Kōsei o Mezashite* [Capitalism and Sexual Discrimination: Looking at Gender and Welfare], Tokyo: Aoki Shoten.
Morita, Akio (1992) '"Nihon Keiei" ga Abunai' ('Japanese Management' is Dangerous), *Bungei Shunjû* (February), pp. 94–103.
Moses, J. (1994) 'Abdication from National Policy Autonomy: What's Left to Leave?', *Policy and Society* 22, pp. 46–61.
Mouer, Ross and Sugimoto, Yoshio (1990) *Images of Japanese Society: A Study in the Social Construction of Reality*, London: Kegan Paul International.
Mouer, Richard and Sugimoto, Yoshio (1981) *Japanese Society: Stereotypes and Realities*, Melbourne: Japanese Studies Centre.
Munakata, Masayuki (1998) 'The End of the 'Mass Production System' and Changes in Work Practices', in Hasegawa, Harukiyo and Hook, Glenn (eds.) *Japanese Business Management: Restructuring for Low Growth and Globalization*, London: Routledge.
Murakami, Yasusuke (1996) *An Anticlassical Political-Economic Analysis: A Vision for the Next Century*, Stanford: Stanford University Press.
Muramatsu, Michio and Krauss, Ellis (1987) 'The Conservative Party Line and the Development of Patterned Pluralism', in Yamamura, Kozo and Yasuba, Yasukichi (eds) *The Political Economy of Japan Volume 1: The Domestic Transformation*, California: Stanford University Press.
Nakano, Koichi (1998) 'Becoming a "Policy" Ministry: The Organization and *Amakudari* of the Ministry of Posts and Telecommunications', *Journal of Japanese Studies* 24:1 (winter), pp. 95–118.
Nakao, Shigeo (1995) *The Political Economy of Japan Money*, Tokyo: University of Tokyo Press.
Nakata, Masaki (1998) 'Ownership and Control in Large Corporations in Contemporary Japan', in Hasegawa, Harukiyo and Hook, Glenn (eds.) *Japanese Business Management: Restructuring for Low Growth and Globalization*, London: Routledge.
Nelson, Joel I. (1995) *Post-Industrial Capitalism: Exploring Economic Inequality in America*, London: Sage.
Nihon Ginkō Kinyû Kenkyûjo (BOJ) (1995) *Waga Kuni no Kinyû Seido* [The Japanese Financial System], Tokyo: Nihon Ginkō Kinyû Kenkyûjo.
Nihon Keizai Chōsa Kyōgikai (1997) *Keizai no Kōzō Henka to Koyō Seido Henkaku: Kanzen 'Nōryoku' Koyō no Jidai ni* [Structural Economic Change and the Changing Employment System: Towards an Era of Real 'Ability'-based Employment], Tokyo: Nihon Keizai Chōsa Kyōgikai.

Nihon Keizai Shinbunsha (ed.) (1997) *Dō Naru Kinyû Biggu Ban?* [What Will Become of Big Bang?], Tokyo: Nihon Keizai Shinbunsha.
Nihon Keizai Shinbunsha (ed.) (1995) *Dokyumento: Nichibei Jidōsha Kyōgi 'Shōri naki Tatakai' no Jisshō* [Documentary Evidence that the Japan-US Auto Accord was a 'Battle without a Victor'], Tokyo: Nihon Keizai Shinbunsha.
Nishinarita, Yutaka (1998) 'Japanese-style Industrial Relations in Historical Perspective', in Hasegawa, Harukiyo and Hook, Glenn (eds.) *Japanese Business Management: Restructuring for Low Growth and Globalization*, London: Routledge.
Noguchi, Yukio (1995) *1940 nen no Seido* [The 1940 System], Tokyo: Tōyō Keizei Shimposha.
Obstfeld, Maurice (1995) 'International Capital Mobility in the 1990s', in Kenen, Peter (ed.) *Understanding Interdependence: The Macroeconomics of the Open Economy*, Princeton: Princeton University Press.
OECD (1996) 'Securitization: An International Perspective', *Financial Market Trends* 61, pp. 33–62.
Ōgata, Shijuro (1996) *En to Nichigin* [The Yen and the Bank of Japan], Tokyo: Chûō Kōron.
Ogita Tamotsu (1969) 'Shingikai no Jittai' [The Realities of Advisory Councils], *Nenpō Gyōsei Kenkyû* 7, pp. 21–71.
Ohmae, Kenichi (1990) *The Borderless World: Power and Strategy in an Interdependent Economy*, London: Collins.
Okubayashi, Koji (1998) 'Small Headquarters and the Reorganisation of Management', in Hasegawa, Harukiyo and Hook, Glenn (eds.) *Japanese Business Management: Restructuring for Low Growth and Globalization*, London: Routledge.
Ōkura, Kazutomo (1996) *MOF-tan no Kokuhaku* [Confessions of an MOF Lobbyist], Tokyo: Appuru.
Osaki, Sadakazu (1996) 'Financial System Reforms', in Hayakawa, Shigenobu (ed.) *Japanese Financial Markets*, Cambridge, UK: Gresham Books.
Ōsono, Tomokazu (1992) *Hitome de Wakaru Kigyō Keiretsu to Gyōkai Chizu* [Business Maps for Understanding Japanese *Keiretsu* Industrial Groups at a Glance], Tokyo: Nihon Jitsugyō Shuppansha.
Ostrom, Douglas (1997) 'Prospects for Economic Reform in Japan: Where is the Safety Net?', *Japan Economic Institute (JEI) Report* 37 (October).
Overbeek, Henk (1990) *Global Capitalism and National Decline: The Thatcher Decade in Perspective*, London: Unwin Hyman.
Ozaki, Tetsuji (ed.) (1993) *Gendai Nihon Keizai Shisutemu no Genryû* [The Origins of Japan's Modern Economic System], Tokyo: Nihon Keizai Shimbunsha.
Padoa-Schioppa, Tomasso and Saccomanni, Fabrizio (1994) 'Managing a Market-led Global Financial System', in Kenen, Peter (ed.) *Managing the World Economy: 50 Years After Bretton Woods*, Washington DC: Institute of International Monetary Affairs.
Palan, Ronen and Abbott, Jason (1996) *State Strategies in the Global Political Economy*, London: Pinter.
Pauly, Louis W. (1995) 'Capital Mobility, State Autonomy and Political Legitimacy', *Journal of International Affairs* 48:2 (winter), pp. 369–88.
Pauly, Louis W. and Reich, Simon (1997) 'National Structures and Multinational Corporate Behaviour: Enduring Differences in the Age of Globalisation', *International Organization* 51:1, pp. 1–30.
Pauly, Louis W. (1988) *Opening Financial Markets: Banking Politics on the Pacific Rim*, Ithaca: Cornell University Press.
Pempel, T.J. (1998a) *Regime Shift: Comparative Dynamics of the Japanese Political Economy*, Ithaca: Cornell University Press.

Pempel, T.J. (1998b) 'Structural *gaiatsu*: international finance and political change in Japan', paper presented to the annual meeting of the American Political Science Association, Boston, MA, 2-6 September.

Pempel, T. J. (1978) 'Japanese Foreign Economic Policy', in Katzenstein, Peter (ed.) *Between Power and Plenty*, Madison: University of Wisconsin Press.

Perraton, Jonathan; Goldblatt, David; Held, David; and McGrew, Anthony (1997) 'The Globalisation of Economic Activity', *New Political Economy* 2:2, pp. 257–77.

Peters, Thomas and Waterman, Robert (1982) *In Search of Excellence*, New York: Harper and Row.

Pharr, Susan J. and Krauss, Ellis S. eds. (1996) *Media and Politics in Japan*, Honolulu: University of Hawaii Press.

Piven, Frances Fox (1995) 'Is It Global Economics of Neo-Laissez Faire?', *New Left Review* 213, pp. 107–113.

Polanyi, Karl (1944) *The Great Transformation*, (reprinted 1980), New York: Octagon Books.

Porter, Tony (1993) *States, Markets and Regimes in Global Finance*, New York: St. Martin's Press.

Porter, Michael (1985) *Competitive Advantage*, New York: Free Press.

Posen, Adam (1998) *Restoring Japan's Economic Growth*, Washington: Institute for International Economics.

Preston, Peter (1995) 'The Socio-Economic Problems of Contemporary Japan and the Limits of Political Reform', *The Political Quarterly* 55:2, pp. 195–204.

Pringle, Robert (1992) 'Financial Markets Versus Governments', in Banuri, Tariq and Schor, Juliet B. (eds.) *Financial Openness and National Autonomy: Opportunities and Constraints*, Oxford: Clarendon Press.

Redman, Deborah A. (1997) *The Rise of Political Economy as a Science: Methodology and the Classical Economists*, Cambridge, MA: MIT Press.

Reich, Robert B. (1991) *The Work of Nations: Preparing Ourselves for 21st Century Capitalism*, New York: Knopf.

Reinicke, Wolfgang H. (1995) *Banking, Politics and Global Finance: American Commercial Banks and Regulatory Change, 1980–1990*, Aldershot: Edward Elgar.

Reinicke, Wolfgang H. (1997) 'Global Public Policy', *Foreign Affairs* (November/December), pp. 127–38.

RIPE (1994) 'Editorial: Forum for Hetrodox International Political Economy', *Review of International Political Economy* 1:1 (spring), pp. 1–11.

Roberts, John (1995) *$1000 Billion a Day: Inside the Foreign Exchange Markets*, London: Harper Collins.

Robertson, Roland (1992) *Globalization*, London: Sage.

Rodkey, Gretchen (1997) 'Domestic Politics, Economic Transitions, and Central Europe's Integration into Global Financial Markets', in Underhill Geoffrey R.D. (ed.) *The New World Order in International Finance*, London: Macmillan.

Rodrik, Dani (1997) 'Sense and Nonsense in the Globalization Debate', *Foreign Policy* 107 (summer), pp. 19–37.

Rosenau, James N. and Czempiel, Ernst-Otto. (eds.) (1992) *Governance without Government: Order and Change in World Politics*, Cambridge: Cambridge University Press.

Rosenau, James N. (1980) *The Study of Global Interdependence*, New York: Nichols.

Rosenbluth, Frances McCall (1993) 'Financial Deregulation and Interest Intermediation', in Allinson, Gary and Sone, Yasunori (eds) *Political Dynamics in Contemporary Japan*, Ithaca: Cornell University Press.

Bibliography

Rosenbluth, Frances McCall (1989) *Financial Politics in Contemporary Japan*, Ithaca: Cornell University Press.

Rothacher, Albrecht (1993) *The Japanese Power Elite*, New York: St. Martin's Press.

Rothkopf, David (1997) 'In Praise of Cultural Imperialism?', *Foreign Policy* 107 (summer), pp. 38–53.

Royama, Shoichi (1986) *Kinyû Jiyûka* [Financial Liberalisation], Tokyo: Tokyo University Press.

Ruggie, John Gerard (1982) 'International Regimes, Transactions, and Change: Embedded Liberalism in the Postwar Economic Order', *International Organization* 36, pp. 379–415.

Rupert, Mark (1997) 'Globalisation and American Common Sense: Struggling to Make Sense of a Post-hegemonic World', *New Political Economy* 2:1, pp. 105–16.

Sachs, Jeffrey (1998) 'International Economics: Unlocking the Mysteries of Globalization', *Foreign Policy* 110 (spring), pp. 97–111.

Saitō Seiichirō, *Ōkurashō ni 'Biggu Ban' wa Dekinai* [The MOF Cannot Implement the 'Big Bang'], Tokyo: PHP Institute.

Sakakibara, Eisuke (1993) *Beyond Capitalism: The Japanese Model of Market Economics*, Boston: University Press of America.

Sakakibara, Eisuke and Noguchi, Yukio (1977) 'Dissecting the Finance Ministry-BOJ Divide', *Japan Echo* 4:4, pp. 98–123.

Sassen, Saskia (1991) *The Global City: New York, London, Tokyo*, Oxford: Princeton University Press.

Schaede, Ulrike (1990) 'The Introduction of Commercial paper: A Case Study in the Liberalisation of Japanese Financial Markets', *Japan Forum* 2:2 (November).

Scher, Mark J. (1997) *Japanese Interfirm Networks and Their Main Banks*, New York: St. Martin's Press.

Scholte, Jan Aart (1997) 'Global Capitalism and the State', *International Affairs* 73:3 (July), pp. 427–52.

Schoppa, Leonard J. (1997) *Bargaining With Japan: What American Pressure Can and Cannot Do*, Ithaca: Columbia University Press.

Schwartz, Frank J. (1997) *Advice and Consent: The Politics of Consultation in Japan*, Cambridge MA: Harvard University Press.

Schwartz, Frank J. (1993) 'Of Fairy Cloaks and Familiar Talks: The Politics of Consultation', in Allinson, Gary and Sone, Yasunori (eds) *Political Dynamics in Contemporary Japan*, Ithaca: Cornell University Press.

Sheard, Paul (1997) *Mein Banku Shihonshugi no Kiki: Biggu Ban de Kawaru Nihonkei Keiei* [The Crisis of Main Bank Capitalism: Changes in Japanese Management under Big Bang], Tokyo: Tōyō Keizai Shinbunsha.

Sheard, Paul (1994) 'Bank Executives on Japanese Corporate Boards', *Bank of Japan Monetary Economic Studies* 12:2, pp. 85–121.

Shindō, Muneyuki (1995) *Gyōsei Shidō: Kanchō to Gyōkai no Aida* [Administrative Guidance: Between the Bureaucracy and the Business World], Tokyo: Iwanami Shoten.

Shindō, Muneyuki (1992) *Gyōei Shido*, Tokyo: Iwanami.

Sinclair, Timothy J. (1994a) 'Passing Judgment: Credit Rating Processes as Regulatory Mechanisms of Governance in the Emerging World Order', *Review of International Political Economy* 1:1, pp. 133–59.

Sinclair, Timothy J. (1994b) 'Between State and Market: Hegemony and Institutions of Collective Action Under Conditions of International Capital Mobility', *Policy Sciences* 27, pp. 447–66.

Sklair, Leslie (1991) *Sociology of the Global System*, Hemel Hempstead: Harvester Wheatsheaf.

Smith, Martin (1995a) 'Pluralism', in Marsh, David and Stoker, Gerry (eds.) *Theory and Methods in Political Science*, London: Macmillan.
Smith, Steve (1995b) 'The Self Images of the Discipline: A Genealogy of International Relations Theory', in Booth, Ken and Smith, Steve (eds.) *International Relations Theory Today*, Cambridge: Polity.
Sobel, Andrew (1994) *Domestic Choices, International Markets: Dismantling National Barriers and Liberalizing Securities Markets*, Ann Arbor: University of Michigan Press.
Soref, Michael and Zeitlin, Maurice (1987) 'Finance Capital and the Internal Structure of the Capitalist Class in the United States', in Mizruchi, Mark S. and Schwartz, Michael (eds.) *Intercorporate Relations: The Structural Analysis of Business*, Cambridge: Cambridge University Press.
Spybey, Tony (1996) *Globalization and World Society*, Cambridge: Polity Press.
Stearns, Linda Brewster (1990) 'Capital Market Effects on External Control of Corporations', in Zukin, Sharon and DiMaggio, Paul (eds.) *Structures of Capital: The Social Organization of the Economy*, Cambridge: Cambridge University Press.
Stockwin, J. A. A.; Rix, Alan; George, Aurelia; Horne, James; Ito, Daiichi; and Collick, Martin (eds.) (1988) *Dynamic and Immobilist Politics in Japan*, London: Macmillan.
Stopford, John and Strange, Susan (1991) *Rival States, Rival Firms: Competition for World Market Shares*, Cambridge: Cambridge University Press.
Story, Jonathan (1997) 'Globalisation, the European Union and German Financial Reform: The Political Economy of "Finanzplatz Deutschland"', in Underhill Geoffrey R.D. (ed.) *The New World Order in International Finance*, London: Macmillan.
Strange, Susan (1996) *The Retreat of the State: The Diffusion of Power in the World Economy*, Cambridge: Cambridge University Press.
Strange, Susan (1994) 'Wake Up, Krasner! The World *has* Changed', *Review of International Political Economy* 1:2 (summer), pp. 209–19.
Strange, Susan (1990) 'The Name of the Game', in Rizopoulos, Nicholas (ed.) *Sea Changes*, New York: Council on Foreign Relations.
Strange, Susan (1988) *States and Markets: An Introduction to International Political Economy*, London: Pinter.
Streeten, Paul (1996) 'Free and Managed Trade', in Berger, Suzanne and Dore, Ronald (eds.) *National Diversity and Global Capitalism*, Ithaca: Cornell University Press.
Sumita, Shōji (1997) *Yakunin ni tsukeru Kusuri* [The Wasteful Spending of Bureaucrats], Tokyo: Asahi Shinbunsha.
Suto, Megumi (1993) 'The Securities Industry in Japan', in Takagi (ed.) *Japanese Capital Markets: New Developments in Regulations and Institutions*, Oxford: Blackwell.
Suzuki, Ken (1997) 'Daiginkō no Shihaiteki Chii to sono Saihen' [The Dominant Position of City Banks and its Reconfiguration], in Yamada, Hiroshi and Noda, Masaho (eds.) *Gendai Nihon no Kinyū: Hatan no Kōzō to Kaikaku no Hōkō* [Contemporary Japanese Finance: Structural Failure and the Direction of Reform], Tokyo: Shinnihon Shuppansha.
Suzuki, Yoshio (1996) 'The Main Issues Facing Japan's Economy', *Japan in the World Economy* 8, pp. 353–60.
Suzuki, Yoshio (1995) *Kisei Kanwa wa Naze Dekinai no ka?* [Why Can't Japan Deregulate?], Tokyo: Nihon Jitsugyō Shuppansha.
Swary, Itzhak and Topf, Barry (1992) *Global Financial Deregulation: Commercial Banking at the Crossroads*, Oxford: Blackwell.

Bibliography

Tadaro, Masayuki (1988) 'Aru Gaiatsu no Kenkyû' [A Case of US-Japanese Financial Friction], *Himeiji Hōgaku* 1, pp. 209–255.

Tago, Hideto; Yamaguchi, Kenichirō; Matsuo, Junsuke; and Ōkubo Tsutomu (1997) *Gurōbaru Sutandâdo: Kinyû Biggu Ban ga Motomeru 'Ishiki Kaikaku'* [Global Standards: The 'Conceptual Revolution' that the Financial Big Bang Demands], Tokyo: Kinyû Zaisei Jijō Kenkyûkai.

Takeda, Masahiko and Turner, Philip (1992) 'The Liberalisation of Japan's Financial Markets: Some Major Themes', *BIS Economic Papers* 34.

Takenaka, Heizō (1997) "Nihon Biggu Ban' de Nani ga Kawaru no ka?' [What will Change with the 'Japanese-style Big Bang'?], *Ushio* (April), pp. 120–7.

Tamaki, Norio (1995) *Japanese Banking: 1859–1959*, Cambridge: Cambridge University Press.

Tanaka, Akihiko (1996) *Atarashii Chûsei: 21seki no Sekai Shisutemu* [New Mediaevalism: The World System in the 21st Century], Tokyo: Nihon Keizai Shinbunsha.

Tanaka, Hitoshi (1997a) 'Ginkōin "Kōchingin"-ron no Mondaiten' [Problems with the Notion of High Wages in Banking], in Yamada, Hiroshi and Noda, Masaho (eds.) *Gendai Nihon no Kinyû: Hatan no Kōzō to Kaikaku no Hōkō* (Contemporary Japanese Finance: Structural Failure and the Direction of Reform), Tokyo: Shin Nihon Shuppansha.

Tanaka Naoki (1997b) *Biggu Ban go no Nihon Keizai* (The Japanese Economy After Big Bang), Tokyo: Nihon Keizai Shinbunsha.

Tavlas, George S. (1993) 'The 'New' Theory of Optimum Currency Areas', *World Economy* 16, pp. 663–86.

Teranishi, Juro (1993) 'Financial Sector Reform after the War', in Teranishi and Kosai (eds.) *The Japanese Experience of Economic Reforms*, New York: St. Martin's Press.

Terrell, Henry; Dohner, Robert; and Lowrey, Barbara (1990) 'The Activities of Japanese Banks in the United Kingdom and United States: 1980–88', *Federal Reserve Bulletin* (February), pp. 39–50.

Thompson, Helen (1997) 'The Nation-State and International Capital Flows in Historical Perspective', *Government and Opposition* 32:1 (winter), pp. 84–113.

Thrift, Nigel (1994 'On the Social and Cultural Determinants of International Financial Centres: The Case of the City of London', in Corbridge, Stuart; Martin, Ron; and Thrift, Nigel (eds.) *Money, Power and Space*, Oxford: Blackwell.

Tsuda, Kazuo (1993) *Kyōdai Ginkō no Kōzō* [The Structure of Giant Banks], Tokyo: Kodansha.

Tsurumi Masayoshi (1991) *Nihon Shinyō Kikō no Kakuritsu* [The Establishment of Japan's Credit Structure], Tokyo: Yûhaikaku.

Tsutsui, William M., (1988) *Banking Policy in Japan: American Efforts at Reform during the Occupation*, London: Routledge.

Underhill, Geoffrey R. D. (1997) 'The Making of the European Financial Area: Global Market integration and the EU Single Market for Financial Services', in Underhill, G.R.D. (ed.) *The New World Order in International Finance*, London: Macmillan.

Underhill, Geoffrey R. D. (1995) 'Keeping Governments Out of Politics: Transnational Securities Markets, Regulatory Cooperation, and Political Legitimacy', *Review of International Studies* 21, pp. 251–78.

Useem, Michael (1996) *Investor Capitalism: How Money Managers are Changing the face of Corporate America*, New York: Basic Books.

Vogel, Steven (1996) *Freer Markets, More Rules: Regulatory Reform in Advanced Industrial Countries*, Ithaca: Cornell University Press.

Vogel, Steven (1994) 'The Bureaucratic Approach to the Financial Revolution: Japan's Ministry of Finance and Financial System Reform', *Governance* 7:3, pp. 219–243.
Volcker, Paul and Gyohten, Toyoo (1992) *Changing Fortunes: The World's Money and the Threat to American Leadership*, New York: Times Books.
Wachtel, Howard M. (1986) *The Money Mandarins: The Making of a Supranational Economic Order*, New York: Pantheon.
Walter, Andrew (1993) *World Power and World Money* (2nd edition), London: Harvester Wheatsheaf.
Watanabe, Takashi (1998) 'The Rise of Flexible and Individual Ability-oriented Management', in Hasegawa, Harukiyo and Hook, Glenn (eds.) *Japanese Business Management: Restructuring for Low Growth and Globalization*, London: Routledge.
Waters, Malcolm (1995) *Globalization*, London: Routledge.
Webb, Michael C. (1991) 'International Economic Structures, Government Interests and International Coordination of Macroeconomic Adjustment Policies', *International Organization* 45:3, pp. 309–42.
Weber, Max (1978) *Economy and Society*, Berkeley: University of California Press.
Weiss, Linda (1997) 'Globalization and the Myth of the Powerless State', *New Left Review* 225 (September/October), pp. 3–27.
Wellons, Philip (1987) 'International Debt: The Behaviour of Banks in a Politicized Environment', in Kahler, Miles (ed.) *The Politics of International Debt*, Ithaca: Cornell University Press.
Williams, David (1996) *Japan and the Enemies of Open Political Science*, London: Routledge.
Yamamura, Kozo (1997) 'The Japanese Economy After the Bubble: Plus Ça Change?', *Journal of Japanese Studies* 23:2, pp. 291–331.
Yoshida, Kazuo (1995) *Gyōkaku to Kisei Kanwa no Keizaigaku* [The Economics of Administrative Reform and Deregulation], Tokyo: Kodansha.
Youngs, Gillian (1996) 'Dangers of Discourse: The Case of Globalization', in Kofman, Eleonore and Youngs, Gillian (eds.) *Globalization: Theory and Practice*, London: Pinter.
Zenkoku Ginkō Kyōkai Rengōkai (Zenginren) (1996) *Wagakuni no Ginkō* [Japan's Banks], Tokyo: Zaikei Shōhōsha.
Zevlin, Robert (1992) 'Are World Financial Markets More Open? If so, Why, and with What Effects?', in Banuri, Tariq and Schor, Juliet B. (eds.) *Financial Openness and National Autonomy*, Oxford: Oxford University Press.
Zukin, Sharon and DiMaggio, Paul (eds.) (1990) *Structures of Capital: The Social Organization of the Economy*, Cambridge: Cambridge University Press.
Zysman, John (1983) *Governments, Markets and Growth: Financial Systems and the Politics of Industrial Change*, Ithaca: Cornell University Press.

NEWSPAPERS AND MAGAZINES

Asahi Shinbun
Banker, The
Economist, The
Economisto
Euromoney
Far Eastern Economic Review (FEER)
Financial Times, The (FT)
Forbes

Institutional Investor
Japan Times, The (JT)
Kinyû Bijinesu
Kinyû Jyânaru, Gekkan
Kokusai Kinyû
Nihon Keizai Shimbun (Nikkei)
Nikkei Kinyu Shinbun
Nikkei Manê
Nikkei Weekly, The (NW)
Tōyō Keizai, Shûkan
Yomiuri Shinbun

INTERVIEWS

Adachi, Nobiru	Senior MOF official and Visiting Professor of International Finance, University of Tokyo
Bebbington, Simon	Nomura Securities (Tokyo)
Duke, Lawrence	Economist, Citibank (Tokyo)
Fraser, Simon	Managing Director, Fidelity Investments (Japan)
Hammerich, Bo	Managing Director, Citibank (Tokyo)
Harney, Alexandra	Tokyo Correspondent, Financial Times
Jones, Russell	Chief Economist, Lehman Brothers (Tokyo)
Kanda, Hideki	Professor of Securities Law, University of Tokyo
Marrantz, Alan	Head of Sales and Trading, Lehman Brothers (Japan)
Ogawa, Alicia	Head of Asian Research, Salomon Smith Barney (Japan)
Okamura, Ken	Strategist, Dresdner Kleinwort Benson (Tokyo)
Okuda, Yasushi	Economist, JP Morgan (Tokyo)
Percy, Keith	Special Advisor, Societé Générale Asset Management
Shina, Yasushi	Financial Markets Department, Bank of Japan
Wait, Jarret	Chief Operating Officer (Asia), Lehman Brothers (Japan)
Wellsteed, Alexander	Corporate Finance Department, Dai-ichi Kangyō Bank (Tokyo)
Whitten, Darryl	Senior strategist, ABN Amro (Tokyo)
Wilkinson, Ralph	Economics and Finance Councellor, EU Delegation of the EC in Japan
Young, Jeffrey	Chief Economist, Salomon Smith Barney (Tokyo)

Index

Administrative Reform Council (ARC) 93, 119
Akio, M. 233
Altman, R. 101–2
Amin, A. 286; and Palan, R. 286
Andrews, 44
Aoki, M. and Patrick, H.T. 339
Arora, D. 295
Arrighi, G. 286
Asher, D. 102, 218, 338
Asian crisis 33, 101–5, 104

Bank of International Settlements (BIS) 104, 153, 159, 183, 184, 228, 292 (56n)
Bank of Japan (BOJ) 60, 62, 64, 72, 73, 79, 85, 87, 92, 95, 96–7, 106, 125, 150, 154, 209, 218, 220, 229, 278
Banking Law 60, 61, 62, 65, 72, 78, 79, 107
Banking and Securities Bureaus 67, 79
banking system 53, 60–2, 63–4, 125, 130–3; assets held by *142*; cost-cutting 157, *158*, 159; distribution of overseas offices *133*; domestically licensed *130*; expansion of foreign 137–8, *139*; failures 279–80; internationalisation *132*; lending *142*; loans 153; offices *131*; outlook 189–90; position in Eurodollar Bond issues *143–4*; world rankings by assets *140*, *141*, see also financial institutions
Baum, G. 288
Beck, U. 15
Berger, S. 288; and Dore, R. 285
Big Bang 3, 7, 35, 100, 105, 109, 110–28, 150, 277; announcement 111, 113; background 113–19; evaluation 125–7; itinerary *112*; as paving way for restructuring 163–4, 166, 168, 170, 179–94; societal implications 245–62; translating concept into policy 119–25
BIS Capital Accord (1988) 140, 148
Black, F. 38
Black-Scholes model 38
Bond Issue Committee 65, 296 (12n)
Boston Consulting Group (BCG) Matrix 286 (11n)
Boyes-Watson, C. 288
Bretton Woods 30, 39, 45, 70, 74
bubble economy 85–7, 105, 132, 136–7, 148, 150, 185, 197, 199, 216, 218, 226, 233
Budd, L. 287
Bull, H. 29

Campbell, J.C. 308
Cerny, P.G. 21–3, 26–7, 28, 29, 55
certificates of deposits (CDs) 72, 73, 108, 298 (29n)
Chandler, A. 25
Christmas Communiqué (1987) 83
Cohen, B.J. 19, 23, 287
Coleman, W.D. 284
Commercial Code 88, 234
competitiveness 154, 157, 184; declining 105–10; global 192–3
convoy system 68–70, 97–101, 154, 297 (22n)
Cooperative Credit Purchasing Company (CCPC) 125
corporate sector 222–35; financing patterns 226, *227*, 228–9; firm-

385

Index

employee relations 230–3; firm-owner relations 233–5; institutional changes 229–35; inter-firm relations 229–30; performance 222–6
Cox, R.W. 4, 12, 23, 28; *et al* 285
'currency-clientele effect' (CCE) 155

De Cecco, M. 289
deregulation 30, *31*, 32–5, 49, 289 (33n); Big Bang case study 110–28; events leading to 70–110; initiatives 72–3; international developments 74–5, 76–87; Nakasone's reform agenda 77; outlook 187–93; problems 73; repercussions of euromarkets 75–6
domestic development, economic maturity 71–3; impact of oil crises 71–3; monetary instability 74–5; Nakasone's reform agenda 77; repercussions of Euromarkets 75–6; transformation 71–6
Dornbusch, R. 207
Drucker, P. 25
Durkheim, E. 14
Duser, J.T. 148

Economic Council (EC) 115–16
economic globalisation 11–29, 288 (31n); competitive innovation 19–21; debates concerning 12–14; economies of scale/scope 19–21; financial structures 21–6; knowledge structures 21–6; nuanced concept 18–29; precursor/postmodern theories 14–18; reconfiguration of state-market relations 26–9; transnational elites 21–6
economic performance 196, *197*, 201–2, 215–16; recession 153; stimulus measures 354–65
Economic Planning Agency (EPA) 115, 119, 120, 124, 203, 205, 232
Economic Sociology 23, 287 (23n)
economies of scale/scope 19–21
Enkyo, S. 346
Epstein, G.A. and Schor, J.B. 287
Esping–Anderson, G. 51–2
Euromarkets 75–6
European Exchange Rate Mechanism (ERM) 22, 207–8
Evans, M. 287
exchange rate 218–20
exchange rates 149–50

Fair Trade Commission (FTC) 90
finance 21–6; financial/nonfinancial institutions 23–4; mobility 21–2; politico-legal aspects 22–3; power/control 24–6, 288 (25n)
financial engineering 86, 304 (72n)
financial globalisation 6–7, 29–42; areas for further study 273–4; challenges 275; competitive deregulation by states 30, *31*, 32–5; competitive innovation by firms 35–8; derivatives market *41*; foreign exchange market turnover *41*; as 'halfway house' 38, 41–2; implications for national institutional convergence 42–54; Japanese insights 266–70; size of markets *40*; understanding Japanese institutions 270–3
financial institutions, all-out cost cutting 179–81; competitive tie-ups 168, 170, *171–8*, 185–7; consumer/investor-friendly products 181–3; convergence 163–4, 166, 168, 170, 179–94; environmental developments 149–52; fall 153–5; foreign 137–9; generalists/specialists 187–9; global competitors 148–55, 157, 159–63, 191–3; home/abroad 130–7; managerial changes 181–3; market perceptions 142, 144–8; outlook 187–94; personnel cuts *158*; position in annual *Euromoney* polls *156*; prioritising profitability 179–81; rankings *162*; restructuring 155, 157, 159–63, *167*; rise 149–53; share of key market sectors 141–2; size *140–1*; strategic choices 152–3; strategic retrenchment 183–5; winners/losers 189–91
Financial Reconstruction Commission (FRC) 278
financial regulation 64–70; administrative guidance 65, 66–8; escorted convoy method 68–70; indirect finance 64–5; international isolation 70; reform 70–110; rigid functional segmentation 65
Financial Services Reform Act (1992) 154, 160
financial strategies 155–63; adoption of Western technologies/learning 159;

386

Index

changes in HRM 161; cost-cutting/staff reductions 157, *158*, 159, *165–6*; geographical diversification 159–60; localisation 161; product diversification 160; retrenchment 183–5; synergetic mergers 160–1
Financial Supervisory Agency (FSA) 92, 94, 125, 184, 278
financial system, changes 70–87; characteristics of postwar regulation 64–70; development 59–70; domestic economic transformation 71–6; historical background 60–2; internationalisation 76–87; legacy of postwar reforms 63–4
Financial System Reform Act (1992) 105, 107
Financial System Research Council (FSRC) 72, 79, 91, 98, 106, 119
Fingleton, E. 297
Floating-rate notes (FRNs) 36, 290 (43n)
Fordism 19
foreign direct investment (FDI) 149, 286 (13n)
Foreign Exchange Law 70, 79, 135
Foucault, M. 25, 288
Frank, A. and Gills, B. 286
Frankel, J.A. 295
Frieden, J.A. 287
Friedman, M. 37
Fuchita, Y. 314

Galbraith, J.K. 288
Garrett, G. and Lange, P. 287
GATT 104; Uruguay Round 103
Gibney, F.B. 295, 335
Giddens, A. 15
Gill, S. 25, 28
Gills, B.K. 13, 286
Glass-Seagal Act (1933) 35
globalisation 87–110; Asian crisis 101–5; concept 1, 54–5; declining competitiveness 105–10; economic 11–29; financial 6–7; impact in/on Japan 2–3; implications for national institutional convergence 42–54; pluralist approach 3–5, 285 (9n); scandals/bureaucratic complicity 88–101; theoretical background 6; US revisionism 101–5

Globex 36
Goldblatt, D. *et al* 29, 285
Goldsmith, J. 284
Goodman, J.B. 287
Goss, J. 288
government policy, direct intervention 210–11; failure of 211–16; fiscal 209–10; monetary 209; regulatory amendments 211; scale of intervention 202–9
gradualism, macroeconomic effects 195–217; microeconomic effects 217–44; societal implications of Big Bang 245–62
Gray, J. 284
Grieder, W. 287
Gyohten, T. 74, 80, 299

Harder, C. 13, 14
Harmes, A. 295
Hartcher, P. 297
Harvey, D. 15
Hayes, S.L. and Hubbard, P.M. 289, 295
Helleiner, E. 30, 285
Henwood, D. 295
Hesei recession *see* recession
Hideki, K. 122
Hirst, P. and Thompson, G. 13, 286, 288
Horne, J. 295, 346
household sector 236–44; employment/personal bankruptcy 237–8, *239*, 240–1; income/consumption 236–7; saving/investment 241–2, *243*, *244*, *245*
human resource management (HRM) 48, 161, 325 (50n)

Ikeda, M. 338
Imai, K. 314
innovation 19–21, 35–8
Inoki, T. 297
insurance companies 191
interest rate 220–2, 302 (60n)
international banking facilities (IBFs) 32
International Finance Bureau 67, 93, 117
International Monetary Fund (IMF) 33, 75, 104, 216, 299 (35n)
internationalisation 76–87; domestic reform agenda 77; financial sector 129–48; global system developments 83–7; Plaza Accord 78–83; Yen-Dollar Agreement 78–83
investment, cross-border 21; trusts 53

387

Ito, O. 59
Iwami, T. 295

Japan Federation of Bankers' Association (JFBA) 166, 181
Japan Offshore Market (JOM) 148, 150
Japanese government bonds (JGBs) 73, 151, 207, 221, 299 (34n)
Jessop, B. 26, 27, 29
joint ventures 168, 170, *171–8*, 183, 185–7, see also mergers and acquisitions
Jones, R.J.B. 12
Julius, D. 26–7
jūsen 91, 95, 98, 100, 308 (95n), 310 (110n)

Kaletsky, A. 207
Kato, J. 308
Kawakita, T. 297
Kazuhito, I. 114, 116
keiretsu 193
Keizai Kikakucho Keizai Kenkyujo 346
Kelsey, J. 287
Kishi, N. 297
Kitaoka, S. 337
Klein, L. 300
knowledge structures 24–6, 288 (25n)
Koike, K. 346
Krugman, P. 27
Kurzer, P. 22

Lash, C. and Urry, 15
Lawrence, 295, 346
legislation 69–70
Leland, H. 38
Leyshon, A. 346
Liberal Democratic Party (LDP) 67–8, 73, 82, 90–1, 92, 93, 94, 95, 96, 101, 107, 115, 118, 124, 211, 213, 234, 276, 278
Lindblom, C.E. 287
Louvre Accord (1987) 45, 83, 149, 303 (64n)
Lyons Summit (1996) 113, 114
Mabuchi, M. 295
McKenzie, 314
macroeconomic effects 195–217; headline international comparisons 196–7, 199–200; Hesei recession 200–9; overview of performance 195–200; policy response to recession 209–17
Maekawa, Y. 340

Maekwa report (1986) 77
Makino, T. 324
Mander, J. and Goldsmith, E. 284
Marshall, D.D. 286
Martin, H.-P. and Schuman, H. 284
Marx, K. 14
Maxfield, S. 23
Meiji Restoration 60–1, 126
Melamed, L. 37
mergers and acquisitions (M&A) 47, 132, 136, 147, 155, 160, 179, 186–7, see also joint ventures
microeconomic effects 217–44; corporate sector developments 222–35; household sector developments 236–44; local implications of policy-induced distortions 217–22
Mills, C.W. 287
Ministry of Finance (MOF) 34, 154, 184, 185, 203, 205, 208, 278, 300 (40n), 304 (76n); Big Bang 118, 120, 121, 122, 123, 124; dominance of 63; moves to break up 347–53; regulatory powers 62, 65–70; scandals effecting 89–97; steps toward deregulation 70–110
Ministry of Health and Welfare (MHW) 236
Ministry of International Trade and Industry (MITI) 67, 102, 119, 120, 219–20, 235
Ministry of Posts and Telecommunications (MPT) 67, 244
Mintz, and Scwartz, M. 24
Miwa, Y. 335
Mizruchi, M.S. and Schwartz, M. 287
monetary instability 74–5
Money Market Certificates (MMCs) 80
Montagna, P. 25
Moran, M. 304, 346
Morita, N. 346
Moses, J. 287
'Mothers' market (Market for High Growth and Emerging Stocks) 282
Mouer, R. and Sugimoto, Y. 295
Multilateral Agreement on Investment (MAI) 45
mutual funds 53

Nakano, K. 297
Nakao, S. 150, 295
Nakasone, Y. 77, 82, 84, 300 (45n)

Index

Nakata, M. 234, 340
NASDAQ (North American Securities Dealers Automated Quotation System) 35, 289 (38n)
National Civil Service Law 97
National Finance Control Organisation 62
national institutional convergence 42–54; financial systems 45–50; regulatory regimes 43–5; social structures 50–4
National Police Agency 95
National Tax Agency (NTA) 88, 89
Nelson, J.I. 25
New Liberal Order 22
Nihon Keizai Shinbunsha 314

Ohmae, K. 12
oil crises 71–3
oil shocks 155
Okubayashi, K. 1
Okura, K. 297
Organisation for Economic Cooperation and Development (OECD) 78, 104, 119, 120, 299 (35n)
Organisation of the Petroleum Exporting Countries (OPEC) 71
Osaka Stock Exchange (OSE) 60
Ostrom, D. 215

Palan, R. and Abbott, J. 29, 286
Pauly, L.W. 23, 295; and Reich, S. 294
Perraton, J. et al 17, 42, 285, 286
Plaza Accord (1985) 45, 78–83, 84, 303 (64n)
Polanyi, K. 29, 288
Portfolio Insurance Theory (PIT) 38
Posen, A. 336
postmodern theories 14–18
price keeping operations (PKOs) 210, 217–18
Pringle, R. 287
products/services, arbitrage 36–7; asset-backed securities 164; automated teller machines (ATMs) 53, 164, 168, 181, 190, 257, 281, 329 (96n); bank sales of straight corporate bonds 254; cash management accounts 53, 189; consumer/investor-friendly 181–3; corporate/private investment trusts 256–7; deregulation of specific injury/illness insurance sales 253;

derivatives 37, *41*, 164, 249, 291 (48n), 292 (53n); discount brokerage services 164, 251–2; diversification 160; electronic money 252, 343 (93n); foreign exchange deregulation 247; foreign–currency–denominated accounts 164, 254–5; general securities accounts 164, 189, 247–8; hi–tech deposit accounts 248; impact *260*; individual stock options 250; investment advisory/evaluation services 258–9; investment clubs 258; multilateral netting services 164; non-financial firms' entry 257–8; off-exchange trading of listed securities 164, 256; over-the-counter (OTC) investment trusts 164, 253–4; over–the–counter (OTC) securities 35; overseas accounts 248–9; personal equity plans (PEPs) 53, 290 (46n); portable electronic money 164; private banking 251; remote banking 164; risk-related 184; securitised financial products 256; shops accepting foreign currency 256; small-lot investment funds 164, 249; sub-divisible insurance policies 164, 255–6; survey of new 246–59; telephone/internet access 53, 164, 281–2, 344 (102n); unlisted stock/venture capital funds 164, 252–3; wrap-around accounts 53, 164, 250
Prompt Corrective Action (PCA) 123, 184, 188, 318 (172n)

recession 200–17; break-down of annual GDP 200–1; leading economic indicators 201–2; policy responses 209–17; rising costs of forbearance 216–17; scale of government intervention 202–9; unemployment figures 200–1
regulatory arbitrage 23, 83–7
regulatory regimes 43–5
Reich, R.B. 25
Reinicke, W.H. 289
return on equity (ROE) 234
Reuter's Monitor system 36, 290 (41n)
risk management 44, 293 (62n)
Robertson, R. 15

Index

Rodrick, D. 12
Rosenau, J.N. 14; and Czempiel, E.-O. 24
Rosenbluth, F.M. 295, 297, 346
Ruggie, J.G. 32

Sakakibara, E. 295
scandals 234; leading to greater legal codification 88–9; restricting MOF's scope for administrative guidance 89–97; undermining convoy system 97–101
Scher, M.J. 339
Scholes, M. 38
Schoppa, L.J. 312
Schwartz, F.J. 298
securities companies 133–7; distribution of overseas offices *134*; domestically licensed *134*; expansion of foreign 138, *139*; internationalisation *135*; outlook 190–1, see also financial institutions
Securities and Exchange Council (SEC) 106, 117–18, 119
Securities and Exchange Law (1948) 65, 84, 107
Securities and Exchanges Surveillance Commission (SESC) 89, 90, 96
securitisation 37, 291 (47n)
Sheard, P. 288, 339
Shindo, M. 297
Sinclair, T.J. 25
Sklair, L. 14
Smith, S. 286, 287
Sobel, A. 295
social structures 50–4
Soref, M. and Zeitlin, M. 24
special purpose companies (SPCs) 124
state-market relations 26–9
stock market 217–18; crash 153, 154; cross-shareholding relations 215, 230; performance 196, *198*
Stockwin, J.A.A. *et al* 297
Stopford, J. and Strange, S. 24
Strange, S. 21, 22, 28, 288, 289
Sumita, S. 337
Supreme Commander for the Allied Powers (SCAP) 63
systemic developments, declining competitiveness 105–10; regulatory arbitrage/bubble economy 83–7

Tago, H. *et al* 336
Takeda, M. and Turner, P. 151
Tavlas, G.S. 287
technology 47–8, 159, 281–2
Third Industrial Revolution 19, 277
Thrift, N. 26, 287, 288
Tokyo Stock Exchange (TSE) 60, 80, 136, 235, 281, 282
Toru, N. 114
total shareholder return (TSR) 162–3
Trade Control Law 79
transnational corporations (TNCs) 28, 287 (13n)
transnational elites 25–6
triple economy 276–82; international competitive export sector 276; new technology 281–2; protected sector 276–81

unemployment 196, *198*, 200–1, 237, *238*, *239*, 240
US revisionism 101–5
US Treasury Bonds 146, 151, 153

Vogel, S. 295, 335, 346
Volcker, P. 304; and Gyohten Toyoo 80
Volcker-shift 51

Waters, M. 14
Weber, M. 14
Wellons, P. 294
Williams, D. 284
World Economic Forum 27
World Trade Organisation (WTO) 45, 104

yakuza crime syndicates 95, 309 (107n)
Yamamura, K. 271–2
Yen-Dollar Agreement (1984) 78–83, 84–5, 137, 199

zaibatsu 63
Zukin, S. and DiMaggio, P. 287
Zysman, J. 296